S
OA
AVA
TIÁN Irún Hendaye
O

FRANCE

ORIA PAMPLONA ANDORRA **Roussillon**
NAVARRE
GROÑO HUESCA GERONA
ORIA **CATALUÑA**
Ebro R. LÉRIDA
SARAGOSSA BARCELONA
ARAGON Ebro R. TARRAGONA
ALAJARA Tortosa
TERUÉL
CUENCA CASTELLÓN **BALEARIC ISLANDS** Minorca
VALENCIA Majorca
STILE VALENCIA
ALBACETE Ibiza
MURCIA Formentera
ALICANTE
MURCIA Elche
Lorca
Cartagena

ALMERIA

ean Sea

elilla

N
W *E*
S

Democracy in Crisis: New Challenges to Constitutional Democracy in the Atlantic Area. E. A. Goerner, ed.

The Task of Universities in a Changing World. Stephen D. Kertesz, ed.

The Church and Social Change in Latin America. Henry A. Landsberger, ed.

Revolution and Church: The Early History of Christian Democracy, 1789–1901. Hans Maier.

The Overall Development of Chile. Mario Zañartu, S.J., and John J. Kennedy, eds.

The Catholic Church Today: Western Europe. M. A. Fitzsimons, ed.

Contemporary Catholicism in the United States. Philip Gleason, ed.

The Major Works of Peter Chaadaev. Raymond T. McNally.

A Russian European: Paul Miliukov in Russian Politics. Thomas Riha.

A Search for Stability: U. S. Diplomacy Toward Nicaragua, 1925–1933. William Kamman.

Freedom and Authority in the West. George N. Shuster, ed.

Theory and Practice: History of a Concept from Aristotle to Marx. Nicholas Lobkowicz.

Coexistence: Communism and Its Practice in Bologna, 1945–1965. Robert H. Evans.

Marx and the Western World. Nicholas Lobkowicz, ed.

Argentina's Foreign Policy 1930–1962. Alberto A. Conil Paz and Gustavo E. Ferrari.

Italy after Fascism, A Political History, 1943–1965. Giuseppe Mammarella.

The Volunteer Army and Allied Intervention in South Russia, 1917–1921. George A. Brinkley.

INTERNATIONAL STUDIES OF THE
COMMITTEE ON INTERNATIONAL RELATIONS
UNIVERSITY OF NOTRE DAME

Peru and the United States, 1900–1962. James C. Carey.

Empire by Treaty: Britain and the Middle East in the Twentieth Century. M. A. Fitzsimons.

The USSR and the UN's Economic and Social Activities. Harold Karan Jacobson.

Chile and the United States: 1880–1962. Fredrick B. Pike.

East Central Europe and the World: Developments in the Post-Stalin Era. Stephen D. Kertesz, ed.

Soviet Policy Toward International Control of Atomic Energy. Joseph L. Nogee.

The Russian Revolution and Religion, 1917–1925. Edited and translated by Bolesław Szcześniak.

Soviet Policy Toward the Baltic States, 1918–1940. Albert N. Tarulis.

Introduction to Modern Politics. Ferdinand Hermens.

Freedom and Reform in Latin America. Fredrick B. Pike, ed.

What America Stands For. Stephen D. Kertesz and M. A. Fitzsimons, eds.

Theoretical Aspects of International Relations. William T. R. Fox, ed.

Catholicism, Nationalism and Democracy in Argentina. John J. Kennedy.

The Fate of East Central Europe. Stephen D. Kertesz, ed.

German Protestants Face the Social Question. William O. Shanahan.

Soviet Imperialism: Its Origins and Tactics. Waldemar Gurian, ed.

The Foreign Policy of the British Labour Government, 1945–1951. M. A. Fitzsimons.

Hispanismo, 1898-1936

Spanish Conservatives and Liberals and
Their Relations with Spanish America

Hispanismo, 1898-1936

Spanish Conservatives and Liberals and
Their Relations with Spanish America

FREDRICK B. PIKE

 UNIVERSITY OF NOTRE DAME PRESS

NOTRE DAME—LONDON

Library of Congress Catalog Card Number: 75-159272
Manufactured in the United States of America by
NAPCO Graphic Arts, Inc., Milwaukee, Wisconsin

To My Children

PAULITA DE LLOPIS, JUNE, AND FREDRICK B. PIKE II

CONTENTS

the Spontaneity, Youth, Vitality, and Economic Potential of Spanish America, 147; Liberal Attempts to Create
the Image of a Progressive Spain, 149; The Altamira
Mission to Spanish America, 1909–1910, 152; The González Posada Mission to Spanish America, 1910, 155;
Shifting Attitudes of Liberals toward the United States,
157; Shifting, Divided Attitudes of Liberals toward
Mexico, 160; Liberal Views on Spanish-American Materialism, 161; Spain's Continuing Image in Spanish
America as a Backward, Decadent Country, 163; Liberal
Disillusionment in Spanish America, 164

PREFACE

In studying Spanish-American history during approximately the past twenty years I have often found myself intrigued by the ideology of conservative intellectuals and statesmen. With some considerable degree of consistency these conservatives have been Hispanophiles. They have, that is, extolled the traditions and values of Spain and acknowledged their spiritual and cultural dependence upon the *madre patria*. In order better to understand the thought of Spanish America's conservatives, therefore, it seemed essential to turn to its origins in the conservatism of the peninsula. As it turned out, it also became necessary to look into Spanish liberalism; for in the peninsula, as frequently also in Spanish America, many liberals seemed just as dedicated as the staunchest conservatives to preserving the traditional social system. Against the background of the social ideology of conservatism and liberalism in the peninsula, I sought to study the conscious efforts of Spaniards and Spanish Americans to establish close cultural and spiritual, and sometimes also economic and political ties, often with the specific purpose of bulwarking the prevailing social system throughout the Hispanic world.

This proved to be a vast project, even though I confined the time span to a period of just under forty years. The present book offers no more than a superficial survey of its far-reaching subject matter, being based primarily on published materials: books, periodicals, and a few—not nearly enough —newspapers. Concerned tangentially with Hispanophiles in Spanish America, it deals primarily with Spanish intellectuals, statesmen, and journalists who showed an interest in Spain's former colonies in the New World and in establishing a close relationship with them; often it ignores the role of Spaniards who were principally or exclusively literary figures. An underlying thesis developed in this book is that the interest of Spaniards in Spanish America often developed directly out of their social and political ideologies. As a result I have chosen to deal mainly with those Spaniards who have clearly stated and explained their ideological positions. Untrained in literary criticism, I am not competent to piece together a writer's social-political credo from inferences lurking in the passages of novels, plays, and poems. In this very fact, admittedly, lies another of the book's many weaknesses.

This study would have been vastly enhanced by research conducted outside of Madrid. Each of the important cities of Spain's periphery, especially Barcelona, Bilbao, Sevilla, and Cádiz, and to a lesser extent La Coruña, Vigo, and Valencia, to cite only a few of the more obvious ones, have developed fairly distinct programs for establishing cultural and economic ties with Spanish America; and each of these programs, as well as the men who formulated and sought to implement them, merit investigation. The relations of various Spanish economic interest groups with the New World republics, treated only in passing in this book, also call for extended research. Moreover, the effects of Spanish emigration to Spanish America, both upon the peninsula and the American republics, should be carefully analyzed. The present book accords only the briefest consideration to this fascinating subject. A particularly glaring omission in this regard, occasioned by the fact that my book deals only with men of the Spanish right dedicated to preserving the established social system, is the lack of reference to Spanish socialist and anarchist immigrants who played a significant role in early organized labor movements in Spanish America. I can only hope that the whole story of the *hispanismo* of the left, of the contacts and relations maintained between Spaniards and Spanish Americans intent upon fundamentally restructuring society through revolutionary violence if necessary, will soon receive the extensive study it deserves.

Hispanismo is a broad field indeed, and many readers will undoubtedly feel that in entering it for a preliminary exploration I have failed to note its most interesting features. Still, it was necessary to begin somewhere in surveying a largely neglected area; and I am by no means unduly apologetic for the results. If the general theme of this book is as important as I think, future researchers will fill in the many lacunae.

The biggest disappointment in preparing this book arose from my inability to use the archives and records of the Spanish Ministerio de Relaciones Exteriores. Rules prevailing at the time allowed one to consult these archives only for the period up to 1900. Had this source been open to me, it might have been possible to discover to what degree the interest of various Spanish intellectuals and statesmen in Spanish America affected the actual functioning of diplomacy between 1898 and 1936. When dealing with this matter I have been forced to rely upon thoroughly inadequate materials and to make inferences and deductions that may not be warranted. In a future research project I hope to carry the subject of this study back to 1808 and am comforted to think that for this purpose I shall be able to use diplomatic records as a principal source.

Preliminary work for this book was conducted in the University of Pennsylvania library; and it was facilitated by a seminar at the University of Texas during the summer of 1968 when, with the collaboration of some excellent graduate students, I worked on the subject of hispanismo. Most of the research, however, I carried out in the Biblioteca Nacional of Madrid during a twelve-month period in 1968 and 1969. A Guggenheim Foundation fellowship and a generous grant from the University of Notre

Dame made this possible. For arranging my grant and leave of absence at Notre Dame and providing every imaginable type of assistance I am particularly grateful to Stephen D. Kertesz, chairman of the Committee on International Relations, without whose support neither this book nor an earlier study on Chile could have been published, and to Vincent P. De Santis, head of the Department of History.

In Madrid I benefited from the attentiveness of Dr. Ramón Paz, head of the manuscripts division of the Biblioteca Nacional, who found a remote and isolated chamber where I could spread materials about at will, flail away at a typewriter, and loudly curse the typing errors sometimes attributable to cold-numbed fingers. Dr. Ramón Bela, executive director of the Fulbright Commission (Commission for Educational Exchange between the United States of America and Spain) did all that I could possibly have expected, and a good deal more, in easing the tasks of investigation.

Gratitude to Miss Matilde Medina y Crespo, then the assistant director of the Fulbright Commission, can never be adequately expressed. Whether the purpose for which I sought assistance involved meeting an intellectual, tracking down a rare book, making travel arrangements, determining where to live and eat, or securing tickets to concerts or bullfights, Matilde's efficiency and resourcefulness were never less than awesome. I often wonder how the children and I would have survived in Spain without her.

Then there was Doña Esperanza Ruiz-Crespo, the señora-viuda de González Ruano, who provided me pleasant office facilities and, far more important, a warm friendship. There was also Encarnación Pachón who proved that Spanish servants today can be just as wise and ingenious as Sancho Panza and also just as free from the groveling demeanor that so many of their class seem to think they must assume—perhaps because they must indeed assume it—in Spanish America.

Even as I began research on this project I was already hoping that if a manuscript resulted it would be subjected to a preliminary reading and appraisal by Arthur P. Whitaker, one of the rare men who is as well versed in and empathetic to the ways, the lore, and the history of Spain as of Spanish America. Such is my respect and admiration for the now legendary Whitaker scholarship that I could not have demurred even if his verdict had been that the manuscript did not warrant publication. To the judgement of no other colleague would I incline to be so submissive. Happily, Arthur returned a favorable critique, together with valuable suggestions that I have attempted to incorporate into this book.

As with several previous publications, I owe a word of thanks to Lewis Hanke. A suitably awed graduate student of his at Columbia University once remarked to me, "Hanke must get up earlier in the morning than the others in this field." Often I have had the same feeling about this amazing person, most recently when he casually brought to my attention some valuable material on hispanismo that had eluded me during a full year of intensive research.

To these and other persons I am vastly indebted. But they have not been able to prevent the errors, weaknesses, and shortcomings of this book, responsibility for all of which I alone must bear.

Fredrick B. Pike

INTRODUCTION: SOME DEFINITIONS AND A DESCRIPTION OF THE SCOPE OF THE STUDY

Hispanismo: A Descriptive Definition

Almost from the time that the Spanish-American republics attained their independence in the 1820s, there has existed a movement known variously as *hispanismo, hispanoamericanismo,* and *panhispanismo*.[1] For the sake of simplicity, this movement is referred to as *hispanismo* throughout the present study.

What is hispanismo? This can best be answered by describing some of the fundamental beliefs of the men who have shaped and guided the movement. Although divided on innumerable matters of detail and even on many issues of fundamental significance, the champions of hispanismo, generally called *hispanoamericanistas* in Spain and *hispanistas* in Spanish America, shared an unassailable faith in the existence of a transatlantic Hispanic family, community, or *raza* (race).

Hispanismo rests on the conviction that through the course of history Spaniards have developed a life style and culture, a set of characteristics, of traditions, and value judgements that render them distinct from all other peoples. Hispanismo rests further on the assumption that Spaniards in discovering and colonizing America transplanted their life style, culture, characteristics, traditions, and values to the New World and then transmitted them to the aborigines whom they encountered there, to the Africans whom they imported, and to the mestizo or mixed blood peoples whom they fathered.

According to hispanoamericanistas, Spaniards (*peninsulares*) and Spanish Americans are members of the same raza, a raza shaped more by common culture, historical experiences, traditions, and language than by blood or ethnic factors. Within the purview of hispanismo, peninsulares and Spanish Americans are further held to be common citizens of a vast spiritual patria made up of all the Spanish-speaking countries of the world. Because of the cultural-spiritual "copenetration"—a favorite word of most hispanoamericanistas—that through the centuries has purportedly taken place between Spain and Spanish America, peninsulares who subscribe to the tenets of hispanismo maintain that they cannot in isolation fully understand or realize themselves. In order to understand themselves as Spaniards they must, they say, study their character as it exists and

1

manifests itself in Spanish Americans; and only in unison with Spanish Americans can they develop the potential of their nature, which clearly reveals certain facets in the New World setting that have only been adumbrated in the peninsula. It follows, in the thinking of hispanoamericanistas, that Spanish Americans cannot aspire fully to understand themselves and to develop the capacities of their nature unless they direct their attention toward Spain and coordinate their efforts and aspirations with those of the peninsulares.

Hispanoamericanistas realize that Spanish Americans have often rejected and bitterly attacked the traditions, culture, and values associated with the madre patria. But they take comfort in the belief that Spanish Americans who appeared to be anti-Spanish were merely exercising the time-honored prerogatives of Spaniards to criticize Spain. Applying this analysis to the Argentine Domingo Faustino Sarmiento, certainly one of the harshest critics of Spain produced in nineteenth-century Spanish America, Spanish classicist Miguel de Unamuno wrote:

> He spoke badly of Spain as a true Spaniard does; he cursed us in the Spanish language and in the Spanish spirit. Thus however much he disliked the fact, there was a deep hispanismo in him. His censure was not of the type made by foreigners who cannot really penetrate into our character or spirit and who cannot fully comprehend our virtues and vices. His censure was that of a man of powerful intelligence who felt in himself what he saw in us and who penetrated with fraternal understanding into our spirit.[2]

Accompanying the belief of hispanoamericanistas in the fundamental unity of character of Spaniards and Spanish Americans was the conviction that Spain had the right to wield spiritual hegemony over the one-time colonies. Peninsulares feared that Spanish Americans, through imitation of alien cultures, especially those of the United States and France, had weakened the genuine and authentic values of the Spanish world and of their own nature. They therefore required the tutelage of Spain, which had remained true to the essential values of "Spanishness." Unless Spanish Americans accepted the spiritual guidance of Spain, they allegedly ran the risk of losing altogether the only culture that was basically in harmony with their character.

A few proponents of hispanismo viewed the movement as a means of achieving spiritual and perhaps even some degree of political and economic unity among the people of Spain, Portugal, Spanish America, and Brazil. Most hispanoamericanistas, however, thought of ties, whether spiritual or political and economic, only between Spain and the Spanish-speaking republics of America. Typically, a Spanish spokesman of hispanismo stated: "the area to which hispanoamericanismo applies, properly speaking, is limited by the language; and although we do not renounce collaboration with Portugal and Brazil, we must recognize that there exists a more intimate bond between Spain and the peoples of America who speak its language."[3] Undoubtedly this widespread viewpoint reflected a recognition that Brazil and Portugal did not want to be included in the "Hispano-American circle but actually felt suspicion and rancor toward Spain."[4] Moreover, most partisans of hispanismo viewed the movement as essentially opposed to Pan-Americanism; and for them the "unwritten alliance" that bound Brazil to Washington-dominated Pan-Americanism automatically excluded the South American giant from their program.

The Time Span of the Study

Throughout most of the nineteenth century, except for the mid- to late 1840s when the United States war against Mexico aroused widespread fear of the Colossus, Spanish Americans worried more over Spanish than Yankee imperialism. They were disturbed by Spanish complicity in schemes of the late 1840s to establish a monarchy in Ecuador; they waxed indignant over Spain's seizure of the Dominican Republic and intervention in Mexico in the early 1860s; and outrage over Spanish occupation of islands off the coast of Peru and the bombardment of Valparaíso and Callao in 1866 brought Hispanophile sentiments to a new pitch of intensity. Moreover, most Spanish Americans objected to the political control that Spain still wielded over Cuba and Puerto Rico; and they sympathized overwhelmingly with the efforts of Cubans to gain their independence. Then came the Spanish-Cuban-American War, and attitudes in the Spanish-speaking republics of the New World changed abruptly.

Stripped of its last colonies in the New World and its military weakness glaringly exposed, Spain no longer loomed as a menace after 1898. From that time on the United States appeared to pose the principal threat to the political sovereignty of Spanish-American republics. A broad spectrum of the press south of the Rio Grande took the war over Cuba as proof of United States desire to interfere in the internal affairs of and even to gain political control over many if not all of the Spanish-American republics. From one end of Spanish America to the other, the warning went out to be on guard against United States imperialism. A close student of these developments has written: "Genuine hispanoamericanismo has as its point of origin the date of 1898. That is the year in which Spain ceases to have a physical, imperial presence in the new world, thereby making possible the strengthening of its spiritual presence. And that is the year in which the naked threat of United States imperialism comes to be seen more clearly than ever before."[5]

A cause largely neglected in the peninsula and frequently reviled in Spanish America, hispanismo in the months immediately following the war over Cuba acquired dozens of enthusiastic new Spanish recruits and even gained a certain modishness among a wide circle of Spanish-American intellectuals and political figures. This is why the year 1898 has been chosen as the beginning point for the study of hispanismo.

A more compelling reason still dictates that this study begin with the end of the nineteenth century, although not necessarily specifically with the year 1898. Virtually all of the peninsula's champions of hispanismo viewed it as a movement aimed at preserving intact the hierarchical, rigidly stratified social order purportedly demanded by the values inherent in Hispanic character and civilization. From the midway point in the nineteenth century, Spaniards, alarmed by signs of revolutionary ferment in their own country, took up the search for new means to safeguard the traditional Iberian social order; and hispanoamericanistas concerned themselves with safeguarding this order not only in the peninsula but in the Spanish-speaking areas of the New World as well. Throughout most of the century Spanish Americans could remain indifferent to the concerns of the peninsulares; for circumstances permitted them to cling to the optimistic belief that in the brave and virtuous New World many of the problems of the Old World, including rancorous class contention, could be avoided altogether. Then, around the turn of the century, signs of a social problem became clearly discernible in much of Spanish America. As a result its leaders began to take some interest in the claims of Spanish statesmen and intellectuals, both conservative and liberal, that they, as the principal heirs and defenders of Iberian values, understood best how to preserve intact the social forms identified with Hispanic nature and civilization. The more apparent the social problem became in Spanish America, the more inclined its directing classes were to investigate the means that Spaniards had for some years been in the process of devising to assure social tranquility and solidarity.

On the whole their cultural heritage rendered Spanish America's directing classes ill-disposed toward liberal, or as it was generally termed, *inorganic* democracy. These classes therefore could scarcely sympathize with the main thrust of turn-of-the-century United States progressivism with its programs for easing the social tensions that had arisen in a democratic setting through the expansion of democratic procedures. The Spanish formulas for avoiding democracy altogether in solving the social problem generally exercised far greater appeal than the models of North American progressivism. Thus the advent of the social problem within their own republics may well have been more crucial than the emergence of United States imperialism in persuading Spanish-American leaders to turn their sympathies away from the Colossus and toward the madre patria.

The logical terminal point for the study is 1936. The civil war that erupted in that year forced Spain to turn its energies inward and to interrupt its consistent efforts of nearly forty years to establish closer ties with Spanish America. Upon the conclusion of the war in 1939, Spain entered into a new era sharply differentiated from that of the late nineteenth and early twentieth centuries. Internal differences within the peninsula were reflected in the post-1939 variety of hispanismo, which even acquired a new name, *hispanidad*. Activists in the hispanidad cause equated Spanishness, the basic set of characteristics, beliefs, values, and attitudes in which all members of the Spanish-speaking world were said to share, with Catholicism and with antiliberal, antidemocratic viewpoints.

Prior to the civil war, hispanoamericanistas had disagreed passionately and profoundly over whether Catholicism was the permanent essence or just a passing accident of authentic Spanishness or whether the two were even basically inharmonious. As a result hispanismo had been characterized more by its divisiveness than its cohesiveness. The degree to which hispanoamericanistas during the 1939–1945 period managed to unify their program around Catholicism, interpreted as a fundamentally antidemocratic faith with an antiliberal social doctrine, gave a new focus to hispanismo. It has not seemed appropriate to extend this study to include hispanismo in its new form of hispanidad. This is a complex topic that could be dealt with adequately only in a separate, book-length study.[6]

Liberals and Conservatives as Rightists

Following the restoration of the monarchy in 1875 at the end of a brief and tumultuous republican period, Spanish politics became a tug of war between liberals and conservatives. For all their bitter differences, however, liberals and conservatives generally found accord in a common devotion to a hierarchically, organically or corporatively structured, stratified, nonopen, nonpluralistic society—the sort of society described by a Spanish nobleman as a "selectrocracy."[7] Because of the similarity of their views on the need for a hierarchical, elitist social structure, liberals and conservatives are often lumped together in this book and referred to as rightists. They stand in contrast to the numerically inconsequential—at least before 1930—leftists who desired fundamental social change, whether in line with the theories of equalitarian democracy, of anarchism, or of Marxian socialism.

Overwhelmingly, Spanish rightists agreed that individualistic, laissez-faire capitalism, especially as practiced within the democratic framework of the United States, would lead ultimately to social upheavals and leveling revolutions. They maintained that a society dominated by huge, aloof, and impersonal corporations reduced the great mass of citizens to anonymous ciphers or atoms. Feeling themselves depersonalized and stripped of individual dignity within this situation, the masses, Spain's rightists argued, would become increasingly alienated from the system that manipulated them and sooner or later strike out blindly against it.

The basic flaw in United States culture, according to this school of thought, lay in its exclusive concern with the material development and progress of the individual and the nation. Only a materialistic society could accept the madness of political democracy based on the concept of one man, one vote. A materialistic society, they explained, was characterized by an exclusive interest in things; and because all men were capable of producing and consuming things—even if not ideas—such a society granted them equal political voice. Within a materialistic society whose hallmark was total indifference to the exalted provinces of the mind and soul, it seemed suitable enough to permit, through the operation of equalitarian democracy, the destruction of the social hierarchies on which depended a hierarchy of values. The products of a materialistic society, Spain's liberals and conservatives charged, did not fret over the fact that when regulated by the half plus one, culture, taste, values, and aesthetic preferences inexorably underwent debasement, plummeting to the level of the lowest common denominator.

Spain's rightists believed that in a society characterized by a mania for material aggrandizement and an indifference to higher human values, the masses would acquire an insatiable appetite for enhancing their physical comfort and multiplying their wealth and possessions. Incapable of experiencing satisfaction regardless of how much they received from society in the way of things, they would eventually destroy society. In the Spanish rightist vision of life, then, capitalism, democracy, and materialism were inseparably linked handmaidens serving, often unwittingly, the cause of social revolution.

Most Spanish rightists concurred in the belief that success in safeguarding the established social order against mounting revolutionary pressures depended upon giving to the masses some "participation"—they used the word again and again—in decision-making processes that vitally affected their immediate interests. How to provide for popular participation in the life of the nation without threatening the final moral, aesthetic, cultural, and political authority of a directing elite was one of the problems that most concerned Spain's rightists. In proposing how to resolve this problem liberals and conservatives consistently disagreed; and this disagreement helped divide Spain into two ideologically distinct camps.

In referring throughout this book to the two Spains, liberal and conservative, I am admittedly distorting and oversimplifying the matter. The two Spains really were not so totally distinct as their respective champions claimed. Moreover, it is probably more accurate to speak about several instead of just two Spains.[8] Still, I suspect that in the course of the period extending roughly between 1808 and the 1920's a significant number of Spanish political and intellectual figures came to believe in the myth-fantasy of the two Spains separated by an unbridgeable ideological chasm. In employing this concept, I am attempting to deal with what Spaniards, seemingly responding to an urge toward national annihilation, came more and more to believe to be true, not necessarily to what was true.

The Two Spains and Hispanismo

Spanish liberals, distinguished by their anticlericalism and confidence in the powers of human reason, had as perhaps their fundamental objective the secularization of society. They insisted, that is, on ending the temporal influence of the Catholic Church. Although they consistently stressed the transcendent importance of spiritual values, they regarded these values as altogether distinct from those of formal, institutionalized Catholicism. Material development when properly conceived and suitably pursued, liberals contended, would not weaken but instead strengthen the spiritual virtues of the populace. On the other hand, most conservatives worried about the adverse effects that material development might produce on Catholicism, which constituted for them the sum and total of all true spiritual values. Conservatives advocated at least some degree of Church influence in temporal society; and a few wished to turn back the secular tide by establishing a virtual theocracy.

Both for liberals and conservatives, hispanismo took as its point of departure the hope to apply to Spanish America the measures deemed essential for preserving social stability and the primacy of spiritual values in Spain. Because liberals and conservatives proposed different measures for providing greater mass participation in society so as to bolster rather than undermine elitist rule and with it the hierarchy of values, they developed two distinct types of hispanismo. In order to understand these two varieties, it is necessary to study liberalism and conservatism as they developed in the Spanish peninsula. Much of the present book, therefore, deals with the two Spains. Specifically, Chapters 4 and 5 deal respectively with conservative and with liberal Spain in the early twentieth century, while Chapter 13 considers the divided Spanish right in the hectic 1930–1936 period. While it might at first appear that such matters have little direct relevance to hispanismo, it is my contention that only against the background of the material discussed in these chapters is it possible to grasp what was involved in the attempt of liberals and conservatives to extend to Spanish America the pet panaceas they had devised for the peninsula.

Hispanismo and Spanish-American Identity

In spite of warnings from both liberal and conservative hispanoamericanistas, many Spanish Americans reacted favorably to the passion for material development and to the democratic ideals associated with the United States. At the same time, however, they remained true, by and large, to the Spanish value system that dictated a hierarchically structured society that would preserve social stratificaton and accord priority status to spiritual and cultural pursuits. Thus Spanish Americans found themselves in an agonizing identity dilemma. They desired to live according to the images they had of two distinct and apparently mutually exclusive cultural worlds. Their difficulties were compounded because their vision both of the United States and of Spain seldom conformed to reality. The United States was neither so exclusively devoted to material progress regardless of consequences nor so thoroughly unconcerned with the preservation of social hierarchies as Spanish Americans often imagined. Nor was Spain so indifferent to material might and development and so steadfastly opposed to social innovation and gradual democratization, defined in accordance with Iberian traditions, as Spanish Americans were wont to assume.

Lured by their vision of the United States, Spanish Americans have frequently adopted democratic procedures. Then, terrified by the likely social consequences, they have acted in accordance with their Spanish, aristocratic, elitist, "selectocratic" norms and aborted the democratic procedures. Spanish Americans have also aspired to duplicate the material development of the United States. At the same time, though, they have not wished to repudiate the Spanish concepts of an aristocratic, gentlemanly society in which social stability is valued above material development and dignity in the face of poverty and adversity more admired than the relentless struggle for affluence. To a considerable degree, despite their rhetoric of economic nationalism, Spanish Americans have allowed foreign, and especially United States, capital to undertake the task of rendering their countries economically productive and modern. They hoped that as a result of this process they could gain at least a façade of material progress and development while avoiding the materialistic, "money-grubbing" qualities believed to account for the physical might of the Colossus. Spanish Americans have desired the end products of both United States and Spanish culture, but they have not been willing to accept the means that are necessary to achieve either of the end products. Therefore they have not developed the character required either to bring about material development or to live with dignity in the face of poverty.

Pan-Americanism and hispanismo have exacerbated the identity problem and the crisis of confidence in Spanish America. Through Pan-Americanism the United States has attempted to attract Spanish Americans to an exclusive emulation of North American life styles and values. And through hispanismo Spaniards have exhorted Spanish Americans to turn to the madre patria for all of their models. What psychological damage must it have had upon Spanish Americans through the years to know that in so many instances even as they are wooed they are at the same time held in contempt and disdain by the United States proponents of Pan-Americanism and the Spanish partisans of hispanismo? Undoubtedly this knowledge has contributed to the pervasive inferiority complex in Spanish America. To some degree Spanish Americans, inclining sometimes toward the United States way of life and at other times toward that of Spain, have tended to accept the view of Yankees and Spaniards that they cannot really measure up in either world. They are haunted by fear that truth may inhere in the common Yankee contention that they are inferior in economic and political affairs and in the Spanish assumption that they are spiritually retarded. Nor is the widely expressed view in which North Americans and Spaniards have concurred through the years that Spanish Americans are racially inferior conducive to the building of confidence in the lands to the south of the Rio Grande. People who believe themselves to be inferior often act as if they were indeed inferior. The inferiority arising from mental attitudes can be just as devastating as that determined by chromosomes.

In order to escape the anguish of their basic identity problem, Spanish Americans have sometimes attempted to reject both the United States and Spain. *Indigenista* movements have often emerged whose leaders insist that the only suitable values and authentic cultural traditions for Indo-America, as they like to call the entire region from Mexico to Tierra del Fuego, are those of the pre-Columbian civilizations. Other Spanish Americans have claimed that their true cultural ties lie not with the United States or Spain, but with France. Still others have insisted that the Spanish Americans are an ethnically new and unique mestizo people, a people in the process of devising an altogether fresh and original culture. Still, however much they have sought to, Spanish Americans have not been able to insulate themselves against the clashing influences of the United States and Spain.

An Invalid and a Valid Claim of Hispanismo

Hispanoamericanists have been arrogantly ethnocentric and thoroughly mistaken in claiming that peninsulares could wield a spiritual hegemony over a united Hispanic patria and raza and devise a nationalism equally serviceable for all countries of the Spanish-speaking world. Understandably, Spanish Americans have insisted upon seeking to emancipate themselves from spiritual and cultural colonialism by devising nationalisms peculiar to their individual republics.

I am persuaded, though, that the peninsulares who guided the hispanismo movement were correct in their claim that Spaniards and Spanish Americans share an imposing body of common values and cultural characteristics. These peninsulares were further correct, it seems to me, in contending as a corollary to this claim that Spaniards could not fully understand themselves unless they studied Spanish America and that Spanish Americans could learn much about themselves by studying Spain. If this is so then even those not of the Hispanic raza, such as this United States historian of Spanish America, should be able to learn a good deal about the Spanish-speaking areas of the New World, and not just their colonial past but their present-moment existence, by studying Spain. This, at least, is the hope that has motivated me in researching and writing my book.

1: THE SPANISH BACKGROUND, 1876–1898

The Politics of the Spanish Restoration

Sixty years of internal divisiveness in Spain, of civil wars and dynastic struggles, of social upheavals and assassinations, of military coups and pronouncements, were capped by yet another revolution in 1868.[1] This was also the year in which the Cubans took to arms in the attempt either to gain sweeping concessions and reforms or outright independence from Spain. Attempts to suppress the Cuban insurrection were seriously handicapped by the disorders that continued in the peninsula in the wake of its new political convulsion.

The principal objective of the leaders of the 1868 revolution in Spain was the ouster of the dissolute queen, Isabella II. Her promptly decreed exile, however, failed to produce the stability for which Spaniards longed. Nor did the importation of foreign royalty yield the desired results. Amadeo of Savoy was lured from Italy to try his hand at exercising the prerogatives of the king of Spain, considerably reduced by the 1869 constitution. But he soon recognized the hopelessness of the venture and retired from the scene, whereupon the first Spanish republic was proclaimed in 1873.

The republic was a fiasco. On this the overwhelming majority of Spanish writers agree, however much they differ on the reasons for the republic's failure.[2] By December of 1875, although little genuine public enthusiasm existed for a return to the monarchical form of government, there was general recognition that republican leadership was incapable of stemming the chaos then gripping Spain. Filled with misgivings and avid only in the desire for peace, Spaniards at the end of 1875 called for the restoration of the Bourbon monarchy under Alfonso XII, son of the recently deposed Isabella II. Indicating just what it was they expected of him, they referred to Alfonso as the pacifier.

The ground rules of restoration were provided by the 1876 constitution, the sixth in a century. This charter was essentially the work of the leading political figure of the day, Antonio Cánovas del Castillo.[3] Born in Málaga in 1828, Cánovas was an amateur historian of some eminence and a writer on social and political issues capable of achieving at least fleeting profundity.[4] As a practical politician who was the preeminent figure in implementing the constitution that he had largely devised, Cánovas "helped provide Spain with a truce among the warring factions that had struggled, particularly after 1808, for political supremacy."[5]

10

If Spaniards were temporarily too worn out to fight for their ideals, and if they found the political system of the restoration at least sufficiently endurable so that they did not feel constrained to dismantle it through violence, they remained, predictably enough, divided in their political ideology. This was clearly demonstrated when various members of the Madrid Ateneo in 1881 and 1882 conducted a spirited debate on democracy and its applicability to Spain.[6] The debate showed that Ateneo membership was divided essentially into three groups, each with important subdivisions. One of the three major groups was made up of Catholic conservatives who were promonarchical and antidemocratic, who proclaimed monarchism to be absolutely incompatible with democracy, and who at the same time expressed admiration for liberty, as defined and understood by the Catholic Church.[7] A second group consisted of republicans thoroughly committed to a type of democracy that they felt to be basically incompatible with monarchy. Finally, there was a group of democratic monarchists. Members of the first group, the Catholic conservatives, appeared to be nearly unanimous in their support of local autonomy and decentralization; but the other two groups were sorely divided over the federalist-centralist issue.

The major accomplishment of Cánovas del Castillo was to fashion a system within which the majority of politically articulate Spaniards, however divided on ideological points, were willing to cooperate in directing affairs of state. The instrument of compromise upon which this system rested had been ingeniously devised by Cánovas. Its essential feature was the alternate wielding of political power by the tamely liberal, staunchly monarchical Fusionist-Liberal Party and the moderately conservative Liberal-Conservative Party headed by Cánovas himself. Cánovas resorted to this procedure, the *turno pacífico*, by permitting the Fusionist Liberals to come to power first in 1881 and then again in 1885 when the death of Alfonso XII initiated the regency of María Cristina that endured seventeen years until Alfonso XIII came of age. In the 1890s the rate at which the two parties alternated increased markedly.

By this time the more flexible and conciliatory Spanish Liberals had accepted the leadership of Práxedes Mateo Sagasta (1825–1903), a shrewd and pragmatic politician from the northern province of Logroño.[8] Upon coming to power for the second time as president of the council of ministers in 1885, Sagasta had vowed to introduce civil matrimony, the jury system, and electoral reform based on universal manhood suffrage. When he relinquished power five years later as the Cánovas-led Conservatives returned to control of the government, Sagasta had accomplished these objectives.

Of all the Liberal innovations, undoubtedly it was universal suffrage that was most obnoxious to the majority of Conservatives.[9] As early as 1871 Cánovas del Castillo, in a congressional discourse, had warned:

When the intelligent minorities, which will always be the property-owning elite, find it impossible to maintain an equality of rights with the multitude; when they see the multitudes utilize the political rights that have been given them so as to exercise a tyrannical sovereignty . . . they will seek from whatever source a dictatorship. And they will find it. Such is the eternal history of the world.[10]

In the 1880s Cánovas no longer foresaw dictatorship as the immediate consequence of the leveling movement that he feared would proceed from universal suffrage. Instead, he predicted that the direct and inevitable consequence of the Liberal folly would be something far worse: socialism.[11]

Once back in power in 1890, Cánovas found it reassuringly easy to curb the dangers of universal suffrage through shrewd manipulation and outright fraud and corruption. Curbing the mounting opposition within his own party, however, proved more difficult.

Although he held an important cabinet post in the Conservative government of 1890, Francisco Silvela (1845–1905) was growing ever more discontent with the leadership of Cánovas. Born and raised in Madrid and appointed to his first cabinet post in 1879, Silvela did not seem the type to present a serious challenge to the leading political figure of the restoration. A serious, academic type and something of a recluse, Silvela was more at home in the libraries of Spain, pouring over seventeenth-century documents,[12] than in the halls of congress and the offices of cabinet ministers. Cánovas del Castillo, moreover, had shown considerable understanding of Silvela's character when he stated: "I know of few men who have such weak will power. Whenever an obstacle appears in his road, he is dismayed and abandons the whole enterprise."[13]

Despite his lack of appetite for sustained political struggle, Silvela had by 1892 become the leader of a serious opposition movement to Cánovas within the Conservative Party (officially, the Liberal-Conservative Party). Silvela felt that without a strong, vital conservative party, the Spanish monarchy itself was in danger, and he worried that Cánovas del Castillo had fallen behind the times and was weakening his party by failing to establish communication with the increasingly restless masses. Feeling that government had to win the commitment of previously ignored groups, Silvela desired sweeping political reform that would begin with the establishment of local autonomy.[14]

Serious political divisions were by no means confined to the Conservative Party. Liberals were torn by the old centralism-federalism debate and by the newer issue of state intervention vs. laissez-faire. The far right of the Spanish political spectrum was also divided, for the Catholic conservative Integristas had separated from the Catholic conservative Carlists over a dynastic issue.[15]

The spring, 1898 elections to the chamber of deputies bore striking testimony to the political divisiveness of Spain. The largest bloc of votes went to the followers of Sagasta, 209 of whom were elected to deputy posts, while only sixty-five Cánovas partisans gained office. In addition, five splinter groups, from both the Liberal and the Liberal-Conservative parties, elected 153 deputies. Six Carlists and twelve Independents were also elected.[16]

By 1898, then, the diversity of its composition tended to impede decisive action by the chamber of deputies. Nor was the makeup of the upper chamber conducive to a concerted approach to the tasks of government. One half of the senators were elected by the major taxpayers and various corporative bodies, including the universities, several academies, and the Church, as well as by certain entities representing industrial, agricultural, and commercial interests. The other half of the upper chamber was formed by lifetime senators appointed by the crown and "senators in their own right," that is ex officio members who included some of the grandees.

Despite many readily apparent difficulties, the politics of the restoration, in outer appearances at least, represented a decided improvement over the earlier part of the nineteenth century. Once the 1878 Treaty of Zanjón ended the ten-year Cuban war, Spain enjoyed an unusual period of peace that endured for fifteen years. And the 1888 Universal Exposition celebrated in Barcelona bore striking witness to that city's industrial progress. It is little wonder that in the period between 1876 and 1893 Spaniards, delighted by the emergence of the much-desired peace, "allowed themselves to believe that the fundamental problems that had brought nearly uninterrupted violence and chaos to the nineteenth century had at last been resolved."[17]

Optimism was rudely shattered by an incident in Melilla that resulted in another African war for Spain. The new African adventure rekindled militarism, disrupted the budget, and increased the frequency of political crises. In the six-year period between 1893 and 1899, four different parliaments governed Spain as Liberal and Liberal-Conservative cabinets succeeded each other with confusing rapidity. In the midst of this period, taking advantage of peninsular instability and preoccupation with Africa, the Cubans and Filipinos launched new insurrections against the motherland.[18]

In an appraisal written in 1945, Pedro Laín Entralgo, a penetrating essayist who has published what is probably the best study of Spain's so-called Generation of '98, points to some of the fundamental weaknesses of the restoration that existed undetected or ignored even during the years between 1876 and 1893. "Beneath the happy surface," Laín writes, "Spain was a body without historical and social consistency. The unity of its members was more fictitious than real. Beneath the surface a real schism between Spaniards was taking place."[19] A principal reason for this schism, Laín contends, was that a governing elite denied the masses any sense of participation in shaping their own and the nation's destinies.

Caciquismo: *the Politics of Nonparticipation*

By the end of the nineteenth century, it had become a commonplace that *caciquismo*, a system of bossism, had been invented by a selfish Spanish oligarchy as a means of furthering its interests and removing the potential dangers from universal suffrage.[20] Bossism, however, was no recent invention in Spain, and its utilization after the law of universal suffrage was simply an adaptation of a time-honored system.

Joaquín Costa (1846–1911), one of the most influential social and political critics Spain has produced in modern times, has been claimed as the spiritual father of virtually every twentieth-century Spanish reform movement. Here is how Costa, writing in 1901, described early and mid-nineteenth-century caciquismo:

> Each region and each province found itself dominated by a certain irresponsible person, sometimes a deputy, sometimes not, vulgarly called a cacique, without whose will or blessing not a sheet of paper was moved, not an order dispatched, nor a judge named, nor a bureaucrat transferred, nor a work undertaken. . . . It was not necessary to ask if you were right, if the law was on your side, in order to know how a legal suit would be judged. . . . It was only necessary to ask if the cacique was . . . with us or against us. When he so desired, a person was declared exempt from military service, with or without making a payment. . . . Justice was administered when he was interested, and if he was not so interested, the law was dispensed with. . . . He would impose fines if it suited his will, whether there was motive or not; he distributed the tax burden not according to the instructions of the treasury . . . but conforming to his own convenience and that of his clients.[21]

The system described by Costa remained essentially intact after the Sagasta-led Liberals succeeded in enacting the law of universal suffrage. The only difference was that the caciques now garnered an additional function, that of organizing at election time a majority for the party then in office. Thus, "the nation continued living without laws, without guarantees, without courts, subject to the same degrading yoke of that nonorganic feudalism that maintained Spain separate from Europe. . . ."[22]

Once Spain had adopted a parliamentary regime based ostensibly on universal suffrage but actually on caciquismo, the political system functioned somewhat along the following lines. The head of the then governing party (the president of the council of ministers) and his minister of interior (*gobernación*) would confer with the opposition and reach a bargain as to the number of deputies that each party would have in the about-to-be elected parliament or Cortes. Once the bargain had been struck, the minister of interior would get in touch with the centrally appointed provincial governors, who would then contact the provincial and local caciques who would see to it that the proper ballot returns were forth-coming when the elections were held. Upon the cacique's ability to deliver the expected vote depended his exercise of a free hand in governing his particular territory.[23]

An astute, turn-of-the-century political observer described the Spanish political system in these terms:

> The cacique cannot prescind from the political parties and the political parties cannot get along without the caciques. Because of the dependence of the parties on the cacique, it is the caciques who run the country as it suits them. From the business that represents millions of pesetas down to the most insignificant matter of some humble town; from the bishop of a diocese down to the least municipal court; from the presidency of the most respectable tribunals down to the most humble doorman, everything is at the disposition of the caciques, who are, more than the ministers and congressmen, those who govern the nation.[24]

Within the system of caciquismo a strictly hierarchical order was maintained. A handful of supreme caciques, holding high positions and enjoying constant access to the royal court, held sway over the second grade functionaries whose jurisdiction extended over a province. The second grade, provincial caciques in turn exercised loose supervision over local caciques who controlled cities and villages. Provincial caciques often enjoyed sufficient power to determine who would be governors, judges, and mayors within their territory; and local caciques were sometimes capable of subjecting their jurisdictions to such despotic control that, as one writer described the situation, "not a leaf on a tree moves against their will."[25]

Turn-of-the-century critics of caciquismo never tired of charging the system with delivering governmental administration to the most ignorant, corrupt, lazy, and cowardly, with guaranteeing the perpetual triumph of personalities over social institutions, of the inferior over the superior.[26] And they agreed that profound and drastic remedies were required to cure the ills of caciquismo. One author went so far as to declare that the only way to do away with caciquismo was to enact a law stating: "A murderer will be declared free from all punishment whenever at least one half plus one of the citizens of the municipality in whose area the deed occurred affirm before the local tribunal that the victim was a cacique."[27]

The critics of caciquismo often exaggerated the evils of the system. Able, efficient, and honest men could find their way into positions of authority in restoration Spain. Moreover, in one of the most balanced appraisals of the system, conservative statesman Pedro Sáinz Rodríguez, writing in 1928, found an important positive element in caciquismo. Between 1808 and 1876, according to Sáinz Rodríguez, politics had been largely under the control of generals and thus determined by military pronouncements. In order to transfer some power into civilian hands, it had been necessary to turn to the cacique, because he was the only available civilian figure that could be utilized in the quest to curb militarism.[28]

If caciquismo for a time produced at least the side effect of challenging unbridled militarism, it did so at the expense of two traditional civilian political institutions, the crown and parliament. The Cánovas del Castillo-devised system of alternating political parties, intended as the main prop of the restored monarchy, in the long run served only to undermine the monarchical institution. As early as 1901 Joaquín Costa recognized this when he noted that caciquismo had absorbed the functions of monarchy and preempted the royal prerogatives. "Now we no longer have an organic balanced system with the crown exercising the moderating power," Costa complained. "All is in the hands of the caciques."[29] Monarchy in the restoration structure as fashioned by Cánovas del Castillo indeed depended upon caciquismo. And as caciquismo came increasingly to be discredited, the less secure was monarchical legitimacy.

Abuses of caciquismo also undermined the legitimacy of parliament. Because parliamentary elections rested ultimately upon the fraud, manipulation, and corruption of caciquismo, Miguel de Unamuno (1864–1936), Spain's great humanist philosopher and classicist, exaggerated only slightly when he declared: "Our parliament is the cathedral of the lie."[30] Marcelino Menéndez Pelayo (1856–1912), the outstanding defender of Catholic traditionalism, was in accord, describing parliamentarism as a "farce as laughable as it is expensive."[31] In 1892 a Spanish sociologist provided a fair echo of public opinion when he wrote that his country's parliamentary system had falsified representative government and "converted it into a shameful market."[32]

When introduced in the nineteenth century, Spanish parliamentarism had lacked the essential foundation of an educated populace, liberated to some degree from a stifling paternalism and living in an environment that permitted the development of civic virtue and the acquisition of expertise in protecting individual and group rights. Because no genuine, authentic foundation for parliamentarism existed, that system came inevitably to rest on caciquismo. Rather than helping to prepare a genuine foundation for parliamentarism, caciquismo served only to divide Spain into a tiny governing group, accountable only to its own members, and a vast non-participating mass that, if at first simply bored with and indifferent to political processes, came to be increasingly hostile to the established order as economic conditions deteriorated.

Whatever their particular political ideology, nearly all reputable and discerning observers of the late nineteenth-century political-social scene were alarmed over the degree to which the prevailing system had separated the ruling elite from the masses, denying any active participation in affairs of state to the overwhelming majority of Spaniards. Eduardo Sanz y Escartín (1855–1938), a political conservative and a devout Catholic, argued that civilization is always advanced by a small group at the top of society that gradually begins to share its new cultural and material accomplishments with the populace as a whole. In the Spain of 1890, Sanz complained, the superior classes were refusing to share their culture, their advances, their ideals with the masses below. No channels of communication between the two Spains existed and the lower classes, denied all sense of participation in the system presided over by the elite, would soon pose a serious menace to that system.[33]

The politically liberal and religiously somewhat irreverent Ricardo Macías Picavea (1847–1899)[34] lamented that incipient democracy and capitalism, vitiated in Spain by caciquismo, were robbing the humbler citizens of all personality and character, reducing them to mere numbers and depriving them of any important, self-realizing role in society. As a result, an overly centralized state that sought to control all from above was cutting itself off from the push and dynamism that the masses could provide if allowed to participate in affairs of the province or local region.[35] Universal suffrage as it has functioned in Spain, Macías stated, "has only served to make the masses indifferent and even hostile to all political processes. . . ."[36]

In a similar vein Segismundo Moret (1838–1913), a leading intellectual and political director of the Liberal Party, complained in 1883 that the civil governors and centrally appointed politicians had no interest in penetrating into the lives of the people and seeking to understand their manner of being, their aspirations and needs. "Because of this," Moret wrote, "I see something that terrifies me in Spanish political life; it is the general indifference of all people."[37]

At about the same time Rafael María de Labra (1841–1918), a moderate republican of decidedly liberal persuasions, observed that Spain had been at its best in 1808 when the country to a man had arisen against the French armies that were trying to establish the monarchy of Joseph Bonaparte. At that time, each Spaniard had had a role to play and a true patria had existed. Since then Spanish citizens had gradually lost a sense of identification with national interests. As a result, Labra complained, Spain was ceasing to exist as a genuine nation; for "when a country is such that some smoke and others spit, you cannot ask those in the second category for greater effort. . . . Such people will not live with all their energy and there will never be achieved a sense of the patria."[38]

To caciquismo, which reduced the citizenry to inert masses that were manipulated and deceived rather than inspired and uplifted, Labra also attributed the blame for the lack of a great national ideal that could excite the enthusiasm of a united nation.[39] Julio Puyol, born in León in 1865 and a lifetime champion of social reform, agreed with Labra. In 1892 he complained about the lack of energetic associations in Spain and the absence of common goals among the populace. "We have less enthusiasm than our fathers and do not want to emerge from inertia. There are no longer present those ideas that in earlier times had the blessed virtue of uniting consciences, of joining consciences and wills, of infusing into souls sympathy for and love of neighbor." According to Puyol, this lack of great, animating ideals was due, at least in part, to caciquismo. The natural leaders of Spain, the men who could be expected to intuit the destiny of the nation and to visualize great national objectives, were cut off from genuine contact with the people by an intermediary horde of mediocre functionaries, the caciques.[40]

Spanish writers of the late nineteenth century generally avoided the attempt to formulate the great national ideals that they agreed were essential for the country's resurgence. On the whole, they confined themselves to drawing attention to the shortcomings of contemporary Spanish life. The case against Spain was well summarized by Francisco Andrés Oliván, a man who since 1847 had devoted most of his life to travel because he found nothing right in his native country. Writing in 1897, Oliván stated that owing to the evils of caciquismo, for which he held Cánovas del Castillo and Sagasta equally culpable, Spain

> had not known how to establish universal military service, for the exceptions are notorious; nor to establish obligatory primary instruction so as to discover the treasures of superior intelligences that remain untapped; nor to establish an effective tax-gathering system; nor to establish a system of irrigation; nor to give impulse to mining; nor to subsidize steamship companies to carry Spanish products to foreign ports; nor to suppress public begging; nor to concern itself with the hygiene of the people so as to raise the life expectancy beyond its present average of thirty-two years and four months; nor to educate the people in practical politics so that by knowing their duties and rights they could bring bad government to account and rid themselves of cacique rule.[41]

Economic and Social Conditions

Spain's political problems were matched by its economic difficulties.[42] For one thing, circumstances forced frequent alterations in the backing of paper money; and this resulted in monetary uncertainty and rapid fluctuations in the value of the peseta.

In the throes of a persistent and prolonged depression and unable to finance gold imports, Spain in 1873 suspended the coinage of gold, going on a de facto silver standard. As a consequence, the amount of paper money issued in 1874 was only 24.5 million pesetas, in comparison with 106.9 million in 1867.[43] Prices fell sharply and not until 1876 did the country begin to show signs of emerging from the depression. In that year Spain reverted to bimetalism; but two years later it was forced to suspend the coinage of silver because of that metal's declining value on the international market. The next year (1879), however, faced with difficulty in obtaining gold to coin because of chronic balance of payments deficits, the treasury resumed the limited minting of silver.

Between 1867 and 1876 Spain enjoyed a favorable balance of payments only in one year: 1873. During this period, moreover, the foreign debt increased from 1,025 million to 4,379 million pesetas.[44] This situation forced Spain to ship gold abroad to meet its deficits. Gold reserves, amounting to 127 million pesetas in 1881, had declined to 36 million in 1883. In that year the government abandoned the redemption of paper money in gold.

Confronted with its balance of payments problem, Spain found it necessary to attract foreign capital in order to have the means for importing gold. Foreign capital inflow, however, came to an abrupt end owing to a depression that began in France in 1882 and soon extended throughout Europe and America. The outflow of gold increased markedly and by 1890 Spain was virtually without this metal. With little if any gold being coined and with a paper money regime essentially in effect, the peseta fluctuated sharply in the 1890s: in 1890, for example, its exchange rate with the United States dollar was approximately 5.2:1, while in 1898 it had declined to 7.8:1.[45]

Internal inflation accompanied these developments as the Bank of Spain, since 1874 the only agency permitted to issue money,[46] emitted more and more paper. Between 1892 and 1901, paper money in circulation nearly doubled, rising from 884.1 million to 1,638 million pesetas. The inflationary process was also fed by the mounting expenses occasioned by the Cuban insurrection that began in 1895. Within two years, the overseas ministry (ministerio de ultramar) had been forced to borrow 397 million pesetas from the Bank of Spain.

Foreign trade deficits compounded the country's monetary problems. In the eighties, only two years, 1888 and 1889, produced small export balances. In the nineties, the total deficit came to 325 million pesetas, with favorable balances recorded only in 1896, 1897, and 1898.[47] This created serious difficulties in meeting the foreign debt and interest payments on foreign capital investments. Between 1890 and 1901 these debt amortization and interest payments came to some 1,000 million pesetas. Had it not been for the approximately 1,000 million pesetas remitted during the same period by Spanish emigrants, living principally in Spanish America, Spain's monetary situation would have been well-nigh hopeless.

Until the early 1880s, the investment of foreign capital, particularly English, French, German, and Belgian, had seemed the economic way out for Spain. It is conservatively estimated that by 1880 foreign capital amounting to 2,000 million pesetas had been invested in Spanish railroads and mines.[48] Although this source of capital input had run dry, Spanish writers began in the 1890s to raise the cry of economic nationalism and to complain about the drain on the economy produced by profits remittances. Thus Ramón Nocedal (1844–1907), the leading voice of the conservative, staunchly Catholic Integristas,[49] denied that Spain's economic problems stemmed from an unfavorable trade balance. The real difficulty, as Nocedal saw it, was that payments for what Spain did export went largely into the hands of the foreign owners of mines and industries.[50] The liberally inclined Julio Puyol concurred. Although Spain appeared to be a richly endowed country, he wrote, its economy was in the hands of foreigners:

> The best sherry lables are controlled by the English; the best mines belong to the Germans, the English, French, and Belgians. Our best fruit from Valencia and Murcia is consumed in other countries. Almost our entire meat production in Galicia is monopolized by the English; our railroad lines are in French hands. The more important credit organizations are not Spanish; similarly, the greater amount of factories do not belong to us.[51]

In the 1890s, however, national capital became increasingly active in the two main industrial centers of Spain: Bilbao and the Basque regions with their mining, metallurgical, maritime, transportation, and banking enterprises; and Barcelona and the surrounding Cataluña areas with their textile plants and diversified light industries. Spanish capitalists productively invested a large part of the paper money generously emitted by the Bank of Spain in industrial pursuits. Furthermore, Cánovas del Castillo and the Liberal-Conservative Party were converted to protectionism in 1891. As a result a new tariff, the rates of which went into effect in 1892, accorded significant protection to a wide variety of Spanish industrial concerns. The combination of paper money and protectionism produced happy results for the Spanish economy. The rhythm of investments and the level of employment remained fairly constant.[52] Although the annual percentage of industrial growth was less in the 1890s than it had been in the halcyon days of foreign investment, it was nonetheless significant; and this time the gains that it represented for the economy remained more consistently in Spanish hands.

At best, however, the Spanish economic situation was spotty. In writing one of the classic studies of the ills of Spain Ricardo Macías Picavea in 1899, with some justification, described the economy in the following terms: "poverty, lack and want, small profits, lack of savings, technological barbarism, unexploited natural resources, flight of the population from liberal or productive professions to services and bureaucracy."[53] In commenting on the rural poverty of Spain, Macías Picavea singled out the credit system for particular censure. "There is no agricultural capital," he stated; "there is no such thing as credit; there is only usury."[54] Ángel Ganivet (1862–1898), whose *Idearium español* was one of the most influential books of the period, corroborated this testimony. The Spanish credit system, he wrote, particularly in rural regions, "is organized on the basis of guerrillas; and it is the small money lenders who are the worst guerrillas."[55]

Usury and lack of adequate credit facilities were, of course, only aspects of the Spanish agrarian problem.[56] The fact was that a large majority of the rural masses lived in misery; and this misery meant that the democratic system and universal suffrage could be nothing more "than a hypocritical, deceiving façade."[57] This misery also prevented significant industrial development and stood as one glaring manifestation of a phenomenon that was beginning to alarm thoughtful Spaniards: the social problem.

One of the earliest voices to warn of an impending social crisis in Spain was that of Juan Donoso Cortés (1809–1853),[58] a volatile Andalusian intellectual. Described as incapable of understanding that in order to love God it was not necessary to hate and depreciate one's neighbors and fellow human beings,[59] Donoso had as a young man been a defender of liberal ideology. By 1848, however, he had become a staunch Catholic reactionary. When he arrived the following year in Berlin as his country's minister plenipotentiary, he had felt stifled by the Protestant environment, and he could not understand why his efforts to unite Russia, Prussia, and Austria in an antirevolutionary bloc dedicated to protecting the papacy aroused little sympathy among German Protestants.[60] In addition to Protestants, Donoso disliked the Jews and Poles whom he encountered in Germany. To the alleged demagogic activities of these two groups Donoso attributed much of the social ferment in Germany.

By the time of his death in 1853, Donoso Cortés was predicting the coming confrontation between atheistic socialism, representing the forces of social leveling, and Catholicism, standing for social stratification, hierarchy, and order.[61]

Addressing the chamber of deputies ten years after the death of Donoso Cortés, Antonio Aparisi y Guajarro (1815–1872), a spokesman of conservative Catholicism and a Thomistic philosopher, also warned about a coming social upheaval. Already, he stated, one could hear the hoofbeats of the galloping horse of Attila. "The spirit of revolution, anarchy, and chaos is mounting," he concluded, and one would have to be blind not to recognize the fact.[62]

The Real Academia de Ciencias Morales y Políticas devoted its 1885–86 sessions to a study of the social problem, hoping to alert the governing classes to its danger.[63] The Marqués de Corvera delivered the inaugural address in this series of conferences. In it the then minister of development (fomento) warned about the dreadful perils of class antagonism generated by the social problem. He referred ominously to the revolutionary doctrines afoot, doctrines that "always deserve the anathemas of men of enlightened judgement and sound heart, terrible doctrines that seek to reform society with the furor of revolution."[64]

Given the predominant climate of opinion, these warnings fell largely on deaf ears. A steady economic liberalism prevailed in the early years of the restoration period, a belief that government could not interfere with the sanctity of property by tampering with the socioeconomic order. There was little idea of the common good, of the social duty of property, and thus statesmen sought to ignore the social problem.[65]

In a predictable reaction to this situation, the resistance societies of Spanish workers, formed after the suppression of the guilds in 1836, began slowly to acquire a revolutionary tone.[66] They turned also to foreign sources of ideas and support in their struggle to improve the conditions of life.

As early as 1870 socialism had appeared as a political force, based initially in Zaragoza. In 1873 the International claimed 300,000 members in Spain. However, the majority of Spanish socialists, whose main strength came to center in Madrid, Andalusia, Asturias, and Cataluña, followed the leadership of Pablo Iglesias and rejected Marx and the International in favor of Bakunin.

In 1882 a Barcelona labor congress established the Asociación Nacional de Trabajadores de España. The Association lasted only a year, but in 1888 another national labor congress convened in Barcelona and established the long-enduring Unión General de Trabajadores, the UGT. Two years later various socialist groups introduced the celebration of May Day in Spain.[67]

At about the same time that socialism was establishing itself among labor elements, anarchism appeared on the scene. An 1881 anarchist congress celebrated in Barcelona founded the Federación Regional Obrera, a forerunner of the major anarchist organization that came into being in 1908, the Confederación Nacional del Trabajo or CNT. From the outset, Spanish anarchism found its principal support in Andalusia and Cataluña.[68]

In 1892 a conservative journal complained that strikes had become the great social sickness of Spain. The remedy, declared the editorial writer, was as yet unknown. Until it was discovered, all the government could do was combat the symptoms: if the sick person asked for something that could not harm him, it should be given him; if he sought absurdities, he should be denied them. Meantime, law and order had to be scrupulously enforced so as to end violence on the streets.[69]

Watchful waiting and stricter enforcement of the law did not strike Liberal-Conservative Party leader Cánovas del Castillo as an adequate response to the social problem. In the 1870s, it is true, he had thought little could be done to resolve the social problem other than to imbue the poor with the "consoling knowledge that this world is not one of absolute justice or equality, but rather one of imperfection, because suffering prepares one and tests one either for eternal salvation or perdition."[70] The Cánovas of the 1890s,[71] having come to accept the need for a protectionist policy, also began to advocate state intervention to ameliorate the social problem. Therefore in 1893 he introduced, unsuccessfully as it developed, legislation to control conditions of child and woman labor.[72]

Other Spaniards, among them progressive-minded republican Rafael María de Labra, saw education as the means of resolving the social problem. According to Labra, education could provide the working classes with a proper set of values in life, eliminate their false, revolutionary orientation, and at the same time impart vocational skills. Also persuaded of the social utility of education, a large group of private business, commercial, and academic associations sponsored the 1890 Madrid Congreso de Sociedades de Educación Popular y Mejoramiento Social. Delegates discussed the contributions that private organizations could make toward easing the social problem by supporting popular education and establishing fraternal contact with workers.[73]

Popular education was a largely unexplored possibility at this time and it is understandable that many Spaniards regarded it as the logical point of departure in seeking solutions to the social problem. In Spain of the mid-nineties, nearly 70 percent of the close to eighteen million population—up from twelve million in 1837—was illiterate.[74] While 1,104,779 children in the five-to-twelve age group were officially inscribed in schools —many of those inscribed did not actually attend classes—2,438,816 were not enrolled. Many school buildings were dilapidated hovels and perhaps as many as one-third of the public primary school instructors lacked the legally required teaching certificate.[75] For the 1897–98 fiscal year, the combined municipal, provincial, and national budget for public primary instruction was only 26.67 million pesetas. Teachers in the public school system almost never received as much as one thousand pesetas a year and in many instances their salaries were long in arears.[76]

Joaquín Costa, he who eloquently exposed the evils of caciquismo, was perhaps the leading critic of contemporary Spain who advocated education as a means of resolving the social problem. But government education projects were expensive and Costa saw little likelihood that Spain would begin to carry them out unless it vastly curtailed its military expenditures. Therefore Costa and his associates in the Cámara Agrícola de Alto Aragón, which he helped organize in 1892, were among the sharpest critics of Spain's military operations in Africa.[77]

The Catholic Reception of "Rerum Novarum"

Unlike Costa, who was generally allied with liberal and republican groups, many traditionalist Catholics tended to think that no amount of money could remedy the social problem. They turned their attention to spiritual solutions[78] and in 1891 they found their program of action in Pope Leo XIII's social encyclical *Rerum Novarum*.

Catholic traditionalists such as Juan Manuel Ortí y Lara (1836–1904),[79] the Thomistic metaphysician at the University of Madrid, Rafael Rodríguez de Cepeda (1850–1918) of the University of Valencia,[80] and Juan Vázquez de Mella (1861–1928), the principal parliamentary spokesman of Carlism,[81] greeted Rerum Novarum as a vindication of the social position they and their associates had been defending for years.[82] Ramón Nocedal of the Integristas, he who had raised the banner of economic nationalism, also hailed the encyclical and demanded that the Liberal-Conservative Party, which he regarded as tainted by secularism, make clear its views on the document. Francisco Silvela replied that Rerum Novarum would guide his party in its program of social legislation[83] and Cánovas del Castillo accorded unstinting praise to the encyclical. Such Catholic intellectuals as Eduardo Sanz y Escartín, who believed that "misery and injustices will always exist on earth,"[84] and the Jesuit Antonio Vicent (1837–1902), who would soon gain distinction as a founder of Church-dominated labor organizations, quickly published books intended to apply the teachings of Rerum Novarum to the social problem as it existed in Spain.[85] Even Gumersindo de Azcárate (1840–1917), an eminent spokesman of anticlerical republicanism, spoke with warm respect of Rerum Novarum, although contending that some of its passages were vague.[86] Finally, enthusiasm over the encyclical gave rise to the famous 1894 workers' pilgrimage to Rome, bringing some 18,000 Spanish laborers to the Eternal City.

Catholics in Spain liked to contend that Rerum Novarum was peculiarly Spanish in content and that its true spiritual father and intellectual precursor was the Catalan Jesuit Jaime Balmes (1810–1848).[87] As early as the 1840's Balmes had pointed to the intensifying social problem, had lamented the suppression of the guilds and the excessive concentration of wealth. He had also criticized classical liberal economic procedures which reduced man to a machine and converted labor into a commodity. Although defending the right of private property, Balmes had drawn attention to its social function. And he had attacked emerging masters of capital as a new species of grandees, more predatory than those of the bygone feudal era. To most Spanish Catholic intellectuals it was clear that Leo XIII had read and been influenced by the works of Balmes.[88]

Spanish Catholics in general applauded the appearance of Rerum Novarum[89] because they understood it for what it was: a thoroughly conservative social pronouncement. In Leo XIII's advocacy of the corporative organization of society, Spanish traditionalists saw a plea for the restoration of the guild system. Among those who were socially conservative in mid- to late nineteenth-century Spain, a category that included in addition to Catholic traditionalists many if not most political liberals, the guild system was regarded as a means of keeping workers securely in their proper place in a hierarchically organized, stratified society. Men of this persuasion believed that the atomized society of individualistic liberalism had removed the restraints and pressures that had kept workers contentedly functioning within their organic associations or corporations. This had, in their view, resulted in the substitution of social competition and flux for solidarity and stability, thereby creating the social problem.[90]

A restored guild system was envisioned as providing opportunity for the participation of workers in directing the affairs of their respective corporations. And this is what the conservative defenders of the guild system understood by "true democracy." Workers, in a true democracy, should have some voice in controlling those affairs that were most immediate and comprehensible to them. Once granted this type of participation, they would cease to demand a share in directing those distant and elevated matters of national administration that they could never be expected to understand.[91]

Long-held views on the need to limit the powers of an all-absorbing government also led Catholic traditionalists to welcome *Rerum Novarum*. To the increasing government intervention that had gradually eroded the control the Church had once exercised over guilds, traditionalists attributed the lamentable collapse of the old corporative system in Spain. If guilds were to be successfully revived, it would have to be under the auspices and control of the Church. In this way the role of the central government, all too often tainted by liberal and secular errors, would be circumscribed. In *Rerum Novarum*'s appeal for the creation of Catholic worker organizations, Catholic traditionalists in Spain professed to find support for their program.[92]

Among Spanish Catholics there existed a traditional antipathy toward capitalism. Capitalism was associated with liberalism, which in turn was associated with the Protestant heresy. Spanish Catholics saw economic liberalism and capitalism as generating a movement of social leveling[93] and as releasing a "flood that was inundating all of Europe, while the only ark of Noah was Catholic traditionalism."[94] Men of this viewpoint were prepared to rejoice at those passages in *Rerum Novarum* that attributed the social problem in large part to the functioning of individualistic, liberal capitalism. And because Donoso Cortés in the early 1850s had attacked liberal capitalism and blamed it for the social problem and the appearance of socialism, he was hailed in the Spain of the 1890s, along with Balmes, as an important precursor of Leo XIII.[95]

Finally, and most important of all, Catholic traditionalists, with their die-hard opposition to all manifestations of the secular society, hailed *Rerum Novarum* because of its insistence that basically the social problem was a moral problem that could only be solved by the force of organized religion. Here, of course, was the point that led Spanish liberals by and large to ignore *Rerum Novarum*, notwithstanding their fundamental accord with the encyclical's social conservatism.

The Religious Issue and the Two Spains

In late nineteenth-century Spain the religious issue was still as bitterly contested and as far from resolution as when it had first come in for serious discussion toward the end of the previous century. Around this issue, Spain had split into two intransigently hostile camps.[96]

In reacting against liberalism, Spanish Catholics had developed "a species of philosophical traditionalism and theocratic absolutism."[97] Out of this school of theocratic absolutism emerged many a Catholic spokesman such as Ramón Nocedal, a champion of *Rerum Novarum* and the guiding spirit of the Madrid daily *El Siglo Futuro*. In a typical editorial published in that paper in 1892, Nocedal demanded a new Spanish reconquest, directed this time not against the Moors but against contemporary heretics whom he identified as the liberals.[98] Nocedal also attacked all Catholics, from Cánovas del Castillo on down, who were members of the Liberal-Conservative Party. These men he charged with the cardinal sin of seeking an accommodation between liberalism and Catholicism.[99]

The notion that liberalism, because it was per se heretical, was not to be compromised with was by no means new among Spanish Catholics. In writing against liberalism at the end of the 1840's Donoso Cortés had stated that its origins lay in the heretical negation of God's direct control over his creatures. The denial of God's sovereignty in the social order and of providential control over history was reflected in the political order, Donoso insisted, by the erroneous formula of a king who was to reign while leaving the actual functions of government to a parliament. In its appraisal of human nature, liberalism, according to the Andalusian philosopher, committed the heresy of affirming the perfection or at least the perfectibility of mankind. As a consequence, liberalism posited the sovereignty of human intelligence, which in turn led to such monstrous practices as universal suffrage and freedom of expression.[100]

Spanish liberals were generally as loathe as their ideological foes to compromise with what they took to be the forces of evil. Any questioning of the belief that morality rested upon natural reason rather than revealed truth[101] or any manifestation of clerical power or influence in the temporal order elicited their blistering anathemas.[102] Little wonder that Unamuno condemned Spanish liberals for operating generally on the same level of dogmatism as their opponents. Dismayed by the "grossness and vulgarity that have always distinguished our progressivism," Unamuno pronounced a pox on both Spanish ideological camps. The one group swears, he said, by St. Thomas, the other by some scientist of questionable merit who happens to be currently in vogue.[103]

The Cádiz assembly that produced the controversial constitution of 1812 provided some of the first evidences in the nineteenth century of the division between anticlerical liberals and conservative Catholics. One group within the constituent assembly wanted to introduce new, European, essentially French, ideas into Spain; another wanted to conserve Spanish traditions in their entirety. Although defeated at Cádiz, the second group managed generally to prevail thereafter until the death of Ferdinand VII in 1833.[104] But in the dynastic wars sparked by Ferdinand's death, the conservative, aristocratic forces of Carlism were defeated by the bourgeois, liberal elements.[105] As the bloody Carlist wars approached their end in 1836, Spain's best-known romantic poet of the period, Mariano José de Larra (1809–1837), made the comment that could easily have been repeated in 1939: "Here lies half of Spain, killed by the other half."[106]

Toward the conclusion of the Carlist wars, the Spanish liberal government confiscated the lands of the clergy and by redistributing them created a new class of landowners. This has properly been described as the most important event in the nineteenth-century liberal-conservative struggle; for it called into being "a bourgeois element that had its roots in the political affirmation of liberalism. The people who bought the goods of the Church had to divorce themselves from the clergy and affirm with their blood and efforts the political regime that had given them social and economic well-being."[107] In this complex process, the Spanish clergy and its numerous lay supporters who never forgave those responsible for and benefiting from the land redistribution, acquired a lasting hatred of the bourgeois society. It is understandable, then, that one of the main characteristics of various right-wing groups in the Spain of the 1930s was their strident denunciation of bourgeois elements and their corrupt, decadent, liberal values.

Following the disentailment episode, the remainder of the nineteenth century witnessed many new skirmishes in the epic struggle of liberalism with conservatism.[108] One of the more interesting occurred when the great republican champion of social reform, Gumersindo de Azcárate, who later accorded mild praise to *Rerum Novarum*, voiced the commonly heard liberal assertion that the Inquisition and Catholic fanaticism in general had been responsible for stifling all scientific study and investigation in Spain and stultifying the general pursuit of cultural and intellectual objectives. Marcelino Menéndez Pelayo, a young student at the University of Valladolid, was encouraged by a professor of his, Gumersindo Laverde Ruiz, to produce a work refuting the Azcárate allegation. The result was *La ciencia española* published by Menéndez Pelayo in 1876, just shortly before his twentieth birthday. The work pointed to many evidences of notable Spanish efforts in the fields of science and general culture and depicted Catholicism as a stimulant to intellectual investigation and the generation of new ideas.

Although initially extremely doctrinaire and even fanatical in his defense of Spanish traditions,[109] Menéndez Pelayo, even as Balmes before

him, mellowed considerably as he matured, coming to recognize the need
for an opening toward innovating forces.[110] Furthermore, in his address to
the Primer Congreso Católico Nacional of 1889, celebrated in Madrid,
Menéndez Pelayo criticized Spanish Catholics for being distracted by
foolish questions and bitter personal recrimination. He urged them to
have recourse to more serious means of bolstering their religion and its
vital interests. They should, he said, turn more to metaphysics, to biblical
exegesis, to natural sciences and history, where they could find the strength
to sustain them in the more significant battles that lay ahead.[111]

In his campaign, Menéndez Pelayo made little headway. He was accused
by his liberal foes of being an obscurantist reactionary, which indeed he
had at one time been. Fellow Catholic conservatives charged him with
contemporizing with error and suffering from the dangerous delusion that
the liberal currents of the Renaissance in Spain had exercised a beneficial
influence.[112] The case of Menéndez Pelayo, who fell into obscurity in the
later years of his life, demonstrates that "the eclectics in Spain have always
died without being understood."[113]

One of the most profound studies on the liberal-conservative issue that
plagued Spain for well over a century was written by Pedro Sáinz Rodríguez, an enthusiastic admirer of Menéndez Pelayo who in 1921 at the
age of twenty-four had won the professorship of Spanish language and
literature at the University of Oviedo and shortly thereafter won a more
coveted chair at the University of Madrid.[114] In the opinion of Sáinz
Rodríguez, quoted earlier in connection with his view that caciquismo had
at least curbed militarism, the real crisis for Spain began when the worldwide revolution in religion finally penetrated the Iberian peninsula. In the
early nineteenth century Spain was at last called upon to meet squarely
two intimately related questions. Is religious faith a matter to be determined by the nation-state or is it a matter of the individual conscience?
Should national policy be one of insisting upon religious unity, even if
this must be attained through an Inquisition, or should it be one of
tolerance?

As Sáinz Rodríguez explained it:

> The struggles of the nineteenth century in Spain are really religious
> struggles of the type that had surged in other European countries at
> the time of the Renaissance, in which the root question is the one of
> tolerance, of individual vs. collective or national faith. These issues had
> been kept out of Spain until the nineteenth century.

The Sáinz Rodríguez analysis, written in 1928, concluded on a pro-
phetic note: "The religious question is still a hypersensitive one in Spain,
because the wars over it have been so recent; in this fact one finds the
possibility of a new civil war."[115]

For one Spain in the nineteenth century, tolerance was indeed the great national objective. A typical spokesman of the liberal school was Rafael María de Labra, the proponent of education as a solution to the social problem and a confirmed republican anticlerical who objected strenuously to the use of the word *God* in the oath administered to congressional deputies. Labra saw religious tolerance as the panacea that would propel Spain out of its backwardness toward progress and modernization.[116] For Labra and men of similar persuasions, religious intolerance was responsible for virtually all of the ills and calamities suffered by Spain since the time of "the Catholic Kings," Ferdinand and Isabella.

To the other Spain, the Spain for which Ramón Nocedal's *El Siglo Futuro* served as a mouthpiece, national greatness in bygone times had been owing exclusively to religious intolerance. National weakness and malaise had appeared only as religious fervor declined and heretical ideas, fomented in the nineteenth century by international Masonry, began to find a favorable climate.[117]

The restoration, with its system of alternating governments presided over by Cánovas del Castillo and Sagasta, simply provided Spain with additional time as it floundered in search of its national destiny and a means of reconciling its fundamental differences.[118] It did little to resolve the "discrepancy between some ardent traditionalists who do not know how to be modern and some fervent progressives who do not know how to make themselves Spaniards."[119]

Spain in the late nineteenth century was a country beset by deeply rooted problems. Sometimes seeking distraction from problems at home that seemed nearly insoluble, sometimes hoping that through the perspectives of newer countries and younger peoples they might better discover their own national destiny, Spaniards increasingly turned their attention toward the lands in America that had once been theirs.

2: AWAKENING INTEREST IN SPANISH AMERICA, 1876–1898

The Unpromising Background for Hispanismo

Given the bitterness generated on both sides of the ocean by the long-enduring and fiercely fought wars of independence, it is understandable that Spain and its former colonies persisted for many years in attitudes of distrust and aversion. As late as 1892 a Costa Rican writer remarked upon the enmity of most Spanish Americans toward Spain. To Spanish Americans, he observed, Spain was a land of decadence and corruption where the lives of foreigners were constantly in danger, a land of fanaticism and inquisitorial intolerance where people were concerned primarily about bullfighters.[1] In the same year a Spanish journalist remarked sadly upon the still nearly universal anti-Spanish prejudices encountered throughout Spanish America. Spain, he concluded, might gradually learn to love its children again, but it did not seem likely that the offspring would reacquire love for the mother.[2]

Against this unpromising background, a few Spaniards at least had labored to establish friendly ties with the new republics of America. Sebastián Lorente, a liberal Spanish intellectual, went to Peru in the 1840s to head the academy of Our Lady of Guadalupe. Soon the disciples of Lorente, who also founded the Faculty of Philosophy and Letters of the University of San Marcos in Lima, included many of the leading figures of Peruvian liberalism.[3] Spanish conservatives also had their representatives in Peru. The Catalan Franciscan Pedro Gual headed a contingent of nineteen missionaries that arrived in 1849 to combat the anticlerical and heretical tendencies purportedly prevailing in the former viceroyalty.[4]

In general, Spanish liberals seemed unlikely agents of hispanismo because of their fondness for picturing Spain as a backward, fanatical land opposed to freedom and progress.[5] The Spanish poet José M. Gutiérrez de Alba (1822–1897) provides a typical example of this. Frequently in trouble with the law because of his advanced ideas, Gutiérrez de Alba found himself temporarily in favor following the triumph of the liberal revolution of 1868. Sent to Colombia on a diplomatic mission, he remained on there in a private capacity after the restoration, indefatigably assailing the reactionary policies that he imputed to Cánovas del Castillo and his associates in the Liberal-Conservative Party.[6]

On the whole, Spanish conservatives tended in the nineteenth century to interest themselves more in Spanish America than did the liberals.[7]

30

Much given to extolling the glories of Spanish accomplishments during the colonial period, they urged Spanish Americans to cling to their one source of greatness by remaining true to unsullied Hispanic values and traditions.[8] Conservatives, though, were seriously handicapped in their efforts to woo the ex-colonies, for what appealed to them was the Spanish America of the past, not the present. Conservative Catholic monarchists could scarcely respond favorably to areas where republican liberalism and rampant anticlericalism flourished.[9] The outburst of the devoutly Catholic poet José Zorilla (1817–1893) against the liberal, anticlerical Mexico of the mid-nineteenth century is scarcely surprising. "Vile and infamous nation, atheistic nation," the Spaniard wrote, "I hope you will be taken over by the Yankees and that I will live to see this happen."[10]

With both liberals and conservatives working under serious disadvantages, Spain was further handicapped in approaching Spanish America because one of its favorite propaganda ploys, often used with considerable success in the twentieth century, made little impact in the nineteenth century. Perceiving that love of Spain in Spanish America depended to some degree on that area's aversion to the United States,[11] Spaniards pointed to the menace of Yankee imperialism and in general sought to foster a climate of Yankeephobia.[12] One colorful agent in this campaign was the eminent poet Gabriel García Tassara (1817–1875), who arrived in Washington in 1855 as Spanish minister plenipotentiary. His efforts to persuade the Spanish-American diplomats in Washington that their countries should enter into a confederation to oppose the Colossus led to the United States demand for his recall in 1865.[13] If García Tassara's efforts had understandably annoyed the country to which he was accredited, they had evoked little sympathy among Spanish-American diplomats who in general regarded Spain as more of an imperialistic menace than the United States.

Early Champions of Hispanismo

The cause of hispanismo, calling for cooperation and friendship and even for political unity between Spain and Spanish America, seemed unpromising if not indeed hopeless in the early years of the second half of the nineteenth century. But Spain has never lacked defenders of hopeless causes and hispanismo was not without its enthusiastic champions.[14]

Antonio María Fabié y Escudero radiated optimism about the prospects of hispanismo. As a thirty-one-year-old conservative deputy he assured his listeners in an 1865 congressional discourse: "We, who have to be always the true depositories of the civilization of Spanish America, ought to be and will be represented there. We will be the channel through which America receives all of the advances and improvements that the old world achieves."[15]

Another Spaniard remaining sanguine about the role of his country in Spanish America was Jacinto Albistur. The author of an optimistic book published in 1861 on Spanish relations with the Río de la Plata region,[16] Albistur had later moved to Montevideo. There he founded and, until his death in 1889, directed the newspaper *El Siglo,* in which he energetically advanced the concepts of hispanismo.[17]

Even Spanish women, scarcely noted for their activity in public affairs at this time, took up the unpromising cause. The most notable case is that of the Granada-born Emilia Serrano del Tornel (1842–1923), who made numerous trips to Spanish America, spending in all some fourteen years there as she conducted research for several books. Glowingly confident about the economic future of some of the Spanish-speaking republics of the New World and a warm apologist for Mexican President Porfirio Díaz, who had befriended her during her stay in Mexico and to whom she dedicated an 1886 publication, Serrano del Tornel labored zealously toward making Spanish America better known—and better liked—in Spain.[18]

Probably the two best-known proponents of closer ties with Spanish America were Rafael María de Labra, the republican who steadfastly insisted on the need for religious toleration, and Juan Valera (1824–1905), a literary critic of real distinction and possibly Spain's most popular novelist in the latter part of the nineteenth century.

Born in Cuba but raised in the Asturias region of northern Spain, Labra since his youth had supported such liberal causes as abolition of slavery and the granting of autonomy to Spain's possessions in the Antilles. From the mid-1860s he had been editor-in-chief of the *Revista Hispano-Americana* and in its pages he published many of his articles urging closer ties with Spanish America as well as liberal domestic reforms.[19]

If Labra's approach to Spanish America was primarily practical, based on belief in the vast economic potential of commercial relations, Juan Valera saw literature as the great bond that would unite the former colonies culturally to their motherland. By the 1880s, Valera was in correspondence with many of Spanish America's leading literary figures and received a considerable number of their publications each year. These works convinced him that Spanish America was by no means "intellectually infecund."[20] In fact, Valera wrote, "although English America has since independence outdistanced Spanish America in matters of the natural and exact sciences, of industry and commerce, it is licit to say that in the field of letters, both in quantity and quality, Spanish has conquered English America."[21]

Valera believed that what was best in Spanish-American literature found its inspiration in Spanish, rather than in French or Italian, culture. Therefore the high quality of Spanish-American literature, in his opinion, reflected credit ultimately on Spanish culture and evidenced the continuing vitality of the Spanish raza.[22]

Understandably, Valera was most pleased by Spanish-American literature that expressed an appreciation of Spanish cultural traditions. Acknowledging receipt of a new work from the Argentine Santiago Estrada, Valera praised the author as a good Catholic who respected tradition and who because of this had written an outstanding set of essays.[23] Valera also praised the Colombian author and statesman Miguel Antonio Caro,[24] accused by some of his own countrymen of being reactionary, obscurantist, and fanatical. Caro's defense of traditionalism and the Spanish colonial past that had occasioned these charges against him was, according to Valera, simply a reflection of the best scientific scholarship "that is gradually dissipating the old legends about the unique cruelties of Spaniards."[25]

Valera's efforts to foster cultural ties between Spain and Spanish America had to some degree been anticipated by the Real Academia Española de la Lengua. In 1861 the Academy, hoping to aid sympathetic Spanish-American intellectuals in the task of preserving the purity of the language and of Spanish culture in general, had begun to confer corresponding memberships. The first such memberships were awarded to Felipe Pardo Aliaga (father of Peruvian President Manuel Pardo, 1872–1876) in Lima and to Bernardo Couto and Joaquín Pesado in Mexico City. By 1865 six Spanish Americans were corresponding members of the Academy.[26]

In the early 1870s the Academy decided to form corresponding chapters in America and proceeded to prepare regulations for their establishment. The first such chapter came into being in Bogotá in 1873, presided over by Miguel Antonio Caro. Within the course of the next twenty years, additional corresponding chapters were founded in Ecuador, Mexico, El Salvador, Venezuela, Chile, and Peru.[27]

Writing in 1889, Juan Valera rendered generous praise to the work of the Real Academia. Through its corresponding chapters it had established, he said, a literary confederation, with Spain as its academic center. From this center, wrote Valera, Spain "exercises a certain hegemony, so natural and subtle that it neither generates suspicions nor arouses jealousies and annoyances."[28]

Despite this optimistic appraisal, the hegemony that the Real Academia sought to exercise in matters of the language and culture did generate suspicions in Spanish America. Moreover, on one important occasion the Academy was responsible for an incident that dealt a serious setback to the cultural goals of hispanismo. This came about when Juan Montalvo, the irreverent and iconoclastic Ecuadoran writer, was proposed during his 1882–1889 period of exile in France for membership in the Real Academia. The membership proposal came from three of the most distinguished men in Spain: Emilio Casterlar (1812–1899), the ardent republican and silver-tongued orator who had long maintained a vital interest in Spanish America;[29] Gaspar Núñez de Arce (1834–1903), a leading poet and literary figure; and Juan Valera. Despite the eminence of his backers, Montalvo's membership bid was rejected, owing primarily to his religious and political opinions. The rejection produced a scandal in literary circles both of Spain and Spanish America.

In 1885 another organization, seeking to combine the cultural approach of Valera and the Real Academia with the practical, commercial concern of Labra, had begun to serve the cause of hispanismo. This was the Unión Ibero-Americana,[30] whose founding was owing largely to the efforts of Jesús Pando y Valle (1849–1911),[31] a member of the board of editors of the review *Los Dos Mundos* that dealt extensively with Spanish America, and Mariano Cancio Villaamil (1824–1894), who had served with distinction as Intendente General in Cuba and who became the Union's first president.[32]

Cancio Villaamil entertained lofty and, given the prevailing climate of opinion, thoroughly unrealistic ambitions; for he saw in the Union the means of forging the political unity of Spain, Portugal, and Spanish America, creating thereby a great and powerful Hispanic nationality with its own constitution, governing council, federal budget, army, and navy.

In the March 22, 1885 inaugural session of the Unión Ibero-Americana, Segismundo Moret, a powerful figure in the Liberal Party that had just returned to power, was only slightly more guarded than Cancio Villaamil in visualizing the future of Spanish-American relations:

> There has arrived, then, the moment for maintaining a contact, a fraternity, a perfect harmony. . . . This cohesion must be established and for this purpose I do not know if the most suitable form would be a federation or if some other model must be sought . . . but in some fashion there must be realized the union of these peoples, who constitute a common raza, so as to arrest the ascendant march of Saxon civilization.[33]

Ever the practical man, Labra was more circumspect in describing the purposes of the Union. In his estimate the Union's mission was to awaken Spanish opinion to the importance of Hispanic America, to explain the history and contemporary circumstances of these New World republics, and to devise the economic means by which Spain could establish more intimate ties with them.[34]

The Unión Ibero-Americana, which ten years after its founding boasted a total of 256 honorable, regular, and cooperating members[35]—up from 134 members in 1892[36]—had in 1890 been officially declared an organization of "public usefulness." As such it was entitled to a state subvention, although by 1895 it had received only the insignificant amount of five thousand pesetas.[37] From its founding the Union had also published the periodical *Unión Ibero-Americana*,[38] an invaluable source on commercial and cultural relations between Spain and Spanish America. Following the pattern established by the Real Academia, the Union also set up corresponding groups in Spanish America. The first of these came into being in Mexico City in 1886 under the presidency of Manuel Romero Rubio, at the time Mexico's minister of interior.

1892: The Fourth Centennial of the Discovery

Spanish interest in Spanish America soared to new heights, at least to new heights of rhetoric, in 1892 with the celebration of the fourth centennial of the Columbus discovery of America.[39] Actually, the Spanish decision to celebrate this event was something of an afterthought, occasioned by the news that the United States was planning to commemorate the event.[40] But once the decision was reached, lavish celebration plans were quickly prepared, largely under the auspices of the Unión Ibero-Americana; and Cánovas del Castillo declared October 12 of the fourth centennial year a national holiday.[41]

Internal ideological divisions prevented Spaniards from presenting a united front as they prepared to manifest their abiding interest in the world that the Columbus discovery had incorporated into the Spanish family. The traditionalist Catholic newspaper El Siglo Futuro declared that the fourth centennial should serve as a reminder of what Spain could accomplish "when guided by the cross of Jesus Christ." Since the days of its glorious achievements in the New World, however, Spain had allegedly been weakened by the forces of Gallicanism, Masonry, rationalism, and liberalism. Only by returning to its Catholic beliefs, the paper editorialized, could Spain reacquire its past grandeur and with it the strength to exercise a significant influence over its former colonies.[42] El Siglo Futuro claimed that Catholics should be exclusively in charge of the fourth centennial; only they could impart to the celebration the religious nature decreed by good taste and proper historical understanding. Above all, Masons had to be excluded from participating in the celebration.[43]

Labra and men of his liberal persuasions approached the fourth centennial in an altogether different light. In the liberal view, the real source of unity between Spain and Spanish America lay in the common struggle that both areas had waged in the nineteenth century for emancipation from authoritarianism and clericalism. In the modern age, liberals asserted, only the mutual quest for liberty, for scientific truth, for economic progress, religious toleration, and the secular society could result in a rapprochement between Spain and "the area that had been discovered because of the bold questioning and scientific daring of Columbus."[44] Altogether unlike the conservatives who wanted the 1892 festivities to commemorate past splendors, Labra and his partisans wished them to mark a commitment of Spain and Spanish America to a bright future—a future that could be realized only through repudiation of the past.

To render homage to the events of 1492,[45] Spaniards and Spanish Americans, together with Portuguese and Brazilians, assembled in Madrid and elsewhere in the peninsula in, among others, pedagogical, juridical,[46] commercial,[47] geographic, and literary congresses.[48] With Labra presiding and with such men of liberal convictions as Gumersindo de Azcárate and Moret playing a prominent role in them, the sessions of the pedagogical congress, attended by 648 delegates, provided some of the liveliest moments of the centennial. After sustained and acrimonious debate, the congress passed resolutions in favor of education for women and laborers. A substantial majority of those in attendance, moreover, subscribed to the Labra view that education must be nonreligious. The delegates further agreed that education could serve as an effective barrier to socialism, the menace of which lay in its ability "to capture the minds of uneducated workers."[49]

In the sessions of the pedagogical congress Spaniards and Spanish Americans learned much about the social problems that were appearing simultaneously on both sides of the Atlantic. And they began to understand the potential usefulness of a united Iberian approach in finding ways to mitigate the social problem so as to stave off revolution.[50] It is significant that La Ilustración Española y Americana, perhaps the most important Madrid periodical then championing hispanismo, gave its main news coverage in 1892 to two phenomena: the Spanish-American rapprochement and the mounting social problems of the Hispanic world. Increasingly, observers would come to see a relationship between these two phenomena, convinced that the directing classes of Spain and Spanish America would have to unite so as to maintain their dominant positions in a hierarchical social structure.

The 1892 celebrations also provided Spain with a new opportunity to pose as the defender of Hispanic interests against the threat of United States imperialism. One conservative Spanish journalist took advantage of this opportunity to remind his readers that while the United States at its Chicago exhibition showed its exclusive concern with material progress and total disregard for more exalted considerations, Spain, in its 1892 celebrations, paid homage to the spiritual glories of the past and present. The journalist admonished Spanish Americans to avoid United States models if they wished to preserve intact the moral values bequeathed by Spain. In addition he established a link between the perils of United States influence and social revolution, warning Spanish Americans that class conflicts would ensue if they followed United States patterns. Exploitative bankers and industrial tycoons of the powerful northern republic were, he wrote, heartlessly crushing the lower classes and jeopardizing the position of the middle class. The United States system was therefore likely to lead to a socialist revolution.[51]

Hispansimo, Its Boosters and Detractors, 1893–1898

In the years following the commemoration of the discovery, Juan Valera continued his work of strengthening cultural ties, convinced that "although the political unity is broken, the literary unity of Spain and Spanish America remains intact; nor can it ever be severed."[52] However, Valera stingingly rebuked Spanish authors, with the exception of Colombians, whom he characterized as being more Spanish than Spaniards, for imitating French literature, "for writing as if they had lived all their lives in Paris." It would be better for the estate of culture in the new republics, he wrote, if their writers would liberate themselves from this obsession with French styles and pay more attention to what was being written and thought in Spain.[53]

Emilio Castelar, the ardent republican who had for some forty years expressed warm sentiments of hispanismo, was less concerned about the Spanish-American veneration of French culture, seeing it as producing only superficial consequences. "Spain made America as God made the world," he wrote in 1898. "The sun will disappear from the heavens before the Spanish essence disappears from the spirit of Spanish America. America will be Spanish eternally."[54]

But the old difficulty remained when it came to defining just what the Spanish essence was. To some it was the rationalism and anticlericalism displayed by the fiery Chilean iconoclast Francisco Bilbao (1823–1865). A new biography of Bilbao, who had gained prominence throughout the Spanish-speaking world of the mid-nineteenth century, was warmly received among Spanish liberal circles in 1895. One reviewer of the biography digressed slightly when he commented upon the sad fate of the anticlerical Chilean President José Manuel Balmaceda, who was pictured as trying to continue the Bilbao tradition and who had been defeated by the congressional forces in the civil war of 1891.[55] Conservatives, on the other hand, continued to regard Bilbao as having been guilty of seeking to destroy the only values that authentically corresponded to the Hispanic world; and they hailed the outcome of the 1891 civil war in Chile.

Liberal elements in the hispanismo movement who wanted to modernize and secularize both Spain and Spanish America welcomed an important new recruit in the mid-nineties when Rafael Altamira (1866–1953), a young professor at the University of Oviedo, which was regarded at the time as a hotbed of advanced ideas, began publication of the *Revista Crítica de Historia y Literatura Españolas, Portuguesas e Hispanoamericanas*.[56] A proponent of cultural exchange between Spain and America, Altamira tried to attract the best writers of the peninsula and the young republics to the pages of his review. Altamira's admission of failure in this endeavor[57] and the comment of Valera that the new review was not attracting subscribers[58] indicated that cultural ties between Spain and Spanish America were still largely nonexistent.

While some Spaniards labored vainly in the late nineteenth century to strengthen cultural bonds with Spanish America, others dreamed of establishing closer diplomatic and juridical ties. They felt they had achieved a considerable victory when in 1895 Colombia, Peru, and Ecuador agreed to submit their boundary disputes to Spanish arbitration. The journal of the Unión Ibero-Americana editorialized that this was the most reasonable course the former colonies could have chosen, for most of the pertinent documents were stored in Spanish archives. Moral considerations, the editorial concluded,

> should also induce the nations that were once an integral part of our empire to turn their eyes again toward Spain; for Spain represents a bond of union between all the nations to which it gave origin; it is the common mother of these nations and as such can in the most impartial and disinterested manner serve as a unifying element, mediating differences in a spirit of equality and sincere affection toward all those who were its daughters.[59]

Animated by similar convictions, some Spaniards felt Spain should become active in formulating a code of Ibero-American international law that would take as its point of departure "the glorious Laws of the Indies." In arguing this point of view, a Spanish legalist declared:

> America, as is proved by the character of its children, its literature, and its institutions is Spanish; and it will always be so, since the Spaniards left their blood and their prodigious spirit there. . . . All of America's originality has in its essence, however much American it is, that which is Spanish. . . . And being united by so many and such strong ties, would it not be possible to form a legal code that would receive the name International Code of Ibero-American laws?[60]

For many Spaniards, the cultural-juridical approach to Spanish America was too nebulous. Those regarding themselves as more practical-minded worked to strengthen economic and commercial relations, particularly with the two countries they considered most progressive and best endowed with resources: Argentina[61] and Mexico.[62] In 1895 Spanish journalist Julio Donón undertook a campaign to inform public opinion about the need for Spain to challenge France, Germany, and Italy for Spanish-American markets. He stressed the urgent necessity of new trade treaties, a subsidized merchant marine, and traveling commercial agents to represent Spanish industries in the New World.[63] At about the same time, under the aegis of Segismundo Moret, official Spanish chambers of commerce in America were chartered[64] and the Commission of Commercial Relations of the Unión Ibero-Americana initiated an endeavor to compile full information on all aspects of trade and commerce with Spanish America and Brazil.[65]

Just as Spain has never wanted for defenders of lost causes, so also it has never lacked skeptics. Lucas Mallada (1840–1921), an engineer and geologist as well as a successful journalist and the author of one of the best known among the dozens of books on Spanish decadence produced in the 1890s, was skeptical about hispanismo. He did not feel that the future of Spain lay in America, least of all in trade ties with the new republics. Writing in 1890, he asserted that imports from Mexico and Cuba had decreased since 1865 and that overall trade with Peru had declined while that with Argentina had barely held its own. Mallada concluded:

> All efforts in the past twenty-five years to increase trade with Hispanic-American countries have been fruitless . . . and there are no grounds to justify hope for future improvement. It is ridiculous to think of close commercial ties between Spain and Hispanic America. The former colonies produce mainly primary goods and import manufactured goods, even as Spain does, for both areas are backward. Thus they cannot develop significant trade; and it is only natural that Argentina, with which Spain enjoys the most significant commercial relations, carries on four times as much trade with Belgium.[66]

So far as Mallada was concerned, the belief that the economic future lay in ties with the former colonies was just another manifestation of the main vice of Spain's national character: fantasy.

> Fantasy makes us dream of the greatest projects and also makes us the laziest people in all Europe . . .; fantasy makes us think that Spain is a privileged country; fantasy induces us to demand a post of honor among the great nations although the English flag continues to fly over Gibraltar; fantasy makes us hope that we will one day be the redeemer of Africa. . . . In our fantasy we think we have an influence in the Americas, that area to which our few products of export have to be carried in English and French ships.[67]

Perhaps the most significant factor that relegated the aspirations of hispanoamericanistas to the realm of fantasy was the at best tutelary and at worst disdainful attitudes of many Spaniards, even those who counted themselves as friends of the new republics, toward Spanish America. Marcelino Menéndez Pelayo, apologist par excellence for Spain's scientific and cultural accomplishments and for national traditions, provides a typical case in point.

Under the auspices of the Real Academia, Menéndez Pelayo between 1893 and 1895 published a four-volume critical anthology of the works of deceased Spanish-American poets. To avoid wounding sensitivities unnecessarily, it had been decided not to include the works of living poets.[68] The Menéndez Pelayo publication, regarded as an important means for strengthening cultural ties between Spain and Spanish America,[69] divided the New World poets according to their countries of origin. For each section in the work, Menéndez Pelayo provided a lengthy introduction

examining the entire literary output of the country under consideration.[70]
He also provided a general introduction to the four-volume work, in which
he stated:

> Today, with renewed fraternity and [with Spain and Spanish America]
> on a path that cannot be blocked, whatever destiny Providence has
> reserved to each one of the separate members of the common trunk of
> our raza, it has seemed opportune to consecrate in some manner a
> reminder of this alliance by gathering into a book the most select
> inspirations of the Castilian poetry from the other side of the ocean,
> thus giving it . . . official entry into the treasury of Spanish literature,
> into which it should have been incorporated long ago.[71]

Actually, this well-intentioned work may have set back rather than
advanced the cause of hispanismo. Although Menéndez Pelayo clearly
admired much of the literary output of Spanish America and although he
looked on this area with pride as building upon what was best in the peninsula's traditions,[72] he also evidenced the typical Spanish tutelary attitude
toward the former colonies. Thus he felt, much like Valera, that Spanish-
American poetry was worthy primarily in so far as it reflected its origin
and inspiration in Spanish culture. Therefore he contended that Spain had
a cultural mission to aid Spanish Americans to become themselves—that
is, to become Spanish and to cease imitating alien models.[73]

Besides this tutelary attitude, understandably resented in Spanish
America, Menéndez Pelayo still evidenced in the mid-1890s some of the
sentiments of disdain toward the new republics that he had expressed in
the seventies and eighties. To Menéndez Pelayo, the basis for Spanish
greatness was its devotion to the true faith, its characteristic unwillingness
to endure the existence of heterodoxy. Spanish Americans he considered
less worthy because of their inclinations toward heresy.[74] Further, he attributed the Spanish American independence movement in large part to
liberal and Masonic conspiracies. Consequently, he tended to dismiss the
area as one conceived in heterodoxy and heresy.[75]

Nevertheless, Menéndez Pelayo did admire those Spanish-American
authors who manifested truly Spanish and Catholic characteristics. One
of his favorite examples of the good Spanish-American writer was Andrés
Bello, the Venezuelan-born intellectual who made notable contributions
to the establishment of higher education and the formulation of legal
codes in mid-nineteenth-century Chile.

> Because the teaching of Bello had been the most effective dike against
> all types of heedless flirtation with the new; because he respected in
> law the traditional element and the eternal source of wisdom of the
> Roman people and of Christianity; because all his life he was con-
> servative . . .; because he represented in America the purest type of
> classical education and the highest teaching authority in regard to

purity of the language, that great master was the target of the ire of all the literary rebels, of all the democratic levelers; and there were those, as the famous Argentine [Domingo Faustino] Sarmiento, who dared to ask in print the perpetual ostracism of Bello for the capital and unforgivable crime of having known too much and been too versed in literature.[76]

Spanish-American writers who did not meet his standards Menéndez Pelayo was apt to attack as "anticlerical, satanical types, fanatics of disbelief."[77] After noting in revulsion the anti-Spanish sentiments of Manuel María Madieto, Menéndez Pelayo concluded that the Colombian author "may have been a man of color."[78] And he referred to Sarmiento, held by some Argentines to be one of their greatest presidents, as a person who always lacked good taste and frequently evidenced the grossest ignorance, a man who in the 1840s had been no more than a "half crazy journalist." The great sin of Sarmiento had been that he had "declared war to the death against the name of Spain."[79]

In preparing the poetry anthology Menéndez Pelayo became thoroughly familiar with the anti-Spanish diatribes that abounded in Spanish-American literature. Better perhaps than any of his countrymen, he recognized the depth of Hispanophobe sentiment in the former colonies and thus realized the extent to which hispanismo was based on fantasy. Understandably annoyed by the prejudices he discovered in numerous Spanish-American writers, Menéndez Pelayo subjected many men who were cultural heroes in the new republics to irascible, scathing denunciations. Little wonder that this work was not, on the whole, favorably received in Spanish America.

If the efforts of Menéndez Pelayo did not succeed in winning sympathy for Spain in Spanish America, they were equally ineffective in enhancing the appreciation of Spanish intellectuals for Spanish-American culture. The author conceded in 1910 that his lengthy anthology was the least known of any of his works in Spain, "where the formal study of the things of America interests very few people, in spite of the vain presentation of discourses in theaters and at banquets of confraternity."[80]

Undoubtedly an important reason for this situation was the prevailing Spanish belief in the irremediable backwardness of Spanish America. However much he regretted it, Labra had to concede the near universality of this belief.[81] Rafael Altamira also acknowledged that attitudes of Spanish contempt were largely responsible for the lack of meaningful ties with Spanish America.[82]

For many Spaniards, Argentina was Spanish America. And as early as 1892 there appeared in Spain a strong attack against this republic, one that would be echoed again and again by later Spanish observers of the Argentine scene. In an article published by El Siglo Futuro in the year of the fourth centennial celebrations, Argentina was described as infected by greed, selfishness, and uncurbed materialism. The "excessive" number of Italian immigrants was blamed to a large degree for this situation.[83]

A writer who prided herself on her Americanist sympathies singled out another republic for censure. She complained about the lack of economic responsibility and foresight, the general profligateness and tendency toward excesses of all kinds that typified Peruvian life.[84] To Spaniards who characteristically praised the stoic qualities of their nature and prided themselves on their gravity and seriousness and concern with spiritual pursuits, charges of materialism and general lack of restraint and self-discipline constituted a serious indictment indeed against the former colonies.

Juan Valera observed in 1889 that most of his countrymen believed the mixture of Spanish blood in America with that of Indians and Negroes had caused the flaws of character that allegedly abounded among the inhabitants of the Spanish-American republics.[85] Valera may have shared this belief himself. At the very least, he regarded the Indians as constituting a decidedly inferior race.[86]

The tumultuous instability of Spanish America was one of the preferred grounds on which Spanish writers maligned the former colonies. Ramiro de Maeztu (1875–1936), who when an older man would write one of the classic defenses of hispanismo,[87] in 1899 was repelled by the political turmoil and chaos of Spanish America. He noted also the common Spanish tendency to attribute these conditions to racial factors. On the other hand, Maeztu recognized that Spanish Americans looked with disdain toward Spain because of the prevalence there of revolutions and military pronouncements. With the example of nineteenth-century Spain before them, Spanish Americans attributed their own blight of political instability to the Spanish racial inheritance.[88]

Here indeed was an unpropitious background for the forging of close ties between Spain and Spanish America, whether cultural, juridical, commercial, whether spiritual or practical. Here also was a far more permanent and profound barrier to the course of hispanismo than the spectacle of an imperialistic Spain trying between 1895 and 1898 to suppress a Cuban insurrection that apparently elicited the sympathy of a majority of Spanish Americans.

Spain and the Cuban Issue, 1895–1898

When José Martí sparked a new Cuban insurrection in 1895, Cánovas del Castillo, president of the council of ministers, announced that Spain would fight "to the last man and to the last peseta." This announcement at first caught the public fancy,[89] for tradition, honor, and prestige seemed to compel Spain to retain its last major outpost in the New World. Smarting, furthermore, from a series of setbacks in the African campaign that had begun with an incident at Melilla in 1893, Spaniards in general seemed in no mood to compromise with the Cuban rebels; and the military longed for a new opportunity to redeem itself.

In addition to honor, prestige, and military reputation, economic considerations impelled many Spaniards to demand the quick suppression of the insurrection. As of the mid-1890s, Cuba was buying annually approximately twenty million dollars worth of Spanish goods. In the entire New World, only with the United States, Argentina, Brazil, and Canada did Spain conduct a larger volume of trade.[90]

From the outset of the new war, Spaniards tended to be almost as irate with the Spanish-American republics, because of their overt sympathy for the insurrection, as with the Cubans themselves. The writer Castro Drocir de Osorno admonished his countrymen not to ignore this sympathy in their misguided statements about Hispano-American unity. Spanish Americans, he stated, were "ingrates," acting in "traitorous, treasonable manner against their mother;" they revealed a "criminal lack of gratitude to the country that had pulled their continent out of ignorance and barbarism, infusing into it the first elements of civilization." All members of parliament, Drocir concluded, express concern over United States encouragement to the insurrection; "but they do not speak out against the equally important moral and material assistance given by the Spanish-American republics, assistance that is greater, in proportion at least to their means, than that of the United States."[91]

Emilio Castelar was typical of the long-time proponents of hispanismo who were sorely troubled by this situation and anxious to find a policy that could somehow, even in the midst of the Cuban insurrection, ingratiate Spain to Spanish America. Because they had created America, Spaniards were, Castelar declared, an American, not a European people. In the future, moreover, "Spain would be a power in the international councils of the world because of its presence in America, not because of ties or alliances with Europe." Accordingly, Castelar urged his country to avoid at all costs becoming involved with Old World powers as it sought a way out of its American crisis. Rather than seeking an association with European countries, he exhorted Spain to find a basis of cooperation with the Hispanic-American republics in resolving its colonial problem.[92]

Cánovas del Castillo with the backing of other Liberal-Conservative Party leaders such as Joaquín Sánchez de Toca, a forty-six-year-old senator long noted for his Americanist interests,[93] devised a policy that seemed intended to achieve the Castelar objectives. The Liberal-Conservative policy was to combat the Cuban insurrection with utmost vigor, sending a large army to the island not only to deal with the insurgents but also to discourage the United States, recognized as the real enemy, from intervention. Having suppressed the uprising and having won the admiration of Spanish America for the manner in which it had stared down the United States, Spain could then make generous concessions to the Cubans, a move that would restore unity to the entire Spanish family of both worlds.[94]

Liberal opponents to the Cánovas program, often led by Labra, demanded the extension of immediate concessions, including such reforms as universal suffrage and proceeding if necessary as far as actual autonomy. Cuba, Labra argued, must be made a showcase of Spanish liberal reforms. Inspired by this example, the rest of Spanish America would assertedly solidify its ties with Spain.[95] Campaigning unsuccessfully for the chamber of deputies in 1897, Joaquín Costa also demanded immediate Cuban reforms. Only through such measures, said Costa, could Spain strengthen its moral bonds with "Mexico, Chile, and the other Hispanic-American nations and thereby proceed toward establishing an alliance that could block the invading and absorbing instincts and contain the rapid advances of the North American republic."[96] Francisco Pi y Margall (1824–1901), a one-time president of the short-lived Spanish republic[97] who had long maintained an avid interest in America,[98] went the full distance of urging immediate independence for Cuba, contending that autonomy would not satisfy the islanders. After granting independence, Spain would be in a favorable position to establish close trade relations not only with Cuba but with the rest of Hispanic America.[99]

To liberal demands, Spanish conservatives customarily replied that internal reforms such as universal suffrage would only alienate the wealthy and respectable classes of the island and thereby make its loss inevitable.[100] They stressed also the racial peril inherent in internal reforms. The motherland, they asserted, had a moral duty to the Spanish settlers of Cuba not to abandon them to the "passions, hatreds, and barbarism of the people of color."[101] Arguing along these lines, an important statesman who had served as overseas minister in the Liberal-Conservative government of 1890 declared that if autonomy or independence were granted Cuba, Spaniards would no longer emigrate to the island. Abandoned to their own resources, the existing Spanish population would be submerged beneath the colored race; Cuba "would become another Santo Domingo, would fall into frightful barbarism and be lost to civilization for centuries."[102] Finally, the leading newspaper of Catholic traditionalism harped on the alleged United States desire to ship some six million Negroes to Cuba as a means of avoiding race war in the southern states. If Cuba lost the protection of Spain, it would be flooded by blacks and subjected to their rule, the paper warned. "Let Cuban Spaniards who begin to incline now toward the United States cause think of this and of the spectacle of black rule in the South during reconstruction, with its frightful results: the treasuries assaulted, the people caught up in an immense orgy of the ignorant and miserable blacks, half-civilized, perverts, absolutely inept."[103]

In combating liberal demands for concessions and conciliation, other conservatives had recourse to religious arguments. They saw the struggle in Cuba as primarily a religious war.[104] Masons and freethinking liberal types were blamed for having ignited the fires of revolution; and the white rebels of Cuba were said to be attracting the blacks to their side through spiritualist religious rites that had been spawned by Masonry. In the cause of religious purity, then, the war had to be waged energetically and Spanish liberals who wished to placate the rebels were, in the final analysis, guilty of heresy.[105]

As the Cuban war continued and mounted in ferocity, liberals and conservatives stepped up their political skirmishing in Spain.[106] Liberals heatedly abused the Cánovas del Castillo government for refusing to accept the April 4, 1896 United States offer of its good offices[107] and complained that war expenses were preventing Spain from undertaking much-needed internal reform and development programs.[108] They objected strenuously to the increasing deployment of Spanish manpower in Cuba, maintaining that no nation of seventeen million could commit 200,000 troops to that island while simultaneously carrying out capaigns in Africa and the Philippines.[109] Opponents of government policy also began to claim that the war had become unpopular in Spain. The continuation of the war, they affirmed, indicated the utter indifference of government officials to public opinion; it afforded proof that the "oligarchy regarded the masses as beasts and slaves" and that a selfish Madrid clique was totally insensitive to the wishes of the provinces.[110] "Never," stated a widely read author, "was a people so much against its will carried, as sheep to a slaughterhouse, to a disastrous war. . . . It has been an antinational war engineered by a few selfish interests."[111]

Predictably, representatives of the incumbent party responded that criticism by the political outs was undermining the war effort; further, it was encouraging the insurgents to maintain their struggle in the hope that a Liberal cabinet would replace the Conservative one then in power.[112] War opponents were also accused of preferring the United States to Spain, and Catholic traditionalist spokesman Juan Vázquez de Mella declared: "The legal insurrection of parliamentary liberalism against our traditions, history, and national honor is at the point of despoiling us of the last remaining testimony to our past glories."[113] With ample justification a Madrid journal observed that Spanish congressmen were spending more time attacking, blaming, censuring, and insulting one another than in criticizing the United States.[114]

On August 8, 1897 in the mountains of Guipúzcoa, Cánovas del Castillo was assassinated by an Italian anarchist. The assassination exacerbated an already existing internal leadership struggle and in the following October the Liberal-Conservatives were replaced in power by the Liberals. Shortly the role of the two parties vis-à-vis the Cuban war seemed reversed. Apparently afraid of being charged with weakness, the Liberal regime maintained a firm policy in conducting the war and in standing up to the

United States. The new administration, moreover, insisted on dealing unilaterally with Cuba and, following the policy that Castelar had counseled, rejected the Conservative-advocated approach of seeking European mediation. As a result, Conservatives began to accuse Liberals of intransigence.[115]

The tensions mounted as the year 1898 began and as Spaniards of both major political groupings fretted more and more over possible United States entry into the war. The anxiety prevailing in Madrid had a deleterious effect, according to one critic, on that city's theater. Madrileños were no longer willing to concentrate on serious, thought-provoking plays. Instead, they sought mere distraction. And producers responded with plays that featured more music and dancing, "and the costumes of the women on stage became scantier so as to reveal more of the body's lines; for this is what now attracts people to the theater."[116]

The year was not far advanced before Spaniards had to curtail the search for distraction and buckle down to austerity. What both the Liberal and Conservative Parties had sought above all else to avoid had come to pass: the United States had entered the Cuban War.

Resignation often characterized the response of Spaniards to the news that war with the United States had actually begun. Many of them seemed to agree with the sentiments expressed by a Madrid newspaper shortly before the declaration of war: "Rather than endure another humiliation, let the war, with all its terrible consequences, come; we know it is inevitable."[117] A column appearing in the March 30 edition of a Madrid periodical must also have reflected the views of many of its readers: "Spain contemplates the bloody possibility of war with the United States with the sad resignation and serenity of the man whose honor and conscience are clear. . . . If there is to be war, better to have it and get it over. . . . For an organism suffers less with violent pneumonia than with a prolonged, debilitating disease."[118]

Two political opponents expressed similar attitudes as they contemplated the reality of war with the Colossus. Ramiro de Maeztu, noted at that time for his liberal doctrines, declared: ". . . if the Yankee cannons have to erase the best of our race, I hope at least, as a Spaniard and as an artist, that our fall will be beautiful. I wish, at the very least, that if we have not known how to say yes to life we will know how to say yes to death, making it thereby a deed glorious and worthy of Spain."[119] Vázquez de Mella, the inflexible defender of Catholic traditionalism, stated:

> This Spanish nation that from the mists of the ocean foam called forth the American continent in order to make of it an altar on which Spain offered its own spirit, consecrated forever to Christ . . . cannot now weakly and through compromise bow out of America. It can leave America only after a gigantic catastrophe, if necessary, or after an immense and definitive victory; but it can never be unworthily expelled.[120]

Nearly identical views were expressed by a politically neutral journal: "Spain cannot withdraw at the bidding of others from the areas it created. The children of Cortés and Pizarro cannot retire as humble lackeys from the region they discovered, populated, and civilized even if all the universe should command it."[121]

If the United States had hoped to have its way with Cuba without war against Spain, it was guilty of a serious misunderstanding of the Spanish character as revealed by these quotations.

In certain quarters, confidence mingled with fatalism and resignation as Spaniards prepared for war with the new opponent. For some time the Spanish press had been reporting on the weakness of the United States military organization.[122] And upon the actual outset of hostilities the periodical *Unión Ibero-Americana* reported: "Public opinion believes in the triumph of our navy and our soldiers. Enthusiastic patriotism prevails in all parts. No one is worried. We will fight with honor and all the world will derive satisfaction as it observes our conduct in this struggle."[123]

The newspaper *El Siglo Futuro* demonstrated that the spirit of Quijote was not dead. It asserted that Spain could win the war by licensing its many owners of sailing ships as corsairs to prey upon both coasts of the United States.[124]

Spanish fantasy had seldom been more remarkably in evidence. But seldom were Spaniards granted so short a period to indulge in their delusions. The rude abruptness with which fantasy was shattered provoked one of the most serious crises of national spirit in Spanish history.

3: SPAIN RESPONDS TO THE DISASTER

1898: The Year of Despair

Disaster was the word with which Spaniards referred to their war with the United States, once the news of its catastrophic consequences began to circulate in the peninsula. Overnight, all previous publications describing the ills of Spain and prescribing remedies had become inadequate and obsolete. Gripped by an all-consuming pessimism, Spaniards concluded that the national sickness was more serious then even the dourest critics of the predisaster body politic had hinted. After the restoration, the question had been "how should Spain live?" Following the disaster, it became "can Spain as an historical entity continue to live?"[1]

Grieving over the shattered Spanish nation in August of 1898, Francisco Silvela declared: "All is undone. Whoever observes public affairs will note that there is no pulse in Spain. Materialism has invaded us; selfishness kills us; the passions disappear because life is extinguished. . . . There is a risk that all bonds of national unity will be totally severed."[2] The following month, in secret senate discussions on responsibility for the disaster, Práxedes Mateo Sagasta is reported to have said that neither he nor Cánovas del Castillo had lived long enough to change the characteristics of the Spanish race, "the source and origin of all our misfortunes."[3]

An anguished Joaquín Costa cried out that Spain was wandering unburied among the tombs of extinct nationalities. His country's fall was so great that he believed it might be impossible for the Spanish people ever to rise again;[4] and he saw the distinct possibility that foreign intervention might make a new Poland of his prostrate homeland.[5] Equally sunk in despair, Menéndez Pelayo for a time stopped answering his mail; and for two years his literary output and creative activity fell off sharply.[6] It was the same with many members of his generation who lapsed into inactivity because they doubted whether Spain could be redeemed by even the most Herculean efforts.

Because the war against the United States had been commonly depicted as the struggle between two races,[7] Spaniards wondered if their own and perhaps even the entire Latin race was doomed. Costa speculated that all nations of the Iberian race might be destined to fall, "grain by grain, before the advances of the Saxon race."[8] Ramiro de Maeztu began to ponder seriously on the question: "In what does the superiority of the Anglo-Saxon over the Latin races consist?" During the fifteen years that he spent in England, his mother's native land, at the outset of the twentieth cen-

48

tury this question was never far from his mind.[9] A former overseas minister asserted just after the disaster: ". . . in its decadence the Latin race now takes a gigantic step toward the abyss of total ruin; everywhere there are now clear signs of this."[10] And a journalist who had long been perturbed by the decadence of Spain asked: "Does providence decree, upon our being overcome in the waters off Cuba, that there disappear from the world our soul, our language, our civilization, our raza, with Spain and all of Spanish America succumbing to the . . . Saxons?"[11]

The literature of despair evoked by the disaster was characterized by the themes of "there isn't" and "we lack:"

> There isn't a school system, there isn't irrigation, wealth, or resources; there isn't industry; there isn't a middle class; there isn't administrative morality; there isn't the spirit of work; there isn't . . . there isn't . . . there isn't. . . . We lack men; we lack willpower; we lack values; we lack virtue, religion, heroism, ideals, a spirit of cooperation; we lack . . . we lack . . . we lack.[12]

A few Spaniards, as they surveyed their ailing nation after the disaster, began rather timidly to suggest rehabilitation programs. But only when they gradually extended their vision so as to encompass Spaniards of America as well as of the peninsula did they acquire animation and confidence as they prescribed methods of recovery. Once viewed in the context both of the New and the Old Worlds, there did seem to be hope for the Spanish raza. Immediately after the disaster, however, Spaniards tended to confine their attention to the peninsula and were lackadaisical as they formulated recovery plans; for they could not shake the haunting fear that they were dealing with an incurable sickness.

Early Prescriptions for the Rehabilitation of Peninsular Spain

ISOLATIONISM AND HISPANIZATION

A common reaction to the disaster was the demand for Spain to dedicate itself to its own affairs and to ignore in so far as possible the outside world. Economic nationalism, propounded by some Spaniards in the early 1890s, found new advocates as it was linked now to a general program of isolationism. Spain, for example, was warned to avoid contracting large foreign loans in its quest for rehabilitation and in general to eschew all foreign economic ties. One writer laid the loss of Cuba to that island's economic connections with the United States; and he advised Spain, in order to maintain its independence, to turn inward economically and develop its own resources with its own money.[13]

As seen by this leading isolationist, Spaniards had only two alternatives: "Either we submit ourselves absolutely to the demands and models of European life, or we retire absolutely and work to form on our own soil an original conception of the national essence, capable of sustaining us in the struggle against exotic ideas. I reject," he continued, "all that would be submission and I have faith in the creative virtue of our land. But to create it is necessary for the nation, like the man, to meditate; and Spain must reconcentrate its efforts and abandon all sterile foreign commitments."[14]

Here was a classic expression of the conviction that Spain's greatest need was to Hispanicize (españolizar) itself: to discover, by turning inward, what truly constituted its national character so that it could then proceed toward reconstruction through means that were compatible with the dictates of that character.

Once he emerged from the apathy brought on by the disaster, Menéndez Pelayo devoted himself with remarkable energy to the task of Hispanicizing Spain. To him, history afforded the best means for discovering the genuine mode of Spanish life and thought that should guide the nation in its struggle for survival and perhaps eventually for rehabilitation. Before history could serve this purpose, however, it had to be written; for in the past, Menéndez Pelayo contended, Spanish history had been either a series of "antireligious blasphemies or else a recounting of pious nonsense."[15] So, he turned again to his books, to the dead with whom he said he lived, convinced that if men of a previous generation had been formed in the cafes and clubs, men of his era in their pursuit of a genuine Spanish history had to be formed in the libraries.

EUROPEANIZATION

To others concerned about the nation's survival, it seemed apparent that Spain had to Europeanize (europeizar) itself.[16] The Europeanizers saw little value in Spanish traditions. Spain, it was reasoned, had been defeated by a country without traditions. What did the United States have? Machines, industries, banks, and money. So then Spain, if it hoped to prolong its existence in the modern world, had to acquire machines, industries, banks, and money. To learn how to accomplish this, a Spaniard wrote, it had to turn not to the United States, with whose spirit it suffered a basic incompatibility, but to the progressive countries of Europe.[17]

Consumed by a faith in Europeanization, Maeztu preached the need for Spain to become an industrialized, bourgeois country. If Spaniards did not learn how to appreciate the beauty of the machine, the stock market, the factory, they "were doomed to become the colonials of the more advanced countries."[18] "We ought," he wrote, "to forget all our history and place our eyes only on the supreme ideal, there in the future. One has to be European, that is, scientific, objective. Europeanization means the march ahead."[19]

The fury with which Spaniards debated the Hispanization-Europeanization issue in the postdisaster era was born of despair and disillusionment. Neither side in the days immediately following the humiliation of 1898 thought it likely that its cause would triumph in time to bring about rehabilitation. Menéndez Pelayo, for example, glumly recognized that he was slipping into obscurity as his mission failed to attract widespread support. And Maeztu remained doubtful that Spaniards were capable of acquiring the traits that had resulted in the superiority of the Anglo-Saxons.

REGIONALISM

The rise of regionalist and even of separatist sentiment in postdisaster days has been described as "the traumatic effect of the loss of colonies suffered in 1898."[20] The *Heraldo de Aragón* noted: "Military triumphs are powerful causes of national integration, just as military disasters disturb the composition of the states that incur them." The Peace of Paris, continued *El Heraldo*, "more disastrous than the war itself," produced in Spain a movement toward disintegration, breathing new life into "the centrifugal forces of regional particularism that have their most radical expression in Catalan and Basque separatism."[21]

Joaquín Costa observed that the colonial disaster heightened the resentment of Spanish provinces against what they considered the misgovernment of Madrid.[22] Spain lost Cuba, Costa continued, because the politicians in Madrid denied the island what rightly belonged to it, that is, autonomy. Because of this the Cubans struck out not for autonomy but for independence. The moral was clear: unless the central government in Spain granted a certain degree of autonomy to the peninsula's political subdivisions, these would come increasingly to insist upon separatism. "If Spain," Costa warned, "continues as an Asiatic regime of the fifteenth century with all power concentrated in Madrid, discontent will mount. The provinces will grow tired of being other Cubas, humiliated and exploited . . .; they will prefer to convert themselves into the well-governed colonies of a London or a Paris."[23]

Stung by the economic losses that the colonial disaster had occasioned and doubtful that they would ever receive from a Madrid government the desired degree of tariff protection,[24] Catalan business groups began to enthuse over the advantages of regional autonomy.[25] They thereby lent fresh impetus to the nineteenth-century school of regionalism in which Catalan disciples of the Prussian statesman Friedrich Karl von Savigny (1779–1861) had contended that regions, possessing their own customs, legal traditions, and ways of life, should be free from the suffocating pressures of centralized power.[26]

MISCELLANEOUS PRESCRIPTIONS FOR PENINSULAR SPAIN

Hispanization, Europeanization, and regionalism were the most important general issues discussed in early postdisaster days. But Spaniards did not confine their attention to broad and general issues as they sought the means to assuage national suffering. To the contrary, they suggested an amazing variety of specific, limited expedients. A few of these will be mentioned in alphabetical order.

Amortization of the Debt and Balancing of the Budget. Alberto Cólogan y Cólogan, the Marqués de Torre Hermosa, pictured amortization of the national debt as a panacea. Once amortization was completed, the state would have adequate funds to stimulate development and create better employment opportunities, thereby banishing social discontent and bringing an end to anarchist schemes. Caciquismo would also disappear, Cólogan y Cólogan claimed, as economic conditions improved, as improve they must once the debt was amortized. In proceeding toward amortization, the Marqués concluded, Spain should follow the example of Porfirio Díaz in Mexico, "our favorite daughter in America."[27]

Before amortization, another Spaniard argued, Spain must concern itself with austerity and budget balancing. If Spanish politicians once found the strength of character to proceed toward the balanced budget, problems of every type would shortly disappear.[28] Liberal journalist Vital Fité suggested an approach to budget balancing for which he guaranteed happy results. Let the government reduce the Church subvention from an estimated forty million to twenty million pesetas. Not only would this step balance the budget, it would force the clergy to acquire the sense of sacrifice that must animate all Spaniards if the country were to survive.[29]

Francisco Silvela, the leader of the Liberal-Conservative Party for some five years following the assassination of Cánovas del Castillo, also demanded an austerity program, a balanced budget, and debt amortization. But he feared that Spaniards would not accept the necessary sacrifices unless inspired by a great national ideal,[30] an ideal that he refrained from specifying.

Education. Among Spanish liberals the outstanding figure in education was Francisco Giner de los Ríos (1840–1915). Shortly after the disaster Giner published one of the most important books in the entire regeneration literature.[31] Repeating and refining contentions that he had long voiced, Giner stated that Spain could achieve regeneration only through the long, slow process of remaking men, beginning at the primary school level. The type of education Giner had in mind was one that was neutral, nonreligious, and essentially progressive in pedagogical methodology.[32] Father Andrés Manjón (1846–1923) agreed that only a long-term educational process could transform Spain into an organism once again viable. For him, though, the proper type of education was the one he had begun in 1889 to impart to the poor Gypsy youth of Granada through his Ave María schools. In these schools the curriculum was built around the catechism. Spaniards could only persevere in their affliction, Manjón claimed, if sustained by the true vision of life that was supplied by the Catholic catechism.[33]

Others concerned about the sick estate of Spain demanded an education that stressed proficiency in practical, technical matters so that love of work would be instilled in the citizenry and "a nation of orators transformed into a nation of laborers."[34] Adolfo González Posada (1860–1944), a pioneering figure in the field of social legislation, believed Spain could emerge from its terrible backwardness only by taking advantage of foreign educational facilities. The country, he stated, must begin to send its engineers, merchants, philosophers, teachers, military men, and even priests, to schools in France, England, Germany, and the United States.[35] To Aniceto Sela, a companion of Posada in many a liberal cause, the only immediate hope for a revitalized Spain lay in university extension work. He called for a vast expansion of the pilot extension projects undertaken by the University of Oviedo in 1899. In university extension Sela saw the means of easing social tensions and restoring class solidarity while at the same time stimulating the economic productiveness of the masses.[36]

Francisco Tomás y Estruch, a Barcelona poet and art instructor, had a different dream of how to save Spain through education. Art instruction, he maintained, would tap the spiritual and aesthetic resources of the people, liberate them from their material appetites, give them new sources of satisfaction and fulfillment and thus ease the social problem.[37]

Feminism. Barcelona sociologist Santiago Valentí Camp was only twenty-three at the time of the disaster, but already he had clear ideas as to how Spain and other Latin nations could triumph in the struggle for survival. He saw salvation in feminism. By liberating its women and placing them on an equal footing with men, Spain could begin to utilize the energy and idealism that would guarantee it a respected position in the modern world. Gathering material in support of this contention, the young sociologist amassed a bibliography of over three thousand titles pertaining to the inability of women in Spain and other Latin countries to contribute to national development owing to discriminatory treatment.[38]

German and Japanese Models. Julio de Lazúrtegui, born in Bilbao in 1859, acquired rather late in life an all-consuming interest in Spanish America and as president of the Centro de la Unión Ibero-Americana en Vizcaya worked tirelessly to increase trade with the former colonies. However, at the time of the disaster Lazúrtegui, who had studied mining and metallurgy abroad, saw Germany rather than Spanish America as the key to Spanish survival. Impressed by what he regarded as the miracle of German industrialization, Lazúrtegui studied the phenomenon in some detail, paying particular attention to the rise of the steel industry. If Spaniards would only follow the German models as he explained them in one of his books, renewed vitality was assured.[39]

The professor of sociology at the University of Madrid, Manuel Sales y Ferré (1843–1910) disagreed with Lazúrtegui. For Sales y Ferré the example that Spain had to study and follow was that of Japan. In contrast to the Bilbaíno, who regarded free enterprise as largely responsible for German achievements, the Madrid-based sociologist saw socialism as the key to the Japanese success.[40]

Literature and Militarism. Literary critic Norberto González Aurioles attributed the disaster largely to a decline in the quality of literature. Rather than a symptom, he believed this to be the cause of decadence. Skepticism and materialism, he maintained, had infected Spain's creative writers. As a result they had abandoned the attempt to uplift and inspire their readers, seeking instead to pander to their sensual appetites. He exhorted Spanish writers to turn to spiritual concepts and pursue exalted ideals through which they could enoble literature. "A regeneration or renaissance of public customs," González predicted, "will follow a renaissance of literature."[41]

To Victoriano Feliz (1880–1936), who began a distinguished military career in the rigorous African campaigns, discipline and organization, not the dreams and visions of the literati, must sustain and redirect the floundering nation. And so Feliz urged the military to intervene more directly in public affairs, to fight social malaise by showing Spaniards how to respond unquestioningly to what was demanded of them in the struggle for national well-being.[42]

Professional Proficiency. Santiago Ramón y Cajal (1851–1933), the largely self-taught medical researcher whose discoveries in the field of histology earned him a share of the Nobel Prize in 1906, thought that Spaniards could best serve their country by developing their own talents in relative isolation from political procedures. When Moret offered him a cabinet post, Ramón y Cajal is reported to have responded that he was too busy to be bothered with such unimportant matters.[43]

Also impressed by the need for each individual to concern himself with perfecting his own talents, Spain's great man of letters José Echegary (1823–1916), a corecipient of the Nobel Prize in literature in 1904, wrote shortly after the disaster:

> If each Spaniard, in his own sphere, large or small, exalted or modest, does what he can, it will be enough. Each man of science must study assiduously and in each moment repeat to himself, "I want to learn so that the wise men abroad will not say that I am ignorant." Each industrialist must work to perfect his industry, repeating always to himself, "I want to progress so that foreign nations cannot say that Spain has no industry." Each agricultural worker . . . must say to himself, "let no one proclaim that the juices of our soil have dried up. . . ." Each merchant must struggle with all his might in the fields of commerce . . . seeking new markets so that no one can think we are lazy. And the least worker, the most modest worker, must offer up all his efforts, thinking with noble ambition: "to work, to work, so that no one can say the Spanish laborer is idle and weak." In short, let all the citizens work as they are capable to improve themselves and gain

proficiency, sanctifying their efforts as they obey that mysterious voice that says: "It is necessary to work individually for the patria."[44]

Public Health, Ruralism, Savings Banks, and Technicians. Surveying the ruins of Spain after the disaster, a prominent medical doctor found that much of what was wrong with the country stemmed from the poor health of the masses. To prolong its national existence Spain, he said, had to embark upon a massive public health program.[45] A Catholic priest, understandably, prescribed a return to the faith. But before that could be achieved, he saw the need for Spaniards to abandon the cities and return to the rural regions. Manifesting a point of view long associated with Catholic traditionalism and one that would strongly influence many elements in the Falange during the 1930s, the priest equated the virtuous existence with the rural existence. To make possible a return to the countryside, he urged a land reform program that would multiply the number of rural property owners.[46]

Claiming to speak for a more practical and feasible approach to national problems, geographer-engineer-journalist Lucas Mallada recommended the establishment of thousands of savings banks in all parts of Spain. Through savings, he reasoned, the masses would acquire economic virtue and security.[47] Francisco Andrés Oliván, the man who had devoted much of his life since 1847 to travel because he could not abide conditions in Spain, envisioned political rather than economic solutions. Spain must rid itself of professional politicians, he proclaimed, and seek leadership from men of proven skill, from businessmen and technicians, from the members of the agricultural associations and the chambers of commerce. What Oliván seemed to be hinting at was the need to replace the parliamentary with a corporative system of functional representation.[48]

Awakening Optimism: Prescriptions for a Transatlantic Spanish Community

From the multitude of Spaniards concerned with narrow and limited expedients for treating national ills, there emerged half a dozen men with broad-range, multiple-remedy programs. Each of the six to some degree shared in the ideal of revitalizing Spain not only in the peninsula but in America as well. Because they contemplated the Iberian raza not just in Spain, where it seemed weak and listless, but in the New World, where it appeared strong and dynamic, they were capable of summoning up far greater optimism than those who observed only the plight of peninsular Spaniards.

JOAQUÍN COSTA AND RICARDO MACÍAS PICAVEA

In his 1896 bid for a deputy post Costa had been soundly defeated. When the disaster struck Spain two years later "a form of creeping paralysis" had already begun to affect his lower limbs. His huge body resting "upon a pair of spindle legs and tiny feet,"[49] Costa seemed more a symbol of Spain's physical degeneration than the guide to rehabilitation. By 1906, living in the humblest of circumstances in Graus, a small town of Upper Aragon, and overcome by financial worries and sickness, Costa thought seriously about withdrawing altogether from public life.[50] When he died in 1911, "everyone seemed sad, but the next day he was forgotten."[51]

Yet it is of this man that Rafael Altamira has written:

> No one in Spain can doubt that Costa is the "regenerator" who exercised the farthest-reaching influence . . . the only one who in the year 1898 and afterward caused a real agitation in the country. . . . His work led to the most profound agitation in our modern history, to the most penetrating analysis of the national psychology, and created the most abundant and specific source of reforms that we have known since 1812.[52]

Maeztu's appraisal was briefer but scarcely less laudatory: "The only men of real importance in the '98 period were Joaquín Costa and Macías Picavea."[53]

Costa's pessimism was still immense in 1900. "In forty or fifty years," he wrote, "Spain has retrogressed two centuries; we are now below the level of 1807 and even that of the time of Charles II [1665–1700]." Yet Costa, two years after the disaster, was not entirely without hope, for he wrote: "It is necessary to improvise a nation, making a revolution from power the work of months or even of weeks."[54]

Probably more than any other individual, it was Costa who popularized the notion of Europeanization. "The government," he declared in a statement that won widespread acquiescence, "must spend less money but spend it more wisely in Europeanizing Spain, that is in making it more productive and modern. In particular," he continued, "it must spend less on defense. Spain needs to defend itself not against the English or the French or other imagined foes in Europe, but against misery, intellectual backwardness, lack of communications, and arid lands."[55]

However much he wanted to Europeanize it, Costa did not want to de-Hispanicize (desespañolizar) his country.[56] Miguel de Unamuno properly recognizes that Costa was profoundly opposed to heedless imitation of European models. Costa, as described by Unamuno, wanted to borrow some European elements, but to make sure that they were properly digested so as to become part of the Spanish flesh and blood. In order for this to happen, Costa believed that Spain had to turn not only toward Europe but also inward so as to discover and then strengthen its own national traditions.[57]

In his desire to strengthen Spain so that it could assimilate and synthesize, rather than servilely imitate European usages, Costa focused his attention on education and food. When it came to education, Costa recommended that schools set themselves the task of producing men with ambition, practical knowledge, initiative, and self-confidence. He called for a war against empty intellectualism and pronounced a plague on current university training with its emphasis on useless knowledge. Spain needed fewer, not more universities, he maintained. Rather than pouring money into archaic universities, the government should establish a vast farm-extension program centering around the farm school.[58]

Undernourishment, Costa contended, had sapped the energies of the populace. In addition to practical education, then, Spaniards had to be provided with an adequate diet. Half the people of Spain, according to Costa, were hungry and the life span was the shortest in Europe. Therefore, the primary concern of the government must be with a "hydraulic policy" that would reclaim thousands of acres of land through irrigation. Once food production was increased sufficiently to provide a nutritious diet for Spaniards, the government would have to seek markets for agricultural exports. National farm production, Costa said, "must be assured eighteen million more consumers than live in the peninsula." The eighteen million he had in mind were the citizens of Mexico and Argentina.[59]

To increase agricultural production and also to strengthen what he felt to be the authentic tradition of Spain in its period of grandeur under the Catholic Kings, Costa recommended the collectivization of agricultural lands. According to his interpretation of the historical past, Spain's one-time greatness had rested to a considerable degree upon the collective holdings of agricultural property. This Spanish tradition had also for a time been strengthened by the feedback effect of the conquest; for the influence of Inca agrarian socialism as discovered by the Spaniards in the New World had nourished Spain's natural predisposing tendencies toward rural collectivism.[60]

If Spain collectivized its rural property while leaving other means of production in private hands it would not only be reviving its traditions, it would, asserted Costa, be preparing a synthesis between European individualistic capitalism on one hand and communism on the other. Costa regarded laissez-faire capitalism and communism, in their pure forms, as equally inimical to the Spanish style of life.[61]

Ever insistent upon the need for an elite to infuse the masses with a great ideal, Costa was by 1900 proceeding toward the formulation of a specific ideal. He declared that mankind needed a strong and powerful Spanish raza, in Europe and America,

> as a counterweight to the Saxon race, to maintain the moral equilibrium in the infinite game of history. . . . To confront the Saxon Sancho there must always be the pure, luminous Spanish Quijote, filling the world with his madness, affirming through the centuries the Utopia of the Golden Age and maintaining perennially here below this spiritual

chivalry committed to belief in something and prepared to sacrifice for
something; a Quijote who through passion and faith and sacrifice makes
the earth become something more than a factory and a market where
things are bought and sold. . . . Therefore I say . . . that not because
of the impulse of vanity and glory, not even for patriotism, but because
of high duties of humanity, we are obliged to foment the growth and
expansion of the Spanish raza.[62]

There had emerged in Costa's mind the concept of a united community
of Spaniards on both sides of the ocean; and for this community Costa
entertained far more exalted hopes than ever he had been able to conjure
up as he considered the future of Spaniards living in the peninsula. Only
by turning his eyes toward the New World did Costa glimpse the ideal
that liberated him at least briefly from his gloom and set him to fancying
a new golden age for the Spanish people. For Costa, Europeanization was
the means of making Spain physically strong enough to support and sustain the dreams of Quijote in the world. Americanization was also essential to the realization of these dreams, for only by acting in concert with
their New World offspring and brothers would the Spaniards of Europe
find the power to fulfill the destiny of the raza.

In many respects the program of Ricardo Macías Picavea for Spanish
regeneration coincided with Costa's. Macías urged hydraulic projects for
reclaiming rural acreage and stressed the need for rule by an elite that was
vitalized by a vision of national destiny.[63] More clearly than Costa, Macías
Picavea asserted the desirability of replacing the parliamentary system
with a corporative structure. Spain, he believed, would remain prostrate
until it uplifted the working classes and incorporated their wills and
energies into the struggle for national rehabilitation. This could best be
accomplished, he maintained, by organizing workers into guilds or corporations and permitting them to participate in shaping guild policy and
in choosing men who would speak for their interests in a functionally
representative national Cortes.[64]

While Macías Picavea did stress the usefulness of religious competition
so as to reanimate Spain's phlegmatic Catholic Church and to combat
the growing tendency toward dehumanizing materialism, he focused primarily on economic means of recovery. Catalan industry, he contended,
should be stripped of its protection and forced to become genuinely com-
petitive in the quest for world markets.[65] Once driven to acquire technical
proficiency, Catalan manufacturers would succeed in finding outlets for
their products in Spanish America. To assist in this process Macías recommended expansion of Spain's consular service in the New World republics
of Spanish origin, the sending of commercial agents, and the establishment
in Madrid of a central clearinghouse of information on conditions and
possibilities of trade between Spain and America. Seeing little hope for
economic recovery in the peninsula unless Spain "secured special relations

with the sister republics of South and Central America," Macías urged "the utilization toward this end of our large colonies of emigrants in those countries."[66]

Costa dreamed on a grander scale than Macías Picavea. A revitalized Spanish community capable of protecting lofty ideals against the creeping materialism of the Anglo-Saxon race was what Costa mused upon. Macías Picavea seemed willing to settle for the establishment of an economically viable transatlantic community. For both men, however, Spain in America was indispensable for the resurgence of peninsular Spain.

Miguel de Unamuno and Rafael Altamira

Spain, as Unamuno saw it, suffered from excessive seriousness and gravity; there was no youth in Spain, only youths. To correct this situation, Unamuno believed it was necessary to reach down to the people and to awaken their latent spirit and spontaneity.[67] At first he thought this could be done only by Europeanized Spaniards; by Spaniards, that is, who had freed themselves from the dead weight of an overly institutionalized past. Therefore in the days immediately following upon the disaster, Unamuno raised his voice in favor of the Europeanization of Spain. He saw salvation in a liberated, Europeanized elite who "would learn consciously what the masses know only subconsciously, so as to be able to guide them better."[68]

Unamuno insisted that a new leadership elite could not come to understand the latent spirit of the masses through the study of history. History dealt only with the surface of human existence; it concerned itself with the waves of the sea and ignored what transpired in the depths below. It was infrahistory, the vast murky area beneath the waves of occurrences recorded by history, that Unamuno wished to explore. The approach to infrahistory, he decided, had to be through the contemplation of the landscapes of Spain, through a study of previously ignored peoples, and through an investigation of "the nonintellectual creations of our spirit," that is, folklore, customs and art works.[69] In studying the second element of the Spanish reality, the masses whose lives had not concerned the historian, Unamuno contended that the romances of the past were a far more valuable tool than all the books of history.

As he concerned himself with the Spanish nation and raza, Unamuno soon concluded that Spain was not confined to the peninsula. What transpired in Spanish America affected the totality of the Hispanic raza, the overall Hispanic community, just as much as what occurred in the peninsula. In contemplating his country after the disaster Unamuno had exclaimed "Spain hurts me." But it was not just the peninsula that hurt him; it was Spain in America as well.[70]

If he was susceptible to being hurt by Spanish America, Unamuno was also capable of being filled with hope and inspired by it. Addressing his Spanish-American readers in 1904, Unamuno declared: "That of my spirit which I cannot realize, you have realized; in you my intimate life revives, in the light and the open air. My blessings upon you." Spain, Unamuno continued, must learn from America; for America had erased sterile Spanish institutions and discarded what was dead and useless of the past, retaining only the pure Spanish essence. "There [in America] our blood, our language are not in the service of purposeless organs, of an imposed body of thought. There lies our future."[71]

Unamuno had by then decided that in order truly to understand themselves and their infrahistory, Spaniards had to turn their attention to the members of their community in the New World. For one thing, Spanish-American literature, particularly a work such as the epic poem *Martín Fierro* by the Argentine José Hernández, constituted an addition to the peninsular romances and thus afforded Spaniards a new means for comprehending their authentic nature as preserved by the masses.[72]

Within just a few years after the disaster, then, Unamuno had acquired a new perspective on Spain. Peninsular Spaniards no longer had to Europeanize themselves; it was sufficient that they Hispano-Americanize themselves.

To a large extent philosopher Unamuno's conception of the Spanish community was shared by historian Rafael Altamira. Noting that he had long meditated upon the Spanish character and soul, Altamira confessed that he had only reached vague and inconclusive theories. The reason, he gradually came to understand, was that he had known no more than half the Spanish soul. To understand it in its entirety, it would be necessary to observe and study the other half across the Atlantic.[73]

Not surprisingly, the historian placed greater faith in the utility of his craft than Unamuno. History, Altamira insisted, could be a useful tool in discovering the real nature of a people and in providing guidelines to direct the slow process of change and progress. He further claimed that "history teaches us that some of the more conservative ideas have absolutely no foundation in past experience, while some of the seemingly most advanced and daring ideas actually are not new at all but have a firm place in history."[74] Altamira believed that the most advanced and daring aspects of the Spanish past could be discovered not only by having recourse to the history of Spain, but by turning to Spain in America, where they were at the moment flourishing and producing new fruits. To him, the history of Spain complemented by the sociology of Spanish America could guide the Hispanic community toward a new and proud destiny in the modern world.

ÁNGEL GANIVET AND JOAQUÍN SÁNCHEZ DE TOCA

Ángel Ganivet (1862–1898) from Granada,[75] considered by some a genial eccentric and by others a sick misanthrope, served in the consular service in various countries, intent upon improving his mastery over many languages.[76] A fallen-away Catholic like so many of his generation, extremely pessimistic and even haunted by despair, Ganivet could nonetheless occasionally exude confidence and enthusiasm. And his mystical faith in a renewed and mighty Spain helped provide a generally despondent era with a basis of optimism.

Alarmed by the early signs of the social problem, Ganivet saw its solution in restoring political and economic power to the municipalities. Only local units of government, he argued, were capable of coping with mounting social discontent. He recommended the return of communal property to municipalities, so as to endow them with the necessary means for feeding the local populace.[77] "Among a people where there exists the possibility of eating every day," Ganivet reasoned, "there would be, it is true, lazy ones, but there would be no dynamiters."[78] In a decentralized regime of local self-rule, workers would also have access to officials whom they knew intimately and perhaps trusted; this would do away with "the fiction of representation in parliament . . ., establishing an effective authority capable of guaranteeing order and territorial cohesion."[79]

Although he recognized the economic requirements of social justice programs, Ganivet had a disdain for the materialistic society and felt Spain could only survive by being true to the stoic traits of its national character. A life of repose he pictured as infinitely preferable to one in which a pressured people "ran incessantly to arrive nowhere."[80] Technological inventions, the Granadan averred, simply enable people to run faster in reaching this destination.[81] Characteristically, he once remarked that the unique form of popular singing that had originated in Cuba was "worth more than all the production of the United States, including its sewing machines and telephones."[82]

Above all, Ganivet admonished Spaniards to avoid the quest for quantitative greatness and to seek instead the spiritual ideal that could bind factious groups and contending regions into a cohesive national whole. "Just as I believe," he wrote, "that in matters of material domination many peoples of Europe are superior to us, I believe also that for the creation of the ideal there is not a people with such natural aptitudes . . . as ours."[83] Quijote, observed the diplomat-philosopher, had had to liberate himself from material preoccupations before he could embark upon his adventures; and he advised a similar liberation for contemporary Spain. "Before enriching a nation," he wrote, "I think it is necessary to ennoble it, because business for the sake of business is a sad thing . . .; if ideals of brotherhood are not inculcated, economic progress will only bring about shameful rivalry."[84]

For Ganivet, ideals of universal brotherhood were utopian. On the other hand, certain peoples in the world were by their very nature brothers because bound together by ties of common interests and values. Spaniards from across the seas Ganivet definitely considered his brothers. "When I

am with a Hispano-American," he confided, "I am in intellectual communication even when we have scarcely exchanged four words. . . . I know
that there exists a community of ideals. . . . On the other hand, with a
foreigner I need a long relationship and sustained efforts to achieve an
understanding."[85] Satisfied as to the natural fraternity of Spaniards on
both sides of the ocean, Ganivet proclaimed: "To think and to work
effectively, we must know that we think and work not only for the peninsula and the adjacent islands, but for the great community in which our
spirit and our language rule."[86]

Having reached these conclusions Ganivet was ready even two years
before the disaster to formulate one of the classic expressions of hispanismo. Upon this feat rested much of the influence he was destined to
exercise upon the men who worked for rehabilitation after 1898. Ganivet's
was a voice of hope because for once his pessimism had vanished as he
meditated upon what a reunited Spanish community could accomplish.
In a way, Ganivet's dream of a resurgent Hispanic community was even
more appealing to Spaniards, with their customary tutelary attitudes toward the former colonies, than Unamuno's. Spaniards, Unamuno thought,
could recapture their vanished greatness by Hispano-Americanizing themselves, by learning from their overseas brothers. Ganivet hoped to arouse
Spaniards from lethargy by holding before them the great ideal of infusing
the genuine Hispanic spirit in America. Rather than asking them to be
saved by America, Ganivet gave to Spaniards the cause of saving America,
or at least the only part of it that mattered, Spanish America:

> No new exterior action can lead us toward the restoration of material
> grandeur, toward the reacquisition of the high rank we once held. . . .
> On the other hand, if by the force of our intelligence alone we could
> manage to reconstitute the family union of all the Hispanic peoples and
> to infuse in them the worship of common ideals, of our ideals, we
> would fulfill a great historic mission and we would give life to a noble,
> original and new invention in the annals of politics. . . . Because we
> have exhausted our forces of material expansion, today we must change
> tactics and bring to the fore those forces that are never exhausted, those
> of intelligence that are latent in Spain and that can, when developed,
> carry us to greater creations. . . . Upon being reborn, we will find an
> immensity of brother peoples whom we will mark with the seal of our
> spirit.[87]

Following the disaster, Joaquín Sánchez de Toca, the Liberal-Conservative Party stalwart who was about to hold important ministerial posts in
several cabinets,[88] gave continuing expression to Ganivet's sentiments. His
unique contribution to hispanismo was to blend these sentiments with a
preoccupation with economic development and seapower.

Because of its uniquely enlightened colonial system, Sánchez de Toca
wrote, Spain through the power of spiritual rather than economic devices,

had established its culture in the New World. As a result, "the Spanish soul still vibrated in Spanish America" even after more than seventy years of independence.[89] Spain's destiny, Sánchez de Toca thought, lay in taking advantage of the continuing existence of the Spanish soul in America so as to call into being a great Hispanic patria.

Spain had begun to decline, in the analysis of the conservative statesman, when under the Hapsburgs it had turned its attention from America toward Europe. The moment was now at hand to rectify that error; but time was fast running out, for the Hispanic-American republics were floundering dangerously, without a consistent orientation, and were therefore highly vulnerable to the imperialistic policies of the United States. Only Spain, he asserted, by reestablishing its presence in America, could provide Spanish Americans with the sense of direction and the unity that would enable them to withstand the Yankee menace.

Sánchez de Toca feared that Spaniards would never be sufficiently aware of their great destiny in America to work and sacrifice for its realization unless they developed practical, commercial, and economic ties with the former colonies. Therefore he called for a massive program of government encouragement to industrial expansion and agricultural renewal. Industrial and farm surpluses would lead to an export economy, and in order to transport Spanish surpluses to the coveted Spanish-American markets, a merchant marine would have to be created through generous government subsidization. With a flourishing export trade and with its own powerful merchant marine, Spain would recognize the necessity of expanding its naval might so as to be capable of protecting its commercial interests. Ultimately, in the statesman's opinion, it was the navy that would protect Spain's presence in America and guard the young republics, reawakened to a sense of their destiny and identity by that Spanish presence, against the incursions of the United States.[90]

Sánchez de Toca had read the works of United States naval officer and historian Alfred Thayer Mahan (1840–1914) carefully and in a spirit of profound accord. Thus he understood the difficulty of creating a strong navy without the previous existence of a formidable merchant marine; and he accepted vast surpluses of national products as the prerequisite for a merchant marine. Colonies and commercial spheres of influence, a vital part of the Mahan blueprint for national greatness, could be obtained by Spain through a strengthening of the spiritual ties with an America that although dangerously neglected could still be incorporated into a great transatlantic Hispanic community. Like Mahan, Sánchez de Toca also realized the grave obstacles to winning the sustained support of the populace to all that was involved in the pursuit of naval power. He hoped to overcome these obstacles by infusing Spaniards with a sense of their mission to make the America they had created a secure haven for Hispanic ideals.[91] "A great nation," he wrote, "needs in order to live and develop

a cardinal and transcendent thought to orient it. . . . Once this orientation is established, there must be subordinated to it in the first place the
foreign policy of the state; . . . and to its foreign policy the nation's domestic policy must in turn be subordinated. . . . For us," he concluded, "the
ideals of the great Hispano-American patria must encompass this thought,
this orientation."[92]

In the Spain of the immediate postdisaster period, the voices of Costa,
Macías Picavea, Unamuno, Altamira, Ganivet, and Sánchez de Toca
raised the plea for a great ideal that would unite Spaniards on both sides
of the Atlantic in a common mission. The plea of this notable half dozen
was echoed by many other Spaniards. What is more, changing attitudes in
America following the disaster seemed for a time to give some substance
to the hopes of these Spaniards for enlisting the energies of a united
Hispanic community in some type of new crusade.

The Rise of Hispansimo in Spanish America

THE SPANISH–CUBAN–AMERICAN WAR AND
A NEW ASSESSMENT OF SPAIN AND THE UNITED STATES

The outcome of the Spanish-Cuban-American War eliminated Spain as
an imperial power from the New World while casting the United States
in the role of an imperialistic aggressor. As a result, more and more Spanish
Americans began to reappraise and to attenuate their traditional Hispanophobe biases.[93] Altamira did not exaggerate when he stated that in the
period immediately following the disaster Spanish Americans, with their
expressions of sympathy toward the madre patria and their growing awareness of the threat of the United States, played a more important role than
did Spaniards themselves in contributing to the rise of hispanismo.[94] Sánchez de Toca went so far as to declare that because of their outpouring of
Hispanophile sympathies in the aftermath of the war, Spanish Americans
were proving themselves to be more Spanish than peninsular Spaniards.[95]

Some three years before the United States had entered the war over
Cuba, Spanish journalist Ángel Salcedo Ruiz writing in the Unión Ibero-
Americana had predicted: "A sharp attack of the Yankees against the
Spanish raza in America would be the signal for a defensive concentration
of this same raza and the beginning of its regeneration in America."[96] Once
the war began, Sánchez de Toca and Rafael María de Labra anticipated
the same sort of Spanish-American reaction as predicted by Salcedo Ruiz.
Spanish Americans would understand, said Sánchez, that the issue involved
not just a conflict between Cuba and Spain, but a confrontation of two
different races and cultures; and Labra claimed that no observer of the
war could doubt that the purpose of the United States was to humiliate
Spain and the entire Latin world that Spain represented in America.[97] It

was not long before the reactions of Spanish Americans began to corroborate these assessments.

Argentine General Mansilla was reported by a Spanish journal to have sought permission to fight against the United States in Cuba, accompanying his request with the following observations:

> So long at the Cubans sought their independence we, who had done the same at an earlier time, were with them. But what we cannot accept is that in order to achieve it they have enlisted against the mother country the help of a foreign nation that is dangerous both to them and to us. The United States lusted for Cuba . . . not only so as to have a sugar factory without rival, but because Cuba is the key to the Gulf of Mexico and the future interoceanic canal and because United States domination there will give them control over the two seas and hegemony over all the continent. . . . We will not be able to do anything in our own home without asking permission of North America. . . . Not only will we have to suffer from this protectorate; Latin Europe, that looks on immobile and is impotent before this intervention so contrary to international law, will also suffer the consequences.[98]

In an open letter to the Buenos Aires newspaper *El Tiempo*, Argentine Professor Calixto Oyhuela declared that the impulse that moved the Yankees to fight Spain, although badly disguised behind the mask of humanity, "is exactly the same impulse that always impelled them against all of Spanish America." Therefore if Hispanic Americans took the side of the United States, they would be aligning themselves against the Hispanic raza and community.[99]

During the war and the months immediately following, Spanish journalist Juan Pérez de Guzmán read the Spanish-American press voraciously, for it consoled him "to see how the ties of culture and blood are now asserting themselves, and how there is a widespread, well-nigh universal reaction in Spanish America in favor of Spain. In this difficult moment, this fact sustains me." The war of the races in the New World was imminent, Pérez concluded, and the Spanish Americans sensed this and so were flocking to the defense of the Hispanic raza and culture.[100]

Commenting upon the mounting tide of pro-Spanish expressions in the former colonies, another peninsular journalist wondered ". . . if the newly evident fraternity will come one day to convert itself into a perfect solidarity of aspirations." If this day should come, it would herald, he said, the launching of an immense crusade by the Latin races "to spread throughout the world the glorious teaching of an ideal to which they have always rendered veneration; a crusade that will conquer the cold calculations of selfish mercantilism, which is the great ideal before which other races of the world, today more powerful, prostrate themselves."[101]

Rubén Darío

In 1888 Nicaraguan poet Rubén Darío (Félix Rubén García Sarmiento, 1867–1916) sent a copy of his book of poems *Azul*, complete with a lavishly laudatory dedication, to Juan Valera. Acknowledging the gift in a letter to Darío, Valera stated that no book arriving from America had so excited his interest and awakened his curiosity.[102] However, for Valera and other Spaniards of this period there was one thing pronouncedly wrong with Darío: his strong anti-Spanish prejudices. Nor did a trip to Spain in 1892 in connection with the fourth centennial festivities rid the Nicaraguan of Hispanophobe inclinations.

In 1898 and 1905 when Darío came again to Spain it was different. Waxing enthusiastic over the spiritual qualities of Spanish culture,[103] Darío established a close contact with such intellectuals and literary figures as Unamuno, Menéndez Pelayo, Maeztu, Ramón Valle-Inclán, and Salvador Rueda. Darío's arrival following the disaster, in fact, "initiated the first truly Hispanic literary movement of encouraging ties among the men of letters in Spain and Spanish America. With Darío there came many other Americans who were going to identify themselves fully with the peninsular group."[104]

Maeztu was immensely impressed that instead of going to Cuba to pay his respects to the newly independent republic, and instead of going to the United States to learn the secrets of that powerful nation, Darío chose in 1898 to have the Buenos Aires newspaper *La Nación* send him as its correspondent to Spain. In this, Maeztu and many Spaniards with him thought they saw Darío's recognition that the true menace in America, that of the United States, could be resisted only by a Hispanic community, united in defense of its unique culture and values. Maeztu praised Darío for appreciating that Spain had been waging a battle in the interest of all the people of Hispanic America and that as a result of the war's outcome the very survival of Hispanic culture in the New World was at stake.[105]

Particularly in his poems published during his 1905 visit to the peninsula, Darío sang the glories of the Spanish raza and expressed confidence in its future. As one Spaniard describes these circumstances,

> Darío appeared at a time when we had sunk into an abyss of sorrow and pessimism occasioned by the disappearance of our empire; he filled us with hope, confidence, and optimism. . . . Darío, with his faith in the Hispanic raza, was like the Archangel Gabriel appearing to Mary to announce great things; this is the effect he had on us.[106]

Still, the nature of Spain's reaction to the Nicaraguan poet and with him the other Spanish-American literary figures who flocked to the peninsula boded ill for the future of hispanismo. Spaniards were proud of the literary feats of their New World offspring because they felt these feats belonged to the cultural history of Spain. Spanish culture, "the matrix of diverse modes of being in those new Spains across the seas," was regarded as being ultimately responsible for the literary flowering in Spanish America.[107] On their side, however much many of them admired Spain in the emotional turn-of-the-century reaction to the war over Cuba, Spanish-American literary figures regarded themselves as the originators of an altogether new style. They did not feel beholden to Spain for their accomplishments; theirs were the accomplishments, they insisted, not of Spaniards, but of Argentines, Colombians, Chileans, Peruvians, or Nicaraguans, as the case might be. Thus they would come increasingly to resent the inclination of Spaniards to judge them culturally as colonials.

José Enrique Rodó

Uruguay's great prose stylist José Enrique Rodó (1872–1917) published his masterpiece *Ariel* in 1900 and Spanish critics quickly voiced their delight with the work.[108] Their response was understandable. In his book, Rodó used the graceful figure of Ariel "as the symbol of reason, nobility and sentiment in contrast to the invisible ogre Caliban, insensitive, sensual and stupid, possessed of the will to perpetrate horrors." Rodó spoke out for the solidarity of peoples of common background, culture, and traditions and argued for a hierarchy of values that placed spiritual and aesthetic considerations at the top. At the same time he warned against the opposing tendencies of utilitarianism, materialism, positivism, and individualism. "He makes clear in *Ariel* who the Calibans of the world are."[109]

Writing one of the first reviews of *Ariel* to appear in Spain, Altamira praised the Uruguayan for being sensitive to and grateful for the substantial Spanish influence on American culture. Altamira also lauded Rodó for having specified the duties of Spaniards in their work of spiritual expansion and the corresponding obligations of Spanish Americans:

> This Ariel, whom Rodó points to as a tutor and guide for the youth of his country, in opposition to Saxon utilitarianism, is also our guide and mentor. Taking his hand, we ought to start out on the road toward tomorrow together with those whom Rodó is leading in America. To the youth of Spain, then, it is as important as to that of America to read and meditate upon this book. . . . It would be well for them to feel in their soul the vivifying contact with the atmosphere of idealism and order, of the noble inspiration of abstract thinking, of disinterestedness, of good taste in art, of heroism in action, of delicacy in customs that is symbolized by the luminous Shakespearian figure called forth by Rodó.[110]

Altamira's advice to read *Ariel* was heeded by the eminent literary figure and liberal ideologist Leopoldo Alas (pseud. Clarín, 1852–1901). Inspired by the book to an ardent faith in "the future unity of the great

Iberian family," Alas wrote the introduction to one of the first editions of
Ariel published in Spain.[111] Antonio Goicoechea, later to emerge as an
important Catholic conservative champion of hispanismo, had completed
his law studies at the University of Madrid just five years before the
appearance of Rodó's book. He read it with avid interest and for the first
time understood the importance of America in "the destiny which it is
necessary for Spaniards to realize."[112]

On both sides of the Atlantic readers long continued to find inspiration
in Ariel. Writing in 1926, Altamira noted that the Spanish youth was still
absorbing the message of Ariel "as the dry land absorbs the redeeming
water showered upon it from the clouds or the careful hand of the cultiva-
tor."[113] And in Spanish America Ariel came to be a work known to all
intellectuals, "quoted, loved and uncritically accepted. Rodó's ideology,
particularly as seen in Ariel, provided a core of values which one finds
repeated in hundreds of later sources."[114]

Darío and Rodó, and their thousands of Spanish-American enthusiasts,
helped restore confidence to a generation of Spaniards and to arouse them
from the pessimism and apathy produced by the disaster. Spain seemed
after all to have a mission to play in the world, one that was recognized
even in the American hemisphere. The ties of the common Spanish culture were proving strong enough to reconcile the two branches of the
transatlantic community, which through united action could survive in
and even transform a hostile world.

Little in the way of tangible achievements resulted from the Spanish-
American spiritual rapprochement occurring in the wake of the Cuban
war. Spanish Americans did not increase their consumption of olive oil
from the peninsula and they continued to purchase more books from Paris
than from the publishing firms of Madrid and Barcelona. On the whole,
economic ties remained virtually nonexistent; and nothing was done to
strengthen juridic bonds through the creation of an Iberian international
law code. In its consular and diplomatic service Spain, according to most
accounts, continued to be underrepresented in Spanish America, while
Spanish Americans continued to regard Madrid as something of a hard-
ship post, mainly desirable because of its proximity to Paris and Rome.

The rapprochement between Spain and Spanish America was confined
to the realm of intangibles and was evidenced primarily by lyrical oratory,
passionate poetry, and elegant prose; it was destined, moreover, to prove
ephemeral. Still, turn-of-the-century Spain was a country remarkably sensitive to intangibles, to the domain of the spirit, to flowery rhetoric and
highly ornamented literary devices that sometimes obscured the line
between sentiment and sentimentality. It is not surprising, then, that
sheer lyricism gave to hispanismo the greatest triumph it was ever to
achieve. In a moment of agonizing doubt, a true dark night of the soul,
Spain received from Spanish America the mystical succor necessary to
emerge from the total crisis of confidence.

The lyricism of hispanismo, which helped provide Spain with a great ideal that in some ways was more important than economic development to national survival, rehabilitation, and pride, was never more unabashedly in evidence than in the year 1900 when the Hispano-American Social and Economic Congress convened in Madrid.

Hispanismo and Lyricism in 1900: The Hispano-American Social and Economic Congress

Like the fourth centennial celebration of the discovery of the New World, held eight years earlier, the 1900 congress[115] came about because of the last-minute intervention and preparations of the Unión Ibero-Americana. Aware that a large contingent of distinguished Hispanic-American delegates would be on hand at the Universal Exposition in Paris, Union president Faustino Rodríguez de San Pedro decided to try to lure the group to Madrid. This would provide Spaniards and Spanish Americans with an inexpensive opportunity to formulate plans for closer cooperation and to study the means for resisting the pressures that the United States was expected to apply at the second Pan-American conference scheduled to convene the following year in Mexico.[116] Rodríguez de San Pedro quickly won the backing of Silvela, president of the council of ministers, who in the following terms petitioned the queen regent to extend government support to the project: .

> A great part of the social and economic future of our country is tied to the necessity of increasing those sympathies of raza that Spain enjoys in America. . . . The indicated congress is most opportune at the present time, because reasons known by everyone ought to stimulate now more than ever the spiritual inclinations of affection toward the Spanish-American peoples. . . . The idea of the congress is complemented with the economic character that its instigators wish to give it. With the energy of the country now totally dedicated to the rebirth of its power, it is indispensable to struggle in those our natural markets to counteract the powerful commercial activity of other nations whose propaganda produces each day a larger decline in our trade.[117]

Queen regent María Cristina approved the petition on April 16 and shortly the government provided 40,000 pesetas to defray organizational expenses for the congress.

Delegates began to arrive in Madrid in early November. The Ateneo and the museums of the city were opened to them without cost and the eminent author and statesman Gaspar Núñez de Arce hosted them at a lavish dinner served in Lhardy's restaurant, at the time one of the favorite haunts of aristocratic Madrileños.

At the sessions that opened on November 10 in the grand salon of the Biblioteca Nacional, fourteen countries were represented by special delegations: Argentina, Chile, Colombia, Costa Rica, the Dominican Republic, El Salvador, Guatemala, Honduras, Mexico, Nicaragua, Paraguay, Peru, Venezuela, and Uruguay. Additional countries were represented by their regular diplomatic or consular officials.[118] During the nine days of sessions, delegates discussed such matters as settlement of disputes among members of the Hispanic community by arbitration, formulation of a common Spanish–Spanish-American–Portuguese international law, conserving the purity of the Castilian language,[119] unification of teaching methods and reciprocal validation of professional titles, establishment of uniform postal and telegraph rates, creation of permanent expositions of the agricultural, industrial, and literary products of Spain and Spanish America, and exchange of books and periodicals.

The candor, the enthusiasm, the give-and-take fraternity and cordiality prevailing among the delegates as the congress came to an end[120] inspired Silvela to declare in the speech that terminated the sessions: "If at one time passionate struggles and misunderstandings about mutual interests have separated us, all this is now completely relegated to history. In the future our only course is to unite ourselves through love, brotherhood, and community of interests."[121]

Although the congress voted with near unanimity on a large number of conclusions and recommendations, these had no binding force on the nations represented, and the governments concerned never took action to put them into effect.[122] Still, the congress helped prepare the way for treaties of arbitration that Spain celebrated with various Spanish-American governments early in the twentieth century.[123] Resolutions adopted by the congress also contributed to the subsequent Spanish attempt to channel its emigration to Spanish-American republics.

Psychologically at least, even if not in the realm of practical accomplishments, the congress was a resounding success; it provided a fruitful opportunity for Spanish Americans to bolster the sagging hopes and faith of the mother country through the all-too-frequently maligned instrument of lyricism. A Spanish observer may have caught the true significance of the congress when he wrote:

> Never had there been seen in the modern age an assembly so powerful, so fraternal, so animated by such high ideals and such profound sentiments. Remembering the glorious past, lamenting the immense misfortunes of the present and looking to the future, the representatives of that great Iberian family promised to unite, on the basis of political equality, their destinies in the world and to strengthen more each day the bonds of Spain with America and of America with Spain.[124]

Silvela found the congress altogether rewarding because it helped him to find what Spaniards of the postdisaster years needed most desperately: a faith in the future, a faith "that cannot be enclosed within the confines of the Spanish peninsula but must extend . . . to that continent of . . . our brothers, where there are the elements of wealth and development of every kind and where our European personality will find an emphasis that we alone, in our interior life, cannot achieve."[125]

Yet even as they found a cause for optimism in their relations with Spanish Americans at the 1900 congress, Spaniards already were unwittingly taking steps to undermine the cause of hispanismo. Silvela himself in one of his addresses to the congress manifested the Spanish tutelary attitude that would become ever more annoying to Spanish Americans. He declared that future development of the Hispanic community depended upon the willingness of Spanish Americans to accept "our representation in Europe of all their interests, of all their hopes, of all their legitimate rights;" it depended also upon their willingness to agree that Spain should be "in Europe the voice of Americans, their representative which will aid them in overcoming all problems, the hand extended across the ocean to assist them in all their needs and difficulties."[126] The young republics of Spanish America, preferring to deal directly with Europe, were not interested in a mediator. To them the Spanish desire to act as a mediator would come in the years ahead to smack of a new and subtle form of imperialism.

The perennial division between the two ideological Spains manifested itself anew in 1900 to cast a further blight on the prospects of hispanismo. Liberals looked forward to the role that a united Hispanic community could play in modernizing and secularizing Spain and Spanish America, but the priest Pedro Martínez Vélez complained that the 1900 congress had forgotten that the Catholic faith is the only basis for forging a Spanish-American community:

> It cannot be denied that the fundamental need of the Latin states is today the power of conservatism that can be provided only by the Catholic faith which, once revitalized, will be the best beginning for a perfect understanding in the political, economic, and social orders. . . . But the [1900] congress could not give to the Church its due position of dominance owing to the errors that have saturated the entire nineteenth-century environment, as much in Spanish America as in Spain. Under these conditions, the congress had to seek the bases of Ibero-American confederation while prescinding from Catholicism, which is the only life and soul of Spanish civilization in the Old and New Worlds.[127]

As of 1900, Spaniards were as far away as ever from reaching a consensus on national purpose that could have brought the two Spains, liberal and conservative, innovative and traditionalist, together into one nation. Important intellectuals and statesmen of the two camps continued as in the past to expound mutually exclusive formulas for setting Spain right. Then, as the twentieth century began, more and more of them were seized by a new dream, that of setting the entire Hispanic raza right by extending the redeeming formulas to America. As the men of the peninsula rushed forth to save Spanish America, not pausing to appreciate the extent to which they had themselves been saved by the message of confidence and spiritual encouragement from the New World, they did so not so much as Spaniards but as either liberals or conservatives. Thus their efforts in behalf of hispanismo can only be understood against the background of early twentieth-century Spanish liberalism and conservatism.

4: CONSERVATIVE SPAIN IN THE EARLY TWENTIETH CENTURY

The Conservative Vision of Spain: The Consubstantiality of Catholicism and Nationalism

Within the conservative purview, Spain had begun to exist as a nation only when a militant form of Catholicism had imbued a common goal among "disparate groups and regions that had never seemed destined to greatness."[1] The birth of the nation had occurred when the fervent spirit of Christianity, as preserved in northern Spain at the time of the Moslem conquest, provided the spark for and gave spiritual nourishment to the mission of reconquest. Spain might well have remained a totally "unnationalized" political entitity as its provinces were gradually "Islamized."[2] But the country escaped this fate because the Church provided it with a *raison d'être* and Catholicism became the "axis of Spanish culture," the one force capable of imparting unity and sustaining it through the centuries. "The Church, rising as a column of smoke that guides the Israelites in their wanderings through the desert, explains everything in Spanish history; without it, the history of Spain is reduced to fragments."[3]

In the conservative view, then, Spain had become a nation only when it assumed the burden of keeping "alive in Europe the sacred ideals of Jesus Christ"[4] and when its citizens came to understand that their land was "the right arm of God" to whom had been entrusted the divine cause of containing the assault of Islam.[5] Thus Catholicism, during the reconquest, forged a nation out of a group of city-states.[6]

Following the successful struggle against Islam, according to the conservative analysis, Spain remained true to its Catholic mission, thereby saving civilization from the "pseudo Reformation that gave to the common masses the right to interpret the Bible, corrupted youth with libertine ways, and provoked wars and disorders. . . ."[7] Sixteenth-century Spain dedicated itself to resisting "heresy and barbarism. This is the true spirit of the post-reconquest period and of the enduring greatness of our raza . . ." for always "the Catholic faith has shaped our undertakings."[8]

For Donoso Cortés, the Counter-Reformation "had provided Spain with its glory, its source of continuing unity and strength."[9] Menéndez Pelayo concurred. Spain, he stated, had solidified its national character and achieved its moments of true grandeur when it had acted as "the evangelizer of half the world . . . the hammer of heresies, the light of Trent, the sword of Rome, the cradle of St. Ignatius."[10] Donoso, Menéndez, and the men of their school maintained that only by resuming its unique mission could Spain reattain its lost moments of glory.[11] If the country rejected this course, if it separated itself from the cross, "its soul would disappear and it would remain only a place on the map with the name of Spain."[12]

Because of the consubstantiality of nationalism and Catholicism in the conservative interpretation of history, Spaniards who cried "Viva España" were in fact saying "Viva religión," and those who insulted the patria were in effect insulting religion, specifically Catholicism.[13] Moroever, if ever they moved to curtail the influence of the Catholic Church Spaniards were thereby knocking at the pillars of national existence. Patriotism and religiosity were synonymous and treason and heresy were one and the same.[14] "A nation for us," as one conservative expressed it, "is a moral unity, and in Spain only Catholicism . . . can provide that moral unity."[15]

Because to them religious tolerance inevitably heralded national dis-unity, conservative Spaniards lauded the historical role of the Inquisition in maintaining orthodoxy. As Menéndez Pelayo put it: "I understand, I applaud and even bless the Inquisition as a formula for safeguarding the unity that rules and governs the national life through the centuries, as the daughter of the genuine spirit of the Spanish people and not repres-sive of it except in the case of a certain few individuals on the rarest of occasions."[16] In the same spirit another conservative arguing against the introduction of religious tolerance asserted: "In other countries the plural-ity of religions as a social fact has always preceded liberty of religions. There is no plurality of cults in Spain, just a few dissident foreigners. . . . Here there is only one religion that flourishes and grows: Catholicism. All others are extinguished and die and do not leave behind more than a trace of agnosticism or, more lamentably still, of atheism."[17] Spaniards, he asserted, rejected the middle ground when it came to religion; either they must be Catholic or else have no religion at all. Thus Spaniards who demanded religious toleration were only clamoring for the religious free-dom of atheists and those who had no faith whatsoever.[18]

The Conservative View of Spanish History

To Catholic conservatives the sixteenth-century theologians who "Chris-tianized the Renaissance"[19] and the soldiers who fought Protestant armies to a standstill were the great heroes who had defended and strengthened genuinely national values. Holy Roman Emperor Charles V (1519–1556, Charles I of Spain, 1516–1556) and even more so his son Philip II of Spain (1556–1598) were admired in spite of the economic ruin they brought to the peninsula through their wars; for they understood that defense of the great national, Catholic ideal was far more important than economic pursuits. Nineteenth-century liberals who censured Charles and

Philip for the economic consequences of their policies were dismissed as rank materialists who failed to understand Spain's true destiny.[20] Because, according to conservatives, these two monarchs had intuited how best to serve the national interest, "Spain in the seventeenth century still conserved its religion, a sense of hierarchy and discipline, and the respect of its citizens for the state. Certain signs of rebelliousness had appeared, but . . . the forces of counterrevolution were still adequate to cope with these dissolving germs."[21]

The eighteenth century produced men and events that were decidedly not to the liking of early twentieth-century conservatives. Never, their version of history goes, had the Spanish race to endure more affronts than in the eighteenth century as hordes of adventurers, courtesans, priests and lackeys from France and Ireland invaded the peninsula "to impoverish us in the name of reform." Moderate economic progress was made, it is conceded, but only at the cost of undermining the national character and dignity, corrupting the language, weakening the culture, and eroding traditions.[22]

Some seventeenth-century Spaniards, observed a conservative writer in 1934, were rightly concerned that their country was inferior to its former peaks of greatness; they still deemed it, though, superior to other countries of Europe. But a group of antinational would-be reformers, insensitive to the true character of the patria, decided in the eighteenth century that Spain was inferior to other European nations and set out heedlessly to imitate foreign models. In the process religious indifference, moral relativity, and anticlericalism were introduced as the spirit of the Encyclopedia, Jansenism, and Gallicanism infected the Spanish populace.[23]

In 1808 the masses of Spain, still uncontaminated by the aberrations of "Frenchified" politicians and intellectuals (afrancesados) arose in the war of independence to oust the invading armies of France that sought to impose Joseph Bonaparte on a Spanish throne. This heroic deed, in the conservative appraisal, represented the reaction of the true Spaniards against the ideas of the French Revolution and the insidious influences of Jews and Masons.[24] But the work of the people, "Catholic and monarchical and enthusiastic supporters of religion,"[25] was undone by the idealogues who framed the liberal constitution of 1812.[26] From this time on the two Spains would be pitted against each other in unending combat: the Spain of the believing masses, who subconsciously at least understood the national character and purpose, and the anti-Spanish intellectual types who wanted Spain to betray itself.

The impious, antinational spirit of 1812 was not confined, conservatives maintained, just to the peninsula; its contagion spread also to the colonies in America. In fact, the entire independence movement there was often attributed to the machinations of Freemasons.[27] Conservatives also denounced Masons, "the declared enemies of altar and throne," for having persuaded Ferdinand VII to choose his daughter Isabella rather than his brother Charles to succeed him in 1833.[28] Upon this development, say the conservatives, right-thinking Spaniards, sensing that Isabella was inclined to compromise with liberal principles, arose to press the claims of Charles to the throne, thereby initiating the Carlist wars.

Regarding themselves as the "true descendants of the people of 1808,"[29] Spain's conservative Catholics, often referred to as traditionalists, suffered a serious blow with the disentailment of clerical properties decreed in 1836 as the civil wars came to an end with the defeat of the Carlists. This action has been pictured as "cementing a dreadful solidarity between ambitious and greedy people."[30] It has also been depicted as the origin of the social problem because it "deprived the Church of its land where there had been maintained charitable institutions to care for agricultural laborers; henceforth the laborers were subjected to the brutal exploitation of private owners as the Church was reduced to a position of miserable, penurious dependence on the state." All of these calamities stemmed from the alleged attempt of the throne to buy the support of a few liberal consciences and to bribe a few conservatives into supporting limitations on Church rights.[31]

Despite setbacks, defenders of the authentic Spanish style and character still held their own, Menéndez Pelayo wrote in 1880, through the first half of the nineteenth century. They were able to do so because the "faith is maintained and Spain does not have a propensity toward heterodoxy." There were, he said, only a few freethinkers in the land and they represented the "worst caste of the impious in the entire world;" they totally lacked originality and were not taken seriously either in the peninsula or abroad.[32] But when he assessed the situation toward the end of the century, Menéndez Pelayo manifested a deep pessimism. He felt that Spaniards were proceeding toward national suicide because, corrupted by foreign influences and cultural traitors on their own soil, they had abandoned interest in the realm of the spirit and become indifferent to Catholicism.[33]

Conservatives on Jews and Masons

Conservatives agreed that the genuine national life style was one of conviction, commitment, and belief. Accordingly, Spain was at its best, was most true to itself and therefore most capable of great and original action, when it was intolerant. It followed that Jews were suspect, for they represented, in the minds of Spanish conservatives, the spirit of skepticism, doubt, questioning, tolerance, and relativity. Perhaps they were acceptable in other countries that had developed different styles of nationalism through the centuries; but in Spain, where the existence of the nation rested upon the profound and unquestioning commitments of militant Catholicism, where the symbol of national greatness was the

Christian knight, Jews must necessarily constitute an antinational force inimical to the established order.

Traditionalists habitually pointed to the alleged materialism of the Jews as contrary to the spiritual essence of Spanish character. One of them wrote that it was not the machine that had corrupted human existence. Had the machine appeared in a better-arranged world, he argued, it would have been a force for good. As it was, though, it appeared in a world where "Judaic materialism had transformed life into the cult of money" and it therefore resulted in the dehumanizing of labor.[34]

By the beginning of the twentieth century conservative types were already equating the menace of communism with that of Judaism. Marx was depicted as typically Jewish in his desire for vengeance against the countries of Western Christendom that had, allegedly with good reason, always suppressed the Jews in the national interest.[35] Jews, it was said, in their everlasting campaign against Christendom, were threatening the civilized world with the social revolution of communism.[36]

Conservatives generally lumped Freemasons together with Jews as constituting a threat to national values and goals. A feature writer in a Jesuit publication typically warned his readers in 1901 that no one could be patriotic and at the same time extend encouragement "in thought, word, or deed to the sworn enemy of every Christian nation, Freemasonry as secretly directed by Judaism."[37] The writer was doing little more than to repeat the 1893 message of a prominent Jesuit priest that Catholics must organize to drive from the national Spanish soil all Masons, freethinkers and their allies who were engaged in a nefarious plot "to persecute religion and to separate the people from their Church."[38]

According to the historical analysis of Menéndez Pelayo, Masonry had originated as a fairly innocent movement in England to serve the cause of the dethroned Stuarts. Gradually, though, it had become a heretical, revolutionary movement, preaching deism, religious indifference, and tolerance and railing against imagined monsters of fanaticism. Introduced into Spain during the reign of Ferdinand VI (1746–1759), the second in the line of the Bourbon dynasty, it had received significant support from the French armies that fought between 1808 and 1814 for Joseph Bonaparte. In 1814 nearly all Spanish liberals affiliated themselves with the more radical Scottish rite branch of international Masonry. From that time on, the conservative historian affirmed, Masons had been either the instigators or supporters of every revolutionary attempt to denationalize Spain by robbing it of its authentic traditions, especially its redeeming commitment to militant Catholicism and the suppression of religious error.[39]

Writing in 1904, liberal historian Rafael Altamira complained of the tendency of traditionalists to attribute all that they did not like in Spanish liberalism to Masonry. To associate with Masonry, Altamira wrote, all

of the modern movement, "so complex and rich in divergent influences;
to believe that all that is urged today in the way of reforming the social and
political order is a product of the mysterious plots of a group of men who
perpetuate that formidable association of other times, is to divorce oneself
altogether from the Spanish reality. . . . Surely," Altamira concluded,
"many of those who preach such nonsense must know that many liberals
and republicans are not Masons—not because they are against Masonry,
but because they do not see the need of being tied to it in order to defend
their ideas."[40]

Suspicious conservatives were not to be put off by such disclaimers. They
took to heart the warning of an Augustinian priest that the devil's most
diabolical ruse had always been to fool people into believing that he did
not exist: "the same can be said of Masonry and Judaism. The most genuinely Masonic plot is to spread the belief that the Masonic-Judaic con-
sortium is doing nothing in the world. Whoever believes this is one who
does not know what Masonry and Judaism really are."[41]

Conservatives on the Need to
Desecularize and Deliberalize Society

"It is essential," a distinguished conservative statesman wrote, "to
undertake the desecularization of modern civilization."[42] In this short
statement he defined the fundamental goal of early twentieth-century
Spanish conservatism; for the distinguishing characteristic of those who
served its cause was dedication to reversing the process of secularization
that had been ushered in by the forces of romanticism, deism, skepticism,
Protestantism, and the other fallacies and heresies said to be ingredients
of liberalism.

To conservatives, liberalism and secularism were necessarily linked forces
of evil. Well into the twentieth century they continued to agree with
Jaime Balmes, who had affirmed that individualistic liberalism, based on
heresy and leading inevitably to anarchism and socialism, could only
flourish in a society that had abandoned itself to secularism.[43] Like Balmes
they called for a crusade to banish secularism by reanimating the spiritual
and enhancing the temporal powers of Catholicism. The Cardinal-Archbishop of Toledo was within the mainstream of Spanish conservatism
when he wrote in 1935 that secularism was the specific microbe of Catholicism, a microbe that was conceived and fostered for no other purpose than
to destroy the true faith. In the confrontation between secularism and
Catholicism, he called upon Spaniards to choose between barbarism and
civilization.[44]

Again and again, twentieth-century conservatives repeated the message
of nineteenth-century statesman and Thomistic philosopher Antonio
Aparisi y Guijarro (1815–1872): secularism, by removing religious influ-

ence from society, undermines hierarchical order and thus challenges the natural and divine positive laws. Only in religion, Aparisi and his later disciples contended, could people find equality. When religious influences were subverted by secularism people sought equality in the temporal and thereby proceeded contrary to the immutable laws of inequality arising from differences in human intelligence and capacity.[45] As an admirer of the influential Thomist expressed it in 1898, if "the deep religious conviction and enthusiasm of the people which have so far presented insurmountable obstacles to the establishment of democratic doctrines" should disappear beneath a wave of secularism, then there would be no means of preventing a leveling social revolution.[46]

Well into the twentieth century, a large group of Spanish conservatives refused to try to work within a secularized society. They regarded secularism as a tide that could still be contained or turned back. Frequently, moreover, they saw no need to compromise with individualistic capitalism, the product, in their view, of liberalism and secularism. Instead, they inclined to lash out blindly against the capitalist system in general, as being tainted by sin and heresy in its very conception, and against the materialistic, "Judaized" bourgeois practitioners of capitalism.

Ramiro de Maeztu in 1927 expressed alarm at this approach of Spanish traditionalists, a group with which he had on the whole come to sympathize and for whom he was beginning to act as a spokesman. Traditionalists, he felt, were doomed to failure unless they learned to accept the permanence of the secular, liberal, capitalist bourgeois society and to work for its modification and alteration rather than its annihilation. Maeztu admired the North American spirit, as exemplified by Benjamin Franklin, which established a moral duty to use wealth so as to generate more wealth. Spaniards, however, not having learned to associate the generation of wealth with ethical obligations, were living still in what Maeztu called a precapitalist stage of development. He admonished Spaniards and the Spanish Catholic Church to come to grips with the secular society and capitalism and acquire a sense of the moral duty to use money in such manner as to reproduce and multiply it.[47]

Most of the conservative ideologues who prided themselves on their devoutness were unimpressed by Maeztu's reasoning, rejecting out of hand the possibility of a wedding between bourgeois capitalism and Catholic morality in a secular society. The suspiciousness if not outright hostility toward modern capitalism exhibited by many Catholic conservatives (an attitude similar to that of the anarchists) continued—up to, during, and after the civil war—to be a point of major significance in dividing them from their country's liberals.

Those Catholics who were convinced that liberal capitalism as it operated within a secular society must inevitably lead to socialism were sometimes bold innovators and revolutionaries with respect to the economic order. Essentially, what they wanted was sweeping economic change encompassing nothing less than the eradication of bourgeois capitalism; they saw no other means of preventing radical social change. Their liberal antagonists were in some ways more conservative vis-à-vis what had become an established order, for they foresaw the possibility of containing social revolution within a secular, capitalistic society.

Conservatives on Religion and the Social Problem

Antonio Vicent was twenty-four years of age when he began in 1861 the training that would lead to his ordination as a Jesuit priest. As a scholastic in the Society of Jesus he fulfilled some of his first teaching duties at the Colegio de San Ignacio of Manresa. While in Manresa he also participated in the founding of a Catholic Workers' Circle.[48] Although in later years when stationed in Valencia Vicent acquired some reputation as a biologist, his most important work always lay in labor organization and in spearheading the Church's drive for social justice. No one played a more conspicuous role in the attempt to implement the dictates of Leo XIII's *Rerum Novarum* as they were understood by Spanish conservatives.[49]

In what was to prove his major publication on the subject closest to his heart, Vicent, writing in 1893, just two years after the appearance of *Rerum Novarum*, devoted considerable space to analyzing the cause of the social problem. He concluded that the cause, despite the explanation of liberal observers, did not lie in economic conditions; for "poverty has existed at all times . . . but not the social problem." In some countries where material progress had been greatest and where the masses had come most fully to enjoy diversions and pleasure, social tensions were at a maximum, with workers consumed by dissatisfaction, bitterness, and hatred. On the other hand, workers in Catholic labor groups, even when poor and in want, were said to be content, because "happiness is not found in material things, it is found in our heart, in our soul."[50] Why did the properly instructed and guided Catholic worker find happiness in his heart and soul? The reason was simple:

For those who believe that angels of God gather the tears of afflicted Christian workers so that one day those tears will shine in a splendor exceeding that of the stars of the firmament, the afflictions and penalties of life are nothing; the Christian who believes this way will pass through life with his head raised, with a smile on his lips and satisfaction in his occupation, even though he is in the midst of the greatest suffering. What is more, in the midst of poverty and afflictions the Christian will enjoy life and find consolation, because he knows what the apostle said: "If we suffer with Him, it is in order that we will also be glorified with Him."[51] . . . Outside of the Christian faith there is no answer to the worker who says it is not right that he labors all day and has barely enough to eat, while others live in opulence. The rationalistic Mason can find no answer to this complaint, no rational means for opposing a leveling social revolution, for those who have ceased to believe in heaven will want to enjoy it on earth.[52] . . . The liberals, who have snuffed out understanding of the true purpose of man in this valley of tears, cannot present rational justifications to the workers for their mounting misery; there is nothing in the liberal creed to justify and excuse this; so, they must rely on force.[53]

The Catholic position on the social problem in turn-of-the-century Spain has seldom been so clearly and frankly stated. Other writers in the Catholic social justice movement who expounded upon the theme did little more than to repeat and to underline the points made by Vicent.[54]

Commenting in 1925 with some disapproval upon the early twentieth-century Catholic approach to the social problem, a man who was himself prominent in the Church's quest for social justice stated that too many of his coreligionists had attributed all of the ills of society to the inevitable consequences of sin. Catholics of this persuasion, he charged, were content "to weep and pray." Others, convinced that the social problem arose from having forgotten the eternal rewards of mankind, totally ignored the present world as they dwelt upon eternity; others attributed the social problem to impiety and sought to remedy it through novenas and other pious actions; still others thought the problem could not be resolved except by a miracle of the Almighty "and they awaited this miracle in inactivity."[55]

By no means all Catholics were content to weep and pray, to attend novenas, and await a miracle. With considerable energy many participated in programs aimed at assuring adequate catechism instruction for the laboring masses. They operated on the assumption that only when the workers understood the purpose of their lives on earth would they cease to clamor against the hierarchical structure of society.[56] Due to the spreading influence of atheistic and materialistic teaching in the public school system it had become virtually impossible, they contended, to speak to the workers about abnegation and sacrifice; hence the need to launch an all-out campaign to educate the proletariat in the principles of the Catholic catechism.[57]

Obsessed by the need to expand the role of the Church in education,[58] Catholics denounced the attempts of liberal politicians "to despoil teaching of all religious character and to convert it merely into an intellectual discipline without any relation to our conduct in life and preparation for eternity."[59] One of the first Catholic intellectuals to publish a book in praise of *Rerum Novarum* asserted in it that talent without morality is a public calamity; "with equal validity," he continued, "one can assert that popular instruction without a religious base will produce, in final terms, grievous consequences for the social order."[60]

The leading organizer of Catholic agrarian syndicates depicted religious instruction for the proletariat as the indispensable means of breaking the iron law of wages. So long as they lacked a sound religious grounding workers would squander their gains on gambling and vices and thus remain in misery. Without moral restraints, he argued, the desires of working classes could never be satisfied, no matter how much salaries were raised; without these restraints, workers would want to work less every day and receive more. Religious instruction, however, would resolve the problem by showing workers how to derive benefit rather than suffering moral decay from material gains. In attacking the social problem, it followed, then, that religious instruction for the workers had to precede economic advances.[61]

José María Salvador y Barrera had long been convinced of the soundness of this analysis. And so in 1913 when he was Bishop of Madrid and Alcalá he lashed out again at those liberal politicans who were supporting legislation to eliminate catechism instruction from public schools and thereby to restrict the teaching of religion "to the mother in her home and the priest in his church." Such legislation, said the bishop, would discriminate against the lower classes by denying them religious instruction; for their parents, both mothers and fathers, had "to slave all day" at their places of employment and thus had no time to impart religious instruction; indeed, they had "scarcely the time to give a kiss of maternal and paternal affection to the child." Moreover, the child of humble parents had "from a tender age" to work for the support of the family; as a result, he had little time to go to church for religious instruction. The bishop saw no need to alter the circumstances that forced parents to slave all day and young children to go to work at a tender age. All he demanded was that instructors in public schools be required to teach the Catholic catechism "so as to give consolation to the lower-class children and thus elevate them to a position of equality with the offspring of the rich," who had ready access to religious education.[62]

In their insistence that religious influences prevail in society as a whole and that religious instruction be guaranteed in the public school curriculum, Catholics depicted a leveling revolution as being, in the long run, the only alternative. Apparently they believed that by trading on the terror of social upheaval they could create a favorable climate of opinion for their campaign to desecularize society and wipe out liberalism. Thus the far right Integristas insisted that the danger of social revolution arose from the Lutheran heresy and could be combated only through Catholicism.[63] An influential priest in the Catholic social movement asserted that thinking persons should be convinced that laic democracy and neutral instruction led to social dissolution. All Spaniards, he said, who sought to avoid social revolution while at the same time prescinding from the Church's influence were wandering aimlessly about like lunatics; for the society that was not Christian was inevitably revolutionary.[64] The same message was repeated in 1936 by a prominent figure in the Falange. He predicted that if spiritualism, which for him in the Spanish context meant Catholicism, did not triumph over rationalism and secularism, then "the inferior in society will triumph over the superior."[65]

Conservatives on Decentralization

Decentralization, as they interpreted and applied the term, was another means, in addition to education, by which Catholics hoped to desecularize society and provide a dike against the tide of social revolution.[66] A number of factors contributed to advocacy by Catholics of decentralization. To begin with, many were dismayed by the degree to which the hated liberals had gained control over the central government of Spain.[67] A Carlist writing in 1897 expressed shocked indignation because "Masons, the sworn enemies of the Church, so often condemned by the Vatican, have served in every ministry of the restoration. . . . How can we Catholics," he asked, "expect from the government of the restoration the protection that is due the Church and its sacrosanct religion?"[68] Decentralization, in which the Church could utilize the strength it ostensibly enjoyed among the masses to gain mastery over local and regional groups as well as over semiautonomous professional organizations, was advanced as the Carlist program for saving Spain from the evils of secularism.[69]

Father Vicent agreed with the Carlists that true liberty would flourish anew in a state organized on the basis of largely autonomous geographic, social, economic, and political subdivisions in each of which the guiding spirit was furnished by the Catholic Church. Once religious influence was restored in this manner, there would be no need "for all of the outer forms of restraint and coaction" that the centralized state had come to rely upon.[70]

In the view of some Catholic ideologists, excessive centralization had arisen from the heretical assumptions that underlay democracy. From the premise of the equality of all citizens, they asserted, there had followed the conclusion that all citizens should be ruled by the same laws and by identical institutions. As a result all "particularisms" of groups and regions had been repressed by a despotic central government.[71] The foolish pursuit of democracy was also blamed for having introduced caciquismo into Spain. Recognizing the need to curb the dangers of universal suffrage, which the utopianist champions of democracy had legislated into existence, Madrid-based directors of the political parties had relied upon caciques to control electoral results and thus Spain had been gripped by an all-absorbing centralism.[72] The consequent abuses as caciquismo came more and more to corrupt political processes had alienated the masses from the government. The only way to regain their interest in and support of the national common good was, according to a priest-journalist, to break down the monolithic structure into its natural subdivisions and to give to the masses some voice in governing those subdivisions.[73]

A society organized on the basis of semiautonomous municipalities, regions, provinces, and professional associations had the enormous advantage, in the eyes of Catholic conservatives, of "guaranteeing the hierarchical constitution of the nation." Here was the type of organization that promised, in the words of a Spanish priest, "to wound to death the individualism of the modern state. And with liberal individualism defeated and sent into retreat, together with its centralizing bureaucracy, we will have stamped out its presumed heir, equalitarian socialism."[74]

The liberal, individualistic state, according to its Catholic critics, destroyed hierarchical organization; for within it each individual circulated as a free atom, participating in decision-making processes at any level. As a result, individuals were allowed and even encouraged to raise their voices on issues that they were incapable of understanding. This unnatural organization was pictured as self-defeating in its democratic purposes; for eventually most individuals, because of their natural inability to understand the complex issues of national policy on which their votes were solicited, would retreat into their own narrow, selfish world of interests and abandon all concern with the nation. By restoring to subsidiary groups some element of autonomy, by regrouping society into natural organisms and replacing an atomistic with an organic structure, it would be possible, conservatives argued, for each individual to find his way into a local geographic group and probably in addition into a professional organization in the management of which he could safely and knowledgeably participate. Individuals would thus fulfill themselves according to the limits of their capacity within subsovereign groups.[75] Content within their own sphere of activity, and politicized therein to the fullest degree permitted by their talents, the masses would happily leave decision making on the higher, national level to an elite that would emerge through careful screening procedures.

From decentralization Catholics hoped not only for preservation of the hierarchical society but also for the gradual desecularization of society. They envisioned the organization of labor and professional groups that would be under the power of the Church and free from the control of a centralized state bureaucracy.[76] They further envisioned within Church-directed labor and professional groups the existence of mutual aid, savings, and cooperative societies that would liberate members from dependence on state-controlled relief programs.[77]

In autonomous, locally controlled schools Catholics saw another means of stemming secularism. A Carlist activist, for example, complained of the impious, Masonic teachers whom many communities had been forced to accept by the centralized state bureaucracy that controlled education. He advised Catholics to band together in demanding local control over public schools so that they could keep Masons and freethinkers out of teaching positions.[78]

The apocalyptic terms in which many Catholics stated the case for decentralization through creation of semiautonomous, subsovereign groups under Church control is revealed by a 1921 publication of Antonio Monedero. A sociologist of sorts and a wealthy livestock raiser who had been enlisted by Father Vicent in the Catholic agrarian syndicate movement, Monedero contended that only decentralization as conceived and directed by the Church could contain the advance of the socialist barbarians "who are better organized each day." Spain, he said, must return to its natural organization, "which is that not of today but of yesterday." Once socially and politically restructured, Spain could summon up the spirit of the reconquest and Lepanto and lead a crusade to save the world "from the new hordes advancing from the East" that threaten to overcome Europe.[79]

Catholic Action in the Service of Conservative Spain

Catholic Action, the apostolate of the laity under the direct control of the ecclesiastical hierarchy,[80] was a principal agency through which the Spanish Church sought to accomplish its goals in the late nineteenth and early twentieth centuries.[81] Through Catholic Action the devout of Spain were expected to mount a reconquest,[82] a new crusade[83] against the secularist forces in society,[84] against all who defended religious tolerance.[85]

In waging the reconquest, Catholic Action was to assume an important teaching role; its members were to be *catequistas*, offering catechism instruction in schools, parishes, labor and professional organizations, always "emphasizing that spiritual succor was more important than material well-being."[86] Two-pronged in its approach to education, Catholic Action was concerned with catechizing the masses and with forming the consciences of the directing classes. In the aristocracy it hoped to reawaken a sense of charity and *noblesse oblige*; it hoped further, as a Spanish clergyman explained it, to persuade aristocrats to be "generous, liberal, and even more than that to be prodigal in extending concessions to the humble; for prodigality is justice and it is also security against social revolution."[87] In this respect, Catholic Action seemed to be following the mid-nineteenth-century advice of Jaime Balmes: "Do you want to avoid revolutions? Then make evolutions."[88]

In the eyes of its partisans, Catholic Action also had a vital role to play in bringing about decentralization by forming labor syndicates that were free from government control but under strict, authoritarian Church direction. Through labor organization Catholic Action hoped not only to achieve decentralization but to combat socialist and anarchist unions and to guard workers against the "debauchery and depravity" that they invariably suffered in nonreligious associations.[89]

Responding to their liberal antagonists, who questioned the right of Church officials to direct a social action movement that would have its principal impact in the temporal realm, Catholic spokesmen asserted that human society is in part a divine society, established on a supernatural, providential order; therefore the Church possessed authority on all questions pertaining to the social order. They further contended that because the spiritual life of man is conditioned by the circumstances of his material existence, the Church had not only the right but also the duty to inter- vene in temporal matters. One Catholic Action militant presented this contention in the form of a syllogism: All social questions are moral questions; morality is based on religion; therefore, churchmen, with supreme power in religion, have authority to pronounce on all social questions.[90]

Because Catholic Action was concerned with implementing the moral teachings of the Church, it followed, in the minds of its leaders, that the movement must function as a firmly disciplined organization within which the laity accepted unquestioningly the direction of the bishops, the pre- siding officials of the institution that claimed supernatural powers and supreme authority in matters of a moral and religious nature. In a 1915 conference the Apostolic Nuncio in Spain expounded this traditional doc- trine. "It is the bishops who, in conformity with the instructions of the Holy See, must resolve and determine in what form it is convenient to establish and develop the distinct organisms and institutions of Catholic Action; it is not licit for any priest, secular or regular, to proceed to this if he does not have beforehand the permission of his bishop."[91] At a later time the Archbishop of Toledo explained: "Catholic Action is not con- ceivable without absolute submission to the authority of the Church . . . the Church that receives all of its cohesion and force from the principle of submission to authority. All who participate in Catholic Action have to do as the Church indicates, without distinction, without reservation."[92]

One of the principal originators of Spanish Catholic Action was the late nineteenth-century Bishop of Madrid and Alcalá, Ciriaco Sancha Hervás, who in spite of considerable obstacles convened a National Cath- olic Congress in April of 1889 to consider the social problem and formu- late solutions that were in keeping with Church teaching.[93] Two years later, following the appearance of Rerum Novarum, the clergy were called together in diocesan assemblies to be reminded of the new social duties imposed upon them by the encyclical. Shortly thereafter regional assem- blies were convened in Valencia, Palencia, and Granada to give a broader basis to the Church's social work and to enlist the laity in certain care- fully stipulated tasks. This activity resulted in, among other things, the publication of five new editions of the catechism which were widely distributed throughout Spain. In rapid succession after this Social Weeks were organized in Madrid, Valencia, Sevilla, Santiago, Pamplona, and Barcelona. In these Social Weeks both priests and laymen discussed the symptoms of the social problem, outlined the Church's social position especially as set forth in *Rerum Novarum,* and took preliminary steps to create organizations to deal with the alienation of the laboring classes from the Church.[94]

Perhaps the most brilliant of all the early Social Weeks was the one presided over in 1910 by Juan José Laguarda, who had been installed only the year before as Bishop of Barcelona. In his address opening the Barcelona Social Week, Laguarda stressed the need for Christians to resolve the social problem by applying the teachings of the gospels; if they did not succeed in this, the world, he predicted, would escape altogether from the influence of Christ.[95] Once the Social Week concluded its sessions, Laguarda worked tirelessly to establish mutual aid societies, cooperatives, and syndicates throughout his diocese. As many other prelates associated with him in the movement, Laguarda believed it was incumbent upon Catholic Action to form good, staunch Catholics who would gradually change the temporal order. Like Donoso Cortés before him, he felt that Catholics could not save society through immediate political action; instead, the Church had to reform the lay members of society and then rely upon them to produce complementary reforms in political institutions.[96]

From the outset, Catholic Action took up the task of establishing industrial and agricultural labor syndicates. Originally joint associations of laborers and ownership-management groups, these syndicates were dedicated "not to economic and social struggle, but to achieving the harmony of classes."[97] Catholic Actionists regarded syndicates as an important means for establishing frequent contact between laborers and the directors of the particular industry in which they were employed or the owner of the farm on which they worked. This, it was hoped, would lead to warm and fraternal relations, once the directing classes had been instructed, through Catholic Action programs, about their Christian obligations to extend charity and offer counsel and advice as well as the examples of good Christian lives to their employees.

Within the Catholic syndicates workers were encouraged to provide for their own security through mutual aid societies and savings accounts. They were also allowed to participate, within a decidedly hierarchically structured system, in decision-making processes that determined syndicate policy. Most important of all, in the minds of the prelates who directed Catholic Action, workers in the new syndicates were to be instructed in the Catholic catechism.

Each syndicate organized under Catholic Action auspices fell under the supervision of a priest, the *consiliario,* appointed by the local bishop. The consiliario exercised what bishops liked to describe as an "indirect"[98] but what in actual practice constituted a quite direct control over syndicate affairs. The most important specified duty of the consiliario was to advise the syndicate on matters of social morality so as to make certain that it remained true at all times to Church teachings.[99]

In 1919 the Cardinal-primate of Spain, Victoriano Guisasola, summoned representatives of all Catholic labor groups to a national congress. This body approved a doctrinal and action program of Catholic worker syndicalism (Programa doctrinal y de acción del sindicalismo obrero Católico) and announced that there were at the time some 500,000 members of the Confederación Nacional Católico-Agraria[100] and perhaps 150,000 members of Catholic Action-affiliated industrial syndicates or circles.[101]

The preponderance of agricultural workers in the Catholic syndicalist movement has led some observers to conclude that by the World War I period industrial laborers were already lost to socialism and anarchism. At least one authority on the matter, however, attributes the situation to the widespread Catholic assumption that greater virtue inhered in rural than in urban settings and that more fruitful work could therefore be undertaken among agricultural laborers. The same authority points out that until World War I industrialization had established only a tenuous foothold in Spain and contends that the pronounced majority of agricultural workers in the Catholic syndicalist movement simply reflected the relative scarcity of industrial laborers.[102]

Arriving in June of 1921 as Apostolic Nuncio, Federico Tedeschini applied his energies, with considerable success, toward incorporating the youth of Spain into Catholic Action.[103] The organization known as Juventud de Acción Católica held its first national congress in 1927 and seven years later boasted two hundred centers throughout Spain with a total membership of ten thousand.[104]

The dynamic, indefatigable Tedeschini infused a new vitality into the entire Catholic Action organization that prior to his arrival had begun to languish. Tedeschini continued to preach the original doctrine of Catholic Action: "The social question is not primarily economic in nature, but rather a moral, religious question that will be resolved morally and religiously in the hearts of each individual; if there is an attempt to solve it by economic means alone, the social problem will be exacerbated."[105] But he brought to his message a new sense of urgency as he exhorted Catholic Action, and especially the youth group within it that he had founded, to rout the forces of evil. The impassioned religious demagoguery of Tedeschini and his firm opposition to the mounting secular spirit in Spain helped inculcate a fanaticism in the Catholic youth of Spain that manifested itself in the years of the second republic.[106]

Catholic Action and Urban Labor Organization: The Catholic Workers' Circles of Father Vicent

Antonio Vicent, the Jesuit who in the 1890s would present a classical defense of the Catholic view that the social problem could be resolved only through religion, had gone to France in 1868 when the liberal Spanish regime established after the overthrow of Isabella II suppressed the Society of Jesus. In France he had been vastly impressed by the work of social solidarity being carried out by Catholic Workers' Circles, within which there had been established close fraternal ties between "rich and poor, between priests and laity, between nobles and plebians, employers and employees."[107] Stationed in Valencia upon returning to his native country, Vicent embarked upon the founding of Catholic Workers' Circles. Soon these circles extended throughout the urban centers of eastern Spain (the Levant).[108]

As of 1893, circles in the Levant either founded directly by, or owing their origins to, the inspiration of Vicent claimed a membership of over 21,000. In addition, the Sunday and night schools operating under the auspices of the circles provided religious instruction for an estimated 20,533 children and adults. Moreover, sickness and other types of social insurance programs set up by the joint employer-employee organizations had accumulated capital holdings of some 287,000 pesetas.[109] Partially so as to tap the economic resources of the rich members of society, who were appealed to on the basis of Christian charity, Vicent always insisted upon the participation of ownership and management in the Catholic circles. Contributions of the well-to-do accounted for most of the 287,000 pesetas that financed social insurance programs. What is more, the funds of rich associates freed circles from economic ties to the government and thus facilitated Church control over them.

The primary purpose of the circles, Vicent always maintained, was to perfect the piety of members; "for what good will it do workers to advance their material interests through association if for lack of spiritual nourishment they run the risk of losing their souls?"[110] All circles provided instruction for members in the Christian concept of life, "teaching them man's duties to God, what they must believe and hope for, what they must do to achieve salvation." Above all, the circles sought "to arm members against false beliefs and to bring to them respect and love for the Church, the common mother of all, and the desire to obey its precepts and frequent its sacraments." Therefore, Vicent's circles refused membership to those who did not confess and receive communion at Easter. Prominent, moreover, within each circle were voluntary associations dedicated to safeguarding the piety of all members. These associations worked to suppress blasphemy, pornographic literature, and suggestive photographs and drawings. Also attached to each circle was a *patronato de la juventud obrera* which was charged with the administration of Sunday and night schools. Another dependent agency of each circle, the voluntary Asociación de Catequistas, furnished teachers for these schools.[111]

To eliminate usury, which had contributed so notably to class animosity, circles encouraged members to open savings accounts and sought to establish credit cooperatives that could extend low-interest loans. And each

circle included in its membership at least two lawyers. In addition to settling disputes among members, the lawyers defended circle interests
against the actions that could be anticipated from a hostile, secular society within which "judges and magistrates did not believe in God or in
an afterlife."[112]

Organized on a strictly hierarchical basis, Father Vicent's Catholic
Workers' Circles were dependent ultimately upon the local prelate and
a diocesan council. A fifteen-member *junta directiva* exercised immediate
control over each circle. Six of the members were representatives of the
owner-management-employer (*patrón*) sector and of the protectors, rich
and esteemed figures of the local community who had been designated
honorary associates of the circle; an additional six represented and were
chosen by the workers; and the last three positions were filled by women,
the wives of either protectors or workers.[113]

Within each circle the major functions of direction fell upon the consiliario, the priest who was appointed by and represented the local bishop
and who presided over sessions of the junta directiva. All junta resolutions
required approval by the consiliario. Should the junta persist in supporting
a policy disapproved by the consiliario, the bishop intervened to resolve
the matter. The consiliario was charged with seeing to it that the circle
complied fully with its religious functions and obligations. All papers that
members proposed to deliver at plenary sessions had to be submitted in
advance for his approval, and the consiliario was to terminate summarily
any discussion in which the dogmas or moral teachings of the Church
were attacked or questioned.[114]

Catholic Action and Agrarian Labor Organization: The Work of Antonio Monedero

In the more fruitful field of agrarian labor organization, the work of
Catholic Action was advanced most conspicuously by Antonio Monedero,
the man who hoped that Spain, once restructured along the lines of
Church-approved decentralization, could summon up the spirit of the
reconquest and Lepanto and lead a new crusade to save the world "from
the hordes advancing from the East."

Against a potentially explosive background of rural discontent that prevailed in many parts of Spain,[115] Monedero continued until 1910 to lead
the life of a socially unconcerned livestock raiser, earning a substantial
income on an estate inherited from his parents in the north-central province of Palencia. All of this changed when he received a letter from Father
Vicent asking for assistance on a small matter. This led to a correspondence between the two men and later to a three-day visit from the Jesuit
priest in the course of which he persuaded Monedero to undertake the
task of establishing Catholic agrarian syndicates. Soon placed in contact
with Ángel Herrera, at the start of a career with the Madrid daily *El*

Debate[116] that would establish him as one of Spain's leading Catholic journalists, Monedero through him was introduced to Father Sisinio Nevares, who became his inseparable collaborator during the next several years in the founding of agrarian syndicates.[117]

Under the inspiration of Vicent and Nevares, Monedero came to believe that the only solution to the "evils spreading out from the cities to infect the countryside was to rewin the rural populace quickly to Christ; to give to them the message of Christian love and sacrifice and to instill in the hearts of the landowners a sense of Christian charity."[118] To accomplish this task he saw the need for an immense crusade, directed and sustained by a few select men of action: "half monks, half warriors, men who without rest would try to save the people, using the weapons of justice and love, teaching to all the catechism and love of Christ."[119]

In the true spirit of Catholic Action, Monedero insisted that the cardinal feature of the agrarian syndicates must be their complete submission to ecclesiastical authorities and their "confessionality." "In such times as these," he averred, "it is necessary to confess one's religion and to advance it against the wave of impiety and secularism so as to return society to the principles that gave it being and that will save it."[120] Applying to a rural setting the formulas developed by Vicent for urban organization, Monedero also professed the need for his agrarian syndicates to include both landowners and rural laborers in their membership.[121] Not only would the association of owners and laborers whose consciences had been properly formed in the Catholic faith ease social tensions; it would also give workers access to the funds of the wealthy in financing credit agencies as well as pension and sickness-insurance plans.[122]

Presiding over each syndicate was a junta directiva, a small group selected initially at a general meeting of all members. The following year and on each successive occasion when there was to be a change in directing personnel, incumbent members of the junta, in collaboration with the consiliario, prepared a slate of two nominees for each post about to fall vacant. A general meeting of the syndicate then selected one of the two men. As with Father Vicent's urban circles, the consiliario controlled matters pertaining to religion and moral behavior; in addition he exercised a veto power, which could be countermanded only by the bishop, over all junta decisions. In the junta and general membership meetings he had a voice but not a vote, "as it would have lessened his prestige had he voted with the minority."[123]

By 1917 the various syndicates founded by Monedero and Nevares in Old Castile had been organized into eighteen regional federations. In that year delegates of the eighteen federations convened in Madrid and created the Confederación Nacional Católica Agraria to wield—with the approval of the bishops, who recognized it as the official instrument of Catholic Action—general supervisory powers over the entire Catholic rural syndicalist movement. Three years later the Confederation claimed a membership of between 500,000 and 600,000[124] and credited itself with having saved Old Castile from socialism. Confederation officials, however, admitted their failure to make appreciable headway in Galicia; they conceded also that in Andalusia, where the need to contain the menace of socialism and anarchism was most urgent, the Confederation had not yet become active.[125]

By 1925 the Confederation was in obvious decline. In that year a Jesuit publication estimated its total membership at no more than 325,000.[126] By 1925, moreover, membership in Catholic industrial syndicates and circles, placed about the end of World War I at some 150,000, was declining; and the socialist Unión General de Trabajadores, considerably below the 100,000 mark until 1920, had climbed to a membership of over 200,000.[127] Catholic Action did not seem to be winning its struggle on the labor front.

Religious Issues and the Dissipation of Catholic Social Efforts

Had the Church and its supporters among the conservative laity focused attention on labor and social projects within an increasingly secularized society as it then existed, had they been willing to accept the insistence of the proletariat on material well-being as a permanent phenomenon that not even a religious revival could totally banish from the world, then Catholic Action programs might have progressed more rapidly. Instead, the Catholic conservative forces decided on the whole that secularism had to be stamped out before meaningful gains toward social solidarity could be achieved.

The men and women of Catholic Action were energetic and aggressive when dealing with religious issues. But when it came to the material world of the flesh, a realm that should not, it was said, be of primary concern to the "true Spaniard," they were often apathetic—especially when dealing with the material world populated by the proletariat. They were convinced that once the masses were won back to the faith they would cease to be so much concerned with their material conditions. In the meantime, the masses in their un-Spanish preoccupation with material needs must be kept in line, by force if necessary.

A clearcut issue of religion that evoked the energetic militancy of Church and Catholic Action groups appeared when a Liberal government at the beginning of the century sought to curtail the number of religious orders legally permitted to operate in Spain. Various Catholic Action associations staged mass protests throughout the land and when the matter was ultimately resolved to the Church's satisfaction a priest, writing in an Augustinian journal, exulted: "These liberals, with their anticlerical hatred of the religious orders, tried to spit at heaven and the saliva has now fallen back on their own faces."[128]

Another clearcut religious issue emerged in 1910 when a Liberal cabinet presided over by José Canalejas (1854–1912) from El Ferrol introduced legislation to grant clearer legal protection to laic schools—schools where teaching of religion was not compulsory[129]—and to permit religious acts and processions during which insignias "other than Catholic" could be displayed.[130] To the Canalejas proposals a theologian writing in a Jesuit periodical responded with the assertion that Catholic dogma prohibits the state from interfering unilaterally in spiritual and religious affairs which do not fall within its competence "as limited by the will of our Lord Jesus Christ to temporal matters."[131] At the same time a leading Catholic lay intellectual darkly warned that a social revolution would ensue if Canalejas succeeded in his attempt to limit clerical influence.[132] Catholic Actionists were called forth to demonstrate in unprecedented number against the government. Writing some time later on these events, a Jesuit gloated that "the brilliant demonstrations of thousands of believers" had helped topple the administration and brought about its replacement by a Conservative regime. On certain occasions, he added, "Catholic Action has to resort to open struggle."[133]

Catholic Action struck again in 1912 and 1913 when Álvaro Figueroa y Torres, the Conde de Romanones (1863–1950), presided over a Liberal cabinet. Not foreseeing the opposition he would incur, Romanones steered through government channels a legal enactment that provided exemption from catechism instruction for non-Catholic children whose parents requested it in writing. Catholics resorted to mass demonstrations, the Bishop of Madrid and Alcalá gathered statistics to prove that the creeping laicization of education, in which the Romanones enactment represented another nefarious step ahead, was responsible for increases in juvenile delinquency and suicide rates,[134] and the Archbishop of Valencia called upon Catholic primary teachers to band together to protect the rights of the Church in matters of instruction.[135]

Romanones, a moderate and reasonable man, expressed amazement at "the veritable army, above all feminine," that the clergy raised against him. When a Catholic women's group called upon him to present its protest, Romanones assured the ladies he would never adopt a permanent policy on religious matters without a previous understanding with the Vatican. Unsatisfied with this assurance, they expressed the fear that the pope might condone a degree of religious tolerance that would not be acceptable to Spanish Catholics. As abuse continued to be heaped upon him, as his adversaries emotionally accused him of attempting to suppress the catechism, and as the left did not rally to give him solid backing, Romanones secured the suppression of the controversial enactment.[136]

Catholic Divisiveness and the Weakening of Conservative Spain

Within Italian Catholic circles there came into being in the late nineteenth century a movement known as Christian Democracy. Pope Leo XIII approved the use of this denomination in the 1901 encyclical *Graves*

Communi. Italian Christian Democracy, originally under the influence of
Giuseppe Toniolo and Romolo Murri, was a strictly conservative movement, willing to accept the absolute control of the hierarchy, intent upon
eliminating the forces of secularism in society, and hoping to achieve
social solidarity by a return to a highly romanticized concept of the
medieval guild system.

Gradually, however, divisions appeared. The priest Luigi Sturzo, born
in 1871, regarded the idea of a clerical movement set up to combat a
secular state in defense of the historical rights of the Church as outdated.
The national democratic state, he was convinced, had established itself as
the necessary context of all social and political action; Catholicism could
find ample freedom for development and fulfillment of its mission within
the regime of democratic freedoms. The Catholic party of the future, as
Sturzo saw it, would be nonconfessional in membership and democratic,[137]
within a corporative organization, in program. The Popular Party that
Sturzo founded in 1919 rejected any notion of a declaredly Catholic mass
party directed by the ecclesiastical hierarchy. Its purpose was to exist as a
political party inspired by Christian social ideals but separated from the
formal, institutionalized Church, a party that would not claim a monopoly of Catholic votes but would appeal to the general electorate on the
merits of its temporal program.[138] The Popular Party approach was resisted
by many Catholics, including not a few who considered themselves Christian Democrats, and occasioned serious divisions within Italian Catholicism. The same situation developed in Spain, where numerous Catholic
intellectuals and politicians closely followed and sometimes imitated
Italian experiments.

By the beginning of the twentieth century a Grupo de la Democracia
Cristiana had appeared in Spain, dedicated to defending the principles of
the papal encyclicals Rerum Novarum and Graves Communi. The Group
established a social school and soon became active in Catholic labor organization work.[139] While it did not attract many figures of note in the
Church's social justice movement, the Group did enlist at least a handful
of distinguished men who through their activities in journalism and teaching created a considerable impact in Catholic circles. One of the most
active leaders of Spanish Christian Democracy was Severino Aznar.[140] Born
in Zaragoza in 1870, Aznar assumed an energetic role in the founding of
workers' organizations, published numerous books as well as hundreds of
articles in most of the Catholic journals and newspapers of the early twentieth century, and taught sociology at the University of Madrid and other
centers of higher education.

By 1910 many of those who regarded themselves as the authentic spokes-
men of the Church's social and political position viewed the Grupo de la
Democracia Cristiana with suspicion and aversion.[141] The Jesuit periodical
Razón y Fe, for example, strongly attacked the Group for its failure to

realize "that it was a part of Catholic Action, directly under the control of the hierarchy." *Razón y Fe* further lamented that many Spanish Catholics, despite Vatican condemnation of their position, persisted in their hope to make of Christian Democracy a political movement not strictly under the Church's immediate and direct authority.[142]

For the next ten years the Jesuit organ and other Catholic publications continued the attack against Christian Democracy. And in 1920 a jubilant Jesuit recounted the setback administered to Christian Democracy in Argentina when the Archbishop of Buenos Aires refused to confer Church recognition and approval on the movement. The sins of Argentine Christian Democracy were the same as those of its counterpart organization in Spain, the priest contended: assuming a political rather than a social role and supporting concrete political reforms instead of working gradually to transform the consciences of individuals; refusing to acknowledge absolute submission to the Church's prelates; competing in the social field with the Church's officially sanctioned agencies of Catholic Action. Quite clearly the Jesuit writer thought it was high time for the bishops of Spain to move toward the official condemnation of Christian Democracy.[143]

As of 1920 the controversial Christian Democrats were deeply involved in the labor organization issue that had begun to divide Catholic ranks. Even as many Italians some twenty years before them, some Spanish Catholics between 1910 and 1920 had begun to fear that mixed, management-labor associations were self-defeating in purpose because they "ignored the psychological value to workers of having an organization of their own."[144] Their critics rightly contended that Catholic Workers' Circles in urban, industrialized areas were not holding their own with socialist and anarchist organizations. The reason for this, the critics asserted, was that workers increasingly regarded the circles as agencies of the capitalists through which they could never win better economic conditions. According to a Spanish priest sympathetic to Christian Democracy, "While Catholics discuss endlessly the licitness of exclusively labor syndicates, the enemies of the Church are organizing them. . . . If we Catholics had opted years ago for the pure trades union, we would not have lost the laboring classes in Spain; but we are always too late in everything we do, and so we have virtually no followers in our urban labor circles."[145]

By the 1920s and even before, Christian Democrats had begun to criticize the concern of Catholic Action labor organizations with religious goals to the virtual preclusion of all other considerations. The object of Catholic Action, complained a priest active in Spanish Christian Democracy, had been to convert the workers into "patient, all-suffering souls, accepting their fate in life, tolerating the greatest injustices in their love of God as they placed all their hopes in eternal reward." There could not have been, the priest continued, a simpler, more painless solution, nor one that was so favorable to the capitalists. Clearly, though, this was no real solution, for religion should be used not just to pacify the workers but rather to give them the strength to demand justice from capitalists. The general apostasy of the workers, he concluded, was the effect, not the cause, of the social question; and this question would endure "even if all the workers were made saints."[146]

Pedro Gerard (1871–1919), a Dominican priest from Zaragoza who in 1910 had been in Belgium to study the social work of Father G. C. Rutten,[147] sought to implement ideas that were more advanced than those of most Christian Democrats, basically a conservative and cautious group. Oppressed by the loss of religion among the working classes, Gerard attributed the situation to the Church's preaching of resignation, a message the laborers were bound to reject as they witnessed the immorality of the capitalist classes. He felt the Church should form exclusively labor syndicates, societies of resistance against the injustices of capital, concerned preeminently with winning material and economic gains for their members. These syndicates, he maintained, should use all licit means, including strikes, to protect their interests and gain concessions from capital and management. Father Gerard also advocated only a very loose Church control over the syndicates and was willing to admit members who were not practicing Catholics.

Although combated by many well-to-do Catholics who accused him of being a socialist, Father Gerard won a large following among the industrial workers of northern Spain, whom he organized into his Sindicatos Libres. The forward-looking Dominican died in 1919, but the movement he had begun continued and in the mid-1920s the Sindicatos Libres boasted a membership of 30,000. These syndicates survived even the 1929 declaration of the episcopacy, obviously directed against Gerard's concepts of labor organization, that "the Catholic trade unions in Spain belong to Catholic Action," that they should be explicitly under ecclesiastical authority and should normally include in their titles the word Catholic.[148]

In condemning the new approach of Christian Democrats to the social problem and the still more advanced one of Father Gerard, traditionalist Catholics lashed out at "demagogic propagandists who told illiterates only about their rights, not about their duties . . . who are always blaming the landowners and telling the peasants that property is robbery; this is not the work of reform, it is the work of subversion."[149] A Jesuit long associated with Catholic Action programs complained that a new breed of social justice spokesmen was making matters worse by encouraging workers to demand what was theirs in justice. It was not justice that would solve the problem, he insisted, but charity. The Jesuit also chided Christian Democrats, entirely without grounds, for tending to ignore the inalienability of property rights as established by the natural law.[150]

In politics, even as in their approach to the social problem, Catholics were sorely divided. Should they support the Carlists or Integristas because of the doctrinal purity of these politically impotent groups?[151] Or should they enlist in the ranks of the politically powerful but "a-Catholic, compromised" Liberal-Conservative Party in the hope that they could persuade this organization to fall into a more confessional mold? Here were questions that were debated almost as heatedly as the social issue.[152] Little wonder that in referring to the early twentieth century an eminent traditionalist statesman commented: ". . . in that time of confusion, Catholics were divided by passionate disputes . . . [concerning] even the interpretation of the documents of authority. . . ."[153]

Political Moderation and Conservatism: The Case of Eduardo Dato

Born in La Coruña in 1856, Eduardo Dato, after receiving his law degree at the University of Madrid, traveled widely through European countries, studying their legal, economic, and, above all, social institutions. Maintaining his youthful slimness but already bald, he held his first important cabinet post in 1899, serving as minister of interior in a Silvela regime. It was in this period that he published a massive study on the social legislation that other countries had enacted[154] and played a major role in drafting and guiding successfully through parliament the first truly significant social law in Spain, one that established employer liability for worker accidents and regulated child and woman labor. Through this legislation, one supporter exclaimed, "Spain entered into the concert of civilized peoples."[155]

His reputation growing as he came to be known as "the great social statesman of his epoch," Dato later served as minister of justice, directing from that post the reform of Spain's penal system. In 1913, 1917, and 1920 he headed Liberal-Conservative Party governments as president of the council of ministers. Then, in 1921, upon entering his automobile to be driven from the parliament building, Dato was gunned down by an assassin's bullets. Those who believed in violence and revolution as the only solution to the social problem could not have chosen a better victim. For Dato may have been the most important political leader of his era who fervently believed in and energetically worked to bring about resolution of the social problem through moderation and gradualism.[156]

Although a Catholic, Dato felt the Liberal-Conservative Party must continue as a nonconfessional party, along the lines established for it by Cánovas del Castillo. Dato also felt that the solution to the social problem lay not in the sectarian approach of private Catholic agencies as they attempted to desecularize society. Accepting a certain degree of secularization as an established and irreversible trend in society, he regarded social legislation, enacted and implemented by a central government in which both believers and nonbelievers collaborated, as the proper approach to restoring harmony and "disarming anarchism." "Unfortunately," he declared, "neither charity nor religion are sufficient solutions for the social problem."[157] Although persuaded that idealism and spiritualism were necessary in addition to economic reforms in meeting the social problem, Dato admired the spiritualism of "Christian humanism" rather than that of Catholic sectarianism.[158] Contending that religious instruction was not the only valuable type of education for the poor, Dato stressed the importance of vocational training. Moreover, he maintained that Spain's upper classes could not adequately prepare for effective leadership roles by immersing themselves in the country's Catholic traditions; rather, they should go abroad to study how foreign countries were meeting their social problems.[159] Altamira expressed the obvious truth when he wrote that many in the Liberal Party would actually be more at home in the Dato wing of the Liberal-Conservative Party, which however moderate "has in some ways gone farther than the so-called Liberals."[160]

Dato argued that "discrete and opportunely exercised" state intervention was the most promising means for achieving social peace, improving capital-labor relations,[161] staving off revolutions "that are always costly and destructive,"[162] and avoiding bloody struggles that would lead society to "a savage estate of barbarism from which it could not emerge except through the imposition of repugnant Caesarism."[163] Through state intervention, which would not only utilize government revenue in improving the lot of the proletariat but would also encourage cooperation between capital and labor in private-sector social security projects, Dato hoped that Spain could avoid the equally distasteful extremes of socialism and individualism.[164] The statesman detested uncurbed individualism because he thought it produced abuses that prevented a great number of the lower classes from realizing their potential; socialism, on the other hand, he condemned as likely to impede men of ability from developing their full measure of talent. He searched for a system in which equality "would mean that every man is free to develop his nature according to its potential;" a system within which "the man of talent and ability . . . has some rights that the others, the men of the less talented classes, do not have."[165]

Dato accepted the secular state and was willing to work within it to establish a nonrevolutionary force of social reform in which Catholics and nonbelievers, clericals and anticlericals could cooperate in a program of Christian humanism. But not until the emergence of the CEDA (Confederación de Derechas Autónomas) in the 1930s at the time of the second republic did his views come to prevail—if the published program and leaders' declarations are to be credited—in a major Spanish political party. In his lifetime Dato, representing the position of the advanced, "leftist" sector of the Grupo de la Democracia Cristiana, was never able to transform his own party into the type of organization he desired. He was fought to a standstill by the many Catholics who remained steadfast in their attempt to convert the Liberal-Conservative Party into the instrument of Catholic Action intransigence. Thus the Conservative Party remained split and partisans of both factions within it were wont to say: "There is only one Conservative Party; the other one is another thing altogether."[166]

Political Intransigence and Conservatism:
The Case of Antonio Maura

Antonio Maura led the Conservative Party that was an altogether different thing than Dato's. Born in Palma de Mallorca in 1853, Maura arrived in Madrid in 1868, studied law, and entered politics as a member of the Sagasta-led Liberal Party. In 1893, his beard and hair already white, Maura served as overseas minister in a Sagasta cabinet, becoming a center of controversy when he introduced legislation calling for virtual autonomy for Cuba and Puerto Rico. The following year he and his brother-in-law Germán Gamazo[167] withdrew from the Liberal Party and for a time pursued a relatively independent policy. Upon the death of Gamazo, in whose shadow he had been content to remain, Maura entered the Conservative Party and served in 1902 as minister of interior in a Silvela cabinet. Upon Silvela's retirement from politics the following year Maura succeeded to party leadership, presiding over several cabinets as president of the council of ministers. He died in 1925 as something of a political outcast because of his implacable opposition to the Primo de Rivera dictatorship.[168]

Maura's dissatisfaction with the Liberal Party in the mid-1890s stemmed partly from his failure to enlist its firm support for his ideas on Cuban autonomy and municipal reform in Spain. More important in bringing about his political switch was Maura's dislike of the virulent anticlericalism of many of the followers of José Canalejas in the Liberal Party. Unbridled anticlericalism, Maura feared, would weaken the Spanish institutional structure and ultimately topple the monarchy.[169]

Maura was one of those who believed that the religious sentiment of the Spanish people was "the historical essence of our nationality." Seeking a political course of action that would stave off revolution from below, he insisted that only those policies that responded to the religious sentiment of the Spanish people were capable of conserving the nation.[170] The prime prerequisite for the "revolution from above" that he hoped to bring about was the moral reform of Spain's elite, an elite that had lost the respect of the masses, he believed, because of its increasingly irresponsible and dissolute ways. Because of his conviction that morality depended upon formal religion, which in Spain meant Catholicism, the Mallorcan maintained that the solution to Spain's social problem lay initially in rekindling Catholic fervor among the directing classes.[171]

Supporters of Maura praised him lavishly for his attempt to transform the Conservative Party, "since the time of Cánovas del Castillo a pragmatic association lacking true ideological and theological convictions," into an organism animated by authentic conservative principles "in harmony with the traditions of the land, preeminent among which is the Catholic faith."[172] On the other hand, Maura's apparent desire to make of the Conservative Party an instrument of Catholicism and the protector of the clergy outraged his opponents. Cánovas, they claimed, would never have dared to commit the Conservative Party to such a policy. What Maura really desired, they charged, was a theocracy.[173] Opponents were further infuriated when Maura's followers organized in 1909 the Maurista Youth Movement (Juventudes Mauristas).[174] Many of the Maurista youths were associated also with Catholic Action. They were being utilized, charged liberal and anticlerical groups, to help Maura, "the incarnation of clericalism," convert the Conservative Party into an agency of Catholic Action.[175]

It was not only owing to his religious convictions that the Mallorcan of aristocratic bearing polarized Spain into bitterly hostile "Maura, sí" and "Maura, no" camps. The strong, dominating Maura personality also figured in the impassioned polemic. Admirers praised his firmness of character and self-confidence; detractors referred to his autocratic ways, to his conceit and arrogance. One of the latter observed: "They used to say of Cánovas that he harbored a certain resentment against God because God had made the world. Maura thinks that he made the world."[176] Another, in comparing Maura to his son Gabriel, wrote: "Maura cannot speak without wounding, even when trying to be suave; his son cannot speak without being suave, even when he wounds. Maura only knows how to convince by falling upon his adversaries and listeners in an unrestrained torrent; his son tries to convince through calm insistence. Maura counts time by minutes, his son by hours."[177]

When glimpsed in his moments of summer repose as he took long walks in the Santander countryside and indulged in his favorite distraction of landscape painting, Maura scarcely looked the part of Spain's most controversial contemporary political figure. Many of his ideas, moreover, seemed innocuous enough. His contention that the masses of Spain had to be given some role of participation in determining policies that most immediately affected them had by this time become commonplace among politicians; so had his advocacy of local autonomy as the means of achieving popular participation.[178] Only extremists on the left would have disputed Maura's insistence on preserving social hierarchies and limiting the masses to "proportional participation,"[179] participation, that is, by people in proportion to their talents and station in life. Many Spaniards, moreover, both of liberal and conservative political leanings, agreed upon the need to proceed toward decentralization by creating, as Maura urged, semiautonomous "organisms of society in which individuals are grouped by class and profession."[180] What made this program the source of impassioned debate was the fear of Maura's enemies that through it he intended to bring about the type of decentralization desired by the Spanish episcopacy in which the Church would gain control over local and functional interest groups and use them to combat the liberalism of central governments and to reverse the secularist trends in society.

Was Maura truly the incarnation of Catholic-Action-style intransigence? This writer does not pretend to know. Nor is the question important. What really matters is that Maura became the central figure around whom the two Spains clashed; for justifiably or not he acquired the image of intransigent clericalism. Automatically, then, he was reviled by liberals. Furthermore, however much they admired him, Catholic traditionalists felt let down by Maura because he did not score a decisive victory over the Dato partisans and thus never succeeded in restructuring the Liberal-Conservative Party along the lines they desired. Many Catholics therefore continued to spurn the Conservative Party, awaiting a new leader and a new political organization that would give them all they wanted.

Religious Indifference and Conservative Spain

Father Vicent, writing in 1893, stated that although it scarcely seemed possible, the majority of Spanish workers "found in their hearts only the most Satanical hatred of religion."[181] In 1907 a Catholic periodical commented upon the decadence of Catholic parish life. Two years later Ciriaco Sancha Hervás, then the Cardinal-Archbishop of Toledo, ordered a survey of religious practices in Madrid. From this it was learned that only 4 percent of the Madrileños complied with their Easter duties to receive the sacraments of penance and communion.[182]

Statistics compiled in the early 1930s revealed a similar situation. Although the state subvention to the Church had increased from the 40 million peseta figure of 1898 to over 61 million,[183] the clergy in many parts of Spain lived in penury and had obviously not found the means of communicating with the masses. In La Mancha only some 2 percent of the men fulfilled their Easter duties. In Alicante less than 1 percent of the male parishioners received communion at Easter time.[184] For Spain as a whole it was estimated that two-thirds of the more than 24 million inhabitants, 99.8 percent of whom were listed as Catholics by the 1930 census, had ceased to practice their religion.[185] Finally, between 1868 and 1935, as the population nearly doubled, the number of Spanish seminarians declined from 23,452 to 10,663; within the same period the number of secular priests fell from 44,735 to 33,587.[186]

Did these statistics indicate that conservative Spain, the Spain whose existence as a nation depended upon its Catholicism, was in its death throes, a victim of the secularism it had sought to annihilate? Not necessarily. At least the programs of Catholic Action and the political crusade presided over by Maura had armed those who already believed with a new degree of fervor and religious intensity.[187] Moreover, the Church's insistence in a steady propaganda campaign enduring for over a generation that only Catholicism could stem social revolution produced an effect even in the consciences of those who considered themselves anticlerical. Once a concerted, overt, and unmistakable drive was unleashed against clericalism and even Catholicism, many in the accommodated classes who had regarded themselves as staunchly liberal would automatically associate this drive with social leveling and would therefore rally to defend the interests of the Church and conservative Spain. And, although the masses were religiously indifferent, so far as this could be determined by outward acts of conformity, this did not mean that they had abandoned their "deep Catholic sentiments" or discarded their "profound, individualistic piety."[188] Nor did it mean that they would respond with overwhelming approbation to governmental policies that were either in fact clearly directed against the Church or that lent themselves to being described as such. To their discomfiture and dismay, many leaders of the second republic learned this lesson too late.

Although the hopes of Catholic Action and Maura had not come close to realization by the 1930s, conservative Spain was not as weak as it appeared to be. Its spokesmen had succeeded in muting the voices of men like Eduardo Dato who believed in the coexistence of Catholicism and secularism and who sought a middle ground between the two Spains. Still, conservatives could not claim exclusive credit for stifling moderation. For many years, for as long a time in fact as the forces of social revolution were kept safely beneath the surface, those who shaped the policies of liberal Spain implacably resisted compromise. In the quest for secularism they insisted that clericalism and Catholicism as a power within the temporal order were not negotiable.

5: LIBERAL SPAIN IN THE EARLY TWENTIETH CENTURY

New-Generation Liberals Reinforce Old Liberal Views of History

Having made up their minds about the kind of present and future they desired for their country, the liberals of early twentieth-century Spain, although not nearly so concerned as conservatives with their country's past and traditions, turned to history to substantiate and confirm their attitudes and prejudices.[1] The national obsession with reconstruction following the war with the United States provided a new stimulus for consulting history; for each prophet of rehabilitation sought in his country's past evidence and analogies that would attest to the likely success of his proposed remedy.

In their interpretations of history written in the postdisaster era, liberals repeated the earlier allegations of their school that Spain had been at its best under "the Catholic Kings" Ferdinand and Isabella, when Spaniards enjoyed liberty and a form of parliamentary government in which the various cortes throughout the nation wielded meaningful power. Liberals also praised the late fifteenth- and early sixteenth-century Spain of the Catholic Kings for having achieved prosperity based on the industriousness of its citizens. "The true greatness of Spain under Ferdinand and Isabella," wrote a Spanish liberal in 1900, "lay in the fact that it was one of the most industrious areas in Europe," a country noted for the output of its manufacturing enterprises, its flourishing commerce, and its agricultural productivity.[2] In the history of this period the writer found not only the story of Spain's past greatness but also the models for attaining future status among the leading nations of the world:

> Let us return to what constituted our true power when we were . . . one of the most industrious regions of Europe. Let us return to our redeeming principles of economy and savings. We do not necessarily have to imitate the nations that have subsequently become prosperous. In ourselves we carry the example, the lesson, the ideal. . . . We were the teacher of the Italians, Dutch, English, and the French in the arts of commerce and industry . . . and now we seem to be no more than the students of African kingdoms in the art of civil war.[3]

However, according to the liberals, even the Catholic Kings bore some responsibility for having initiated policies that, when carried to extremes

103

at a later time, started Spain on its path toward decadence. Abandoning the practice of religious tolerance that had contributed to Spanish dynamism, Ferdinand and Isabella had introduced the Inquisition, expelled the Jews, and, under the influence of Cardinal Francisco Jiménez de Cisneros (1436–1517), opted for a policy of forced conversion of the Moors.[4]

With the arrival of Charles I—later, Charles V, Holy Roman Emperor —in Spain (1516) and the beginning of Hapsburg rule liberals saw the quickening of Spain's march toward ruin; they saw also the lessons which if properly applied would enable the country to recover from its decadence. Even more than their nineteenth-century predecessors, the new generation of liberals sympathized with Juan de Padilla and the comuneros, who rebelled against the absolutist tendencies of the new monarch and lamented the end of municipal liberties that resulted from Charles's triumph over the comuneros (1520–1521). They also censured Charles, and much more so his son Philip II, for having fanned the spirit of religious fanaticism and squandered lives and treasure in wars against Protestantism. According to an 1899 analysis widely applauded in liberal circles, Spain was denationalized by the Hapsburgs and forced to undergo "Germanization." In this process the developments that should have stemmed from and built upon the accomplishments of the Catholic Kings were impeded; "infected by the introduction of a foreign body into its organism, Spain suffered a paralysis of its natural historical evolution." This interpretation, condemning as antinational some of the features that conservatives praised as most genuinely Spanish, concluded with the following observation:

> Caesarism is not Spanish, but German; dogmatism and obsession with theology are not Spanish traits but German; fanaticism and intolerance are not Spanish, but German; being more papist than the pope is not a Spanish characteristic, but rather a reflection of the German heresy; the favoring of mercenary adventurism over industriousness is not Spanish, but German. . . .[5]

Turn-of-the-century liberals further disagreed with conservatives in appraising the Spanish colonial venture in America. In the conquest and colonial period liberals saw the tragic manifestations of religious fanaticism as Spaniards, set upon spreading the gospels by the sword, perpetrated the cruel slaughter of native races. According to the liberals, economic exploitation during the colonial period, often abetted by a parasitical Church, impeded development and accounted for Latin America's backwardness in the postindependence period. On the other hand, and again in contrast to the conservatives, liberals tended to admire the British colonies in America, where "people were encouraged in the arts of self-government which in turn stimulated their initiative and encouraged them to become economically productive."[6]

In the postdisaster era liberals continued to express admiration for French civilization, as a result of which they were contemptuously categorized by their conservative adversaries as afrancesados. According to Rafael María de Labra, the tireless campaigner for laic education and religious toleration, France was the intellectual vehicle "through which there comes to this Euro-African people . . . the currents of modern thought."[7] Labra and other liberals persisted also in lauding the eighteenth-century Bourbon rulers of Spain, particularly Charles III (1759–1788), who had introduced new ideas from France in the attempt to banish "superstition, fanaticism, and laziness."[8] In addition liberals expressed admiration for the framers of the 1812 Cádiz constitution, whom they saw as reviving the spirit of the sixteenth-century comuneros. And they extolled the leaders of the Spanish-American independence movement, picturing them as struggling to free their people from "the excesses and restrictions of the old regime." The success of these leaders was contrasted with the failure of peninsular Spaniards to overcome the force of darkness.[9]

Finally, the new generation of liberals bitterly assailed the consequences of the restoration. They blamed the restoration for having saddled Spain more securely than ever with the religious intolerance, the political ineptness, the educational backwardness, and the economic stagnation that had generally typified national existence since the Catholic Kings.[10] To restoration politics they also attributed the fact that the promising beginnings of secularism and anticlericalism, as manifested by the 1836 disentailment and the revolution of 1868, had not come to fruition.

Liberals on Catholicism and Secularism

A perceptive English author has written: ". . . the Spanish Church . . . remained until the twentieth century the embodiment of the Spanish nature. When the Church declined, the chief unifying force in the country lost its vitality."[11] Spain's turn-of-the-century liberals would not have agreed with this statement. So far as they were concerned the Church had long ago lost its vitality as a source of unity. It was, and had been for generations if not centuries, barren, ritualistic, given to vain and petty disputes over empty issues.[12] In the liberal view, religion survived in Spain "only through lies"[13] and for more than a century the majority of those who made a public confession of their Catholicism as they assumed public office "were living a lie;"[14] the sooner, moreover, that the lie of Spanish Catholicism was acknowledged, the more quickly the country could become Christian.[15]

According to Ricardo Macías Picavea, who analyzed national problems in considerable depth in the bleak period following the disaster, Spaniards were the most irreligious people, the most "atheistic in practice" in all of Europe; "they have religion so much on their lips because there is so little of it in their hearts."[16] Macías Picavea conceded, though, that at the time of Ferdinand and Isabella religion had been the most important and vital national force. What then had gone wrong? In his analysis, the Church in the latter sixteenth century had become excessively ultramontanist and overly ambitious to create a theocracy. The quest for theocracy corrupted the priest, turning him into a politician. In this process the Church became just one more political organization. Equally disastrous, he stated, had been Philip II's insistence on maintaining Catholicism as the one established religion for reasons of political expediency. The imposition of religious uniformity by the state, said Macías, had brought about Spain's expulsion from the company of the civilized countries of the world. Moreover, government support of Catholicism had weakened and corrupted the clergy, "for struggle and competition are necessary to strengthen and purify men and institutions."[17] Predicting the flowering of a true Christian spirit if complete religious liberty were to be introduced, Macías Picavea concluded:

> Neither the nation nor the Spanish Church will be great, powerful, happy, and prosperous so long as both fail to place themselves amidst the conditions that obtain today among all civilized peoples; the state must be thoroughly secularized and the Church made national, that is popular, with all important posts held by Spaniards, as in the best times of the past that witnessed the formation and growth of our nation.[18]

Completely in accord with this analysis, Labra declared that the history of the world from the fifteenth century had been essentially the story of the emancipation of men from religious tutelage, "better said, from the theocratic thought that infused the great epochs of the Middle Ages, serving then at least to some degree the cause of civilization and progress." At the present time, however, according to Labra, the temporal interests and aspirations of the Church were no longer compatible with progress.[19] It was necessary, therefore, to initiate a "titanic struggle against the theocratic power so as to emerge from the suffocating oppression of its ideals." To end theocracy, he asserted, it was necessary for the state to block all of the Church's temporal pretenses.[20] Joining with Macías Picavea in the plea for secularization, Labra declared: "Progress in modern life is inevitably dependent on secularization; it is secularization that molds nationalities. The Church should be just one element among many in modern life, stripped of all monopolies and special privileges."[21]

Gumersindo de Azcárate, a great leader in liberal Spain's campaign for social reform in the early twentieth century,[22] joined in the demand to deny special privileges and temporal powers to the Church. In a penetrating essay on the subject he explained what laicism meant to him. It did not imply, he stated, the exclusion of God from society; it sought merely to bar the priest from a sphere of action that was not appropriate to him. "It is important," he asserted, "not to confuse secularization of the state with secularization of one's inward life. The latter can appeal to those who consider religion as something transitory and destined to disappear, not to those such as I who consider religion a permanent end in constant evolution." Azcárate continued:

> It can happen that upon being secularized, the state will be more religious than before. . . . To the state there corresponds properly the pious work of attaining justice; and he who serves justice serves God and walks with God; while he who works in a manner contrary to justice works against God, even though he has God's name on his lips a hundred times a day. . . . On the other hand the state that includes a budget for the clergy, that stages religious processions headed by public officials and accompanied by the national troops, that has members of the war council hear mass before arriving at decisions, the state that does all of this and at the same time disdains justice and morality is in reality a state that is atheistic in practice.[23]

In concluding, Azcárate pointed out that there was no unanimity among the past and present doctors of the Church, or among the Catholic bishops in countries outside of Spain, on the need for religious intolerance and exclusivism. The advocates of intolerance in Spain, he contended, were just one sect within the Church, deserving to be heard but not to be blindly heeded.[24]

Even more directly than Azcárate, Miguel de Unamuno challenged the conservatives on their most fundamental belief concerning Spanish nationalism. Catholicism, Unamuno flatly stated, was not consubstantial with Spanish nationalism. The "disastrous doctrine" that to de-Catholicize Spain was to denationalize it had resulted in untold damage, said Unamuno, both to the patria and to Christianity. "Since the emergence of the principle of the consubstantiality of Catholicism with the national Spanish traditions, there had begun the decadence both of the nation and of Christianity."[25]

However much he fought for secularization and denounced clericalism and all manifestations of intolerant, militant Catholicism, Unamuno fervently believed that Spain's primary concern must be with spiritual rather than material values. Described by one observer as thinking that Spain could be saved through a new form of "laic religion,"[26] Unamuno, having by 1906 given up his earlier infatuation with Europeanization, disparaged progressive Europe's obsession with science. The object of science, he wrote, is life, while the object of wisdom is death; "Science says it is necessary to live and seeks the means of prolonging life; wisdom says it is necessary to die and seeks the means of preparing us to die well." Expressing his preference for Spanish wisdom over European science, Unamuno denied that Spaniards were overly concerned with death. In his view, their concern was a healthy one that indicated a recognition of the primacy of spiritual over material values.[27]

The truth is that most Spanish liberals were wracked by internal conflicts of values. However much they tended on the whole to admire, they also saw the shortcomings of the material development of progressive European countries; and however devoutly they desired desecularization, they seemed dubious about some of its likely effects. Pedro Laín Entralgo in a classic study notes that the members of the Generation of '98, notwithstanding their religious indifference and their anticlericalism, were all of them either repulsed to some degree by modern, progressive civilized life in itself or else by the manner in which Spaniards sought to imitate that life. Fascinated by and at the same time disdaining technological proficiency and mechanization, they generally ended by opting for rural Spain over the city, the landscape over the factory.[28]

Few Spaniards better demonstrated this inward dichotomy than Macías Picavea. In his best-known book he urged Spain to modernize and industrialize. Yet, in the same book he stated: "It is evident that the civilized world is dominated more each day by industrialism, the symbol as well as the product of the base, mediocre bourgeoisie that directs it." The whole system, he added, was mad; its insatiable greed led to the creation of more and more industrial plants and to massive overproduction, which necessitated an ever more frantic search, utilizing fair means and foul, for new markets.[29]

Although ambivalent toward many characteristics of the more progressive countries, Spanish liberals accepted almost unequivocally the modern principle of free discussion as the means of arriving at truth; hence their demand for tolerance and their willingness to import ideological systems that might lack deep roots in national experience. Still they were convinced, perhaps as much as the conservatives, that moral, ethical, and spiritual truth should take precedence over that deriving from applied science and concerned exclusively with material consequences. The main difference between the two ideological camps was that liberals felt the higher truths had yet to be discovered and accepted in Spain, while conservatives thought they had merely to be recalled from Catholic dogma and reacknowledged. A lesser difference was that some liberals believed that out of individual morality and inward, spiritual progress there might flow a dignified, seemly, and well-ordered type of national economic development. Conservatives, on the whole, were less interested in a possible connection between spiritual and material development.

In their attitudes toward secularization, morality, religion, and material development, as well as in their interpretation of the historical past, Spanish liberals of the early twentieth century were still under the influence of Krausism. Some of the major liberal-conservative intellectual skirmishes of the nineteenth century had been fought over Krausism. And Krausism's lingering influence gave rise to some of the battles that liberals and conservatives waged for ever higher stakes in the years between the disaster and the civil war.

The Krausist Origins of Early
Twentieth-Century Spanish Liberalism

According to Rafael Altamira, who succinctly summarized the majority liberal view on the matter, Krausism embodied the entire spirit of Spanish liberalism. From Krausism had stemmed the concern with individual liberty, with intellectual freedom and religious tolerance, with science and material progress. From it there proceeded also the "virile doctrines of Costa, proclaiming juridic autonomy of regions and agrarian collectivism; from it came the notion of decentralization based on the autonomous municipality. . . . What doctrine," inquired Altamira, "is more suited to save Spain from the selfish atomism of individualism" than Krausism, with its insistence upon the "organic structure of society?" The historian concluded by praising Krausism as an open, flexible, tolerant ideology and, above and beyond that, as a "religion of rational virtue."[30] Another of the ideology's admirers contended that although Krausism aimed at the construction of a religion of rationality based on natural rather than supernatural virtues, it was in keeping with the Spanish temperament because it accepted the importance of intuitive and even mystical experience in arriving first at morality and then at religion.[31]

How was there initiated the infatuation of Spanish liberals with a German philosophical-moral-religious system that stressed the freedom of the individual's mind and conscience but sought to mitigate the social effects of atomistic individualism through an organic, essentially corporative sociopolitical structure; that valued economic progress for the nation but only as an outgrowth of the moral perfection of individual citizens; that urged a morality of rational virtue but left a role for intuitive mysticism in formulating it; that attacked existing religions but dreamed of man's future union with God through a new and universal faith; that accepted and extolled science but primarily as a means of bringing man to a higher plane of ethical and religious beliefs?

Interested in learning about new trends of philosophical thought in Europe, the Spanish government in 1843 commissioned Julián Sanz del Río (1814–1869), a metaphysician from a small village near Arévalo in the region slightly northwest of Madrid, to study the German intellectual scene at first hand. Sanz del Río undertook his first trip to Germany in 1844, meeting in Brussels, on his way there, the German philosopher Heinrich Ahrens (1808–1874).[32] Through Ahrens the traveling Spanish scholar learned about and acquired his first enthusiasm for the philosophy of Karl Christian Friedrich Krause (1781–1832), a little-known German intellectual who, despite repeated efforts, had never won an important university teaching post. Imbued with a strong desire to improve the situation of humanity, Krause had originally turned to Masonry as the most promising instrument for effecting sweeping reforms. Rebuffed by most German Masons, Krause had then developed his own intellectual-moral-religious system, one that has most frequently been described as idealistic pantheism.

Although he was eclipsed by Fichte and Hegel and other German philosophers and died in obscurity, Krause attracted at least a few disciples, the most enthusiastic being Ahrens. Following Krause's death his disciples edited his largely unpublished works and through their efforts gained for him a degree of fame that, although slight, was considerably more than he had enjoyed in his lifetime.[33]

Visiting Germany for a second time in 1847, Sanz del Río spent in all some three years in that country, mainly in Heidelberg, his admiration for Krause and Krausism growing all the time.[34] Once back permanently in Spain, he spread the doctrines of Krausism from his chair of philosophy at the University of Madrid. Although he incurred the implacable opposition of Catholic Thomists led by the Dominican priest Ceferino González and the philosopher-politician-journalist Juan Manuel Ortí y Lara,[35] he also won a considerable number of converts to Krausism. Among those converted either totally or in part were intellectuals and professors such as Francisco Giner de los Ríos and University of Sevilla rector Federico de Castro,[36] politicians such as Liberal Party leader José Canalejas and the republicans Azcárate and Nicolás Salmerón,[37] a former president of the first republic who in addition to his duties in parliament taught metaphysics at the University of Madrid.

It is not surprising that liberally inclined Spaniards, anxious to end the influence of the Catholic Church in the temporal realm and yet convinced generally of the primacy of spiritual and moral over material considerations, passionately dedicated to religious pluralism yet just as fervently opposed to social pluralism, responded approvingly to Krausism as expounded by Sanz del Río. Had Krausism not appeared in mid-nineteenth-century Spain, liberals would have found it convenient and even essential to invent something very much like it.[38] As it was they were given a ready-made apologia of their position that had the prestige value of proceeding from the country that was widely hailed as the leader in contemporary philosophical thought.

KRAUSISM: THE MORALITY OF SUBJECTIVE INTUITION, RATIONALITY AND SCIENCE; THE UNIVERSAL RELIGION OF TOLERANCE

One of the most popular features of Krausism as it was disseminated in Spain by Sanz del Río was its Kantian contention that belief in God sprang from morality, not morality from belief in God. The moral law was said to exist independently and on its own, awaiting discovery by the unfettered human intelligence; it did not depend upon religion, revealed truth, and supernatural grace. After the moral law had been discovered, then religion might come into play as a means of fortifying ethical precepts through "the majesty of the divine legislator." But before associating morality with a divine origin, it was thought necessary to discover moral precepts.[39]

Spanish Krausists, then, believed in the primacy of a system of moral law, from which a religious faith could later come as a natural result. Because of this they have been described as centered, "despite all their pretensions as innovators, within a fecund national tradition, standing as perhaps the last link in the moralist chain that began with Seneca and that illuminated with its light the greatest creations of the artistic genius of our raza."[40]

As expounded by Sanz del Río, Krausism taught Spanish liberals that man, if released from all restrictions of dogma, could discover a morality based on rationality. But that morality was not to be discovered only by rational inquiry and empirical investigation. Initially, in fact, it was to be approached through an intuitive, subjective, almost mystical process by means of which man cut through the trappings of old beliefs and taboos and, prescinding from all sacraments and supernatural accouterments, communed with the perfection within him that in turn reflected divine perfection and attested to man's basic oneness with God.[41] Once vaguely grasped, the moral law would be bolstered by legitimate self-love as proclaimed by humanism, by the noble aspiration for public esteem, by love of work and the impulse toward artistic creativity, and finally by the discoveries of science, arrived at in an intellectual climate distinguished by the unregulated and "unceasing battle of ideas."[42]

As he came to understand his true nature and the means of developing it to its full potential, man, the Krausists believed, would freely choose to curb his base desires and passions; no longer would coaction, violent repression, and force be necessary to assure moral conduct. As Sanz del Río explained it:

> You cannot achieve morality through the force of the state, through censorship and inquisitorial means; it must come from within us, through education for morality that trains the will. . . . Through education the will of the people can be awakened to act toward the full development of human nature. Action aimed at the development of one's nature . . . is only worthwhile when freely chosen without the threat of compulsion and sanctions.[43]

Krausists contended that in the quest for his moral perfection, for the harmonization of all the instincts and inclinations of his nature and for the maximum development of his natural capacity, man could avail himself of the various religions of the past, each of which, Christianity included, presented a perspective, a limited aspect of truth. Accordingly they urged complete religious tolerance so that man could benefit from partial truths and go on from these in search of ultimate and complete religious truth.[44]

Religions of the past, Sanz del Río charged, had never achieved liberation from historical and nationalistic particularisms. Consequently, they
had bred intolerance and generated ethnocentric, chosen-people com-
plexes. The challenge of mankind was to gain release from all factors that
had restricted tolerance and to work toward the development of a universal
religion of humanity.[45] The ideal church of the future, according to Krause
as translated by Sanz del Río, was one of complete tolerance; for "the
true religion embraces all men in a universal spirit of charity, recognizing
the fundamental unity that joins mankind together in the divine goodness." The ideal church desired by Spanish Krausists was, then, a truly
catholic church, the church of "natural virtue and of social religion."[46]

But before men could proceed to the founding of this church, they had
to make their heaven on earth by achieving moral purity and coming
thereby first to resemble the nature of God and ultimately to become one
with it;[47] for by developing their potential, by harmonizing all opposing
forces within themselves, men inevitably came to share and participate in
the divinity of God.[48] Only a few individuals, however, a truly select elite,
Sanz del Río assured his readers as he interpreted the doctrines of Krause,
could arrive fully at the state of moral perfection that would allow them
to undertake the creation of a new and universal religion.[49]

Krausism: Social Hierarchy, Social Solidarity, and the Decentralized Organic Structure

Krause, in a passage that exercised enormous appeal to his Spanish
admirers, observed that the saddest phenomenon in contemporary society,
and the one that most militated against realization of the ideals of
humanity, was class struggle and competition. As the solution to this
saddest of all social phenomena, he envisioned the organization of men
into subsovereign, subsidiary, semiautonomous municipal and professional
associations. The municipality and each association could then impart to
those participating within them a sound understanding of their proper
function in society as a whole. Once the citizens of each municipality and
the members of each association were afforded the satisfaction of shaping
the policies that affected them most immediately within their group and
were at the same time trained to see the function served by their subsidiary entity in the overall social scheme, they would accept the need for
divisions and stratification; and thus "the prevailing competition of classes
and professions would disappear."[50]

In establishing associations, Krause maintained that it would be absurd
not to distinguish between the various professions on a hierarchical basis
as "obviously the man who works with his mind is above the one who
works just with his hands; the more fully a man employs all his human
gifts, the higher is his status in life." In his view of society, then, Krause
saw a hierarchical structure at the base of which were the manual laborers

"who rented their arms to others." Above them were the free artisans who worked for themselves; and at the very top stood the "profound scientists" and the men of "poetic genius."

While each man, according to Krause, was on earth to pursue his end through his particular vocation he should also, however lowly his estate, participate to some degree in "the higher callings of human nature." Thus he should be taught to enjoy the beauty of nature and given a liberal education that included instruction in art, literature, and music so as to awaken in him a regard for the world of aesthetic pleasure. By learning to perceive, however dimly, and to appreciate, however imperfectly, the higher truths and beauties of life, man would gain liberation from material desires, from base passions and appetites, from selfish inclinations and resentment and rancor against others. Man thus liberated would attain a more harmonious and fully developed character while at the same time finding the solace and joys necessary to make him content and resigned within his station in life. However, man should be trained in science, art, and aesthetic appreciation only to the degree appropriate to the profession he practiced and the level he occupied in society. Only a few men, Krause declared, could master their profession and in addition comprehend its full relationship to the world of scientific, artistic, aesthetic, and creative human undertakings. Such men were clearly those whom Krause viewed as the directing elite that should preside at the very top of an organically structured society.[51]

Krause maintained that the superior classes had a duty to establish warm and fraternal contact with the inferior classes. Not only should the directing classes practice traditional forms of charity; they should in addition take a hand in cultivating, in so far as they could be cultivated, the higher human faculties of the humble.[52] Thus within the municipality and professional organizations, the upper classes must supplement the public educational structure by helping to stimulate the appreciation of the laboring classes for the fine arts. A cultural dialogue of this sort would in the long run, it was maintained, contribute to the artistic creativity of society's elite.[53]

As they began in their limited way to interest themselves in the higher things of life, the humble classes would come to revere the hierarchy of values in which the artistic and spiritual and aesthetic took precedence over material considerations. They would come to revere this hierarchy because in their leisure time, when they rested from the physical labor that gave "no nourishment to the spirit and that chilled the heart,"[54] they would find an exhilirating, stimulating, and rewarding world as they immersed themselves in the higher pleasures to which they had been introduced through their liberal education and the solicitude of the upper classes. Coming to appreciate a gradation of values, the laboring classes would tolerate and even welcome social gradation, understanding that only the better men could fruitfully pursue the better things in life and realize new works of artistic creativity that would eventually add to the pleasure of the humble, noncreative classes.

However much Spanish Krausism underwent transformation as positivism came to influence it late in the nineteenth century,[55] it retained its insistence upon the organic, corporative organization of society as well as its anti-individualistic and antimaterialistic orientation. Therefore, despite fudamental differences with their principal ideological opponents over the means to achieve it, Krausists and their twentieth-century intellectual offspring sought a social organization remarkably similar to the one desired by conservative, traditionalistic Catholics.[56]

The Social Conservatism of Spanish Liberalism and the Advocacy of Reform through Decentralization

Intellectuals in the Spanish-speaking world of Europe and America often reacted to positivism by accepting many of its philosophical concepts while at the same time spurning its pretensions as a new religion. Spanish liberals frequently reacted similarly toward Krausism. Ignoring its theological implications and rejecting it as a pantheistic religion of humanity, they nevertheless continued for two or three generations to propound its philosophical concepts and its social doctrines. Thus they reiterated again and again the demands of Krausism for a temporal order free from Catholicism's influence, for religious tolerance and the free discussion and teaching of all ideas on the assumption that truth would prevail over error. They accepted further the Krausist contention that the social problem could best be solved not by Catholicism but rather by a morality based on unaided human reason and intuition.[57] Likewise, they approved of the importance that Krausism attached to art, poetry, and to the entire world of aesthetic and cultural creativity and enjoyment. And they regarded with satisfaction the strong implication inherent in Krausism that a virtuous working class would be a productive working class, capable of bringing about national material development. Perhaps above all else, Spanish liberals clung to the social conservatism of Krausism.

Pío Baroja, one of Spain's more popular turn-of-the-century novelists, presented credentials of liberalism that could scarcely be faulted; for he was a Mason and an impassioned anticlerical.[58] He was also an outspoken foe of democracy on the grounds that it would result in social tumult and chaos by encouraging the mad ambitions that led men to seek to rise beyond their proper place. "Rule by the people?" asked Baroja. "Ridiculous. They have never commanded, not even in the most revolutionary times, and they will not command in the future." Quite to the contrary, there must at all times be rule by aristocrats, because in power they have "fewer impatiences, fewer appetites, and are more courteous and gentlemanly."[59] For one aspect of democracy Baroja confessed admiration: its encouragement of charitable benevolence toward others "which is an expression of humanity." But democracy as a political system in which the masses dominate through the absolutism of numbers "made him smile and even fear that he might die of laughter."[60]

Manuel Sales y Ferré, a professor of sociology at the University of Madrid and the key intellectual figure in modifying Krausism to positivist doctrines[61] agreed with Baroja on the absurdity of rule by the masses. "No," he responded to a question he had posited on whether democracy was a feasible form of government. "The masses are incapable of contributing either ideas or solutions; it is not their function. The masses can only express their needs and aspirations; devising the means to satisfy these corresponds to the men of talent and genius."[62]

Even José Canalejas, a man of "advanced democratic ideas,"[63] an advocate of universal suffrage, the jury system, and liberty of conscience,[64] whose liberalism was further demonstrated by the fact of his excommunication,[65] detested the "submission of capital to labor" that he felt would result from the tyranny of the masses in a system of absolute democracy.[66] In his distrust of democracy, Canalejas has been described as typical of "the most progressive liberals."[67]

Canalejas believed in government intervention to resolve the social problem—only the man of the forest rejected this concept, he declared in 1903[68]—precisely because he feared that otherwise there might occur a revolution as a result of which the tyranny of the few would give way to the tyranny of the many. In order to mitigate the tyranny of the few, and thereby to forestall revolution, Canalejas hoped to achieve cooperation between capital and labor, beginning at the level of municipal and other subsovereign, subsidiary groups.[69]

Initially the anticlericalism of Canalejas had helped drive Antonio Maura from the Liberal Party.[70] But in 1912 similarity in views over the proper form of social organization and the common desire to head off radical change led to an accord between the two men.[71] Nothing came of this, for shortly after the Liberal and Conservative came to their understanding Canalejas was assassinated by an anarchist. A commentator on this tragic event showed striking perceptiveness when he speculated on why Canalejas, who held some of the most advanced ideas among statesmen of his era, had been chosen as a victim by the anarchist. The reason, the writer suggested, was that Canalejas, with his receptiveness to innovation, was one of the men most likely to contribute effectively to preserving the monarchy and the system of elite rule, to which he was wholeheartedly devoted.[72]

In his celebrated book *España invertebrada*, published in 1921, nine years after the Canalejas assassination, José Ortega y Gasset (1883–1955), whose views on religion and Spanish traditions made him one of the intellectuals most despised by his country's Catholic conservatives, presented few new ideas on the desirable forms of social and political organization. He simply set forth the consensus arrived at much earlier by Spanish liberals as he stated: ". . . when in a nation the masses refuse to be masses—that is, to follow a directing minority—the nation is unmade, society is dismembered, social chaos prevails. . . . In summary, where there is not a minority that acts upon a collective mass, and a mass that is capable of accepting the influence of a minority, there is not a society."[73]

Generally in firm accord with conservatives on the need for elite rule, Spanish liberals further concurred with their philosophical-theological adversaries on the need for fraternal relations and continuing dialogue between governing and governed classes. To the lack of this contact and dialogue they attributed the social tensions and the inability to work toward a common national goal that had resulted in Spanish decadence.

Addressing the Real Academia de Ciencias Morales y Políticas, sociologist Adolfo González Posada, a leading liberal intellectual who dedicated much of his life to working for government-administered social justice programs, urged the establishment of local assemblies and professional associations in which men of all social classes would come together to discuss the problems most vital and immediate to them. The advantage of such assemblies and associations, Posada stated, was that they would provide "a social means adequate to produce a select minority, an elite. Government by an elite, rising spontaneously and freely through circumstances of open and unobstructed discussion, fulfills in my judgement the exquisite condition of a regime of organic democracy."[74] Posada argued essentially for the restoration of social harmony by encouraging the association of all classes in assemblies and groups that would, through decentralizing and subdividing the prerogatives of an impersonal central government, bring participation in power down to the grass roots level. Here was a social and political formula that appealed widely to liberals.

The Conde de Romanones, the Liberal Party leader whose enactment making it possible for some non-Catholic children to be excused from catechism instruction had precipitated a political storm that took him by surprise, consistently urged the creation of privately organized, non-Church-affiliated associations of management and labor, employers and employees. In these associations, which, in the spirit of the medieval guilds, would constitute intermediate groups between government and the individual, classes hitherto opposed would come to realize their mutual dependence and would work in a spirit of cooperation toward advancing the interests of their enterprise. It was impossible, said Romanones, to think in terms of independent labor organizations, because of the prevailing lack of culture among the working classes. The upper classes had an indispensable tutelary role to play, a role they could best assume within mixed capital-labor associations.[75]

Segismundo Moret, a fervent admirer of British institutions, a popular professor at the University of Madrid and one of the most studious and best-informed leaders of the Liberal Party, also advocated intermediate, mixed capital-labor associations.[76] Within them the directing classes could undertake various projects, demanded by justice and counseled by charity, aimed at bettering the material lot of laborers while at the same time instructing them in an environment of fraternity as to their duties. In exercising their tutelary role among laborers, the directing classes, Moret insisted, had to rest their claims to authority on morality, a morality arising from natural virtue and the lessons of Christian humanism rather than from the dogmas of Catholicism. Finally, Moret—as so many of his liberal associates—urged enactment of local autonomy legislation so as to revitalize the life of the municipality. Within the freely functioning town unit the laboring classes, enlisted in government-supported rather than Church-directed community-development projects, would benefit from the opportunity "to participate in municipal life."[77] As Joaquín Costa at an earlier time, both Moret and Romanones advocated the return of communal properties to municipalities so as to endow them with financial resources under their own control.

In their approach to the social problem liberals, by insisting on mixed rather than purely labor organizations, imposed upon themselves the same handicaps from which Catholic Actionists suffered. Operating on principles apparently more in line with the aspirations and psychological needs of workers themselves, socialists and anarchists proved far more successful in organizing labor than either Catholic conservatives or anticlerical liberals, both dedicated to defending a hierarchical, paternalistic structure in which workers received benefits because of the enlightenment and charitable inclinations of their superiors, not because of their power to demand and wrest concessions from the established system.

Ultimately realizing their tactical mistake, liberals began to accept the concept of exclusively labor syndicates within each profession, hoping to offset their power by management organizations within the same profession and bargaining committees between the two groups in which each was represented on the basis of numerical equality. In some ways this appeared to be the same approach that many Catholics had settled upon by the 1920s. There were important differences, though. Liberals desired laic, nonreligiously affiliated labor syndicates and were often willing to deal even with socialist unions; generally, moreover, they envisioned management associations that had a fairly close relationship to the government and bargaining committees that were responsive to pressures that might be applied by the state. Catholics, on the other hand, wanted labor unions, management groups, and joint committees that were basically a part of Catholic Action. In the liberal concept, then, it was a carefully screened laic elite presiding over affairs of state at the highest level that should exercise the moderating power in resolving the clashes of interest within and among various subsovereign groups. In the Catholic conservative concept the exercise of the moderating power had to be in conformity with the teachings of religion and therefore it devolved upon the bishops as princes of the Church.

The Conservatism of Spanish Liberalism: Advocacy of Reform through Education and Social Legislation

Catholic conservatives feared that out of ideological, philosophical, and theological pluralism would come social pluralism. If there were not a sacrosanct body of thought beyond discussion and debate and also beyond the ability of the multitudes to comprehend, then the masses would not recognize the need for a hierarchical organization in which a select elite existed to guard the purity of essential truths and to pass them on intact to succeeding generations. The uninhibited give-and-take competition of all ideas on a basis of equality would, according to conservatives, lead to the unrestrained give-and-take competition of all men and classes on a basis of equality; ideological anarchy would, in short, produce social chaos.

Liberals believed that ideological, philosophical, and theological plural-ism would not lead to social pluralism because inevitably some people would prove to be so superior in handling the free and open discussion and analysis of ideas that their mastery would be acknowledged by the less talented multitudes. But the masses could never recognize the superiority of some men and classes, and at the same time acknowledge their own inferiority, unless given some chance to share in, on the crude level of their competence, the pursuit of truth through open examination of all ideas. Ideological pluralism, the liberals believed, instead of leading to social pluralism was the best means for preventing it.

Basically, the assumptions of the liberals rested upon their blind faith in the inferiority of the masses. At the same time, and rather paradoxically, liberals remained optimistic in their appraisal of human nature. They assumed that the masses were sufficiently endowed with basic goodness and virtue to be able to recognize and willing to acknowledge their inferiority in pursuing the highest objectives of which the human spirit was capable. Acknowledgement of this inferiority would result as the masses came, through education and associations of various kinds, into consistent contact with those who were superior to them in the exalted realm of cultural and spiritual pursuits. For conservatives, on the other hand, the doctrine of the basic goodness and virtue of the masses signified primarily a faith in the ability of even the lowliest of human beings to attain supernatural salvation. But conservatives, on the whole, doubted that the masses possessed sufficient discernment and virtue, within a strictly humanistic frame of reference, to be able to recognize and voluntarily accept their inferiority on this earth. It followed, then, that the permanent hierarchical structure of temporal society demanded unassailable religious dogmas and spiritual-intellectual authoritarianism. To men of this persuasion, education based upon free competition of ideas was contrary to the laws of human nature and destined inevitably to foment social revolution.

Through education, Spanish liberals believed, the masses could be at least minimally exposed to the wonders of the levels of existence above them. A few of these wonders they could absorb and as a result their lives would acquire a new fullness, a new treasury of inward resources. As they came to appreciate the higher existence that they had never before known even remotely of, the masses would learn that they could claim only a few of its blessings because of their incapacity to assimilate more. In the process they would lose their resentment against those who occupied higher stations in life, coming to comprehend that social stratification was the result of differences in capacity among human beings to understand and creatively to add to the wealth of the mind and spirit. Here, then, was the intellectual-cultural corollary to the political process of allowing the masses to participate in decision-making processes at the level of the municipality or regional professional group. The appetite of the masses, it was assumed, both for cultural and political realization could be easily and safely sated.

From a number of different perspectives, liberals converged to extol popular education. One of them explained that university extension work could exercise a "wonderful pacifying force." By providing the masses with their first rudimentary acquaintence with cultural life it would give them a new source of pleasure.[78] Exposure to the higher world of culture would, declared another, lead workers to be more moderate and reasonable in their material demands.[79] Still another described how a liberal education in the humanities would enable the workers to find inward happiness and to live in harmony with the superior classes.[80] Education of this type, he also asserted, by giving the worker interests other than material would bring an end to crime.[81] Little wonder that a conservative Catholic accused the liberals of thinking that through an education stressing art, aesthetics, and natural morality they could achieve with the working classes what right-thinking men knew could only be accomplished through religion.[82]

Some liberals stressed the nonspiritual aspects of education as they concerned themselves with resolving the social problem. The more educated the worker, they reasoned, the more productive and therefore better off he was. Developing this point of view, a liberal statesman explained that the intelligent, educated worker could labor more effectively and produce more and thus his employer could afford to pay him a better remuneration.[83] Generally, liberals recognized the need for a combined approach to mass education. Workers, they argued, should be given vocational training so that they would become more proficient within their assigned position in life and simultaneously instructed in the humanities so as to have a source of spiritual succor.[84]

Because the vocational and cultural education of the workers was recognized as a long-term process, liberals often added to their educational recommendations a wide variety of state-supported social security proposals aimed at the immediate alleviation of tensions. In the long-term approach of remolding the character of the Spanish masses by providing them with a well-balanced technical and liberal education free from the dogmatic claims of any one religion, Francisco Giner de los Ríos was the acknowledged leader of his era. In the endeavor to relieve the social problem through government protection of the worker, no one matched the zeal and total dedication of Gumersindo de Azcárate.

Liberal Reform through Education: The Work of Francisco Giner de los Ríos and the Institución Libre de Enseñanza

Open-minded, tolerant, and eclectic in his intellectual interests, Giner de los Ríos (1840–1915) found a great deal that appealed to him in Spanish Krausism.[85] He was also influenced by Herbert Spencer's theories on social evolution, although rejecting outright the Spencerian belief in the necessity of unregulated competition and conflict among men and classes. Giner was further attracted to certain tenets of positivism, however much he combated what he considered its excessive intellectual rigidity and inclination toward dogmatism.[86]

Giner always stressed the obligation of select spirits—he preferred to describe them as an aristocracy of character rather than of talent, for the latter word implied only worldly success to him and was associated with intelligence rather than the will—to establish a close rapport and uninterrupted communication with the masses. Success in this, he felt, depended upon the ability of the elite to deal with the masses as associates in a common venture rather than as their mentors. And it was in this spirit that Giner approached his students. He appeared to be as much interested in their opinion as in his own; he sought to win their confidence and to awaken their intellectual curiosity by the example of his own dedication to the search for truth rather than to overwhelm them with his already accumulated fund of knowledge. Even Catholic conservatives, who sometimes studied under him, tended to admire this mild and moderate man "who had no idols but hated no one, who found his example in St. Francis, who lived quietly and happily in austerity."[87]

The story is told that one day a student inquired of Giner de los Ríos: "Don Francisco, what would you do if you should come to wield political power?" "What would I do?" mused the teacher. "Perhaps nothing. It is necessary to make men; this is slow and sure work, yes; but also the most difficult."[88]

Even as in the approach of Catholic Action, Giner believed it was essential to remake the men of Spain. Political reforms imposed from above would always in the long run, he believed, prove ineffective. "Institutions do not initiate the purifying and reforming impulses," he once wrote; "they receive these impulses from the people."[89]

Liberalism, triumphant in 1868, had erred, according to Giner, in attempting to impose new laws and various reforms through external force. He was convinced that new laws could be effective only if they arose in response to the demands of the gradually changing consciences of the populace.[90] Laws, he asserted, must come to prevail in an almost mystical manner as the masses somehow intuited, at least vaguely, the need for them. The nation that depended upon coaction for the observance of its laws faced a continuous threat to survival.[91]

Giner detested the "absurdity of inorganic democracy"[92] because this political system allegedly threatened the rights of minorities.[93] Owing to the very nature of the men who comprised them, he explained, minorities were sharply differentiated from one another and thoroughly uncohesive in internal composition. This was so because it was the more exalted human endowments and resources, which were exploited and developed only by the most able men who ideally made up minorities, that imparted distinctive characteristics to human nature. In contrast the masses, to whom inorganic democracy based on universal suffrage gave control over a country's destiny, were uniform and undifferentiated; for they had not risen appreciably above the lowest level of human nature, that of animality. Within a democratic structure, then, the masses, united in the lowest common denominator of human existence, would prevail over the minorities whose members, because they had more fully developed their potential, were highly diversified.

Given these circumstances the way to protect the status of superior minorities was not through tyranny and force but rather through awakening the higher capacities of the masses by teaching them to appreciate the same things that the select few had already come to treasure. As the masses were awakened in their higher human calling, they would themselves, to some degree at least, emerge from their amorphous uniformity and become individualized;[94] as a consequence they would accept and defend a social organization that safeguarded a wide variety and complex gradation of groups. Once individualized through education, the masses would spontaneously, of their own volition, reject egalitarian, leveling social movements seeking to reduce all men to the same level. In such circumstances minority rights within a hierarchical organization would be secure; for these rights would arise from the natural preferences of the people rather than deriving from an ever-precarious imposition from above.[95]

Instead of acquiring a common class-consciousness in which they simply regarded themselves as constituting the lump sum of labor, masses that had been individualized through education would, Giner believed, recognize their distinct functions and band together into different functional-interest groups, syndicates, or corporations. And, understanding that they were joined by common cultural values and economic purposes with the director-employer sector of their particular occupation, they would reject organizations that were exclusively labor in membership.

Giner's ideal was not a pluralistic society. Each group or syndicate would not rely upon its own power in obtaining its goals through a system of open competition. Nor, of course, would it struggle for its ends through appeal to a mass electorate. Rather, each group would select from among its members the most able men, who would exercise at the level of the national parliament a moderating power that harmonized the conflicting interests of the country's functional associations. The rank and file in each corporation would accept the national moderating power, content that in its exercise they were represented by trusted peers who had their mutual interests at heart.[96]

Because he believed that the more uniform a people was the more easily it was subjected to tyranny, Giner championed religious diversity. Unity in Catholicism allegedly made people identical on the basis of their lowest common intellectual denominator, the blind acceptance of memorized formulas. On the other hand the individual search for theological truth through the free comparison of different faiths, all of them approached with respect as containing at least a partial glimpse of ultimate truth, would introduce infinite religious diversity into society; and religious diversity would in turn complement the ideal liberal education in individualizing and differentiating men, in evoking their hostility against movements aimed at conformity. Catholicism to Giner was a leveling force that reduced men to anonymous ciphers in an amorphous mass. In the final analysis Catholicism as an imposed state religion might be conducive to socialism, which required as a prerequisite a conforming, nonindividualized mass base.[97]

In the Institución Libre de Enseñanza, Giner de los Ríos found the means to introduce into Spain the sort of laic edcuation that would change the nature of the populace, that would safeguard and perpetuate the aristocratic organization of society by turning the masses into replicas, as perfect as their spiritual endowments and stations in life permitted, of aristocrats.[98]

The Institution came into being in 1876, founded by Giner de los Ríos and other professors, among them Moret, Costa, and Azcárate, who had been ousted from their regular teaching posts in the wake of a purge that accompanied the restoration.[99] Providing its members with the opportunity to teach freely in accordance with their consciences, the Institution by its very existence registered a protest against state or clerical control over education. Operating funds for the Institution derived from private support and from tuition collected by its secondary school—*colegio* or preuniversity lycée that granted the bachelor's degree—which was soon expanded to encompass the primary level. Even when readmitted to their university posts, the Institution's founders often stayed on in a part-time capacity to staff the school, in many instances offering their services gratuitously.[100]

With an educational approach that stressed the development of the whole man and an intimate, fraternal relationship between student and teacher—presaging the ultimately hoped for warm relationship between labor and capital—the Institution's school sought to develop the artistic abilities and spiritual interests, the vocational competence and physical strength and dexterity of its pupils. Above all, the Institution tried to encourage the spirit of independent, personal investigation. Its school was to be a laboratory in which the child learned through his own experiments, not by listening to the discourses of teachers and memorizing exercises. Periodic examinations were abolished and students were graded on the basis of the teachers' daily observations. Thereby, according to Giner, an anonymous, cold, and detached method was replaced by a personal, warm, and human system of examination.[101]

Not all of the work was carried out in the classroom. Giner and the other instructors of the Institution's school led their wards on field trips in which the students were introduced to the natural beauties of Spain, shown locales of historical significance, and trained in the ways of the woodsman and outdoorsman.

Because of the Institution's success in placing graduates of its school in teaching positions it became to some degree the great normal school of Spanish liberalism. On these grounds it was indignantly denounced by Catholic conservatives for undermining the morals of the entire nation.[102] To combat the Institution and its mounting power as a training center of teachers, Catholics founded in 1914 a new Madrid seminary. The teachers to be trained in this seminary were seen as the servants of God who would challenge the lackeys of the devil produced by the Institution. Dedicated to Christ, they would save children from the "Anti-Christ, from the apostasy and perdition to which they are attracted by the products of the Institution."[103]

If opponents were alarmed by its success, sometimes friends of the Institution questioned whether its program was adequate to the tasks confronting liberal Spain. Writing in 1900 an admirer of Giner asked if the gradual redemption of Spain through the slow formation of individual minds and consciences would stave off the threatened social revolution. "Can we wait?" he asked. "Will not the remedy arrive too late? An external, forceful justice that extends from above . . . would not this give us strength to await the effects of individual redemption?"[104]

Convinced that the masses must indeed be sustained by certain remedies administered from above, Gumersindo de Azcárate, the man who hoped Spaniards would not confuse secularization of the state with secularization of their inward lives, took the lead among liberals in securing enactment of social legislation and in initiating government programs to protect workers and minister to their most pressing material needs.

Liberal Reform through Government Intervention: The Work of Gumersindo de Azcárate and the Instituto de Reformas Sociales

Moderation was one of the key characteristics of Azcárate (1840–1917), the tall, slender, and ascetic professor-politician of decided Krausist leanings who at different times in his distinguished career was rector of the Institución Libre de Enseñanza as well as president of the Ateneo of Madrid and of the Real Academia de Ciencias Morales y Políticas. Although a staunch republican, Azcárate hoped that Spain would evolve gradually and peacefully into a republic. Cautious both in his approach to politics and the social problem, he wanted above all else to avoid what he considered the always exorbitant price of revolution.[105] He believed that if the "revolutionary hypothesis" was banished from the land the social problem could be slowly resolved in a spirit of tolerance and mutual respect as capital and labor came to forget past grievances.[106] In the process, he asserted, the capitalist classes would have to make the major sacrifices in a spirit of stoicism and abnegation, for primary responsibility for having produced the social problem lay with them.[107]

European society in general, Azcárate believed, had not yet recovered from the destruction of institutions perpetrated in accordance with the principles of the French Revolution. His concern lay with the creation of new institutions that would achieve harmony in class relations and effect a compromise between socialism and individualism. Individualism, he wrote, was predominant at the turn of the century. It was necessary, then, to curb its absolute reign by the creation of "free, private associations" in which both capital and labor were represented. These associations would, he hoped, revive the spirit of the old crafts guilds. Ever since the destruction of these guilds, he lamented, the worker had been forced to function as an isolated atom and thus had been incapable of defending his interests. The state could not create these entities; but it could and must provide a more propitious atmosphere for amicable capital-labor relations by enacting and enforcing social laws that protected the worker. Once the worker was provided with some element of material security, society could proceed toward the emancipation of his spirit.[108]

By 1904 Azcárate headed an agency that was as effective in implementing some of his ideas as was the Institución Libre de Enseñanza in fulfilling the dreams of Giner de los Ríos. Azcárate's good fortune resulted from a chain of events reaching back to 1883 when the then minister of interior, Segismundo Moret, founded the Comisión de Reformas Sociales.[109] The function of the Commission, whose members received no salary, was to study all aspects of capital-labor relations. Although the Commission published interesting studies in 1884 and 1902 and presented carefully prepared suggestions for legislation on employer responsibility for industrial accidents, Sunday rest, and safe and hygienic working conditions, liberals at the turn of the century had come to regard it as altogether inadequate for carrying out the degree of state intervention that the times seemed to demand. In 1902, therefore, José Canalejas called upon Adolfo González Posada[110] and Adolfo Álvarez Buylla,[111] two professors of Krausist persuasions active at the time in the extension work of the University of Oviedo,[112] to assist him in preparing plans for an institution that could expand the government's social role.

The outcome of this collaboration was a bill introduced by Canalejas, modeled to a large extent on recently enacted Italian legislation, calling for the creation of a government institute of labor whose functions would be to gather information on capital-labor relations, to compile labor and social statistics, to study means of improving working-class conditions, and to prepare appropriate legislation for consideration by the Cortes.[113]

Although the Canalejas bill did not win parliamentary approval, its essential features were incorporated into legislation successfully steered through the Cortes the following year by a Conservative government headed by Silvela. The 1903 law, for which Liberals and Conservatives could claim joint credit, created the Instituto de Reformas Sociales within the ministry of interior. The Institute was charged with conducting investigations on the social question, preparing social and labor legislation for submission to the Cortes, and supervising the enforcement of existing and future laws bearing on capital-labor relations.[114] Representatives both of capital and labor were to collaborate within the Institute in carrying out its purposes.[115]

The spirit of Liberal-Conservative cooperation that led to creation of the Instituto de Reformas Sociales carried over into the operating procedures of the new agency, within which Krausist liberals and conservative Catholics—particularly the Christian Democrats—collaborated, often united by their common advocacy of an organic, corporative social structure.[116] The spirit of cooperation was very much in evidence when Maura, who had succeeded Silvela as leader of the Conservative Party, called upon Azcárate to head the Institute when it commenced its functions in March of 1904. Azcárate, who would remain the president of the Institute and its guiding spirit until his death in 1917, quickly summoned Posada and Buylla to aid him "in the lovely work of social pacification."[117]

One of the most important and fruitful endeavors undertaken by the Instituto de Reformas Sociales was that of encouraging workers to establish savings accounts and to organize credit cooperatives and mutual aid societies.[118] To coordinate and to expand the scope of these efforts the Institute early in the century helped bring into being the Instituto Nacional de Previsión (National Savings and Insurance Institute).[119] Under the leadership of José Maluquer y Salvador, an insurance expert who helped prepare its charter,[120] and José Marvá y Mayor, a sociologist-engineer who, upon retiring from his army career, became its president,[121] the new Institute undertook an extensive campaign to encourage savings habits among the working classes throughout Spain.

Liberalism's Failure to Resolve the Social Problem

In spite of Azcárate's Herculean efforts in the quest of social harmony, abundant evidence at the time of his death in 1917 indicated that the social problem was worse than it had been when the Instituto de Reformas Sociales came into being in 1904. González Posada was deeply perturbed by the Spain that he observed in 1917. The general strike of that year, allegedly instigated by Marxism and other dangerous foreign ideologies,[122] constituted a warning, he declared, of greater calamities to come; it might even presage a catastrophic social upheaval.[123] Additional warning signs abounded. Ever since 1910 strikes, many of them accompanied by violence, had averaged more than a hundred a year.[124] Between 1917 and 1922 the government struggled in vain to curtail the mounting tide of labor violence and anarchist-inspired street wars in Barcelona.[125]

Conditions spawned by World War I heightened social tensions in Spain. Aware of the need for maximum industrial output to meet the demands of the wartime market, men in government resorted to immediate intervention whenever strikes threatened to interrupt production. Strikes were averted or settled on the basis of generous concessions to labor, with the result that management raised prices to cover increased operating costs. Between 1913 and 1920 the price level index rose from 100 to 228.[126] Hard-pressed consumers inclined more and more to believe the charges of management that an unwholesome collaboration between government and organized labor was responsible for the spiraling costs of living.

Against this background the Instituto de Reformas Sociales recommended, but did not enthusiastically urge, that the government decree an eight-hour day for most industrial workers. Somewhat to the surprise of the Institute, the government responded almost at once with a decree of April 3, 1919, establishing the eight-hour day.[127] To the spokesmen of most management and consumer interests, here was the final proof of the unreasonableness of the labor-government complex. As they saw the situation, labor and its allies in government, not satisfied with previous gains that were economically unjustifiable and notwithstanding the prevailing shortage of goods and continuing price increases, had struck yet another blow against the public interest, one that could only result in worse shortages and sharper price markups.

Serious attempts at capital-labor collaboration, favored for over twenty years both by liberals and conservatives, came virtually to an end following the eight-hour day decree, as management adopted a stance of intransigent opposition to worker demands. Within the Instituto de Reformas Sociales the representatives of capital refused all further discussion with labor delegates.[128] The Institute entered upon a period of fatal decline and scarcely a voice was raised in mourning when dictator Miguel Primo de Rivera abolished it in 1924.

By this time, moreover, the accommodated classes had begun to worry more and more about the communist menace. It was a sign of the times when Fernando de los Ríos in *Mi viaje a Rusia soviética*, published in 1922, dwelt upon the threat to Spain posed by recent events in Russia. In this atmosphere it became ever easier to attribute worker demands to communist influence and to insist upon resolution of the social tension through stricter law-and-order expedients. The establishment of rapport and harmony between capital and labor in a setting of expanding political and cultural freedoms began to seem a utopian hope.

In part because they had expended so much of their time and energies in fighting one another over religious issues, neither conservatives nor liberals had by the early 1920's advanced toward their common goal of ending the social crisis by coopting working classes into an established order that, although considerably modified by certain reforms, would be characterized as always by a hierarchical, rigidly gradated, nonpluralistic structure of society. Having failed in their respective programs that were almost always at cross purposes in regard to means, both conservatives and liberals were on the whole disposed to welcome the attempt of Primo de Rivera, beginning in September of 1923, to cope with the social problem and contain the revolution that it threatened by dictatorial means.

But the disillusionment that led to the welcoming of dictatorship was over twenty years in developing. At the beginning of the century, filled with burgeoning confidence and optimism that resulted partly from increasing contact with their brothers across the Atlantic, conservatives and liberals alike dreamed not only of remaking Spain in line with their ideals but of remaking the Spanish world in America as well.

6: THE SPANISH RAZA AND SPAIN'S MISSION IN AMERICA

Spanish Belief in the Existence of a Spanish Character

A fundamental characteristic of Spaniards has always been the unassailable conviction that there are fundamental characteristics of the Spanish people. Cutting across the ideological divergencies of the two Spains, this conviction is shared by conservatives and liberals alike. And it has never mattered in the least whether there is scientific evidence to support the view that there are basic character traits of the Spanish people or of any other national group. Spaniards tend to be convinced that there are things science knows not of and that one of these is the existence of a character, a nature, a temperament in a particular people or raza.[1] Rafael Altamira, for example, states unequivocally that each national populace, for reasons or causes unknown to science, acquires through the centuries a special character.[2]

Expressing his belief in the distinguishing characteristics of a people or raza, Juan Valera wrote:

> They say that I am a skeptic. But I believe in a multitude of things in which those who pass as believers often have no faith. Among other things I believe, in however vague and confused a manner, in the collective spirit. My fantasy transforms into a substantial reality that which is called the genius or spirit of a raza. That which is a rhetorical figure of speech for the generality of men for me is a vital reality.[3]

For Pedro Martínez Vélez, a conservative Agustinian priest, the national character or genius was just as real as it was for the somewhat anticlerical Valera:

> National character is the totality of those common properties which in the midst of physical and moral differences of individuals marks the natural and special constitution of a people. From this definition it arises that when the national character is formed, especially in homogeneous peoples, thanks to a long influence of the same physical and moral causes, of the same sentiments, it exercises a transcendent influence in the life and history of nations.[4]

The anticlerical, predominately liberal, irreligious and sometimes even antireligious Generation of '98 was typically Spanish in assuming that something rendered Spaniards different from other men.[5] And Víctor Pradera (1872–1936), the spokesman of Catholic traditionalism, was no less certain than his ideological foes that the Spanish people was stamped with a unique character. This character stemmed, he asserted, from the fact that as man passes through life he is influenced, "if he does not in fact receive these influences from the cradle, by the accumulated life and legacies of previous generations; these mold his character, direct him and perfect his spirit." As a result, Pradera concluded, "man is the son of his nation, involved in a relationship with his ancestors, who were, and his descendents, who will be. The nation is the patria just as the woman who conceived us is the mother."[6]

As a young man Menéndez Pelayo contended that national characteristics were determined largely by raza as understood in a biological sense. Thus he stated that semitic peoples had a proclivity toward pantheism, while Spaniards, because of their Aryan blood, resisted this heresy. On the other hand he was also willing to admit the importance of the geographic environment in determining the characteristics of a people. "The national genius," he wrote, "is defined biologically through blood and through soil, through raza and through the geographic medium. It is materially impossible, given the laws of transmission and inheritance . . . that thinkers of the same blood, born on the same soil, subject to the same physical and moral influences, would not demonstrate a similar manner of being . . . although they might contend against one another in diverse and even hostile schools."[7]

As he advanced in years Menéndez Pelayo increasingly discounted the biological aspect of raza.[8] He thereby brought himself more into line with the generally prevailing Spanish viewpoint that assumes nonbiological factors to be of paramount importance in molding the characteristics of raza. This viewpoint was well summarized in a 1904 address by the president of the Spanish Chamber of Commerce in Mexico: "When we speak of raza we must say we do not allude precisely to the common ethnic origin, but to a certain psychological identity which consciously or subconsciously impels certain collectivities toward the realization of specific goals. . . . In any event," the speaker concluded, "the recognition and study of this phenomenon carries us to the conviction that, whether or not it is the fruit of the will, there exists a positive, indestructible moral affinity among the Iberian peoples."[9]

Spanish Views on the Basic Traits of Spanish Character

For Ramón Menéndez Pidal (1869–1968), the philologist, historian, and all-around scholar of the Renaissance type, the most distinctive traits of Spaniards, and at the same time their most characteristic virtues, were sobriety, gravity, and seriousness.[10] Unamuno agreed. The saddest thing for him, he once wrote, would be to see Spaniards become frivolous and jovial in the way of other Europeans. In that case they would cease to be Spaniards. "We would then have perhaps better wines, more refined wines, less asperous oil, better oysters." But, he concluded, "we would then have renounced the possibility of a new Quijote, of a Velázquez, and above all the possibility of a new Saint John of the Cross . . . of a new Saint Teresa, of a new Loyola, whether orthodox or heterodox, which would all be the same."[11]

Spanish sobriety and gravity were traced back by Ángel Ganivet to Seneca's stoicism, the fundamental precept of which was to maintain oneself upright and with dignity at all times "so that at the very least it can be said of you that you are a man."[12] Menéndez Pidal states, as he develops a theme that virtually all commentators on Spanish character have remarked upon, that in their stoic qualities Spaniards recognize that life is not the supreme good: "The ancient Spaniard gave up his life with patriotic enthusiasm . . .; he gave it up to fulfill high duties of honor and fidelity. . . . We do not know," the philologist continued, "specifically to what religious, political or social principles this preferring death to other evils corresponds, above all preferring death to loss of liberty. But in all this we see pulsating something analogous to stoic thought. Seneca praised suicide as liberation, understanding that death is nothing to fear, that it is the end of evils and the beginning of true liberty in the eternal."[13]

Another Spanish writer attributed to stoicism his countrymen's alleged lack of concern with material goods, their ability to understand that "the poor person is not he who has little, but rather he who wants more than he has; because material necessities are very few, while vain ambition is inexhaustible."[14] To whatever they may attribute the phenomenon, Spaniards agree with remarkable unanimity that theirs is not a materialistic raza. Typically, Ramiro de Maeztu commented upon the nonmaterialism of Spaniards in contrasting them with Anglo-Saxons. The latter, he wrote, seem "to prefer wealth to poverty even at the cost of maximum labor," while Spaniards appear "to prefer idleness, once their most elemental needs are satisfied, even at the cost of remaining indefinitely in poverty."[15]

One of Maeztu's contemporaries advanced a widely held opinion when he asserted that among Spaniards imagination was valued over rationalism, beauty over truth, theory over practice, and spirit over matter.[16] Ganivet concurred, stating that Spaniards tended naturally to put the ideal and the spiritual ahead of material considerations. "If we give a primarily economic or material goal to our actions, we will always be servile imitators."[17]

As a young man the Spanish intellectual Federico de Onís, who in 1916 commenced a distinguished teaching career at Columbia University, worried that Spain's characteristic inattentiveness to material considerations might render it permanently incapable of achieving progress and a respected status among the modern nations of the world. Upon more mature reflection, however, he decided that the apparently progressive members of international society were coming to be more and more disillusioned with the barrenness and emptiness of the type of civilization resulting when pursuit of material goals became the primary goal. Ultimately, he predicted, the countries once thought advanced would be forced to seek solace in the wisdom of Spain, whose people had known how to remain true to medieval roots and had thus preserved the ideal of civilization that was destined to triumph in the future.[18]

"Unconquerable individualism"[19] is another trait that nearly all writers on the subject have attributed to Spanish temperament. "Always independent, never docile,"[20] the Spaniard has been described as basically inclined to resist organization, as willing to endure anything so long as left free from attempts "to coordinate him into mass procedures."[21] In the 1930's a Spaniard predicted that communism would not attract his fellow citizens because of their innate horror of eating in a collective dining room.[22] During the same period another Spaniard explained that his countrymen preferred charity to justice because of their ingrained individualism. Spaniards, he declared, regarded as sacred only those obligations that they imposed upon themselves.[23]

Individualism may account for the tendency of Spaniards to prefer sentiment to logic, intuition to rational deduction, mysticism to painstaking investigation in the search for truth and meaning in life.[24] In the Spanish approach to truth man is absolutely on his own, unfettered by rules, regulations, and laws of rigid philosophical systems; he is free "to palpitate," not required "to calculate" in accordance with the dictates of impersonal, external systems and methods.[25] Because of necessities imposed by their very nature Spaniards, according to Ganivet, always approached truth and religion through mysticism and intuition; they preferred "to fly on the wings of inward faith" rather than "to crawl through libraries" in search of objective, rational systems of thought.[26]

Quite possibly Spanish individualism, inducing them at all costs "to avoid the vulgar" and "to resist succumbing to the mediocrity of the common,"[27] has fostered their distrust of democracy conceived of in terms of inorganic, universal suffrage. The Spaniard might occasionally choose to curb his individualism so as to serve the overall interests of groups to which he felt intimately connected on the basis of warm, interpersonal relationships, such as family, municipality, and professional associations or guilds; but he abhorred doing so in order to serve the interests of a mass, numerical majority with which he did not feel personal ties. All life for the Spaniard was "a prolongation of the patriarchal family;" he was willing to accept order, but only an order based upon "the intimacy of the regulated, patriarchal family."[28]

Inclining in their preferences toward a corporative social and political structure, Spaniards could scarcely imagine that other people might accept an order determined by the desires of a numerical majority. Rule by majority represented to them a dictatorship in which citizens were forced by outward and impersonal pressures to limit their options for action. Spaniards seemed to feel that, wherever it existed, the impersonal tyranny of majority rule would result ultimately in social anarchy as men rebelled against the cold and detached forces that regulated their lives.

Because they could see inorganic democracy based on universal suffrage as leading only to social chaos and leveling revolution, Spaniards of both the conservative and liberal schools wondered how they could protect themselves against the spreading democratic contagion. They feared that on their own they probably lacked the strength to preserve the type of social and political organization suited to their character. That is why they longed to act in concert with the Iberian peoples of America. A united Iberian family could summon up the strength to conserve its cherished way of life while a divided Hispanic world would succumb to the evils of modern civilization. According to this line of reasoning, or of feeling, peninsular Spaniards could not maintain a style of life that corresponded to their basic characteristics and values unless their brothers across the sea shared with them the same characteristics and values. Therefore in the early twentieth century Spaniards of the Old World turned with some urgency to ascertaining whether Spanish Americans genuinely shared in the temperament of the Spanish raza. With their wishes shaping the reality, they soon discovered in the New World precisely what they had hoped to find.

Spaniards on the Characteristics of a Transatlantic Spanish Raza

It was easy, Juan Valera observed, to forgive Spanish Americans for having rebelled against Spain in quest of political independence. What could not be forgiven was their sacrilegious and inevitably vain endeavor to rebel psychologically, to turn against the genius or spirit of Spain, which was, whether they accepted the fact or not, the only authentic genius and spirit they had.[29]

Two Spanish writers in the early twentieth century shared Valera's willingness to forgive Spanish Americans for gaining their political independence. After all, these writers remarked, the revolutionary wars begun in 1810 did not constitute a break with, but rather arose out of, the Spanish spirit; they were not carried out by Indians, but by white men and mestizos in whom Iberian blood, culture, and values predominated. Thus the independence fighters manifested anew "the audacity and vision, as well as the cantankerousness and selfishness, of the original Spanish conquerors."[30] Writing in 1904, a Madrid journalist pardoned even the Cubans for their recently concluded independence struggle on the grounds that it had originated not in the desires of the island's populace but in the "intervention of a vile rapist more interested in wealth than beauty, intent only upon ripping from the Cuban neck its strand of pearls."[31] The three cited writers all agreed that having obtained their political sovereignty, Spanish Americans were more and more abandoning their unnatural insurrection against the Spanish spirit.

Six years after the disaster Francisco Silvela averred that Spanish sentiments and values showed a greater strength and vitality in Spanish America than in the peninsula. In the New World, he said, the polemics that characteristically divided Spaniards were largely events of the past. Because they had surmounted superficial sources of divisiveness, Spanish Americans had learned to treasure and guard what was most basic in the Iberian temperament and value system.[32] At about the same time Rafael María de Labra declared that Spain and Spanish America had in the course of modern history copenetrated one another and achieved thereby a moral and intellectual intimacy.[33] The copenetration of Spain and Spanish America also impressed Menéndez Pidal. Owing to it, he stated, Spaniards always felt at home in Spanish America.[34] All Spanish-American civilization, he added, "rests principally on its Spanish bases, at times surprisingly archaic; for it even preserves Spanish customs that have disappeared in the peninsula."[35]

Unamuno, who saw Simín Bolívar as the incarnation of the spirit of Quijote, continued in the days following the disaster to believe that Spanish traits and values exercised the paramount influence in Spanish America, even in Argentina with its large colony of Italian immigrants and its infatuation with French culture. The Italians, the French intellectuals and literary figures had exercised a superficial influence, but beneath the surface the values of the Spanish world prevailed.[36] By no means always inclined to do so, Ortega y Gasset agreed with Unamuno in this instance. Argentina had been Spain, Ortega asserted as he addressed an Argentine audience, and what something has been it continues inevitably to be.

> The Spain that Argentina was endures then, whether this is desired or not, in the most subterranean depths of your being, and it persists there, tacitly, creating its mysterious chemical effects. During the century that followed the attainment of your country's independence, in spite of the decided and deliberate will among wide groups of your countrymen to seal themselves off hermetically from Spanish influence, Spain, as had to be the case, continued to influence you, although in a less visible manner . . . in a process of osmosis. . . .[37] This has nothing to do with . . . political approximation; it has instead to do with something of far more fundamental importance: the progressive coincidence in a determined style of life.[38]

The mounting conviction, arising out of the fervent hope, that the New World republics founded by Spain continued to be purely Spanish in essence[39] found characteristic expression in 1924 by a University of Barcelona professor of political geography. "Upon directing my eyes toward the New World," he wrote, "I perceive with indescribable pleasure that our spirituality endures there; that through the veins of the Americans circulates Spanish blood; that there they think, feel, and speak as we do."[40]

What was the most important evidence that Spaniards and Spanish Americans were indeed members of the same raza, of the same "community of culture?"[41] According to most Spanish analysts, it was the common concern with spiritual rather than material, utilitarian values.[42] Joaquín Sánchez de Toca evidenced this typical attitude when he wrote in 1898 that what bound Spain to Spanish America was the unique attentiveness to things of the spirit and the mutual agreement that material objectives were not the most important in life.[43] Writing some fifty years later, a Spanish author returned to this constantly recurring theme in nearly all works alluding to hispanismo. Because spiritual considerations stood at the top of their hierarchy of values, he wrote, Spaniards and Spanish Americans were homogeneous peoples, forming a "moral, mystical, spiritual whole; a supranational entity, clearly defined and delineated, whole and united, integral and complete."[44]

Regarding their overseas brothers as members of their own raza, Spaniards naturally found encouragement in the accomplishments of the Spanish Americans. Every triumph of Spanish Americans, in whatever field of endeavor, proved that the Spanish raza was not decadent, and, in the apparently bright future of Spanish America, where they enjoyed an abiding spiritual presence, Spaniards saw their own future.[45] At the same time, because they believed they had bequeathed their spirit to Spanish Americans, Spaniards perceived a paternal duty to nourish and sustain that spirit, to keep it pure and uncontaminated so that those formed by it could realize a destiny in keeping with their nature, rather than being led astray by alien values.[46] Moreover, their self-assumed responsibility to safeguard the purity of the Spanish spirit in America logically imposed upon Spaniards the obligation to preserve the purity of the language in the New World.

Spain, Spanish America, and the Purity of the Language

Spain, the Liberal statesman the Conde de Romanones declared in 1904, has a "providential mission to fulfill" in its relations with the people on the other side of the ocean who speak a common language; "it is to maintain the purity of that language."[47] Conservative leader Antonio Maura concurred. To him, in fact, this mission seemed no less important than that undertaken by sixteenth-century Spaniards to preserve the purity of Spanish blood, both in the peninsula and the Indies, against the contamination of Judaism.[48]

Spanish concern with maintaining the purity of Castilian arose basically from the belief that the language and spirit of a people were intimately connected, that when the language was corrupted the spirit likewise suffered debasement. As Altamira saw it, language reflected the spirit of a people;[49] those who spoke the same language belonged inescapably to the same intellectual community, a community that could not be penetrated by those who had grown up speaking a different tongue.[50]

According to Unamuno, language carried in itself "a vision and a view of the universe, a conception of life and human destiny, of art, philosophy, and even religion."[51] Language, he often repeated, is "the blood of the spirit;"[52] it is "the basis of our spiritual patria; and to this day Cervantes gives us firmer claims of possession over America than Columbus gave to our forefathers."[53] People who speak the same language, the classicist added, "feel life" in the same way. And however much the physical blood of Spaniards was mixed with that of Indians in the New World, so long as Spanish Americans retained undefiled the "blood of the spirit" bequeathed them by their ancestors, they would continue to feel life in a Spanish manner.[54]

Men of liberal persuasions such as Romanones, Altamira, and Unamuno would not have agreed with Menéndez Pelayo that the English language represented the spirit of Protestant individualism, while Spanish was the natural vehicle of the Catholic, integrated, organic concept of life.[55] However, they would have agreed with a prominent member of the Real Academia Española who described language as "the great psychological archive that conserves the common values of peoples."[56] They would further have agreed with Rodolfo Reyes, a Mexican who lived many years in Spain, when he declared: "as Spanish Americans we can never be strangers in Spain; and Spaniards can never be strangers in our lands. For we speak the same language and because of this we think with the same spirit and feel with the same heart."[57]

Among Spanish intellectuals, then, there existed a broad consensus that language reflected and was in turn a vehicle for the spirit of a people, that language was more important than any other single element in transforming different peoples into a raza, into a cultural community.[58] Therefore they stressed that their community with Spanish America, on which rested so much of their hope for achieving a proud destiny, depended upon preserving the Spanish tongue in relatively uncorrupted form in the New World. As a result they reacted with dismay to the influence of English, Italian, and French on the spoken and written Spanish of the former colonies.[59] In particular they saw the alleged desire of the United States to supplant Spanish with English throughout the American hemisphere as a calculated endeavor to stamp out all vestiges of Hispanic culture.

The Spanish spirit was in danger in America, Altamira warned, because the Spanish language was in danger. "Our influence there," he added, "is the last card we have to play in the doubtful game of our future as a human group." Therefore he urged his countrymen not to delay a moment in taking up the defense of their language, for in so doing they would be protecting their spiritual presence in America.[60]

In 1900, the very year in which the Bishop of Barcelona issued a pastoral letter urging his clergy to preach in Catalan rather than Castilian,[61] a noted Spanish advocate of hispanismo hailed the appearance of a new book by Ernesto Quesada. In it the Argentine statesman spoke out strongly in favor of preserving the purity of the Castilian tongue. Upon this purity, Quesada argued, depended the unity between Spain and Spanish America "that could make our raza invincible."[62]

Also in the year 1900 a celebrated dispute between Juan Valera and Rufino J. Cuervo approached its peak. Cuervo, a distinguished Colombian philologist who in 1886 had published the first—and, as it turned out, the only—volume in a projected multivolume Castilian dictionary,[63] feared that the Spanish language was about to break down into various tongues, the sad fate that had overtaken Latin upon the collapse of the Roman Empire. To prevent such a catastrophe, Cuervo, writing from Paris, where he lived in virtually a self-imposed exile, sought to imbue his fellow Spanish Americans with a horror of even minor departures from the proper norms of Castilian usage. "Aside from those who work to conserve religious unity," he wrote, ". . . no one does so much to achieve the fraternity of the Spanish-American nations and their rapport with Spain as those who develop studies that tend to conserve the purity of the language and to destroy all the barriers that differences in dialects pose to the exchange of ideas."[64]

On the other hand Valera saw little likelihood that the language he so loved was on the brink of the disaster foreseen by Cuervo. Unlike the Colombian, he detected no danger in the gradual modification of the introduction of new usages into the Spanish language. In fact, Valera seemed to feel that the spiritual unity of Spain and Spanish America could best be conserved if the overzealous peninsulares who tended to lionize Cuervo did not chide Spanish Americans too severely over the alterations they introduced in certain details of the language.[65]

For some years the issues involved in the Valera-Cuervo debate continued to divide both Spaniards and Spanish Americans. The Spanish Jesuit historian Constantino Bayle took a position on the Cuervo side, complaining that he could not read with pleasure the works of Argentine historians because of their improper use of the language. He exhorted Argentines resolutely to resist all further linguistic corruption.[66] In the same spirit, a defender of the work of the American branches of the Real Academia Española declared that Spanish Americans had to turn to the motherland as the final arbiter in all matters pertaining to the proper forms of language. Only Spain, he stated, could supply the controls required to keep the "exuberant imagination of the Spanish Americans" within the limits of linguistic good taste.[67] Another Spaniard argued that Spanish Americans must be guided by the peninsula in matters of language if they hoped to gain a rank of distinction in international society. "Preservation of the original language is the stamp of great peoples," he declared; "imitation of foreign usages is the sign of weak and decadent peoples."[68]

Claims of absolute Spanish sovereignty over the Castilian language were also advanced when a dispute arose over acceptable pronunciation in talking movies. A self-appointed authority on the matter stated it was all right for Spanish Americans to employ "the local pronunciation" in films depicting life in a particular New World republic; but in talking movies "that did not have a determined locale, it was imperative that *proper* Spanish pronunciation be employed."[69]

Understandably, this approach infuriated many Spanish Americans. In 1907 the Chilean Julio Saavedra bitterly assailed the pretensions of the Real Academia Española to infallible authority in all matters of the language both in Spain and Spanish America. "We are tired," he asserted, "of being told that our language is bad because it reflects French influence and sentence structure; our language is proper in Chile and it is not for you to criticize us because you do not consider it proper in Aragon or Castile. . . . We are tired of incurring your disdain because in our pronunciation we do not distinguish between the s and the z."[70]

Unamuno agreed with the indignant Chilean. Spanish Americans, he said, should not take the Real Academia seriously, for only a handful of stuffy and pedantic Spaniards did so. He advised Spaniards to abandon altogether their claims on monopolistic control over the language. Since Castilian, he reasoned, had been extended to many nations, "each of these has an equal right in transforming and bringing greater flexibility to the language."[71] At the same time he expressed enormous satisfaction that Spanish Americans had desisted in "the ridiculous attempts" of some turn-of-the-century Argentines and Chileans to establish "national languages" prescinding from Castilian.[72]

Looking back on the whole issue some years later Menéndez Pidal also voiced immense relief that Spanish Americans had refused to consider seriously the formation of national languages. Obviously, he observed, Cuervo's fears of a breakup of the Spanish language had been groundless. The Spanish Americans had preserved their language essentially intact. In the process, Menéndez concluded, they had maintained their spiritual affinity with Spain[73] as a result of which Spaniards and Spanish Americans continued to be members of the same raza. It followed in the minds of most hispanoamericanistas that Spaniards had a right to assert themselves in Spanish America in all matters pertaining to defining and preserving the Hispanic spirit.

The Spanish Concept of a Mission in America

While Spaniards by no means disregarded the possible economic consequences of closer relations with Spanish America, many of them, especially in the period prior to World War I, preferred to stress the spiritual goals of hispanismo. Thus Altamira advanced as the primary argument in favor of hispanismo the need to maintain in the New World the spiritual values of the Spanish raza. The continuing disunity of this raza would, he said, result in the disappearance of these values, thereby mutilating all of humanity. Any other argument in favor of closer ties between the different components of the Hispanic raza, the historian asserted, was apt to be stained by self-interest.[74]

It was the spiritual foundation of the envisioned Spanish-American rapport that in the eyes of most Spaniards conferred upon the peninsula the right to exercise hegemony over a more closely united Iberian raza. Peninsulares assumed that Spain had maintained the true Hispanic spirit in relatively pure form, while in the former colonies it had been weakened by Indian influences and the constant assault of foreign values, especially those of the United States.

Severino Aznar, a devout Catholic and staunch defender of the Church's rights and privileges, frankly stated that Spain must exercise a tutelary role in calling into being and watching over a Spanish-American collectivity. He based his assertion on the claim that Spanish America had gone astray in the nineteenth century, renouncing much of its true spirit as it borrowed from foreign usages. "We," he said, "must help Spanish America find its way again."[75] Gumersindo de Azcárate, the Krausist liberal who saw Spanish progress as dependent upon secularization, presented a parallel analysis. Spanish America, he asserted, "has to seek its soul by prescinding from all the pressures and lures of countries that are foreign to its spirit;" and Spain had to lead and assist the New World republics in the search for self, because Spain had never allowed foreign influences to weaken and distort its Iberian personality.[76]

Once they had begun to strengthen the languishing spiritual essence of Spanish America, Spaniards expected to proceed toward more tangible accomplishments; they could, it was hoped, begin to translate into practical effects the ties of spirit by forging some semblance of unity of political action among the various components of the Spanish raza. Carlist ideologist Juan Vázquez de Mella envisioned a United Spanish States of South America, bound loosely to Spain and accepting from the madre patria its overall orientation in international affairs. The Iberian world would thereby acquire its own equivalent of Pan-Germanism.[77] Sánchez de Toca also longed for a confederation of diverse, independent, and sovereign states, bound together by similarity of ideas, sentiments, interests, beliefs, blood, and language; this confederation would become the great fatherland (patria grande or patria mayor) of the Spanish raza.[78] Another Spaniard, who seems not to have been taken seriously in the peninsula, looked forward to a federally organized collectivity composed of Spain, Spanish America, and the Philippines. The name for this federation would be Espérica, formed from the first syllables of España and the last three of América.[79]

Common even to the more moderate Spaniards who expected ties of the spirit to result in practical consequences was the belief that a more closely united Spanish raza could acquire status among the major centers of international power.[80] More immediately, however, it was hoped that through a concerted effort the Hispanic raza could preserve the cherished patterns of hierarchical social organization and gain the strength to stem the social revolution that seemed likely to engulf the component nations one at a time if they did not band together. In a united Spanish raza other hispanoamericanistas saw an effective barrier against United States imperialism in Spanish America.

A United Hispanic Raza in Defense of the Hierarchical, Organic Social Order

Writing in 1905 after a tour through several of the New World republics, a Spaniard with a lifelong commitment to hispanismo sounded an alarm on the growing gulf between rich and poor in Spanish America. Social revolution there, he warned, was a distinct possibility.[81] Following a tour of the area in 1911 Adolfo González Posada also warned of the increasing likelihood of social violence in Spanish America.[82] Three years later a journalist in Cádiz wrote that although Spanish Americans seemed generally blind to the fact, the social problem had become the most acute challenge they faced. Only through an intelligent policy, he opined, could they avoid social revolution. He further hinted that Spanish advice and collaboration would be essential if the Spanish Americans expected to devise an intelligent policy.[83]

Other Spaniards gave more direct expression to this viewpoint. For example, an unidentified writer in a 1904 special edition of the Unión-Ibero-Americana stated that Spain's greatest contribution to Spanish America would be to show those republics, "with their restless democracies," how to preserve social tranquility and solidarity.[84] Writing some twenty years later two prominent Spanish authors agreed that their country's mission was to provide leadership to the entire Spanish raza in the endeavor to avoid class struggle and social upheaval. Spain, they maintained, through the Laws of the Indies, had demonstrated a unique ability to devise an institutional structure that guaranteed social peace and hierarchical organization, keeping the Indians and the various castes contentedly in their assigned places. Twentieth-century Spain, the authors agreed, knew how to repeat its success of the colonial period.[85]

Conservatives professing a militant Catholicism understandably contended that Spaniards must lead Spanish Americans in the endeavor to stave off social revolution by demonstrating to them how to revitalize the raza's authentic religion. Only through a religious revival, warned the conservative secretary general of the Unión Ibero-Americana in 1907, could the forces of individualistic materialism be overcome in Spanish America; and, he added, the inevitable consequence of individualistic materialism was economic exploitation that would call forth the reaction of social revolution.[86] A few years later a Spanish Augustinian serving in Peru reported that the threat of social revolution in that country stemmed from the fact that the lower classes were beginning to emulate the anarchy that they observed in the conduct of the godless upper classes. The solution to the problem, he asserted, lay in winning back the upper classes to God, and in this Spain would have to take the leading role. Peruvians, he explained, were not up to the task themselves because they had suffered too serious a spiritual collapse and had proceeded too far in their experiments with dangerous democratic practices.[87]

Men of this outlook responded approvingly to the 1922 statement of a bishop in Argentina that social upheaval had become a danger in the country because spiritual had been subordinated to material values. Spain, the bishop stated, having remained insistent upon the primacy of spiritual values, would have to assist the former colonies in emerging from their subservience to materialism.[88] Spanish conservatives reacted also with satisfaction when an Argentine prominent in Buenos Aires social work declared that the Catholic syndicalist movement as initiated and developed in Spain offered the best hope for a solution to his country's social problem—a problem, he added, that could never be met through material means.[89]

Anticlerical liberals in Spain, although not in accord on the means to be employed, agreed with conservatives on the need for a concerted, Spanish-Spanish American effort to head off leveling revolutions be easing the social problem. Labra, in fact, declared in 1912 that the appearance of the social problem throughout the Spanish world was largely responsible for the rapprochement between Spain and Spanish America, for the increasing favor with which the former colonies were coming to regard the old motherland.[90]

At the turn of the century liberals such as the writer Leopoldo Alas, the educator Giner de los Ríos, and the historian Altamira had hailed the appearance of Ariel, a book in which the Uruguayan writer José Enrique Rodó gave considerable indication of Krausist leanings. To them the book revealed that Spanish Americans were beginning to recognize the need for a broad, humanistic education for the masses, as well as for constant fraternal contact between the elite and the multitude, in order to combat the leveling forces of materialism and utilitarianism.[91] Alas declared that to him the main message in Rodó's book, although he admitted it appeared implicitly rather than explicitly, was that Spain and Spanish America must strengthen the bonds of unity in the common effort to escape the plague of leveling democracy that resulted from the pursuit of utilitarian values.[92]

The liberal belief that Spain had a mission to play in staving off social revolution in Spanish America found perhaps its most succinct exposition in a 1914 article by Manuel Rodríguez-Navas (1848–1922), an eminent philologist and the political associate of such men as Labra, Canalejas, and Nicolás Salmerón. In the article Rodríguez-Navas, who devoted the last years of his life to working for a closer community between Spain and Spanish America, observed:

> Materialism, the desire to gain wealth without working for it, is largely responsible for modern revolutionary pressures in society. In [Spanish] America the danger of social revolution is greater than elsewhere because of the materialism and lust for wealth of the peoples who have emigrated there. This danger in America is indeed grave unless a vivifying spiritualism comes to the nations of the new continent to compensate for the disequilibrium resulting from excessive materialism. . . . Spain can supply this spiritualism because it still represents the fine arts, the secular humanist tradition, and chivalry. The spirit of Spain can be spread in Spanish America through the spiritual union of all the Hispano-American countries. . . . Without Spain, [Spanish] America would be an immense portion of the planet dedicated exclusively to material pursuits, without art, ideals, spirituality, that is to say, without a human end or destiny.[93]

Certain influential Spanish-American intellectuals agreed on the need for Spanish collaboration in the attempt to preserve the social status quo. Thus the Argentine sociologist Carlos Octavio Bunge (1875–1918) noted the similarity of the Spanish and Spanish-American social problems. Accordingly, he advised Spanish Americans to turn their attention to the "old motherland" so as to discover the methods being developed there to cope with social pressures.[94] And the Mexican Rodolfo Reyes asserted in 1910 that one of the primary purposes of Spanish–Spanish-American rapprochement was the formulation of joint social-economic policies that would preserve harmony and solidarity among the classes.[95]

Such expressions were naturally pleasing to those Spaniards who believed their country had a mission to aid the former colonies in avoiding social disaster. So was the fact that the labor and social laws steered through the Cortes in 1900 by Eduardo Dato exercised considerable influence on subsequent legislation in Argentina and other Spanish-American republics.[96] All of this suggested to those who served the cause of hispanismo in the peninsula that they were progressing toward realization of their desire that Spanish Americans find unity in identifying with the culture and values of Spain. If they did so identify, then it was assumed that they would learn the secrets of how to avoid social revolution. Out of the unity resulting from identifying with the Spanish culture and spirit, Spanish

Americans would also, their peninsular brothers hoped, derive the strength to defend themselves against the political imperalism of the United States and the cultural penetration of its materialistic values that allegedly contributed to radical social change.

A United Spanish Raza to Contain the United States Menace

The major threat of the United States, most Spanish observers insisted, was not to the political independence of Spanish-American republics; rather, it was to their spiritual independence.[97] If the material success of their powerful northern neighbor seduced the Spanish-speaking New World republics into emulating its spirit and character, they would, according to their solicitous observers in Spain, "denationalize" themselves,[98] betray "the law of their origin,"[99] and therefore cease to exist as true members of the Hispanic raza without ever basically acquiring the characteristics of Anglo-America. In such circumstances they would become spiritually moribund, even though they continued to exercise a meaningless form of political sovereignty.[100]

The United States, as seen by its Spanish critics, posed a danger to the Hispanic raza in America because it lacked spirituality,[101] was concerned only with material triumphs, and dedicated to "equality in mediocrity."[102] The Yankee ideal, wrote a Spanish journalist as he recorded an impression widely held among his countrymen, "must always be the exact opposite of the Spanish ideal. To assert otherwise is not to know the two ideals in their essences."[103] And a distinguished Spanish geographer, who through his efforts on both sides of the Atlantic contributed enormously to the cause of hispanismo, extended this warning to the Spanish Americans: "The Yankees are . . . the enemies of our soul, of our civilization, of our character, of our independence; imitation of the Yankees in whatever respect should be hateful to us for it will destroy us."[104]

Spanish writers delighted in painting the consequences of United States materialism and utilitarianism in darkest colors. That physically powerful republic, a journalist affirmed in 1908, was rapidly becoming the country with the world's highest rates of crime and lawlessness. He offered the following explanation for this development: "in the Saxon race selfish individualism, nourished by the [United States] educational process, destroys sentiment and brings about the surrender of moral principles to material obsessions; thus the people become slaves to an insatiable desire for wealth that leads them to their doom. . . ."[105] At about the same time an important official of the Unión Ibero-Americana charged that the "masters of the United States have nothing but their bank accounts to justify their position." In order for social structures to be firm and secure, he continued, the directing classes must base their right to command on their moral excellence. Because moral qualities had been replaced simply by moneymaking expertise in United States leadership, he predicted that a social revolution was likely to occur.[106] A collaborator of this official in the Union agreed without qualification. The United States, he said, was closer to social revolution than any other country in the world because of its rampant materialism and total lack of social morality. United States civilization as it presently existed, he declared, would disappear through violence. "Happily," he concluded, "this opinion is coming increasingly to be shared by Spaniards across the sea as they begin to understand the mission of the raza."[107]

Whether this viewpoint was indeed becoming widespread in Spanish America would be difficult to determine. Certainly, though, many Spanish journalists reflected it, among them one who in 1915 ended an article on the United States with the statement that social revolution "is the inevitable fate of countries that are attentive only to material pursuits and discard their moral, spiritual orientation and values."[108]

Influenced by the example of their neighbor to the north and by the practices of North American business firms as they operated to the south of the border, Spanish Americans, according to many Spaniards, had taken to vicious forms of social and economic exploitation which they justified by utilitarian and materialistic criteria.[109] Because of their receptivity to United States values and economic models, Spanish-American leaders were, it was charged, unwittingly inviting social revolution. According to a Spaniard writing in 1904, the only way to contain the dangerous influence of the United States, with its "inorganic democracy," was for Spanish America to enter into an ever closer relationship with its motherland, so as to receive from it the spiritual strength that its own directing classes lacked.[110]

In short, the social problem to most Spanish analysts was a spiritual problem; and the single most important contributing factor to social unrest in Spanish America was contamination by the alien United States spirit, a contamination that could best be contained by a Spanish raza united under the spiritual leadership of Spain.[111] Giving typical expression to this viewpoint, two Altamira disciples in 1924 registered dismay at the spectre of social revolution that still confronted Spanish America because of its infatuation with the alien values of the United States. By uniting on the basis of the "spirit that derives from Spain," they wrote, ". . . the Hispanic Americans, confronting the united and powerful Anglo-Saxon republic, can avoid . . . extinction."[112]

While Spaniards worried primarily over the threat of the United States to the authentic spirit of the Hispanic raza, they did not totally ignore the menace that that country purportedly posed to the political independence of the Spanish-American republics.[113] One writer charged in 1904 that the United States had its "covetous eyes" on colonies and markets in the Far East; consequently, it would seek to guarantee the security of the Isthmian trade route that would be opened with the completion of the canal by assuming political control over the entire Caribbean and Central American region.[114]

In the early twentieth century United States political intervention was seen as a greater danger than ever before because Europe, intimidated by the brandishing of the Monroe Doctrine, was no longer an effective check on the ambitions of the Colossus.[115] Spanish Americans must therefore, Hispanoamericanistas concluded, resist United States imperialism by joining together under the leadership of Spain, which could then plead their cause in Europe and arouse world opinion in their favor.[116] Segismundo Moret at the 1912 centennial commemorating the controversial Cádiz constitution stressed the need for this type of united front if Spanish America was to preserve its political freedom.[117]

In pursuit of this goal, Spaniards tried to convince Spanish Americans that Pan-Americanism represented a threat to the full exercise of their political and economic independence. Pan-Americanism, they insisted, could only be counterbalanced by hispanismo, a spiritual movement that in no way impaired rights of national sovereignty. And Spaniards enthused when Argentina, from the very outset, responded to the Pan-American menace by assuming a role of leadership among South American republics in a drive to nullify Yankee influence. In the light of this, Spaniards often suggested that the campaign against Pan-Americanism would be most fruitful if concentrated in Argentina.[118]

Encouraged by the headway they imagined they were making in uniting Spanish America under their leadership so as to resist the multiple dangers of the United States,[119] Spaniards in increasing numbers came to hope for fulfillment of a prophecy made at the beginning of the twentieth century by Luis de Armiñán, director of Unión Ibero-Americana:

> The day will come when, from Mexico to Cape Horn, there will be an autonomous people, confederated by the ties of blood, language, and history, that will be able to prevent brutal Saxon conquests. Then, as sentinels in Europe, Spain and Portugal . . . will work in accord, united by the vital interests of the raza, stretching a helping hand across the Atlantic to those children who were conceived for the purpose of advancing human progress.[120]

Liberals Prepare for a Campaign in America: Their Underlying Assumptions

Unfortunately for those desiring fulfillment of Armiñán's prophecy, many Spanish Americans continued to be attracted by United States models, in part at least because of that country's remarkable material progress.[121] To offset the lure of the United States, Spanish liberals active in the hispanismo movement tried to create the image in Spanish America of a Spain that was progressive, interested in science, and beginning to achieve notable economic development.[122] At the same time they tried to impress upon the New World Spaniards that mere material progress resulting from United States patterns would lead in the final analysis to social chaos and revolution. Only Spain, they proclaimed, could help Spanish America match the physical might of the United States while at the same time avoiding leveling democratic practices.

Spanish liberals expected not just to give to but also to receive from Spanish America. Fascinated and even awed by the physical potential of the New World, by the dynamism of its inhabitants, by their exuberant confidence and optimism that had not been diminished by centuries of adversity and economic stagnation, liberals hoped to receive from Spanish America a decisive impetus toward the material development to which they had in many instances committed themselves. Moreover, through association with Spanish Americans, who had, it was assumed, escaped from most traces of religious fanaticism, Spanish liberals looked forward to gaining reinforcements in the battle for secularization, in the campaign to banish the otherworldliness of conservative Spain that was inimical to economic progress.

Spain's liberals envisioned a united Spanish raza that would be spiritually and materially powerful. Spain would provide the basis for spiritual grandeur; Spanish America would contribute the basis for material greatness. This projected division of labor afforded clear indication of the supremacy that Spaniards assigned to themselves within the Spanish raza. Scarcely a Spaniard, be he liberal or conservative, doubted the superiority of a spiritual over an essentially material contribution.

Conservatives were less given to optimistic fantasies as they surveyed turn-of-the-century Spanish America. To them the new republics seemed dishearteningly godless, weakened in spirit by monstrous anticlerical legislation, and, with the notable exception of Colombia, irreversibly committed to the values of the secular society. They found little of what they regarded as the true spirit of the Spanish raza—the Catholic spirit, that is—in the former colonies. Instead the spirit of the Institución Libre de Enseñanza, of Krausism, and of positivism seemed to prevail there. By and large, then, notwithstanding important exceptions, liberals rather than conservatives provided the main thrust of hispanismo in the days immediately following the disaster.

7: LIBERALS AND HISPANISMO, 1900–1930

Krausism and Positivism as Stimulants to
Liberal Interest in Spanish America

Spanish liberals under the influence of Krause had ample grounds for assuming that their country had a role to play in stimulating and strengthening the spiritual values introduced into the New World by the motherland during the conquest and colonial period but allegedly allowed to atrophy since independence. Krause, and after him his Spanish disciples, had stressed the duty of an elite in each country to penetrate among the masses so as to awaken in them appreciation of aesthetic and spiritual values. Communication between the elite and the masses, Krause argued, would not only develop the aesthetic senses of those below but at the same time would augment the artistic creativity of those above. According to the German metaphysician, this process had a corollary in international affairs. The educated, advanced nations, he wrote, should take upon themselves "an uplifting contact with the younger, less advanced nations and countries."[1]

In his writings Krause had even developed what Spanish liberals could take as the rationale for their claims to spiritual hegemony over Spanish America in order to save the republics from the United States:

> Immature people who do not know how to rule themselves . . . become dependent in one way or another, according to a law of history, on mature people, upon people who are more cultivated and more advanced in the political art. This relationship can be advantageous to the dependent people when it awakens in them the moral sentiment that leads to development of their political personality. But this relationship becomes damaging and inimical to full human development when under it the dependent people is allowed to remain immature or when, as the consequence of an abuse by the dominant people, the dependent people are physically added to a foreign state so as to be absorbed into it.[2]

Krause and his disciples viewed humanity as evolving ultimately toward a fraternal unity that would embrace all peoples of the world. Before this distant goal could be achieved, however, the peoples of similar culture had to band together. "Free societies of peoples," Krause wrote, "are formed . . . when by natural reasons people who are friendly and similar in culture establish among themselves a free exchange of ideas. . . ." Through this free exchange of ideas, Krause asserted, peoples of common culture

146

could best develop their own capacity while at the same time creating strong and dynamic supranational groupings, which at a later time could be federated with similarly formed groupings into one common family of humanity.[3]

The influence of Krause, then, both in Spain and Spanish America, seemed naturally destined to encourage interest in hispanismo. The same was true of positivism, which became one of the main intellectual forces among late nineteenth-century Spanish-American liberals and which also wielded a considerable impact on Spanish Krausists. Positivism challenged the romantic, utopian concepts of the French Revolution that were anathema to so many of the socially conservative liberals of the Spanish world on both sides of the ocean; it challenged also the "sophistry of parliamentary democracy"[4] and thus provided a basis for uniting liberals of the Spanish world in defense of the hierarchical, organic social-political structure. As adapted to the Spanish-American scene, positivism also challenged the earlier romantic, liberal concept of the Indians as noble savages. Positivism, in fact, often nourished an attitude of disparagement toward the Indians, who were dismissed as obstacles to national development. Because of this positivism furnished a link between Spanish Americans and the vast number of peninsulares who believed that the Indian was incapable of contributing to the cultural and material progress of the one-time colonies.

Liberal Fascination with the Spontaneity, Youth, Vitality, and Economic Potential of Spanish America

Returning home after a tour of Spanish-American republics, a Spanish businessman-journalist-politician reported that his faith in the raza had been restored, for he had observed many Spaniards who, although failures in the peninsula, had amassed fortunes as their vitality and energies gradually returned in the New World setting. This proved to the writer that there was nothing wrong with the Spanish raza; once artificial restraints and restrictions were removed, it would flourish anew in the peninsula. Meantime, the Old World Spaniards were admonished to learn from their offspring in America as they sought to sweep away the institutional and intellectual deadwood that had been accumulating for centuries.[5]

Novelist Vicente Blasco Ibáñez (1867–1928) looked with awe on the dynamism and energy of Spanish Americans. Spain, he wrote in 1909, was in a state of decline because it had transmitted its drive and force to so many New World offspring. It was "anemic because of its excesses of creation; it had lost its own force because of having transmitted it to its children. . . . But the noble matron, sick and exhausted, smiles the smile of the proud mother, seeing her robust children, all of them future giants

. . . who grow and grow until there will come the moment when they will dominate the world."[6]

Writing these lines, Blasco Ibáñez seemed to doubt that Spain itself would ever reacquire its old drive and push; it must content itself, therefore, with contemplating what it had created in the New World. But Luis Palomo, a liberal politician and ardent apostle of hispanismo, thought otherwise. Palomo, who under the aegis of his friend Canalejas[7] founded in 1910 the Centro de Cultura Hispano-Americana as a clearinghouse of information and the principal liberal agency for encouraging cultural exchange, believed that the revitalization of peninsular Spain would result from closer contact with Spanish America. "I feel," he wrote in 1908, "that the ties with America must be constantly strengthened . . . because it is indispensable that we recover our youth there, our health, and our life; for our people lack sufficient energy to emerge alone and unaided from the oppression that suffocates us. . . . The future of Spain is in America. Spain must be rejuvenated through contact with those young people who breathe in an atmosphere of modern progress."[8] Ortega y Gasset, writing several years later, concurred with Palomo. In the young people of Spanish America, he stated, who "are still in a processs of formation," the Spaniard catches a glimpse of his future. The optimism of the Spanish Americans, their freedom from prejudices, their tolerance for new ideas would, the Spanish philosopher proclaimed, ultimately produce a salutary impact in the peninsula, an impact whose strength would be in proportion to the intimacy of cultural ties maintained between the New and Old Worlds.[9]

Spanish liberals tended uncritically to accept the assertion made in 1909 by the thirty-five-year-old Venezuelan literary figure Rufino Blanco-Fombona that "we Spanish Americans have redeemed ourselves from servitude. . . . Our . . . legislation guarantees civil equality, liberty of thought, and freedom for all religious beliefs. . . ."[10] Consequently a liberal like Luis Palomo, who regarded Spain's religious intolerance as "the cause of the backwardness that has always suffocated us," hoped that from an alliance with the New World republics Spain would receive the necessary impetus for carrying out the desired policies of secularization.[11] And a liberal visitor to Buenos Aires in 1917 recorded his delight that on the city streets, although flies and prostitutes abounded, he did not see "beggars, dogs, or priests." Here was the type of country, he implied, that could teach Spain a great deal.[12]

In addition to anticlericalism, Spanish liberals expected hispanismo to serve the cause of economic progress in the peninsula. In glowing, and frequently wildly exaggerated, terms they described the material development and the bright economic future of the Spanish-American republics. Close ties with the economically ambitious, imaginative, and capable Spanish Americans would inevitably, they assumed, lead to major developmental breakthroughs in Spain itself. Even Ecuador—which appealed to Spanish liberals because of the sweeping anticlerical program carried out in the early twentieth century, particularly under President Eloy Alfaro (1896–1901, 1906–1911)—was pictured as a country well on the way toward economic progress, one "called to a glorious destiny in the great future of the Latin race"; it was further described as among "the most progressive countries in Spanish America because of its desire for development, its hardworking habits, its modern spirit and culture."[13] Most often, though, the liberal press in Spain singled out Mexico and Argentina for its accolades.[14]

Liberals agreed generally with the 1904 assessment of Mexico made by a Colombian diplomat serving at the time in Spain. According to him Mexico had become a great and sovereign nation, one that provided a friendly home for all those with the desire to work; it had passed beyond the experimental stage and its future was assured.[15] In the same year a Spanish journalist hailed the new electoral triumph of Mexican strongman Porfirio Díaz, the dominant political power in his country since 1876. The reelection, the journalist asserted, constituted additional proof of how much the Mexican people idolized their president, who had transformed a disorganized republic into a formidable nation.[16] Writing also in 1904, still another liberal newspaperman praised the positivist spirit of Mexico under Díaz. The country exhibited, he said, "the thirst for a full life and the ambition for wealth. Upon these two axes rest morality, peace, and culture."[17]

Traveling through Argentina in 1910, González Posada commented upon its apparently unlimited economic potential. By cultivating its ties with the progressive young country, Posada predicted that Spain would necessarily facilitate its own material development.[18] A few years later a liberal journalist who had just spent a month in Buenos Aires expressed his unbounded admiration for a new generation of Argentine millionaires who struggled incessantly, "day and night, allowing themselves no relaxation, to add yet another million to their fortunes." He pictured these men as the spiritual descendants of the conquistadores, "who had not been content with conquering just one village." In this new age, the journalist continued, "men cannot manifest their greatness in conquest and warfare; instead it is in the field of business that they must prove their superior human values." Spaniards, he concluded, could learn much by observing the Argentine nation builders, whose greatness arose from their ability to adapt the Spanish character to new times and challenges.[19]

Liberal Attempts to Create the Image of a Progressive Spain

Spanish liberals assumed that success in establishing close and mutually advantageous ties with the republics of the New World, whose youthful zest and spirit of tolerance and freedom of intellectual inquiry and whose economic attributes they vastly admired, depended upon creating the image of a progressive, increasingly liberal Spain. They feared that if the new breed of nation builders regarded Spain as mired still in medievalist obscurantism, they would turn from it in repugnance.[20]

Writing in 1905 Labra presented the typical liberal analysis when he asserted that if Spain insisted upon clinging to archaic prejudices and practices it could never hope to establish harmony with "the progressive spirit of the Latin American republics." These republics, he added, had fought for and attained their independence precisely so as to escape from the influence of a medievalist, conservative Spain; and if Spain hoped now to be taken seriously in Latin America, it must abandon its conservatism.[21] Seven years later, upon the celebration of the centennial of the 1812 Cádiz constitution, Labra claimed that Latin Americans vibrated to the liberal spirit that had inspired that instrument; they had rejected Spain at the time of the independence movement because of the attempt of King Ferdinand VII and other Spanish reactionaries to suppress that spirit. Only by reanimating the liberalism that had produced that notable charter, Labra maintained, could Spain hope for a rapprochement with the former colonies.[22] He concluded by urging Spaniards to lauch a propaganda campaign, by means of books, magazines, pamphlets, letters, and cultural exchange programs, to convince Latin Americans that the old motherland had assumed a modern, progressive, liberal spirit.[23]

Ramiro de Maeztu was less optimistic than Labra about the immediate prospects of hispanismo. He felt that before a successful propaganda campaign could be undertaken Spain had to achieve certain successes worthy of being widely advertised. "At the moment," he wrote in 1911, "the problem of Spain in America seems to me above all else to be an internal Spanish problem; it is a problem of Spanish renovation, of Spanish culture. In order to participate effectively in America we Spaniards . . . have to rise to the first rank as economists, technicians, merchants, financiers, industrialists, and inventors."[24] Francisco Grandmontagna, a Basque emigrant in Argentina who early in the twentieth century pursued a distinguished career in journalism there, agreed with Maeztu, asserting that the work of Spain in America had to be the work of progressive industrialists and merchants, who, with the exception of a handful of men, had not yet appeared in the peninsula.[25] And Avelino Gutiérrez, a Spanish medical doctor living in Buenos Aires, declared in the early 1920s that Spain had first to develop a great, modern, scientific and literary culture before it could aspire to a role of leadership in Spanish America.[26]

If Maeztu and other Spaniards remained somewhat skeptical about Spain's having earned the right to be considered a modern and progressive power, other peninsular liberals followed the Labra line in exuding confidence. The Conde de Romanones asserted in 1905 that Spain was already a different country than the one it had been before the disaster. "No one can doubt that; we have opened our eyes, we have begun to see the light of the twentieth century." One saw signs of progress everywhere, Romanones claimed, as well as an encouraging disdain for the past.[27] The following year Unamuno commented with pleasure on the degree to which the emergence of a new, progressive Spain was coming to be recognized in Spanish America. In reading the books and pamphlets of American authors, he stated, he found increasing evidence of their awareness of the rise of a new Spain and also of their continuing disenchantment with the Spain of the past.[28] The Argentine Manuel Ugarte (1871–1951), concerned most of his life with awakening Latin Americans to the dangers of United States imperialism, was lauded at this time by one of his Spanish admirers for his recognition that "Spain was on the march again, advancing toward becoming a progressive, productive state."[29] Another Spaniard praised Bolivian sociologist Alcides Arguedas (1878–1946) because of his appreciation of recent Spanish cultural and economic development.[30]

Anticlericalism remained one of the cardinal features of liberalism in the early twentieth-century Spanish world. As a result, liberals of the peninsula understood that they had to present evidence of anticlericalism if they hoped to gain a following among their ideological colleagues of Spanish America. González Posada, for example, wrote that "in order to win the respect of those people who today regard themselves as without religious prejudices and free from all intransigent attitudes . . . Spain must more and more affirm the spirit of tolerance . . .; it must open itself with spontaneity and love to all the intellectual and spiritual winds of the world."[31] Apparently a victim of wishful thinking, Altamira assured Spanish Americans in 1916 that the liberal concept of religious toleration had already gained such strong roots among the masses that another armed uprising in defense of religious intolerance was inconceivable.[32]

Altamira sought further to base Spain's right to be heeded and respected by Spanish-American liberals on the success his country was said to be achieving in solving the social problem. In one of his books he noted that government-supported schools of arts and crafts had appeared throughout Spain. In these schools students received instruction in drawing and other subjects that "opened their imaginations" and "expanded their intellectual horizons." He went on to describe the warm relations between the laboring and upper classes who "worked together as brothers in these schools." This relationship, he said, was producing results referred to as "socially very beneficial;" owing to it, the working classes were losing some of their "rough edges" and acquiring "a certain delicacy in tastes, a desire to cultivate good habits, and an appetite to know what others know." He further described in his book, intended largely for a Spanish-American audience, how the Spanish government had established a program for the performance of fine plays before the working classes, noting that audience response had been overwhelmingly favorable. "A beautiful spectacle," he enthused, "that of the artist and the workers in a spirit of unison engendered by art." He praised also the circulating libraries that the government had established in order to introduce the humble classes to the great works of literature.

Through their interest in beauty and the higher things of life the Spanish lower classes, Altamira contended, were gaining new strengths that rendered them less clamorous and revolutionary than when left to their own resources and exposed to seduction "by purely material considerations." Here was proof, the historian implied quite clearly, that Spain was a progressive country that could by its example contribute toward economic development that would not bring social upheaval in its wake.[33]

The journal of the Unión Ibero-Americana in a 1924 edition devoted considerable space to documenting the story of Spanish progress.[34] An editorial writer observed that in 1898 there had been only five Spanish cities with populations of over 100,000; in 1923 there were nine. During the same period total merchant marine tonnage increased from 448,000 to 1,300,000; money in circulation rose from 1,433 million pesetas to 4,326 million; and the value of savings deposited in banks throughout the land climbed from 300 million to 700 million, "manifesting the frugality of our humble classes." Against this background of material development, Spain's crime rate, according to the writer, had decreased. This situation, described as unique in the world, was offered as proof that Spain knew how to achieve development and progress while at the same time maintaining social solidarity and peace.[35] Little wonder that a liberal hispanoamericanista writing in 1924 declared: "The truth is that if they can teach us something in Spanish America, they can learn more from us. . . ."[36]

The Altamira Mission to Spanish America, 1909–1910

As early as 1909 various professors and officials at the University of Oviedo evidenced concern with calling the attention of Spanish America to the progress within order that Spain was achieving. By so doing they felt they could renew and strengthen the spiritual influence of Spain in America. As the initial means for accomplishing this purpose, the Oviedo group proposed sending the University's professor of law, Rafael Altamira, on a cultural mission to Spanish America.

Seeking support for this plan, Altamira wrote to the minister of public instruction and to the heads of various educational institutions in Spain as well as to the officials of Spanish emigrant colonies in America. In these letters he stressed the importance of making Spanish America aware of the new Spain, of the hardworking and industrious Spain that was bringing itself up to the level of the progressive European countries. This was the Spain, he averred, that for most Spanish Americans was the unknown motherland.[37] Altamira also recommended cultural exchange, which he hoped to initiate with his tour to the New World, as "the surest means of conserving in Spanish Americans the unity of the spirit of the raza and of protecting them against the influences that rob them of their nature to our disadvantage."[38] He noted that already the United States had begun to develop cultural exchange with Spanish America through the trips of professors such as William Shepherd and Leo S. Rowe. In this development he saw the danger that the United States would assume a commanding influence over higher education in Spanish America, thereby producing "the disastrous consequences for the true Spanish nature foreseen by Rodó and others."[39] In the Altamira analysis, then, the United States was beginning to use cultural exchange as an arm of Pan-Americanism, and Spain must respond to the menace by enlisting cultural exchange in the cause of hispanismo.

The proposal of Altamira and his Oviedo associates elicited no government, and very little private, support until it was warmly endorsed by the Madrid newspaper *El Imparcial* in an April 14 editorial. Emphasizing the need to convince Spanish Americans, as they prepared to celebrate the one hundredth anniversary of the inception of the independence movement, of their continuing spiritual ties with Spain, *El Imparcial's* editorialist ended his column with these words:

> It is indispensable for us to demonstrate to those people, called into being and civilized by us, that we live on something more than memories; that we represent something more than a glorious tradition; that the marvelous force, never exceeded by anyone in history, which the Spanish nation brought to bear in the New World did not so exhaust her energies and vitality as to render her incapable of collaborating actively and fruitfully in the work of improvement and progress which the Hispanic raza must undertake. . . . The dispatching of Spanish professors would be a wonderful means of enabling Spanish Americans to know and appreciate us better, thereby facilitating our efforts on behalf of the Hispanic raza, threatened in the new continent by the growing Anglo-American predominance.[40]

Following the appearance of this editorial, some private financial backing for the mission materialized, although the government still refrained from offering assistance. The private funds obtained allowed Altamira to plan an itinerary that took him to Argentina, Uruguay, Chile, and Peru in late 1909, and concluded with stops in Mexico and Cuba early in 1910.

On the eve of Altamira's departure a declaration of support for his mission attracted signatures and endorsements from some five thousand Spaniards, among them senators, provincial deputies, municipal officials, teachers, judges, engineers, lawyers, public employees, merchants, and military officers. The declaration included a typical presentation of the assumptions that underlay hispanismo at the time:

> Spain is America. To the splendid world, which it called forth from the seas, Spain gave all that it had: its enthusiastic heart, its ardent blood, its vigorous faith, its august mysticism . . . its love for independence . . . its whole soul with its diverse virtues and its human defects. It made this world so much its own that it was bone of its bone, blood of its blood, soul of its soul.[41]

In the various discourses welcoming Altamira to the New World, Spanish Americans alluded both to spiritual concerns and to practical considerations as they commented upon the significance of the cultural mission. Spiritual concerns prevailed in the speech of the Cuban Rodolfo Rodríguez de Armas. He saluted "the community of blood, the solidarity of the spirit, the affinity of culture, the similarities of temperament and sensitivities." These factors, he declared, "form the essential bases of nationalities and create close and intimate ties . . . among men of identical origin and development, ties that are eternal and indestructible even when events bring about the dissolution of political union." The spirit and soul of Spanish America, the Cuban concluded, would be strengthened by Spain's reawakened interest in the New World as evidenced by Altamira's tour.[42]

University of La Plata rector Joaquín V. González, in contrast, stressed the practical results he anticipated from cultural exchange. Spain, he asserted, could make its best contribution by having its most competent scholars cooperate in training modern, research-oriented faculties for Spanish-American universities. The González-recommended approach was followed at once, for Altamira offered a three-month course on historical methodology for University of La Plata professors. In other countries, the visiting professor assisted in preparing new and modernized university curricula in which courses were to be based on the most recent sources and newest research techniques.[43]

In carrying out his mission, Altamira attempted to point up the connection between practical results and spiritual considerations. Thus he insisted that cultural exchange programs would not produce fruitful results in modernizing higher education unless those collaborating in them shared the same culture. In upgrading the educational structure of Spanish America, he contended, Spain could play a far more effective role than the United States, "because Spaniards have a solidarity with you that is superior to all others, that of spirit and that of language, which signifies not only a common means of expression but a common manner of thinking."[44]

Surprised, upon his return, at the widespread interest his tour had aroused, Altamira accepted invitations to address audiences in many parts of Spain. In these lectures the historian reported he had discovered abundant evidence of the continuing spiritual affinity between Spain and Spanish America.[45] New World Spaniards longed, he said, for common action with their Old World brothers in the quest of strengthening the unique spirit of Hispanic culture and defending it against the assaults of alien influences. He reported further that his description of a new, resurgent Spain had always evoked an enthusiastic response from Spanish-American audiences. Because Spanish Americans were coming to understand that there was a new Spain, he contended, they recognized the right of the former motherland "to call at their door." The itinerant lecturer further observed that Spanish Americans were intrigued by the efforts of Spaniards to resolve the social problem and convinced of the utility of collaborating with Spain in easing their own class tensions. The time had come, he suggested, to establish branches of the Instituto de Reformas Sociales throughout Spanish America. The Institute, he said, might well prove to be "the most valuable organ in bringing Spain and Spanish America together."[46]

In his conferences, Altamira generally tempered optimism with the warning that the propitious climate for Spanish-American rapprochement would not contribute toward beneficial results unless specific cultural exchange programs were promptly undertaken and financed at least in part by government funds. He called for exchange not only of professors but of students as well. Beyond this, the historian urged the exchange of workers and farmers so that Spaniards and Spanish Americans might come truly to know one another.[47]

These ideas attracted the attention of the minister of education in 1910, the Conde de Romanones. As a result Romanones arranged for two conferences between King Alfonso XIII and the staunchly republican professor. Altamira reported that the king appeared to be highly interested in and favorably disposed toward his proposals.[48] A short time later, though, he conceded that the Spanish government continued to be reluctant to commit funds to cultural exchange.[49]

The González Posada Mission to Spanish America, 1910

Among the government agencies whose personnel Altamira conferred with upon his return from America was the Junta para Ampliación de Estudios e Investigaciones Científicos, recently created to encourage and support cultural exchange programs between Spain and various foreign countries. Altamira tried to persuade the Junta's directors to reserve for Spanish-American students a certain number of places in Spain's centers of higher education, to provide fellowships for Spaniards to study in Spanish America, to encourage exchange of professors and scholarly publications, and to finance studies of the former colonies that would neces-

sitate utilization of Spanish archival materials. To these suggestions the
Junta's administrators responded in very limited manner, agreeing only to
contribute some funds to the proposed mission of Adolfo González Posada.
A long-time associate of Altamira's at the University of Oviedo and an
important official of the Instituto de Reformas Sociales, Posada had been
invited by the University of La Plata to conduct a three-and-a-half month
course on politics and government.[50]

Arriving in Buenos Aires in June of 1910, Posada discovered that the
centennial celebrations of the independence movement tended to distract
attention from his cultural mission. Nevertheless, he reported that any
number of university students and professors had approached him to confess disillusionment with their countrymen's obsession with the pursuit
of wealth. Contending that Spanish Americans ought to pay more attention to inward development and affairs of the soul, these men frequently
commented to Posada on the need for Spain to act as a guide in weaning
their republics away from an excessive materialism.[51] Posada expressed
encouragement at this and other evidences of pro-Spanish sentiments
(españolismo) that he came upon in the New World. Commenting upon
how history, language, and a "certain spirit of the raza" bound the members of the Spanish world together, he maintained that the Spaniard felt
at home at once in Spanish America: "The Spaniard simply does not feel
that between Buenos Aires and Cádiz there is an ocean."[52]

Particularly in Uruguay, Posada enjoyed a striking example of españolismo when José Enrique Rodó, orating at a banquet in Montevideo,
praised the work of cultural exchange:

> The moment is apt for this work. The American conscience begins
> clearly to recognize—and there are a thousand signs that reveal this—
> that if there is one type of collective self-love that is necessary and
> fruitful, the love, that is, of the patria, there is another type of collective
> self-love that is no less necessary and fecund, the love of the raza. The
> sacred sentiment of the raza, of common origin and historical ancestry,
> will enduringly unite the American and the Spanish consciences. Spain
> and America . . . feel the ever more pressing need to reconstitute in
> the spiritual realm, in the realm of the soul, the unity that has been
> broken in the political order. This inspiration . . . for cultural exchange
> that has come from the renowned University of Oviedo must be carried
> forward with accelerating intensity and animation.[53]

Just as for Altamira, so also for Posada, one of the most promising fields
for Spanish-American cooperation lay in a combined effort to resolve the
social problems that were common to the Hispanic raza on both sides of
the Atlantic.[54] In Argentina, Posada was particularly impressed by the
efforts of evolutionary, gradualist socialists, among them Carlos Octavio
Bunge, Juan B. Justo, and Alfredo Palacios, to devise a synthesis between
Spencerian thought and socialism. These Argentines hoped, through a

program of liberal as well as vocational instruction for the masses, to persuade workers in the course of the next several generations not to destroy but rather to seek to join the bourgeoisie. Much in the approach of Giner de los Ríos, the Argentines saw in education the means whereby the worker would be led to develop himself as an individual, ceasing in the process to regard himself as a member of a proletariat mass. And, in the approach of Azcárate, these Argentine socialists hoped for enactment of reforms that would remove artificial, unnatural restraints on which the current system of stratification rested, facilitating thereby the eventual emergence of a more rational order in which inequality and hierarchical gradation reflected the greater or lesser talents and capacities of individuals.[55]

In Argentina, Posada also responded favorably to the work of the Departamento Nacional del Trabajo presided over by Marco M. Avellaneda, son of Nicolás Avellaneda, who was president of the republic from 1874 to 1880. The Spanish professor praised the Department's "mission of social peace," its efforts to establish fraternal relations between management-ownership sectors and those of labor. And he lauded Marco Avellaneda for understanding that labor organizations, provided they were closely associated with and controlled by the government, were not to be feared as contributing to anarchy but rather to be welcomed as a means of attaining social peace by "putting a brake on the ambitions of a plutocracy, which if unchecked in its blind greed would cause disaster."[56]

Shifting Attitudes of Liberals toward the United States

Altamira, Posada, and most of the liberals, who for the next several years continued the efforts initiated by the two cultural missions, alluded consistently to the menace posed by the United States to the genuine spirit as well as to the political independence of Spanish America.[57] Then, in the World War I period and immediately thereafter, many liberals began to advance new theories concerning the possibility of collaboration between the Spanish world and the United States.

A number of factors contributed to the changing of attitudes. For one thing, conditions attendant upon the war had enabled the United States clearly and definitively to replace Europe as the main foreign economic power in Spanish America. Under these circumstances, the old liberal attempt to encourage Spanish Americans to live virtually in isolation from the Colossus began to seem hopeless. Then too, the long-predicted social revolution had not overtaken the United States; quite to the contrary, various reforms of the progressive era seemed to have contributed to social tranquility. Moreover, indications had appeared that instead of trying to obliterate Spanish culture in the American hemisphere, the United States was becoming interested in and sympathetic toward it. Perhaps, then, liberals seemed to conclude, the United States was not quite the social and cultural menace it had once appeared to be. Finally, in a tradition dating back to the eighteenth century, many of Spain's liberals were afrancesados; as such they sympathized with the French cause in the war and appreciated the military intervention of the United States, which swung the balance in favor of Latin over Teutonic elements in Europe.

As early as 1916, Altamira, Labra, and some of their associates began to acknowledge the inevitable economic dominance of the United States in Spanish America. To some degree they even began to believe that good results might stem from increased United States economic penetration.[58] Perhaps disillusioned by rates of economic development that did not match turn-of-the-century expectations, at least a few Spanish liberals seemed to have concluded that without the stimulus of United States capital and technology the Spanish Americans were incapable of transforming their lands into modern and progressive republics.

Liberals of this outlook abandoned the hope of many early hispanoamericanistas that Spain could serve as the mediator between Spanish America and Europe and thereby encourage the flow of European capital and cultural influences into the New World so as to block United States hegemony. Instead they envisioned a role for Spain as the intermediary between the United States and Spanish America. Specifically, they recommended a series of joint Spanish–United States capital investment ventures. Besides contributing funds to these ventures, Spaniards would serve in a public relations capacity, taking advantage of their cultural affinity with Spanish Americans so as to minimize the hostility that Yankees on their own seemed always likely to incur.[59]

Through economic collaboration with the United States certain Spanish liberals hoped to expand their sphere of action in the spiritual realm, thereby helping Spanish America to remain true to its authentic character and traditions.[60] As two disciples of Altamira explained it in the mid-1920's, Spain could help Spanish America to acquire the material development associated with Yankee capital and technological expertise without in the process being contaminated by the utilitarian "equality in mediocrity" that characterized the United States. In short, the two writers asserted, if Spanish America accepted Spain as a middleman in dealing with the United States, it could accomplish economic expansion without abandoning "the poetic instincts of our raza and the ideal of the beautiful."[61] Or, as Altamira himself summarized this viewpoint in 1927, through economic collaboration with the United States, Spain could maintain its monopoly in the field of Spanish-American culture.[62]

A few Spanish liberals believed that transformations in United States cultural values had reduced, and in the future might eliminate, that country's threat to the Hispanic spirit. Thus Federico de Onís, teaching at Columbia University since 1916, commented in 1920 upon the awakening interest of the United States in Hispanic culture. He took the hispanista movement in the United States as a happy indication that the country was beginning to appreciate and to seek for itself a more spiritually oriented culture.[63] Spain, he stated, should respond to this development by establishing ties with the United States, emerging thereby from its isolationism. And he predicted that mutual interest in Spanish America would contribute toward a Spanish–United States rapprochement.[64]

In the early 1920s the Conde de Romanones also observed that the United States had begun to enrich its culture and to compensate for its early excessive materialism by learning something of the land and spirit of Quijote. This would lead the United States, Romanones believed, to a greater understanding of Spanish America and to a recognition of the fact that friendly relations with that area depended upon a closer relationship with Spain.[65] The initial mistake of Pan-Americanism, the statesman declared, had been its attempt to prescind from Spain in its dealings with Spanish America. The United States, he predicted, would soon rectify that error and thus Pan-Americanism would cease to be a menace.

Because of its timing, the partial shift in liberal attitudes toward the United States proved decidedly counterproductive to the cause of hispanismo. The 1920s witnessed the rise of nationalistic fervor throughout most of Spanish America. Against this background, Spanish Americans came to consider United States intervention the greatest affront to national dignity. At the sixth Pan-American Conference held in Habana in 1928, spokesmen of the southern republics resolutely insisted upon the principle of nonintervention as the United States haughtily refused to abandon the interventionist rights that it claimed were sanctioned by international law. The impasse threatened to bring about the collapse of the entire Pan-American movement. At this precise moment, then, just when Spanish Americans had decided that the United States and the Pan-Americanism that it manipulated in its own interests posed a maximum threat to nationalistic aspirations, some of Spain's liberals had opted for collaboration with the Colossus.[66]

Argentine Manuel Ugarte as early as 1920 registered his indignation over the shifting policy of Spanish liberals.[67] By 1928, a growing number of Spanish Americans felt that Spain had let them down in the struggle to protect their honor against the United States. In this frame of mind, Spanish Americans often agreed among themselves on the need for a united front against the Colossus. But the united front they desired was one of New World republics, which excluded Spain.[68]

With nationalism on the rise, Spanish Americans found doubly insulting the common Spanish liberal assumptions that the former colonies were incapable of material progress without the assistance and guidance of the United States and unable to protect their culture without the tutelage of Spain. Moreover, just as they had earlier rejected Spanish claims that the motherland should act as a mediator between Europe and Spanish America, in the 1920s they repudiated Spain as an intermediary between them and the United States. In whatever intercourse they had either with Europe or the United States, they acknowledged no need for Spanish middlemen.

Shifting, Divided Attitudes of Liberals toward Mexico

Liberal response to the Mexican Revolution of 1910 was divided. Some writers hailed the anticlerical features of the movement and lavishly praised the 1917 constitution that eliminated every vestige of Church influence in the temporal order.[69] Others complained about the anti-Spanish spirit unleashed by the Revolution, about the number of Spaniards killed or imprisoned in the course of the early years of violence, and about the amount of land confiscated from Spanish citizens.[70] A Spanish authority on the matter who was a prominent member of the liberal school claimed that Spaniards numerically headed the list of foreigners who had been killed or despoiled of property. He went on to charge that corruption had accompanied the redistribution of seized properties with the result that those who had the greatest need for land generally remained landless. This, he concluded, was the inevitable result of revolutionary movements that spew forth greedy adventurers who manage to take advantage of initially idealistic impulses to serve their selfish ends.[71]

The dictatorial regime of Miguel Primo de Rivera, which governed Spain from 1923 to 1930, inclined to follow the lead of the United States government in demanding adequate compensation for lands taken from citizens, and the liberal press generally supported these demands. In some instances Madrid seemed to be even more intransigent than Washington in pressing claims. In the eyes of the Mexican government, then, and probably in the view of a broad spectrum of informed Spanish Americans, Spain came to be identified as a force basically hostile to the national Revolution, as a country inclined to pursue, if it had the means, an interventionist policy similar to the one associated with the Colossus.[72] Understandably, the New World republics that had come to regard nonintervention as the cardinal objective of their foreign policies could not regard Spain as a natural ally.

Although El Sol, Spain's leading liberal newspaper, tended to defend the Mexican Revolution,[73] other liberal organs seemed to find positive satisfaction in reporting the decline of agricultural productivity that followed land redistribution; and one liberal journal claimed the economic disasters of the Revolution proved that only deposed dictator Porfirio Díaz and his associates had understood how to govern Mexico.[74] Moreover, a liberal writer declared that Mexico's economic failures of the 1920s raised the possibility that the Indians, declared by Mexicans to be the principal beneficiaries of the Revolution, were "an inferior species."[75]

Writing in early 1929, a liberal Spanish journalist praised the Mexican philosopher-educator José Vasconcelos (1882–1959), who, following a tour through Spain which won him many admirers, had just entered his country's presidential campaign. Vasconcelos was described as a true Hispanophile, as a genuine representative of Spanish liberalism owing to his convictions on the primacy of spiritual values. If Mexicans rejected him and chose instead the businessman Pascual Ortiz Rubio they would indicate, the journalist suggested, that they had rejected the Spanish liberal tradition, sold out their inherited values, and embarked upon a course of unbridled materialism. The journalist concluded that he could not imagine that such an event would come to pass.[76] The fact that Ortiz Rubio triumphed over Vasconcelos by an official tally of one million some odd votes to about twenty thousand may well have strengthened the belief of many Spanish liberals—a belief which, shared by many conservatives, constituted a serious drawback to the cause of hispanismo—that Spanish Americans were a basically undesirable people because of their hopeless materialism.

Liberal Views on Spanish-American Materialism

The bustling energy and dynamism of Spanish Americans as they engaged in the pursuit of wealth had appealed to some turn-of-the-century Spanish liberals. Others, however, had been appalled by the frenetic quest of material success, taking it as a symptom of serious spiritual illness if not inherent inferiority. González Posada in 1911 noted that a Spanish philosopher commenting upon developments in the United States had observed: "They are building a palace there; later, perhaps, there will come a spirit to live within it." In Posada's opinion, Argentines and Spanish Americans in general were building the same sort of palace; and he wondered if on their own, without the mentorship of Spain, they could find a spirit to occupy the gaudy material shell.[77]

Some years later the well-known Spanish physicist Blas Cabrera, liberally inclined in his political preferences, also commented disapprovingly on the materialism of Spanish Americans. Because of their obsession with material success, he opined, Spanish Americans could not produce good scientists. In order to dedicate themselves selflessly to scientific pursuits, he explained, men had to understand that satisfaction within the moral order was superior to that within the economic order. Spaniards, he added, understood this truth; but Spanish Americans did not. Therefore, they seemed doomed to the role of parasites and colonials as they sought to enjoy the material comfort that only the scientific investigations of people with more fully developed moral character made possible. "To think that it is possible to enjoy passively the advantages that rest on the achievements of others," he concluded, ". . . seems to be absurd and immoral."[78]

In 1924 Ortega y Gasset expressed certain mild doubts—doubts that he would feel much more strongly as he grew older—about the ability of the Spanish-American youth, given their alleged obsession with material comfort and success, to develop the strength of character, the "Seneca-like discipline" that was always necessary in the pursuit of scientific as well as moral truth.[79] It was Unamuno, though, who pronounced the classical liberal denunciation of Spanish-American materialism. He did so in an essay published in 1905.

Spanish Americans, declared Unamuno, had no ability in metaphysics; as philosophers they were nearly always rank dilettantes. The reason for this, he suggested, was that they had little interest in the eternal religious problems pertaining to the ultimate end of the individual and of the universe. No people, he asserted, could acquire a vision of its mission and its role in the world if it lacked a collective conscience that responded, in however obscure a manner, to "the great and eternal human problems of our final end and destiny."[80] Because they avoided thought and speculation on eternity, the classicist declared, Spanish Americans lacked a collective conscience, they had no vision of their destiny in the world, and thus they had never developed the strength of character, "the austerity of sentiment and the profundity of spirit" that were essential to transform heterogeneous groups of people into a nation-state. All the literature of Spanish-Americans revealed that there had not passed "over them the life-giving breath of great and noble concerns."[81]

An individual, according to Unamuno, might be able to lead a good and beneficial life without ever worrying about eternity and the next world; this was so because the people among whom he lived could provide him with "the necessary moral juices" that would enable him to live "as a parasite lives in the digestive tract of a superior animal. But an entire people cannot live without a preoccupation with the eternal."

It was clear to Unamuno that Spanish Americans lived without this preoccupation. In back of their barren, semihuman existence, lay their overriding concern with material goals and objectives, their monumentally mistaken belief that "in order to progress in this world it is necessary to ignore the other world."[82]

Unamuno, and like him many Spanish liberals well known for their interest in Spanish America, could never dispel their doubts concerning the authentic Spanishness of their overseas brothers. Because of the excessive materialism spawned in the New World setting as environment somehow gained mastery over heredity, it was feared that, however much peninsulares might try to guide them, Spanish Americans could not contribute effectively toward achieving the future greatness of the Hispanic raza. This gnawing, abiding fear seriously diminished the enthusiasm with which Spaniards served the cause of hispanismo. As conceived by Spanish liberals, and conservatives as well, hispanismo was often the hybrid creature of love and contempt.

Spain's Continuing Image in Spanish
America as a Backward, Decadent Country

If Spanish liberals had their doubts and fears about Spanish Americans, liberals in the New World had their reservations and misgivings about Spaniards. In spite of the efforts of Spanish liberals to create the image of a Spain that was new, resurgent, modern, and progressive, Spanish Americans tended to regard the one-time metropolis as backward and fanatical, a country in which the spirit had "somehow been imprisoned and impeded from attaining the breadth and vision of humanity, tolerance, and fraternity that this same European civilization has attained in the New World."[83]

A Peruvian active in promoting Spanish-American ties and well acquainted in peninsular liberal circles conceded in 1917 that the greatest obstacle to hispanismo was the disparaging attitudes that Spanish Americans continued to hold toward Spain; they felt, he contended, that Spain was unprogressive, even hostile to progress, and had nothing to teach them.[84] Some seven years later a Spaniard who had lived many years in Spanish America confirmed this impression. Spanish Americans, he reported, regarded Spain as backward in every respect; whatever their country of birth, they assumed it to be infinitely more progressive and advanced than Spain. Part of the reason for this, he affirmed, lay in the defamatory attacks against Spain written by many Spaniards themselves, particularly those of liberal outlook who purposely exaggerated their country's ills in the hope of shaming fellow citizens into attempting cures. In addition, he blamed French, English, and North American news media for conducting throughout Spanish America an unrelenting campaign of anti-Spanish propaganda.[85]

In 1926 another Spaniard who had lived for some time among them described Spanish Americans' views on Spain in this way. The upper classes, he said, felt only disdain for Spain as they abandoned themselves to imitation of French fashions and cultural tastes; the middle classes reacted with a certain compassion or pity, imagining Spain to be governed by priests and religious fanatics; and the working classes detested Spain, having heard only bad things about that country from its indigent emigrants.[86] Spanish liberals, he continued, had at the beginning of the century made some headway in persuading Spanish Americans that Spain was entering a new era. Spanish Americans had responded enthusiastically to Canalejas and his attempts to introduce a modern spirit. He contended, though, that all of this good work had been undone by the Spanish execution of Francisco Ferrer, the well-known freethinker, educator, and anarchist, because of his purported complicity in the July, 1909 violence in Barcelona, which produced some one hundred fatal casualties and resulted in the burning or damaging of forty-two convents and churches. The Ferrer execution, touching off anti-Spanish riots and demonstrations in many parts of Spanish America, was said to have confirmed the view that Spain had not truly emerged from the era of the Inquisition.[87]

According to Venezuela's Rufino Blanco-Fombona, the disillusionment of Spanish-American liberals with Spain had not come until 1923. Prior to that year, he maintained, Spain enjoyed increasing respect owing to the attempts of several governments to curb the power of the clergy and to the mounting acceptance of organized labor movements, including those directed by socialists. Then came the September coup that ushered in the military dictatorship of Primo de Rivera. This convinced Spanish Americans that Spain had not changed after all, that it persisted in its backwardness, opposed "to all that implies liberty and represents the future."[88]

Undoubtedly, Blanco-Fombona exaggerated the initial damage to the Spanish image resulting from the Primo de Rivera coup; for many Spanish-American liberals admired the dictator's early steps toward economic modernization and his willingness to deal with socialist labor groups as a result of which he seemed to be moderating their early tendencies toward violence and winning them to gradualist policies; they admired also his success in ending the Moroccan War by late 1925. During the course of military rule, however, there can be no doubt that the virulent antidictator and even antimonarchical campaign undertaken by eminent Spanish liberal intellectuals, among them Blasco Ibáñez and Unamuno, severely tarnished Spain's image in liberal circles of the New World. Seldom was a more unrestrained campaign of defamation carried out by Spaniards against Spain. Spanish propaganda that vastly exaggerated the evils and abuses of the dictator's regime was disseminated widely in Spanish America, where it convinced many readers that Spain had indeed returned to the darkest days of medieval fanaticism and inquisitorial terror.[89]

Liberal Disillusionment in Spanish America

If Spanish-American liberals tended toward increasing disillusionment in Spain between 1923 and 1930, Spanish liberals had by that last year approached the point of abandoning hope in Spanish America. The reasons went far beyond the aversion to the purported materialism of the New World republics that had disenchanted many liberals at a much earlier period.

By 1930, the optimistic appraisals concerning the Spanish-American future made by many turn-of-the-century Spanish liberals seemed utterly without basis. Most of the republics had remained economically backward, and the vaunted prosperity of a few had collapsed like the proverbial house of cards before the first winds of the great depression. Clericalism and religious fanaticism showed greater strength than ever in Colombia, while elsewhere, as in Peru, the influence of Catholicism seemed on the ascent. Most republics appeared not to have advanced toward political stability, responsibility, and rationality. Mexico was in the throes of a revolution strongly criticized in many liberal circles; Argentina, Peru, and Chile were among the countries ruled by military dictatorships; and indigenista rather than hispanista sentiments were uppermost in many programs expounded by a new generation of avant-garde intellectuals.

Spaniards concerned with hispanismo, whether liberals or conservatives, found further cause for discouragement in the traditional disputes that continued to strain relations between Peru and Ecuador, Peru and Colombia, Chile and Bolivia, and Bolivia and Paraguay. Apparently the common ties of the raza, of language and tradition, were not strong enough to bind even the New World republics together, let alone bind them to Spain. It was further disheartening to Spanish devotees of hispanismo that in successfully resolving their boundary dispute in 1929, Chile and Peru had turned not to the motherland but rather to the United States.

Still, the cause of hispanismo was not dead. What had occurred between 1900 and 1930 was that leadership in the movment had passed largely from Spanish liberals to conservatives.[90] And many of the losses sustained by liberals in their attempt to strengthen ties with Spanish America had been matched by gains of Spanish and Spanish-American conservatives in working toward rapprochement.

Spanish-American conservatives had ever inclined toward suspiciousness of the present and admiration of the past. As of 1930 they seemed to have ample grounds for arguing that the distant past was indeed preferable to the recent period that had been distinguished in most New World republics by the vogue of liberalism. Since the beginning of the depression liberalism was on the defensive and even discredited in many parts of the world. More than ever, then, Spanish-American conservatives turned toward Spain for the models that might guide them back to the grandeur of the past. The continuing image of Spain as a country essentially unchanged through the centuries thus enhanced the case of hispanismo among Spanish-American conservatives just as much as it had damaged that cause among liberals.

Meantime in Spain, conservatives had come to look with more hopeful eyes on Spanish America; for, with the most notable exception of Mexico, much of the rampant anticlericalism and secularism of the nineteenth and early twentieth centuries seemed to have been tamed by a revival of Catholic influence. Collaboration among members of the Spanish raza to defend the values of the conservative Hispanic world had become a definite possibility even as the likelihood of a common effort to defend Hispanic liberalism had receded into the background.

8: CONSERVATIVES AND HISPANISMO, 1900–1930

Catholicism and Hispanismo in the Conservative View

Spain's chief title to greatness in "the book of human progress," according to a devout Catholic journalist writing at the turn of the century, consisted in having imparted Catholicism to the New World. In so doing it had given to America its soul.[1] Here was the common point of departure from which Spanish conservatives approached Spanish America. They were bound to the New World republics, they insisted, because they shared the same Catholic soul, "the only perfect basis of solidarity."[2] Liberals, they maintained, would always and inevitably fail in their labors in the field of hispanismo because they prescinded from the one true source of unity between Spaniards of the New and Old Worlds.[3]

Spanish conservatives were certain that "the unity of spirits arising from the same religious faith is the best source of fraternity among nations in all orders of their existence."[4] They were certain too that "Spanish and Spanish-American culture in all its aspects is the work almost exclusively of the Church and its ministers."[5] It followed, therefore, in their analysis that Catholics and especially the clergy must take the lead in creating anew a harmonious brotherhood among the members of the Spanish raza.

As a means of encouraging solidarity among the priesthood of Spain and Spanish America and making its members aware of the role they had to play in achieving Hispanic unity, the young clergyman Donaciano Martínez Vélez founded early in 1901 the Revista Ibero-Americana de Ciencias Eclesiásticas.[6] The untimely death of Martínez halted publication of the Revista within a year of its appearance; but in January of 1903 Spanish Augustinians established the periodical España y América to unite the clergy of Spain and Spanish America in the coming struggle against "the dark errors generated by sick and disturbed minds and sustained by the brutal and unthinking force of human passions."[7] Its editors hoped that, by encouraging the Spanish clergy on both sides of the Atlantic to act in unison, the new review would contribute to social tranquility both in the peninsula and the new republics;[8] they hoped further that a united Spanish–Spanish-American priesthood could ultimately form the vanguard in a movement leading to "the rehabilitation and rebirth of the grandeur of the Latin race."[9]

The spirit that animated conservative apostles of hispanismo throughout the first third of the twentieth century was well summarized by a Spanish clergyman writing in 1930. Spain, he asserted, was God's chosen instrument to preserve Catholic values in the world; and this objective Spain could best achieve through a close union with Spanish America, a union that would bring international prestige and power to the Spanish raza.[10]

In spite of the Utopian hopes expressed by a few of their spokesmen, most Spanish conservatives, when they contemplated the reality of Spanish America in the days immediately following the 1898 disaster, saw little hope for restoring grandeur to a united and Catholic Hispanic raza. Instead, they showed concern about how to isolate themselves from the pestilence of the New World republics that seemed intent upon repudiating their Catholic origins and traditions. Spanish conservatives singled out two republics in particular as representative of the evil and debauchery toward which Spanish Americans, in their unnatural attempts to deny their Catholic origins, were assumed to have a predisposing tendency. Understandably, these republics were the two that—in addition to turn-of-the-century Mexico—most appealed to liberals: Ecuador and Argentina.

Conservative Animosity toward Ecuador and Argentina

Between 1860 and 1875, when the devout Gabriel García Moreno exercised the dominant political influence, Ecuador had been the supreme example of a country in which it was official government policy to equate nationalism with Catholicism. To some degree this continued to be the case for about twenty years following the 1875 assassination of García Moreno as Ecuadoran conservatives managed to remain in power. Then in 1895 liberal forces headed by Eloy Alfaro, who would twice serve as the country's president until his death in 1912 at the hands of an enraged mob of Quiteños, staged a successful revolution and initiated one of the most sweeping anticlerical programs that the New World had witnessed since Mexico's La Reforma of the 1850s and 1860s. Dismayed by the sudden turn of events, Spanish conservatives freely vented their indignation against the Ecuadoran liberals and, by implication at least, against the liberals of the peninsula who, if they had their way, allegedly would bring to Spain the same catastrophes that had overtaken the once happy South American republic.

Writing in 1897, a Franciscan contrasted the serene and progressive Ecuador of García Moreno, the "Philip II of America," with the ruin and decay into which it had fallen under Alfaro.[11] The moral to be drawn from Ecuador's misfortune, he claimed, was that no country could be happy and socially tranquil unless it followed the teachings of the Catholic Church. In 1905 a Jesuit asserted that Spaniards must take to heart the example of Ecuador and intensify their campaign to suppress the promulgation of erroneous, heretical ideas and pornographic materials by the liberal press. The gradual relaxation of censorship in Ecuador, he maintained, had prepared the way for the liberal revolution.[12] Two years later the Spanish Augustinian Eusebio Negrete denounced the "odious crimes" that he said had become the order of the day in Ecuador. As an example of such crimes he pointed to a new law establishing "laic, secular education" in all government-supported schools.[13] Six months later Negrete reported on the "brutal and savage tyranny that dictator Alfaro exercises in the name of the canaille, contrary to the will of the honorable, cultured, hardworking, and patriotic classes. Youths are assassinated and religious centers where they apply for instruction in their faith are assaulted. . . . All of those who do not burn incense before the throne of Alfaro are jailed." Fortunately, the priest continued, Ecuador seemed to have tired of this shameful spectacle of crime and violence; its citizens were abandoning pacific protest and, he predicted, soon would arise in arms against the tyrant so as to end by violence "the state of things that if allowed to continue much longer would bring about the republic's moral and material dissolution."[14]

The Augustinian's prediction of an antiliberal revolution was not fulfilled and so the Catholic press of Spain continued to fulminate against Ecuador. Owing to the triumph of liberals there, a Spanish Jesuit wrote in 1929, the directing classes had become thoroughly corrupt and debauched. Since the 1895 revolution, he charged, Ecuador's presidents had been fatuous, dishonest merchants and drunkards and the country had won distinction as the most decadent in all Spanish America.[15] The following year the Jesuit periodical *Razón y Fe* described Ecuador as sunk in "ignorance and corruption" owing to the neutral education insisted upon by its liberal rulers. "All that is required to gain a teaching post in the public system is to be anti-Catholic. In the public schools free love doctrines are taught and the directors of the schools put the doctrines into practice with girl pupils and lady teachers."[16] A situation such as this, as well as decadence and retrogression of every sort, were inescapable, the journal contended, when liberalism held sway over latin countries.[17]

Spanish Catholics also waxed indignant over the anticlericalism manifested by most Argentine governments beginning in the 1860's. They charged that the "atheistic curricula" of the public schools, where religious instruction was prohibited, had contributed to the republic's rampant materialism, and they complained about the spirit of tolerance that was leading, as it always must, to complete religious indifference. Owing to pernicious freedom-of-the-press laws, they further alleged, Argentina's youth was becoming ever more depraved. Worst of all, according to one Catholic journalist, "Masonry, that reprobate and immoral sect, so many times condemned by the Church, publicly displays its repugnant figure in Argentina, exercising more power than is generally recognized and managing at times even to stain the office of the chief executive."[18]

In 1901 a Catholic writer compared the liberals of Buenos Aires, who had attacked a group of worshippers returning from a pilgrimage to the shrine of the Virgin of Luján, to the Spanish freethinkers of Zaragoza who had recently assaulted a group of the faithful on their way to the shrine of the Virgin of Pilar.[19] A few years later another Spanish Catholic expressed a conviction, widespread at the time in conservative circles, that Argentine events were a harbinger of things to come in Spain if anticlericalism and secularism remained uncurbed. He attributed the exploitative capitalism and social unrest said to prevail in Argentina, as well as an electoral system that elevated only the worst elements to power, to an educational establishment controlled by Masons and to a government that had forgotten that only "divine charity and Catholic prudence" can produce social justice.[20]

In the view of early twentieth-century Spanish conservatives, then, Ecuador and Argentina were scarcely countries to be enlisted in a Catholic crusade to reanimate the Hispanic raza. They were useful only in a negative sense, because of the examples they presented of the horrors that would come to Spain if liberalism and secularism were not banished.

Still, all did not appear bleak to Spanish conservatives at the beginning of the century as they surveyed Spanish America. Colombia seemed still to be as devout as the Ecuador of García Moreno had been. Elsewhere in Spanish America there were clear signs of a Catholic revival that would soon provide substantial encouragement to the peninsula's conservatives who continued to be lured by the vision of hispanismo.

A Catholic Revival in Spanish America and Its Impact on the Hispanismo of Spanish Conservatives

Out of the Plenary Council of Latin American prelates, convoked in Rome by Pope Leo XIII in 1899, arose an effort to reinvigorate the Church in Latin America and to improve the channels of communication between it and Rome. The Plenary Council also provided the impetus for a series of provincial councils within the various Latin American republics, one of the first of which was held in Caracas in 1904. A Spanish witness to the event hailed the Venezuelan council as a clear indication of the growing strength of the Church in Spanish America, and he greeted the *Instrucción Pastoral del Episcopado Venezolano al clero y fieles de la república*, issuing from the council, as a program of action suitable not just to Venezuela but to Spain as well. Apparently what most appealed to him in the statement of the Venezuelan bishops was the condemnation of the liberal press and the denunciation of Masonry and neutral education.[21]

The resurgence of the Catholic Church in Venezuela, dating from the 1904 provincial council, continued during the lengthy dictatorship of Juan Vicente Gómez (1908–1935). Some twenty years after Gómez came to power, a Spanish journalist commented upon the flourishing estate of Catholicism in Venezuela and noted that the Church was "properly grateful to the president, who had always favored it."[22]

The 1899 Plenary Council also gave rise to several provincial councils in Colombia. The third of these, held in Bogotá in 1916, produced a joint pastoral in which the Colombian hierarchy condemned the liberal press for advocating separation of Church and state, for favoring neutral education, for asserting that morality stemmed from natural reason rather than revealed religious truths, for encouraging a "vague and absurd" distinction between religion and clericalism so as to deny "to sacred ministers" a role in civil society, for claiming that ecclesiastical authorities had no power to control the reading habits of the faithful, for proclaiming the validity of civil marriage, and for affirming that the interests of the nation came before those of the Church. In their pastoral the prelates also instructed the faithful to vote only for political leaders who would protect the interests of the Church and allow the clergy a role of "moderate intervention" in the public life of the country.

Upon the conclusion of the council a Spanish writer complimented the bishops for their efforts, which had, he said, increased the already appreciable strength of the Church in Colombia, establishing it as the most formidable "bulwark of the existing social order." He added that the joint pastoral resulting from the council laid down principles that were just as essential for the well-being of Spain as for that of Colombia; consequently, the pastoral merited recognition as an important basis for the concerted action of Catholics in the Old and New Worlds.[23]

The Church's gradual acquisition of prestige and influence in Venezuela following a period of rampant anticlericalism in the late nineteenth century[24] and the strengthening of its already considerable power in Colombia were signs of a general revival of Catholic influence in most parts of Spanish America. In a way Catholicism's resurgence can be traced to the turn-of-the-century reaction against positivism and utilitarianism. This reaction was initiated by men like José Enrique Rodó who were religiously indifferent and convinced that humanism afforded an adequate foundation upon which to base the higher values they extolled. But roughly between 1910 and 1930, with the situation differing considerably from country to country, a new pattern became discernible. Increasingly the leaders of the spiritual reaction against the vogue of utilitarian and mechanistic criteria began to return to the Catholic Church, persuaded that the higher human values, if they were to prevail, required a theological and supernatural basis. Only in Mexico, where intellectuals after the beginning of the 1910 Revolution preferred to flirt with radical anticlerical and sometimes with atheistic doctrines, and in Uruguay, where the Church had never enjoyed more than the most tenuous existence and agnosticism was a significant intellectual force, did the reaction against positivism and materialism fail to evolve into a resurgence of Catholic influence. Even in Uruguay, Luis Alberto de Herrera emerged as perhaps the most eloquent lay spokesman of Catholic and Hispanic values ever produced in his country.[25]

In this changing intellectual environment a Catholic university movement began to flourish in certain countries. The year 1917 witnessed the establishment of a Catholic university in Peru, while in Chile an older Catholic university, founded in Santiago in 1888, began for the first time to acquire academic respectability in the early twentieth century.[26] Both of these universities aimed primarily at forming an elite that could appreciate, guard, and nourish the most exalted human values; largely they eschewed practical studies as beneath the dignity of a privileged intellectual class. By the 1930s, in Peru at least, the new Catholic university could claim greater social prestige than the venerable national institution (San Marcos), which—under the pressure of the university reform movement originating at Córdoba, Argentine, in 1918—was opening its doors to students of humble origins. In contrast, the Catholic university reserved its instruction for members of the aristocracy.

Early in the twentieth century, understandably desiring to capitalize on the increasingly favorable circumstances in which they found themselves and at the same time hoping to ease social tensions, the Spanish-American episcopacy launched an effort to organize the laity into Catholic Action groups. As in Spain, the primary purpose of Catholic Action was to quicken the social conscience of the upper classes and to induce them, under the hierarchy's direction, to take paternalistic measures to mitigate the suffering and isolation of the masses. This little-studied development in Spanish-American Catholicism produced consequential results in reducing social pressures and undoubtedly curtailed the impact of the advocates of violent revolution.

Even Argentina, over which Spanish conservatives had tended to despair at the beginning of the century, provided a fertile ground for Catholic Action.[27] A Spanish Augustinian serving in that country noted in 1903 that the ten recently founded Catholic Workers' Circles already claimed some thirty thousand members.[28] In addition, he praised a Christian Democratic organization that had staged a huge Buenos Aires celebration in honor of the tenth anniversary of *Rerum Novarum*.[29]

In 1915 a Spanish Jesuit saluted Argentina's Ladies of St. Vincent de Paul on their twenty-fifth anniversary. According to him the 29,000 ladies enrolled in the association made over 11,000 visits each month to poor families, supplying them with clothes, food, and Christian counsel. The Ladies of St. Vincent de Paul were, he said, playing a leading role in routing the forces of secularism and winning Argentina back to the Church.[30]

During the World War I period the Spanish Jesuit Gabriel Palau, an outstanding figure in his own country's Catholic Action, transferred to Buenos Aires, where he collaborated for some years with the local clergy in combating the impiety and secularism of the sprawling Argentine capital.[31] Palau played an active role in the Buenos Aires Centro Católico de Estudiantes and in 1925, in collaboration with Spanish clergyman Zacarías de Vizcarra, organized a series of courses on Catholic culture in which young Argentines were instructed in the principles of Thomistic philosophy and Catholic Action and trained to serve as catequistas among the laboring classes.[32]

As in Spain, so also in Spanish America the appearance of radical revolutionaries urging class warfare helped give rise to the Catholic Action movement. Sooner than in Spain, moreover, the specter of social revolution in the New World republics contributed to a liberal-conservative rapprochement. For years Spanish-American liberals and conservatives had been in accord on many social and economic issues, remaining separated largely by traditional disagreement over Church-state issues. Faced with what appeared to be an immediate threat to the established order, liberals began to curb their anticlericalism and to present a common front with conservatives against the forces of sweeping change. Even during the late nineteenth century Bolivia's liberals and conservatives had managed to arrive at a mutually advantageous modus vivendi. By the 1920s this pattern was spreading to Ecuador, where the "out" conservatives learned to cooperate with the incumbent liberals and in return received many important political posts, and to Colombia, where the "out" liberals found a basis of cooperation with the incumbent conservatives. By the early 1930s Chilean liberals and conservatives, ignoring issues that had divided them for decades, had joined to form an alliance that would remain one of the country's most powerful political forces for the next thirty years.

Conservatives in Spain were gratified by these developments, for they seemed to indicate that New World liberals, once feared and reviled as the wildest and most godless secularizers of their entire breed, were coming to accept the traditional conservative contention that without Catholicism and some degree of Church influence in the temporal order social harmony could not exist.

Conservatives and "La Fiesta de la Raza"

In connection with the celebration of the fourth centennial of the discovery of the New World in 1892, Conservative Party leader Cánovas del Castillo suggested that all nations of the Spanish-speaking world set October 12 aside as a national holiday. For some years nothing came of this suggestion, but in 1899 the Catholic Church did at least move to encourage an annual religious commemoration of the Columbus discovery. The Plenary Council assembled in Rome that year obtained the pope's approval for celebrating in all parishes of Latin America a mass of thanksgiving and a solemn Te Deum on the Sunday closest to October 12. From an early date, then, the Church became intimately associated with the rendering of tribute to the discoverer whose most enduring claim to immortality was considered to have been his opening of a new world to the redemptive grace of Catholicism.[33]

For still another reason Catholics could claim a religious significance for October 12 throughout the Spanish-speaking world; it was the feast day of the Virgin of Pilar, widely venerated in Spain as a national patroness. Spanish Catholics regarded it as providential that their nation embarked upon its great mission of bringing the true faith to millions of souls living previously in spiritual darkness on the feast day of their patroness. For them, October 12 necessarily signified "the religious brotherhood of all Iberian nations,"[34] serving as an annual reminder that religion, synonymous with patriotism throughout the Hispanic world, was the only basis for enduring ties between "the madre patria and its children in America."[35]

Early in the twentieth century, certain Spanish-American republics began to commemorate October 12 with privately organized festivities. Thus in 1912 members of the Spanish community joined with local social and political leaders of the Dominican Republic to celebrate el día de Colón. Three years later Spaniards and Uruguayans joined in Montevideo to celebrate el día de América. Already, then, disagreement over the proper designation of the October 12 celebration had become apparent.

In 1913, the Unión Ibero-Americana, generally leaning toward conservatism in political and religious attitudes,[36] in contrast to Luis Palomo's Centro de Cultura Hispano-Americana, undertook a campaign to have the government declare October 12 an official holiday under the denomination of el día or la fiesta de la raza.[37] For this proposal the Union gained support from the municipal government of Madrid, from some members of the national Cortes, and from various representatives of the Spanish-American diplomatic corps in Spain.[38] Finally in June of 1918 the government responded to the campaign that the Union spearheaded[39] by decreeing October 12 a national holiday to be known as la fiesta de la raza. The June decree bore the signature of Antonio Maura, serving then as president of the council of ministers.

One year before Spain the governments of Argentina and Peru had proclaimed October 12 a national holiday. Chile followed suit in 1921, and by the end of the 1920s the custom had become firmly established in most of the Spanish-American countries. Although not always officially designated el día or la fiesta de la raza, the holiday came generally to be known by one of these names.

Because the custom of celebrating October 12 came into widespread use at the time of the Catholic revival in Spanish America, and because in Spain the impetus for its celebration had come largely from Catholic groups, the term raza increasingly acquired a religious connotation. In the hispanismo movement, therefore, conservatives scored a victory over liberals as Catholicism came to be recognized, at least by most October 12 orators each year, as the essential factor in uniting the various components of the Hispanic raza.

Certain Spanish Catholics, however, registered dissatisfaction with the name día de la raza. The priest José María González, for example, initiated a campaign in 1918 to change the designation of the October 12 holiday to el día de Colón y de la paz. In his mind the term raza denoted ethnocentrism and lack of Catholic universalism.[40] Zacarías de Vizcarra, the Spanish priest who together with Gabriel Palau worked in behalf of Catholic Action in Buenos Aires during the 1920's, agreed completely with González. Spain, he averred, owing to its Catholicism, was the most universalist and least racist of any nation in the world. As the term race acquired a narrower, more restrictive, more strictly biological connotation in many parts of the world during the 1920s and the early 1930s, Vizcarra objected all the more strenuously to its continuing use in connection with commemorating the Spanish discovery of America. In 1926 he led a press campaign in Buenos Aires to celebrate October 12 as el día de hispanidad. According to him the term hispanidad had been employed as early as the sixteenth century; its meaning was basically the same as hispanismo, he explained, and it connoted a unity based upon religion, customs, and language rather than upon common ethnic origins.[41]

Under whatever name, the celebration of October 12 contributed toward strengthening the bonds of sentiment among conservative Catholic groups of Spain and Spanish America. At the very least the annual holiday must have facilitated the efforts of the hundreds of Spanish clergymen in the New World to tighten the ties of Catholicism that predisposed at least some elements of the peninsula and New World republics toward cooperation and copenetration.

The Spanish Clergy in Spanish America: Their Contributions to Hispanismo

Desolate over the loss of Cuba and Puerto Rico in 1898, an infanta of Spain found consolation in the thought that Spain would continue to send missionaries to Spanish America. In this way the motherland would maintain the bond of religious unity with the New World, a bond that was, she said, far more important than political connections.[42]

In one of its first editions in 1903, the Augustinian journal España y América echoed the infanta's sentiments.[43] Because religion constituted the principal link between Spain and the New World, clergymen, it asserted, should naturally be recognized as the men best qualified for leadership in bringing about the unification of the transatlantic Spanish community.[44] Particularly to the missionary fell the task of "defending our influence in Spanish America, undermined each day by the arrival of emigrants from other countries." Because the Spanish missionary, next to his sacred religion, most loved his "far-off patria," it followed logically that he should serve as the principal instrument for "stimulating the noble currents of sympathy toward mother Spain," thereby enhancing the prestige of Spaniards among people who will come to admire "the abnegation and culture of the wandering Spanish clergymen."

Considerable disagreement existed among Spaniards as to which elements of the Spanish-American populace stood in greatest need of the motherland's missionary solicitude. There could be little doubt of the need of unassimilated Indian tribes for the missionary, and, since the late nineteenth century, Spanish clergymen, especially Franciscans, had undertaken the main burden of keeping the Catholic faith alive among the Indians of eastern Peru and Bolivia.[45] A Jesuit, manifesting the typical superiority attitude of peninsulares vis-à-vis Spanish Americans, saw another fruitful field for mission activity. According to him, the upper classes of the former colonies most desperately required the services of Spanish missionaries. Theosophism, he contended, "spawned and nourished by Masonry," had had virtually no impact in Spain; in contrast it had by the mid-1920's made considerable headway among the upper classes of Spanish America. The reason for this, the Jesuit maintained, was the lack of religious formation among the educated circles of Spanish Americans. Spanish clergymen therefore had a sacred obligation to conduct missionary work among the accommodated classes of the New World, who would otherwise succumb to the blandishments of Theosophism and Masonry, of Protestantism and spiritualism.[46]

As of 1920, some 308 Spanish religious, including 169 regular clergymen, 13 secular priests, 49 brothers and 77 nuns, were active in missionary work in Spanish America, particularly in Peru, Bolivia, Ecuador, Colombia, Nicaragua, and Honduras. The regular clergy in this group were principally Capuchins, Franciscans, Augustinians, Dominicans, Carmelites, and Recollects. Among other activities missionary personnel ran 165 rural schools, in which 6,781 students were enrolled.[47]

In all, some 4,258 Spanish religious were in Spanish America as of 1920, a high percentage indeed of the total number of 6,758 religious from the peninsula stationed abroad.[48] The great majority, then, of Spanish religious in the New World served in a nonmissionary capacity. A large part of them staffed the fashionable private Catholic schools that abounded in most of the important urban centers. Probably most of the personnel so employed agreed with the Spanish Augustinian who stated that the primary objective of his country's religious teaching in Spanish America was "to instill in the students a love of Spain and a pride in her accomplishments" so as to prepare the way for "an ever closer spiritual, commercial, and political relationship between the motherland and the former colonies."[49]

Perhaps even more effective in serving the cause of hispanismo were the few Spanish clerical educators who concerned themselves not so much with cultural propaganda as with genuinely advancing scientific knowledge within the countries to which they were assigned. Such a man was the Jesuit Francisco Cerro, who arrived in La Paz, Bolivia, in 1893, where he taught mathematics, physics, chemistry, and natural history at the Colegio de San Calixto. Father Cerro also taught science courses at the Higher War School in La Paz. Proceeding to Sucre in 1911, he established and for years directed a meteorological observatory. Back in La Paz in 1926, he founded the country's only seismographic station. For his notable contributions to scientific knowledge, the Bolivian government in 1931 awarded the Jesuit the Condor of the Andes medal.[50]

Other Spanish clergymen made their contribution to hispanismo by undertaking brief lecture tours in Spanish America. In 1927, for example, the well-known Spanish Jesuit astronomer Luis Rodes, director of the Ebro observatory, gave a series of conferences in Argentina and Chile, providing his audiences with "persuasive evidence of Spain's advanced position in scientific knowledge."[51] Two years later the Unión Ibero-Americana sent Father Zacarías García Villada to Colombia on a similar cultural mission. Upon his return, García reported that "the sons and daughters of Spain who are the most loyal in spreading the love of the madre patria in the New World are, without question, the Spanish religious, male and female."[52]

None of the short-term tours of New World republics by Spanish clergymen came close to matching the impact of the 1923–1924 visit of Cardinal Benlloch. Even the anticlerical Luis Palomo lauded Benlloch on his return to Spain for having "reconquered the Spanish soul in America."[53]

Born in Valencia in 1864, Juan Benlloch y Vivó was ordained to the priesthood in 1888, preconized Bishop of Burgos in 1919, and named a cardinal in 1921. The following year he was appointed president of the Unión Misional del Clero en España and personally broke ground for a seminary in Burgos dedicated to training Spanish missionaries. By this time Benlloch had assumed a vital interest in Spanish America, regarding it as the most important theater for Spanish missionary activity.[54]

A group of Spanish Mercedarians serving as missionaries in Chile petitioned in 1923 for the elevation of their church in Santiago to basilica status. When Rome acceded to this request, the Mercedarians asked Benlloch to come to Chile to officiate at the ceremonies. The cardinal agreed at once and, when additional invitations were received from groups in other Spanish-American countries, expanded his itinerary so as to visit

Uruguay, Argentina, Peru, Ecuador, Panama, Colombia, Venezuela, Cuba, and Puerto Rico.

Following a brief stop in Montevideo and eight days in Buenos Aires, filled with an uninterrupted round of receptions and public appearances, Benlloch journeyed by rail to Santiago, arriving there on October 2, 1923. After being received in imposing style by Santiago's popular Archbishop Crescente Errázuriz, he presided over the ceremonies conferring basilica status on the Mercedarian church and remained on in the Chilean capital for what was probably the most lavish and emotion-packed celebration of la fiesta de la raza up to that time.

Proceeding by sea to Peru, Benlloch was greeted by large and enthusiastic receptions in Callao and Lima. When the cardinal's ship touched in Guayaquil, the president of Ecuador journeyed down from Quito to offer his personal welcome. In Panama he was also greeted by the president, while in Cartagena, Colombia, he was received as a chief of state and declared "the modern apostle of the missions." Benlloch completed his American tour at the beginning of 1924, arriving back in Spain by mid-January.[55]

At a huge reception in Segovia to welcome him upon his return, Benlloch was, not surprisingly, hailed by the conservative alcalde of the city as a man who, thanks to divine inspiration, "had been permitted to realize perhaps the most transcendent work in contemporary history: the rewinning of the hearts of those brothers across the seas."[56] What was surprising was that Cultura Hispano-Americana, the official journal of the Centro de Cultura Hispano-Americana, an organization founded under the inspiration of Canalejas in 1910 as the principal liberal agency of hispanismo and consistently dedicated since that time to anticlerical policies, saluted Benlloch as one of the greatest apostles that Spain had ever sent to Spanish America. The liberal journal went on to concede the place of Catholicism in maintaining the bonds of unity between Spain and Spanish America and suggested that the government arrange as quickly as possible to send Benlloch on a follow-up tour.[57]

At precisely this time Cultura Hispano-Americana was engaged in a campaign to expose the horrors of the leveling, socialistic, atheistic revolution in Mexico. Perhaps there was a connection between the journal's treatment of the Benlloch mission and the Mexican Revolution. Alarmed by events in Mexico, a few Spanish liberals, even as a larger number of their counterparts in Spanish America, may have begun to take to heart the traditional conservative warning that without Catholicism as a buttressing force the established, hierarchial social order would always be in danger.

Following his rapid tour of New World republics, Cardinal Benlloch devoted all of his energies to fostering Spanish interest in Spanish America. His desire was to have the motherland begin more fully to reciprocate the great love for it that he had discovered among the Spanish Americans. Only if acting out of a sincere and intense love, he believed, would Spain undertake the heroic missionary labor necessary to cause Catholicism to prevail and flourish anew in Spanish America, an area that suffered from an appalling scarcity of native priests. "What we began in the sixteenth century," the cardinal declared, "we must complete today."[58]

Exhausted by his arduous efforts in behalf of Spanish-American rapport, Benlloch began to fail in health. The medical help he sought in Madrid was to no avail and he died in that city in 1926. As one admirer has observed, "it could be fairly said that he died of hispanismo."[59]

Benlloch's death deprived hispanismo, as a conservative, Catholic movement, of one of its most effective leaders. But conservative hispanismo had by then received new strength and vitality from the favorable attitudes and policies of dictator Primo de Rivera.

The Primo de Rivera Dictatorship and Conservative Hispanismo, 1923–1930

When Primo de Rivera seized power in September of 1923, most conservatives welcomed him as the saviour of traditional Spain. With warm approval they greeted the dictator's often-proclaimed dedication to patria, religion, and monarchy, his decision that there should be obligatory instruction in religion and patriotism in all primary schools,[60] and his declaration that the Spanish raza, in order to fulfill its mission in history, had to base its action on "the foundation of solid Christian morality."[61]

Primo de Rivera was decidedly interested in hispanismo.[62] And he delighted conservatives by his conviction that Catholicism was the essential basis of hispanismo. Spiritual relations between Spain and Spanish America must first be encouraged; only after they were established could fruitful intellectual and commercial ties be anticipated.[63] Conservatives also accepted as an important indication of the dictator's official policy the manner in which Alfonso XIII, in his November, 1923, audience with Pope Pius XI, juxtaposed an avowal of Spain's Catholicism with a declaration of his country's dedication to hispanismo. "If," the king said, "the cross of Christ did not project its shadow upon Spain, then Spain would not be Spain."[64] Alfonso then expressed "the most vehement aspiration of Spain to extend a warm embrace of affection to all of those republics that were previously its colonies in the New World, so that with all Spaniards, on both sides of the ocean, united, the Hispano-American raza would arrive at the zenith of the greatness that rightly corresponds to it in the world."[65]

To some extent Spain's conservative hispanoamericanistas managed even to turn to their advantage the antidictatorship campaign waged in the Spanish-American press by Spanish liberals. In an effective propaganda counteroffensive, conservatives pictured liberal defamation of the dictator fundamentally as an attack against religion, inspired, supported, and financed by Masonry and communism. Spaniards who spoke badly of Spain did so not just in order to criticize its form of government, they said, but in order to attack the very essence of Spain, its Catholicism. This contention gained credence among Catholic conservatives in Spanish America, endearing to them all the more the Spain of Primo de Rivera, subjected to villification for no other reason than its steadfast devotion to Catholicism.[66] On the other hand, many liberal hispanistas in Spanish America were repulsed by the dictatorship as described to them by its harsh critics. During the years, then, of Primo de Rivera's rule, conservatives advanced toward a position of monopolistic control over hispanismo. This process was abetted by the skill of José María Pemán in setting forth the aspirations of conservative hispanismo[67] and by the diplomatic expertise of Ramiro de Maeztu in seeking fulfillment of these aspirations in the republic of Argentina.

The young Pemán was the principal ideologue of conservative hispanismo during the dictatorship. The vice-director of the conservatively oriented Real Academia Hispano-Americana of Cádiz, Pemán presented his views on hispanismo principally in a book published in 1927 and in a discourse delivered two years later at the fiesta de la raza ceremonies held in Sevilla and presided over by Primo de Rivera.[68] In his book and discourse, both lavishly praised by the dictator, Pemán drew upon the writings of Ángel Ganivet in maintaining that material expansion and political imperialism were childhood diseases of nations. Having already suffered from these sicknesses, Spain was in a stage of convalescence and thus advanced beyond other nations, such as France, England, and Germany, which still manifested the symptoms of traditional imperialism. Because the more mature Spain had abandoned all thought of material expansion and political imperialism, it was ready to pass to a higher form of national activity, that of spiritual, idealistic expansion.[69] The great ideal of Spain, Pemán asserted, must be to "radiate its spiritual presence" in America.[70]

Traditionally, the young writer maintained, statesmen had concerned themselves with the sovereignty of the family, the city, the region, and the nation; but now they must devote themselves to a higher sovereignty, "that of the raza." The object of hispanoamericanismo, he declared, was to create a new form of international law and a new climate of "interfamily" relationships that would be conducive to the realization of the highest destiny of the Hispanic raza, whose members were united by a common religion, language, spirit, and culture.[71]

The United States, Pemán acknowledged, had contributed to the initial establishment of cooperation and to the preliminary stages of New World unification through Pan-Americanism. It had also facilitated the rise of universal order through its intervention in the Great War and through the concern of President Wilson with the creation of a League of Nations. But the United States lacked spiritualism; because of this its Pan-Americanism was incapable of making further advances toward American-hemisphere unification and its international policies in general could render no further service to the cause of worldwide order and peace. On the other hand the Spanish raza possessed the most abundant reservoirs of spiritual resources in the world. Therefore, it was the "apostolic mission of the Hispanic raza to help the world proceed toward a new international order based upon peace, justice, and Christian morality."

Pemán urged the Hispano-American youth to become "wildly idealistic" as they enlisted in this cause, to acquire "a blind faith in their mission" so that they could supply the spirit that is missing "in the narrower, more traditional organization in Geneva. . . . Yes," he declared, "there must be formed a society of Hispano-American nations that will provide the world with the model of the new international life; this is an imperative of history and of the spirit." Of course, he added, in establishing the unity that would point the way for the rest of the world, Spain and Spanish America had to recognize the primacy of the Christian—by which he obviously meant the Catholic—element, for this was the only true source of fraternity.[72] Echoing the assertion of Primo de Rivera, Pemán observed that after Spain and Spanish America had attained spiritual rapport, commercial and "practical" ties would multiply rapidly, leading, among other results, to the establishment of a customs union.[73]

Ramiro de Maeztu also believed in the primacy of spiritual ties in hispanismo. Pan-Americanism, he contended, was directed only toward economic objectives; but Spaniards, who preserved the proper priority of values, approached Spanish America on the more exalted level of religion.[74]

Maeztu had not always felt this way. As a young member of the Generation of '98 he had been concerned principally with the material development of Spain, had urged the need for its Europeanization, had fallen into habits of religious indifference, and had wondered if the apparent incompetence of Latins in matters of economic productivity evidenced their inferiority to Anglo-Saxons. By 1927, however, when at the age of fifty-three he was appointed ambassador to Argentina, Maeztu had long since abandoned his youthful liberalism to become an eloquent spokesman of Catholic traditionalism. As a member of the board of directors of the Unión Ibero-Americana he had also established some fame as a proponent of conservative hispanismo.

Arriving in Argentina in February of 1928, Maeztu maintained correct relations with the Hipólito Irigoyen administration. But the ambassador felt little affinity to the elderly Argentine president, who in his political ideology acknowledged his indebtedness to Krause and who seemed intent upon making his Radical Party an instrument of secularization. Therefore Maeztu established his closest ties with a group of young Argentine rightists who advocated a nondemocratic republic, organized along corporative lines, in which the Catholic Church, in collaboration with the military, would serve as the keeper of the public conscience and impose moral rectitude upon the populace through authoritarian methods. In *La Nueva República*, the journal published by his rightist friends, Maeztu often was pleased to find the texts of such political philosophers as Juan Donoso Cortés, Louis de Bonald, and Charles Maurras. The Argentine rightists frequently visited the Spanish Embassy and dined with the ambassador in his residence. In 1930 when Irigoyen resigned his office under pressure and was shortly replaced by José Félix Uriburu, a lieutenant general with corporativist leanings and closely associated with the *Nueva República* group, Maeztu must have exulted at the contribution he had made toward facilitating a warm relationship with the conservatives who appeared to be in charge of Spanish America's most powerful republic.[75] This development was all the more gratifying in view of the fact that conservative hispano-americanistas had about given up hope on Mexico, the other republic of Spanish America that through the years had most aroused the interest of Spaniards.

The Response of Conservative Hispanismo to the Mexican Revolution

Conservative Spaniards had tended to admire, at least grudgingly, the Mexico of Porfirio Díaz. Although they regretted the influence of positivism in the country, they at least felt that the Porfiriato represented a distinct improvement over the days when liberalism and anticlericalism had been at their apogee under Benito Juárez. A one-time Spanish minister to the republic wrote approvingly in 1904 that although Díaz governed according to the ideals of a republic, Mexico under him was nourished by a force that was "energetically conservative."[76] Some years later an Augustinian priest praised Díaz for having known how to keep in check for thirty years the instincts of a race that, "sunk in misery and ignorance, could not otherwise ever have interrupted the series of civil wars that had begun with its independence. . . ." Mexico, the priest concluded, required the Díaz type of heavy-handed rule because its population was only 20 percent white and the nonwhite castes were inherently inclined toward comitting "all types of disorders and absurdities."[77]

Once the Revolution began, however, and quickly acquired its pronouncedly anticlerical and even antireligious orientation, Spanish conservatives became outspoken in their denunciations of Mexico, referring to the country as godless and barbaric. Commenting in 1915 on the "notorious cruelties and ferocious persecutions" directed against the Church,[78] *Razón y Fe* declared "the crucifixion of Mexico is one of the greatest tragedies in history."[79]

The same journal in 1920 attributed the Mexican catastrophe to the manipulations of President Wilson, the Protestant sects, and New York Masonry allied with Mexican Masonry. Most of the leaders of the Revolution, the journal informed its readers, had been trained in the Protestant schools of Mexico. "No wonder," the editorial writer concluded, "banditry, murder, including the killing even of children, and tyranny and social upheaval prevail in Mexico; for these are the natural fruits of liberal revolutions and Protestantism."[80]

Some years later the Jesuit publication found still another villain in addition to the United States, Protestants, Masons, and liberals to which it attributed the plight of Mexico: the Jew. Mexico, it charged, had opened wide the doors to Jewish immigration, with predictable results; for "this race is never assimilated in a country, it never produces anything but instead syphons off what others produce. It never identifies with the nationality . . .; it constitutes an insidious force that seeks to destroy the nationality of others. It does not have its own patria and therefore it does not want other peoples to have one."[81]

Catholic writers in Spain also attributed Mexican developments to the international socialist movement and charged that events both in Russia and Mexico clearly demonstrated the social consequences of assaults against formal religion.[82] In describing the plight of revolutionary Mexico, a Catholic journalist wrote: "I hope by these chronicles to enable Spain to witness a sad but instructive spectacle: the ruin of a Christian civilization as it is gradually destroyed by barbarous liberalism and its still more savage children, socialism and communism."[83]

Through skillful propaganda, carried on against a background of mounting social restlessness in the peninsula during late 1929 and early 1930, conservatives, using Mexico as their object lesson, brought a new urgency to their traditional warning that liberalism, Masonry, and Protestantism were allied forces in producing communist-style revolutions. Meantime, Spanish liberals were sorely divided in their response to Mexican events, with only socialists and extreme leftists consistently supporting the Revolution.

Liberals in the 1920s were also shifting and divided in their attitudes toward the United States. Conservatives, on the other hand, because they remained steadfast in their traditionally hostile sentiments toward the Colossus, were able to take advantage of the rising anti-Yankeeism in Spanish America to strengthen their hold over the hispanismo movement.

Conservative Hispanismo and the United States

Catholicism, a Spanish priest declared in 1904, was the one force that could prevent Spanish America from being absorbed by the United States and from disappearing "politically, culturally, and socially."[84] Through the years, Spanish conservatives continued to make similar statements.[85] The

United States, an eminent conservative statesman warned in 1917,[86] the very year in which many liberals began to advocate rapport and cooperation with the Colossus, had as its ambition nothing less than the complete cultural and spiritual absorption of Spanish America; and it was up to Spaniards to protect their religion in the New World, for its disappearance would result in the annihilation of the Hispanic raza and culture in the lands that Spain had called into being.[87] Conservative hispanoamericanista Antonio Goicoechea, writing in 1928, just two years after two of Altamira's disciples had published an influential book proposing active collaboration with the United States,[88] described the Spanish mission as being that of "perfecting the nationalization of the Spanish American spirit." Only through Spain, he asserted, could the new republics obtain the "awareness of a common past" and of a spiritual grandeur that they must defend "tooth and nail." The essential factor to the survival of Hispanic culture in the New World, he concluded, was the militant Catholicism of the peninsula; for without it "Ariel could not survive and triumph over Caliban in the struggle of the two cultures in America."[89]

In the mid-1920's Jesuit historian Constantino Bayle registered grave apprehension about the threat to Spanish culture posed by United States missionaries in Spanish America. President Theodore Roosevelt, according to the Jesuit, had once conceded that the absorption of Spanish America by the United States would remain difficult so long as the southern republics retained their Catholicism. Manifesting their tacit accord with this appraisal, Bayle maintained, the Protestant sects were sending hordes of new troops to Spanish America to soften the area for the ultimate conquest by Yankee imperialism. To protect its interests in the new struggle between the followers of Luther and the defenders of the true faith, the priest declared, Spain must rush auxiliary troops into battle.[90]

Another Spanish writer with a deep interest in Spanish America pointed to a different kind of United States menace. In his opinion the indigenista movements radiating out from Mexico and Peru, characterized always by a virulent strain of Hispanophobia, were consciously conceived and abetted by the United States. The Colossus recognized, he insisted, that unity based on hispanismo, on common religion, language, and customs was the only effective defense of the Spanish raza in America. As a result, the United States sought to undermine the cultural unity of Spanish America by fomenting indigenista movements. The writer lamented that many Spanish Americans were falling into this trap and called upon Spaniards to redouble their efforts to help the former colonies resist the United States menace in its many guises.[91]

Spanish conservatives were consistent in their anti-Yankee attitudes, in part because they associated Catholicism—for them the very essence of hispanismo—with anti-Yankeeism. This consistency unquestionably helped the conservatives to eclipse, by the late 1920's, their liberal rivals in the competition for control over hispanismo. In many ways the conservatives thereupon proved to be gracious victors, probably because their rivalry with liberals within the hispanismo movement had often been, despite the barking and howling rhetoric sometimes employed, a friendly one. On many occasions conservatives and liberals had collaborated closely in working to achieve a more intimate spiritual-cultural relationship with Spanish America. The experience of collaborating in the common quest of the goals of hispanismo may even have helped prepare the way for the cooperation that some conservatives and liberals entered upon during the second republic in their common desire to protect, this time not Spanish America, but Spain itself against the menace, real or alleged, of "denationalization," materialism, utilitarianism, Marxism, and leveling social revolution.

9: LIBERALS AND CONSERVATIVES IN QUEST OF CULTURAL-SPIRITUAL TIES WITH SPANISH AMERICA, 1900–1930

Early Twentieth-Century Comments on the Lack of Cultural-Spiritual Ties

Spaniards, and for that matter all Europeans, complained Venezuela's Rufino Blanco-Fombona in 1909, were indifferent to or disdainful toward Spanish America. "They do not understand us, they do do not care about us. They report only our earthquakes and revolutions. It is as if we were to judge Spain only by its anarchist activities and Europe by the scandals of courtesans, the Dreyfus affair, and the homosexuality of German generals and princes."[1]

Writing three years before the Venezulan, Unamuno had described the situation in similarly bleak terms:

> I will tell you truthfully that here in Spain scarcely anyone interests himself in the affairs of Spanish America or regards the people of America as important. The men of letters scarcely ever open an American book. The newspapers of America, if they are received in Spain, are not read. This is the pure truth. . . . Those who talk the most about union with Spanish America usually do not know where Paraguay is or if Bogotá is an ocean port. . . .[2] Nor do Spaniards know anything of Spanish-American history in the period since independence; the only men of the new republics about whom they may have vague ideas are Juan Manuel de Rosas of Argentina, Dr. José Gaspar Rodríguez de Francia of Paraguay, and Gabriel García Moreno of Ecuador.[3]

Spaniards, Unamuno had further lamented, were as ignorant of the literature of Spanish America as they were of its history: "When I recommend the work of a Spanish-American author to a Spaniard, he replies, 'see here, this writer may be a shining light in America but here among us he would be just one of many, isn't it so?' "[4] Expressing his frustration and pessimism over the situation, Unamuno concluded he did not know what could be done to dispel the nearly total disdain in which the literary, artistic, and scientific production of Spanish America was held.

Undoubtedly the disdain in which many Spaniards held the culture of Spanish America arose from their attempt to repay in kind the contempt with which many Spanish Americans regarded Spain. Unamuno noted this contempt when he complained that those Spanish Americans who wished to praise him did so by saying he was "the least Spanish of those

185

now writing in Spain;" when they wished to insult him, they accused him of being "typically Spanish."[5]

A member of the Spanish aristocracy declared that he never bothered to read historical works written in Spanish America because their sole purpose seemed to be to malign and insult Spain.[6] A Spanish journalist expressed a similar attitude, adding that most Spanish-American writers evidenced the desire to deny their ties of blood with Spain, considering the peninsula to be poor and backward and dismissing Spaniards as belonging to an inferior race.[7]

Colombians, at least, provided certain welcome exceptions to this pattern. Writing in 1907 a Spaniard noted that Colombian history textbooks, which once had instilled in the youth a spirit of hatred against Spain, were undergoing sweeping revision. Owing particularly to their bitter disillusionment with the United States occasioned by their loss of Panama, Colombians, the Spanish writer explained, were coming to understand that their true destiny lay in identifying with the values of Hispanic civilization. As a result they had acquired objectivity in their works of history and had begun to give due credit to the accomplishments of Spain in introducing a spirit, a soul, into the New World. Here was a hopeful development, the Spaniard concluded; for once Spanish Americans discarded their warped, prejudiced interpretations of the colonial period they would be ready to establish enduring cultural and spiritual ties with modern Spain.[8]

According to a conservative journalist, Spanish liberals could not be expected to participate in efforts to revise the history of the colonial period so as to present Spain in a more favorable light. Liberals, he asserted, were ever wont to denigrate their country's past and had thus been largely responsible for inspiring the unflattering opinions that most Spanish Americans held of the motherland.[9] To a considerable degree, however, the conservative observer proved to be wrong. Spanish liberals interested in hispanismo realized they could not establish cultural fraternity with Spanish Americans unless "the wall of hatred resulting from calumny and poisoned history" was torn down.[10] Just as energetically as conservatives, then, they set themselves to the task of refuting poisoned history and rectifying the so-called Black Legend, according to which Spaniards had been uniquely cruel in the conquest of America and singularly fanatical, despotic, and opposed to all cultural advances throughout the colonial period.

Spanish Conservatives and Liberals
Unite to Combat the Black Legend

Spanish conservatives had long recognized that "legend masquerading as history had been one of the main elements in preventing Spanish— Spanish-American rapprochement."[11] Even before the end of the nineteenth century Menéndez Pelayo set out to place the history of Spanish exploits in the New World in proper perspective. According to him Spaniards in America did for humanity what no other people had ever done: "they discovered a new world and offered it to God as an altar. Through the transmission of their blood, their language, their faith and their culture, they brought into being a new civilization." Spanish deeds, said Menéndez Pelayo, stood in stark contrast to those of other peoples who were interested in nothing save exploiting, enslaving, and killing less-developed human beings, whose imperial adventures were motivated solely by selfishness, who were not interested in converting newly discovered groups of men but only in carrying off the material wealth of virgin lands.[12] In 1912, the year in which Menéndez died, another conservative developed a similar theme: "The Spanish nation can rightly be proud of having carried to completion the most humanitarian colonization that any country has ever undertaken. . . . The Spanish colonization manifested from its beginnings a moral level much more elevated than that of other European colonizing nations; for it was always guided by . . . the Catholic, humanitarian spirit. . . ."[13]

In singing the praises of Spanish conquest and colonization, conservative authors often referred to the racial tolerance purportedly displayed by Spaniards in the New World. One of them asserted it was owing to Spanish civilization, with its foundation of Catholic humanitarianism and tolerance, "that some of those republics have had men of the colored race and of the castes as their governors, caudillos, poets, and business leaders."[14] Another maintained that Spain in the colonial period bequeathed to Spanish America the belief in racial equality, while "on the other hand the horrors of racial segregation, consequences of Protestant thought, were introduced into the United States by Anglo-Saxon colonization."[15]

The leading Spanish conservative historian in challenging the Black Legend—a term that he appears to have coined—was Julián Juderías y Loyot (1877-1918), a disciple of Menéndez Pelayo and the son of a literary figure who translated into Spanish some of the works of Thomas Macaulay. An expert linguist, who lived in many foreign lands to study their languages and social customs, Juderías in 1913 received a prize from the Madrid review La Ilustración Española y Americana for a work entitled Leyenda negra y la verdad histórica. A revised and expanded version in book form, published in Madrid in 1914, bore the title La leyenda negra y la verdad histórica: contribución al estudio del concepto de España en Europa, de las causas de este concepto y de la tolerancia política y religiosa en los países civilizados.[16]

In the expanded version of his work Juderías dealt not only with the enlightened policies of Spanish colonialism in America; he considered in addition the character of the Spanish raza, the evolution of the Spanish people during the Middle Ages, Spain's domestic and foreign policies of the sixteenth and seventeenth centuries, and the contributions of Spaniards during those and subsequent centuries to literature, the arts, and sciences.

In the words of Juderías, his work on the Black Legend found its inspiration in the ambition to prove "that the great work of Spain through the centuries, its contributions to civilization and progress, is not matched by the history of any other people."[17] Indignant that many of the studies dealing with Spain and its American colonization had been written by foreigners with an obvious anti-Spanish bias, he had, he said, set out to prove both to Spaniards and Spanish Americans that they could be proud of the past accomplishments of Hispanic peoples and optimistic about the future of the raza.[18]

By the time the Juderías work appeared, Spanish liberals had become just as convinced as the conservative historian that there could be no cultural-spiritual unity with the New World unless Spanish Americans were weaned away from the Black Legend and made to feel pride and satisfaction in the Spanish accomplishments of the colonial era.[19] During the year 1914, for example, Cultura Hispano-Americana, the periodical published by the liberal-oriented Centro de Cultura Hispano-Americana, presided over by Luis Palomo, published a series of articles aimed at refuting the Black Legend. Its efforts at historical revisionism stemmed, in the words of Palomo, from a recognition of the fact "that in order to achieve Hispano-American fraternity it is indispensable that our brothers on the other side of the Atlantic begin to discard and reject all the calumnies against the name of Spain that have been raised in a spirit of envy and to understand that the civilizing work of Spain, although not perfect, was superior to that of any other nation of the world."[20]

The following year Rafael María de Labra eulogized the "humanitarian nobility" of the Laws of the Indies and maintained that Spain's colonizing ventures were carried out on a higher moral level than those of any other country.[21] He further insisted that throughout the colonial period Spain was concerned not just with material and economic objectives in America; its principal preoccupation lay with spiritual considerations, for it desired to give to the New World its own beliefs and values. Labra exhorted his Spanish readers to continue this work begun in the sixteenth century; but he conceded that Spaniards could anticipate little success in this mission unless Spanish Americans came to respect the unique contributions made to the New World by Spain during the colonial period.[22]

Particularly in dealing with the Laws of the Indies, conservatives and liberals tended to speak with one voice as they praised Spain's colonial achievements in America.[23] Thus a conservative spokesman wrote: "An opinion contradicted by no one, and one that can in consequence be elevated to the category of uncontested truth, is that the laws which Spain gave to its overseas possessions are one of the most glorious monuments in its national history."[24] And liberal hispanoamericanista Rafael Altamira declared: "One of Spain's greatest contributions to the world's progress has been that it recognized, as no other civilization, the human rights that correspond to so-called inferior peoples; the Laws of the Indies are the highest example of paternalistic and tutelary legislation."[25]

One of the features of the Laws of the Indies that most appealed to Spain's hispanoamericanistas, be they conservative or liberal, was the formula they contained for keeping all citizens in their proper station within a hierarchically organized, paternalistic social structure. And, although Spaniards liked to stress their universalism and lack of racial prejudice in their imperial experience, they could at the same time praise the wisdom of colonial legislators in devising an order that was to some degree a "pigmentocracy," with men of color, aside from a few exceptional ones to whom channels of upward social mobility were never completely closed, confined to the lower strata of the social pyramid.[26] Conservatives and liberals alike also tended to praise the corporativist provisions of the Laws of the Indies as an inspired formula for guaranteeing tranquility and harmony. If Spanish Americans wished to avoid social revolution, Spanish apologists of the Laws of the Indies clearly inferred, then let them be guided by the wisdom of the colonial legislators who had best understood how to establish and maintain organic stability in an ethnically heterogeneous and socially gradated society.[27]

Demonstrating a considerable spirit of collaboration, Spanish conservatives and liberals came together with numerous representatives from the New World republics in 1912 to celebrate the first centennial of the Cádiz constitution. At the festivities to which Argentina and Peru sent former presidents, José Figueroa Alcorta and Andrés Cáceres respectively, Spanish liberal statesman Segismundo Moret pleased conservatives by stating he always insisted upon the instruction of his children "in their holy religion." Moret also maintained that the 1812 Cádiz constitution had not been antireligious in its provisions; Spaniards and Spanish Americans recognized then, as they still did, he asserted, that in order to unite in defense of liberty, they had ever to defend their faith and creed.[28]

Numerous orators took advantage of the assembly to stress not only the laudable feature of the constitution, but to strike a blow against the Black Legend by pointing with pride to Spain's overall accomplishments in America during the entire colonial period.[29] At the conclusion of the celebration, a Cádiz periodical called upon Spaniards of all political persuasions to continue their efforts toward reaching an understanding with "those peoples across the sea who proceed from the same origin, who speak the same language, who share credit with us for the uniquely enlightened achievements of the colonial period, and whose destinies must in the future be linked to Spain's for the good of humanity and its progress."[30]

Spanish conservatives and liberals continued their efforts to dispel the Black Legend at the First, Second, and Third Congresses of Hispano-

American History and Geography held at Sevilla in 1914, 1921, and 1930 respectively. At the 1914 congress, Colombian delegate Luis Herrera presented a paper defending Spanish treatment of the Indians in America and picturing Spain as having worked constantly for the good of her colonies.[31] Understandably, Spaniards responded warmly to Herrera's paper. They were gratified also by two resolutions that the 1914 congress adopted. The first declared that Spain as a nation "was not responsible for the excesses committed during the American conquest and colonization." The second proclaimed that Spanish colonial policy had protected the Indians and had been conducive to "the progress of the colonies."[32]

At the Second Congress of Hispano-American History and Geography, whose sessions were devoted about equally to propaganda and serious papers,[33] delegates approved a resolution urging Spanish-American governments to provide public school courses that set forth "justly and adequately" the history of Spanish conquest and colonization. By dispelling error, the resolution concluded, the way would be prepared for achieving a spiritual communion among the Hispanic peoples of the world.[34]

The first of the congresses lent impetus to the founding in 1914 of the Centro de Estudios Americanistas, housed in the Archivos Generales de las Indias building and affiliated with the University of Sevilla. The purpose of the Center was to promote historical research by Spanish and Spanish-American scholars in the Archivos, described by one enthusiastic hispanoamericanista as "the bank where Spain had on deposit its titles to ownership over the spirit of America."[35] During its early years, the Center led a precarious existence. In 1919, for example, the Spanish government curtailed the modest subvention to the research institution, apparently for no other reason than that a Catalan, who saw no need to spend public funds on cultural activities centered in Sevilla, replaced an Andalusian as minister of public instruction.[36]

The cause of refuting the Black Legend in the interests of hispanismo may not have been sufficiently compelling to induce Spaniards to put aside regional prejudices. To a surprising degree, however, this cause did produce unity of action among conservatives and liberals. And, as they united to revise the prevailing interpretations of the history of Spain's conquest and colonization of America, the peninsula's hispanoamericanistas, regardless of politico-ideological commitments, came to agree that the culprit primarily responsible for the inception of the Black Legend was Bartolomé de las Casas, the sixteenth-century Dominican who in order to awaken the conscience of the crown to the need for protecting the Indian races had, allegedly, wildly exaggerated the cruelty of the early conquistadores.

According to Menéndez Pelayo, Las Casas was "violent and asperous in his mental condition; irascible and choleric in his temperament; intractable and rude in the fanaticism of his school; hyperbolic and intemperate in his language, a mixture of scholastic pedantry and brutal injustices. . . .

Such was the ferocious controversialist whom some . . . would convert into a reasonable man and a philanthrophist." While Menéndez admired the concern of Las Casas for the Indian, he contended that the Dominican could have achieved his purpose without having blackened the reputation of Spain. A patriotic Spaniard, the conservative idealogue inferred, would never have permitted the publication of reports on Spanish cruelty, even had they been true. But, because Las Casas did publish his accounts and because they were eagerly seized upon by all enemies of Spain, "the patria has had to pay very dearly for the glory of having produced a philanthrophist."[37]

Luis Palomo agreed wholeheartedly with Menéndez Pelayo's views on Las Casas. The Dominican's lying histories, according to the director of the Centro de Cultura Hispano-Americana, had for centuries contributed to the campaign of defamation conducted against Spain by its enemies throughout the world; what is more, they were responsible for the unfavorable image of Spain in Spanish America. Thus, he contended, a primary goal of all concerned with a cultural-spiritual approximation between Spain and the former colonies must be the destruction of the exalted reputation that Las Casas continued to enjoy in Spanish America as a historian and philanthropist.[38]

The Impact of the Anti-Black Legend Campaign in Spanish America

Spanish emigrant colonies often assumed a key role in extending to America the campaign to refute the Black Legend so as to prepare a climate of opinion conducive to the flourishing of hispanismo. In 1904, for example, Spaniards living in the Buenos Aires area inaugurated an annual series of *juegos florales* in which prizes of gold or silver flowers were awarded authors of the best essays or poems glorifying Spanish colonial traditions. The distinguished jury selected to judge the contest was presided over by Roque Saenz Peña, long identified with pro-Spanish and anti–United States sentiments and destined to serve as his country's president between 1910 and his death in 1914.[39] Joaquín V. González, rector of the University of La Plata and the man who would prove to be one of the staunchest supporters of the Altamira and Posada cultural missions, served as a member of the jury.[40] The following year, 1905, the Casino Español, an association of the Spanish community in Habana, Cuba, paid for the preparation and publication of a Spanish edition of Edward Gaylord Bourne's *Spain in America*, a revisionist work of fundamental importance by a Yale University professor who presented the Spanish colonial period in a favorable light.[41] Spaniards resident in Habana also instituted the annual Juegos Florales Hispanoantillanos and by the 1920s these literary contests, which rewarded both Spaniards and Spanish

Americans for writing kindly about the Spanish past and extolling the spiritual ties that united members of the Hispanic raza, had become social and cultural events of major importance.[42] Similar functions were performed by the corresponding chapters of the Real Academia Española de la Lengua, commissioned in 1919 by the mother organization in Madrid to award annual prizes to the literary works that best demonstrated appreciation for Spanish values and the correct use of the Castilian tongue.[43]

For their efforts in behalf of hispanismo Spanish emigrants and those who supported them in the peninsula were rewarded with indications that some Spanish Americans at least were coming gradually to reject the legend of Spain's cruelty and depravity during the colonial period. When a Costa Rican writer, upon the occasion of his country's independence day in 1917, published an article insulting to Spain, a fellow Costa Rican, Hernán S. Peralta, retorted with a series of articles. In his passionate defense of the Spanish colonial period and Spain's cultural legacy in America, Peralta made frequent references to the revisionist works of United States historians Edward Bourne and Charles F. Lummis[44] and praised the Latin American studies program at the University of California for its efforts in repudiating the Black Legend. The delighted Spanish community of San José quickly financed the publication of the Peralta articles in the form of a short book.[45]

In the same year that Peralta sprang to the defense of the madre patria and the Spanish heritage, hispanismo won a major convert in Peru: Javier Prado y Ugarteche. One of Peru's leading social, intellectual, and political figures, Prado (1871–1921) as a young man had himself contributed to the Black Legend by publishing one of the most stinging indictments of the Spanish colonial past ever to appear in his country.[46] However, in a 1917 address before the Academia Peruana he acknowledged his mistakes, noted his indebtedness to the work of Juderías, and "presented such cogent arguments that no one from this time on can believe in the intellectual backwardness of the Spanish colonial period."[47]

Because many Spaniards regarded Argentina as the most important republic in Spanish America, indications that its intellectuals were rejecting the Black Legend caused particular satisfaction to hispanoamericanistas. And, beginning in the World War I period, leading Argentine figures afforded evidence of just such a rejection. Dr. Estanislao S. Zeballos, for example, an Argentine parliamentarian, former minister of foreign relations, and an influential university professor, came in for warm praise in a 1913 address by the president of the Real Academia Hispano-Americana of Cádiz. According to him, Zeballos was gradually rectifying the false history of the colonial period and helping to create a genuine affection for Spain among Argentines.[48] Returning from an Argentine lecture tour in 1916 the Spanish writer Mariano Belmás referred not only to Zeballos but also to Manuel Gálvez[49] and Carlos Octavio Bunge as eminent intellectuals active in dispelling the Black Legend in the rapidly developing young republic.[50]

In 1919 Spaniards were heartened when Argentine professor José Antonio Amuchástegui initiated a campaign to revise the teaching of history in his country's public schools so as to stress that the essence of Argentine life and character came from Spain, not France, Italy, or England.[51] They were further encouraged by the hispanista sentiments displayed by Roberto Levillier, who took advantage of his four-year diplomatic assignment in Spain (1918–1922) to conduct extensive research on the colonial period and who upon his return to Argentina became perhaps his country's most important historian in attacking the Black Legend.[52] Another Argentine historian converted to Hispanismo during the course of his research in Spain was Juan Carlos García Santillán. His work on Spain's sixteenth-century Indian legislation was described by Jesuit historian Constantino Bayle as "the kind of book that is necessary to establish close intellectual ties, the only basis for enduring Spanish–Spanish-American unity; it is a work based on true research, one that is moderate, objective, and judicious, not a panegyrical volume in the Lummis style, in which the general tone makes one suspicious as to its truthfulness."[53]

In spite of signs of an anti-Black Legend movement, a statement made by an Argentine in 1907 was probably as applicable in the 1920's as when originally made—and applicable not only to Argentina but to Spanish America as a whole. According to the Argentine, who regarded himself as a fervent Hispanophile, Spain's initial endeavors up to 1907 to revise the historical treatment of the colonial period had made a difference in his republic: "Until just a few years ago, Argentines hated Spain and Spaniards; now they just hold them in general disdain, while a few look with pity and compassion toward the old metropolis."[54]

Cultural Ties and the Book Trade

Spaniards concerned with hispanismo had always recognized the importance of an extensive exchange of books in creating ties of mind and spirit between Spain and Spanish America. And, with ample justification, they complained again and again, year in and year out, about the insignificance of the book trade between the peninsula and the Spanish-speaking republics of the New World.

Juan Valera commented in 1890 on the virtual impossibility of obtaining Spanish-American books in Spain; he observed that only because friends occasionally shipped him books did he come into possession of any Spanish-American publications.[55] Numerous delegates to the 1900 Hispano-American Congress held in Madrid referred to the urgent need to expand the book trade. Seven years later, though, a Spanish Augustinian serving in Colombia complained that Spanish America still imported virtually no books from Spain. Because of this, he asserted, Spain was almost totally unknown in the New World: "Spanish Americans seem to think that Spain is concerned only with fiestas and bullfights. They do not know that our nineteen million inhabitants have major industries; that within a short period of years our production of cereals, wines, oils, livestock, fabrics, and other products has quadrupled and quintupled."[56]

The situation continued to be as bleak in 1910 when Spanish America imported an estimated 40 million pesetas worth of books, only 5.7 million of which came from Spain. Worse still, according to one concerned observer, Spanish presses had a bad reputation, one that was well-earned, for defrauding Spanish-American authors.[57] Two years later a prominent Cuban complained that no Spanish–Spanish-American book trade worthy of the name existed.[58] And in 1915 a prominent official of the Centro de Cultura Hispano-Americana noted that although Spain during the preceding year had produced books worth 67,582,751 pesetas, the value of books exported to Spanish America had amounted only to 7.5 million pesetas.[59]

A considerable increase in the book trade did occur during the World War I period and in 1922 the Spanish government moved to consolidate these gains by creating the Cámara Oficial del Libro de Barcelona to act as a central clearinghouse of information in stimulating the exchange of books between Spain and Spanish America.[60] The following year book fairs were held in Barcelona, Madrid, Sevilla, and Oviedo in the hopes of augmenting the sale of Spanish books in foreign markets. Also in 1923 the press association of Santander sought to enhance interest in literary contact between Spain and the New World by organizing a contest exclusively for Spanish-American authors. The prize of 25,000 pesetas went to the Venezuelan poet Andrés Eloy Blanco.[61] By the mid-1920's, moreover, a well-established Spanish novelist could count upon selling as many copies of his books in Spanish America as in Spain.[62]

According to one of the closest students of the Spanish–Spanish-American book exchange at this time, however, the situation was still disappointing. True, the author conceded, the net value of books exported by Spain to Spanish America in 1925 came to just under 50 percent of the total net value of books published in the peninusla;[63] but Spain exported nearly exclusively works of literature while other countries sent scientific works and textbooks. "Our books," he stated, "entertain the Spanish Americans but do not teach or educate them."[64] It was particularly damaging to the cause of hispanismo, he asserted, that Spanish America imported history textbooks written mainly by Englishmen, North Americans, Germans, and Frenchmen with notorious anti-Spanish prejudices. Textbooks, he added, "are the best instrument that a country can utilize to exercise a spiritual ascendency. . . . Spain has virtually none of this market in Spanish America. That is why the Black Legend continues there."[65]

Cultural Ties and the Origins of Exchange Programs, 1910–1914

By 1910, distinguished Spanish visitors were somewhat less a rarity than they had been throughout most of the years since the attainment of independence in Spanish America.[66] In 1907 the well-known political figure Alejandro Lerroux, a leader of Spain's moderate, pragmatic left, visited Argentina. The following year Vicente Blasco Ibáñez, soon to gain international fame as one of Spain's foremost novelists, presented a series of conferences in Argentina and Chile; and in 1909 the eminent poet Juan Antonio Cavestany lectured in the New World on the need for closer cultural ties between Spain and Spanish America. Generally concluding his lectures with the reading of some of his poems, Cavestany received an enthusiastic response in Mexico (where President Díaz was in the audience), Cuba, Guatemala, Chile, and Argentina. El Heraldo de España, the Spanish-colony newspaper in Santiago de Chile, commented: "In recent times Spain has sent us Altamira, Blasco Ibáñez and Cavestany. We prefer the last to the others."[67]

When Spanish America celebrated in 1910 the centennial of the inception of its independence movement a new spirit of rapprochement with the madre patria was much in evidence[68] and Spain was represented at the festivities by a distinguished group of emissaries. Alfonso XIII's aunt, the Infanta Isabella, headed the Spanish delegation to the centennial ceremonies in Buenos Aires.[69] The Marqués de Polavieja, a distinguished military and political figure who had sought a policy of conciliation with Cuba in the 1890's, led the Spanish mission to Mexico. Reportedly, he received the warmest reception of any of the foreign dignitaries. As proof of the cordial relations prevailing between Spain and Mexico, Polavieja, in the name of Alfonso XIII, decorated President Díaz with the chain of the Order of Charles III.[70]

Heading the Spanish delegation to Venezuela was Aníbal Morillo, a grandson of General Pablo Morillo, who had commanded the royalist forces against Simón Bolívar's patriot armies. In 1820 General Morillo had exchanged an abrazo with Bolívar at Santa Ana as the two leaders agreed on the terms of a cease-fire. In connection with the centennial celebration the Spanish community in Venezuela, through the Asociación Patriótica Española, presented to the government of the republic a statue depicting the two military leaders in their famed abrazo. As General Morillo's grandson looked on, the governor of the federal district of Caracas accepted the statue as a fitting symbol of "the origins of the close cordiality that today exists between noble Spain and the people of Venezuela."[71]

It was well and good for Spain to send important personages to Spanish America on notable state occasions and for the one-time colonies and metropolis to engage in gestures of mutual respect and affection in commemorating historical events. But the Spanish community in Buenos Aires

rightly perceived that enduring effects could result only from institutional-
izing cultural exchange programs on a permanent basis. As its small contribution toward this objective it arranged in 1914 to finance through its
newly created Institución Cultural Española a Menéndez Pelayo chair in
the University of La Plata. To fill this chair the Institution hoped each year
to bring a distinguished Spanish intellectual to present a lecture course
dealing with some aspect of Spain's cultural achievements, past or present.
These courses were inaugurated by Ramón Menéndez Pidal, previously
a visitor to Colombia, Peru, Chile, Argentina, and Uruguay in search of
"romances of the Spanish type written in America,"[72] who lectured on
Menéndez Pelayo and the revisions he had made in his own writings in
the unrelenting search for truth.[73] In the same year Spain was represented
both in Argentina and Chile by Vicente Gay, a young, conservative professor at the University of Valladolid who subsequently would devote
much of his energies to the attempt to refute the Black Legend.[74] Gay
presented a series of university conferences and returned to Spain with
glowing impressions of Spanish America and of hispanismo's future.[75]

As of 1916, cultural exchange programs, financed with difficulty by private organizations, had touched off no massive wave of interest in Spain
among Spanish Americans. As proof of this one of Spain's dedicated hispanoamericanistas observed in deep frustration that in all Spanish America
there were only thirty-eight corresponding members of the Real Academia
Española.[76] Nevertheless, during World War I privately supported cultural
exchange programs between Spain and the former colonies underwent
considerable expansion. As a result, more than a few Spaniards were
encouraged to believe that a lasting basis for cultural-spiritual copenetration had at last been established.

Hispanismo during the World War I Period

When at the outbreak of the war a government presided over by Eduardo Dato proclaimed Spain's neutrality and when a majority of Spanish-
American administrations opted for neutral status,[77] a rare opportunity
seemed at hand for proponents of hispanismo. The peace-loving nations
of the great Hispanic family could, it was believed, by defying pressures
from the traditional centers of world power and maintaining a strict
neutrality, take a giant stride toward a permanent moral and even political
union that would guarantee them great-power status in the postwar
world.[78] Even the usually realistic Conde de Romanones, president of the
council of ministers between 1915 and 1917, was beguiled by this dream.
The time had at last arrived, he asserted, when Spain could "aspire to preside over the moral confederation of all the nations of our blood."[79]

The neutrality pursued by the leading nations of Hispanic America
was particularly gratifying to Spanish conservatives for it reflected, in their

judgement, an anti–United States spirit and a desire to escape once and for all from the subordinate position to which they had been relegated by Pan-Americanism.[80] Ever convinced that the rise of hispanismo depended upon the decline of Pan-Americanism, conservatives applauded the anti-Yankee sentiments to which in large degree they attributed the neutrality of Mexico, Chile, and Argentina.[81] One of them, for example, announced that the Hispanophile convictions of Argentine President Hipólito Irigoyen (1916–1922) were proved by his hatred of the United States, which had inspired his intransigent insistence upon neutrality.[82] Conservatives also liked to believe that the neutrality of the New World republics arose from their pro-German feelings. Although the majority of Spanish conservatives approved their country's neutral stance, they made little effort to disguise the fact that their sympathies lay with Germany rather than with liberal, anticlerical France. Undoubtedly the role of the United States in ultimately swinging the tide of battle in favor of France and the Allies "in a foolish crusade for democracy"[83] served to intensify conservative dislike of the New World Colossus.[84]

Spanish liberals on the other hand, although generally agreed on the advantages of neutrality,[85] leaned more often than not toward the Allied cause.[86] Thus the world conflict to some degree heightened divisions among Spanish conservatives and liberals, preventing them from taking optimum advantage of the neutrality maintained by the leading nations of the Hispanic family to wage a concerted campaign in the interests of hispanismo. However, hispanoamericanistas by no means totally neglected the opportunities presented them during the course of the war.[87]

New periodicals dedicated to the purposes of hispanismo appeared in confusing abundance and old ones flourished as never before.[88] Closely following the completion of hostilities still another review was founded, Raza Española.[89] In its first edition Blanca de los Ríos de Lampérez explained that the times were uniquely propitious for establishing close ties between Spain and Spanish America. She quoted with approval the assertion of Argentine intellectual Calixto Oyhuela that one could not be integrally American without being integrally Spanish;[90] and she added that one could not be fully Spanish without simultaneously feeling Spanish American. Concluding her article she stated: "our [common] nationality is a nationality of raza. All of this great family, which is nourished by our spirit as embodied in our language, all this vast geographic world . . . comprises our raza . . . : the Hispanic raza, one and integral, united and animated by the . . . spiritual essence of its glorious and magnificent language and called to the highest of destinies in the very near future."[91]

By the end of the war Rafael Vehils, a leading figure among the Barcelona businessmen who had for years struggled to augment Spain's commercial and cultural ties with Spanish America, was so encouraged by recent progress that he thought the time had come to proceed toward political unification. He advocated the establishment of an interparliamentary committee to be comprised of representatives of the Spanish American legislatures and the Spanish Cortes. The committee, Vehils predicted, would quickly bind the Hispanic nations together on the basis of common objectives and policies in the international order. Apparently only three recognized Spanish-American personages expressed public support, but Vehils professed to be encouraged by the "enthusiastic New World response" to his proposal.[92]

A person certainly no less dedicated to hispanismo, Altamira, introduced a note of realism as World War I drew to a close. In spite of ties of language and a common past and in spite of the large and active colonies of Spanish emigrants in the New World republics and the marked hispanista orientation of many intellectuals there, he said, "Spain is losing ground in America."[93] Perhaps an important consideration inspiring this appraisal was the fact that notwithstanding a spirited campaign waged by virtually all Spaniards interested in hispanismo, the Spanish-speaking people of the New World seemed increasingly inclined to refer to their America as Latin rather than Spanish America. That Latin America was becoming the preferred denomination among people who should, according to peninsulares, have understood that they were Spanish Americans living in Spanish America constituted a serious setback to the hopes of hispanoamericanistas.

The Name Issue: Latin America or Spanish America

As early as 1888 Juan Valera had objected to the use by the Argentine poet Olegario Andrade of the term Latin America. The words Latin America, Valera wrote, offended him as a Spaniard and wounded him, "just as an old man would be wounded upon learning that his son, emancipated, rich, and with a bright future, living in a remote country and filled with well founded ambitions, had denied his paternal name. . . ." When those of Spanish origin in America call themselves Latin, Valera continued, "it is because of disdain for the blood that runs in their veins. The only common bond among the people of those lands cannot be found in what is Latin, but in what is Spanish."[94]

Not until the World War I period, however, did Spaniards manifest widespread opposition to the use of the term Latin America. At this time Menéndez Pidal and Mariano de Cavia, a university professor and journalist, joined in a largely successful campaign to have the Spanish press discard the offensive term.[95] Spain and Spain alone, they argued, had created the spiritual substance of the Spanish-speaking area of the New World; France and Italy had exercised only a superficial influence and therefore Latin America was not an accurate or acceptable denomination for the area.[96] A Spanish journalist asserted that French and Italian influence in

Spanish America was not only superficial but also antinational, directed toward diverting Spanish Americans from the true essence of their nationalisms.[97] Blanca de los Ríos de Lampérez reiterated this theme as she wrote: "Yes, if the peoples of our America . . . do not wish to deny themselves and us, the Catholic faith and the Hispanic tongue . . . they will maintain for the dignity and glory of our great family the name of Spanish America."[98]

In the 1920s Spaniards continued their efforts to suppress the term Latin America. At the 1921 Congress of Hispano-American History and Geography they gained passage of a resolution stating that the word Hispanic was the proper one to use when speaking of things common to Spain, Portugal, and Spanish and Portuguese America.[99] The following year an editorial writer for the periodical La Unión Hispano-Americana contended that the campaign in favor of the Latin American denomination was being waged by France and Italy in the hopes of persuading the New World republics to regard close ties with the Latin countries of Europe as their best defense against United States imperialism. The writer warned Spain's overseas brothers not to fall into this trap. Spain, he said, alone among the countries of Europe, was not the puppet of the United States; therefore the only source of protection against the expansionist tendencies of the Colossus lay in Spanish–Spanish-American unity.[100]

An influential political leader, alarmed at the increasing use of Latin America in the New World, reasserted in 1924 the claims long advanced by Spain in the name dispute. Spanish America, he insisted, owed its formation, its character, its attitudes and values exclusively to Spain: "It was Spain that planted the seeds out of which all Spanish Americans have sprung. . . . It was not the Latin, it was only the Spanish raza that shaped the continent that now amazes the world with its civilization and wealth."[101] Two years later a Spanish writer denounced the efforts of the Italian colony in Argentina to gain universal employment of the term Latin America. These efforts, he charged, arose from commercial greed; and he objected with particular indignation to the manner in which Italians in serving their avaricious purposes sought to "downgrade our literature, theater and actors, and our music."[102]

Spaniards objected further to Italian attempts to wrest some of the glory from Spain on the annual celebration of the October 12 fiesta de la raza by stressing Columbus's Genoan origins.[103] It may well have been resentment over Italian attempts to share with them some of the credit for the Columbus expedition, and to advance the national origins of Columbus as justification for referring to the area he discovered as Latin America, that drove some Spaniards to the endeavor to prove that the intrepid navigator was born in Spain.[104] At the 1930 Third Congress of Hispano-American History and Geography the Spanish priest Adrián Sánchez, according to a fellow clergyman, the Jesuit historian Pedro Leturia, "showed care neither for scientific methodology nor for the correctness of conduct that should be followed at a scientific congress" as he petulantly insisted that Columbus was born in Extremadura.[105]

As was often the case in the pursuit of the objectives of hispanismo, Spaniards in their attempt to convince Spanish Americans on a particular point succeeded only in convincing themselves. By the mid-1920's the Spanish-speaking peoples of the New World preferred in a large majority to designate themselves Latin Americans. Spaniards grudgingly acknowledged this fact,[106] even as they continued to insist upon referring to members of their raza across the sea as Spanish Americans.

Hispanismo and Cultural Exchange in the Early 1920s

In the years immediately following World War I Spain continued to send distinguished political delegations to join with Spanish Americans in commemorating auspicious historical events. In 1920, for example, the government appointed a delegation, whose members included the Infante Ferdinand, to represent Spain at the fourth centennial of the Spanish passage through the Straits of Magellan which was being celebrated in Chile. José Francos Rodríguez, a novelist, dramatist, and theater critic as well as an important liberal politician, headed the mission that made official visits to Panama, Argentina, and Uruguay in addition to Chile. Francos was delighted to discover that "there is something of Spain in every aspect of Spanish America; Spanish Americans are constantly aware of Spain and have never discarded their ties of loyalty to the old metropolis."[107] Particularly encouraging to him was an assembly in Valparaíso where some twenty thousand Chileans, "mainly of the working classes," filled the principal plaza to render homage to Spain and Alfonso XIII.[108]

The Francos mission, with its uninterrupted series of banquets and lavish receptions, probably contributed less in a fundamental way to the purposes of hispanismo than the less spectacular and indeed rather plodding efforts that the Unión Ibero-Americana continued to wage. By 1921 the Union sent an annual average of over 83,000 pieces of correspondence to Spanish America as it carried on its campaign to strengthen cultural and commercial ties.[109] At this time the Union's little-heralded activities received unusual recognition from a Spanish American. Víctor Raúl Haya de la Torre, president of the Federación de Estudiantes of Peru and later the founder and head of the Alianza Popular Revolucionaria Americana (APRA), which had an indigenista and therefore an anti-Spanish orientation, hailed the Union "whose work is looked upon by the young generations of the old Spanish viceroyalty with the most fervent sympathy." The youth of Peru, Haya continued, saluted the Union for its labors in behalf of the "ample and effective spiritual unity of the peoples of the Columbian continent with the glorious Spain that lives in our blood."[110]

In 1921 the Real Academia de Ciencias Morales y Políticas, acting at last on a suggestion made by its secretary Eduardo Sanz y Escartín in 1909, began to confer corresponding status on various Spanish-American organizations. The first association to receive this status was the Academia Católica de Ciencias Sociales de la Habana, presided over by the Cuban university professor Mariano Aramburo, a corporative state advocate much admired by Spanish Catholic Action leaders.[111] By conferring corresponding rank on New World associations, the Real Academia, founded in 1885 to study the social problem in Spain and devise means for preserving stability and order, hoped to contribute to a joint Spanish–Spanish-American endeavor to contain the threat of leveling revolution.[112] In the same year of 1921 Spain made another move to assist Spanish Americans in the maintenance of order by sending a mission of the Guardia Civil to train and reorganize the police of Peru.[113]

All the while the Institución Cultural Española of Buenos Aires continued its little-publicized but nonetheless effective work begun in 1914. It brought Ortega y Gasset to Argentina in 1916 to occupy the Menéndez Pelayo chair at the University of La Plata for a series of lectures. In subsequent years it arranged for the coming of such distinguished Spaniards as the dramatist Jacinto Benavente, the essayist Eugenio d'Ors, the historian Américo Castro, the mathematician Julio Rey Pastor, the medical doctor and physiologist Augusto Pi y Suñer, and the gynecologist-obstetrician Sebastián Recaséns.[114]

Unhappily, a number of unauthorized Spanish lecturers also appeared in Spanish America, claiming status as eminent men of letters or science and demanding huge fees for conferences. Sometimes these lecturers persuaded the Spanish colonies to meet their exorbitant honorarium demands and then proceeded to set the cause of hispanismo back by delivering discourses of such low quality as to drive most listeners from the auditorium. *Unión Ibero-Americana* reported that one of the worst offenders in this regard was a certain Carlos Angulo Cavadra, who wandered through Spanish America posing as a representative of the Union, collecting inflated fees from unsuspecting Spanish-community associations, and then offering presentations in which he read his "dreadful verses, which seemed to be the result of mental aberrations," or pronounced discourses "as empty of ideas as they were full of commonplaces." To make the matter worse, the journal charged, the self-styled savant generally concluded his appearances by insulting Spain; at this point, though, only a few members of the audience were still on hand to hear the defamatory remarks.[115]

In the post–World War I era Spanish-American respresentatives, fortunately officially authorized ones, began to appear more regularly in Spain. A large group of prestigious Spanish Americans came to Madrid in 1920 in connection with a postal congress that achieved notable success in its efforts to lower postal rates and make them uniform among the nations of

the Hispanic world. Among the many organizations holding special receptions for the Spanish Americans was the Real Academia Española de la
Lengua, presided over at the time by Antonio Maura. On this occasion
Maura presented an eloquent address filled with sentiments of hispanismo.[116] Two years later Argentine president-elect Marcelo T. de Alvear
visited Santander, San Sebastián, and Vigo, delivering some of the pronouncements undoubtedly expected of him. Argentina, he said on one
occasion, was also Spain, because "in it the madre patria has left something of its soul."[117]

Spanish intellectuals, fearing that only superficial results ensued from
missions that were primarily political, diplomatic, and ceremonial in
nature, anticipated more lasting benefits from programs that attracted
Spanish Americans to Spain to pursue their university studies. In 1919
the Asociación de Amigos de la Universidad, made up mainly of conservative University of Madrid professors and directed by Adolfo Bonilla y
San Martín, urged the government to establish a program of scholarships
for Spanish-American students.[118] In response to this and several other
similar requests, the government in 1921 resolved to set aside 100,000
pesetas each year for this purpose. It initiated the program by awarding
twenty-five scholarships to students from Argentina, Bolivia, Chile, Colombia, Costa Rica, Cuba, the Dominican Republic, Ecuador, El Salvador, Guatemala, Honduras, Mexico, Nicaragua, Panama, Paraguay, Peru,
Uruguay, and Venezuela.[119]

In spite of this beginning, Altamira and Posada, precursors of Spanish–
Spanish-American exchange programs, and numerous of their professor
colleagues continued to complain that the government made little more
than token gestures, leaving the main burden of encouraging cultural flow
in either direction between Spain and America to private initiative.[120]
Complaints of this type seemed to produce results during the Primo de
Rivera regime as the dictator took important steps to extend government
support to cultural exchange.

Hispanismo and Cultural Exchange during
the Primo de Rivera Dictatorship

Late in 1925 Primo de Rivera made public a brief exposition in which
he urged that the present political section within the ministry of state be
subdivided so that there would be one section specifically concerned with
America and another to deal with the rest of the world. Creation of an
American political section, Primo argued, would provide an agency for
augmenting and channeling government endeavors to improve cultural
relations. "It is in the sphere of culture," the Spanish strongman continued, "that the sister peoples of the same raza ought to maintain their
closest interchange. The language constitutes a very powerful bond of

union between peoples; but it does so only when it serves as a vehicle of spiritual communication and when the raza maintains intact its common mentality and ties of culture . . . its elevated and generous moral sense, which transcends the individual differences among sovereign political personalities."[121]

Alfonso XIII acted upon Primo de Rivera's request on December 21, issuing a decree that subdivided the political section along the lines advocated by the dictator. Shortly thereafter the Spanish government added to the new American political section an office of information charged with providing for the exchange of reviews, periodicals, and general cultural information between Spain and Spanish America.[122]

In 1927 still another agency was added to the ministry of state, the Patronato de Relaciones Culturales. Awarded an initial subvention of 15,000 pesetas each year, the Patronato's prime objective was the fostering of cultural relations between Spain and Spanish America. Toward this end it was to bring the "leading cultural figures of America to Spain" and to organize schools for Spanish children and adults living in the New World republics. In this way the patriotism and "true Spanish spirit" of the emigrant colonies would be bolstered and overseas Spaniards would become more effective "cultural emissaries for the madre patria."[123]

Gradually expanding its activities, the Patronato de Relaciones Culturales created a Hispano-American professorship in the University of Madrid to be held each year by a prominent Spanish-American intellectual figure, established a professor exchange program between the Universities of Madrid and San Marcos in Lima, and encouraged with a small annual subvention the projects of the Federación Universitaria Hispanoamericana. Formed in 1925, this Federation—made up of the approximately 150 Spanish-American university students in Spain, most of whom were pursuing programs in law or medicine under grants either from the Spanish or their national governments—had as its objective the realization of a wider degree of "cultural copenetration" between Spain and America. Among its many activities, the Federation conducted an information service to encourage a larger number of Spanish Americans to study in Spain and published a periodical entitled *Patria Grande*.[124]

As a further indication of its interest in broadening cultural contact, the Primo de Rivera regime held the long-delayed Ibero-American Exposition in Sevilla. Although concerned primarily with fomenting trade and commerce, the 1929 exposition also included art and historical exhibitions and provided the occasion for many meetings between Spanish and Spanish-American intellectuals. Finally, the government slightly increased the subvention to the Unión Ibero-Americana, enabling it to augment the size and expand the coverage of its official review,[125] to establish corresponding associations in Spanish America,[126] and to send two or three lecturers each year to the New World.[127]

To the accelerating tempo of cultural exchange during the dictator-ship,[128] the revised journal of the Unión Ibero-Americana attributed the fact that Colombians chose the Spanish sculptor Julio González Pola to execute a monument in commemoration of the hundredth anniversary of the battle of Ayacucho, in which patriot armies had defeated Spanish forces in Peru at the end of 1824, thereby guaranteeing the success of the independence movement.[129] At the same time Peru's eminent Catholic intellectual and diplomat Víctor Andrés Belaúnde speculated upon the future effects of rapidly expanding cultural relations between Spain and Spanish America. The result, he said, seemed likely to be the triumph "of the supreme values of the spirit and of the ethical sense of life over the utilitarian philosophy of the Anglo-Saxons. . . ." The ocean divides Span-iards and Spanish Americans, he declared, "but there exists . . . the one great spiritual patria: our mother Spain."[130]

Contributing to the rapport between the one-time metropolis and colonies reported on by many observers both in the peninsula and the New World was Spanish America's mounting alarm over United States imperialism. Against this background many eminent Spanish intellectuals and politicians added their voices to those of Spanish Americans in pro-testing United States intervention in Nicaragua during the Coolidge administration.[131] And Spaniards applauded the various Spanish-American republics that challenged the Colossus in its interventionist pretensions at the 1928 Habana Pan-American conference. Expressing a hope then widespread in the peninsula, a Spanish journalist predicted the end of the entire Pan-American movement; its demise, he said, would guarantee the permanence of the spiritual rapprochement that had taken place between Spain and Spanish America.[132]

For years, various Spaniards had been urging a tour by Alfonso XIII through Spanish America. The king's presence there, they contended, would touch off such an explosion of hispanista sentiments as to doom once and for all the prospects of Pan-Americanism in the New World.[133] In many ways 1928 might have been the ideal year for a royal visit because of the rising tide of anti–United States feeling. However, the visit could not be undertaken, in part because the anti–Primo de Rivera campaign waged in Spanish America by many important Spaniards and frequently directed against the institution of monarchy itself had stimulated repub-lican sympathies among many members of the Spanish communities and also among numerous intellectual circles in Spanish America. Still, another type of Spanish mission, carried out in 1926 by four previously unknown Spaniards, was probably about as successful—at least for a few emotion-filled weeks—as a royal visit could have been in awakening His-panophile enthusiasm in Spanish America. The four Spaniards were Ramón Franco, Julio Ruiz de Alda, Manuel Durán, and Pablo Rada; and they evoked a tumultuous response in the Hispanic world by crossing the

Atlantic in a hydroplane christened the *Plus Ultra*.[134] The pilot on this flight was Ramón Franco, brother of the future caudillo of Spain.

The fliers, who touched first in Pernambuco, Rio de Janeiro, and Montevideo before proceeding to Buenos Aires, aroused the admiration of Spanish Americans, who regarded them as symbols "of a new Spain in which scientific progress is combined with traditional courage and valor."[135] According to one delighted Spaniard, the flight of the *Plus Ultra* joined Spain and Spanish America in "an effusive spiritual embrace;"[136] in the words of a Dominican Republic statesman, it meant "the boundaries between Spain and her American sisters have disappeared."[137] Throughout Spanish America local citizens joined with members of the Spanish communities in hailing the aviators and paying homage to the spiritual ties that the flight symbolized. Even in Mexico, whose relations with Spain were strained, the sudden demand for Spanish flags precipitated by the Atlantic crossing rapidly exhausted the supply.[138]

In Buenos Aires, 397 different Spanish-colony organizations of the Río de la Plata area collaborated in preparing the welcoming receptions, banquets, processions, and parades in honor of the four triumphant Spaniards. Then, with the celebration at its height, an incident occurred that offset to some degree the boon to hispanismo provided by the flight and proved that virtually no cause could induce Spaniards to put aside their political rancors and feuds.

Shortly after their reception in the presidential palace, the plaza in front of which was "so filled with deliriously happy people that they were in danger of crushing one another,"[139] the Spanish fliers received a telegram from the government in Madrid ordering them to terminate their flight in Buenos Aires and to return to Spain by ship. The *Plus Ultra* was to remain in Buenos Aires as a gift from the Spanish government to Argentina. Franco, who had expected to continue the flight to the other Spanish-American republics, was furious and made no attempt to hide the fact from journalists, some of whom reported that Primo de Rivera, allegedly jealous of the pilot, had decided to prevent him from being accorded a hero's welcome in additional Spanish-American countries. Other reports had it that radical political pronouncements made by the impetuous Franco had induced certain members of the conservatively inclined Asociación Patriótica Española, which claimed to be the Spanish community's most important association in Buenos Aires, to send a telegram to the Primo de Rivera regime urging the grounding of the *Plus Ultra* and its crew. Apparently Franco believed this account, for he referred to the Buenos Aires Spanish community as being "little worthy of our raza."[140] On his part Félix Ortiz y San Pelayo, for many years the major figure in the Asociación Patriótica Española, indignantly denied that any telegram had been sent.

Whatever the truth of the matter, the entire incident divided the Spanish community of Argentina more bitterly than ever into two camps, one rightist, prodictator and monarchical, the other leftist, antidictator, and republican. The controversy over the termination of the *Plus Ultra* flight also occasioned derisive treatment of Spain's government and its Buenos Aires community by the Argentine press.[141]

Two other Spaniards, Ignacio Jiménez and Francisco Iglesias, crossed the Atlantic in 1929, flying the hydroplane *Jesús del Gran Poder*. Again, an unfortunate incident marred the goodwill effects that should have resulted from this feat. The Spanish colony in Mexico, which had prepared a lavish reception for the fliers, who after visiting other republics of Spanish America were expected to end their flight in Mexico City, reacted with undisguised anger when Primo de Rivera ordered Jiménez and Iglesias to terminate their tour in Cuba. The handling of the matter, with the dictator offering a weak and unconvincing explanation, did little to improve relations between Spain and Mexico.[142]

The Weaknesses and Failures of Cultural-Spiritual Hispanismo

In 1926 a Spanish intellectual lamented that hispanismo had so far produced only empty lyricism and unfulfilled promises; as a result, no one really believed in the movement. Worst of all, he concluded, after years of attempting to establish cultural and spiritual ties, Spaniards and Spanish Americans still did not regard themselves as members of a common community.[143] In the same year one of Spain's most steadfast advocates of hispanismo reported that service as a military attaché in Spanish America had led to his discovery that Spanish books were still scarcely to be found in that part of the world. "Book dealers will not handle them and the newspapers do not report on them." Spanish art, he added, "in contrast to that of France and Italy, is unknown. And the same is true of Spanish musicians; Spanish Americans have never heard of them. When [Pablo] Casals went on tour in Spanish America he played to half-empty houses and expressed the wish never to return."[144] One year before this, in 1925, the Spanish mathematician Julio Rey Pastor, returning from Buenos Aires, where he had offered a course in his specialty, had reported that Italy and especially France enjoyed far greater prestige than Spain in cultural and intellectual circles. In the field of science, the mathematician had added, Germany was supreme and the only contribution made by Spaniards was to translate German sources for Spanish-American readers.[145]

In the early 1930s the author of one of the few regular news columns on Spanish America appearing in the Spanish press[146] indicated his discouragement. Spanish America, he declared, was as much as ever an unknown quantity in the peninsula. Spanish newspapers reported only the natural catastrophes, the political corruption, and the revolutions of the republics; consequently, "the Spanish-American diplomatic corps in Spain remains on the verge of despair."[147]

Apparently Spanish–Spanish-American cultural copenetration continued to be in the 1920's and early 1930s as distant and elusive an objective as when conceived by such men as Altamira and Posada in the early twentieth century. Spanish cultural missions to the New World had, it is true, become more numerous. Sometimes, though, they produced results decidedly counterproductive to the objectives of hispanismo; for those Spaniards who conducted them were as apt as not upon their return to publish accounts critical of and therefore highly resented in Spanish America.

Once back in Spain after lecturing in Buenos Aires on his specialty of economics, Luis Olariaga contended that Argentina had not made notable progress toward becoming a true nation or toward developing a higher culture. Part of the reason for this, he maintained, was that Argentina had chosen European utilitarianism as its favorite credo of life. "Utilitarianism has worked in Europe," the economist wrote, "only because it has a subcore of values, a firm foundation of beliefs and action patterns, out of which the ideology has emerged. Included in this foundation are habits of savings and sacrifice and the strength of character to curb conspicuous consumption. In importing only the end product of utilitarianism without its underlying values," the Spaniard observed, "Argentina has left itself dependent upon European capital, for it is Europe that has acquired the character necessary for capital formation."[148] Olariaga did not believe it likely that Argentina would quickly develop the character on which capital formation depended; therefore he regarded the bold pronouncements of economic nationalism made by some Argentines as empty rhetoric.

The comments of Olariaga stand as a penetrating analysis not only of Argentina but of Spanish America as a whole. Naturally enough, though, they caused deep resentment in Argentina and elsewhere in the Spanish New World.

Undoubtedly one of the main setbacks to the campaign to establish a cultural-spiritual community resulted from the inability of Spanish propagandists and serious historians to dispel the Black Legend in the New World republics. According to a Spanish priest writing at the end of 1926, "in spite of the magnificent flight of Ramón Franco and his three associates, which demonstrates the resurgent power of Spain, the historical textbooks of most Spanish-American countries continue to defame the madre patria by propagating the Black Legend."[149]

The twenty-sixth Congreso Internacional Americanista, held in Madrid in 1935, demonstrated the degree to which Spaniards and Spanish Americans still disagreed on the central figure in the Black Legend controversy, Bartolomé de las Casas. Rómulo Carbia, a professor of the Universities of Buenos Aires and La Plata and the first New World citizen to receive his doctorate in the history of America program at the University of Sevilla, was scheduled to present a paper on Las Casas at the October 20 plenary session. Well in advance it became known that the Argentine would seek to demonstrate that Las Casas had purposely falsified much of the data in his histories. Five days before the Carbia paper, various Spanish-American delegates began to deliver lavishly laudatory statements about Las Casas, sustaining his reliability as a historian and thus by inference manifesting their belief that the Black Legend was no legend. Upon every mention of the name Las Casas, numerous Spanish-American delegates burst into applause and this caused a Spaniard to arise and angrily proclaim that no one could take the Dominican seriously as a historian. Reporting on these incidents, Spanish Jesuit historian Constantino Bayle described how "a supposedly scientific congress was converted into a chamber of deputies."[150]

The historical revisionism undertaken by Juderías and many other writers contributed significantly to the mounting national pride of Spaniards as they struggled to regain confidence in the years following the 1898 disaster. In Spanish America, though, the Black Legend continued to live and to receive new stimulus, especially in such republics as Mexico and Peru, where strong indigenista movements appeared. Thus the climate for a cultural-spiritual reconciliation remained largely unpropitious.

Some Spaniards were in no manner surprised by the apparent failures of hispanismo as a cultural-spiritual movement. All along a group of intellectuals and businessmen had dismissed as "lyricism" every pronouncement on the cultural-spiritual ties that supposedly united the members of the Hispanic raza. According to those who disdained the lyricism of hispanismo, countries of common language and origin were as likely to live in conflict and warfare as in harmony and fraternal cooperation. The only meaningful ties of fraternity, they declared, were practical ones, based on commercial intercourse and economic self-interest. If Spain and Spanish America were ever to achieve relative unity, they insisted, it would be owing primarily to trade relations. Therefore in the years following the disaster they exhorted the government, the Spanish diplomatic corps, and the emigrant colonies in Spanish America to direct their energies toward realizing the practical objectives of hispanismo.

10: PRACTICAL HISPANISMO: TIES OF TRADE AND ECONOMIC INTEREST, 1900–1930

The Case for Practical Hispanismo

Writing in 1905 a Spaniard long noted for his interest in the New World rejoiced that lyricism, by which he meant a preoccupation with cultural-spiritual-racial ties, was giving way to a sense of reality in Spain's relations with Spanish America. "We have learned," he said, "that without the community of interest, the community of the raza serves for little or nothing. In commercial treaties and tariff agreements are to be found the means for achieving a community of interest toward which oratory, politics, and literature have never contributed significantly."[1] At about the same time a former minister of the treasury wrote: "Our relations with America have to be essentially commercial."[2] And a Catalan journalist-businessman declared: "The time has come for deeds, not words. Let financiers, industrialists, and merchants . . . take a role: deeds, not words, to realize the ideal of hispanoamericanismo so that the Spanish raza will come to have a decisive influence in the destinies of the world."[3] Summing up the views of the early twentieth-century advocates of practical hispanismo, a Barcelona journalist wrote: "Down forever with lyricism, with discourses, and with other 'intellectualities' that accomplish nothing because they do not correspond to the modern, eminently utilitarian spirit that infuses America."[4]

The years 1904 and 1905 witnessed the first important outbreak of anti-lyricism in the hispanismo movement.[5] For the next decade, though, anti-lyricists generally occupied a subordinate position, with proponents of cultural-spiritual bonds serving as the main spokesmen for hispanismo. Then at the time of World War I, when a uniquely opportune moment for augmenting Spanish–Spanish-American trade seemed to be at hand, the partisans of practical ties asserted themselves with renewed vigor. The Conde de Romanones, president of the council of ministers in 1916, seemed to place himself on their side when he stated: "There is only one base for developing the relations of one collectivity of peoples with others, and this base is practical interest. . . . Because we have not talked specifically in terms of interest, but have stressed the other factors that might link us to Spanish America, we find today that ours is the country in all of Europe that has the least influence in America."[6]

That Spanish liberals, concerned with material progress and generally the proponents of Europeanization following the disaster, should eschew lyricism and pronounce in favor of practical ties as the basis of hispanismo is in no way surprising. Canalejas seemed to be expressing the viewpoint logically to be expected of liberals when at the 1912 centennial celebration of the Cádiz constitution he maintained that "commerce is the basis of the most enduring ties" among nations.[7] However, the issue of whether hispanismo should be primarily a cultural-spiritual or a practical, economic movement did not produce a clear-cut division between liberals and conservatives. Many liberals, among them Altamira and González Posada, initially expressed more concern with the ties of spirit than with those of economic interest. And, although tending by and large to stress the ties of a common religious faith, conservatives by no means ignored the practical side of hispanismo. Conservative statesman Eduardo Sanz y Escartín, for example, declared that the notion of a spiritual community among the Hispanic nations of the world to oppose the expansionist tendencies of the United States could only make the practical leaders of Spanish America, such as Presidents Porfirio Díaz of Mexico, Pedro Montt (1906–1911) of Chile, and Julio Roca (1880–1886, 1898–1904) of Argentina, laugh in derision. "It is commercial relations that must be intensified," Sanz insisted, "if Hispanic unity is to become meaningful."[8] Moreover, when the short-lived Real Academia Hispano-Americana de Ciencias y Artes de Madrid was founded after the end of World War I, its largely conservative membership approved the suggestion of its president, Gabriel Maura (son of conservatism's leading statesman Antonio Maura), that discourses at all sessions be prohibited. Discourses, Maura and the membership maintained, were associated with the empty and discredited lyricism of hispanismo and not conducive to the forging of ties of economic interest and commerce. At all official sessions, therefore, Academy members could express themselves only through ordinary conversational means.[9]

If the issue of whether hispanismo should be principally a spiritual or a practical movement did not appreciably widen the gulf between the two ideological Spains, conservative and liberal, it did further separate the two geographic Spains, center and periphery. Spaniards of the periphery, especially of the industrialized port cities of Barcelona and Bilbao, tended to embrace the practical approach. They ridiculed the allegedly Quixotic endeavor of central Spaniards to establish a union with Spanish America that depended on nebulous ties of spirit and "the blood of the spirit," as Unamuno described the Castilian language. How, after all, could Catalans, Basques, and even Galicians be expected to respond appreciatively to the notion that language was a principal bond between Spain and Spanish America when so many of them were striving to suppress Castilian as the official language within their own regions?

What concerned civic leaders in the cities of Spain's periphery at the turn of the century was expanding trade with Mexico[10] and Spanish South America so as to offset the loss of the Cuban and Puerto Rican markets following the war with the United States.[11] Between 1891 and 1895 the annual average value of total trade between Spain and Cuba, exports and imports, had been in excess of 166 million pesetas (between 1890 and 1930 the value of the peseta fluctuated between approximately 7.5 and 5.5 to the dollar),[12] while the value of overall trade with Puerto Rico had averaged about 49.5 million pesetas. With both of these island possessions Spain at this time had enjoyed a substantial export balance of trade.[13] As of 1900, the value of total trade between Spain and Cuba was down to 62 million pesetas; between Spain and Puerto Rico it stood at 13 million.[14]

Little wonder that the Spanish diplomatic corps in Spanish America began in 1899 and 1900 a desperate search for new markets so as to make up for the staggering loss to Spanish commerce occasioned by the Treaty of Paris that definitively deprived Spain of Cuba and Puerto Rico, in addition to the Philippines.[15] Little wonder also that various patriotic associations of the Spanish communities in Spanish America intensified their efforts to open new channels of trade with the stricken motherland.[16] The main burden, though, of augmenting Spanish commerce with the New World following the disaster fell upon the businessmen of the Spanish periphery.

The Practical Hispanismo of the Periphery: Barcelona and Bilbao

By the beginning of the twentieth century Cataluña, particularly in its major city of Barcelona, had developed a thriving textile business that required foreign markets for its surplus production. Barcelona had also become a primary port for the shipping of Spanish oils. Moreover, in supplying emigrants to the New World, especially to Argentina, Cataluña was second only to Galicia. According to a Barcelona periodical, Catalans in 1904 made up some 30 percent of the Spaniards living in Argentina, estimated with considerable exaggeration at 400,000.[17] It was only natural, then, that Cataluña and especially the maritime center of Barcelona would be a focal point of Spanish commercial interest in Spanish America.

The periodical *Mercurio: Revista Comercial Hispano-Americana*, soon to emerge as the principal journal of practical, trade-oriented hispanismo, began publication in Barcelona in 1901, its principal founders being José Zulueta and Federico Rahola. Zulueta led the early twentieth-century liberal campaign in the national chamber of deputies to commit the government to a program of augmenting trade with Spanish America.[18] Rahola, a politician, businessman, and poet who became director of *Mercurio*, agreed with Zulueta that trade with Spanish America provided the only hope for "the regeneration of our commerce and agriculture."[19]

With the spirited support of many members of the Barcelona business community,[20] Zulueta, Rahola, and a colleague of theirs on the *Mercurio*

staff, José Puigdollers y Macía, undertook a mission to Argentina and
Uruguay at the end of 1903 for the purposes of gathering commercial
information, apprising industrialists and merchants in these two republics
of the possibilities of trade with Spain, and enlisting members of the
Spanish communities there in a campaign to increase imports from Spain.
As the three trade emissaries prepared in late November to embark on
the *Reina María Cristina,* they received from Liberal Party leader Raimundo Fernández Villaverde, then president of the council of ministers,
a telegram expressing his "ardent desires for the success of the interesting
undertaking to increase among those people whom we so much love the
consumption of our products. . . ."[21]

Once in Uruguay and Argentina, the three Spaniards attended a series
of receptions, banquets, and luncheons offered them by local political and
industrial leaders and by the various associations of the Spanish community; in addition the commercial ambassadors, as they called themselves,
visited dozens of factories. Wherever they went they repeated their message that if in the past Spain had been known by its heroism, it wanted
now to be known by its products.[22] The products they constantly referred
to as the ones most likely to make Spain favorably known in the New
World were oils, wines, textiles, canned foods, and iron.[23]

Returning home early in 1904, the Spanish trade promoters failed in
their endeavors to inaugurate commercial expositions and to establish a
permanent museum of Spanish and Spanish-American products.[24] To a
large degree, however, they succeeded in stimulating Catalan investment
in and emigration to Argentina. In addition, they helped spark a concerted Catalan challenge to the virtual Italian monopoly over the olive
oil market in that republic. As a result, Catalans managed, according to
Altamira, to gain the upper hand over their Italian competitors by the
outbreak of World War I.[25]

Following up on suggestions contained in two 1909 articles published
in *Mercurio* by Rafael Vehils, who was beginning to rank with Zulueta
and Rahola as a leading Catalan spokesman of hispanismo, a group of
Barcelona business and commercial leaders came together with many
Spanish Americans living in the city to found the Sociedad Libre de
Estudios Americanistas. The Society, which intended to hold study sessions, organize conferences, expositions, and information centers so as
to enlist more widespread public support for attempts to stimulate trade
between Spain and Spanish America, included on its board of directors
such distinguished hispanoamericanistas as Labra, Vehils, Zulueta, and
Rahola.[26] In 1910 the ministry of public instruction authorized Vehils to
undertake a mission to establish a loose confederation between the Society
and various other associations throughout Spain dedicated to the objectives of practical hispanismo. As a result, the Society entered into agreements to collaborate with groups in Valencia, Málaga, Bilbao, Cádiz,
Sevilla, Huelva, and Madrid.[27]

Meantime, owing to the efforts of the Puerto Rican José G. del Valle, a group of Spanish-American residents of Barcelona had come together to form the Club Americano. By organizing social events, holding classes, sponsoring concerts and founding a library, the Club provided opportunity for more contact between Spaniards and Spanish Americans. Soon the directors of the Club reached an accord with the Sociedad Libre de Estudios Americanistas to combine the two associations and as a result there came into being early in 1911 the Casa de América. In its first official function on March 10 it received the special emissary sent by Mexico, returning the official visit made by a Spanish delegation the previous year in connection with the republic's centennial celebration of the beginning of the independence movement.[28]

In September of 1911 the Casa de América named a delegation, headed by its secretary general Vehils and officially supported by the Spanish government, to visit Uruguay, Argentina, Paraguay, and Brazil in the attempt to expand trade between those countries and Spain. The Casa de América delegates spent some sixteen months on their trip, in the course of which they conversed with political and business leaders of Spanish America, collected books and pamphlets dealing with economic conditions and commercial laws, and established contact with numerous Spanish-colony organizations, especially chambers of commerce.[29] The Casa de América emissaries enjoyed a particularly warm reception in Uruguay, where President José Batlle y Ordóñez (1903–1907, 1911–1915), distantly related to Vehils, promised wholehearted cooperation in the endeavor to increase commerce with Spain.[30]

While other port cities, such as Vigo, Valencia, and especially Cádiz, looked with intense interest on the possibilities of expanding trade with the New World, it was the northern port of Bilbao, capital of the province of Vizcaya, that most nearly approximated Barcelona's ventures into the field of practical hispanismo. As with Barcelona, the interest of Bilbao in the New World was heightened by the number of residents from its hinterland who utilized its port facilities as they departed Spain in search of new opportunities in America. Between 1900 and 1917 an estimated 62,047 Vizcayans embarked at Bilbao, some 43,000 of them destined for Argentina and most of the remainder for Cuba and Chile.[31]

Bilbao, the heavy-industry center of Spain and the major city in an area that produced three-fourths of the peninsula's iron,[32] completed the construction of new port facilities in 1903. The following year exports to Spanish America, consisting mainly of wines, canned foods, and firearms destined for Cuba, Mexico, Uruguay, and Chile, reached a value of over eight million pesetas, while imports from Spanish America were valued at slightly more than seven million.[33]

By this time a group of Basque businessmen—headed by Julio de Lazúrtegui, who had studied mining and metallurgy in France, England, and Germany—had become convinced that the future of their region depended upon "the constant exchange of the products of their [Spanish America's] industries with ours."[34] To encourage this exchange the northern businessmen in 1904 founded the Centro de la Unión Ibero-Americana en Vizcaya.[35] Working through it and other agencies, the industrialists and merchants of the north succeeded to a considerable degree in increasing the commerce between Bilbao and Spanish-American ports. By 1912 the value of this trade stood at nearly forty million pesetas.[36] The northern businessmen failed, however, in their bid to obtain government support for an Ibero-American international exposition. By 1913 Sevilla had been chosen as the site for this exposition, which was delayed again and again and did not open until 1929. They failed also in endeavors to establish a Spanish–Spanish-American industrial-commercial museum and information center in Bilbao, in spite of the offer of José Rufino de Olaso, an important director of the Centro de la Unión Ibero-Americana en Vizcaya, to donate the land on which the museum could be constructed.[37]

Trade and Commerce between Spain and Spanish America, 1900–1913

With Barcelona and Bilbao providing much of the impetus, trade between Spain and Spanish America made solid but by no means spec-

CHART 1

SPAIN'S COMMERCE WITH ITS PRINCIPAL TRADE PARTNERS
IN SPANISH AMERICA, 1903
(in millions of pesetas with exchange rate of 6.8 to the dollar)

	Spanish Exports to	Spanish Imports from
Argentina	17.1	22.4
Chile	2.0	1.5
Colombia	3.5	.8
Costa Rica	.2	.5
Cuba	66.1	6.6
Dominican Republic	.4	.1
Ecuador	.5	4.3
El Salvador	1.0	1.1
Guatemala	.1	2.4
Mexico	12.0	3.1
Peru	.2	.8
Puerto Rico	4.5	5.8
Uruguay	5.5	4.3
Venezuela	2.2	5.1
Total:	115.3	58.8
Brazil	2.2	7.5

SOURCE: Mercurio, no. 37 (December 1, 1904), p. 292.

CHART 2

SPAIN'S COMMERCE WITH PRINCIPAL BUYER-SELLER NATIONS, 1903
(in millions of pesetas with exchange rate of 6.8 to the dollar)

	Spanish Exports to	Spanish Imports from
Great Britain	315.7	184.5
France	219.7	160.6
United States	26.0	118.4
Germany	42.6	94.9
Portugal	42.9	45.6
Belgium	25.8	39.7
Italy	40.7	24.1
Russia	3.3	36.9

SOURCE: Mercurio, no. 37 (December 1, 1904), p. 292.

tacular progress toward compensating for the commercial catastrophe brought about by the war with the United States.

In 1903 Spain exported to its principal trade partners in Spanish America—excluding Brazil—goods worth some 115.3 million pesetas. From these republics Spain imported goods valued at 58.8 million pesetas. Thus the total value of Spanish–Spanish-American commerce in that year came to about 174.1 million pesetas (see Chart 1). Prior to the disaster, in 1897, the value of that trade had been 432.3 million pesetas: 284.2 million in exports and 148.1 million in imports.[38]

Overall Spanish trade with Spanish America in 1903 was not only less than 40 percent of what it had been in 1897; it was a relatively insignificant percentage of Spain's total foreign commerce, estimated at 1,924.4 million pesetas and conducted primarily with Great Britain, France, the United States, and Germany (see Chart 2). One factor at least was encouraging to Spain in its trade with Spanish America: an export balance of 56.5 million pesetas that contrasted with an import balance of 32.6 million pesetas in its total foreign commerce.

By 1908, the value of commerce between Spain and Spanish America rose to approximately 209 million pesetas, with exports amounting to some 141.4 million and imports to 67.7 million pesetas.[39] By this time Spain's total trade with its four best commercial partners in Spanish America, Argentina, Uruguay, Cuba, and Mexico, was worth approximately 40 percent of what it was with Great Britain and slightly less than 60 percent of what it was with France; and the value of Spanish commerce with the four New World republics was nearly double that with Germany and close to four times greater than that with Italy.[40]

Nevertheless, Spain's overall role in Spanish-American commerce was still an insignificant one. Argentina, for example, was second only to Cuba as the major Spanish-American purchaser of Spain's exports; and it was the leading supplier of Spanish imports from Spanish America. Yet as of

1908 Spanish commerce with Argentina, exports and imports, amounted to only one-nineteenth the value of Argentina's trade with England, one-ninth the value of that trade with Germany, one-fifth the value of that trade both with Belgium and the United States, and slightly better than one-half the value of Argentine trade with Brazil.[41]

Between 1908 and 1913 Spanish trade with Spanish America inched up at such a slow rate as to discourage and frustrate the advocates of practical hispanismo.[42] For that last year estimates were that Spain supplied Spanish-American republics with barely 3.5 percent of their overall imports. From Spanish America Spain purchased no more than 2 percent of the republics' total exports.[43] Why, the business leaders especially of the Spanish periphery wanted to know, had Spain made such little progress at capturing the markets of Spanish America in the fifteen years following the disaster?

As early as 1904 José Zulueta, in a national chamber of deputies discourse, listed some of the factors that impeded the expansion of trade between Spain and Spanish America—factors that concerned parties would continue to point to during the ensuing quarter of a century. Zulueta mentioned first the lack of adequate transportation facilities, noting that railroad rates for shipping goods from the interior to Spanish ports were excessive. Part of the reason for this situation he traced to foreign ownership of much of Spain's railway system; he charged the Spanish government, though, with still greater responsibility because of the high transportation taxes it imposed. Once goods arrived at a port, the deputy continued, it was next to impossible to send them overseas on Spanish ships, because of the decline of the national merchant marine. To compound these difficulties, virtually no credit was available for financing Spanish–Spanish-American commerce, tariff provisions were often prohibitive, and the Spanish diplomatic corps allegedly assumed no initiative in seeking more advantageous trade treaties. This last problem Zulueta attributed to the lack of selectivity in assigning personnel to Spanish America, to serious understaffing, and to massive red tape that frustrated the efforts of the few diplomats and consuls seriously committed to augmenting commerce.

The bleak situation, Zulueta concluded, need not endure, for once Spaniards acquired the will to improve it they could do so literally overnight: "Where did Italy and Germany stand some thirty years ago in regard to trade with Spanish America? It is only through desire and will that they have achieved their present eminence in exports. Spain has all of the economic potential to achieve similar ends once it puts itself to the task. The day that Spain wishes to do so, it will arise."[44]

The situation proved somewhat more complex than Zulueta believed. Spaniards indeed showed considerable will at this time, but what they willed was often at cross-purposes. Thus when a minister of the treasury, at about the time of Zulueta's discourse, actually introduced a bill calling for reduction of transportation taxes, a hue and cry went up from all those concerned with maintaining a balanced budget and the stability of the peseta. As a result, the matter was dropped.[45] And so it continued in many instances to be more expensive to send goods by rail to a Spanish port than to transport them by sea from there to Buenos Aires.[46]

To support its merchant marine the Spanish government had before the turn of the century decreed a subvention for the Compañía Transatlántica with its headquarters in Barcelona. Owing in part to this subvention the Compañía by 1903 sent one regularly scheduled ship each month to the La Plata area. Up to the World War I period, however, by far the greatest amount of Spanish trade with Spanish America depended on foreign shipping facilities.[47] As a result proponents of practical, commercial hispanismo increasingly demanded that the government up its subsidization of the merchant marine and take other steps to expand maritime services.

One advocate of government action to expand the merchant marine lamented that virtually all increases in Spanish–Spanish-American commerce between 1900 and 1907 had resulted from the private initiative of Spain's shipping companies. The resources of private companies were severely limited, however, and unless the government responded to the situation with general outlays no substantial growth of commerce with Spanish America could be anticipated. Ending on a note of realism, the writer of this analysis conceded that the niggardly subvention to the Compañía Transatlántica, already under severe criticism by those who followed the current vogue of demanding reduced expenditures and a balanced budget, enjoyed no immediate prospects of a raise.[48]

One of the greatest disadvantages of having to rely on foreign shipping companies, according to most observers, lay in the fact that these firms relabeled Spanish products, selling them in Spanish America as French, English, Italian, or German goods. As a result, Spanish Americans remained totally unaware of the high quality of Spanish products and tended automatically to order goods from other countries.[49] A frustrated Spanish consular agent serving in Concepción, Chile, commented upon this situation: "We have only one aspiration, and that is to see our country emerge at the top of all other nations on this soil made fecund by the blood of thousands of Spanish heroes. . . ." But, he gloomily concluded, so long as Spanish Americans remained ignorant of the existence of Spanish finished goods and agricultural products because of fraudulent labeling by commercial intermediaries, "this aspiration has no possibility of fulfillment."[50]

In his 1904 chamber of deputies discourse Zulueta had mentioned lack of credit facilities as a serious obstacle to Spanish–Spanish-American trade. Fellow spokesmen of practical hispanismo agreed with him that an anachronistic and underfinanced commercial credit structure indeed contributed enormously to Spain's continuing commercial underrepresentation in Spanish America. Merchants in the New World republics who imported through the firms of most European nations obtained six- to nine-month credit arrangements, beginning at the time goods were actually delivered. Under the best of circumstances importers dealing with Spanish-American firms could hope only for ninety-day credit, calculated to begin upon the signing of papers of sale rather than upon delivery of goods. Importers anxious to purchase Spanish goods often found it impossible to obtain credit even of this unsatisfactory type.[51] Persisting in tight-money policies so as to contain inflationary threats, the Spanish government turned a consistently deaf ear to the pleas for expansion of commercial credit.[52]

Many hispanoamericanistas concurred also in Zulueta's 1904 indictment of diplomats and consuls for indifference to the opportunities available to them in Spanish America for expanding trade.[53] Other observers, however, attributed Spain's inability to capture Spanish-American markets to the general ineptness of its manufacturers and merchants.[54] Manufacturers and merchants were accused of refusing to package goods attractively and to adapt products to market demands; they were further charged with failing to dispatch well-informed commercial agents with a full line of samples; and they were criticized for excessive greed that led them to spurn profit rates deemed satisfactory by English, French, German, Italian, and United States firms.[55]

Perhaps more fundamentally important than the reasons alluded to by Zulueta and other hispanoamericanistas for the paucity of commerce with the former colonies was the fact that Spain found sources of economic rehabilitation in fields that had nothing to do with Spanish America. Between 1905 and 1913, for example, Spain benefited from a foreign capital input of close to 800 million pesetas.[56] As a result, it could maintain almost painlessly a favorable balance of payments and thus did not have to go to the considerable trouble of seeking a major expansion of trade with Spanish America. Also of basic importance in explaining Spain's failure to achieve significant breakthroughs in practical hispanismo was the continuing contention between the two Spains, center and periphery.

A Vizcayan businessman expressed a belief widespread in his region when in 1915 he blamed the unsympathetic attitudes of the Madrid government for the relatively slow rate of development in northern Spain. A stiflingly centralistic government, he contended, dominated by individuals with little business acumen, consistently imposed policies counterproductive to economic development, policies that weighed with particular onus upon those areas of Spain that had economic drive and expertise—that is, upon the periphery.[57] Proponents of Catalan regionalism spoke out in the same manner. The centralistic restrictions of a government basically unsympathetic to material progress, they maintained, prevented Cataluña's economic development. In particular Catalan businessmen liked to blame the failure of their industries to capture Spanish-American markets on the unwillingness of the central government to afford adequate tariff protection.[58]

Some political and intellectual leaders of the geographic center, of course, agreed with the assessments made by spokesmen of the periphery. One Madrileño referred to the businessmen of Barcelona and Bilbao as the only true standard-bearers of progress: "It is necessary for us in Madrid," he added, "where we suffer from the mortal sickness of infecund rhetoric, to pay attention to these men; for they are the heralds of the new Spain that wishes to renew the old."[59] A more typical reaction of the center to the claims of the Spanish periphery was voiced by a nobleman from the province of Soria in Old Castile. He decried the excessive materialism of the industrial periphery and attributed Barcelona's inability to compete successfully for Spanish-American markets to the unwarranted protection its industries already enjoyed. If tariff protection were removed, he opined, the Catalan industries would be forced to increase their efficiency, after which they could compete successfully for the markets of Spanish America.[60]

Even had they received full cooperation from the central government, the industrial-commercial cities of coastal Spain might not have been able to achieve the gains in Spanish–Spanish-American commerce anticipated by many hispanoamericanistas between the disaster and World War I. Undoubtedly, though, the periphery's performance suffered from friction with the center where many of those interested in hispanismo were preoccupied with spiritual and cultural ties and content to allow Spain's principal commercial relations to continue to be with the countries of Europe and with the United States.

For a brief period, however, at the outset of World War I, Spain's center seemed to become almost as interested as the periphery in the expansion of commercial relations with Spanish America. This new development is readily explainable: the drying up of foreign investment threatened Spain with an economic crisis at the precise time that opportunities for trade with Spanish America suddenly became more promising than ever before.

Practical Hispanismo during World War I and the Immediate Postwar Era

Spain's minister of state declared in 1915 that the strengthening of commercial ties between his country and Spanish America should constitute the principal objective of every administration; "but now," he added, "the necessity is more urgent than ever before," because, owing to the disruption of normal trade between Europe and America occasioned by the war and owing also to the opening of the Panama Canal, "Spain has a golden opportunity to capture the Spanish-American markets."[61] At the same time Altamira beseeched Spaniards to concentrate all their efforts in taking advantage of the uniquely propitious moment to expand trade with Spanish America. Such a moment, he said, might never come again.[62] And a Spanish senator, referring to the potential boon of the war and the canal[63] to trade relations with the former colonies asserted: "We must take advantage of these conditions. One could well repeat the phrase, 'it's now or never.' "[64]

With his usual moderation, Labra warned Spaniards against holding exaggerated hopes. "These are not the times," he said, "for the fantasies of El Dorado and the Fountain of Youth. One cannot think of monopolizing the American markets for Spanish production and commerce. Nor is it reasonable to dream of a Spanish political and social hegemony across the Atlantic strong enough to annul the influence of the rest of the world and of the mosaic of foreign populations in America." Short of these exaggerated hopes, however, Labra contended, Spain could at least aspire to fill a good part of the commercial vacuum in Spanish America, which he estimated at a thousand million francs, caused by the disruption of trade with Great Britain, France, Germany, Italy, and Belgium.[65]

A new periodical dedicated to the purposes of practical hispanismo made its appearance in 1916, La Unión Hispano-Americana.[66] In the first edition its editorial staff contended, like Labra, that Spain could justifiably hope to fill permanently at least a part of the commercial vacuum created by the war. And it raised anew, although in a different context, the concept that Spain should serve as the intermediary between Europe and Spanish America. In the past, most hispanoamericanistas had envisioned Spain as the cultural intermediary between Europe and Spanish America. Now, according to the editorial writers of the new review, Spain must become the commercial link, taking advantage of its neutrality so as to sell to Europe the products of Spanish America, and to Spanish America the goods of Europe.[67]

Above all, though, Spaniards thought about the exchange of their own products with Spanish America. Such an exchange appeared to be the means to survival in the postwar era, when Europe might impose boycotts in retaliation against Spain's neutrality.[68] Anticipation of boycotts prompted the leading proponent of practical hispanismo in the north, Julio de Lazúrtegui, to proclaim that more than in European markets, "the future of Vizcaya lies in Latin America."[69]

Lack of merchant ships continued to present a formidable impediment to fulfillment of hopes for a dramatic burgeoning of Spanish–Spanish-American trade.[70] Luis Palomo recognized this and urged the creation of a joint Spanish–Spanish-American merchant marine.[71] Nothing came of the Palomo proposal. Nor did any practical results ensue from the 1915 visit of former Colombian president (1904–1906) Rafael Reyes to Spain. Reyes, who as so many others at this time was fond of referring to "the providential, never-to-be repeated moment" for establishing economic ties, hoped—in vain, as it turned out—for the formation of a huge steamship company financed by capital from Spain, Spanish America, and the United States.[72]

Despite imposing obstacles, Spain, as the war continued, began to score certain gains in its commercial relations with the New World republics. By 1916 Spanish exports to Spanish America, excluding Brazil, were up to 200.7 pesetas; imports from Spanish America registered 133.4 million pesetas. Thus the total value of this trade stood at 334.1 million pesetas, up from approximately 209 million in 1908 but still well below the 432.3 million mark of 1897 (see Chart 3).

CHART 3

SPANISH–SPANISH-AMERICAN TRADE, 1916

(in millions of pesetas with an exchange rate of 6.45 to the dollar)

	Spanish Exports to	Spanish Imports from
Argentina	84.9	60.0
Bolivia	.1	.1
Colombia	5.5	1.6
Costa Rica	.2	.3
Cuba	70.8	19.5
Chile	6.5	10.2
Dominican Republic	.3	negligible
Ecuador	1.6	4.3
El Salvador	.5	.1
Guatemala	.4	.7
Honduras	.4	negligible
Mexico	1.8	5.4
Panama	6.1	.4
Peru	1.7	.4
Puerto Rico	2.3	7.3
Uruguay	13.0	12.1
Venezuela	4.6	11.0
Totals:	200.7	133.4
Brazil	4.3	16.1

SOURCE: *La Unión Hispano-Americana*, no. 77 (March, 1923), p. 37.

As of 1919, the value of Spanish exports to Spanish America had declined to 147.2 million pesetas; but the following year it soared to 230.3 million. In the same two years Spain imported from Spanish America goods worth 212.4 and 235.8 million pesetas. In these two years, then, total Spanish–Spanish-American trade figures came to 359.6 and 466.1 million pesetas, respectively. However, an export balance of 67.3 million

CHART 4

SPANISH–SPANISH-AMERICAN TRADE, 1919, 1920
(in millions of pesetas with an exchange rate of 6.45 to the dollar)

	Spanish Export to		Spanish Imports from	
	1919	1920	1919	1920
Argentina	67.2	96.2	121.5	134.3
Bolivia	.1	.1	neg.	.2
Colombia	1.5	2.8	4.5	4.3
Costa Rica	.2	.5	.6	.6
Cuba	44.2	81.0	14.2	17.0
Chile	4.6	3.6	15.1	33.0
Dominican Republic	neg.	.1	neg.	.1
Ecuador	.3	.5	4.0	2.3
El Salvador	neg.	.1	.1	.4
Guatemala	neg.	neg.	.1	neg.
Honduras	neg.	neg.	neg.	neg.
Mexico	7.2	13.5	8.0	9.9
Panama	5.6	10.5	.3	neg.
Peru	1.3	2.1	.1	.3
Puerto Rico	1.6	3.0	6.1	6.2
Uruguay	11.3	13.2	21.1	7.7
Venezuela	2.1	3.1	16.7	19.5
Totals:	147.2	230.3	212.4	235.8
Brazil	4.3	8.0	14.1	28.7

SOURCE: La Unión Hispano-Americana, no. 77 (March, 1923), p. 37.

pesetas in 1916 had been converted into an import balance of 65.2 million pesetas in 1919 and 5.5 million in 1920 (see Chart 4).

During the four-year period 1916–1920, Spanish trade, exports and imports, with all Spanish America averaged approximately 15 percent of its total foreign commerce, in comparison to 23.2 percent with France, 20.7 percent with the United States,[73] and 15.9 percent with Great Britain (see Chart 5).

Although World War I seemed to contribute to a marked expansion in Spain's trade with Spanish-American republics, an expansion that apparently continued in the immediate postwar period, the above statistics are in some ways deceptive. They attest to a sizeable increase in the absolute value of trade; but they do not reveal the fact that Spain failed to make appreciable headway in capturing a larger percentage of Spanish America's overall commerce. In 1913 Spain had supplied about 3.5 percent of all Spanish-American imports. As of 1918 this percentage had risen to approximately 4.5. By 1920, however, it had reverted to the 1913 level. Spain in 1918 had purchased about 2.5 percent of Spanish America's total exports;

CHART 5
Spanish Foreign Commerce, 1916–1920
(in millions of pesetas)

	Spanish Exports to			Average Annual Percentage of Total Value of Exports during Five-Year Period
	1916	1919	1920	
Spanish America	200	147	230	15.49 percent
Rest of America, excluding United States	5	6	9	0.55 percent
United States	96	98	78	6.72 percent
France	567	492	280	35.1 percent
Great Britain	285	206	219	17.0 percent
Rest of World	273	424	279	25.1 percent
Totals:	1,426	1,373	1,095	

Average annual value of exports during five-year period: 1,262 million pesetas.

	Spanish Imports from			Average Annual Percentage of Total Value of Exports during Five-Year Period
	1916	1919	1920	
Spanish America	133	213	236	14.46 percent
Rest of America, excluding United States	27	28	43	2.6 percent
United States	454	392	331	34.77 percent
France	110	111	219	11.2 percent
Great Britain	326	183	214	14.77 percent
Rest of World	279	207	461	22.18 percent
Totals:	1,329	1,134	1,504	

Average annual value of imports during five-year period: 1,198 million pesetas.

Source: *La Unión Hispano-Americana*, no. 78 (April, 1923), p. 59.

but, by 1920 these purchases were down to their 1913 level of 2 percent or under.[74]

Most of the hopes that World War I inspired among Spaniards for an increased share of the Spanish-American trade had been shattered by 1920. Spain still did not have what it considered to be its fair share of Spanish America's foreign commerce. By running very fast during the war it managed only to retain, as hostilities ended, the lowly position it had occupied when the fighting erupted. Still, the gain in the absolute value of this trade was not negligible; it mitigated the seriousness of Spain's economic position in the immediate postwar years, which registered a considerable decline in the absolute value of its total foreign commerce, especially with the countries of Europe.[75]

As the war drew to an end and as the postwar period began, the propo-

nents of practical hispanismo in the northern periphery remained dissatis-
fied with accomplishments. In the hope of stimulated trade with Spanish
America, the provincial assemblies of Vizcaya, Guipúzcoa, Álava, and
Navarra in 1922 commissioned Lazúrtegui to undertake a fact-finding and
contact-establishing mission to the New World. Lazúrtegui visited fourteen countries and explored possibilities for more intensive commercial
relations in thirty-three cities, from New York and Philadelphia to Santiago and Buenos Aires. The *Informe y memoria* that he issued upon his
return is one of the most valuable documents pertaining to postwar trade
relations between Spain and Spanish America.[76]

In the same year that Lazúrtegui was touring the principal countries of
the New World, Argentine President-elect Marcelo T. de Alvear visited
several ports of northern Spain. In Santander he conferred with the president of the council of ministers and suggested that the leading businessmen of the Spanish communities in America be brought to Spain to participate in a commercial congress through which they could instruct the
manufacturers and merchants of the peninsula on the most effective means
for capturing a larger share of Spanish America's foreign commerce.[77]
To this suggestion the government responded with a royal decree creating
a committee to organize a Primer Congreso Nacional del Comercio
Español en Ultramar. Rafael Vehils served as secretary general of the committee, which drew strongly on the advice and assistance of the Casa de
América in Barcelona and the Unión Ibero-Americana in Madrid.[78] The
Spanish government contributed 450,000 pesetas toward financing the
congress and private business in Spain and Spanish America raised an
additional 125,000 pesetas.

Sessions of the congress, which attracted business leaders of the Spanish
communities from nearly all parts of America and the Philippines, were
held in three cities: Barcelona, March 21–27, 1923; Madrid, April 1–7;
and Sevilla, April 10–16. Alfonso XIII personally inaugurated both the
Madrid and Sevilla sessions. Delegates to the congress made the usual
points about the need to reorganize the Spanish consular service, to provide better credit facilities, to secure commercial treaties and tariff reductions, to establish trade museums and information centers, to expand
advertising on Spanish products, to dispatch commercial agents on a regular basis, and to modernize Spanish manufacturing and selling techniques.[79] In addition, they pursued one relatively fresh approach to the
problems of Spanish–Spanish-American trade by deliberating at length on
how to convert Spanish emigrant colonies into effective agencies for
augmenting commerce.

The congress produced several practical results. After studying some of
the suggestions contained in the resolutions, the government responded
on May 15, 1923, with a royal decree that lowered tariffs on some Spanish-
American products.[80] A subsequent royal decree of July 12 stipulated that

official status should be conferred on all overseas Spanish chambers of commerce (*cámaras de comercio*)—more than twenty of which had by this time been organized by emigrant colonies in Spanish America) that could meet certain minimum conditions laid down by the ministry of state. Once recognized by the ministry, overseas chambers of commerce qualified for modest government financial support so long as they continued to perform designated functions. They were, for example, to gather commercial information and forward it to various ministries of the Spanish government as well as to private business associations; in addition, they were charged with assisting traveling commercial agents from the peninsula, with organizing permanent expositions of Spanish products, and with supplying groups in Spain with samples of Spanish-American goods. In order to receive continuing state support overseas chambers of commerce had also to arrange expositions of Spanish books and periodicals and to maintain up-to-date information on all aspects of business and commercial laws in the republics where they were located. Finally, the chambers were obliged to send an annual *Memoria* to the ministry of state providing detailed information on their activities.[81]

In mid-1923, the Spanish government also created a Junta Nacional del Comercio Español en Ultramar. Based in Madrid, the Junta was presided over by the minister of labor, commerce, and industry and its members included the heads of numerous private and government associations concerned with business, manufacturing, and commerce, as well as delegates from such agencies of hispanismo as the Casa de América and the Unión Ibero-Americana.[82] In addition several private citizens gained appointive posts on the Junta, among them Altamira, González Posada, Lazúrtegui, Palomo, and Gabriel Maura.[83]

Intended to provide liaison among business groups of the peninsula and the Spanish colonies in Spanish America and the Philippines, the Junta would, its founders hoped, become the principal clearinghouse of commercial and economic information and the major link between government and private endeavors to expand trade between Spain and the rest of the Spanish-speaking world. Another objective of the Junta, one which it did not fulfill, was to convene an annual Conferencia Nacional del Comercio Español en Ultramar to be attended by delegates of each officially accredited Spanish chamber of commerce in Spanish America and the Philippines.[84]

In the early 1920's the Spanish government also manifested its interest in practical hispanismo by encouraging through modest subventions those groups engaged in laying plans for an Ibero-American Exposition. Originally conceived by Bilbao merchants early in the century, the exposition project had subsequently been taken over by business and academic groups in Sevilla. Scheduled at one time for 1913 or 1914, the exposition had been postponed upon the outbreak of the World War.[85] After the successful Primer Congreso Nacional del Comercio Español en Ultramar, political, social, and business leaders grew more optimistic about the feasibility of the exposition, envisioning it as likely to be a major stimulus to Spanish–Spanish-American commerce. Thus by the time Primo de Rivera seized power in September of 1923, hispanoamericanistas had begun to overcome their disillusionment occasioned by the scarcity of results achieved during the war and were entering with renewed energy into the quest for a closer economic relationship with Spanish America.[86]

Practical Hispanismo during the Primo de Rivera Dictatorship

In one of its first acts the Primo de Rivera government expanded the activities of the Junta Nacional del Comercio Español en Ultramar and raised its subvention—later in his regime Primo declared the Junta an official adjunct of a newly created ministry of national economy.[87] In defining the broader responsibilities of the Junta, the administration relied heavily upon the advice of the Casa de América. To this Barcelona association it also entrusted much of the preparatory work in connection with the second Congreso Nacional del Comercio Español en Ultramar, scheduled originally to convene in 1927 but subsequently postponed for two years.[88]

Concerned from the outset of his regime with seeing that Spanish shipping companies utilized state subventions with greater efficiency in providing service to Spanish America, the dictator could by 1927 point with satisfaction to the fact that ships of the Compañía Transatlántica made, among other regularly scheduled voyages, sixteen round trips each year between Bilbao, Santander, Gijón, and La Coruña and Habana and Vera Cruz, sixteen round trips between Barcelona, Málaga, and Cádiz and Montevideo and Buenos Aires, fourteen round trips between Barcelona, Valencia, Málaga, and Cádiz and New York, Habana, and Vera Cruz, and eleven round trips between Barcelona and Pacific coast ports of South America.[89] By this time also Ibarra y Compañía, with headquarters in Sevilla, sent ships, departing from Genoa the twenty-fifth of each month and servicing Spain's Mediterranean ports, to Rio de Janeiro, Montevideo, and Buenos Aires.

Not only by means of steamship navigation but through communications services in general Spain was united more directly and effectively to Spanish America during the dictatorship. In 1925 Spain established a direct telegraph link with Argentina, Uruguay, and Brazil. Late in 1929 came the opening of radio-telegraph communications with Argentina, Brazil, Cuba, and the United States; and the same year witnessed the inauguration of airmail service between Spain, Argentina, Brazil, Paraguay, Uruguay, and Chile. It may have offended national pride that a French line handled this service, but businessmen were delighted that a letter mailed in Alicante or Barcelona could be in Buenos Aires or even Santiago de Chile in approximately eight days.[90]

At a Madrid banquet in late 1927 the Cuban ambassador to Spain noted that in the realm of practical matters and trade relations Spanish America was becoming more firmly bound than ever to the one-time metropolis. As evidence of this and of Primo de Rivera's attention to "practical deeds and tangible realities," the ambassador pointed to a recently celebrated commercial treaty between Spain and Cuba, to Spain's loan of 100 million pesetas to Argentina and its sale to that republic of two cruisers, and to a treaty of arbitration with Chile.[91]

Encouraged by the progress, actually more imagined than real, in creating economic ties between Spain and Spanish America, one of the peninsula's leading hispanoamericanistas predicted in 1926 that the time was at hand when the Hispanic nations, united under the influence of Madrid, could force the United States to abandon its imperialistic ways under threat of nonpurchasing agreements.[92] Two years later another Spaniard, no less renowned in the field of hispanismo, declared that in the near future Spain would be able to liberate Spanish America from United States imperialism by extending to the New World republics the loans they had previously had to obtain from Wall Street.[93] These predictions, which indicate that as much fantasy inhered in practical hispanismo as in its cultural-spiritual counterpart, were never fulfilled. But a dream long entertained by practical hispanoamericanistas was realized when the Ibero-American Exposition opened in Sevilla in 1929.

In November of 1923, Primo de Rivera had petitioned the crown to declare Sevilla the site of an exposition that would "strengthen the ties that happily exist between Spain and the countries of . . . America."[94] The king, of course, had consented to the dictator's request, and as a result the government shortly committed itself to match the six million pesetas that the local administration of Sevilla was pledged to contribute toward financing the exposition. Ultimately, the central government would contribute at least an additional fifteen million pesetas, not including the annual subsidy of 300,000 pesetas that it had allotted between 1923 and 1929 to the committees and associations charged with planning and organizing the exposition.[95] Private investment had contributed the remainder of the estimated fifty million pesetas expended on construction of the exposition's palaces and pavilions; private capital had also augmented public funds, national and municipal, in paying for the laying out of the magnificent María Luisa gardens and the building of the luxurious Alfonso XIII hotel that would house many of the important visitors to the exposition.

With Alfonso XIII, Primo de Rivera, and numerous dignitaries from Spanish America and Portugal on hand, the exposition opened on Ascension Thursday in the spring of 1929. In his address on this occasion Primo de Rivera emphasized that the exposition demonstrated the modern progress and material advances achieved by the Hispanic raza. Immediately following the grand opening Alfonso XIII traveled to Barcelona to inaugurate that city's International Exposition. In his address at this ceremony the king stressed that the Sevilla exposition looked toward America, the one in Barcelona toward Europe. Developing one of the constantly recurring themes of hispanismo, Alfonso declared it was his task as king to convert Spain into the great link between Europe and America.[96]

Practical hispanismo, based on ties of trade and economic investment, desperately needed the boost that many hoped the 1929 expositions would provide. As of 1929 Spain's total trade, exports and imports, with its eight major buyers and sellers among the Spanish-American republics had risen to 534 million pesetas (see Chart 6). While this sum might have seemed substantial, it was considerably less than the value of Spain's overall trade with the United States, which in the previous year had amounted to an estimated 678.436 million pesetas.[97] Furthermore, the increase in value of trade over 1920, when Spain's commerce with all Spanish America reached a value of 466.1 million pesetas, was not altogether a real one; for between 1920 and 1929 the exchange rate of the peseta to the dollar had worsened, passing from 6.45:1 to 7.5 and even 8.5:1. Finally, the year 1929 witnessed an import balance of 45.8 million pesetas in Spain's trade with Spanish America, compared to trade deficits of 65.2 million in 1919 and 5.5 million

CHART 6

SPANISH TRADE WITH EIGHT PRINCIPAL SPANISH-AMERICAN BUYERS AND SELLERS, 1929
(in millions of pesetas at an exchange rate of 7.5 to the dollar)

	Spanish Exports to	Spanish Imports from	Total Trade	Difference between total trade value for 1920
Argentina	121.1	166.1	287.2	56.7 increase
Chile	4.8	46.0	50.8	14.2 increase
Colombia	2.6	1.3	3.9	3.2 decrease
Cuba	63.7	29.4	93.1	4.9 decrease
Mexico	10.8	27.2	38.0	14.6 increase
Peru	2.4	1.2	3.6	1.2 increase
Uruguay	32.1	3.1	35.2	14.3 increase
Venezuela	5.1	17.1	22.2	.4 decrease
Totals:	242.6	291.4	534.0	

Net increase in value of total trade with eight principal Spanish-American buyers and sellers in 1929 over the 1920 value: 92.5

SOURCE: Carlos Ibáñez de Ibero, *La personalidad internacional de España* (San Sebastián, 1940), pp. 134–35.

in 1920 and, more significantly, compared to a traditional export balance that had prevailed until the late stages of World War I. Meantime, between 1922 and 1928, Spain's overall unfavorable balance of trade in its total foreign commerce had declined.[98]

Between 1920 and 1929 Spain seldom supplied any Spanish-American country with more than 4 or 5 percent of its total imports; in the great majority of instances, Spanish goods amounted to less, considerably less, than 4 percent of the value of products imported by Spanish-American republics. During the same period, moreover, Spanish-American countries seldom sent to Spain goods worth more than 1 or 2 percent of their total exports.[99]

The world depression destroyed the hopes of those who had looked to the 1929 expositions as the means for stimulating Spain's disappointing trade with Spanish America.[100] A writer for *Razón y Fe* observed that the Sevilla and Barcelona expositions, which remained open until June of 1930, might have been good for Spanish pride but had constituted a "financial catastrophe." Owing to the depression, he said, Spain could never hope to recoup through commercial profits the huge sums invested in them. Not only had the exposition in Sevilla been a financial catastrophe, he added, it had also been a moral outrage because of the sale of Protestant Bibles on the premises and the shameless display of nudity in the statues and paintings on exhibit. In addition, Spanish sensitivities had been offended, he claimed, by the emphasis on Indian culture found in some of the Spanish-American displays.[101]

Even had the depression not occurred, factors purely internal to Spain probably would have doomed the attempts to establish important ties, commercial as well as cultural, between Spain and Spanish America during the dictatorship. In order for the dreams of binding Spain to Spanish America to have become a reality, it would first have been necessary for the different Spains to become more united among themselves. The cleavage between liberal and conservative Spain was probably less pronounced in 1929 than twenty or thirty years earlier. But the growing strength of a new, radical, socially revolutionary left had brought into being another Spain whose peaceful assimilation by the older ones did not seem likely. Moreover, the divisions between the two geographic Spains, center and periphery, had broadened between 1923 and 1929. Primo de Rivera infuriated the Catalans by denying, perfidiously, they claimed, their aspirations for greater autonomy. Catalans, and Basques as well, who felt almost no affinity with the central government of Madrid, could muster little enthusiasm for the ties with Spanish America that the dictator's government sought either to forge or to strengthen. Most decidedly hispanismo had not become the great ideal which was envisioned by Ganivet and numerous Spaniards since him and which would restore national cohesiveness to Spain, bring about unity with brothers in America, and assure the Spanish raza a position of international power.[102]

While Spaniards within the peninsula struggled without notable success between 1900 and 1930 to bring to life the aspirations of hispanismo, many of their fellow citizens labored in behalf of the same aspirations in Spanish America. Spain's diplomats and emigrants in the New World often rendered distinguished service to the cause of hispanismo. But, as was the case with proponents of hispanismo in the peninsula, their efforts as often as not proved counterproductive to the movement they hoped to advance.

11: SPANISH DIPLOMATS AND EMIGRANTS AS AGENTS OF HISPANISMO, 1900–1930

Alleged Inadequacies of Spain's Diplomatic-Consular Representation in Spanish America

A Spaniard living in Montevideo threw up his hands in dismay as he contemplated the prospects of hispanismo in 1906. Spain, he contended, had been unable to establish any real presence, either cultural or economic, in Spanish America. On the other hand the United States, Great Britain, France, Italy, and Germany were penetrating more deeply every day into every aspect of life in the new republics. The reason for this, he stated, was that of all foreign countries Spain was the least well served by its diplomatic and consular service in Spanish America. Legations maintained by his country, he charged, were among the shabbiest buildings to be found in the capitals of Spanish America; and the men who worked in them were no better than the buildings. Diplomats from the peninsula, he concluded, were useless and consuls were even worse because "they collected the highest duties and enforced the most antiquated regulations in all America."[1]

In the same year an unidentified writer lamented, in the columns of Barcelona's *Mercurio*, that neither ties of sentiment nor of economic interest existed between Spain and Spanish America. He attributed this situation to the poor quality of the Spanish diplomatic service in Latin America: "We do not send first-rate men there. It is a sort of testing ground to see if a man can qualify for an important post. We maintain legations there on a penurious basis, while on countries of the Old World in which Spain has no vital interest and in which an ambassador serves only a decorative role we lavish great sums of money."[2]

Ten years later the Conde de Romanones blamed the lack of preparation and the poor quality of Spain's diplomatic and consular service for the failure to progress, in spite of the opportunities presented by the war, toward cultural-commercial approximation with Spanish America. "Service in America," the Liberal Party statesman declared, "is regarded as a punishment. When a diplomat leaves for America, he thinks only of returning in the shortest time possible. . . ."[3] Worse still, according to Rafael María de Labra, Spain's diplomats maintained an insufferable superiority attitude in virtually all their dealings with citizens of the New World republics. Until Spain's representatives dropped this approach,

231

Labra concluded, it would be difficult indeed to achieve Spanish–Spanish-American rapport.[4]

If, as Labra contended, Spanish diplomats made themselves unpopular among the citizens of Spanish-American republics, they were often equally inept at winning the confidence and respect of Spanish immigrant communities in America. Javier Fernández Pesquero, a leading figure of the Spanish community in Chile, observed that as of 1910 only about 10 percent of Spain's immigrants had bothered to register with their country's diplomatic representatives in the republic. "The truth is," Fernández observed, Spain's representatives have never done anything to establish contact with the Spanish community; and what little contact is made often leads to mutual hostility." One reason for this situation, he said, was Spain's total indifference to the quality of its diplomats in Spanish America. As an indication of this, Fernández told of two Spanish ministers to Chile in the early twentieth century who could not even speak Castilian properly, apparently because both had been educated and lived long years outside of Spain. "You can imagine," he said, "what effect it produces among the members of the Spanish community in a Spanish-speaking republic to hear the minister of Spain mispronounce the language and speak it with the difficulty of an Englishman or German." Even when they could speak the language properly, Fernández averred, Spain's diplomats established a close relationship with just a handful of their fellow citizens and generally managed to exacerbate the feuds and jealousies that characteristically divided Spanish communities.[5]

By no means all of the alleged shortcomings of Spain's diplomatic-consular representation in Spanish America could be attributed to lack of preparation and qualification, for there was also a glaring lack of quantity.[6] At the end of the nineteenth century Spain was officially represented in Spanish America—excluding Brazil—by eight ministers, thirteen legation secretaries,[7] and eleven consuls, a total of thirty-two individuals. The only first-class minister was assigned to Mexico. Second-class ministers were stationed in Buenos Aires and Santiago de Chile; another second-class minister was accredited to the governments of Peru, Bolivia, and Ecuador. Resident (third-class) ministers served Spain in Montevideo, Bogotá, and Caracas; another resident minister represented his country before the five Central American republics (Costa Rica, El Salvador, Guatemala, Honduras, and Nicaragua). Moreover, first-class consuls were stationed only in Valparaíso, Buenos Aires, San José (Costa Rica), Quito, and Vera Cruz.[8]

In a 1904 chamber of deputies discourse Faustino Rodríguez San Pedro, president of the Unión Ibero-Americana and then serving as minister of state, complained of Spain's diplomatic underrepresentation in Spanish America. Owing to this, he said, ministers could not attend adequately to their business.[9] His plea for an increase in diplomatic personnel produced no effect in the economy-minded Cortes. As late as 1923 Spain still maintained only one minister to represent it before the governments of Peru, Bolivia, and Ecuador.[10]

Spain's understaffed diplomatic-consular service did not suffer with indifference the charges of responsibility for the overall failure of the hispanismo movement. With considerable justification its members lashed back against their critics, insisting they were doing all that could reasonably be expected of them, given their lack of manpower and economic resources. Diplomats complained also that their best efforts generally came to naught because their reports went unread by government authorities in Madrid; and they contended that their ineffectiveness in dealing with Spanish communities sprang from the notorious lack of patriotism exhibited by Spaniards living abroad, in stark contrast to the example of German and Italian immigrants. In addition, as representatives of a monarchical government they were handicapped, they claimed, by the republican sympathies of so many members of the Spanish communities, particularly the younger elements.[11]

Spanish consuls were especially outspoken as they defended themselves against allegations of inefficiency. The failure of Spain to capture a larger share of Spanish-American markets they attributed to the "incredible ineptness and stupidity"[12] of Spanish manufacturers and merchants. United States, German, Italian, French, and English firms understood, they said, the need to send traveling commercial agents to Spanish America with a full line of samples and reliable price lists. Spanish enterprises, however, refused to send such representatives. And often when the energetic work of the consuls actually resulted in the placing of an order for Spanish goods, firms in the peninsula allegedly sent goods far below the quality stipulated in the sale contract; sometimes they even sent products entirely different from those ordered by the Spanish-American importer.[13] A consul in Asunción (Paraguay) expressed the viewpoint of most of Spain's consular service in Spanish America when he complained that merchants and industrialists of the peninsula "simply do not understand modern ways. Because of this, all of the ties that are based on our common raza, customs, and language can produce no practical results."[14]

In 1910 a particularly disgruntled Spanish consul in Valparaíso, after leveling the usual complaints against his country's industrialists and merchants, and after charging the Spanish community with lack of patriotism because of its willingness and even eagerness to purchase non-Spanish imports, concluded there was really no hope for expanding commerce between Spain and Spanish America. "Those who see the economic regeneration of Spain in Spanish America are," he declared, "grossly mistaken." Spanish-American republics, according to his analysis, were incapable of industrialization; as a result for all of the foreseeable future they would have to import finished goods, which meant they would inevitably trade with the more advanced manufacturing countries of the world. The consul recommended that Spain lower the priority of Spanish America in its foreign policy and abandon the vain endeavor to increase its share of that area's commerce. Spain should instead, he advised, concentrate on its more natural markets in England, Holland, Germany, Denmark, Sweden, and Russia. Spain's failure to augment its economic stake in Spanish America, he testily concluded, could not be attributed to the consular service. Instead, it was the result of natural and inexorable market conditions and also of the unreliability and irresponsibility of Spanish-American governments which rendered trade relations with them most difficult even under the best of conditions.[15]

The Economics of Spanish Diplomatic-Consular Representation in Spanish America

If the number of diplomatic-consular personnel in Spanish America and the percentage of the foreign service budget allotted to their support provide accurate indicators, then Spain did not follow the 1909 advice of its consul in Chile to downgrade the importance of the former colonies. In 1898 Spain had expended a total of 625,150 pesetas on the salaries and expenses of its thirty-two diplomatic and consular representatives in Spanish America; by the end of 1898 personnel had increased to thirty-three.[16] In 1915 the total salary and expense allowances for the twenty diplomatic representatives (nine ministers, including first-class ones both in Mexico and Argentina, in addition to five first-class and six second-class secretaries) came to 487,350 pesetas, while twenty-seven consular representatives received 298,225 pesetas. Thus, during a seventeen-year period, 1898–1915, diplomatic and consular personnel had increased from thirty-three to forty-seven and the money allotted for their salaries and expenses had risen from 625,150 to 785,575 pesetas.[17] Moreover, by 1915 examinations for all persons entering the diplomatic service had come to include extensive and detailed questions on Spanish America and Brazil.

As of 1915, about 22 percent of Spain's entire, worldwide budget for the salaries and expenses of diplomatic personnel was allotted to its legations in Spanish America. And the government assigned approximately 26 percent of its entire budget for the salaries and expenses of consular personnel to agents serving in Spanish America;[18] this at a time, moreover, when trade with Spanish America constituted only about 15 percent of the value of Spain's worldwide commerce.[19] So far as expenditure of money is concerned, then, the charges of hispanoamericanistas that Spain neglected Spanish America in the fields of diplomacy and consular relations do not appear to be warranted. Given the limitations of its foreign policy budget, Spain may well have been underrepresented throughout the

world. In expending its inadequate funds, though, the Spanish government seemed actually to award priority status to Spanish America.

By 1925, a total of twenty-three diplomatic personnel, including first-
class ministers in Buenos Aires, Mexico City, and Habana, represented
Spain in Spanish America. The sum total of their salaries and expense
allowances came to 814,022 pesetas, up 326,672 pesetas since 1915 and
constituting about 27 percent of the total allotted to all diplomatic personnel serving overseas.[20] The percentage of the budget allocated to consulate personnel in Spanish America had also increased; and out of the
total personnel of 113 in the Spanish consular service with the rank of
second-class consul or higher, twenty-eight served in Spanish America.[21]

The interest that dictator Primo de Rivera assumed in Spanish America
is clearly manifested by the statistics on diplomatic and consular representatives assigned there. By the time the dictator fell from power in 1930,
three of Spain's ten ambassadors were accredited to Spanish-American
republics, and Spain's total diplomatic personnel in these republics stood
at thirty-four, up from twenty-three in 1925. Moreover, 1,516,000 pesetas,
approximately 28 percent of the entire amount budgeted for salaries and
expenses of overseas diplomats and the maintenance of legation buildings,
was allotted to personnel and post buildings in Spanish America.[22]

By 1930 consular personnel had climbed to forty-five, approximately
a 30 percent increase since 1925. Their salaries and expense allowances
came to about 1,057,000 pesetas, constituting some 28 percent of the
amount budgeted by Spain for the remuneration of its entire consular
service.[23] Furthermore, by 1929 funds appropriated for the support of
overseas Spanish chambers of commerce had risen to 200,000 pesetas,
twice the amount allocated for this purpose in 1923.[24]

If the complaints of hispanoamericanistas about government indifference to the diplomatic-consular service in Spanish America seem groundless, at least when judged by economic criteria, much additional research
remains to be done before it will be possible to gauge accurately the persistent criticism of the quality of Spain's representatives. Preliminary investigations indicate to this writer that personnel transferred to Spanish
America from other foreign service posts received promotions more regularly than personnel transferred to other theaters. This could suggest,
although there might be other explanations based on such considerations
as time of service prior to transfer, that Spanish-American posts were
assigned to individuals who might not have been considered competent
to hold corresponding positions in other parts of the world.[25]

Whatever the truth of this matter may be, a Romanones government
moved in 1916 to enhance the stature and prestige of the diplomatic
corps in Spanish America by elevating the legation in Buenos Aires to
embassy status.[26] Primo de Rivera took further steps along these lines as
his government entered into reciprocal agreements with Cuba and Chile

to raise diplomatic representatives to the ambassadorial rank. In addition the dictator's minister of state, José María Yanguas y Messía, won a substantial budgetary allocation that permitted him to purchase more imposing legation buildings in numerous countries, particularly in Spanish America.[27]

The Lack of Impact of Spanish Diplomacy in Spanish America

Despite the fact that governments were not so indifferent to the matter as critics accused them of being, Spain's diplomacy in Spanish America, whether conducted by legation or consulate personnel, did not produce a notable impact. Beginning with Argentina in 1902 Spain did, it is true, sign a series of copyright and patent treaties with a number of Spanish-American republics, and between 1902 and 1929 Spanish governments entered into arbitration treaties with a majority of the republics as well as agreements of mutual recognition of academic and professional titles.[28] The same period witnessed the signing of numerous customs agreements. But Spanish diplomacy never remotely approached realization of one of the more exalted dreams of hispanismo, for Spain most definitely did not come to be regarded as the natural arbiter in international disputes involving Spanish-American republics.

At the turn of the century it had seemed that Spain might be about to make its diplomatic presence felt in Spanish America. In 1898 Guatemala chose Spain to arbitrate its differences with certain Italian citizens. Then, in 1905, Nicaragua and Honduras, as well as Ecuador and Peru, submitted their boundary disputes to the arbitration of Alfonso XIII.[29] In the Nicaragua-Honduras proceedings, however, Spain was accused of undue procrastination;[30] and in the Ecuador-Peru case Liberals muddied the waters by attempting to create a political scandal as they accused Antonio Maura of having accepted an unconscionably large fee to represent Ecuadoran interests.[31] Following this, the Spanish-American republics generally ignored the mother country when seeking outside assistance in resolving international disputes.

In the early 1920s when a boundary controversy flared between Colombia and Peru,[32] Spain managed to incur the enmity of both disputants. The Spanish government first agreed to sell warships to Colombia; then, in the face of irate protests from Peru it canceled the agreement, only to be roundly denounced by Colombia. Moreover, when Chile and Peru finally settled their boundary dispute of nearly forty year's duration in 1929, the purportedly menacing Colossus of the North, rather than the supposedly revered madre patria, played the role of arbiter.

Nor did Spain have the opportunity to bolster its diplomatic impact by dispatching important military missions. The Spanish-American republics on the whole sought technical assistance in training their armed forces and national police bodies from other countries in Europe or from the United States. In the first thirty years of the twentieth century, only seventeen Spanish officers participated in the nine relatively insignificant military missions that Spain undertook in Spanish-American countries.[33]

In the League of Nations many hispanoamericanistas had seen the means for effecting a new diplomatic unity between Spain and Spanish America. Within the League, they reasoned, Spain, and perhaps Portugal as well, could come together with the Spanish-American nations to form a bloc to contain the imperialistic menace of the United States and to facilitate the creation of a regional trading group among the nations of the Hispanic world.[34] Great Britain, however, refused to see the League employed as a counterweight to the United States in the American hemisphere; and the Latin Americans made it apparent that their main hope was to use the League to facilitate unity among themselves, but not with Spain or Portugal.[35] Moreover, in 1926 Spain announced its withdrawal from the international organization when it failed to obtain the necessary unanimous backing for permanent membership on the League council. Subsequently it reconsidered, settling for a newly created status of semipermanent council member. But the entire incident weakened Spain's already miniscule power within the League and just at the time when Spanish Americans seemed most in need of effective European allies in their mounting determination to oppose United States intervention.[36]

By the end of the 1920s, Spain had taken steps to bolster its diplomatic and consular representation in Spanish America. But all of the grand schemes of diplomatic approximation remained unfulfilled. And it was still fashionable for hispanoamericanistas to blame Spain's diplomatic and consular corps for the failure to establish meaningful ties, either of spirit or interest, between the members of the transatlantic Hispanic world.[37]

Understandably, Spain's nonofficial representatives, its emigrants, had a far greater impact in Spanish America, if for no other reason than their numbers. Frequently by their presence they contributed enormously to the realization of hispanismo's objectives. On balance, though, their presence may have done more to estrange Spanish Americans from Spaniards than to draw them together. Nevertheless, in their customarily unrealistic manner, Spain's hispanoamericanistas looked to the emigrant to play a major role in bringing about the permanent rapprochement and copenetration of the one-time colonies and metropolis.

Estimated Numbers and Some of the Activities of Spanish Immigrants in Spanish America

In a book published in 1912, the usually restrained and realistic Labra asserted: "Spain cannot live without Spanish America. . . . The old metropolis must again conquer the New World. How and in what sense?

It must conquer through the sweat and love of the Spaniards who work in America, respected there and identified with the undeniable sovereignty of those . . . splendid countries with their good fortunes and happy futures. . . ."[38]

The Spaniards whom Labra envisioned as the new conquerors were indeed a formidable army. According to official statistics for 1900, approximately 350,000 Spaniards resided in Spanish America, nearly 200,000 of them in Argentina, some 67,000 in Cuba, and about 56,000 in Uruguay. Labra insisted, however, that the official statistics were inaccurate. "All informed persons," he stated, "believe that there are no fewer than 300,000 Spaniards in Argentina alone, an additional 129,000 in Cuba, and perhaps 120,000 in Uruguay."[39] In all, according to Labra, some 800,000 Spaniards lived in Spanish America at the turn of the century. And in the immediately ensuing years the sizeable Spanish communities received numerous reinforcements; for Labra calculated that between 1904 and 1913, 1,617,-614 Spaniards emigrated, two-thirds of them going to America.[40]

Statistics published by *Unión Ibero-Americana* in 1912 placed the number of Spaniards living in Spanish America at over four million, with better than 35 percent of them located in Argentina.[41] However, another periodical of hispanismo, *La Unión Hispano-Americana*, estimated in 1923, notwithstanding a vast influx of new immigrants during the past decade, that the number of Spaniards residing in Spanish America totaled "just under four million." The journal observed that this was indeed a tremendous number in view of the fact that the total Spanish population stood at slightly under twenty million in 1910 and at 20,719,598 in 1918.[42]

Following his extensive New World tour at the beginning of the 1920s, Julio de Lazúrtegui guessed that there were not quite two million Spaniards in Spanish America. Of these, about 1.2 million lived, he said, in Argentina; and he added that only in two or three cities of the peninsula were there more Spaniards than in Buenos Aires. Lazúrtegui calculated that at least 350,000 Spaniards resided in Cuba; in Mexico, about 80,000 and a similar number in Chile; in Uruguay, 60,000; in Colombia, 15,000; in Venezuela, 12,000; in Peru, 10,000; in Ecuador and Bolivia, about 5,000 each. In the five republics of Central America, according to Lazúrtegui, there were some 6,000 Spaniards, while an additional thousand lived in Panama and just under a thousand in Paraguay. The Vizcayan proponent of practical hispanismo estimated that 83,500 Spaniards resided in Brazil.[43]

However great the discrepancies in emigration statistics, there is no doubt that the greater number of Spaniards destined for the New World departed from Galicia, the Basque provinces,[44] and Cataluña. Thus in 1924 when 60,198 men and 26,722 women officially emigrated to America, 33 percent departed from Vigo, 27 percent from La Coruña, a combined total of 7.8 percent from the two ports of Gijón and Bilbao, and 7.5 percent from Barcelona.[45] This situation arose in part from the fact that Vizcaya had the highest population density in Spain, followed by Cataluña and Guipúzcoa.[46] A more important reason was that the manual laboring classes, who provided the overwhelming majority of emigrants until the 1920s, when more and more middle sectors began to seek their fortunes in America,[47] were less impoverished in the north and also less apt to be illiterate[48] than in Andalusia and the south, where agrarian problems were more severe. As a result, it was mainly northern Spaniards who could take advantage of the New World opportunities; and the repercussions of emigration in the peninsula, both adverse and favorable, were most pronounced in the north.

Once settled in the New World, Spaniards engaged in a great variety of activities, some of which won them the enmity and others the respect of local citizens. Throughout most of the nineteenth century, because of their readiness to intervene in local political affairs, Spaniards were regarded with suspiciousness and outright hostility in most Spanish-American republics.[49] In the 1890s resentment against the Spanish colonies intensified because of the Cuban issue. Most Spanish Americans sympathized with the insurrection and resented the fact that Spaniards contributed a sizeable proportion of their American earnings to the support of Spain's military operations. In Buenos Aires, for example, Spaniards organized the Asociación Patriótica Española primarily for the purpose of soliciting contributions from fellow citizens living throughout the La Plata area for the war effort in Cuba.[50] By 1898 the Association had collected enough money to pay for the construction of a new cruiser, the *Río de la Plata*, which was eventually delivered to the Spanish government but only after the termination of hostilities over Cuba.[51] The Spanish colony in Mexico also remitted large sums to Spain to help sustain the endeavor to suppress the Cuban insurgents. Not only because of these remittances, but also because of the propaganda activity of the Spanish-community newspapers in defending Spain's cause in Cuba, Spaniards incurred the contumely of New World citizens.

By the end of the war, however, Spanish Americans began increasingly to sympathize with the defeated motherland. After 1898 when they concerned themselves with the Cuban question it was no longer Spain but rather the United States that they accused of frustrating the island's quest for genuine independence. By this time, moreover, Spanish immigrants had largely abandoned their proclivities toward political intervention in the American republics; instead of dangerous subversives, they were coming to be recognized as hardworking individuals with considerable skill and shrewdness who could contribute to the material progress of the areas in which they resided. As a result, by the beginning of the twentieth century Spanish immigrant colonies had won a degree of acceptance in Spanish America that contrasted sharply with the discrimination from which they had previously suffered.[52]

The rags-to-riches success stories of many Spanish immigrants resulted in a growing respect for the business acumen of the new arrivals among the citizens of the American republics. At the same time these stories, widely publicized in the Spanish-community newspapers in Spanish America—by 1918 seventeen of these newspapers appeared regularly[53]—and repeated in the press of the peninsula lured additional waves of Spaniards to the New World.

In Buenos Aires, Francisco R. Alcobendas had by the early years of the twentieth century become a legendary figure. Arriving as a poor immigrant from Spain, he had within a remarkably short time become a rich *estanciero*, celebrated for the modern methods of agriculture that he introduced on his estates, and an influential member of the board of directors of the Banco Español del Río de la Plata.[54] In Cuba, Secundino Baños, born in humble circumstances in Galicia, had by 1907 become one of the island's wealthier merchants and the president of the Centro Gallego de la Habana. Another poor Spaniard, Ignacio Nazabla, had within a few years become a prosperous merchant in Habana and a member of the board of directors of the Banco Nacional de Cuba. And Pedro Landeras, born into a poverty-stricken family in Santander, rose within a brief time following his arrival on the island to a position on the board of directors of the flourishing banking and commercial house of Landeras, Calle y Compañía; he also became a leading figure in Cuban society as well as the vice-president of the Sociedad Montanese de Beneficencia, a paternalistic organization concerned with the protection of impecunious immigrants from northern Spain.[55] Arriving as an indigent immigrant in Mexico toward the end of the nineteenth century, Íñigo Noriega quickly established himself as one of the republic's wealthier *hacendados*; in addition, he became an intimate friend of President Díaz, a director of an important export-import firm, and a member of the board of directors of the Compañía de Seguros La Fraternal.[56]

Disembarking in Valparaíso in 1879 at the age of nineteen, Fernando Rioja Medel was almost totally without funds. But before the passing of many years he had established a tobacco enterprise, become active in the export-import business, founded an insurance company, as well as a nitrate and other mining firms, and a textile industry. By the World War I period he had become one of the leading livestock raisers in southern Chile. For three years, moreover, he had been president of the Banco Español de Chile; in addition he had founded the official Spanish chamber of commerce in Chile as well as the Asociación Patriótica de la Peseta Española, which supported commercial and industrial schools in Spain for youths contemplating emigration to America. By the time of his death in 1924 Rioja had gained a place within the Spanish nobility with the title of Conde de Rioja de Neila.[57] Another poor Spaniard, Antonio Montero, reaching Valparaíso at about the same time as Rioja, soon accumulated a fortune in industrial and commercial ventures. In the course of twenty years he founded the following Spanish community organizations in Santiago: El Centro Español, La Unión Ibero-Americana Beneficencia y Socorros Mutuos, and La Bomba Española, the last a group of volunteer Spanish firemen. In recognition of his work in behalf of the Spanish colony, the crown awarded Montero the cross of Isabella the Catholic.[58]

Although the great majority of Spanish emigrants departed the peninsula as impecunious laborers, nearly 9,000 of the 60,000 Spaniards living in Uruguay at the turn of the century were, according to the Spanish consul in Montevideo, local property owners.[59] Statistics gathered in 1909 by one of the best-informed members of the Spanish community in Chile showed that of the approximately 17,000 Spaniards, 3,319 were merchants, 2,218 white-collar workers, and 232 industrialists. Fewer than three thousand were listed as manual laborers.[60]

A Spanish journalist in 1907 recorded a typical impression of the impact of emigration to Spanish America: "The Spanish emigrant . . . is a constant reminder of the superiority of the Spanish raza. Spaniards have a role to play in every successful and large financial institution in Spanish America. You find them in high positions of prestige and success in every district and town. In all areas they are members of the directing classes."[61] A Spaniard who visited countries of Central and South America in 1921 depicted a similar scene: "In most places I had been in, the most vital, industrious and fruitful element was the Spanish colony—the Spaniards of today, who were also among the most influential and prosperous in every walk of life."[62] The following year the Conde de Romanones declared that practical hispanismo was progressing as never before, owing to the examples of hard work and business expertise presented every day by Spain's emigrants to the New World.[63]

The success stories of Spaniards in America, however, often contained decidedly unattractive chapters. Spanish novelist Ramón Valle-Inclán in 1922 drew a devastating picture of the corruption that underlay the accumulation of most quick fortunes in the New World. Spaniards of the type described by Valle-Inclán, and there must have been many of them in Spanish America, did little to win esteem for Spain. Moreover, a substantial part of the Spanish-American social and economic leaders came to look with suspiciousness if not aversion on Spanish immigrants because of the numerous socialists and anarchists from the peninsula who struggled to give a revolutionary orientation to early organized labor movements in many of the New World republics.[64]

Most Spanish immigrants in Spanish America neither achieved notable economic success nor participated in revolutionary movements. By far the larger proportion arrived poor, remained poor, and led inconspicuous, drab, and unadventurous lives. To attend to the needs of poverty-stricken immigrants, many of whom clearly desired to return to Spain but lacked sufficient funds, well-to-do elements of the Spanish communities founded hospitals and countless charitable institutions. Seldom in history have Spaniards practiced greater charity toward fellow Spaniards. But the fact that a large number of immigrants subsisted in America on the charity of beneficence and mutual aid societies led some Spaniards to wonder if their government did not have a duty to warn its citizens of the perils awaiting them in the New World and even to enact measures restricting emigration.

Spanish Attitudes toward Emigration

In 1904 a journalist writing in Mercurio noted the rising tide of criticism directed against Spanish emigration. Emigrants, according to numerous Spaniards, were impoverishing Spain's natural resources by making their productive contributions not to their own nation but to the New World countries in which they settled. The journalist sought to refute this charge. Emigrants did not, he contended, impoverish Spain. The largest number of them came, he pointed out, from Galicia, Vizcaya, Cataluña, and the east coast, "the richest and most flourishing parts of Spain." By encouraging rather than restricting emigration, he insisted, Spain would place itself in a favorable position to capture new markets in America and would at the same time "maintain the continuity of the Spanish spirit in those republics."[65]

Complaints about emigration and about the conditions often faced by the unsuspecting emigrant continued to be voiced. In 1907 the Spanish government responded with a law aimed at providing the potential emigrant with more accurate information about circumstances in the country where he intended to establish residence, at curbing the fraudulent advertising resorted to by many recruiting agents, at improving conditions of marine transportation, and at establishing a fund to facilitate the return of sick and indigent Spaniards living abroad. Two years later a congress convened under private auspices in the Galician town of Santiago de Compostela to discuss problems of emigration. Delegates to the congress, who elected Labra as presiding officer, Palomo as one of the vice-presidents, and Federico Rahola as one of the secretaries, conceded that emigration entailed many disadvantages and often subjected Spaniards to cruel and exploitative situations. At the same time a vast majority agreed that emigration provided the only means whereby thousands of northerners could escape poverty and find employment opportunities. Emigrants, the delegates further agreed, aided Spain by remitting money to the peninsula and, in the case of those who prospered abroad, founding schools in their native communities. In their resolutions the delegates concluded it would be nice if Spain could end emigration, for with only eighteen million citizens the country was underpopulated. For the immediate future, though, they contended that problems arising from caciquismo and usury in Galicia and elsewhere in the north were not likely to be resolved. Therefore emigration was inevitable as Spaniards sought to flee "hunger and injustice."[66]

Certain Spaniards continued to demand a curb on emigration. Thus in 1915 a journalist reported that within the past twelve months some fifty thousand broken and disillusioned citizens had returned to their peninsular homes from America. Spain, he said, had had to spend millions of pesetas in repatriating them, whereas if only half of this amount had been invested internally vast programs of soil reclamation and colonization might have been initiated within the peninsula.[67] Apparently, though, the majority of Spaniards agreed not only with the explicit statement of the 1909 congress that emigration was inevitable but with the implication that emigration was a less painful way of mitigating the social problem than the undertaking of domestic reforms.

The Lyrical and the Practical Aspects of Emigration

Typical elements of both the lyrical and the practical approach to hispanismo provided a rationale for the refusal of Spanish officials to interfere with the flow of emigration to America. On the level of lyricism, Spaniards maintained that emigration would preserve the Hispanic culture and raza in America. In the practical approach, they pointed to the role that emigrants could play in encouraging the importation of Spanish goods into the New World. They drew attention also to the remittances of Spanish emigrants that were well-nigh indispensable in maintaining the peninsula's economic stability.

Those concerned with culture and the raza expressed apprehension because the young republics had "not solved their basic problem by assimilating different ethnic elements into a unified whole." As a result their inhabitants remained uncertain as to their identity. If Spaniards did not take steps to increase enormously their physical presence in the New World, then Spanish Americans would, it was feared, be tempted to repudiate their true heritage, traditions, and character and to guide themselves in the search for identity by the cultural models of the United States, France, Italy, and indigenous groups.[68] According to a prominent statesman writing in 1922, not only Hispanic culture but the raza itself in the New World had to be bolstered by a continuing wave of emigrants from the peninsula; otherwise that culture and raza might well be annihilated.[69]

Hispanoamericanistas fretted especially over the danger that Italian immigration posed for Hispanic culture and the raza in Argentina. Following his visit to Argentina in 1910, González Posada expressed amazement at the degree to which Italians had influenced the cultural environment and even the language in Buenos Aires. As a result, Argentines faced the

danger of losing their Spanishness, the only true essence of the national
character, and becoming a confused, hybrid product totally lacking a sense
of national cohesiveness, purpose, and direction. If Argentines were to
prosper and attain the happy future that destiny might have in store for
them, then they must guard against de-Hispanization by nourishing themselves with Spanish blood.[70]

Federico Rahola worried about Argentina's neighbor, Uruguay. The
Uruguayan race, he asserted, had been weakened by excessive inbreeding
in Montevideo and by the blood of the fierce Churrúa Indians among the
inhabitants of the interior. The solution was to renew the blood of the
Uruguayans by crossing it with that of waves of Spanish immigrants.
Through this process, he predicted, the natural instincts of Uruguayans
for revolution and violence would be restrained.[71]

Spanish emigration to Cuba was encouraged on the grounds that it
would enable that island republic to resist cultural absorption by the
United States.[72] To some degree Spaniards in Cuba fulfilled the expectations of the peninsula's hispanoamericanistas; for through their various
organizations they actively disseminated anti-United States propaganda.[73]
Although the matter requires extensive research, it is possible that the
Spanish community in Cuba contributed in no small degree to the
anti-Yankee sentiments which Cuban political leaders, the last and most
notable being Fidel Castro, exploited so successfully through the years.

Peninsular writers pictured Spanish immigration as the means not only
of enabling Cubans to resist absorption by the United States but also
of preventing a social revolution led by the island's blacks. A Spanish
priest, for example, wrote that the white race was in danger both in Cuba
and Puerto Rico as a result of the increasing political activity of blacks
and the virus of democracy exported by the United States. Only additional
Spanish immigration, he contended, would enable the two islands to preserve the supremacy of the white race.[74] Another Spaniard maintained
that the future of the Dominican Republic, with its dark-skinned populace, was bleak unless its race could be improved by large-scale Spanish
immigration.[75]

Elsewhere in Spanish America, according to peninsular writers, large
Indian populations hampered development possibilities. In their analysis,
the alleged laziness and shiftlessness of the Indian could be corrected
only through crossbreeding with new armies of Spanish immigrants. The
Basques, one writer observed, had a unique facility for crossing with
Indians and thus they had a particular responsibility to fulfill in raising
the population quality of the Indian republics of Spanish America.[76]

The Conde de Romanones expressed a widely held attitude throughout
the first third of the twentieth century in Spain when he wrote in 1915
that the peninsula's emigrants to America were protecting "the Spanish
raza and its values against the inroads and incursions of other races."

"They are continuing," Romanones added, "the work begun by the Spanish conquerors and making it possible, on some remote day in the future, for all the people of Spanish America to say 'We are Spaniards.' "[77]

To many Spaniards, the views on Spain's cultural-racial mission in the New World smacked of lyricism. Men of this outlook placed their interest in practical matters, particularly in the sums of money that Spanish immigrants in America remitted to the peninsula each year.

At the turn of the century the annual average value of remittances to the peninsula from Spanish immigrants living in Spanish America and Brazil was estimated at around 240 million pesetas; of this amount some 65 percent came from the Spanish colonies in Argentina and Uruguay, and about 18 percent each from the colonies in Mexico and the Antilles.[78] By 1906 some estimates placed the value of these remittances at 335 million pesetas.[79] According to one well-informed source, "three quarters of the people of rural northwest Spain live off the money received from relatives and friends in America."[80] Moreover, this capital inflow enabled Spain to resolve its monetary crisis following the disaster; and, until 1908 when European investment in the peninsula began to increase sharply, it played the major role in enabling Spain to avoid serious balance of payments deficits.[81]

Apparently the annual value of remittances from Spanish America and Brazil held steady at between approximately 200 and 300 million pesetas during the 1904–1915 period.[82] Toward the end of World War I remittances fell off slightly,[83] only to soar to new highs during the 1920s. For the 1924–1926 period, estimates of the value of remittances from Spanish America, excluding Brazil, ranged from 250 to 520 million pesetas. Even assuming that the lower estimate is the more accurate, the value of these remittances still came to about 10 percent of the Spanish government's national budget during these years.[84] In addition, Spanish colonies in Spanish America imported goods from the motherland valued at over fifty million pesetas each year. Countries without large Spanish colonies imported virtually nothing from Spain.[85]

The Spanish Government and the Emigrant

In spite of the role they were supposed to play in safeguarding the raza in Spanish America and in spite of the contribution they were expected to, and actually did, make to the Spanish economy, emigrants to the New World were largely ignored and abandoned by their government. The Instituto de Reformas Sociales, principally because of the efforts of its secretary Julio Puyol,[86] made some attempt to provide prospective emigrants with reliable information concerning the conditions they would encounter in America;[87] and in 1907 Pedro Sangro y Ros, active both in the Instituto and in Catholic social action projects, published a useful manual for the emigrant describing accurately the labor situation in Argentina.[88] However, virtually no serious and sustained effort was made to enforce the provisions of the 1907 emigration law. One of the main objectives of the law had been to protect Spaniards against unscrupulous emigration agents. Yet on the Consejo de Emigración, created by the 1907 legislation, representation was provided for twenty-eight foreign and domestic firms, most of them navigation and steamship companies whose principal concern was selling passages to as many Spaniards as possible.[89]

Spaniards emigrating to the New World often traveled on ships that did not provide even minimal sanitation facilities and arrived in lands where unemployment was high and where inflation robbed apparently generous wages of purchasing power.[90] Those finding employment frequently suffered exploitation by management owing to their ignorance of local labor protection laws or because these laws applied only to the native-born. And, because of their willingness (often through necessity) to work for cut-rate salaries, they incurred the hostility of local laborers.[91] According to a leading member of the Spanish colony in Chile, only a small percentage of Spaniards appreciably improved their lot in the New World. The success legends of the *Indiano*—the term applied to Spaniards who had lived in America—only obscured the fact, he said, that the life of the average immigrant was filled with "thorns, disillusionment, and bitterness."[92]

Miguel Toledano Escalante, a successful journalist in Barcelona who made many trips to America, composed in 1915 an impassioned warning to Spaniards not to emigrate to Argentina. He counseled them in the first place not to believe the propaganda of emigration agents, most of whom, he said, were in the pay of Argentine firms seeking cheap labor and of steamship companies greedily eager to sell passages to the unsuspecting. Such a paid agent, he charged, was the Spanish novelist Vicente Blasco Ibáñez, who in 1910 had published in Madrid a book entitled *Argentina y sus grandezas*. Intended to attract Spaniards to Argentina, where Blasco Ibáñez had spent a brief period, the book described the New World republic as a veritable paradise.

The great majority of Spaniards living in Argentina, Toledano contended, would never have come to the land had they not been deceived by the "lying tongues of the propagandists," against whom the Spanish government made no attempt to protect them.[93] Once in the new land they encountered widespread unemployment; when they did find work it was of the sort that only "animal men" could perform.[94] They also found a high crime rate and a corrupt, venal police and court system that would not protect the rights of poor foreigners. The Spanish immigrant also discovered that he was contemptuously dismissed by the natives as a *Gallego* (someone from Galicia), a term that connoted far greater opprobrium than *Gringo*. "I have passed various times through that inhospitable country," Toledano wrote, "seeing how they disdain Spaniards and Spain, ridiculing its accomplishments, twisting its history, denying its virtues and denigrating its men."[95] Worse even than native Argentines in this respect, the journalist contended, were the sons of Spaniards born in the young republic; these blighted individuals seemed to feel that their first obligation was to deny their father and his land of origin.[96] Toledano concluded:

> Only for the person who has never had anything, material or cultural, is Argentina a country of hope. For a man of culture and conscience, for one who has the desire to work but is not accustomed to cheating ways, to one who cannot accommodate himself to servility, to one who is not avaricious, Argentina is a land of disenchantment. . . . It is impossible for real men to live in that country where the only ideal consists in making oneself rich through a continuous struggle that awakens the brutal qualities in those who accommodate to it.[97]

Responding to the pressures brought by journalists like Toledano and by numerous Indianos who wanted their fellow citizens to be spared the disillusionment they had suffered in the New World, the Spanish government passed a law in 1918 expanding some of the protective devices included in the largely unobserved legislation of 1907.[98] Just prior to the enactment of this law Catholic groups had established the Asociación Española de San Rafael to try to dissuade prospective emigrants from leaving Spain and to assist those who insisted upon going to America.[99] Particularly alarmed by the high percentage of Spaniards who abandoned their faith in the New World, the founders of the Association hoped to create agencies through which the large number of Spanish clergymen resident in America would begin to minister to the spiritual needs of their fellow immigrants.[100] Unfortunately, few practical results ensued from the 1918 law or from the plans of the Catholic Association. By and large Spanish immigrants in the New World continued to suffer from, and keenly to resent, the abandonment by their government and Church.

In 1921 a Spaniard well informed on the situation because of the years he had spent in Argentina complained bitterly about his government's abandonment of the emigrant. Owing to this situation, he wrote, "the Spanish emigrant has virtually no citizenship."[101] Five years later one of the peninsula's most active hispanoamericanistas lamented that a large percentage of Spain's immigrants in America, despairing of ever receiving assistance or even attention from their country's diplomatic and consular representatives, became citizens of the republics in which they had taken up residence.[102]

The Primo de Rivera regime did make some attempt in the mid-to late 1920s to improve the situation by augmenting the diplomatic and consular representatives in America—the fifty-seven diplomats and consuls in Spanish America as of 1925[103] could scarcely have been expected to minister adequately to the needs of between two and four million immigrants. Toward the end of 1924 the dictator's government also produced a comprehensive new emigration law, creating a Dirección General de Emigración within the ministry of labor, commerce and industry. To advise and assist the Dirección, a central junta was established in Madrid while local juntas were set up in each of the ports from which substantial numbers of emigrants embarked. To aid the Dirección further in its work of properly supervising emigration, the government created juntas in the principal cities of Spanish America and charged them with assisting consular agents. These juntas included representatives of the local Spanish chambers of commerce and of the various Spanish-community organizations.[104]

Under Primo de Rivera the government also at long last moved to provide schools for Spanish colonies in America. To implement this new program it awarded an annual subvention of 500,000 pesetas to the Patronato de Relaciones Culturales, created in 1927 and described in Chapter 9.[105]

Efforts of the Spanish government to attend adequately to the needs of its emigrants and to enroll them as effective agents of hispanismo came late and proved largely ineffective. Not until the successful conclusion of the Moroccan campaign toward the end of 1925 were funds available for financing new programs; and even after that date a good part of Spain's revenue went into pacification programs in northern Africa. With the 1929 depression and the overthrow of the dictator the next year, followed by six years of turmoil and chaos during the second republic and then by three years of civil war, Spain reverted to a policy of neglect and abandonment vis-à-vis the emigrant.

Emigration and Hispanismo: An Assessment

The failure of Spanish governments to safeguard and assist the overseas colonies of its citizens and to utilize them effectively as goodwill missionaries in America probably arose in part from the disdain in which many prominent intellectual and political leaders held the emigrant. The classicist Miguel de Unamuno and the poet Juan Antonio Cavestany provide typical examples of this. Both contended that the least desirable elements of the peninsula emigrated to America.[106]

If the average emigrant was dismissed as a wastrel by many of his fellow Spaniards, he was apt to be held in equal if not greater scorn if he returned to Spain as a wealthy man following his labors in America. Numerous authors have commented upon the contempt exhibited by most Spaniards toward the Indiano.[107] To some degree Spaniards rejected the Indiano because he had allegedly been contaminated by the brutal materialism assumed to prevail in the New World republics.[108] The tendency to reject the Indiano because he had purportedly been corrupted and brutalized by the New World environment, occupied by people suspected of cultural and racial retardation, reveals the basic Spanish attitude of superiority toward Spanish America. So long as this attitude prevailed, the cause of hispanismo could hardly have flourished, even had the Madrid government conscientiously sought to maintain close contact with its citizens living in the New World.

The Spanish emigrant in America seldom performed as an agent of hispanismo. In America, he was not apt to contribute toward creating a favorable image of Spain because he felt aggrieved by his government. If he developed real affection for a New World republic and returned to the peninsula as a successful Indiano, he could contribute little toward enhancing the image of Spanish America because of the contempt in which he was held just for having lived there. And if upon his return he brought with him a dark-skinned wife, the scorn he encountered was apt to be still more intense.

Moreover, when it came to the possibility of advancing the purposes of hispanismo, Spain's largest colonies seemed to be located in the wrong places. Spanish immigrants resided in the largest number in Argentina; but even had they been effectively utilized by their home government, their influence would still have been largely eclipsed by the huge Italian colony. Present also in formidable numbers in Cuba, Spanish immigrants saw their influence offset by that of the United States. And the power that they had once exercised in Mexico, in part because of the close ties that many maintained with President Díaz, declined temporarily with the 1910 Revolution that ousted the strongman and soon acquired a pronounced indigenista and anti-Spanish orientation.

On numerous occasions Spaniards in America reflected discredit on their motherland by the unseemly disputes in which they engaged. In 1897 when the Spanish colony in Buenos Aires was ready to send to the government in Madrid the first large installment on the purchase of the cruiser *Río de la Plata*, a heated controversy erupted as to which leader of the various groups and associations was entitled to sign the draft. The wrangle delayed the sending of the installment for some two months and made the Spanish community a laughing stock in Buenos Aires circles.[109] A few years later a financial scandal which saw the secretary-treasurer of the Asociación Patriótica Española of Buenos Aires fleeing the country to avoid criminal prosecution led to bitter accusations and counteraccusations and further divided the Spanish community.[110]

The journal *Unión Ibero-Americana* referred in 1907 to the "mortifying discords" that divided the Spanish colony in Mexico City.[111] Some time later González Posada declared that lack of solidarity was the most typical characteristic of all Spanish immigrant oranizations in Spanish America.[112] In the 1914 *Memoria* that he prepared for the Spanish chamber of commerce in Guatemala, of which he was president, Felipe Yurrita pleaded with the members of the Spanish community not to speak so badly of each other. By their ceaseless rancor, he said, they imparted a bad name to Spain. The following year the Club Español of Montevideo issued a manifesto to all Spaniards living in Uruguay calling for harmony and unity and proposing the establishment of an arbitration council to settle pending and future disagreements among them.[113] Because the Spanish communities in each of the New World republics suffered from severe divisions among their members, it is not surprising that efforts undertaken in 1913, 1919, and 1922 to establish a confederation of all Spanish groups in America came to naught.[114]

In addition to insulting one another, Spaniards in America seemed to delight in voicing affronts against the motherland, often because emigrants to the New World had been associated with unsuccessful political causes in the peninsula. Thus after the collapse of the first republic and the defeat of the Carlists in their second uprising in the 1870s, large groups of republicans and Carlists emigrated to America. There they began, according to a Spanish journalist with long experience in the New World, a campaign of vicious anti-Spanish propaganda. In the years between the late 1870s and 1916, the journalist reported, Spaniards, disaffected by the course of events in their native land, did far more than the Italians and French to sully the reputation of Spain.[115]

The attempts of Primo de Rivera's government to foster closer ties with emigrant communities in America did not induce Spaniards either to cease internal feuds or to attenuate attacks against Spain. The 1926 flight of the *Plus Ultra* touched off a dispute among the Spanish residents in Buenos Aires, as described in Chapter 9. At the same time, moreover, the verbal and written condemnations of the Spanish government actually intensified; for most of the immigrants came from Galicia, the Basque provinces, and Cataluña and resented what they considered the dictator's endeavor to stamp out regional autonomy.

When it came, then, to strengthening Spanish Americans against alleged cultural and ethnic menaces and to establishing closer bonds of spiritual sympathy and cultural affinity between Spain and Spanish America, emigration from the peninsula probably exercised a negative effect. When it came to practical hispanismo, however, emigration was strikingly effective. The Spanish communities in America provided new markets for Spanish goods and their remittances helped substantially to maintain economic equilibrium in the peninsula. Perhaps most important of all, emigration provided Spaniards who might otherwise have formed a hotbed of revolutionary ferment the chance to earn a living, and sometimes even to prosper beyond their wildest dreams, in countries that were congenial at least in language and certain customs.

For some fifty years in the late nineteenth and early twentieth centuries, America was Spain's, especially northern Spain's, frontier. This frontier provided Spain with many of the advantages but only a very few of the drawbacks of colonial possessions; for the Spanish government paid virtually nothing for the privilege of exporting hundreds of thousands of men, who might otherwise have been unemployed, indigent, and burningly resentful, to lands where some of them could prosper and in the process support countless families in Spain and help sustain the entire peninsular economy. Had it not been for its frontier in Spanish America, which cost it next to nothing, Spain would have had to invest huge sums in internal colonization ventures and other domestic reforms or would have faced perhaps uncontainable revolutionary pressure from unemployed masses demanding an escape from misery.

Then suddenly at the end of 1929 the depression struck Spanish America with devastating fury and Spanish emigrants, even had they been able to afford the journey, would have been unable to find employment in the New World republics. In the 1930s, moreover, restrictive immigration quotas, only rumored in the 1920s, became a reality in Argentina.[116] All at once Spain confronted a situation which brooked no further delay in the inception of internal socioeconomic reforms. The crisis of the 1930s highlighted the failure of both liberals and conservatives, pursuing the methods they had developed at the turn of the century, as well as the failure of Primo de Rivera, to remove revolutionary pressures by providing adequate material and spiritual compensation to the working classes of the peninsula within a paternalistic, hierarchically organized society.

12: THE SOCIAL PROBLEM AND THE RESPONSE OF SPANISH CONSERVATIVES AND LIBERALS IN THE 1920s

From World War I to the Dictatorship: Signs of Social Crisis

Between early 1914 and late 1916, the average price in Spain for a dozen eggs rose from ten to fourteen pesetas; the price of ham tripled and for beef it increased sixfold; for a pair of rabbits, it soared from three-and-a-half to twenty pesetas. Seizing upon these circumstances, Spanish socialists began to make the high cost of food their principal issue in attacking the government and the entire established order.[1]

In 1917 lower-class discontent touched off violence in Madrid; and the authorities reacted by attempting "to suffocate this discontent in blood."[2] From the pages of the prestigious Madrid newspaper *ABC* the Duque del Infantado in 1918 called upon the nobility to take action to stave off social revolution. After referring ominously to the recent overthrow of the monarchy in Portugal and to the revolution in Russia, the Duque reminded his readers of food shortages in Spain, cost-of-living increases, violence in Barcelona, and the threat of a general strike. He exhorted Spain's noblemen to unite in defense of the monarchy and to initiate lavish charitable projects to ease the material suffering of the masses. Otherwise, he warned, the nobility, together with the monarchy, would be swept aside in a veritable bloodbath.[3]

The situation seemed no better in 1920. *Razón y Fe* complained that Spain was deluged by conflicts, agitation, and protests: "protests against the increase in the cost of all articles; protests against the lack of living facilities . . .; protests against the higher taxes threatened by new budgets; protests of rural renters against property owners . . .; protests of workers against management and management against workers." No longer confined to manual laborers, revolutionary syndicalism, the Jesuit journal continued, had begun to infect intellectuals, the teaching, medical, and other professions. *Razón y Fe* concluded, "there are anarchist strikes accompanied by assassinations and bombings; there is general impunity for crime, and fear invades the directing classes; authority is disdained and trampled underfoot by the canaille. Power like a ball passes from hand to hand without achieving even a moment of repose."[4] In the final sentence the publication alluded to the fact that since Alfonso XIII had come to the throne in 1902 the average duration of cabinets had been approximately nine months.[5]

A prominent intellectual writing in the pages of the official journal of the Institución Libre de Enseñanza agreed with *Razón y Fe* about the existence of a crisis. Laborers had become lazy, he contended, and had been pampered by the eight-hour-day legislation that reduced productivity and contributed to inflation. Meantime a vulgar, new-rich class had arisen; and the spectacle of its conspicuous consumption and social irresponsibility inflamed the hatred of the proletariat.[6]

Writing in 1920 in the pages of a liberal Madrid newspaper a member of the national chamber of deputies complained that the custodians of the law lived outside the law, giving to the lower classes the example of anarchy. The people, he charged, "are given sermons on submission and examples of indiscipline. . . . Not one of the urgently needed reforms has been enacted. . . . It would be rash to predict revolution. But it is certain that today there exist in our nation all the historic conditions of a revolutionary ambience."[7] Three years later González Posada wrote: "We find ourselves already in the torrents of a veritable revolution."[8]

In 1918 Spain was gripped by 256 strikes, up from 176 the previous year. One of the 1918 strikes involved the personnel of the ministry of the treasury and resulted in the total suspension of ministry services. "Such indiscipline cannot be permitted," *ABC* editorialized in connection with this strike. "Reality demands extraordinary and exceptional action."[9] Strikes, however, continued. In 1919 there were 403 of them involving 178,469 workers; and the following year there were 424, involving 244,684 workers.[10] A spokesman for the Catholic labor movement admitted in 1922 that the Church had lost the industrial worker either to socialist or anarchist unions.[11] As of that year the socialist Unión General de Trabajadores de España (UGT) claimed over 200,000 members. Although the anarchist Confederación Nacional del Trabajo (CNT) opposed compiling and publishing statistics, it may have had nearly as many members as the socialist organization.[12] As a respected Spanish economic historian has pointed out, it remains to be determined if anarchism developed at this time "as a consequence of the lack of vision and the severity of the management class in Spanish capitalism, or if this class adopted its hard position of strong resistance in the face of the anarchist tendencies of syndicalism."[13] Whatever the truth on this cause-effect issue, in the post-World War I days a confrontation seemed closer than ever before between the defenders of the established social-economic order in Spain and those intent upon its destruction.

The unpopular war that the Spanish government continued to wage in northern Africa contributed to the signs of social crisis in the early 1920s. For years socialists and republicans had urged withdrawal from Africa so that the government, by reducing its military expenditures, would have additional funds for domestic reform programs.[14] Discontent over the protracted African campaign reached new peaks in July of 1921 when Spanish troops fighting the Riff war sustained a bloody and humiliating defeat at Annual in Morocco. Francisco Cambó, a highly successful businessman and leader of a conservative regional-rights political group in Cataluña, was one of many influential Spaniards who joined the antiwar protesters following this setback. The war was unpopular, he stated, and the lower classes were justified in resisting conscription because "Spain will never reap important advantages from this effort; and meantime it prevents Spain from carrying out important social reforms and undertaking the work of regeneration."[15]

At the beginning of the critical year of 1922, the Catholic hierarchy issued a document, signed by all the prelates of Spain, proclaiming that the country and the Church were in danger. "Order," the bishops declared, "is disappearing, social peace is under attack from evil ideas and actions; the family is being weakened, the workers are suffering; authority is impotent to contain the spread of vices, ambitions, and the spirit of vengeance." The prelates called for a vast social campaign "to construct a dike against the diffusion of revolutionary syndicalist ideas." They called further for an increase in state subsidization for the clergy so as to enable parish priests, living in abnegation and penury, to play a more effective role in containing the menace of social revolution. "The cause of the nation and of the Church are one and the same," the bishops concluded, as they besought government support for the social campaign that Church officials, in collaboration with the lay faithful, stood ready to launch.[16]

The liberal intellectual Ortega y Gasset found other symptoms of Spain's sickness at this time and proposed different cures. Even as the Catholic hierarchy, though, he believed that Spain faced a grave social crisis. As Ortega y Gasset saw it, the crisis of Spain arose from its particularism. In times of national well-being, the philosopher asserted, classes and groups within the nation that desired something for themselves sought it by reaching accord with other classes and groups. Under such conditions, interest groups, instead of proceeding directly and immediately to the satisfaction of their desires, believed themselves obliged to seek the approval of the general will; and thus they proceeded through legal channels.[17] In contrast the Spain of his day, he affirmed, suffered from particularism, "that state of spirit in which we believe we do not have to take others into account. Sometimes because of excessive esteem for ourselves, at other times because of excessive disparagement of our neighbors, we lose the realization of our own limits and begin to feel ourselves completely independent."[18] The mentality of particularism, he observed, led to direct action and often violent action; for a class or group infected with particularism felt humiliated when in pursuit of its desires it had to have recourse to the institutions and social-political organisms that represented the interests of other classes and groups.[19]

How to emerge from the crisis of particularism that threatened to bring about a total collapse of the political, social, and economic order? "It is necessary," the philosopher averred, "to maintain alive in each class or profession the awareness that there exist about it many other classes and professions, . . . which are just as respectable as it is, which should be tolerated, and at least known, . . . even though they have other customs and ways." Ortega was convinced that only an exalted national ideal that cut across class and interest lines in capturing the allegiance of the entire populace would enable Spaniards to overcome the curse of particularism.[20] Unlike Catholics, who also stressed the need for a national ideal, Ortega did not associate the redemptive ideal with the traditional faith.

No ideal capable of facilitating Spanish unification was forthcoming and the atmosphere of crisis continued. In the first nine months of 1923 there were 411 strikes and bombings and acts of violence and terrorism occurred on a record-breaking scale in Barcelona. Early in September *ABC* complained of an epidemic of separatist sentiment in Cataluña and the Basque provinces, of sedition in Málaga, of violence on the streets of most Spanish cities, of the spread of banditry, of the multiplying of professional gunmen and thugs of every kind, and of notorious fraud in the public services. "Disorder and violence," in the words of the editorial, "result from the total lack of fear of authority and law. Little by little the state and its organs have come to be no more than a fiction."[21]

Later in the same month of September, specifically on the twenty-third, Miguel Primo de Rivera staged his coup d'etat. For the moment, at least, most Spaniards rejoiced. The preceding years had seemed to threaten so cataclysmic an upheaval that the majority of men with some stake in the prevailing system, however disparate their political views, accepted the need for dictatorship to preserve a hierarchically organized, stratified, "organic" social structure. And, general satisfaction with the dictator peaked in September of 1925 when Spanish troops, benefiting from French collaboration, effected a daring landing at the Bay of Alhucemas that brought a virtual end to the unpopular African war.

The Conservative Prescription for Rehabilitation and Social Harmony: The Vogue of the Corporative State

If Catholic conservatives tended initially to support the dictatorship, they regarded it as no more than a stopgap expedient which, having aided them in bringing about the fundamental reforms and restructuring that Spain required, would give way to a new era of monarchical institutionalism. What were the fundamental reforms that conservatives expected the dictator to help them implement? In essence, they involved the transforming of Spain into a corporative state, as defined by Catholic traditionalists.

The social prescriptions of conservatives in the 1920s differed very little

from the formulas laid down by their ideological forefathers in the nineteenth century. Society was sick, they said, because all of the intermediary
groups between individuals and government had been destroyed in accordance with the heretical principles of liberalism. As a result the isolated,
atomized individual had no means of making his voice heard in governing
circles. Under these circumstances the great majority of people lived outside of the political life of their country and had no dialogue with their
government. They were "bored and disillusioned with all political processes; they were skeptical of them and felt deceived by them."[22] They
hated the caciques for relegating them to the role of bribed, political non-
entities; they hated themselves for the fact that they had been corrupted
and politically emasculated by the caciques; and they hated the established system for having forced this degradation and impotence upon them.

Even as at the turn of the century, conservatives of the 1920s insisted
that the remedy for this situation lay in giving to individuals a decision-
making role in those functions that were most immediate to them and
about which they were likely to be well informed. To accomplish this,
they advocated sweeping decentralization. Autonomy, they said, should
be restored to the municipality; and corporations, that is semiautonomous
class- and functional-interest groups, should be reestablished in line with
medieval traditions. In this way the inorganic, atomistic society would be
transformed into the organic society. By the organic, corporative society
conservatives essentially meant one in which the individual participated
within the organisms or corporations appropriate to and intimately related
to his station and function in life.[23]

Once intermediary associations between the state and individual were
restored, guaranteed against overweening centralistic control, and given
a semiautonomous existence of their own, and once individuals were
allowed to participate in determining the policies of those groups with
which they were naturally associated because of social position and professional vocation, then the citizenry would shake off its indifference and
skepticism and assume a vital interest in directing those aspects of the
national life in which they could claim some competence. "With an awakened citizenry," one conservative Catholic wrote in the 1920s, "no system
of government is bad, not even absolutism or dictatorship."[24]

Conservatives, and for that matter liberals as well, clearly recognized
the dangerous alienation that resulted when Spaniards, with their traditional hypersensitive concern for their individual dignity regardless of
their social station, were forced to lead a depersonalized existence that
robbed them of that dignity. The alienation that the Spanish masses felt
from a society that in effect denied them the possibility of maintaining
an individual personality would, conservatives realized, bring on social
revolution. One of them stated: "The only thing we owe to Marx and
for which we can be grateful is his warning of a social revolution. And as

the means of avoiding it there has come into being the [concept of the] corporative state."[25]

In the view of Spanish conservatives, the authentic national values as traditionally propounded by the Church and accepted in previous centuries on all levels throughout the land, encouraged individuals to seek realization and gratification within the station in life into which they were born. When Spain was at its apogee under the Catholic Kings, its institutions, said the conservatives, had been in consonance with these values, for they had permitted the individual to achieve realization within his station. Inorganic democracy on the other hand, charged the conservatives, did not permit this and instead perpetrated a series of affronts and outrages against the personal dignity of those comprising the lower social groups. These affronts and outrages eventually would provoke revolution. Only within the corporative state, spokesmen of the right maintained, could the individuals of the lower social strata retain their dignity and therefore their willingness to heed the directing classes.

Anarchists also understood the degree to which Spaniards were alienated from an impersonal society that diminished their sense of individual dignity. They took advantage of this alienation to win thousands to their cause, promising them participation in new socio-economic organisms. But whereas many anarchists wanted a decentralized system without a governmental superstructure rising above autonomous local and interest groups, conservatives most definitely desired a highly complex superstructure. By giving to the masses the right to participate in the control of subsidiary groups, they hoped to impart to them a sense of political realization. The masses, they hoped, would not proceed from this to demand a voice in the more exalted realms of national administration that lay beyond their sphere of understanding.

Rising above the semiautonomous groups in the corporative state and empowered to resolve conflicts among those groups would be a national government, the legislative branch of which was chosen not by universal, inorganic suffrage on the basis of one man, one vote but rather by the semiautonomous groups or corporations. Congress would thus be made up of delegates chosen by the members of a peer group competent to judge the capabilities of the men they elected. In consequence, congressional posts purportedly would fall to men of recognized ability rather than to those whose only talent lay in political demagoguery and manipulation. Under these conditions the wielders of authority at the highest national level would constitute a "government for the people; but there would not at that level be government by the people."[26]

Deeming the functions of capital and labor to be of equal importance in the productive processes, conservatives hoped to award equal votes to these two sectors within each corporation in the selection of delegates to a national congress. This procedure, by providing capital with a weighted vote, would protect the hierarchical organization of society and guard against the leveling concept of one man, one vote. Moreover, in affairs of statecraft other vocations were considered just as essential as those associated with capital and labor. Therefore, according to conservative ideologists, intellectuals and members of the liberal professions should be represented in equal numbers along with capital and labor at the highest level of legislative power. Again, the result was to give to certain small elites a decidedly weighted vote. Conservatives defended this on the grounds that in the truly organic society each organ was as vital to the existence of the whole as any other; its importance did not depend upon its size.[27]

In the corporativist outlook on life, the preservation of higher values and the safeguarding of art and culture depended upon placing ultimate political power in the hands of an elite. "He who says democracy," Maeztu proclaimed in an utterance typical of his school, "says mediocrity."[28] In a similar vein, philosopher Manuel García Morente declared that one of the greatest and most enduring of all Spanish characteristics was the obsession with avoiding vulgarity. Democracy, however, encouraged and deified vulgarity and destroyed culture; it was therefore inimical to Spanish character, whereas corporativism, García implied, was congenial to that character.[29]

Spain's conservatives may or may not have been right about democracy's inclination toward mediocrity and vulgarity because of its assault against elites and its encouragement of social flux and mobility. They may or may not have been right in their contention that inorganic democracy inevitably crushed individual dignity and personality. They may or may not have been right in prescribing decentralization and the creation of intermediary, semiautonomous groups between government and individuals as the means for preventing the dehumanization of the masses and, in the wake of this, social revolution. These are the issues, though, that make the corporative ideas of Spanish conservatism in the 1920s relevant to the situation of the 1960s and 1970s in many advanced countries of the Western world.[30] The prescience of many Spanish intellectuals, beginning with Balmes and others in the nineteenth century, in foreseeing the consequences of an affluent but depersonalized capitalist, democratic society is well-nigh frightening. This prescience moreover, often shared in by imitative Spanish-speaking thinkers of the New World, helps account for whatever vogue Spain's conservative ideology has enjoyed through the years in Spanish America.

Catholic Spokesmen of the Corporate State in the 1920s

Early Spanish advocates of decentralization and the corporative state, as described in Chapters 1 and 4, had included Balmes, Donoso Cortés, and Vicent.[31] In the early twentieth century Maura was the leading conservative statesman identified with this position. In vain, he tried to put the ideas of the Catholic right into effect by bestowing relative autonomy on municipalities and providing for municipal councils based upon corporative or functional representation.[32] Other Catholic proponents of the corporative state attracted attention in the 1920s.[33] Two of the principal ones were Juan Vázquez de Mella (1861–1928), the outstanding intellectual figure of twentieth-century Carlism,[34] and Víctor Pradera (1872–1936), for many years a leading representative of Catholic traditionalism in the national chamber of deputies.[35]

Vázquez de Mella justified the corporative state on the grounds that it was the structure within which governing officials in high positions could best seek out the wisdom of the masses. The system in effect in restoration Spain, he maintained, based upon inorganic democracy, had resulted in an inversion of the proper political processes. He referred to caciquismo, the most characteristic product of restoration democracy, as an inverted plant that had its roots in the ministries, while its branches and leaves reached into the last recesses of rural town councils. To correct this inversion, Mella declared, "we aspire to establish the corporative life in which the municipalities will reacquire the land which the centralizing state took from them. . . . We desire that classes and interest will be organized hierarchically so that they will again have the intense life that is born initially in the bosom of the family and natural organizations and that does not depend upon the public power." The corporative organization, he added, would end centralism and encourage regionalism; and it would guarantee that within every sphere of activity, power would rise from below to above.[36]

Further developing his ideas, Mella observed that when all sovereignty is concentrated in an oligarchy that constitutes the national government and political parties, then every particle of political control is in the hands of a few men: "they possess all of the preeminences and rights; and those who are not a part of this narrow oligarchy must submit abjectly to it."[37] This being the case, all who do not share in power or sovereignty on the highest national level, the only level on which any meaningful vestige of political power exists, desire somehow to acquire a role in the exercise of sovereignty. The engineer, the priest, the doctor, the lawyer, the military officer, men of all vocations, in fact, cease to operate within their proper spheres and covet a share in political sovereignty at the very highest national level. This desire leads, Mella warned, to unbridled ambition and concupiscence, encourages corruption, and erodes the specialization essential at all times to the properly organized social-political structure.[38]

In all organically ordered societies, Mella contended, there are five categories "that express the great collective interests." These categories are material interest, represented by the men engaged in agriculture, industry, and commerce; intellectual interest, represented by the men of the schools, universities, and scientific-cultural organizations; moral and religious interest, represented by the priesthood; the defense interest, represented by men of the army and navy; and finally the historical political interest, represented ideally by a class that is not only an aristocracy of blood but that actually embodies the "social superiorities and virtues." "If you wish to reproduce in a parliament these categories that are natural and self-evident," Mella wrote, "you will have to do so in such a way that all these social forces or interests are condensed and reproduced as in a mirror. Take one away, and society is mutilated; take all away, and society disappears."[39]

According to Mella a great virtue of the corporative society he envisioned was that it would do away with equalitarian democracy, "one of the monumental failures in the modern world."[40] True democracy for him was "hierarchical democracy." It rested upon the natural selection of superior people by various associations or corporations where subsidiary power resided. In the true or hierarchical democracy the masses below did not have the right to govern, except within their own limited interest groups; they had instead "the right to be well governed and to demand that they were well governed."[41]

Writing in the 1920s, Víctor Pradera asserted that society was naturally organized into classes and that in order to function properly political institutions must reflect class divisions. According to him the five major classes were those comprised of industrialists, landowners, merchants, members of the liberal professions, and manual laborers. Each of these classes, he said, should be represented within the national Cortes.[42]

By the early 1930s Pradera had arrived at certain refinements in prescribing for the ideal, corporative or organic national assembly. It should, he said, be divided into nine sections, with fifty representatives for each. Seven of these sections Pradera designated as agriculture, commerce, industry, property, manual labor, professional labor, and regions. An eighth section was made up of the five natural bodies of the state: clergy, aristocracy, magistracy, diplomatic service, and armed forces. Each of these five bodies would elect ten representatives to the eighth section within the Cortes. Finally, the national legislature would include a ninth section of fifty deputies representing "national corporations" whose ends were moral, intellectual, or economic. Most of the business of the Cortes, Pradera explained, would be conducted not by all 450 deputies assembled together but by homogeneous groups of fifty, within which each deputy would have firsthand knowledge of matters under discussion.[43] Essential to the smooth functioning of this system was a monarch who would exercise a moderating power in resolving conflicts among the various sections so as to synthesize all their efforts into a concerted, national policy.[44]

Pradera argued that the corporative society as he outlined it would do away with the monstrous foolishness of asking an inorganic electorate to decide issues about which the constituency had no understanding. When people voted only within their own class or interest group they could cast an intelligent ballot. In contrast, the formula of one man, one vote within an inorganic, amorphous, undifferentiated mass electorate was tantamount to "one animal, one vote . . . [for] within the structure of inorganic democracy, voting could not be an intelligent act."[45]

In the 1920s Spain's Christian Democrats continued their strong advocacy of the corporative state.[46] Manuel de Burgos y Mazo, one of the movement's leaders, ascribed the social ills of Spain to the fact that the functions of natural organisms, by which he meant social classes, interest groups, regions and municipalities, had been absorbed by a centralistic state. As a result the natural organisms had lost their freedom of action and their dynamism; the "spark of the people had been snuffed out," for within the absorptionist state there was no opportunity for their participation. Spain, he declared, could not begin to progress toward fulfilling its destiny until the state recognized the existence of "collectivities with their own and autonomous personality, not dependent upon the state for their existence and for the laws that govern their essential functions."[47]

In the Spanish Christian Democratic concept, the corporative state was to rest upon distinct syndicates for labor on the one hand and for the capital-management sector on the other. Every entity of economic production throughout the country was to organize two syndicates, one for labor, the other for capital-management. Local syndicates of each distinct economic enterprise, such as mining, manufacturing, transportation, services, agriculture, defense, liberal professions, and the like, would then be linked together with syndicates of similar function into regional and ultimately into national confederations. At each level of this hierarchical structure, the labor and capital-management syndicates of the particular economic enterprise would elect an equal number of representatives— note the weighted vote for capital-managment—to a corporation. In this scheme, then, corporations were joint labor, capital-management groupings. Every sector of the entire productive spectrum would have its distinct corporations, local, regional, and national; and these corporations would set policy for and resolve disputes within the various producing concerns of the country. In addition, corporations would elect the members of the national legislative assembly, thus substituting suffrage by class and interest group for inorganic universal suffrage.[48]

At every level of this organic structure envisaged by Christian Democrats, syndicates, whether representing labor or capital-management, would be Catholic in spirit and under the influence, although not the direct control, of the priesthood. Throughout the 1920s, Christian Democrats continued to criticize, as they had been doing since early in the century,[49] the insistence of many Catholic leaders upon forming joint labor-capital syndicates under overt Church control. Unless encouraged by Catholic officials to form strictly labor syndicates enjoying freedom from direct internal intervention by capital-management and the clergy, Spain's laboring classes would, Christian Democrats maintained, increasingly spurn the Church and drift into socialist, anarchist, and other radical organizations.[50]

Into the Catholic literature advocating the corporative society, Antonio Goicoechea introduced the concept of proportional representation. Goichoechea, who had completed his law studies at the University of Madrid in 1895 and who had served as minister of interior in 1919, when Maura presided over the council of ministers, had by the 1920s emerged as a leading spokesman of Catholic conservatism. He was also one of his school's most ardent hispanoamericanistas.

According to the diagnosis offered by Goicoechea in 1925, the infirmities of Spanish politics resulted from two things: the "absenteeism" of the people, of the masses, from participation in any of the processes of decision making; and the domination of the majority over the superior minorities.[51] As a cure, Goicoechea prescribed a two-house national legislature, the upper chamber to be corporatively structured so as to represent class and interest groups. The lower house was to be constituted by delegates of political parties elected on the basis of proportional representation. Goicoechea thought that political parties, as many as possible and the more the better, should present themselves before the general electorate; and the number of votes each party received would determine the proportion of its representation in the lower chamber. The leadership of each party would then designate the men who would fill the assigned number of deputy posts. Thus the wishes of the uninformed majority would be tempered and interpreted by the informed minorities that directed the nation's political parties. The result, Goicoechea argued, would be a higher level of competence, morality, and intelligence in the chamber of deputies. At the same time the general electorate would feel more involved in the political process because presented with more options and alternatives by the numerous competing parties. Many of these parties would be purely local or regional in scope and thus more directly related to voters than the distant and aloof handful of parties that ever since the restoration had relied upon caciques to turn out the electorate.[52]

Liberals and the Corporative State

Whether in the mid-nineteenth century when influenced by Krause or at the turn of the century when under the spell of positivism, liberals, almost as consistently as conservatives, criticized the atomistic individualism said to result from an inorganic political structure.[53] As briefly related in Chapter 5, some liberals hoped to remedy the alarming isolation of the individual from the state by infusing the municipality with renewed vigor and restoring the various corporations, guilds, and semiautonomous groups that had flourished in medieval Spain. Except for the fact that so far as they were concerned the religious influence had been too pervasive, liberals tended to admire the Spanish Middle Ages as much as conservatives.[54] A fundamental reason for this was the widespread liberal approval of the organic, corporative society.[55]

Ramón Menéndez Pidal always maintained that inorganic universal suffrage must inevitably fail in Spain because it produced results inimical to the Spaniard's sense of individualism. He complained, moreover, that not enough Spanish statesmen concerned themselves with how to make an "organic adaptation" of universal suffrage so that it would be appropriate to Spaniards.[56] In the light of conservative preoccupation, from at least the time of Balmes through the 1920s, with restructuring Spain along corporativist lines and in view of persistent liberal activity directed toward the same end, this complaint hardly seems warranted.

The concern of conservatives and liberals with effecting the "organic adaptation" of universal suffrage is one of the few constants in restoration politics. But this concern produced few if any results because although both ideological camps saw the corporative state as a desirable means for preserving the hierarchical society and avoiding equalitarian, majoritarian democracy, they differed decidedly on one fundamental matter. Conservatives viewed the corporative state as an instrument for increasing the Church's temporal influence and liberals saw it as a means for achieving the secular society. As a result each side sought zealously to block the corporativist aspirations of the other. Not until the religious issue had been resolved, therefore, or until a dictatorship capable of ignoring both conservative and liberal wishes had been established, could Spaniards have succeeded in remaking their society in the organic, corporative mold.

As early as 1885 Labra had urged a modified guild system, adapted from Spanish medieval traditions, as a means of ending proletariat alienation by encouraging worker participation in mixed labor-capital groups.[57] In the same period Eduardo Pérez Pujol, a Krausist and at one time the rector of the University of Valencia, advocated a corporativist solution to the socioeconomic and political problems of Spain. As so many of his school, Pérez Pujol vastly admired his country's medieval institutions, especially the guild system.[58] In 1892 Julio Puyol y Alonso, an historian and sociologist whose spirit of secularism qualified him as a liberal, published a book in which he criticized the failures of inorganic democracy and urged that Spain adopt a corporativist organization.[59]

By 1898 Joaquín Costa was advocating a corporative society organized on the basis of syndicates and crafts guilds; and the General Assembly of Spanish Chambers of Commerce that met in Zaragoza in November of that year adopted resolutions that reflected the Costa program.[60] Another liberal, Vital Fité, came out in 1899 in favor of the corporative society based on class- and functional-interest groups.[61] In 1902 the liberal politician-sociologist-historian-journalist José Cascales y Muñoz published a book that was lavishly praised in a prologue by José Canalejas. In this work Cascales maintained that the old liberal dream of democracy, resting upon universal suffrage, was thoroughly discredited. Economic and class interests were the only vital forces in society, he declared, and the political system should reflect this fact. Each profession, he advised, should organize itself into a league in which workers and management were equally represented; and each professional league should then select its candidates for local and national elections. The number of representatives for each league, Cascales explained, would be set in accordance with the principles of proportional representation—but he did not go into detail as to just how this representation would be determined and allotted. Within a system such as he advocated, Cascales wrote, people would again become interested in and participate in the processes of government. Except for one brief sentence as he described the ideal corporativist structure, Cascales sounded remarkably like his conservative contemporaries. In that one sentence he maintained that religious beliefs were no longer an influence in modern states and that harmony in social and economic relations could only be obtained by prescinding from religion.[62]

Canalejas himself favored the corporative features for municipal elections included in the local reform projects that Maura presented unsuccessfully to the Cortes during the 1903–1904 sessions. And in the municipal legislation that he in turn unsuccessfully introduced in 1906 and 1912, Canalejas also provided for partial corporative representation on the local level.[63] In this he appeared to be evidencing his conviction that "the majority can be oppressive, tyrannical, erroneous and there is a need to protect minorities against it."[64]

In 1917 González Posada complained that the system of universal suffrage had collapsed in Spain.[65] Six years later he came out unequivocally in favor of the corporative senate. "It is important," he wrote, "that the senate cease to be a high chamber of nobles and of other types of archaic notables and undergo conversion into a body resting on a syndical base in which all the organized social and interest elements can make themselves heard and can collaborate in the . . . tasks of ruling the economic life of the country and determining the political course of this nation." Posada maintained that this transformation could be achieved without provoking dangerous convulsions. "The most dangerous thing would be to leave the nation constituted as it presently is."[66] In justifying his stance, Posada noted that Francisco Giner de los Ríos, the animating spirit behind the Institución Libre de Enseñanza and in many ways the leading intellectual of Spanish liberalism in the late nineteenth and early twentieth centuries,[67] favored the corporative organization of the senate. Giner, in fact, referred to the corporative senate as an instrument of conservatism "in the highest sense of the word, in a pure Krausist conception."[68]

New liberals appeared on the scene in the 1920's to add their voices to those of older colleagues in calling for the corporative state.[69] One of them, Antonio Zozaya, published an interesting article in the journal of the Institución Libre de Enseñanza in which he asserted: "It is necessary to choose a new path, and the approach to this path has to be by way of an organic, corporativist constitution."[70] Like the earlier liberal proponent of corporativism Cascales Muñoz, Zozaya spoke out in favor of the secular state. With considerable passion he proclaimed there could be no education worthy of the name until Spaniards gained release from authoritarian influences as perpetuated by confessional instruction.

Primo de Rivera and the Corporative Organization of Spain

Revealing the degree to which he was influenced by the organic concepts both of conservatives and liberals, Primo de Rivera early in his dictatorship wrote: "The principal cell of the nation has to be the municipality and the family; the nucleus is the province; and the vertebrae which give shape to the whole system is the state. Not, however, an absorbent, centralized, bureaucratized, and inert state, but one that inspires, stimulates, and lends impulse to the natural organisms."[71] No modern state could exist, the dictator continued, without "the intense intervention" and "active participation" of its citizens "in the collective life." Therefore, he declared, his state would organize various institutions and tribunals through which citizens could give effective voice to their demands and seek redress of grievances.[72] In achieving this goal the dictator attached priority to the restoration of municipal autonomy. The autonomous municipality, he wrote, not the central state, could best undertake the task of "enlisting the interest and participation of citizens," of arousing the concern of the people for the common good of Spain, and of "tapping new energies that will be economically advantageous to the nation." Above all, Primo stressed, the autonomous municipality would provide Spaniards with the opportunity "to participate in public life on the level at which they can best understand that life."[73]

On minister of the treasury José Calvo Sotelo, a Galician born in 1893 who had been a follower of Maura and a member of the Grupo de la Democracia Cristiana,[74] Primo de Rivera conferred the responsibility of revitalizing the country's municipalities. When informing his treasury minister about what he was expected to accomplish, the dictator had perceptively noted the similarity in plans for municipal reform developed early in the century by the Conservative Maura and the Liberal Canalejas.[75] And Calvo Sotelo's program for restoring some measure of autonomy to local governments and ending the control that caciques had for decades exercised over them drew heavily upon the plans both of Maura and Canalejas.[76]

Calvo Sotelo's program, enacted into law in 1924, provided that corporative bodies, grouped under the three main headings of capital-management, labor, and culture, would select one-third of the members of each municipal council.[77] In actual practice the municipal reform law, as was true of so many of the enactments of the dictatorship period, did not produce the ostensibly intended results because its provisions were ignored. Thus instead of being selected by corporation membership and the municipal electorate at large, as provided by the 1924 law, town councilmen were appointed by higher authorities.[78]

Early in his regime Primo de Rivera also proposed the formation of a corporative system that would bring labor and management "face to face and endow each with equal rights and identical responsibilities" in regulating the economic life of the country.[79] Such "an authentic Spanish system," Primo wrote, would not only prevent class struggle by guaranteeing harmony between capital and labor, "the supreme aspiration of our people;" it would in addition create among the participants in each of the professions and activities of the country a "clear consciousness of citizenship."[80]

To prepare legislation for the restructuring of Spain along corporative lines Primo turned to Eduardo Aunós Pérez, his minister of labor, commerce, and industry. Born in Lérida in 1894, Aunós Pérez, together with his younger brother Antonio, had for some time been active in various Catalan Catholic groups working to adapt Spain's medieval, corporative traditions to contemporary circumstances.[81] A decree law of November, 1926, prepared by Aunós provided for the "national corporative organization" of Spain. The key element in the corporative structure was the *comité paritario*, a committee on which labor and capital-management were equally represented.[82] Each producing firm, enterprise, or business in Spain, outside of agriculture, that contributed in whatever way to the gross national product was to maintain separate syndicates for labor and capital-management. These syndicates were to elect an equal number of representatives to the comité partiario. Presiding over each of the committees was an official appointed by the government. Thus in the likely event that delegates of labor and capital-management should deadlock on a particular issue, the government representative would cast the deciding vote.[83]

Above the local comités paritarios rose a complex hierarchical superstructure. The entire Spanish economy was compartmentalized into twenty-seven groups, including primary industries, processing industries, various types of services, and the like. Each one of these twenty-seven groups constituted a corporation and each corporation was controlled by a *consejo de corporación.* This council was made up of an equal number of labor and capital-management representatives, chosen by the comités paritarios of the local, subsidiary firms and enterprises included in the particular corporation. The councils were empowered to issue binding decrees determining conditions of labor and to set salaries and production quotas. As with the comités paritarios, the president of each consejo de corporación was appointed by the government.

At the very top of this structure was the *comisión delegada de los consejos de corporaciones.* The commission was constituted by an equal number of labor and capital-management delegates selected by the consejos de corporaciones. Its function was to resolve disputes among the twenty-seven corporations and to fuse and synthesize the policies of each into one national economic program. It served further as an advisory commission for the ministry of labor, commerce, and industry.

The syndicates most widely recognized as the authentic representatives of labor in each of the twenty-seven economic groupings and empowered to elect worker delegates to each of the local comités paritarios were those affiliated with the socialist Unión General de Trabajadores. Favored with official government recognition, and benefiting from the fact that the state official on the comités and consejos often voted on the side of labor, the UGT moderated its early radicalism, resolving to collaborate with rather than to seek the destruction of the capitalist system. To a considerable degree, then, the dictator succeeded in co-opting, at least temporarily, the once dreaded socialist labor movement into the established order.[84]

The corporative organization of Spain during the dictatorship was more *de jure* than real and substantive. For example, of the twenty-seven envisioned corporations for industry and services, only two were actually organized. Many of Spain's rightists, both conservatives and liberals, who were favorably disposed toward the corporative reorganization of Spain understandably complained about the dictator's lack of accomplishments in pursuit of this goal. Many of them also took issue with the theories and the rationale of corporativism as developed by Primo de Rivera and his partisans.

The Spanish Right and the Dictatorship

Several years before the Primo de Rivera coup, Vázquez de Mella had begun to advocate establishment of a military dictatorship to preside over the transformation of Spain into a corporative society. In his view the only alternative to this was likely to be a leveling social revolution.[85] When Primo seized power, then, Mella looked on with enthusiastic approval. So did Víctor Pradera. To him the dictatorship meant an end to revolutionary uprisings and the introduction of corporative principles in social, economic, and political organization.[86] Pradera's satisfaction with the course of events increased when Primo de Rivera, shortly after the September coup, asked him to prepare four position papers, three of which had to do with the corporative restructuring of Spain.[87]

The approving attitudes of Mella and Pradera typified the initial conservative reaction to the dictatorship. Antonio Maura was one of the few representatives of Spanish conservatism who from the outset expressed opposition to the military regime.[88] He foresaw the failure of the dictator's programs; and he feared that as the general disgraced himself the monarchy would in turn be discredited because of the manner in which Alfonso XIII had appeared not just to accept but to welcome the military regime. Some of Maura's fears were speedily confirmed, for the antidictator campaign waged by many Spanish liberals, among them Unamuno and Blasco Ibáñez, soon developed into one of the most serious antimonarchical movements that Spain had witnessed since the restoration.

If at first Maura stood as a relatively isolated figure in his opposition to the dictatorship, it was not long before an increasing number of conservatives began to come around to his position. By 1928, three years after Maura's death, Pradera was complaining that Primo, in spite of his rhetoric, had not moved effectively to transform Spain into a corporative state. Spain, he charged, had only the superficial trappings of corporativism; beneath a veneer, it still clung to the old and discredited ways of regulating its economic and political life.[89]

Spain's Christian Democrats, already beginning in the 1920s to incline toward political accidentalism, the view that the form of government was not of essential importance and that a republic could be as suitable for Spain as monarchy, did not share Maura's great concern lest the dictatorship ultimately undermine royal legitimacy. At first, with some notable exceptions,[90] they welcomed the dictator with enthusiasm. Five years after the Primo coup, however, El Debate, the Madrid daily that increasingly had come to reflect Christian Democratic views, had resorted to veiled criticism not only of the dictator's failure to establish true corporativism but of the overly centralized manner in which he was pursuing the corporative goal. By this time the staunchest and most consistent supporters of the dictatorship among the Catholic right were men of fascist leanings and the admirers of Mussolini, among them Calvo Sotelo and the Aunós Pérez brothers, who favored the corporative state because they regarded it as an instrument of a strong central government, with power imposed from above instead of rising from below.[91]

In criticizing Primo de Rivera's corporativism, Christian Democrats and other Catholics pointed out that the comités paritarios and consejos de corporaciones did not reflect the wishes of the syndicates which they supposedly represented; instead they were the puppet creatures of the government, manipulated by their presiding officers appointed by a centralistic state.[92] An influential priest noted that the Church did not give blanket approval to corporative principles. Some corporative systems, he maintained, were good, others were morally indifferent, while some were actually evil. Those that encouraged centralism, rather than the dispersal of power among subsidiary, semiautonomous groups, were evil.[93]

Catholics who criticized Primo's corporativism did so not only because it failed to create a decentralized structure within which individuals could reacquire a sense of dignity by participating meaningfully in shaping those decisions that most immediately affected their interests; they criticized it also because it frustrated the Church's aspirations to strengthen its temporal influence and to rout the forces of secularization. Thus they censured Primo de Rivera for recognizing the numerically strong UGT rather than the weak and demoralized Catholic syndicates as the principal agency for selecting labor's representatives on the comités and consejos.[94] Because socialists and government officials suspected of indifference and even hostility toward religion, rather than men of good Catholic conscience, had gained control over the corporative machinery, a large number of Spanish Catholics denounced the dictator for having subverted true corporative principles.[95]

As Primo de Rivera continued in office and showed decreasing interest in relinquishing power, some Catholics began to demand a return at any price to constitutional procedures. Contemptuously dubbed the New Right[96] by their detractors, these Catholics maintained also that the Church was not doctrinally committed to the corporative state. Democracy based upon universal inorganic suffrage should, they argued, be modified slightly and tamed, perhaps by means of a two-house legislature in which one chamber would be directly chosen by the electorate at large, the other by class and interest groups. Given the popularity of democracy and universal suffrage throughout the world it was not realistic, according to this school, to seek their total suppression.[97]

In its position, Spain's Catholic New Right shared a common ground with some of the country's liberals who had grown disillusioned with corporativism because of the way in which a dictator, seemingly intent upon retaining power indefinitely, was imposing it. The Liga Constitucional, formed by Liberal leader Romanones to combat the dictatorship, advocated a program strikingly similar to that of the New Right. Demanding a return to constitutional government and the convoking of a Cortes elected by universal suffrage,[98] the League did not rule out the possibility that one house could be chosen by corporative procedures.

The Fall of the Dictator and Increasing Polarization in Spain

Shortly before the dictator's fall a Catholic writer quoted Primo de Rivera to the effect that the basic purpose of his government was to devise a system for achieving social solidarity suitable not only to Spain but also to Spanish America. The writer complained that the specific fault of

Primo's government lay in its failure to produce a system. The search for social solidarity had been carried out through opportunism and improvisation, he said; whatever partial success it had achieved was owing to the prosperity of the times, not to the soundness of administration plans and programs.[99]

Discontent with the dictator had been mounting for some time in Spain, spearheaded by intellectuals who objected strenuously to curbs on freedom of expression and to Primo's reluctance to formulate plans for a return to constitutional procedures. The depression struck the mortal blow against the regime, depriving it of the funds to carry out its various development programs which, however much they had suffered from improvisation, had contributed to social tranquility. Menaced by an army conspiracy and having lost the confidence of the king, Primo de Rivera resigned on January 29, 1930, and went into immediate exile in Paris, where he lived out the remaining three months of his life.

Spain again faced the social and economic problems that had so alarmed the directing classes in the early 1920s and led them in general to welcome the dictator when he had seized power; only now these problems were exacerbated by the effects of a depression. The dictator had done little more than buy time for the established order and lure certain of its leaders into a sense of false security about the ease with which that order could be preserved. He had not contributed to a lasting resolution of Spain's social crisis.

A Catholic writer who had devoted much of his life to advancing the Church's social program noted in early 1930 that the agrarian laborers of Córdoba, and of all Andalusia for that matter, were on the verge of revolution. He pointed also to a remarkable resurgence in the strength of the anarchist labor organization among industrial, urban workers. Anarchist unions had been weakened by the repressive measures of the dictatorship and by the official support that Primo extended their traditional rival, the socialist UGT. With this support removed, however, the temporarily tamed and domesticated socialists were being eclipsed by the revolutionary anarchists.[100]

In mid-1930 a journalist for a Madrid periodical reported in alarm on the "commercial catastrophe" in Bilbao. The social problem created by this catastrophe was, he said, producing terrifying consequences, for the communists were gaining control over organized labor and threatening to launch a social revolution.[101] In Madrid people were said to be dying of cold and hunger as the winter of 1930 began, and the streets were inundated with hordes of beggars "such as had not been seen in years." Reporting on these conditions for a local journal, another writer raised the question as to how much longer peace could be maintained between rich and poor.[102]

Spanish liberals had traditionally voiced their confidence in a process of social evolution that would lead to constantly improving cultural and material standards of living for the masses, thereby eliminating the danger of class warfare. Other countries of the world, liberal Europeanizers assured their fellow citizens following the disaster of 1898, had already discovered the best processes for facilitating this natural evolutionary development, whereas Spain's archaic institutions and customs allegedly impeded it. Therefore liberals had called upon Spain to imitate the more rapidly advancing countries of Europe. The depression, however, seriously challenged the liberal belief in straight-line evolutionary improvement in all countries that enjoyed enlightened rule, for even those countries that were most advanced and assumed by Spanish liberals to be most enlightened faced crises that threatened the very survival of their traditional institutions and social-economic patterns.

In the 1870s, the appearance of a social problem in Spain had alarmed the liberal intellectual José de Moreno Nieto to the point that he had renounced his former anticlericalism and begun to urge cooperation with the Church in the struggle to maintain social harmony. He declared: "We must with all speed reestablish the great moral forces and religious beliefs, whose influence we have sought until now to reduce and even to suppress."[103] Shortly before his death in 1903 Práxedes Mateo Sagasta, the Spanish Liberal Party's principal leader, had, at least according to the author of a biographical sketch, come to realize the socially catastrophic consequences of anticlericalism and universal suffrage. As a result, the writer maintained, Sagasta had in his last years withdrawn in disillusionment and dismay from the political arena.[104]

In the 1870s Moreno Nieto's ideological transformation had been practically unique among Spanish liberals. Nor did Sagasta's questioning of his old beliefs—assuming without conclusive evidence that this questioning took place—set a pattern that other liberals emulated. In the early twentieth century, Spain's liberals were confident as never before of the soundness of their convictions. They were optimistic that as an inevitable aftermath to the 1898 disaster the traditionalist Catholics would be repudiated and swept from the field of intellectual and political contention. By 1930, however, as they faced an explosive situation liberals were wondering if Donoso Cortés could possibly have been right when he wrote: "The most total remedy against the revolution can only be Catholicism, because Catholicism is the one doctrine that is its absolute contradiction."[105] The rise of communist influence also gave wavering liberals food for thought, for conservatives had always depicted communism as the unavoidable consequence of liberalism.

Writing in 1935, one of Catholic conservatism's most perceptive analysts of Spain's historical past and its contemporary problems stated that his country's liberals had never desired the consequences of their doctrines of universal suffrage and anticlericalism. Liberals, he contended, had

always been as much opposed as conservatives to any leveling social movement that threatened the existence of hierarchies. Given the conditions of
the early 1930s they were purportedly being forced into an awareness of
the results that must inescapably flow from their ideology. As a result, he
concluded, liberals had turned back toward the nation's traditional formal
religion as they endeavored to contain the forces of social revolution.[106]
Perhaps the retreat of liberals from their historic position was not as massive as the Catholic writer implied. However there were indications to
suggest that the trend had developed.

At the outset of the 1930s Gregorio Marañón y Posadillo (1887–1960),
a medical doctor and Renaissance-type cultural universalist who had once
clearly identified with Spanish liberalism, objected to the movement's
time-honored anticlericalism.[107] At the same time that Marañón voiced his
objection an article appeared in one of Madrid's journals that had for
years maintained a classically laissez-faire attitude on economic questions
and an anticlerical orientation on Church-state issues. The author of
this article asserted: "Without a moral and ethical sense based on Christianity, no social harmony is possible; and social harmony must be the
great, overriding concern of all governments."[108]

Increasingly disposed to accept Catholicism as an important force for
preventing social upheaval, liberals were ready to associate any move
directed against the traditional rights and privileges of the Church as
heralding an attack against the social order. Thirty, twenty, even ten years
earlier, liberals would have delighted in the anticlerical measures enacted
during the second republic. In the 1930s, however, many one-time liberals
had come, even as Catholics had for years been telling them they must
rationally and logically do, to equate anticlericalism with revolutionary
objectives for social reorganization.

Traditional, Catholic Spain had demonstrated remarkable staying
powers and had for the moment at least begun to assimilate the other
Spain. Historical liberalism was becoming less and less visible in the
intellectual-political landscape. Its proponents in large numbers merged
into various conservative groups; others took up with the more moderate
elements supporting the republic. In either instance the effect was to rob
Spanish liberalism of its existence as a separate, independent intellectual
and political movement.

Before the threat, real or imagined, of a massive, thoroughly radical
and revolutionary assault against the social structure, the two ideological
Spains had drawn together. Spain was polarized at the beginning of the
1930s, but not as it had characteristically been since the eighteenth century. At one pole there now stood the previously contending elements,
conservative and liberal, which had always had much in common because
of a similar vision of the organic society as a Spanish ideal. At the other
pole stood those who advocated either the inorganic, open, pluralistic

society, or a Marxist dictatorship of the proletariat, or an anarchist republic of one type or another.

Those who took their stand around the pole on the right were determined to maintain the hierarchically structured organic society in Spain. Many of them hoped also to contribute to the preservation of such a social order in Spanish America. But underneath their willingness to cooperate toward realizing these supreme objectives, they were divided and disconnected on virtually every secondary issue.

13: A DIVIDED SPANISH RIGHT IN DEFENSE OF AUTHORITY, HIERARCHY, AND ORDER, 1930–1936

The Right's Apocalyptic Vision of the Struggle between Good and Evil

At the beginning of 1930 a Catholic intellectual long active in the Church's social program noted that nine rightist political associations had appeared in Spain, each aspiring to become a major political party. None of the nine groups, he said, could ever hope to establish itself as a powerful force, let alone gain a majority in a national Cortes. Unless the country's rightists united, he foresaw disaster for them at the next election.[1]

The right remained divided and at the municipal elections of April 12, 1931, sustained a stunning defeat from the combined republican-socialist forces. The main issue in these elections, the first held in over eight years, was whether Spain should continue as a monarchy. Forty-six of the fifty largest towns voted republican and the following day Alfonso XIII, under the urging of the Conde de Romanones, leader of the constitutional monarchists, left Spain so as to spare the country bloodshed.[2] Taking advantage of the confusion and institutional disarray accompanying the collapse of the monarchy, anarchists in May spearheaded the first of several widespread sprees of church and convent burnings.

A constituent Cortes that assembled in Madrid in July of 1931 was a predominantly anticlerical body.[3] In October it approved, by a vote of 267 to 41, Article 3 of the proposed republican constitution, stipulating "The Spanish state does not have an official religion." Shortly after the vote of approval Manuel Azaña, leader of the Left Republicans and minister of the army in the provisional government, arose in the Cortes and began a speech with the words: "Spain is no longer Catholic." On October 14, the day after the Azaña speech, the Cortes, by a vote of 178 to 59, approved Article 26 of the draft constitution. This article provided for the suppression of the Jesuit order, called for the total extinction of state subvention to the clergy within a maximum period of two years, and prohibited all religious orders from engaging in teaching activities, thereby striking at the base of the Church's educational system.[4]

Responding to Article 26, the man who would shortly become Spain's primate as the Cardinal-Archbishop of Toledo took up his pen "to defend a most sacred cause," affirming that the state subvention to the clergy was "justified by history and by the divine positive and natural laws . . .

which are prior and superior to those of the state."[5] Almost simultaneously a priest who was a widely read journalist denounced the provision that forbade religious orders to engage in teaching:

> The height of injustice is that a dozen Moors, Jews, Protestants, or Buddhists, without academic title, could form a community or association and found a school and teach in it; while on the other hand a dozen religious cannot do this, although they possess the titles. If, however, they took off their habits and delivered themselves to scandalous lives, then they would be allowed to educate. These are the juridic and pedagogical monstrosities that inflame the blood and incite us to struggle to the death against those who impose them.[6]

So far as a civilian leader of conservative Catholicism was concerned, republican Spain had, because of its anticlerical program, ceased to be a genuine patria and become instead an antipatria. "The Spanish state," he wrote, "could never have come into existence if it had not been united by the Catholic concept of civilization; and we cannot reconstruct a genuine Spanish nation unless we become once more the paladins of the same Catholic civilization. For Spaniards there is no alternative. A laic state is an antinational state. . . ."[7] He added, "The republic is based on three antinational principles: laicism, regional separatism, and Marxism. It is therefore only a provisional, transitory state that cannot endure."[8]

Catholics soon pointed to actions of the constituent Cortes as proof of their oft-advanced contention that an attack against the Church must inevitably be associated with an attack against property and the prevailing social order. The legislative assembly approved an agrarian reform that exceded the land redistribution provisions favored by the provisional government, thus demonstrating, in the words of a leader of the Catholic opposition, "the destructive passion of the revolutionary left" and its "explosive radicalism."[9] Commenting on this new development a Spanish priest declared: "Rightists now face the worst possible disaster in the economic order. Agriculture and industry are receiving rude and mortal blows because of iniquitous spoliation, unjust taxes, and in general a mad and suicidal despoilment of the inherent right to property."[10]

Catholic rightists delighted in describing the situation in apocalyptic terms. One of them asserted that the unbridled lust for material gain, resulting from the elimination of higher values as elites succumbed before the masses, had removed all order and restraint in the economic sphere and had thus helped bring on the depression, which was the final proof of the failure of liberal institutions. The Western world, in the throes of the depression, was said to confront a communist revolution spearheaded by "Asiatic barbarism."[11] According to another spokesman of the Catholic right the advent of the republic signified that the time bought by the restoration had run out. Spain had now to confront a titanic struggle "between Masonic Judaism and Catholicism, between those revolutionaries on one hand who are against the natural order of society and who deny the existence of . . . an all-imperious God of the moral order, and, on the other hand, the antirevolutionaries of diametrically opposed ideals."[12]

A Spanish bishop wrote in 1931 that the crisis spawned by the French Revolution and economic liberalism would be resolved, one way or another, much more quickly than was commonly realized; it would be resolved in favor of "Satanical forces or in favor of the defenders of Spanish Catholicism."[13] In a similar spirit a priest with a high position in Catholic Action declared, "The history of the enemies of Christ is about to be repeated. It is the eternal drama of the diabolical emissaries of evil. The grotesque persons, the clowns of the circus, present themselves again with new disguises, receiving the hearty congratulations of Masonry."[14] And again he stated:

> The threat today is posed by the communist youth, the sons of Satan, atheists who have nothing to curb their lust and evil instincts, who glorify in their bad lives and evil customs, always looking for new sensual pleasures, exalting the gross passions and respecting nothing that exists. . . . But they are resisted by the Catholic youths, the knights of the ideal, willing to become martyrs for the ideal. . . . One group looks to Christ and the Church, the other to Russia, that snow-covered Colossus of the North.[15]

Behind the challenge to good and virtue in their own country and throughout the world, Spanish rightists saw not only liberals, Masons, and communists, but their old enemy, the Jew.[16] In the subconscious essence of Marxism, one of them wrote, "there is an ethnic element, and this ethnic element is the Jew."[17]

> The semitic hatred against Europe and the desire to submerge it have given continuity to Marxism and prevented it from splintering. . . . Communism is today a great crusade which the Jewish race wages against the European world and its culture with all the zeal of the Christian missionaries.[18]

Since the mid-nineteenth century a host of idealogues of the counterrevolution had contended that liberal institutions and values led inexorably to communism. By the 1930s, in the frenzied setting of the second republic, a large mass of Spaniards had come to accept the myth-fantasy conceived by Spanish rightists nearly a century earlier and perpetuated since then by several generations of believers. By the 1930s, in fact, enough people accepted this myth-fantasy to make its prophesy self-fulfilling.

The Divisiveness of the Traditional Right

Spain's traditional rightists agreed almost unanimously that the triumph of the forces of good over godless social revolutionaries depended upon maintaining the power, prestige, and privileges of the Catholic Church; and they agreed generally, but by no means unanimously, that the restoration of monarchy was essential to their cause. Beyond this they found very few matters on which they could concur. As a result they divided into a number of contending groups.

Returning in 1930 from Argentina, where he had served as his country's ambassador, Ramiro de Maeztu quickly became convinced of the need to form a counterrevolutionary bloc of Catholic rightists.[19] The following year, with the enthusiastic backing of such political and intellectual personages as Víctor Pradera,[20] Pedro Sáinz Rodríguez,[21] José María Pemán, Antonio Goicoechea,[22] and Eugenio Vegas Latapié,[23] he helped found Acción Española and became its first president. Described as a society and study club rather than a political party,[24] the new organization disseminated its views through a series of conferences and lectures and through a periodical entitled *Acción Española*.[25]

In its program Acción Española called for a return to traditional, Catholic, monarchical Spain, the Spain that Spaniards had turned away from in their infatuation with liberalism and Krausism and in their obsession with Europeanization. Only by turning toward their own past, Maeztu argued in the first edition of *Acción Española*, could Spaniards discover the formulas for "harmonizing, as we succeeded in doing during our great centuries, the principles of authority and hierarchy, necessary for civilization, with those of love and humanity, demanded by the heart of man."[26] Concerned as they were with making Spain return to itself, "to discover thereby its life,"[27] the members of Acción Española recognized Marcelino Menéndez Pelayo as their precursor and spiritual-intellectual guide; for Menéndez Pelayo had always proclaimed that Spain would be nothing until it resolved to be itself by turning back to its authentic traditions and accepting Catholicism as the essence of national existence.

To members of Acción Española, monarchy was almost as consubstantial with Spanishness as Catholicism. "Monarchy," Sáinz Rodríguez wrote, "is absolutely essential to a true Spanish nation. . . . There must be continuity and a single source of command which can only be provided by monarchy. . . . Permanent victory over the revolution cannot be achieved in Spain except within the monarchical organization of government."[28] Pradera elaborated upon this argument by explaining that only a monarchy, guided and counseled by the Catholic Church, could, by consistently imposing those policies demanded in the interest of the common good, maintain social harmony and solidarity. Republics had to cater to uninformed majorities. Monarchies on the other hand, he stated, could protect the majority against their own follies; for the legitimacy of monarchs did not depend upon the approval of the half-plus-one and they could thus remain steadfast in the pursuit of the common good, as defined by the divine positive and natural laws, even though thereby incurring the opposition of the majority. By its very nature, Pradera concluded, the republican form of government was inimical to the preservation of higher, immutable values, to an elitist structure, and to hierarchical stratification; therefore it was inescapably revolutionary in its social consequences.[29]

Spanish Carlists agreed with Acción Española that Catholicism and monarchy were basic ingredients of Spanishness. But they differed heatedly as to who should occupy the throne once monarchy was restored. The Maeztu-directed association favored either the deposed Alfonso or a son of his. Carlists, on the other hand, backed the elderly uncle of Alfonso XIII, Alfonso Carlos. Not only were his dynastic claims to the throne more legitimate, they maintained; he had not been contaminated, as Alfonso allegedly had been, by political liberalism and admiration for French culture.[30] Carlists contended that the restoration of Alfonso or the crowning of a son of his would represent a compromise with liberalism, a compromise that would ultimately lead to socialism. And so toward the end of 1931 Carlists, refusing to collaborate with Acción Española, formed the Comunión Tradicionalista Carlista which shortly began to publish the militant journal *Boletín de Orientación Tradicionalista*.[31] Two years later another Catholic monarchist association appeared, Renovación Española, organized by Antonio Goicoechea.[32] By this time, then, a Spanish rightist who felt that Catholicism and monarchy were essential to preserving his ideals, could associate himself either with Acción Española, at least during those periods when the government permitted it to function legally, the Comunión Tradicionalista, or Renovación Española.[33]

A fairly numerous group of Catholic monarchists could not find a congenial home in any of these three associations. This group, similar to the one described as the New Right in the late 1920s, was made up of parliamentary rather than traditionalist monarchists, successful and "comfortable Catholics who accepted the democratic-bourgeois system,"[34] confident that within its framework they could through astute bargaining and manipulation protect their interests. Catholics of this type rejected the corporativist organization of society, for they had prospered in a noncorporative structure and feared that any basic changes in the body politic might jeopardize their status;[35] they advocated a political constitution in which the king would exercise his moderating power in collaboration with a parliament chosen by inorganic suffrage and representing parties of the type that had functioned between 1876 and 1923. They recommended also a political order within which such liberal principles as freedom of expression were respected. Furthermore, they downgraded ideology and declared in favor of tolerance, compromise, and a pragmatic spirit.[36] Men of these persuasions did not form a separate political association but they did possess in the newspaper *ABC* an important instrument for propagating their views.[37]

In addition the Spanish right included "fascist types,"[38] men who in ideology and actions conformed, though not in every respect, to the classical, and grotesquely oversimplified,[39] description of fascism as the attempt of a beleaguered bourgeoisie to defend their interests against a rising proletariat. Francisco Cambó, the millionaire Catalan industrialist and entrepreneur and leader of a conservative, regional political association, was a fascist type.[40] Devoted to the bourgeois, industrial capitalist society that had devloped in Cataluña, Cambó wished to protect it against the menace posed by a radicalized proletariat. He favored the corporative state as the best means for co-opting the working masses into the bourgeois system by giving them a role of participation at a level appropriate to them within the socioeconomic and political order.[41] He favored also a glorification of historical traditions as a means of fostering a passionate nationalism that would win the commitment of the workers to the patria and instill in them a willingness to sacrifice for its well-being. Because of Mussolini's apparent success in using both the corporative state and nationalism to head off the threat of the proletariat, and because of the degree to which he had won the backing of bourgeois elements by enlisting them in a campaign to augment industrial output, Cambó expressed warm admiration for the Italian dictator.[42]

In his advocacy of regionalism, however, Cambó departed from Italian models. He advanced the right of Spain's regions to enjoy economic autonomy; for he feared that within a centralized structure a government bureaucracy dominated by the values and prejudices of the Spanish center would be incapable of understanding, let alone responding favorably, to the needs of industrialized Cataluña. Economic autonomy, Cambó felt, which would leave the Catalan bourgeoisie free to control the business of their region as they saw best, could coexist with political centralism. In his political scheme, a strong, almost dictatorial president would exercise the moderating power, with the king serving as little more than a figurehead.[43]

Another fascist type was the Galician José Calvo Sotelo, former minister of treasury for dictator Primo de Rivera, whose French exile ended in mid-1934. Influenced in France by Charles Maurras and Action Française,[44] Calvo Sotelo returned to Spain singing the glories of the totalitarian state[45] and announcing that the times called for a true Caesar. "Modestly, he seemed willing to offer himself for this role."[46] In part because the ideology of Acción Española—which had been suppressed by the government for an extended period—and of the Comunión Tradicionalista, stressing the importance of subsidiary, semiautonomous associations, was not in harmony with his conviction that the corporative state should be highly centralistic with power rigorously imposed from above, Calvo Sotelo formed a new group called the Bloque Nacional.[47]

Through the Bloque, Calvo Sotelo hoped to enlist Spanish rightists in a crusade to save the bourgeois, capitalist society, which actually he equated with the Christian society.[48] To lessen the danger of a revolution directed against bourgeois capitalism he urged a highly centralized, state-administered system of social justice calculated to win the gratitude of the working classes.[49] He insisted, though, that before Spain could bring about a redistribution of wealth in the interests of social justice, it had to produce more wealth. His implication seemed to be that in the short run at least the state should collaborate principally with the capitalists who knew how to produce, giving to the workers just enough in the way of protection and services to tame their revolutionary impulses. Determining how much was enough to give the workers was obviously a delicate matter, for in the struggle to emerge from the depression Spain could not be overly generous with the workers. Indeed, in the immediate future they would have to accept a decrease in remuneration.[50]

The former treasury minister and one-time Maurista recognized the value of Catholicism in keeping the workers in line during the critical period. "Skeptical positivism"[51] and Masonry purportedly placed too great a stress on material gratification and did not encourage heroic sacrifice and abnegation. Therefore Calvo Sotelo through the Bloque Nacional demanded the formation of a Catholic state that would refuse resolutely to accommodate any man or group desirous of limiting the Church's temporal influence.[52] In seeking the synthesis of bourgeois capitalism and Catholicism, the Galician conservative was attempting to fuse two forces and value systems that many Spaniards considered mutually exclusive.

The preceding outline falls far short of listing the varieties of men, groups, and splinter groups that comprised the forces of the traditional, Catholic right in the early 1930s.[53] Somehow, though, the men of the right, of the counterrevolution, achieved sufficient cohesion to outvote the left and to gain control over the national Cortes elected in November of 1933. Largely responsible for the outcome of the elections was the Confederación Española de Derechas Autónomas (CEDA), a new kind of rightest group that departed considerably from many of the time-honored positions of Spanish conservatism.

Deviant Groups from the Traditional Right: The CEDA

José María Gil Robles, thirty-two years of age at the time, was dismayed by the outcome of the April, 1931, elections in which the republican-socialist forces scored impressive victories in the major cities, thereby toppling the monarchy. Raised in a devout home and much influenced by his father, a professor of political law at the University of Salamanca and a Carlist in his political affiliation, Gil Robles as a young man had earned his living as a lawyer and as a journalist for various Catholic publications.[54] In 1922 he had begun an association with El Debate, the newspaper backed in part by Jesuit money and directed by Ángel Herrera, one of Spain's most energetic figures in Catholic Action youth programs.[55]

Conferring together in the *El Debate* offices following the 1931 municipal elections, Gil Robles and Herrera began to formulate plans for defending the Church and the established social order within the newly proclaimed republic. The two men collaborated in founding Acción Nacional —later, in April of 1932, rechristened Acción Popular because the government refused to permit groups lacking official character to use the denomination "national."[56] Acción Popular's motto was religion, family, order, work, and property.[57]

Seeking a broader backing in early 1933, Acción Popular helped create, and then merged with, the Confederación Española de Derechas Autónomas, a party whose main core of support came from the Christian Democrats. Gil Robles and the men of Acción Popular had by then decided that the principal issue facing Spain was not whether it should be a monarchy or a republic, but rather whether it could avoid succumbing to Marxism. They viewed the CEDA as an instrument for uniting all rightist groups in the struggle against Marxism.[58] In the 1933 elections the CEDA emerged as the third largest group in the new parliament with a key position among the right-wing parties.[59]

In its platform the CEDA announced its general goals as: defense of religion and spiritual principles; defense of the family, currently threatened by forces of dissolution; defense of property, increasingly under attack by radical enemies; and defense of the social order, "which is on the verge of slipping into anarchy."[60] The CEDA also advocated the ultimate restructuring of Spain along corporative lines.[61] A more immediate goal, it affirmed, was a vast program of social justice assuring each worker an income adequate to support himself and his family in frugal comfort. To achieve this objective the CEDA advocated a redistribution of property to substantially increase the number of rural landowners; it further proposed that workers share in the profits and direction of industry.[62]

In one fundamentally important respect the CEDA departed drastically from the traditional right, for its paramount concern seemed to be nothing less than a compromise with Spanish liberalism. In the pronouncements of its leaders it came close to accepting a secular society in which the Church would not enjoy an all-dominant position but would have to make its way by bargaining and reaching understandings with various groups and forces that it had once sought to exterminate. Spain, Gil Robles maintained, had been ruined by the tendency to reduce all issues to matters of dogma. "One should have fundamental faith and convictions," he said. "And the more solidly planted they are, the more one should be able to compromise on accidentals, on the matters not essentially related to the overall faith and basic convictions. Saying this I know I wound the sensibilities of those who have waged a high-minded and disinterested struggle against compromise of any sort."[63] Gil Robles added that the CEDA would collaborate with any party and within any regime that seemed to have the best chance of maintaining the type of social order that corresponded in its key features to the most deeply rooted national traditions.

Applying the accidentalist doctrine to the monarchy-republic issue, the CEDA maintained that either form of government was compatible with its basic goals. Moreover, it expressed the desire to collaborate within the republican regime; and in the political arena it allied with the once extremely anticlerical Radical Party.[64] The CEDA leadership apparently felt that in view of the Liberal and Radical willingness to compromise on their historic positions by accepting the Church as one important force in preserving the established social order, the right should modify its stance by dropping the intransigent insistence on monarchy and by accepting certain aspects of the secular society.

For Liberals and Radicals, though, there remained fundamental questions as to whether they could accept the CEDA pronouncements at face value. Did the existence of the new party evidence a true shift in the politics of the Spanish right, pointing to the triumph of the Christian Democratic element over its more conservative critics? Was the CEDA truly independent in spirit and willing to reach a permanent accommodation with a secular society? Or was it firmly under the control of the prelates and simply pursuing an opportunistic policy of temporary conciliation with secularism until the times became more propitious for claiming a monopolistic position for the Church in the setting of social policy and public morality? These questions received no unequivocal answers, for it never became altogether clear whether the ultimate source of authority lay within the CEDA itself or outside of it in the Catholic hierarchy. Many Catholics who sympathized with or belonged to the CEDA, and Ángel Herrera is a striking example, were also militants in Catholic Action. As Catholic Actionists, they stressed the supreme authority of priests and bishops and the need for absolute obedience on the part of the laity.[65] Could Catholics such as this, asked many suspicious Spaniards, maintain a separate identity as members of Catholic Action and of the CEDA? Or would they always in the final analysis regard the CEDA as a political arm of Catholic Action, dedicated to seeking by means however devious, subtle, and disguised the ultimate triumph of the Church over the forces of secularism?

Spaniards dedicated to preserving the established social order and at the same time committed to the republic could also wonder as to the sincerity of the CEDA in its pronouncements of political accidentalism. If the form of government was really a matter of indifference to it, then why did not the CEDA accept the republic as an established fact and publicly declare adherence to it? Throughout its existence, the CEDA refused to do this.

The CEDA had hoped to complete the fusion of the two Spains, conservative and liberal. The first faltering steps toward this fusion had been taken at the outset of the twentieth century when Catholics, especially those of the Grupo de la Democracia Cristiana, had joined with products of the Institución Libre de Enseñanza to seek, through the Instituto de Reformas Sociales, a solution to the social problem. The cause of fusion had received new impetus from the collaboration between conservatives and liberals in the hispanismo movement. More significant progress toward fusing the two Spains was achieved by the moderate wing of the Conservative Party led by Eduardo Dato; and the most important gains occurred when characteristically anticlerical groups began to accept the utility of the Church in stemming the forces of social upheaval. But the two Spains remained mutually suspicious. The Christian Democratic spirit which generally prevailed within the CEDA did not calm the misgivings of the socially conservative Liberals, Radicals, and Republicans. The CEDA could not calm these misgivings because much of its constituency lay among the members of the traditional right; and traditional rightists resolutely refused the sort of concessions that would have won the confidence of the political groups of liberal Spain with which the CEDA sought to collaborate.

Even had they desired to do so, the leaders of the CEDA could not entirely have dissociated their party from the precepts of Catholic Action, for to have done so would have totally alienated the partisans of intransigent, intolerant Catholicism, thereby dangerously splitting the forces of the right and rendering them less effective in the campaign to save Spain from the alleged Marxist threat. And, even had a majority of its members so desired, the CEDA could not have openly embraced the republic, for this would have brought upon them the implacable hostility of the many rightists who were die-hard monarchists.[66] Thus the CEDA failed in its principal objective of devising a program that could win the support of all those Spaniards dedicated to defending the traditional social order. Defenders of this order inclined hesitantly toward cooperation with one another, but so long as armed confrontation between the forces of counterrevolution and revolution was avoided, they could not sufficiently put aside the prejudices acquired through decades and generations to act upon that inclination. It would take a civil war, and Franco, to accomplish what Gil Robles had hoped to bring about in peace.

Deviant Groups from the Traditional Right: The Falange Española and Its Origins

In many ways it is incongruous to include the Falange Española in a discussion of rightist groups; for the FE attracted many men with Marxist and even anarchist leanings.[67] Moreover, José Antonio Primo de Rivera

(1903–1936), the stunningly handsome, indulgently raised son of the dictator who founded the FE in October of 1933[68] and then provided it with charismatic leadership, can scarcely be compared to the general run of Spanish rightists.[69]

One of the few figures in modern history to whom there does seem to be a basis of comparison is Fidel Castro. Both José Antonio and the Cuban revolutionary professed a sincere hatred of the bourgeois capitalist society, attitudes in part attributable to the influence during their school years of values associated with one traditional current of Hispanic Catholicism. In developing a rabid nationalism, both men to some degree utilized the myth-fantasy that the existence of the hated bourgeois capitalist society within their own countries was owing in large part to the plots and manipulations of powerful interventionist republics to the north. Both men used their mesmerizing oratory to urge the need to bring political awareness to the masses; both felt that only the uncontaminated youthful generation could be entrusted with the political mobilization of the masses; both saw the need for violence in changing the established order—although José Antonio came only gradually and reluctantly to this conclusion—and both men, as they entered their thirties, showed tremendous naiveté as they underestimated the economic difficulties standing in the way of the social justice to which they were fervently committed. Both leaders, moreover, turned to foreign ideologies to rationalize their own revolutionary positions—José Antonio to fascism,[70] Castro to Marxism-Leninism. Yet neither man, least of all José Antonio, was willing to become the abject servant of foreign ideological currents; attracted to them largely through expediency, they utilized them principally as accidental ingredients in their political and social philosophies. The two men regarded themselves as nationalists rather than as cogs in an international movement. Yet neither was an isolationist. In order to nourish the nationalism they sought to inculcate in their people, they turned to dreams of extending to all Ibero-America the new style of civilization they believed they were creating.

If José Antonio developed into a radical and a revolutionary when it came to means, he remained unwaveringly conservative in his vision of what the good society should ultimately be—and here the similarity with Fidel Castro may or may not end. In the concept of José Antonio and of the Falange, the good society was one that was organically, corporatively, hierarchically organized, with sovereignty ultimately residing in the hands of a small elite.[71] For this reason the FE is included in the discussion of the Spanish right.

Much of José Antonio's political ideology, and also his gradual shift toward advocating revolutionary means rather than those of reformism, can be traced to the influence of Onésimo Redondo and Ramiro Ledesma Ramos, two young men who in November of 1931 founded the Juntas de

Ofensiva Nacional Sindicalista (JONS),[72] later affiliated with the FE.

The son of a poor family of Valladolid, Redondo was born in 1905. Passing his youth in extremely humble circumstances and working hard in most of his spare moments, he managed to earn his law degree at the University of Salamanca and in 1928 went to Germany, where he spent slightly more than a year, teaching Spanish in Manheim and Heidelberg.[73] Before returning to Spain Redondo, who visited Munich briefly, became aware of and considerably interested in the rise of Hitler[74]—although he later repudiated fascism both of the German and Italian varieties.[75]

Back in Spain Redondo founded an agrarian labor syndicate and began to play a role in Catholic Action. In Valladolid he established the weekly *Libertad*, the first number of which appeared on June 13, 1931. In the pages of this journal he began to develop his thesis that since the eighteenth century France had plotted to weaken Spain by turning it away from its true character and values, often enlisting Jews and Masons in this endeavor. The French design, he suggested, contributing initially to the establishment of bourgeois capitalism, was now in its final stages; for under the influence of insidious forces manipulated in the country to the north an antinational republic,[76] a "Marxist-Jewish-Masonic republic," had been imposed on Spain.[77]

To combat the antinational republic Redondo called for a movement that was Castilian and agrarian: Castilian, because through the centuries only Castile had understood how to bring unity to Spain and even to an empire that had embraced the races of a distant continent;[78] agrarian, because only agricultural laborers by their work and sacrifice had sustained the Spanish nation, in spite of which they had never received reward or recognition and were always victimized by less authentically Spanish interest groups.[79] "The idea that Spain requires industrialization," Redondo wrote, "is no longer in vogue. Industrialization has been a failure. All of the artificially protected industries have helped bankrupt Spain. What is necessary is to develop the rural economy, paying particular attention to improving the living conditions of the peasants."[80] Through vast reclamation projects Redondo envisioned the "reconstruction" of Spain's soil. Once this was accomplished, an extensive internal colonization program could be launched to lure people out of the cities and away from the perversion and falseness of urban life.[81]

To implement his program and to preside over the creation of a corporative state, Redondo hoped to call into being a "new right," equally distant from its adversaries on the left and from the traditional bourgeois right, vitiated by "countless corruptions." Far more important than the unity of the old right, he declared, was "the intensity of the new right." Only the Spanish youth, he believed, could form a new and intense right, for the older Spaniards who identified with the right were inert and listless, "no more than shells motivated by selfishness" and incapable of being inspired by great ideals.[82] A youthful, impetuous, and fervent right, sincerely committed to social justice, would understand how to accomplish the main task facing Spain: "reconciling the working classes" and "binding the masses to the nation."[83]

Meantime in Madrid a group of young men headed by Ramiro Ledesma Ramos and Ernesto Giménez Caballero, the latter an ardent hispanoamericanista,[84] had founded the weekly *La Conquista del Estado*.[85] Shortly afterward Giménez Caballero went abroad and Ledesma became the principal guiding spirit of the weekly that had published its first of twenty-three numbers in March of 1931.

Born (1905) in a small town in the province of Zamora close to Redondo's native Valladolid, Ledesma Ramos was the same age as the founder of *Libertad*; both men had grown up in poverty and both would meet violent deaths in 1936 in the early days of the civil war.[86] At the age of fifteen Ledesma moved to Madrid. There he found employment in the post office and eventually saved enough money to study philosophy and mathematical sciences at the University of Madrid. Attracted particularly to German philosophy, he was much influenced by Nietzsche. To some degree he fell also under the spell of Mussolini. However much he admired Italian fascism, he also criticized it for affording a favored position to the bourgeoisie.[87]

Ledesma, in contrast to Redondo, did not equate Spanish nationalism with Catholicism. In fact, he tended to ridicule the religious devoutness of Redondo and to chide him for "continuing his intimate contact with the Jesuits."[88] And Ledesma desired a state far more centralized than the one conceived by Redondo. He seemed also to accept the need for industrialization and he frequently stressed the duty of the state to transform Spain into an economically efficient country. In other ways, though, the thought of Ledesma coincided closely with Redondo's. Thus Ledesma saw the need for a new and militant right; and he believed that the traditional monarchists, the conservative republicans, the bourgeoisie, and the aristocracy were very nearly as much traitors to the true Spain as the leftists.[89]

Writing in *La Conquista del Estado* Ledesma urged considerable autonomy for the municipality and the creation of a social-economic order based on syndicates or guilds. Within the municipality and the syndicates citizens could participate "in the proper and traditional functions of their competence, which are of an economic and administrative character."[90] Ledesma justified the corporativist or national syndicalist organization of society on the grounds that it would guarantee a hierarchical structure of values and classes.[91] Further, he advocated the formation of a youthful, militant association to fight for the basic changes Spain required. "The first duty today . . ." he wrote, "is the duty of war. The cowardly pacifists have to retire before the push of the heroes."[92] He proposed that the organization be structured on the base of syndical cells and that membership be composed of persons between the ages of eighteen and forty-five."[93] Only people in this age group, he maintained, could "understand and serve the revolutionary imperative that animates us. It is necessary to celebrate in Spain the cult of vigor and force; this is the only policy that can attract and provide nourishment to youth. We adopt the procedures of violence; we want direct action of the people, represented by civil bands that possess military discipline."[94]

In November of 1931 the youthful editors of *Libertad* in Valladolid joined with the Madrid-based directors of *La Conquista del Estado* to found the Juntas de Ofensiva Nacional Sindicalista (JONS). Then, in February of 1934, following a period of extended and delicate maneuvering, the JONS merged with the Falange Española to form the Falange Epañola de las Juntas de Ofensiva Nacional Sindicalista.[95] A triumvirate made up of José Antonio, Ledesma Ramos, and Julio Ruiz de Alda, one of the four Spaniards who crossed the Atlantic in the 1926 flight of the *Plus Ultra* and a founding member of the FE,[96] presided over the new organization.

From the outset the FE-JONS—for the sake of simplicity often referred to hereafter as the Falange—was an uneasy alliance. So far as many Jonsistas were concerned José Antonio had not lived down the affluence of his upbringing and his youthful conservatism; in their view he was too intellectual and therefore too timid and vacillating, not sufficiently inclined to direct action and violence. How, wondered the Jonsistas, could the señoritos, the effete, idle, parasitical sons of landowning families who held many high posts in the FE, be expected to become tough revolutionaries.

Ledesma contrived to pull José Antonio increasingly toward the left and more into line with militant Jonsista policies. However, tension and friction continued between the two men and in January of 1935 Ledesma was ousted from the triumvirate. From that time on the FE-JONS came under virtually the exclusive control of the dynamic José Antonio, as the quiet and self-effacing Ruiz de Alda retired more and more into the background. Increasingly, though, the eclectic founder of the FE adopted the viewpoints originally advanced by Ledesma and Redondo.[97]

The Ideology of the Falange

José Antonio originally entered Spanish politics to defend his father's reputation and policies. The young Primo de Rivera, however, conceded that the dictator had not been able to forge "a great, central ideal, an exalted and fervent doctrine."[98] In their hopes to arouse Spaniards to the quest of national greatness, José Antonio and the members of the Falange saw their principal challenge to be the creation of a great ideal that could incite the ardor of a broad spectrum of Spaniards, regardless of class and occupation.

José Antonio condemned the liberal state precisely because it did not produce the unassailable faith and conviction that could inspire men to action and sacrifice in the service of the patria. "The liberal state," asserted the Falange leader, "does not beieve in anything . . .; it is a state without a faith . . .; it allows everything to be placed in doubt, including its own existence. And it lacks a scale of values. In the liberal state values, because they are established by counting votes, are constantly changing."[99]

Spanish rightists, José Antonio maintained, had in recent years been as incapable as liberals of creating an animating faith, of "awakening and calling forth the great spiritual resources of Spain."[100] In particular, he criticized the bland, conciliatory, compromising tone of the CEDA and of the newspaper *El Debate*. The spirit of Spanish Christian Democracy, he complained, was cold, sterile, and unemotional. He dismissed *El Debate* as "a prodigious refrigeration machine."[101]

Because of their ambition to imbue the greatest possible number of citizens with fervent devotion to a great ideal, Falangistas professed indifference as to whether Spain remained a republic or restored the monarchy. Justifying political accidentalism, Ledesma wrote: "Communism presents a creative myth that stirs people. What Spaniards must realize is that neither the monarchy nor the republic any longer has connected with it a creative myth; both have lost their mystique." He concluded that communism must therefore be opposed by a new set of passion-evoking loyalties.[102] Ledesma, however, did not rule out the possibility of an eventual restoration. He simply felt that the issue was not important enough to claim the immediate concern of the Falange. Onésimo Redondo, many of whose ideas found their way into the ideology of the FE-JONS, was in accord. "Our movement is neither monarchist nor republican," he wrote. "The form is accidental. When people are reanimated and placed on the march, reincorporated into the state and aroused from inertia, they will know, moved by an authentic conviction, which form is most convenient to the substance of the redemptive ideal."[103]

Occasionally José Antonio sounded more inclined to abandon the monarchical cause altogether. The monarchy, he said, had fallen "like an empty shell," because it had fulfilled its cycle. "We can regret its fall; but we cannot expect to fire youth with enthusiasm to recover an institution that we consider to have perished, however gloriously. . . . It served its purpose; it was the instrument, at one time, of maintaining the empire; but its mission is finished."[104]

Preoccupied with creating a national ideal that could appeal to a vast cross section of Spaniards, especially to the youth, the Falangistas-Jonsistas recognized that the secular spirit of liberalism and Krausism had advanced too far ever to be completely extirpated. They understood, therefore, that they could not base their nationalism on an intolerant, exclusivist form of Catholicism. Ledesma explained that Catholicism could serve as an effective stimulus to exalted national deeds "when it is the religion of all the people, when religious unity is a fact." Religious unity had been a fact, he continued, in the sixteenth century and at this time Catholicism had to a large extent been the whole substance of Spanish nationalism. "Today," he contended, "Catholicism only influences a part of the country and it includes in its bosom a great proportion of people lacking a fervent national spirit." Under these conditions, he reasoned, Catholicism was "not only ineffective for envigorating the spirit of the Spanish people; it could in fact convert itself into a debilitating agent."[105]

Even the devout Redondo agreed with this analysis. Nationalism, he said, should be nonconfessional but by no means antireligious. "We can recognize that the greatness of Spain is tied to its Catholicity and accept that nationalism cannot be anti-Catholic and still maintain . . . that nationalism ought not to be confessional, ought not to be equated with Catholicism."[106] Defending this position, Redondo argued that nationalism must envelop a nation entirely and completely, that it must be totalitarian. Most Spaniards, he candidly conceded, were not militantly Catholic. Therefore they would not take up the violent struggle against Marxist traitors in the name of Catholicism. "An immense sector," he wrote, "without doubt a majority of Spaniards of all regions and social classes is not inclined to enter parties that have the specific end of the defense of religion. You cannot reject this majority by making the national program a confessional one."[107]

If Spaniards were not in their majority militantly Catholic, neither, Redondo averred, were they anti-Catholic. Thus the great ideal for Spain, the basis of an animating nationalism that could unite and inspire vast numbers of citizens, had to be one that respected the Church. "Nationalism," the young Valladolid intellectual affirmed as he summarized his position, "for today's Spain cannot be confessional. This does not mean that nationalism is neutral. It is the declared enemy of the forces that are neutral: liberalism and Masonry."[108]

José Antonio evidenced similar attitudes on the issue of nationalism and religion. Those who wished to reconstruct Spain had to be guided, he said, by the essential traditions of Catholicism, for these traditions through a long historical process had become associated with the genuine and authentic values of the Spanish nation. But, he insisted, religious persecution and monopolistic exclusivism could not be revived. "The times of religious persecutions and intolerance are past. . . . Nor . . . will we countenance those interventions of the Church that could damage the dignity of the state or undermine national unity."[109]

Rather than on a narrow, exclusivist, confessional Catholicism the Falange hoped to base the great ideal of Spanish nationalism on the antimaterialism assumed to be one of the constants of Spanish character. José Antonio and other Falange leaders admired the antimaterialistic spirit that they found in certain currents of Spanish socialism; at times they even envisioned a coalition of their forces with those of socialist leader Indalecio Prieto.[110] But Falangistas and Jonsistas abhorred the materialism of Marxian socialism. According to José Antonio, socialism had originated as a laudable protest against the injustices engendered by liberalism; but then "a cold and impassive German Jew" who had no real sympathy for workers, "who regarded them as cattle, diverted socialism, giving it a hard, impersonal, cold orientation, hoping to use the workers only as the means of proving his doctrines." In its new form socialism became "completely materialistic" and therefore completely inharmonious with the Spanish character and national values.[111]

Although anticommunism was one of the main components of their national ideal, Falangistas-Jonsistas denounced bourgeois capitalism with the same zealousness as Marxists. To a considerable extent their movement represented the attempt of self-declared elitist groups to enlist the support of the proletariat, small landowners, and artisans[112] not only in stamping out communism but in dismantling the world of bourgeois capitalism.[113] In this the FE–JONS clearly had its antecedents in Juan Donoso Cortés, in Carlism and Catholic traditionalism, and in many of the Church's social justice movements of the late nineteenth and early twentieth centuries. In this it also had a close connection to the ideology of Acción Española, Renovación Española, and, to a lesser degree, of Christian Democracy; at the same time it was basically opposed to the spirit of such fascist types as Cambó and Calvo Sotelo.

In condemning the evils of bourgeois capitalism, José Antonio declared: "It is necessary to end the immense blotter effect of the idle, privileged classes who nourish themselves on the small producers; it is necessary to transform this absurd capitalist economy in which he who produces nothing takes everything, while the laborer who works and creates wealth does not receive even the least participation in it."[114] José Luis de Arrese, probably the leading economic theoretician in the Falange, described capitalism's basic formula as "I lend, you work, I profit."[115] He further criticized capitalism for bringing about the organization of huge and anonymous corporations that dehumanized private property and deprived the laboring classes of a sense of individual dignity and importance.[116] In his view, corporation capitalism was "the Masonry of money. It hides itself in order to act. As the Mason assumes the mask of mystery so as to disguise his deeds, so the capitalist covers himself with his cape and hides behind some titles or shares so as to be able with impunity, from the shadow of his anonymity, to dictate his will upon the small proprietor."[117]

Because of its cruel exploitation of the masses and its robbing them of a sense of dignity, José Antonio contended, capitalism as practiced by a heartless bourgeois plutocracy—which, in contrast to genuine elites, was incapable of charitable instincts—led inevitably to communism. Therefore, in order to prevent communism in Spain it would be necessary to do away with capitalism, in the process reducing its bourgeois practitioners and defenders to impotence.[118] Once bourgeois capitalism had been swept aside by violent revolution, it would be possible, he thought, to forge a paternalistic, organic or corporative state capable of withstanding the threat of communism. Although necessitating bloodshed, José Antonio believed that the type of revolution he envisioned had a greater chance for success in Spain than in other countries. This was so because Spanish capitalism was comparatively undeveloped, its bourgeoisie relatively weak. "Spain," he exclaimed, "blessed be your backwardness!"[119]

If superimposed upon the existing capitalist-bourgeois structure the corporative state, José Antonio affirmed, would simply contribute to perpetuating the dominance of capital over labor. To Spanish rightists, he said, the corporative state signified the organization of capitalists into one group and laborers into another, with the state always intervening to aid the capitalists.[120] In contrast, he advocated a revolutionary corporativism necessitating destruction of the capitalist system as it then existed.

The ideal national syndicalist or corporative structure as conceived by José Antonio and his Falangista-Jonsista associates required the forming of joint capital-labor syndicates. This would remove the need for the comité paritario, an institution which, according to the Falange, arose from a belief in the inevitability of class struggle.[121] Within the Falange-type syndicates, the distinction between capital and labor would little by little pass away, with the two functions coming to be combined in the same men.[122] This would be accomplished through profit-sharing devices resulting in the distribution not just of money but of shares in each enterprise to the workers. Eventually, then, ownership of each firm would pass to the laborers.[123] In this way private property and capitalism as they had previously existed would disappear.[124] As a consequence of this revolutionary restructuring of the economic order, Falangistas admitted the possibility that some workers might be materially less well off than under the traditional capitalist system; but, "the worker would live with dignity, and that is what he wants."[125]

In the analysis of José Antonio, the then prevailing system of private property and bourgeois capitalism was doomed; in one way or another, it would be swept aside. If Marxian revolutionaries toppled the system, they would destroy more than the material order of Spanish life, they would destroy also the spiritual-cultural order. If Falangistas demolished the present material order, they would do so in the interest of preserving "the essential values of the spirit . . . from the new Barbarian invasion."[126] The essential values of the spirit, in the Falangista-Jonsista concept, could be conserved only by elite groups. The continuing existence of these values depended therefore upon the hierarchical organization of society. And the viability of a hierarchical society could be assured only by imparting to the masses below a sense of individual dignity. This sense of dignity could not obtain among the masses unless the old capital-labor distinction, always pejorative to labor, was removed by transforming workers into capitalists. Finally, in the view of the FE–JONS, members of the working masses would not gain an adequate sense of dignity unless afforded the opportunity, when endowed with exceptional talent, to rise to the very top of the veritically organized local, regional, national syndicalist structure and to gain a seat in the national legislature, constituted on the basis of functional representation.

In essence, then, the great ideal of the Falangistas-Jonsistas was the creation of a society in which the individual dignity of the masses and their rights of participation in decision-making processes were reconciled with an elitist structure, with "authority, hierarchy, and order."[127] Such a society would enable Spaniards to recapture the great and unique values of their civilization as molded by Catholicism but inadequately sustained by Catholicism alone in modern times.

Rightists and Hispanismo

The participation of the masses as a means of giving them a sense of dignity and an accompanying resignation to their position and function, and the preservation of authority, hierarchy, and order within the socio-economic-political system: these were the objectives that appealed to the men of Acción Española, the Comunión Tradicionalista, Renovación Española, the Bloque Nacional, the CEDA, Catholic Action, and the FE–JONS, and also to men imbued with the characteristic values of Spanish liberalism. The different groups, however, seemed incapable of agreeing on how to proceed toward attaining these objectives; nor could they concur on whether the main stress should be on the participation and dignity of the masses, or on authority, hierarchy, and order. Moreover, these very terms meant different things to different rightist groups.

As the 1930s began, each of the groups within the divided Spanish right felt that a moment of destiny had arrived; for, to judge from many indications, the world of inorganic democracy, of mechanistic utilitarianism, had collapsed at the onset of the depression. The time seemed propitious, therefore, for Spain to regenerate itself in line with its authentic values, believed always to have been incompatible with inorganic democracy and mechanistic utilitarianism. Perhaps the moment was also at hand, rightists mused, for Spain to exert an international influence in leading such powers as France, England, and even the United States out of their crises and in attenuating the pagan materialism of fascism and national socialism. Alone and isolated, Spain could scarcely expect to play this role; but if it took its place at the head of a vast confederation of the Spanish raza, then it might be able to take up the mantle of international leadership.

Leaders within each of the rightist groups of Spain, as had been true of the most distinguished prophets of national regeneration following the disaster of 1898, hoped to arouse their fellow citizens to action and sacrifice by instilling in them a sense of mission not only to rehabilitate Spain but the entire Spanish raza. In a way this mission seemed more promising in the 1930s than at the turn of the century, for a variety of signs suggested that Spanish Americans had themselves become increasingly apprehensive about leveling social movements and willing to experiment with new programs of mass participation so as to preserve authority, hierarchy, and order. Many Spanish Americans seemed, moreover, to have grown more resolutely hostile to United States-style inorganic democracy and mechanistic utilitarianism, fearful of the menace that the values of this way of life posed to the essence of their existing social order. Thus they might be more disposed than at the beginning of the century to eschew the influence of the northern Colossus, to reject Pan-Americanism, and to take up the cause of hispanismo by seeking the aid and counsel of Spain's rightists in forging a Hispanic world united by the only values and traditions that were authentically its own. This at least was the assumption of many Spanish rightists who in the midst of adversity even more severe than that of the immediate postdisaster years turned with quickened interest toward Spanish America. For these men, even as for some of their ancestors of the Generation of '98, hispanismo was a contributing element to the myth-fantasy, to the great ideal, with which they hoped to spark a redemptive nationalism.

14: HISPANISMO, 1931–1936: RIGHTISTS AND THE REPUBLIC IN COMPETITION FOR THE ALLEGIANCE OF SPANISH AMERICA

Spanish Rightists and Hispanidad

Writing from Madrid on Peruvian preparations for the fourth centennial of the founding of Lima, a Spanish Augustinian in 1934 decried the sorry estate of affairs both in the former viceroyalty and in the madre patria itself. The anti-Catholic spirit, he asserted, that swept over both Peru and Spain in the eighteenth and nineteenth centuries, the product of "the pagan Renaissance, the false Protestant Reformation, and the Satanical French Revolution," had destroyed the order, stability, and material well-being that depended upon a robust Catholicism. The Augustinian was not without hope for the future. Spaniards, he stated, had already begun to strike back against diabolical forces. Meantime Peruvians, following the example of peninsular rightists and led by the "genuinely Spanish Peruvian" José de la Riva Agüero,[1] "noted for his exemplary Catholicism both in public and in private life," had shown signs of preparing to challenge "the falsity of modern liberalism, the principal cause of evil in the contemporary world, and to return to the Catholic values that had guided Spain during the Siglo de Oro."[2]

Following the 1898 disaster, Spanish Catholics had hoped to lead a crusade to save Spanish America from the liberalism, from the crude materialism, the mechanistic utilitarianism, and the inorganic democracy of the United States. In the 1930s they saw their mission as being to protect Spanish America not only from the "gigantic tentacles of the United States"[3] and its financial imperialism,[4] but also from communism, "the natural result of the Renaissance, of Protestantism, and liberalism."[5] Spanish America, they said, could only be saved from Marxism through what was Spanish and Catholic; and they expressed encouragement over the mounting number of intellectuals and political leaders in the New World republics who had begun to realize this.[6] All Spanish Americans who opposed hispanismo—or hispanidad, as Catholics in the peninsula came increasingly to call the movement in the 1930s[7]—were dismissed as Marxists in the service of a foreign government, intent upon betraying the interests of their own countries.[8]

International Marxism had, in the view of Spain's Catholic rightists, already established its first beachhead in Spanish America; the scene of this tragedy was Mexico, a country described as having joined Russia as one of the "Satanocracies of the world."[9] Liberal democracy, a Spanish Jesuit journal editorialized in 1935, had produced in Mexico its natural offspring, atheistic socialism. As a result Catholics were being indiscriminately killed and religious instruction had been replaced by sex education in all schools. In the course of their sex education Mexican boys and girls allegedly bathed together in the nude and encountered other procedures aimed at arousing their carnal appetites. Already the contagion was spreading, the journal concluded, for signs of Marxian revolutionary ferment had appeared in Cuba and Ecuador.[10]

In the eyes of Spanish Catholics, the situation in Spanish America posed particularly grave problems because insidious and diabolical forces had more effectively weakened the religious conscience there than in the motherland. Consequently, Spain had to take up the task of saving the hapless former colonies.[11] Spaniards of this persuasion reacted with dismay to blows struck against the clergy in Spain. If the clergy, and especially the religious orders, were weakened in the peninsula, this would mean that Spanish priests could not spearhead the anti-Marxist crusade in Spanish America; it would mean that Spanish culture might disappear in the New World with the Castilian tongue being replaced by English.[12]

Perhaps the most eloquent Spanish Catholic rightist urging fellow citizens to save not only themselves from the Marxist menace but Spanish America as well was Ramiro de Maeztu.[13] The former ambassador to Argentina and one of the founders of Acción Española set forth his views in the book *Defensa de la hispanidad*, first published in Madrid in 1934. By *hispanidad* Maeztu meant Spanishness, or the qualities of soul, acquired through historical experiences as synthesized and integrated by Catholicism, in which all members of the Hispanic raza shared and by which they were united into a vast transatlantic community.[14] Hispanidad, Maeztu believed, was threatened by the final consequences of naturalism, materialism, and liberalism, spawned through the generations by traitors who had tried to "foreignize" their culture. The peninsula, he contended, was beginning to save itself by returning to its Catholic spiritualism; and Spain, which understood how to cure its sickness, had to share this understanding with sister republics in the New World suffering from the same malady.[15]

Maeztu believed that the masses of Spanish America had gradually lost a sense of dignity and thereby had become disposed toward revolution, because the spread of "liberal humanism" had fostered the notion that "men who are successful are superior and owe nothing to inferior men."[16] The solution lay in counteracting liberal with Catholic humanism, which taught that all men are equal in their souls, that all of them are endowed with sufficient grace to win salvation by their own merits.[17] It is essential, Maeztu wrote, "that the poor cease to be regarded as something distinct from and inferior to other men. And it is precisely this truth that Spaniards have proclaimed as no other people. They have known how to make the most humble feel that between men there is no basic difference."[18] If Spaniards helped Spanish-American elites to reacquire the values of Catholic humanism, then these elites would cease to disparage the Indian, the mestizo, and all the dark-skinned citizens of their republics who in general comprised the proletariat; they would begin to treat the dark-skinned individuals of the lower classes as complete men who shared fully in the grace of God and whose salvation was as likely as that of the aristocrats. Once the directing classes recognized the spiritual dignity of the lower classes and treated them accordingly, and once the lower classes gained an appreciation of their innate spiritual dignity and equality, the proponents of class struggle would cease to find an attentive audience in Spanish America.

Spain, Maeztu affirmed, possessed an understanding unmatched by any other country of the nature and workings of the spiritual humanism "that affirms the essential equality of all men within those circumstances that are most adequate to preserving their inequality."[19] In these words Maeztu expressed his conviction that faith in spiritual equality would lead the masses to accept their inequality in intellectual ability, in social and political status, and material wealth. Men who duly appreciated the significance of their spiritual equality and their spiritual liberty—their capacity, that is, to merit salvation by their own efforts—would accept rule by the "secular hierarchy" that understood how to carry out the work of "redemption and regeneration based on the ideals of hispanidad. . . ."[20]

An equally ardent proponent of hispanidad was Isidro Gomá y Tomás. Because of the impassioned address that he delivered on October 12, 1934, at the International Eucharistic Congress assembled in Buenos Aires,[21] he has been referred to as "the prince of hispanidad."[22] On that occasion the recently preconized Archbishop of Toledo, soon to be named a cardinal, defined hispanidad as a union established by a common Catholicity "within the great limits of a grouping of nations and ethnic groups. It is . . . of the divine and human order at the same time," Spain's primate stated, "because it comprehends the religious factor, Catholicism, and also a catholicism that includes tradition, culture, collective temperament, and history. From all of this results a civilization, a specific civilization, with an origin, a historic form, and certain tendencies that can be classified within universal history. . . ." Hispanidad, the churchman explained, owed its existence to the fact that "the spirit or genius of Spain has entered into other lands and races and, without destroying their own natures, has elevated and purified them and made them similar to Spain itself . . . marking them with the stamp of the Spanish soul."[23]

For Gomá y Tomás, hispanidad signified the integral union of Spain and Spanish America resulting from a fusion of blood, language, and culture. It followed that Spain's America, an America "invented,"[24] "engendered and nourished by Spain for civilization and for God,"[25] could not deny its Spanish essence without destroying itself; for "all the spiritual values of Latin America are originally Spanish."[26] Nor could Spain's America deny its Catholicism without committing suicide, because hispanidad and Catholicism were one and the same.[27]

In the social and political realm hispanidad entailed, according to Archbishop Gomá, "harmonizing all around God so as to produce order and well-being in the world."[28] Because they had been fused together by common allegiance to the values of Catholicism, the prelate maintained, Spaniards and Spanish Americans were above all other peoples imbued with a sense of hierarchy.[29] But Spain and Spanish America alike were threatened by "the infiltration of the culture of distinct peoples." Such an infiltration, Gomá declared, inevitably heralded moral conquest, "the sort of annexation of spirits that results in their servitude."[30] He made it clear that so far as he was concerned the United Sates and Russia were the main cultural infiltrators against which the Hispanic world must defend itself.[31] Exhorting Spaniards and Spanish Americans to unite in opposing the spread of the values associated with the materialistic concept of life, he told them that together they could "preserve the spirit of discipline without which a healthy society cannot conceivably exist. . . . This spirit of discipline is part of the Spanish genius and it was imposed in America by kings, hidalgos, and missionaries. . . ."[32] Predictably, the archbishop concluded that all would be lost in the Hispanic world unless the spark of Catholic fervor was rekindled. "Today as always it is only Catholicism that can unite Spain and Spanish America. Family . . . authority, the school, property, even liberty, today have no other guarantee than Catholicism."[33]

Francisco Cambó, a "fascist-type" conservative concerned with protecting an industrial bourgeoisie, showed relatively little interest in alleged spiritual ties between Spain and Spanish America. In the early years of the republic he urged the need for greater investment of peninsular capital in Spanish-American businesses in order to realize the objectives of practical hispanismo[34]. On the other hand liberal philosopher Manuel García Morente seemed much closer to such traditionalist Catholics as Maeztu and Gomá y Tomás in stressing the primacy of spiritual ties.

The son of a distinguished medical doctor who practiced in Granada, García Morente was born in 1886 in a small town in the southern province of Jaén. He studied philosophy at the Sorbonne and at the University of Madrid under Giner de los Ríos. An authority on Kant and other German philosophers, he spent considerable time in Germany. In addition to publishing works of his own García Morente, who for a time taught philosophy at the Institución Libre de Enseñanza, prepared a Spanish translation of Oswald Spengler's The Decline of the West.[35] Long associated with the relativistic philosophical school of Ortega y Gasset, García Morente in the 1930s demonstrated the receptivity to the values of the Catholic right that had become typical of many Spanish liberals.

Four epochs, the philosopher theorized, had been crucial in shaping the Spanish nation and character. During the period of the Roman Empire Spaniards, knowing how to assimilate what was necessary while conserving their own popular traditions, had hispanicized their invaders at the same time they were being latinized by them.[36] Then, at the time of the Arab invasion, Spaniards in the mountains of Asturias had saved Christianity "and with it the essence of European culture. . . . This is when the Christian religious spirit comes to constitute a special element of the Spanish nationality. Christianity from that time becomes something that is consubstantial with hispanidad."[37] In the third crucial epoch, Spain had spread its culture and values to America and originated many of the Western world's concepts of imperialism.[38]

As a result of experiences acquired during these three epochs, García Morente explained, Spain became a nation, which is to say it developed a style. This style determined by collective preference and antipathies, likes and dislikes, as they evolved during the centuries, gave to Spain, and to its colonies, a special homogeneity, an intangible, indefinable common character.[39] Important features of the Spanish style included the ability to maintain the primacy of spiritual considerations, the talent not to confuse pleasure and comfort with values, and the wisdom not to become so engrossed with material progress as to suffer dehumanization and to abandon the pursuit of inward development.[40]

The fourth crucial epoch for hispanidad was, in the analysis of García Morente, the contemporary one in which the "Communist International of Moscow" sought to dehispanicize the Spanish community. Russia's ultimate goal, he warned, was "to erase hispanidad from the world."[41] By overcoming this menace in the peninsula Spaniards would, he declared, help make it possible for Spaniards of the New World to maintain their only authentic and natural style. Alarmed by the revolutionary-counter-revolutionary confrontation in Spain, Spanish Americans would, he predicted, come to recognize communism as the product of values that were incompatible with their own style. Reasserting their true identity, they would join in the struggle to preserve the style of hispanidad. Upon its preservation, he said, depended the survival of the highest values in the Western world.

The CEDA also paid at least passing attention to the need to establish closer bonds between Spain and Spanish America and to devise a common set of policies for the two branches of the raza. One important conservative South-American newspaper, taking cognizance of this attention, recognized in the CEDA the party that had a "complete vision of what is required in the times in which we live; a vision of the new program that must arise from the ruins of liberal democracies . . . and that is based on a conviction that there is a mission to do more than maintain order and balance the budget; a vision of a program that attends to the spiritual, political, and social problems that are present today among all people."[42]

The political accidentalism of the CEDA may well have been a positive factor in its pursuit of hispanismo—distinguished from hispanidad, which was ideologically more intransigent and theologically more dogmatic, more militantly Catholic; whereas the traditionalist right, with its insistence that monarchy was the only form of government morally consonant with Hispanic values, tended to assume an insufferable attitude of superiority toward the New World republics and thereby limited its own effectiveness. In Spain proper, however, the CEDA suffered from the fact that, as in its approach to virtually all issues, it was bland and conciliatory, rational, restrained, and moderate in its advocacy of hispanismo. It did not view the movement in such apocalyptic terms as traditionalist rightists in groups like Acción Española and Renovación Española and revolutionary rightists in the Falange. In a period that saw Spaniards inclined to seek Quijote-like ideals, the tepid hispanismo of the CEDA created little impact in the peninsula.

There was nothing tepid about the Falange program, either as it applied to domestic affairs or to relations with Spanish America. Ernesto Giménez Caballero, active in the group that established the JONS and a collaborator with many of the founding members of the Falange, contributed a great deal to the emotional fervor that revolutionary rightists brought to their hispanismo; until taken over by Franco and incorporated into the Nationalist Movement, Falangistas generally preferred the less religiously charged term hispanismo to that of hispanidad.

The Falange and Hispanismo

For some time previous to his participation in the founding of "the authentically Catholic periodical" La Conquista del Estado,[43] Giménez Caballero had worried over the identity problem in Spain. His country had fallen into decadence, he believed, because there had occurred within it "a crossing of the medieval, Catholic, and transcendent world with the heretical, individualistic, and materialistic world."[44] As a result Spaniards had become the children of two mothers and did not know with which one to identify. To emerge from this crisis they had to realize that "the secret of all nationalism . . . the solution of national life, is always in the dead. The only life, eternally alive, that a nation possesses is in its dead. . . ." Once Spaniards understood this and desisted from their attempt to deny and betray the dead they would, Giménez asserted, solve their identity problem.[45]

Giménez Caballero exhorted Spaniards to turn to their dead for guidance so that they could live once more in harmony with their true nature as Spaniards; and he admonished them to reject the idiocies of the "social-democratic" state and to replace it with a strong, corporatively organized state "in which the masses are hierarchized."[46] In learning how to live through reverting to the values of the dead, Spaniards would rediscover the need for natural rather than hereditary aristocracies;[47] they would come to value "hierarchy over capitalism;"[48] they would begin to see that it was indispensable to abandon "that great vanity, the concept of the rights of man," and cling to "the heroic concept of service, of duty, of being obliged to do something."[49] By constructing a social and political system based upon the wisdom of "the living dead" Spaniards would in effect be creating the sort of state that Mussolini described as fascistic. Fascism, Giménez declared, had existed in Spain long before Mussolini appeared upon the scene; it had originated, in fact, at the time of the Catholic Kings.[50]

For Giménez Caballero the genius of Mussolini lay in his ability to discover the essential values on which the Roman Empire had once rested and to incorporate them into Italian fascism. As a result, the movement emanating in Rome seemed likely to forge a new catholicity that would bind together all those Latin countries of Europe that had once been integral parts of the Roman Empire. Fascism, the Spanish idealogue of the revolutionary right believed, was synonomous with the universality or catholicity of the Roman world. The religion of Catholicism, however, was not to be equated with catholicity. Through the years Catholicism had become narrow and sectarian, losing the ecumenical vision that had once distinguished it. A new generation of mystic reformers was needed, according to Giménez, to counteract the constraining effects of the clerical bureaucracy and to restore to Catholicism a catholicity that would guarantee it a vital presence in all of the countries into which the Latin world had split. Once it had undergone this renovation, Catholicism would again become an essential ingredient of the catholicity or fascism that Giménez so admired.[51]

Hitler's Germany, though much praised by Giménez Caballero, represented in his mind a heresy against the universalist vision of the old Roman world. The heresy consisted in the belief in the superiority of the Nordic race, in contrast to the Mediterranean, Catholic, universalist concept of the equality of races. Because the racial exclusivism of Germany's national socialism clashed with Italy's universalism, an ultimate struggle between the two powers seemed likely.[52] However, it could be avoided, Giménez asserted, by Spain. Assuming "the providential role of conciliator and synthesizer," Spain, he said, could reconcile the spirit of racial pride with that of racial fraternity.[53] In this way fascism could fully and completely acquire and become one with the catholicity that was necessary to reintegrate the countries of Europe once joined by Rome.

Spain qualified for its "providential role" because of all countries in the world, said Giménez Caballero, it was the most thoroughly universalist in its attitudes toward race. Spaniards, he believed, had been able to incorporate the New World into the cultural patterns initiated by the Roman Empire precisely because they were not obsessed by notions of eugenics.

As a result Spain, "a fecund, genital country," had created a new populace in America[54] but a populace infused with cultural values that were very old.

In spite of his glorification of universalist concepts, the catholicity that Giménez Caballero anticipated as the product of the synthesis which Spain would effect between German and Italian fascism was not really universalist; it would apply, with a single exception, only to continental Europe. The exception was Spanish America. Most decidedly Giménez's catholicity or fascism was not to encompass the United States; for that country had been conceived and formed in a spirit of rejection of Europe.[55] Giménez believed this rejection to be basic, natural, and unalterable.

Between Spanish America and Europe, on the other hand, there existed spiritual highways, first established by the conquerors.[56] Spanish Americans had, according to Giménez, foolishly attempted to close these highways and to deny their true spiritual heritage; as a result they had fallen into a way of life characterized by "permanent insurrection."[57] But, he predicted, Spanish Americans would return to their senses and repudiate all the "toxic notions," the "false traditions" and "political mirages" that had led them to spurn Spain; they would eventually realize that their true spirit was the Spanish spirit and they would then be rejoined to the revitalized Europe, united once more in a catholicity that owed much to the universalist, synthesizing genius of Spain. "This moment gets closer all the time" the visionary Spaniard wrote. "We will await it silently and anxiously, all of us who . . . believe in an inexorable resurrection of the spirit of genius in history." Until this moment arrived Giménez counseled Spaniards to pursue a policy of watchful waiting in regard to Spanish America. Concluding an article on hispanismo, he stated: "I believe that the Hispano-American problem is for Spaniards a question of patience."[58]

Ramiro Ledesma Ramos, the principal collaborator with Giménez Caballero in founding La Conquista del Estado, seemed less resigned to patience. The Hispanic peoples both of the peninsula and America, he declared, were dissipating their talents and energies by discussing matters of secondary importance. He clearly felt that the bold and innovative minds associated with him in producing the periodical and later in forming the JONS had discovered what the vital issues were. Therefore he and his colleagues had a duty to share their discovery with Spanish Americans. Rather than contenting themselves with watchful waiting, he implied, Spain's youthful elite should assume a tutelary role vis-à-vis the former colonies. "The people of Spanish America," he wrote, "are for Spain the perpetual manifestation of its imperial capacity. We have a role in Spanish America that is more than that of simply a friendly people; we are always obliged to be something more than this, for we are a part of them and they will always be a part of us."[59] Ledesma and his associates insisted, therefore, that Spain "affirm itself" as an international power by undertaking a positive mission in Spanish America.[60]

Onésimo Redondo, together with Ledesma a principal director of the

JONS, fully agreed in regard to the imperial mission of Spain in America.[61] "We proclaim," he wrote, "our veneration for the great traditions of the patria and for the community of raza and destiny that unites us with the Iberian nations overseas."[62] On another occasion Redondo observed: "There are eighty million people overseas joined to us by language and raza who have a right to share in the renaissance and redemption of Spanish culture. There are imperial duties, then, that Spain recognizes and the national youth that enters into the life of the new state will be seriously resolved to fulfill them."[63]

As for the leaders of the JONS, so also for the founders of the Falange "unity among all the lands and all the men of the extended Spanish world" always constituted a major goal.[64] For this reason José Antonio saluted the efforts of Argentine foreign minister Carlos Saavedra Lamas to unite Latin America against the imperialism of the northern Colossus. "He works," José Antonio wrote in June of 1935, "for the formation of the old spiritual empire. Today, from our modest position, we give him thanks. Tomorrow we will contribute to his labor."[65]

Leaders of the Falange stressed that national syndicalism was a program applicable to all men formed in the values of Hispanic culture "and for this reason it has to be the glue of our future empire."[66] When they spoke of their "future empire," however, Falangistas made it clear that they had in mind spiritual, not political, imperialism. "Our future empire," one of them wrote, ". . . will not be concerned with the expansion of material frontiers but with the extension of spiritual frontiers. . . . There will continue to be territories with distinct names; but they will be united in the same feeling, the same essence, in the same national syndicalist organization . . . in the same soul."[67]

This concept of hispanismo found its way into the official program of the FE-JONS, one of the points of which affirmed: "With respect to the Hispano-American countries, we seek the unification of culture, of economic interests and power. Spain advances its condition as the spiritual axis of the Hispanic world as a title of preeminence in universal undertakings."[68] Early in 1935 José Antonio paraphrased this point in one of his newspaper articles: "America," he wrote, "is for Spain not only the extension of a world that is open to her cultural influence, but also . . . one of the best titles that Spain can advance for reclaiming a preeminent post in Europe and in the world." The Falange's leader concluded: "All efforts however vast to strengthen our ties with America seem scarcely adequate to us."[69]

The importance of Spanish America in the Falange program arose in part from the fact that José Antonio and his partisans foresaw the day when the world would be led "by three or four racial entities." Spain, they affirmed, could be one of these if it placed itself at the head of a spiritual, Spanish-American empire. Fulfillment of this dream, which had fired the imagination of Ángel Ganivet in 1896,[70] would mean that for Spaniards the Atlantic ocean would become the mare nostrum[71] and that Spain would participate "with a preeminent voice" in directing the spiritual affairs of the world.[72]

The endeavors of Spanish rightists, whether traditionalist or revolutionary, to accomplish the time-honored objectives of hispanismo were seriously weakened during the 1931–1936 period by the divisiveness that continued to prevail among their various groups and associations. An equally important debilitating factor was the attempt of the republican regimes in charge of Spain's official relations with Spanish America to minimize the influence of the basically conservative organizations that had become the primary instruments of hispanismo. Thus the Unión Ibero-Americana, which at the beginning of 1932 had chosen overtly antirepublican Antonio Goicoechea for its president, sustained a severe diminution of its state subvention and suffered from further acts of government harassment. This situation, according to an article published by the Union's journal at the beginning of 1934, had caused the organization during the previous year to lose over one hundred members, leaving membership in the peninsula at slightly over two hundred, and had forced it to suspend many important activities.[73] Apparently the Casa de América in Barcelona fared even worse under the republic, for as of 1935 its subvention had been suppressed altogether.[74]

Having virtually eliminated the groups traditionally concerned with hispanismo, the Unión Ibero-Americana complained, the republican regimes for their own part had shown nothing but indifference toward Spanish America. Allegedly the government had reduced scholarships for Spanish-American students and suppressed the schools for Spanish emigrants established in the New World under the Primo de Rivera dictatorship. The Union also complained that officials appointed by the republic to shape its policies for Spanish America knew absolutely nothing about the area. Finally, the government was charged with encouraging emigrants to interfere "as never before" in the internal affairs of Spanish-American republics.[75]

The Union exaggerated considerably in accusing the republican administration of gross neglect of Spanish America. The accusations are significant primarily in that they reveal the degree to which the conflict between the right and the republic extended into the field of hispanismo and thereby impaired Spain's efforts to strengthen its presence in Spanish America.

The Second Republic and Spanish America

In its relations with Spanish America the second republic was seriously handicapped by the depression. The effects of the depression fell with particular harshness on those unofficial ambassadors of goodwill, the Spanish emigrants, in whom so many hispanoamericanistas had customarily placed unrealistic hopes. Owing to the lack of employment opportunities, Spanish immigrants in Spanish America found that they were more and more resented by local laborers. Soon the republican government was deluged with requests from its citizens in the New World for assistance in arranging for repatriation.[76] A long-time resident of Cuba reported on a phenomenon observed by many fellow immigrants throughout the New World republics: "There is a xenophobia here," he wrote, "that makes life impossible for the Spaniard. No Spaniard can survive the rampant spirit of Cuba for the Cubans."[77]

In the sphere of trade relations the effects of the depression were catastrophic. Spain's total trade, exports and imports, with its eight principal Spanish-American buyer-seller nations stood at 534 million pesetas in 1929.[78] By 1932 the value of this trade had plummeted to 169.3 million pesetas. Two years later, as Chart 7 shows, it was down to 109.6 million.[79]

CHART 7

SPANISH TRADE WITH EIGHT PRINCIPAL SPANISH-AMERICAN
BUYERS AND SELLERS, 1932, 1934[80]
(in thousands of pesetas)

	1932		1934	
	Spanish Exports to	Spanish Imports from	Spanish Exports to	Spanish Imports from
Argentina	38,975	59,304	22,368	18,393
Chile	655	12,589	1,330	14,551
Colombia	997	735	681	1,003
Cuba	15,246	9,282	13,562	8,718
Mexico	4,223	11,263	4,811	12,263
Peru	450	110	319	86
Venezuela	1,626	5,873	1,267	5,684
Uruguay	6,533	1,407	2,337	2,251
Totals:	68,705	100,563	46,675	62,949

Attempting to augment trade with its principal Spanish-American buyer-seller republics, Spain in 1935 ratified a new treaty with Argentina, calling for substantial mutual tariff reductions.[81] In a less significant move, the republican administration in mid-1935 offered members of officially recognized overseas Spanish chambers of commerce a one-third fare reduction on Spanish lines when they came to the peninsula on commercial missions.[82] In spite of these and other measures, cargo and passenger business was so light in 1935 that the Compañía Transatlántica sharply curtailed services to America and suppressed some runs altogether.[83] Persuaded that the government was not taking adequate steps to stimulate commerce with the New World republics, a group of private businessmen, industrialists, and merchants came together in Madrid in the summer of 1935 to found the Bloque Ibero-Americano.[84] The Bloque's endeavors to expand trade with Spanish America proved no more effective than those of the government. The hard reality of this situation forced most Spaniards during the period of the second republic to abandon hope in practical hispanismo based on commercial-economic ties.

A considerable reduction in Spain's consular service in Spanish America afforded one indication of this loss of hope. The total number of consular personnel in the Spanish-American republics and Puerto Rico stood at thirty-two in 1935, down from forty-five in 1930. Moreover, only 11 percent of the overall consular service budget was allotted to Spanish America, down from 28 percent in 1930.[85] While engineering this cutback in the consular service in Spanish America, the republican government maintained personnel in other foreign posts at very nearly the 1930 level.[86]

To some degree the republican government hoped to compensate for the decrease in Spanish presence brought about by the reduction in consular personnel by dispatching to Bolivia the largest single military mission assigned by Spain to duty in the New World since independence. Headed by artillery commandant Enrique Fernández Heredia y Gastañaga, the five-man mission was charged with nothing less than the complete reorganization of the Bolivian army and military academy.[87] Arriving in La Paz in March of 1932, the mission remained in the Bolivian capital for one year, thus suffering the extreme misfortune of being in Bolivia when that country became involved with Paraguay in the Chaco War. Rumors soon circulated that the Spaniards were in the front lines directing the Bolivian operations. Although totally groundless,[88] these rumors gained widespread credence in Bolivia. By the time the government of the second republic withdrew the mission many citizens of the landlocked republic blamed the Spanish officers for the series of disastrous defeats sustained by Bolivian armies.[89]

In the area of cultural-spiritual hispanismo, the Spanish government made serious efforts to improve relations with the New World republics, thereby belying the charges of neglect often brought against it by right-wing hispanoamericanistas. To begin with, officials of the Spanish republic made rhetorical commitments to cultural-spiritual hispanismo. Thus minister of foreign relations Luis de Zulueta at a 1932 banquet in Geneva for the Spanish-American representatives to the League of Nations declared that spiritual were more important than economic ties. The way to Spanish-American copenetration lay, he insisted, through cultural programs, through exchange of teachers and students, through common scientific investigations, through meetings of teachers and intellectuals. This, he stated, is how solidarity is achieved among nations; "once spiritual understanding is realized, commercial ties will follow."[90] Zulueta's convictions, much in line with those of Altamira and González Posada in the early years of the century[91] and with those of dictator Primo de Rivera in the mid-1920s,[92] sprang in part from his personal experience with the sort of cultural exchange programs in which he saw the immediate future of hispanismo. Brought to Mexico in 1927 by the Instituto Hispanomejicano de Intercambio Universitario, he had presented a course on pedagogy. Following this he had lectured in Habana at the invitation of the Institución Hispanocubana de Cultura. Both sponsoring organizations had been founded by Spanish emigrant communities.

A collaborator on various Spanish liberal newspapers and on the *Boletín* of the Institución Libre de Enseñanza, Zulueta, who considered himself a disciple of Rousseau and who steadfastly opposed all religious influence in education, had at the outset of the republic been named Spanish ambassador to, but was refused acceptance by, the Holy See. Understandably, his ideological leanings led him to single out revolutionary, anticlerical Mexico—reviled by the right as a marxist "Satanocracy"—as the country with which the republic could establish the closest ties of spiritual understanding.

About a year after Zulueta stated the case at Geneva for spiritual ties, the Spanish government made another friendly gesture toward cultural spiritual hispanismo. This occurred early in 1934 at the official celebration of the third anniversary of the founding of the republic. On this occasion one of the featured speakers read a long selection by Emilio Castelar rendering homage to the intimate bonds of spirit that drew Spain and Spanish America together into one family and raza.[93]

By deeds as well as words the republican government demonstrated an interest in cultural-spiritual hispanismo. In 1933 the government budgeted one million pesetas for support of teaching and study centers abroad, particularly in Spanish America. In the same year it allocated to the Patronato de Relaciones Culturales, founded in 1927 with the primary objective of fostering cultural relations between Spain and Spanish America and charged with organizing schools for Spanish children and adults living in the New World republics, a subvention of 900,000 pesetas.[94] Although certain restrictions were introduced, the republic also continued the program initiated under the monarchy for granting fellowships to Spanish Americans to enable them to study in the peninsula.[95] Shortly after its inception, moreover, the republic established the Centro de Estudios de Historia de América within the University of Sevilla. The new center offered lecture and seminar courses on Spanish-American history, geography, and archaeology.[96]

Far more than most governments of the restoration period, administrations during the republic cultivated hispanismo through means of diplomacy. In 1935 the republic dispatched a special mission to award decorations to the presidents of Argentina, Uruguay, Chile, and Peru. Before this, in 1932, it had elevated its representative in Mexico to the rank of

ambassador,[97] manifesting thereby its special sympathy for that republic—
a fact noted with due appreciation in 1934 by Genaro Estrada, Mexico's
ambassador to Spain.[98] With Mexico as well as with Peru and Chile, moreover, the Spanish government entered into new bilateral agreements in
which the countries mutually undertook "to prevent the commerce, circulation, and exhibition of all classes of motion pictures considered offensive by the contracting parties."[99]

Although the republican government drastically curtailed its diplomatic
representation in most foreign posts,[100] it avoided personnel cuts in Spanish America. Thus in 1935 the number of ambassadors (stationed in
Argentina, Cuba, Chile, and Mexico), ministers, and secretaries totaled
thirty-four, the same as in 1930. Even more significantly, Spain allotted
nearly 40 percent of the total amount budgeted for the salaries and expenses of foreign service personnel and for the maintenance of legations
abroad to its diplomatic service in Spanish America, up from 28 percent
in 1930.[101] Perhaps, though, the effectiveness of representation suffered
from the "republicanization" of the foreign service following the abortive
right-wing coup of August, 1932, led by General José Sanjurjo. The extensive purge of diplomatic personnel and, frequently, their replacement by
men who lacked experience disrupted Spain's foreign service for some time.

The republic's attempt to serve the cause of hispanismo through cultural
exchange and diplomacy suffered further from the propaganda campaign
that Spanish rightists waged throughout Spanish America in the attempt
to depict the administration as dangerously radical if not out-and-out
communist. Even when presented in the best light, as socially conscious,
progressive, and non-Marxist, the republic was seen in Spanish America as
definitely liberal, democratic, and anticlerical. This redounded in many
circles to the republic's disadvantage, for at the time Spanish America
evidenced a growing disillusionment with liberal, democratic ideals, as
well as a widespread willingness among intellectual and political figures to
accept the Church as an indispensable force in staving off social revolution.

Obstacles to Hispanismo, 1931–1936

In Argentina an antidemocratic, proclerical, right-wing movement
showed signs of mounting strength as the 1930s began. Furthermore,
between 1930 and 1932 José Félix Uriburu, a general with decided corporativist leanings, served as president. Ramiro de Maeztu delighted in Argentine developments during this period, a fact that boded ill for the success
of the republic's hispanismo campaign.

Elsewhere the situation was similar. The crisis of the depression brought
Uruguay's much-vaunted democratic processes into disrepute, facilitating
the installation of a mild military dictatorship in 1933 and swelling the
right-wing forces of Luis Alberto de Herrera, who ideologically shared a

common ground with the traditionalist Catholic right of Spain.[102] In Chile a Catholic corporativist movement registered significant gains and a Nazi party proved surprisingly successful in recruiting members from the upper-class youth. In 1933 Chile's Liberals, abandoning their characteristic anti-clericalism, entered into an alliance with the proclerical, Church-dominated Conservatives. In the 1930s, then, Chileans were by and large less in sympathy with a liberal, democratic, and anticlerical government in Spain than they would have been thirty, twenty, or even ten years earlier.

Peru, beginning in 1933, was governed by General Óscar R. Benavides, who paid lip service to corporative ideals and who early in his regime appointed as prime minister the reactionary Catholic and fascist-sympathizer José de la Riva Agüero.[103] In Colombia throughout the 1930s the Catholic Church continued to enjoy its customary exalted position and control over education and public opinion media. Colombian Liberals, moreover, even as those of Chile, had attenuated their anticlericalism and accepted the Church as an important bulwark of the prevailing social system; and, among Conservatives a strong antidemocratic and corporativist movement apparently finding its inspiration in Spain's Catholic conservative position had arisen under the leadership of Laureano Gómez.

In the early twentieth century, right up to 1929 in fact, it had been fashionable in most Spanish-American republics to pay at least verbal respect to liberal, democratic concepts, to advance anticlerical ideas and discourse upon the need to end the Church's temporal power. In the 1940s, with the triumph of "democratic forces" over fascist totalitarianism, it would again become modish to render obeisance to liberal democracy. Furthermore, in the 1940s the influence of Catholicism, resurgent in the previous decade, entered upon a serious decline. It was the misfortune of the Spanish republic, then, to conduct its spiritual courtship of Spanish America at the one point in the twentieth century when it was most certain to be rebuffed.

In the 1930s the ideological climate of Spanish America, with the striking exception of Mexico, was singularly propitious for the flourishing of hispanismo as conceived by Spain's Catholic rightists. But at this precise period the rightists, very much on the defensive during the second republic, had lost a great deal of their political influence and were unable to bring Spain's policies into line with their concepts of hispanismo. Within five years after the rightists regained their power upon the conclusion of the civil war in 1939, their opportune moment had passed; for the outcome of World War II brought the antidemocratic, corporativist, Catholic right into disrepute in Spanish America. Thus in pursuing hispanismo, Spanish rightists were as unfortunate in their timing as the directors of the republic.

Spain's hispanoamericanistas, whether of the Catholic, conservative right, of the revolutionary right, or of the republican center and left, suffered also during the 1931–1936 period because of the gains of Pan-Americanism. Spaniards had consistently recognized that the success of hispanismo in the New World depended to a considerable degree upon the failure of Pan-Americanism; for if Spanish Americans identified with the values of the New World, as encapsuled, according at least to United States enthusiasts, in the programs, goals, and vision of Pan-Americanism, then they would automatically reject hispanismo and the values upon which it rested. By the mid-1930s the unmistakable surge of Pan-Americanism augured ill for hispanismo.

Shortly after the Franklin D. Roosevelt inauguration at the beginning of 1933, the United States began to acquire a new image among Latin American leaders. The social reforms of the New Deal seemed to ease the threat of revolution. This made it difficult to take seriously the contention of Spanish rightists that the United States style of life led inevitably to social upheaval. To many Latin Americans it seemed increasingly likely that by cooperating with the United States, perhaps by learning something from New Deal programs, while at the same time maintaining close economic-commercial ties with the tamed Colossus they could "muddle through" without having to resort to any of the fanciful and sweeping innovations suggested by Spanish idealogues as the only way of combating communism. Cooperation seemed all the more feasible in view of United States retrenchment from interventionism and the apparent willingness of its leaders, in their new mood of humility born of adversity, to respect Latin American traditions and to abandon attempts to "reform" them in line with Yankee values. When, under Woodrow Wilson, the United States had sought to make the world safe for its type of democracy, it had loomed as a menace in the eyes of Latin America's conservative directing classes. The new, noninterventionist, live-and-let-live stance of the United States under Roosevelt was one of the most engaging features of the Good Neighbor policy in the eyes of many Latin American elite groups.

An important Latin American diplomat predicted that the United States, in line with its changing attitudes, would abandon altogether its former ways of economic, political, and cultural imperialism.[104] His prediction seemed to undergo at least the first stage of fulfillment at the Seventh Pan-American Conference that convened in Montevideo in December of 1933. Secretary of State Cordell Hull agreeably surprised Latin Americans there by accepting the general principle of nonintervention, although he incurred some displeasure by stating his country would insist upon certain reservations—subsequently dropped at the 1936 Buenos Aires conference at which the United States committed itself virtually unconditionally to nonintervention.

Immediately after the dramatic events in Montevideo a South American newspaper noted for its anti–United States position acknowledged that the Seventh Pan-American Conference had been the most successful of them all and conceded that the fresh attitudes displayed by the United States were responsible for this fact.[105] The Good Neighbor policy gained new adherents for Pan-Americanism when in 1934 the Roosevelt administration secured abrogation of the Platt Amendment, which had given the United States the right to intervene in Cuba's internal affairs, and withdrew the last marines from Haiti.

In 1934 Manuel Ugarte, an Argentine who had dedicated most of his life to warning Latin Americans about the dangers of United States imperialism and whose activities had won the frequent plaudits of Spain's hispanoamericanistas,[106] published an article in which he evidenced a drastically revised viewpoint. United States actions at Montevideo, he wrote, heralded a true change in that country's policies, a change initiated by Secretary of State Henry Stimson during the presidency of Herbert Hoover. The altered United States approach, he suggested, was partially economically motivated, for the northern industrial power, desperately in need of new Latin American markets, had discovered that "you can't expect people to buy from you unless you are their friend." Ultimately, though, the change in United States policies, the Argentine contended, rested upon something deeper than economic considerations. "There is a spiritual basis. The United States continues being the country of Jefferson and Lincoln, a country of high ideals, in spite of imperialistic aberrations. The spirit of Monroe has now been repudiated."[107]

Observing events in the New World, an eminent Spanish diplomatic historian who was an ardent hispanoamericanista reached the conclusion that if the Good Neighbor Policy succeeded, "the moral position of Spain in America will suffer irreparable harm."[108] As of 1935, many signs indicated that the Good Neighbor policy was indeed succeeding. Even the Yankee-baiting Argentine foreign minister Carlos Saavedra Lamas, counted on by José Antonio to play a major role in uniting Spanish America against the imperialism of Anglo America, was temporarily mollified by the attentions and courtesies of Hull at Montevideo and had begun to evidence a guarded willingness to cooperate with the United States.

In their chronic dilemma of whether to respond to the lure of the Colossus or of the madre patria, Spanish Americans in the 1930s found the case for the United States decidedly more compelling than the one for Spain. The reasons for the weakness of hispanismo at this time are numerous, extending far beyond the resurgence of Pan-Americanism and reaching back a long way into the history of Spanish–Spanish-American relations. Still, as of the 1930s, hispanismo had by no means suffered a total collapse in the New World, and, just as for its debility, many reasons account for its powers of survival. An extended assessment of the causes for the frailty and strength, for the failure and success, of hispanismo is in order.

15: THE WEAKNESSES AND STRENGTHS OF HISPANISMO: A CONCLUDING ASSESSMENT

Sources of Weakness in Spain: Attitudes toward Spanish America

In 1905 Rafael María de Labra observed that one of the most serious obstacles to the advance of hispanismo resulted from Spanish claims to the right to exercise spiritual hegemony over Spanish America. Labra saw little hope for the cause that he steadfastly championed throughout a long life unless Spaniards accepted the cultural as well as the political sovereignty of Spanish America and approached the republics as equals.[1]

The observations of Labra produced little effect. As material in the preceding chapters attests, Spaniards continued to manifest their tutelary attitudes vis-à-vis Spanish Americans. The case of Carlos Badía Malacrida provides a further illustration of this fact.

In the period immediately following World War I, geographer Badía served in the consular corps in Mexico. He acquired at that time an abiding interest in hispanismo. With considerable eloquence he lamented the damage inflicted upon Spanish-American relations by those Spaniards who demanded a tutelary role for their country. In a book published in 1919 he wrote, "Spanish America must be approached in a spirit of equality. We must be brothers, not tutors. We are no longer the mother country dealing with her children; we are sisters, descended from the same family trunk. . . ."[2] Badía then proceeded to advise Spanish Americans on how to reconstitute their national boundaries along sensible geographic lines. If they followed his advice, he modestly suggested, Spanish Americans would be able finally to resolve their foolish boundary disputes and to find a "supranationality on the basis of what is common to them all, their Hispanic origins and foundations."

The tutelary attitude of Spaniards arose in part from their conviction that the Spanish-American republics, because of their extreme youthfulness, were still in a process of formation and therefore in need of friendly direction from a mature adviser. In the late nineteenth century Juan Valera chided Spanish Americans on their youthful impatience,[3] and Menéndez Pelayo informed them that "a new people can improvise everything except an intellectual culture."[4] In a statement typifying the reaction of many Spaniards to Spanish America as a whole, Miguel de Unamuno observed that because Argentina was still in a stage of formation[5] it had been unable to assimilate either the men or the ideas of foreign countries and to "synthesize them into a national whole. . . . There is not," he asserted, "a collective spirit in Argentina and this is why the Argentines have been unable to assimilate the colonies of foreign immigrants, just as the intellectual classes have been unable to assimilate the variety of ideas in the world today; they imitate, juxtapose, and superimpose these ideas, but they do not digest them."[6]

Unamuno did not presume on this occasion to state explicitly that the New World, because young and in formation, required direction and leadership from Spain. His restraint was not matched by most Spaniards who concerned themselves with hispanismo. More typical of this group was an authority on international law who wrote in 1939, more than thirty years after Unamuno had published his analysis: "America, with its people who are still young, needs perhaps even more than we ourselves a tradition that provides the necessary historical orientation. This tradition can only be the one that was created by our genius in the course of four centuries of mutual relations."[7]

In a spirit of ethnocentric arrogance bearing striking similarity to the attitudes of some of the less temperate U.S. proponents of Pan-Americanism, hispanoamericanistas saw in hispanismo a nationalism, conceived, defined, and interpreted by Spaniards, that would provide the animating spark for all the countries over which they claimed the right of cultural-spiritual guidance. It was one thing for Spanish-American republics to be in many respects culturally colonial and for their thinkers indiscriminately to borrow ideas from abroad and even to a great extent to borrow from Spain. It was something else, though, for Spanish-American intellectuals publicly to confess the cultural colonialism of their lands. Hispanismo, at least in the hands of its more zealous Spanish spokesmen, demanded little less than this public confession.

Spanish attitudes toward Spanish America did not always rest upon a benevolent and paternalistic assumption that the former colonies required guidance simply because they were young, immature, and in the process of national character formation. Often Spaniards contemplated "their" area of the New World with undisguised disdain. This disdain was rooted in several pejorative assumptions concerning Spanish Americans. To begin with, the representatives of the Catholic right, for whom national virtue and traditions were synonymous with Catholicism and in whose view hispanismo rested ultimately on faith in the Church of Rome, had their doubts as to just how Catholic Spanish Americans were. Thus a Spanish priest asserted in 1926 that Mexico was a long way from being a Catholic country and that the same could be said of "almost all Spanish America." He continued:

> We, who spread the Catholic faith with all the force of sentiment and all of the vigor that distinguish us in enterprises of this sort, did not have time to consolidate the faith in those new races so that it would become an overwhelming conviction of the soul. Therefore in America,

generally speaking, religion is emotional rather than intellectual; emotional because it is practiced in a manner not yet purified of a pagan residue.[8]

In colonial times, Spanish administrators had exempted Indians from the direct jurisdiction of the Inquisition and had also excluded them, with certain exceptions more freely granted in Mexico than in South America, from ordination to the priesthood and from reception of the sacrament of the Eucharist. The primary reason for this was the widespread belief that Indians, as spiritually and intellectually inferior beings, could not fully grasp the Catholic doctrine. Indicating that this belief still prevailed early in the twentieth century, *Razón y Fe* observed in 1910 that throughout the Philippines and Latin America, no matter how favorably disposed toward the Church a vast majority might be, only a small minority could be considered fully practicing Catholics because "men who do not have more than one-half European blood are properly exempted from various obligations and privileges" ordinarily attaching to the faithful.[9] This statement suggests that among many devout Spaniards, the people of Spanish America continued to be regarded as less than full Catholics and therefore as less than full human beings.

Considerations of a spiritual nature also led liberal, anticlerical Spaniards to hold Spanish Americans in disdain. Argentines, according to Unamuno, had fallen victim to a crude materialism. As a result, they were allegedly obsessed with wealth and did not scruple as to how they acquired it. Moreover, they falsified the hierarchy of values and held in contempt all exalted and noble undertakings.[10] On another occasion Unamuno wrote: "Mammonism is the great American peril. Material prosperity, without a counterweight, threatens to denaturalize Americans and to convert them into true, Byzantinized savages. . . ."[11] The classicist so disliked the materialism and spiritual laziness of the people of Spanish America[12] that he opposed Spanish emigration to the area. He feared that Spaniards, contaminated in the New World setting, would upon returning to their native land spread the contagion of materialism.[13]

José Ortega y Gasset shared Unamuno's concern over the vices, particularly the materialism, of Spanish Americans.[14] Because of their spiritual weakness and their excessive covetousness, the philosopher charged that Spanish Americans "carry in the deepest confines of their collective soul a source of immorality."

> We will not discuss how this source has been formed. The fact is that it exists and so long as it is not cast out and replaced with an energetic set of moral reactions which function automatically on all occasions, the Spanish Americans cannot entertain illusions of ascending to the rank of select peoples, even if one of their countries, such as Argentina, might possess not a few of the rarest endowments required for such a feat.[15]

Spain's hispanoamericanistas, whether conservative or liberal, repeatedly warned that the example of the United States and the cultural imperialism practiced by that country might lead Spanish Americans to betray the higher spiritual virtues received from Spain. As often as not, moreover, their interest in having Spain assume a tutorial role arose from their desire to save the Spanish raza in America from the threat of cultural annihilation at the hands of the Anglo-Americans. However much they talked about the need to preserve their culture in the New World, many Spaniards seemed in their hearts to feel that the battle had already been lost.

Spaniards often despaired over Spanish Americans not only because of their reputed spiritual backwardness but because of their racial inferiority as well. In 1898 Spaniards had looked with hope and optimism toward the anticipated accomplishments and progress of Spanish America. The deeds of their New World progeny would prove that the Spanish raza was not, after all, decadent. But development in Spanish America during the first third of the twentieth century did not in general justify the high hopes that many Spaniards had entertained in the days immediately following the disaster. Events in Spanish America, in fact, suggested to peninsulares that there might be something basically lacking in the Spanish "race" in America. Perhaps this is why not a few peninsulares, in spite of hispanismo's lyrical rhetoric about a common, transatlantic raza basically the same in America as in Spain, began to assume that the "race" in America was not after all Spanish, that instead it had been hopelessly debased by inferior elements. Such an assumption fed on and in turn helped perpetuate the beliefs common among Spaniards of the conquest and colonial period concerning the inferiority of Indians[16] and mixed-blooods—beliefs that had led Spain to fashion a "pigmentocracy"[17] in its American empire.

In describing the natives discovered in America by the conquerors, Spanish writers of the late nineteenth and early twentieth centuries used such terms and phrases as "apathy and laziness,"[18] lack of understanding, extreme mental and physical laziness."[19] Ortega y Gasset wrote of the Indians: "In their culture they were so inferior to the colonizers that it was as if they did not exist except as exploitable items."[20] And the Catholic intellectual José María Peman, one of the most important hispanoamericanistas during the Primo de Rivera dictatorship, wrote: "Spaniards went to a New World and found an inferior race; but they then applied themselves to the task of whitening the faces of that race and of opening up their limited craniums so as to introduce into them the luminous and civilizing thought of the blessed Castilian race."[21]

Many Spaniards, though, believed that the Indians had not been essentially uplifted or improved by their continuing contact with the forces of civilization. In a 1915 editorial a leading periodical organ of hispanismo referred to Mexican Indians as "basically ungovernable, in perpetual rebellion, incapable of understanding law, justice, and liberty."[22] In 1927

Ramiro de Maeztu—notwithstanding the fact that in *Defensa de la hispanidad*, published in 1934, he would praise Spaniards for their unique commitment to a belief in racial equality—attributed Spanish America's lack of progress to the presence of the aborigines.[23] "The Indian," he wrote, "is the son of nature. He lives in lands infinite in extent and infinite in beauty. He thinks these lands cannot be changed or improved, that nature can only be made worse through foolish human intervention. Thus he is dedicated to enduring and to resisting, never to changing or improving. This is his soul."[24] Finally, writing in 1932, one of the peninsula's spokesmen of hispanismo concluded that the agrarian reform program in Mexico might well prove that the Indian is "refractory to civilization, that he belongs to an inferior species."[25]

Other Spaniards approached the issue by contending that the Indian had ceased to exist as a cultural influence in Spanish America, having been absorbed by the superior colonizing race.[26] A typical expression of this belief appeared in a book published in 1896: "The pre-Columbian history of America has only scientific interest; but the real history of the area does not begin until the arrival of the Spaniards. The Indian ethnic element is little by little disappearing and its cultural remains have long since disappeared beneath the waves of immigration of a dominant race."[27] Thirty years later a Spanish priest revealed a similar viewpoint as he wrote:

> Thanks to the good treatment received from the Spaniards, those [Indian] races have not disappeared from the map, as in other parts of the world; but they do not count for anything at all, except to lend a bit of color to the white race in America. The truth is America belongs today, and will belong still more in the future, to the Spanish race and civilization. The Indian race will little by little be absorbed without leaving a history to be continued or glories to be celebrated. The glories of America begin with the discovery and colonization by the Spaniards.[28]

For all their avowals of the disappearance of Indian cultural elements in Spanish America, Spaniards may well have continued to suspect the survival of the "inferior" culture of people "refractory to civilization." To some extent their characteristic disdain toward Spanish America reflected this suspicion.[29] To a more considerable degree, however, attitudes of disdain sprang from Spanish beliefs concerning the instability of character, the unreliability, and the general inferiority of the mestizo.[30]

According to a Spanish Augustinian who was an active hispanoamericanista in the early twentieth century, racial mixture in order to be fruitful required one essential condition: that the races undergoing mixture "are not of very different mental or physical constitution. . . . When the races are very dissimilar . . . no advantageous mixture is possible." Race mixture, the priest contended, had been a success in Anglo-America, because there the Yankee had bred only with European nationalities of the white race, "which is the superior and dominant race par excellence."

In Spanish America, on the other hand, the consequences of race mixture purportedly had been catastrophic.[31]

Whether the Augustinian realized it or not, he was virtually paraphrasing an earlier Unamuno pronouncement. According to the classicist, the crossing of basically similar races produced good results; but, "the crossing of very different races is damaging and even infecund in the long run."[32] Unamuno, in turn, acquired his views of race, at least in part, from various Latin American sociologists, among them the Argentine Carlos Octavio Bunge and the Bolivian Alcides Arguedas, who had developed complex and nonsensical theories about the inferiority of the mestizo.[33] Unfortunately, just as many of the views of Spanish Americans on Spain were shaped by Spaniards who pursued the time-honored tradition of writing venomously on Spain, the views of Spaniards on the New World republics were often influenced by Spanish Americans who wrote deprecatingly of their own people.

Spaniards, however, did not need the help of Spanish Americans in forming their attitudes on the results of race mixture or mestizaje in Spanish America. Their biased views seemed to come naturally to them and to persist long after Spanish Americans had begun to find virtue in mestizaje. In 1918 a Spanish author declared that the only progressive countries of Spanish America were those that had killed off their Indians and escaped the coming of "large waves of Africans." Argentina, Chile, and Uruguay he held up as examples of truly progressive Spanish-American countries. In particular, he singled out Uruguay for praise because it "presented the best demonstration of what the Spanish race can accomplish when allowed to mix with foreign elements of quality."[34]

Four years later a Spanish writer often featured in the Ibero-American page of the liberal newspaper El Sol asserted that the New World republics had not achieved political stability because they were unable to overcome the psychological instability that stemmed from their "unresolved ethnic and historical problems."[35] In the following year, 1923, that old hand at practical hispanismo Julio de Lazúrtegui commented upon the inability of the Spanish-American republics to achieve stability. He attributed this to problems that were "simultaneously ethnic, geographic, and topographical—oh! the fatal influence of volcanic soils."[36] One year later Germán Latorre y Setién, a respected professor of geography at the University of Sevilla, urged Spaniards essentially to confine their New World ties to the republics of Argentina, Chile, and Uruguay. The other countries, he asserted, were still in a state of "embryonic organization, without national conscience, without a sense of civic duty and public rights and responsibilities, inhabited mainly by Indians, mestizos, Negroes, and mulattoes . . . disrupted by frequent revolutions and coups and suffering from caudillismo . . . and disorganized treasuries and therefore the easy prey of foreign interventionists."[37]

Whether based on cultural and spiritual pretensions, on racial prejudices, or on any one of a variety of other causes, the Spanish attitude of disdain toward most Spanish Americans was so strong and so candidly expressed as to call forth deep resentment in the New World republics. In addition, attitudes, beliefs, and prejudices that had originated in the New World and did not represent a response to Spanish haughtiness militated strongly against the cause of hispanismo.

Sources of Weakness in Spanish America: Indigenismo, New Worldism and Nationalism, Latin Americanism, and Pan-Americanism

With obvious approval a Spanish writer commented in 1922 on a statement published by a Chilean journalist. "One thing is certain and undeniable," the journalist had written, "and this is that each Chilean aspires to prove that he is of pure Spanish blood. To call him an Indian is to offend him. Even the humblest persons do not recognize as their ancestors anyone except Spaniards."[38]

If the situation as described actually obtained in Chile, elsewhere it was clearly different. In Mexico, for example, Spaniards observed with alarm the increasing glorification of Indian culture and traditions and the mounting concern with incorporating the natives into society. One Spaniard at least comforted himself by suggesting that, in the final analysis, the "Spanish spirit" was responsible for the "whole surge of the Mexican Indians." Spaniards, he said, and Spaniards alone had discovered and begun to extol the more positive features of Mexico's Indian cultural heritage, and only the Spanish directing classes were capable of "molding and leading the Indian masses in the endeavor to transform Mexico into a great brown power."[39]

In his interpretation of the "brown power" movement in Mexico, this Spaniard indulged himself in false comfort. The spirit of the indigenista movement sweeping not only Mexico but also Peru and to a lesser extent Guatemala, Ecuador, and Bolivia, was more accurately captured by a Latin American writer. "Who is the Indian?" he asked. "Is he a being capable of serving as an efficient instrument in a renovating social revolution?" Not only is he capable of this, the writer responded to his own question, but "the Indian is the most valuable factor in our entire socioeconomic organization. . . ." He continued: "Only the Indians and their mestizo descendants, sensitive to their own ideals, can vindicate themselves. Vindication will not be accomplished by the slow and rusty machinery of education, as the white-skinned lords of the land imagine. It will come about through a sudden blow, struck in manful posture, in the same way that man reaches out and takes what is essential for survival. . . ."[40] Seen in this light indigenismo was incompatible with hispanismo, and the rise of the Indianist movement boded no conceivable good for the aspirations of hispanoamericanistas.

For indigenistas, the future greatness of the American republics depended upon their adherence to the models of pre-Columbian civilization, especially the communal, collectivist features of Indian life. Typical of this school was the Peruvian Luis E. Valcárcel, who insisted that only the Indian could redeem and regenerate his country. He saw Peru's future in the imposition by the Indian of his allegedly collectivist civilization on the entire country. "European culture," he wrote in 1927, "has never truly affected the Indian. Peru is Indian and will be Indian. . . . The only true Peru is Indian Peru."[41] Another indigenista of the period avowed: "Peru will not emerge as a nation until power is transferred into the hands of the majority, the Indians of the sierra. Peru will not begin genuine political life until these socialists of the sierra take the capital."[42]

Spaniards and hispanistas in Spanish America dismissed the indigenista movement as childish and ridiculous. They described it also as a communist plot, and one South American hispanista asserted that a combination of "Jewry, communism, and Protestantism" was trying to take advantage of the Indian issue in order to force alien forms of life and culture on the Andean republics.[43]

The Peruvian poet José Santos Chocano thought it possible to reconcile admiration for the Spanish past and traditions with a respect for and a fascination with Indian cultural values. He indicated this in the lines he wrote when dedicating a book of verse to King Alfonso XIII:

Sir: I have another muse, which is not the Hispanic muse,
although in its blood there is the blood of the Spanish scion.
It feels at times Indian and at times Castilian;
it is the daughter of a Catholic Queen and of the sun.[44]

But ardent hispanoamericanistas insisted upon an exclusive devotion to Spanish traditions and values. Thus they were hopelessly at odds with the spirit of the New World, which impelled most people living there to want to be something other than carbon copies of Spaniards.

Convinced they were destined to be something different and unique, something never before known in the world, Spanish Americans tended to stress the influence of environment over that of race, language, and traditions. They viewed themselves, in many ways at least, as the products of the New World setting, not of their Spanish hereditary origins.[45] This being the case, an Argentine contended, Spaniards "do not and cannot know us; they should not concern themselves with us."[46]

Unlike the Argentine who felt Spaniards should not even concern themselves with Spanish Americans, the Venezuelan Rufino Blanco-Fombona welcomed close ties with the peninsula. At the same time he maintained: "We are the land of the future, so proud of our common New World patria that we would not exchange it for the most glorious nationality of the Old World."[47] Blanco-Fombona roundly criticized Spaniards for demanding cultural hegemony over the New World. America, he insisted, was creating a new culture, and only the foundation of that culture was Spanish.[48]

Similar ideas found expression by the Argentine socialist Alfredo Palacios: "Our America until today," he wrote, "has lived from Europe, accepting Europe as its guide. . . . Let us now look to ourselves. Let us recognize that the paths of European culture do not serve us. We stand before new realities. Let us emancipate ourselves from the past and the European example. . . . Our program is the . . . elaboration of a new culture."[49] And Ricardo Rojas, one of Argentina's most revered writers, began in the early 1920s to propound a cultural nationalism that paid homage to the contributions of Spaniards, Indians, and recently arrived immigrants. All of these components, he felt, shaped by the influence of the American environment, could be fused to create an Argentine product new and different from any of its components.[50]

The greatest error of hispanistas, according to a perceptive South American writer, was to consider the Spaniard as the single, exclusive progenitor of Spanish-American culture and peoples. From the earliest times, he stated, those Spaniards who decided to establish themselves permanently in the American Andes became "Indianized Spaniards" and soon acquired "a new orientation in life. . . . They became men of the Andes. . . . These historic Andes, where human values are largely imposed by the Indian soul, enveloped the Spaniard and submerged him in their essence, at the same time developing in him a personality distinct from that which he brought from Spain." The result of this process was, the writer contended, the emergence of a new people, a mestizo people; and he concluded: "The mestizo soul, in spite of the disdain commonly attaching to the term mestizo, is the beginning of total Americanness. It is the germ of a new personality."[51]

Especially in the 1920s Spanish Americans, instead of lamenting the allegedly adverse effects of race mixture, as Bunge and Arguedas had done and as so many Spaniards continued to do, began to extol the purportedly superior qualities of mixed races, or mestizo peoples. Such a person was the Mexican José Vasconcelos, who in 1925 published La raza cósmica: misión de la raza iberoamericana y notas de viajes a la América del sur. In the book Vasconcelos urged, among other things, the crossing of Asiatic or Oriental and Spanish-American blood. Only a people that already enjoyed the advantage of being mestizo in its makeup, he contended, could undertake this task of creating a "cosmic race."[52]

Ortega y Gasset was scarcely a conforming figure in the hispanismo movement precisely because he sympathetically understood the awe and fascination with which Spanish Americans contemplated themselves as the youthful, energetic, ethnically distinct citizens of a new world, capable of developing fresh and original life styles.[53] On the other hand, most

hispanoamericanistas remained utterly insensitive to this awe and fascination. Exasperated by this fact a Mexican who had spent many years in
Spain and in many ways admired Spanish culture, pleaded with Spaniards
to face up to the reality that Spanish Americans were different. The
inability or unwillingness of Spaniards to comprehend the fact that Spanish Americans were not the same as Spaniards and their tireless efforts
to prove the sameness were, the Mexican asserted, "a source of deep
resentment and misunderstanding in America."[54]

Not enough Spaniards heeded the pleas of the Mexican. In 1926, for
example, when the Unión Ibero-Americana launched a new journal to
serve the cause of hispanismo and to report on events both in Spain and
Spanish America, it chose the title *Revista de las Españas*. The Union's
directors thereby demonstrated remarkable insensitivity to the fact that
Spanish-American republics, most of them gripped by a burgeoning spirit
of nationalism,[55] did not wish to be regarded as other Spains. Many hispanoamericanistas joined the directors of the Union in failing to recognize
that the day of the atomized nationalism of individual countries was not
yet about to give way to the supranationalism of an extended spiritual-
cultural patria. Apparently they believed that because the Spanish-American republics had not succeeded in becoming true nation-states, it would
be easy to incorporate them into a supranational collectivity. In this frame
of mind they were incapable of considering the possibility that the directing classes of pre-nation entities had first to acquire and for a time luxuri-
ate in the satisfaction and confidence arising from the successful transformation of their countries into genuine nation-states before they could
think in terms of overtly relinquishing some of the perquisites, whether
cultural or political, of national sovereignty.

However much they stressed the importance of the New World environment in shaping their nationalisms, values, and life styles, many Latin
Americans conceded that their culture had its foundation, its origin, and
point of departure in Spanish culture or at least in the culture of the
Romanized part of Europe. Men who made this concession considered
themselves permanently distinct from the Yankees, whose cultural origins
lay in England. In order to defend the unique cultural patterns they
believed they were developing against the absorptionist tendencies of the
alien and distinct United States, these Latin Americans often stressed the
need to achieve a united front through some loose form of political and
economic cooperation. However, in contrast to Spain's disciples of hispanismo who contended that only a Spanish-led league could offset the
menace of the United States, Latin Americans as often as not desired
to confine cooperation to their own New World republics.

Latin Americanism (some intellectuals preferred to call it Indo-Ameri-
canism), conceived of as a defensive grouping of the republics to the
south of the Rio Grande, was based to some degree on a view of contin-

ental cultural isolationism. As such it was obviously in conflict with the objectives of hispanismo. Latin Americanism existed also under a different guise in which, if less directly hostile to the program of hispanismo, it was nonetheless opposed to the exclusivist spirit of the peninsula's more ardent hispanoamericanistas. To many intellectuals of the lands extending from Mexico to Tierra del Fuego, Latin Americanism was a term that denoted the existence of special cultural bonds between their countries and Latin Europe—Spain, Portugal, Italy, and most especially France.

Still other Latin Americans, wishing to keep all international options open, resented the assumption that they were bound by special ties to any one area of the world. When Argentine statesman Roque Saenz Peña proclaimed in 1890, "Let America be for humanity," Spaniards hailed him for having repudiated the spirit of Monroeism with its underlying credo that America was for the Americans, specifically those of the United States. But the Saenz Peña pronouncement was just as inimical to the narrow spirit of hispanismo as to the pretensions of Pan-Americanism. Through the years the Latin Americans who have been guided by Argentine's exhortation have been equally opposed to the contention that conditions of consanguinity bound their republics in a unique way to Spain,[56] to the claim that cultural antecedents tied them to Latin Europe, and to the allegation that geographic location within the American hemisphere joined them in a peculiar manner to the United States.

Through the years, moreover, and not just in the 1930s when the Good Neighbor produced certain spectacular if ephemeral results, hispanismo has suffered from the fact that not a few Latin Americans have felt themselves strangely attracted toward the United States—even when at the same time they have often been repulsed by the Colossus.[57] Uruguayan President Baltasar Brum (1919–1923) perturbed Spain's champions of hispanismo considerably[58] when he asserted in 1920 that there was absolutely no reason for Latin Americans to try to isolate themselves from the United States. "The community of our forms of government and of our ideals of justice and democracy with those of the great sister of the north," he stated, "are powerful factors which foment ties of solidarity." The Uruguayan further contended that differences in language did not constitute an obstacle to the establishment of close bonds among peoples: "We have seen this in Europe, where countries of the most diverse languages and races associated themselves for purposes of common defense." Necessary for international harmony and accord, Brum insisted as he defended Pan-Americanism, "is a community of ideals and the coordination of interests; and it is undeniable that our ideals are similar to those of the United States and that our interests do not exclude theirs."

Brum acknowledged that the United States had in the past been guilty of unjustifiable acts of imperialism. But this did not imply to him that Latin America should try to quarantine itself from the northern republic.

Instead, it should collaborate, he believed, with the United States in "multilateralizing" the Monroe Doctrine so that all the countries of the New World would participate equally in interpreting, enforcing, and expanding the Doctrine's precepts.[59]

Equally disconcerting to Spain's hispanoamericanistas were the views of the distinguished and widely read Argentine poet-essayist Leopoldo Lugones. According to him the notion of community arising from language was a delusion. In spite of common language, the republics of Spanish America engaged in unsavory commercial competition and even in cruel wars, "while the accomplishments up to now in the realm of hemisphere accord have been owing to the initiative of the United States." The presence of the United States in Latin America, culturally and economically was, Lugones stated, inevitable, and he advised Argentines and all Latin Americans to accept this fact and not be lured by visionary schemes of Hispano-American unity. Referring to Argentina and equating the adjective *American* with United States, something rarely done by Latin Americans, he wrote:

> Our political organization is an adaptation of the American system; our federal justice is organized along American lines; our normal schools are of the American type; our monetary system has the dollar as the standard of reference; our industry and even our kitchens function on American models. The greatest part of our commerce is with the United States. The influence that all of this exercises over our organization and our thought is great and in general, we believe, beneficial. . . . We have no reason or valid motive to change this.[60]

The Staying Power of Pan-Americanism and Hispanismo

In spite of all the blunders of United States statesmen and in spite of the steady opposition to it among a wide circle of Latin American intellectuals and political leaders, Pan-Americanism did not wither away as hispanoamericanistas hoped it would. The ambivalence with which Latin Americans regarded it, attracted to it at the same time they were repelled by it, helped enable Pan-Americanism at least to survive and occasionally to flourish in unexpected manner. With hispanismo it was the same. The blunders, the misconceptions, the arrogance of Spaniards who labored in its cause, combined with the numerous forces in Latin America basically hostile to its assumptions and objectives, might well have been expected to result in the total collapse of hispanismo at almost any moment in the 1898–1936 period. But hispanismo survived, after a fashion at least, because Latin Americans maintained the same ambivalence toward it as toward Pan-Americanism.

A fundamental reason for hispanismo's survival lies in the fact that its value system was consonant with the apparently natural preference of

Spanish Americans for the hierarchically, organically structured, stratified, generally nonopen and nonpluralistic society—even if impaired economic progress was the price that had to be paid for this society. In this preference Spanish Americans seemed decidedly to be more influenced by their Spanish heritage than by their propinquity to the pragmatic innovators of the "Great Republic of the North" with their faith in inorganic democracy and obsession with material progress.

In their attempt to maintain the sort of social structure inherited from their colonial past, Latin Americans understood that they could combine the ideals and values of hispanismo with the fruits of Pan-Americanism. They rejected the validity of the sharp dichotomy presented by Ramón Valle-Inclán in one of his novels. In this work the distinguished peninsular writer sketched a scene in which a member of the Spanish colony in a mythical Spanish-American country conversed with a United States businessman. The Spanish immigrant insisted that the directing classes of the country realized that in order to avoid social upheaval they had "to turn their eyes once more toward the madre patria." With considerable scorn the Yankee businessman replied: "If the creole elements endure as the directing classes it will be owing to the ships and cannons of North America."[61]

Spanish Americans apparently felt that preservation of their social system depended both upon nourishing the ideals and value judgements of the madre patria and in utilizing not just the ships and cannons but also the capital and technology of the United States. They skillfully mixed the two forces, one Spanish and essentially spiritual, the other North American and basically material, as they effected superficial alterations of the social, economic, and political system in the first third of the twentieth century in the endeavor to keep the established order fundamentally intact. Latin American appreciation of the value of the two forces in defending the status quo accounts in part for the endurance and occasional flowering of Pan-Americanism and hispanismo. Situated at "the crossroads between two worlds,"[62] Latin Americans ingeniously managed to make the best of the situation and to utilize both worlds.

Social Stratification and Stability at the Cost of Economic Progress: Spanish America in the First Third of the Twentieth Century

The rapidly shifting styles, currents, and vogues of ideology in Spanish America have often been attributed to the quest of its intellectuals for originality and for an authentic cultural nationalism tailored to the needs, tastes, and unique traditions of their individual countries. In some ways, though, Spanish-American thinkers seem to have been less concerned with originality and nationalism than with fashioning the intellectual models and guidelines for systems, institutions, and processes intended to strengthen the status quo; at other times they appear to have been mainly preoccupied with rationalizing such devices after they had been arrived at pragmatically. In their principal endeavors the social ideologists of Spanish America have been almost constantly eclectic and imitative, and moreover apparently undisturbed by this fact.

Intellectually the rationale which seemed best suited for the social and economic system desired by Spanish America's directing classes in the late nineteenth century was a combination of Auguste Comte's positivism and Herbert Spencer's social Darwinism. Positivism, even as liberalism with its traditional anticlericalism, justified an attack against the paternalism and charity that constituted key elements of the Church's role in temporal society. Departing from Comte, who wished to replace Church-controlled charity with a paternalism imparted by the secular priesthood of a new religion of humanity, Spanish Americans generally rejected the religion of positivism and embraced only its temporal precepts, particularly those stressing order, authority, and elitist rule. They seemed hostile to all forms of paternalism, and to warrant this stance they turned to social Darwinism and glorified a process in which the fit, by refusing to pamper the unfit, would gradually through evolutionary stages eliminate allegedly inferior classes altogether.

The social doctrines derived from a mixture of the teachings of Comte and Spencer, combined with a Spanish-American tendency to recognize dark skin and Indian or Negro blood as proof of unfitness, encouraged unabashed exploitation of the lower classes by the directing elite and inevitably resulted in an intensifying social problem with a frightening revolutionary potential. About the turn of the century, then, positivism—social Darwinism had run its course as a suitable manual of conduct for an elite intent upon maintaining the established order basically intact. Consequently, an ideology that can best be described as neopositivism came into vogue.

Neopositivists retained the stress of positivism on empirical, scientifically demonstrable truth, upon order and progress. But they rejected social Darwinism by insisting upon the need for government action to protect the laboring classes. In this attitude the neopositivists strongly resembled those Spanish liberals, discussed in Chapter 5, who at the turn of the century abandoned laissez-faire doctrines, came out in favor of government intervention to ease the social problem, and in the attempt to apply their new concepts collaborated with Gumersindo de Azcárate in the work of the Instituto de Reformas Sociales.

At least one of the Spanish American neopositivists, the Argentine Manuel A. Bermudes, also showed a striking similarity in his thought to Francisco Giner de los Ríos and to the pedagogical theories derived by Spaniards from the teachings of Krause. Through education, according to

Bermudes, the poor man would come to accept his situation as the natural result of his limited talents. Gradually recognizing his lack of capacity for participating with understanding in the realms of higher cultural pursuits, he would become reconciled to performing his menial tasks, and he would no longer resent the elevated status of the gifted men who could operate effectively on more exalted levels.[63] Viewed in this light, mass education could become the instrument for safeguarding inequality.

As the positivists, so also the neopositivists were vitally concerned with development and progress. Unlike their ideological predecessors, however, the neopositivists argued that progress depended upon making the masses productive and therefore virtuous, not upon eliminating them as unfit. One of South America's most typical neopositivists asserted:

> It is necessary . . . to educate, and to educate people through labor, through industry, which is the greatest medium of moralization. There is nothing which will better elevate the character of the man of the masses today, nothing which will make him interest himself more effectively in the future of his country, than to educate him to be practical and prudent and to desire to acquire wealth by means of his personal efforts.[64]

Until the lower classes had acquired material ambitions and the skills requisite for their fulfillment, neopositivists demanded that they be protected by government-administered social programs.

Other members of the Spanish-American ruling class and intelligentsia denied that social stability depended upon imparting to underlings a desire for material aggrandizement and then teaching them how, after an initial, transition period of government protection, to fulfill their ambitions through their own efforts. Instead, they maintained, social stability and solidarity depended upon minimizing the material aspirations and economic self-sufficiency of the lower classes while making them permanently reliant on the paternalism of an interventionist government. In the outlook of these men—who, because their concepts largely reflect the values of the colonial past, can be referred to as traditionalists—lack of material progress was the price that had to be paid for maintaining rigid social stratification. As it turned out, Spanish America, excepting Mexico, developed in the first third of the twentieth century more along the lines desired by traditionalists than by neopositivists.

The Mexican constitution of 1917 stands as a landmark in the ideological, social, economic, and political development of Spanish America. Its basic significance lies in its repudiation of the individualistic, classically liberal spirit of the preceding constitution, the charter of 1857, and its establishment of an interventionist state, one of the primary duties of which was to enforce the social obligations of property and to protect the laboring classes. The 1917 constitution emerged from the political Revo-

lution that had erupted in 1910 and gradually evolved into a social movement. And the Revolution was in many ways the result of the fact that
Mexicans, steadfastly refusing to challenge the prevailing concepts of
positivism-social Darwinism, had allowed a social problem to generate
uncontainable pressures. After the Revolution, Mexicans retained the
preoccupation with material progress that had shaped national policies
during the long period (1876–1911) when Porfirio Díaz had wielded
political power and when the theories of Comte and Spencer had held
sway. In the post-Revolutionary period, the approach of Mexicans to
their country's problems seemed often to be at least partially in line with
the precepts of neopositivism.

Elsewhere in Spanish America the directing classes responded more
quickly than had the Mexicans to the early signs of a potentially revolutionary situation; and, by ingeniously adopting state interventionist policies they managed to stave off upheaval. The methods they resorted to
were more in accord with the prescriptions of the traditionalists than of
the neopositivists.

Beginning with the first presidential term of José Batlle y Ordóñez
(1903–1907) Uruguay gradually adopted and implemented a series of
social and labor laws that for a time made it, in matters of social security
and worker protection, the most advanced country in the American hemisphere. Similar though far less sweeping programs were introduced in
Argentina following the victory of Hipólito Irigoyen in the 1916 presidential election. A representative of urban middle sectors and intellectually under the influence of Krausism, Irigoyen in that year triumphed
over the candidate of the conservative landowning oligarchy that had
dominated Argentine politics since the 1860s. To a considerable degree,
however, the temporarily eclipsed oligarchy, motivated by enlightened
self-interest in its desire to preserve as much as possible of the old order,
collaborated in the new interventionist policies and helped guarantee
their relative effectiveness. Analagous developments took place in Chile
during the first presidential term of Arturo Alessandri (1920–1925) and
the dictatorship of Carlos Ibáñez (1927–1931). Even as early as 1907
the trend toward neopaternalism, through which the lower classes were
protected not by the charity of private institutions such as the Church
and of individual landowners and industrialists but rather by the social
and labor programs of the government, had become unmistakable in Chile.
In that year the powerful Radical Party had abandoned its customary
laissez-faire stance, coming out squarely in favor of state intervention.

When the Liberals of Colombia came to power in 1930, they introduced
fairly extensive social legislation. Well before the Colombians, Peruvians
had come into line with the Uruguayan, Argentine, and Chilean patterns
by enacting various labor laws culminating with the eight-hour-day legislation of 1919. During the eleven-year dictatorship of Augusto B. Leguía

(1919–1930), who viewed his mission as being to stave off a communist revolution, additional social measures were enacted and as a result middle and lower sectors came to benefit from a variety of new services and protective devices. The Indian masses, however, did not share in these benefits, in spite of the provisions of newly enacted laws. The club, as wielded by the army, instead of the carrot, as offered by new bureaucratic agencies that administered social programs in coastal Peru, continued to be regarded as the best means for dealing with the remote and isolated Indians.

As a result of Spanish America's social and labor programs introduced at varying points during the first third of the twentieth century, laboring classes, particularly in the cities where the means of organization were more available to them and where therefore they seemed potentially more dangerous than in isolated rural regions, were won over to the established system of government by being made increasingly reliant upon it. Labor was permitted to organize but almost always under the careful regulation and control of the government. Generally labor leaders were simply intermediaries between the rank and file and government, and their success depended upon their friendly connections with government. When concessions were won they resulted not from the autonomous strength of unions but rather from the ability of labor leaders to make advantageous deals with their government contacts. As it became apparent that worthwhile gains could be achieved in this way, labor settled into the pattern of dealing with and seeking accommodations from the government rather than of challenging it directly.

As often as not, the gains of organized labor took the form of wide-ranging fringe benefits instead of increases in real wages. Thus workers gained protection against arbitrary, and sometimes even well-warranted, firing. Athletic fields, parks, kindergartens, and subsidized housing became available to them. Exhibitions and various forms of entertainment were arranged for them and on certain holidays they were eulogized in the flowery discourses of government and social leaders. Sometimes vacation and rest centers as well as local travel tours were provided them. In addition the government provided them and their families with numerous medical facilities, one consequence being a notable reduction in infant mortality that would later contribute to a staggering population problem. Increases in real wages would have brought genuine power to the workers. But the granting of innumerable fringe benefits made them all the more dependent upon the government, the source of all favors and concessions.

In many Spanish-American countries the inflationary spiral fitted in conveniently with this pattern—perhaps fortuitously, perhaps premeditatedly. Inflation discouraged workers from saving, and thus they remained without the power and security that derive from capital accumulation. Unable to save and living in an inflationary setting, workers had to rely upon the government each year to give them an increase in wages that would at least come close to matching the rise in living costs. With some regularity they received this increase. In the process, as it operated year after year, the dependence of workers upon the government and the system it served became all the greater.

Spanish-American directing classes, whether motivated by the respect for the individual dignity allegedly inhering in the Hispanic value system or simply by enlightened self-interest, seemed to make the conscious decision not to submit the working masses to the intense degree of exploitation that accompanied the industrial revolution in Europe, and later in the United States, and later still in Russia. In a way this decision impeded industrial development. At the same time it proved conducive to social solidarity and to the maintenance of the established order. In the eyes of the Spanish-American elite the price of foregoing economic development was not an excessive one to pay for the desired social advantages.

The social services programs by which Spanish-American governments won the allegiance of the laboring classes, or at least bought their quiescence, required imposing capital outlays. As the system developed, in fact, soaring social overhead seriously reduced the capital that might otherwise have been available for economic development. Probably Spanish-American governments could not have funded their social programs had it not been for the fact that foreign capital relieved them to a considerable degree of the necessity to invest in economic development. The overall process enabled the Spanish-American directing classes to avoid social revolution and to remain true to the social ideals of Spain, as urged by the Spanish immigrant in the conversation reported by novelist Valle-Inclán; but in order to do so the elite had to accept a dependence on the ships and cannons mentioned by the Yankee businessman and also upon the capital and technological expertise of the United States.

When it came to incorporating new middle sectors into the established system and even pressing them into service as the watchdogs of that system, Spanish-American leaders were just as successful as with the urban lower classes. The aristocracy remained to a considerable extent open, permitting successful middle groups to enter it through marriage, through membership in exclusive clubs customarily reserved to those recognized as aristocrats, and through acquiring rural property and the social prestige uniquely associated with it. The dream of joining the aristocracy—and the number of persons who actually fulfilled this dream made it seem a reasonable one—provided a safety valve that relieved the pressures which middle sectors might otherwise have directed against the established class system.[65]

Judged according to economic indices, Spanish America in the first third of the twentieth century had begun to acquire a substantial middle sector. On the basis of attitudes, of psychological criteria, however, Spanish America remained a two-class society; for the middle sectors identified by and large with the aristocracy or upper class. Men of the middle sectors did not regard themselves as constituting a permanent class. Instead, they saw themselves as in transition, as being about to join the upper class. And while they awaited admission, either for themselves or their heirs, they did all in their power to protect and preserve the perquisites of the upper class, so that these perquisites would be available to them once they completed the process of upward social mobility.

The society and the economy were so structured as to make the waiting period agreeable for the middle sectors. Spanish Americans of the middle sectors could go to the university, enroll in overwhelming numbers in the prestigious law school and be assured upon graduation of finding a position in the government bureaucracy or in other rapidly expanding services. Work of this sort did not attach a stigma to those who performed it. The manner in which governments expanded their bureaucracies, absorbing energies that might otherwise have been applied to basically productive sectors of the economy, perpetuated an inefficient economic system that had appeared during the colonial period as a reflection of the one established in the peninsula during the sixteenth century. At the same time the uneconomic burgeoning of the bureaucracy guaranteed social stability by making it possible for middle sectors to gain gentlemanly employment and to live in accordance with their basic values, which were not production oriented.

Middle-sector men found further opportunities available to them as industrial entrepreneurs, beginning especially about the time of World War I, when Spanish-American governments, facing the fact that their countries could no longer purchase finished goods from the old sources, had introduced vast import substitution programs. Not drawn toward industry by their traditional values, middle sectors had almost to be bribed into the field through lavish concessions, through promises of various immunities, and through generous tariff concessions. The whole process was repeated at the outset of the great depression when governments once more had to resort to import substitution on a massive scale. As with labor, success for industrialists depended upon government concessions. And just as with labor, industrialists who won concessions from government became beholden to the system that government served.

Centuries before this in Europe, the spontaneous, natural rise of an autonomously powerful industrial class had unleashed revolutionary forces which threatened and, eventually, thoroughly transformed the established order. In Spanish America, the forced, unnatural, hothouse creation of a new industrial class strengthened the status quo.[66]

In the Spanish-American setting, according to Maeztu, industrialists sought the "money of power." Avoiding direct involvement in purely economic affairs, they sought access to power, to the government, in order to win the privileges that would make it possible for them to acquire money without risk. In the United States on the other hand, Maeztu contended, people pursued an economic, not a political, approach to money. To them, moneymaking meant entering directly into economic ventures. Utlimately they welcomed and rejoiced in the power that money gave them, but they did not think initially of turning to the wielders of power to obtain opportunities for amassing wealth.[67] Undoubtedly Maeztu exaggerated the degree to which the "money of power" concept was absent from the United States. Still, it seems hard to deny that this concept had stronger roots in Spanish America. The result, once again, was to impair economic development but to strengthen the control that government exercised over society in the interest of the established order.

During the first third of the twentieth century, Spanish America underwent considerable change. To a remarkable degree this change achieved its calculated objectives; for the more the area changed, the more it remained the same. This fact bears striking testimony to the ingenuity of the Spanish-American directing classes. At the same time it demonstrates the enduring strength of the values originally bequeathed by Spain to the New World and upon which the hispanismo movement largely rested.

Continuity and Hispanismo in Spanish America

The most vital concern to Spanish rightists, whether conservatives or liberals, was the preservation of the hierarchical, stratified society, which was threatened, so they believed, by the leveling forces of inorganic democracy and communism. Outside of its practical aspects—the concern, that is, with trade and commerce—the great animating ideal of hispanismo was to unite the Hispanic raza against all the pressures and forces that threatened to disrupt the traditional social hierarchy and with it the prevailing hierarchy of values. Accompanying this ideal was the conviction that Spaniards had to serve as the mentors of Spanish Americans in the crusade to preserve the sort of social organization and values consonant with the essential character of the raza.

Spanish America's directing classes, naturally with some exceptions, remained unwaveringly dedicated to preserving basically intact the type of social structure bequeathed them by their colonial experience. The steadfastness with which they applied themselves to this objective evidences their accord with the fundamental values of hispanismo. But their very success in attaining their goal weakened hispanismo as a formal, Spanish-led program of action. What need had the Spanish Americans for guidance and direction from Spain when they proved so sucessful in their own way in transforming the details of the established order so as to maintain its essence and guarantee the continuity of tradition? With their own methods working so well within the framework of a hypocritical adaptation of the democratic-liberal system, what possible inducement could there have been for Spanish Americans to turn to the corporativist schemes of Spain's mainstream rightists or to the desperate expedients advocated by the revolutionary right?

Spain in the first third of the twentieth century was far less successful than many Spanish-American republics in assimilating new groups and forces into the old structure. The proletariat as well as many middle-sector groups remained outside of this structure and grew increasingly alienated from it. Not until the civil war had been fought, in fact, would Spaniards prove to be as adept as Spanish Americans had been during the first third of the twentieth century in incorporating new groups into a traditional social structure.

Spanish Americans had no need for the leadership of Spain implicitly assumed in the hispanismo movement. At the same time they did have a decided need for the kind of close economic collaboration with the United States which was frowned upon by the great majority of hispano-americanistas—with the most notable exception of a few liberals in the immediate post-World-War-I period. Economic collaboration with the United States, Spanish Americans realized full well, helped make possible the preservation of that social system that was in line with the values of hispanismo.

Given their geographic location in the New World and the inescapability as well as the profitability of ties with the United States, Spanish Americans realistically saw the need to reject the organizational structure that Spaniards associated with hispanismo. Precisely by rejecting a Spanish-led confederation, whether loose or formal, cultural, economic, or political, Spanish Americans have been better able to fashion a New World adaptation of the spiritual essence of hispanismo. The failure of the organizational program of hispanismo was in fact a necessary prerequisite for the triumph of its spirit and values in Spanish America between 1898 and 1936.

NOTES

NOTES TO INTRODUCTION

1. An excellent study of the early stages of this movement is Mark J. Van Aken, *Pan-Hispanism: Its Origin and Development to 1866* (Berkeley and Los Angeles, Calif., 1959).

2. Unamuno, "Sobre la literatura hispanoamericana," a 1905 essay included in his *Alqunas consideraciones sobre la literatura hispanoamericana* (Madrid, 1968, 3rd ed.), p. 77. Unless otherwise specified, all books and periodicals cited are published in Madrid.

3. Eduardo Gómez de Baquero, "Nacionalismo e hispanismo," *Revista de las Españas*, no. 29 (March, 1929), p. 75. The author, an eminent journalist and literary and theater critic, was received into the Real Academia Española de la Lengua in 1925.

4. Francisco Anaya Ruiz, "Ilusiones y realidades del hispano-americanismo," *ibid.*, no. 25 (September, 1928), p. 432.

5. Gómez de Baquero, "Nacionalismo e hispanismo," p. 73.

6. William Baker Bristol has written an excellent doctoral dissertation on this topic: "Hispanidad in South America, 1936–1945" (unpublished doctoral dissertation, University of Pennsylvania, 1947).

7. See Luis Marichalar, the Vizconde de Eza, *Vivero de selectorcratas* (1940).

8. This matter is treated authoritatively by Arthur P. Whitaker in the third chapter of *Spain and Defense of the West: Ally and Liability* (New York, 1961). The chapter is entitled "How Many Spains?" See also Juan J. Linz and Amando de Miguel, "Within-Nation Differences and Comparisons: the Eight Spains," in Richard L. Merritt and Rokkan Stein, eds., *Comparing Nations: The Use of Quantitative Data in Cross National Research* (New Haven, Conn., 1966).

NOTES TO CHAPTER 1

1. A valuable general survey of nineteenth-century Spanish history is found in Raymond Carr, *Spain, 1808–1939* (Oxford, Eng., 1966). Penetrating insights abound in Gerald Brenan, *The Spanish Labyrinth: An Account of the Social and Political Background of the Spanish Civil War* (Cambridge, Eng., 1943). Salvador de Madariaga, *Spain: A Modern History* (New York, 1958), is a useful work but often biased in favor of the liberal position. Luis Sánchez Agesta, "Sentido sociológico y político del siglo XIX," *Revista de Estudios Políticos*, LI, 1945, pp. 23–43, is a brief but perceptive analysis. A pessimistic appraisal by an important

literary critic, poet, novelist, and dramatist is Juan Tomás y Salvany, *España a fines del siglo XIX* (1891, 2nd ed.).

2. A sympathetic account of the first republic is found in John B. Trend, *The Origins of Modern Spain* (Cambridge, Eng., 1934), esp. pp. 20–24. See also John T. Reid, *Modern Spain and Liberalism* (Stanford, Calif., 1937) and Rhea Marsh Smith, *The Day of the Liberals in Spain* (Philadelphia, 1938).

3. Useful and newer works on Cánovas del Castillo include: J. L. Comellas, *El sistema político de Cánovas* (1961); Melchor Fernández Almagro, *Cánovas: su vida y política* (1951), perhaps the best available biography; José María García Escudero, *De Cánovas a la república* (1951); Fernando Suárez de Tangil y de Angulo, *Antonio Cánovas del Castillo* (1946), a volume in the series *Los presidentes del consejo de la monarquía española, 1874–1931*.

4. The best-known historical study by Cánovas is *Historia de la decadencia de España desde el advenimiento al trono de don Felipe III hasta la muerte de Carlos II*. His *Problemas contemporáneos*, vols. XVII, XVIII, and LXXXI in *Colección de escritores castellanos*, 160 vols. (1880–1915), contains many valuable insights.

5. Pedro Laín Entralgo, *Menéndez Pelayo: historia de sus problemas intelectuales* (1944), p. 120. Laín is one of Spain's most perceptive historian-essayists. Conservative and Catholic in outlook, he is generally objective and moderate in judgment. See also his *Menéndez Pelayo* (Buenos Aires, 1955).

6. See Manuel Pedregal y Cañedo, *Concepto de la democracia: resumen de la discusión sostenida en la sección de Ciencias Morales y Políticas del Ateneo de Madrid* (1882). The author (1832–1896) was an important figure in Spanish liberalism. Extremely valuable material on nineteenth-century intellectual, social, economic, and political history is found in *La España del siglo XIX: Colección de conferencias históricas celebradas durante el curso de 1885–1886, en el Ateneo Científico, Literario, y Artístico de Madrid*, 3 vols. (1886–1887).

7. A representative of this school was the extremely conservative Catholic Thomist Alejandro Pidal y Mon (1846–1913). Only after much soul-searching did Pidal y Mon decide to collaborate within the ranks of the Liberal-Conservative Party, regarded by many of his fellow Catholic conservatives as irremediably vitiated by liberalism. See Pidal's *De la consubstancialidad de la monarquía y la patria* (1890).

8. A highly favorable study of Sagasta was written by his partisan Natalio Rivas Santiago, an energetic journalist, politician, and bibliophile who assembled a most imposing private library. See Rivas, *Sagasta* (1932), a volume in the series *Los presidentes del consejo de la monarquía española, 1874–1931*. Another useful study is Álvaro Figueroa y Torres, the Conde de Romanones, *Sagasta, ó el político* (1903). Romanones (1863–1950) was for many years a leading figure in the Liberal Party. A statesman of balance and moderation, he wrote extensively and objectively on the Spain of his day. Other works of his dealing with Sagasta and the turno pacífico period in general include *Notas de una vida, 1868–1911* (1934)

and *Las responsibildades políticas del antiguo régimen de 1875–1923* (1924). The latter sets forth in masterful manner the strengths and weaknesses of the restoration period.

9. Suffrage was restricted to men who were twenty-five years of age or older, in full possession of civil rights, and citizens for at least two years of the municipality in which they resided.

10. *Diario de sesiones del congreso*, November 6, 1871, quoted in Severino Aznar, *Las encíclicas "Rerum Novarum" y "Quadragesimo Anno:" precedentes y repercusiones en España* (1941), p. 27.

11. See Pedro Sáinz Rodríguez, *La tradición nacional en el estado futuro* (1935), p. 13.

12. Silvela's most notable historical work is *Las cartas de Sor María de Ágreda y Felipe IV* (1885).

13. Cánovas, quoted in Diego Sevílla Andrés, *Antonio Maura: la revolución desde arriba* (Barcelona, 1953), p. 82. See also Enrique de Tapia, *Francisco Silvela, gobernante austero* (1968), p. 160 ff. No truly satisfactory biography of Silvela has been written.

14. See Tapia, *Silvela*, pp. 170–71.

15. See the Integrista newspaper *El Siglo Futuro*, August 23, 1892, for a good resume of the split between Integristas and Carlists. For a general coverage of Carlism and Catholic traditionalism see *Biblioteca Popular Carlista: Publicación mensual de propaganda* (Barcelona, 1896–1897); Melchor Ferrer and José F. Acedo, *Historia del tradicionalismo español*, 25 vols. (Sevilla, 1941–1959); Santiago Galindo Herrera, *Breve historia del tradicionalismo español* (1956); Vicente de Manterola, *El espíritu Carlista* (Madrid, 1871), a good exposition of Carlist ideology by a priest who was important in the movement; F. Martínez Lumbreras, "El pensamiento y la acción tradicionalista en España durante el siglo XIX," *Boletín de la Universidad de Granada*, X, 1938, pp. 29–58; Román Oyarzún, *Historia del Carlismo* (Bilbao, 1939). See also note 49.

16. Vital Fité, *Las desdichas de la patria . . .; insurrecciones de Cuba y Filipinas . . .; pérdidas y responsabilidades. Nuestro regeneración* (1899), pp. 260–61.

17. See Laín Entralgo, *La generación del noventa y ocho* (1956, 3rd ed.), p. 46. The original edition of this brilliant study, *La generación del 98*, appeared in Madrid in 1945.

18. See Luis Morote, *La moral de la derrota* (1900), pp. 5–15. A staunch liberal in his beliefs who once reputedly referred to himslf as "a personal enemy of Jesus Christ," Morote (1864–1913) was one of Spain's better-known journalists.

19. Laín Entralgo, *La generación*, p. 47.

20. See Sevilla Andrés, *Antonio Maura*, p. 171.

21. Joaquín Costa, *Oligarquía y caciquismo como la forma actual de gobierno en España: urgencia y modo de cambiarla* (1901), pp. 7–9.

22. *Ibid.*, p. 10.

23. See Juan Sánchez Rivera, *El sufragio universal y el parlamentarismo* (1929), pp. 5–9.

24. Lucas Mallada, *Los males de la patria y la futura revolución española* (1890), p. 191. In spite of the title, this work deals only with the

current or contemporary evils of Spain, principally caciquismo, and does not take up the matter of a future revolution. Mallada (1840–1921), an engineer, geologist, and linguist, wrote frequent columns for a number of Spanish newspapers.

25. *Ibid.*, p. 193. See also Costa, *Oligarquía*, pp. 17–20, and Ricardo Macías Picavea, *El problema nacional: hechas, causas, y remedios* (1899), pp. 257–58. Macías Picavea taught such subjects as psychology, logic, ethics, Latin, Spanish geography and history at the University of Valladolid. As many men of his period, he held highly pessimistic ideas on Spanish decadence.

26. See, for example, Costa, *Oligarquía*, p. 20, and Macías Picavea, *El problema nacional*, pp. 224–25.

27. Mallada, *Los males*, p. 193.

28. Pedro Sáinz Rodríguez, "Interpretación histórica de la España contemporánea," *Revista de las Españas*, nos. 22–23 (June-July, 1928), pp. 251–53. Sáinz Rodríguez (b. 1897), often balanced and objective but occasionally inflexibly conservative in his views, was a staunch defender of right-wing nationalism who denied that Spain was a decadent country. See his *La evolución de las ideas sobre la decadencia española* (1924).

29. Costa, *Oligarquía*, pp. 37–39.

30. Unamuno quoted in Laín Entralgo, *La generación*, p. 94.

31. Menéndez Pelayo, *Estudios y discursos de crítica literaria e histórica*, 7 vols. (1941–1942), VI, p. 336. Authorities seem equally divided as to whether the proper form of the name is Menéndez Pelayo or Menéndez y Pelayo. I have chosen to omit the y.

32. Julio Puyol y Alonso, *La vida política en España* (1892), pp. 22–23. For additional contemporary criticism of the parliamentary system as it operated in Spain see Gumersindo de Azcárate, *El régimen parlamentario en la práctica* (1889).

33. Sanz y Escartín, *La cuestión económica: nuevas doctrinas; socialismo del estado* (1890), pp. 64–65. Sanz y Escartín, the Conde de Lizárraga, was a lifetime senator who once served as minister of labor. For many years he held the secretary general post of the Real Academia de Ciencias Morales y Políticas.

34. See L. Legaz Lacambra, "Las ideas político-sociales de Ricardo Macías Picavea y su visión del problema nacional," *Estudios de historia social en España* (1952), II, pp. 7–61. See also note 25.

35. Macías Picavea, *El problema nacional*, pp. 468–72.

36. *Ibid.*, p. 473.

37. Moret writing in *El Día*, March 6, 1883, quoted in Costa, *Oligarquía*, p. 34–35. A great admirer of the English and French parliamentary systems and generally considered the man of broadest cultural interests and knowledge in the Liberal Party, Moret wrote extensively on the social problems of Spain. On him see Antonio González Cavada, *Segismundo Moret* (1947), a volume in the series *Los presidentes del consejo de la monarquía española, 1874–1931*, and Luis Antón del Olmet and Arturo García y Caraffa, *Los grandes españoles*, 9 vols. (1913–1914). Vol. V is dedicated to Moret.

38. Rafael María de Labra, *Discursos políticos, académicos, y forenses*, 2 vols. (1884, 1886), I, pp. 98, 101.

39. *Ibid.*, I, p. 100.

40. Puyol, *La vida*, pp. 182–84.

41. Francisco Andrés Oliván, *Por España y para España: querer es poder. Ensayo económico-político* (Zaragoza, 1899), pp. 59–61.

42. The economic history of Spain remains largely to be written. With the assistance of several well-qualified collaborators Jaime Vicens Vives (1910–1960) has prepared a valuable survey, *Historia social y económica, de España y America*, 5 vols. (Barcelona, 1958–1960). Vol. IV of this work (1959) deals with the nineteenth century. Statistical information on the late nineteenth century is found in Dirección General del Instituto Geográfico y Estadístico, *Censo de la población de España según el empadronamiento hecho el 31 de diciembre de 1887*, 2 vols. (1891).

43. Juan Sardá, *La política monetaria y las fluctuaciones de la economía española en el siglo XIX* (1948), pp. 167–69. Much of the material in this significant, carefully documented study deals with the period extending up to World War I.

44. *Ibid.*, pp. 164–65.

45. *Ibid.*, p. 219.

46. See Juan Antonio Galvarriato, *El Banco de España: constitución, historia, vicisitudes, y principales episodios en el primer siglo de su existencia* (1932).

47. Sardá, *La política monetaria*, p. 220.

48. This is the estimate found in *ibid.*, p. 220. Other authorities have estimated that 2,500 million pesetas had been invested in Spanish railroads alone by foreign capitalists. On this matter see also Jaime Vicens Vives, *Aproximación a la historia de España* (Barcelona, 1952).

49. Ramón Nocedal, whose father Cándido (1821–1885) was a leading figure in the Carlist movement, abandoned Carlism to form the Partido Integrista, which he always regarded as the only authentic instrument of Catholic traditionalism. His many published works generally touched off bitter polemics.

50. See Luis Morote, *El pulso de España: interviews políticas* (1905), pp. 334–36.

51. Puyol, *La vida*, pp. 202–203.

52. Sardá, *La política monetaria*, pp. 226–27.

53. Macías Picavea, *El problema nacional*, p. 207.

54. *Ibid.*, p. 169.

55. Ángel Ganivet, *Idearium español* (1942 ed.), p. 57. This book originally appeared in 1897.

56. One of the principal Spaniards to concern himself with the nineteenth-century agrarian problem was Álvaro Flórez y Estrada (1769–1853), who in his major work, *Tratado de economía política*, urged collectivization of rural lands. Another important work by this pioneer economist, who exercised considerable influence on Joaquín Costa, is *La cuestión social: origin, latitud, y efectos del derecho de propiedad* (1839).

57. Vicens Vives, *Aproximación*, p. 167. See also Vicens Vives and

J. Pérez Ballestar, *El problema social: génesis, planteamiento, soluciones* (Barcelona, 1958).

58. The principal work by Donoso Cortéz is *Ensayo sobre el Catolicismo, el liberalismo, y el socialismo* (1851).

59. Juan Valera, *Nuevas cartas americanas* (1890), p. 198.

60. Carl Schmitt, *Donoso Cortés: su posición en la historia de la filosofía del estado* (1930), pp. 2–4.

61. *Ibid.*, p. 5. Had Donoso lived a year longer, he would have been all the more disturbed by the appearance in 1854 of Francisco Pi y Margall's *Reacción y revolución.* This book presented to Spanish readers a synthesis of the ideas of Proudhon.

62. Aparisi y Guajarro, quoted in Tapia, *Silvela*, p. 30. A poet and dramatist as well as a Thomistic philosopher and politically active Carlist, Aparisi published prolifically. His five-volume *Obras completas* was published in Madrid, 1873–1877. Even as Donoso Cortés and Jaime Balmes, Aparisi continues to influence Spaniards of conservative inclinations and many anthologies of his works have appeared during the years.

63. A rich mine of information on the vital questions of the day is found in Academia de Ciencias Morales y Políticas, *Discursos de recepción y de contestación leidos ante la Real . . . al dar posesión de sus plazas a los individuos de número de la misma, 1860–1888*, 4 vols. (1875–1889) and *Memorias y discursos de la Real Academia de Ciencas Morales y Políticas*, 14 vols. (1861–1890). Additional material on the late nineteenth-century social problem is found in: Gumersindo de Azcárate, *Resumen de un debate en el Ateneo: el problema social* (1881), the first attempt in Spain at a serious, scientific study of the subject; Andrés Borrego, *Historia, antecedentes y trabajos a que han dado lugar en España las discusiones sobre la situación y el porvenir de las clases jornaleras* (1890); Miguel Fernández Jiménez, *El problema obrero y los partidos españoles: estudio de política contemporanea*, with a prologue by Eduardo Dato (Granada, 1904); Rafael María de Labra, *Estudios de economía social: la escuela contemporánea; el problema obrero; la educación popular* (1892); and A. Marvaud, *La cuestion sociale en Espagne* (Paris, 1910), the classic study of the subject written by a French observer.

64. The Marqués de Corvera, quoted in S. Aznar, *Las encíclicas*, p. 4.

65. See León Martín Granizo, "A modo de prólogo: El Vizconde de Eza y su tiempo," *Antología de las obras del Excmo. Sr. Vizconde de Eza* (1950), p. xx. The work is a valuable compilation of the writings of the conservative Catholic statesman Luis Marichalar y Monreal, the Vizconde de Eza.

66. On early Spanish labor organization see Antonio Ruméu de Armas, *Historia de la previsión social en España: cofradías, gremios, hermandades, montepíos* (1944) and Francisco Guillén Salaya, *Historia de sindicalismo español* (1941).

67. See Miguel Sancho Izquierdo, Leonardo Prieto Castro, and Antonio Muñoz Casayus, *Corporatismo: los movimientos nacionales contemporáneos* (Zaragoza, 1937), p. 38. See also Álvaro Calzado, *Doctrinas colectivistas y breve historia de las teorías comunistas, socialistas y colectivistas* (1909) and Matías Gómez Latorre, *El socialismo en España:*

del tiempo viejo. Colección de artículos (1918), written by an early leader in the social reform movement.

68. See Pedro Sangro y Ros, Crónica del movimiento de reforma social en España (1925), p. 11 ff. The author (b. 1878) was a devout Catholic who collaborated with many liberals in working for government amelioration of the social problem. A man of great tolerance, he did not think Catholics should eschew cooperation with anticlericals in the quest for social justice.

69. La Ilustración Española y Americana, January 30, 1892, p. 58, and March 22, 1892, p. 174.

70. Cánovas del Castillo, Problemas contemporáneos, III, p. 585.

71. As early as 1884, Cánovas in his La sociología moderna y el socialismo had hinted at the need for government intervention.

72. See Sanz y Escartín, El estado y la reforma social (1893), pp. 180–81, and Aznar, Las encíclicas, pp. 29–32.

73. See Labra, El congreso pedagógico hispano-portugués-americano de 1892 (1893), pp. 152–55, 171.

74. See Macías Picavea, El problema nacional, p. 152. In 1860, illiteracy was estimated at 75 percent; by 1910 it had declined to 59 percent. See Mallada, Los males, p. 44, and Unión Ibero-Americana, Año XXX, no. 8 (August, 1916), p. 4.

75. Mallada, Los males, p. 44; Morote, La moral de la derrota, pp. 467–68, 695, and La Gaceta, March 26, 1895.

76. Morote, La moral de la derrota, p. 467. See also Labra, El congreso pedagógico, pp. 171–74.

77. See Morote, La moral de la derrota, pp. 412–33.

78. See Joaquín de Encinas, La tradición española y la revolución (1958). The work of a Spanish priest, this is a defense of Catholic traditionalism. Contemporary books tending to view the social problem purely as a moral issue that could be resolved only by a return to formal religion and Christian charity include: Ceferino González, La economía política y el cristianismo (1874), one of the many works by the prolific Dominican Thomist who was the Cardinal-Archbishop of Sevilla; Narciso Martínez Izquierdo, Pastorales, circulares, y discursos, 2 vols. (1889), a work in the same spirit as that of González by the Bishop of Salamanca, who in 1885 was elevated to the Madrid-Alcalá see; José Salamero y Martínez, La crisis religiosa, causa principalísima de la crisis social, tiene en el Catolicismo su remedio mas eficaz (1890), a typical book by the priest known as "El Padre de los Pobres" who was active in charitable work and directed La Lectura Católica: Revista Decenal Religiosa, Científica y Política (1879–1885).

79. On Ortí, who was the director of La Ciencia Cristiana: Revista Quincenal (1877–1882) and whose opposition to universal suffrage and other democratic concepts is expressed in his La sofistería democrática (1861), see Damián Isern, Ortí y Lara y su época: estudio sociológico necrológico (1904, 2nd ed.). In addition see the introduction by Ortí y Lara to Franz Hitze, El problema social y su solución (1880). Ortí was also the translator of this work by an eminent German priest active in social work and in combating Bismarck's anticlerical program.

80. Works of Rodríguez de Cepeda include *Las clases conservadoras y la cuestión social* (1891), *Concepto cristiano del derecho de propiedad* (Valencia, 1895), and *Organización del movimiento Católico contemporáneo* (Valencia, 1897). His *Tratado de derecho natural*, purporting to advance the social doctrines of St. Thomas and Pope Leo XIII, first appeared in a two-volume Valencia edition of 1887–88. Already in its seventh edition in 1918, it was for a third of a century a popular university textbook.

81. Vázquez de Mella's most significant work is considered the *Filosofía de la eucarista*. A nineteen-volume edition of his *Obras completas*, including many previously unpublished articles, appeared in Madrid in 1946. Various anthologies of his publications have also been compiled. On him see: S. Aznar, "El pensamiento social de Vázquez de Mella," in vol. XXIV of *Obras completas* (1946), and Rafael García y García de Castro, *Vázquez de Mella, sus ideas y su persona* (Granada, 1940).

82. See Maximiliano Arboleya Martínez, *XL aniversario de la "Rerum Novarum," la Carta Magna de la justicia social* (Barcelona, 1931), pp. 169, 183–85. A prolific author and for a time director of the periodical *Renovación Social*, Arboleya was one of the most active clergymen in the Catholic social justice movement of the early twentieth century.

83. Severino Aznar, *Las encíclicas*, p. 46–47. Born in Zaragoza in 1870, Aznar was perhaps the leading lay exponent of early Christian Democracy in Spain. An active journalist and author of many books, he played an important role in the Catholic labor movement.

84. Sanz y Escartín, *El estado y la reforma social*, p. 201.

85. The book of Sanz y Escartín was *El estado y la reforma social;* that of Father Vicent, *Socialismo y anarquismo: la encíclica de León XIII . . . y los Círculos de Obreros Católicos*.

86. Aznar, *Las encíclicas*, p. 11.

87. On Balmes see: Maximiliano Arboleya, *Los orígenes de un movimiento social: Balmes, precursor de Ketteler* (Barcelona, 1912); M. Fraga Iribarne, *Balmes, fundador de la sociología positiva en España* (Vich, 1955); José María García Escudero, *Política española y política de Balmes* (1950); Miguel Sancho Izquierdo, *Filosofía política de Balmes* (1949).

88. See Arboleya, *XL aniversario*, p. 101; Aznar, *Las encíclicas*, p. 13; and Juan Mir y Noguera, S.J., *El triunfo social de la Iglesia*, 2 vols. (1910), I, pp. 300–301.

89. For indications of the enthusiastic Catholic reception of *Rerum Novarum* see: Ramón Albo y Martí, *La caridad, su acción y organización en Barcelona* (Barcelona, 1901); Domingo Enrique Aller, *El estado y las clases obreras* (1894); Pedro Armengol y Cornet, *La participación de beneficios, bases de armonía entre capital y trabajo* (1896); Alberto Martín Artajo and Máximo Cuervo, *Doctrina social Católica de León XIII y Pío XI* (1939, 2nd ed.); Ramón Martínez Vigil, Bishop of Quevedo, *Pastorales*, 3 vols. (1898); Juan Maura y Gelabert, Bishop of Orihuela, *La cuestión social: pastorales* (1902); Alejandro Pidal y Mon, *La iglesia y los problemas políticos y sociales* (1893); Ciriaco Sancha Hervás, Bishop of Madrid-Alcalá, *La cuestión social: discursos y opiniones* (1891). A few Catholics grumbled that *Rerum Novarum* was too ad-

vanced and dangerous in its social thought, as Arboleya, XL aniversario, esp. pp. 30, 126, points out; but this was decidedly a minority position.

90. See M. Fernández Jiménez, El problema obrero, pp. 117–20.

91. See Lorenzo Moret y Remisa, Del cristianismo en España como elemento de nacionalidad (1899), p. 10 ff.

92. See Aznar, Las encíclicas, p. 43, and Arboleya, XL aniversario, pp. 57–58.

93. Fernández Jiménez, El problema obrero, p. 117.

94. Aznar, Las encíclicas, p. 36.

95. Ibid., pp. 20–21. Aznar feels that Donoso's attacks against liberalism because of the social abuses spawned by it qualify the Andalusian thinker for recognition as a precursor of Leo XIII's social message. However, Aznar concedes an important distinction between the approaches of Donoso and the pope. For Donoso, charity and alms are synonymous. For Leo, charity is love; the employer who loves his workers will not deny them a just wage, and workers should never be reduced to such misery that they are forced to rely on alms. Leo is concerned with justice, but Donoso, in his obsession with alms and charity, seems to ignore justice. Aznar, furthermore, concedes that many Spanish Catholics who professed to be in accord with the spirit of Rerum Novarum actually followed the Donoso approach of relying on charity as equated with alms.

96. Literature on the Spanish religious issue is vast. Some of the useful titles include: Francisco Blanco García, La literatura española en el siglo XIX, 3 vols. (1891–1894), an important work by an Augustinian priest (1864–1903) that is an indispensable source on intellectual currents; José Castillejo, War of Ideas in Spain: Philosophy, Politics, and Education (London, 1937), from the liberal point of view; Católicos y conservadores (1885), sketches of prominent men and their views; Rafael García y García del Castro, Bishop of Jaén, Los apologistas españoles: 1830–1930 (1940); Francisco Gutiérrez Lasanta, Pensadores políticos del siglo XIX (1949), a biased study by an extremely conservative priest; F. Pérez Embid, "Los Católicos y los partidos políticos a mediados del siglo XIX," Nuestro Tiempo, XLVI, 1958, pp. 387–409, and "Los Católicos españoles ante la restauración liberal," ibid., XLVIII, 1958, pp. 643–69, carefully researched articles; Federico Suárez Verdaguer, La crisis política del antiguo régimen en España, 1800–1840 (1958, 2nd ed.), Conservadores, innovadores, y renovadores en last postrimerías del antiquo régimen (Pamplona, 1955), Los partidos políticos españoles hasta 1868 (Santiago de Compostela, 1951), and "Planteamiento ideológico del siglo XIX español," Arbor, X, 1948, pp. 57–69, skillful expositions of the conservative Catholic point of view.

97. Menéndez Pelayo, Estudios y discursos de crítica literaria e histórica, V., pp. 214–15.

98. El Siglo Futuro, September 6, 1892, p. 1.

99. Ibid., January 12, 1892, p. 2; August 4, 1892, p. 1, and April 8, 1892, p. 1. A useful bibliographical source on this period is Juan Pedro Criado y Domínguez, Las órdenes religiosas en el periodismo español (1907), listing the newspapers and periodicals published by religious orders at the turn of the century. For an exposition of the conservative

view see also Juan García Nieto, *Apuntes sobre el problema religioso* (1904). Somewhat better balanced is Edmundo González Blanco, *Democracia y clericalismo: estudios de política aplicada* (1901).

100. See Rafael Calvo Serer, *España sin problema* (1957, 3rd ed.), pp. 61–62, and J. de Encinas, *La tradición española*, p. 166, both works by conservative Catholics highly favorable to Donoso Cortés.

101. On the liberal-Catholic debate over the issue of whether morality could be based purely on natural reason, see the work by the Carlist priest Vicente de Manterola, *Afirmaciones Católicas* (1884), p. 143 ff. The book is a strong defense of the Catholic position, singling out for condemnation some of the liberal, opposition literature.

102. See, for example, Adolfo de Castro y Rossi, the liberal Gaditano (native of Cádiz) who with his Quaker friend Luis Uzos conducted extensive investigation into Protestanism in Spain, *Católicos y conservadores* (1885), *Examen filosófico sobre las principales causas de la decadencia de España* (Cádiz, 1852), a dogmatic, inflexible work attributing decadence to Spain's dogmatic, inflexible Catholicism, and *History of Religious Intolerance in Spain, or an Examination of Some of the Causes which Led to that Nation's Decline*, translated by Thomas Parker (London, 1853). See also John William Draper, *Los conflictos entre la ciencia y la religión* (1876). This work, translated anonymously, exhibits a marked hostility to Spain and attributes its alleged backwardness to Catholicism. It has an enthusiastically laudatory prologue by Nicolás Salmerón, briefly a president of the first republic and long a leader of Spanish republicanism and anticlericalism. The work called forth spirited rejoinders by Tomás Camara, Bishop of Salamanca, *Contestación a la historia del conflicto entre la religión y la ciencia de Juan Guillermo Draper* (Valladolid, 1883, 3rd ed.) and Father Miguel Mir y Noguera, *Harmonía entre la ciencia y la fe* (1881).

103. Unamuno quoted by Laín Entralgo, *La generación*, pp. 94–95.

104. The best study on the period of Ferdinand VII's rule is Miguel Artola Gallego, *La España de Fernando VII*, vol. XXVI in the *Historia de España* series directed by Ramón Menéndez Pidal (1968). The work stresses the mounting challenges to absolutism, 1808–1833, and deals with the introduction of liberal ideas and the rise of French influence, the appearance of a bourgeoisie, and the increasing role of the masses.

105. See José María Gil Robles, *Cartas del pueblo español* (1966, 3rd ed.), p. 16. This work resulted from the efforts of a team of men assembled by Gil Robles to consider contemporary Spain and the problems likely to arise in the post-Franco era. The interpretation of the early nineteenth-century history of Spain at the beginning of the book is excellent.

106. Larra, quoted in *ibid.*, p. 19.

107. Sáinz Rodríguez, "Interpretación histórica de la España contemporánea" (see note 28), p. 250.

108. One series of skirmishes was touched off by the efforts of Englishman George Borrow to distribute Protestant bibles in Spain. His efforts led to frequent stays in Spanish jails. See Borrow, *The Bible in Spain*,

3 vols. (London, 1842). The work was translated into Spanish by Manuel Azaña, *La biblia en España*, 2 vols. (1921).

109. This tendency is seen in Menéndez Pelayo's *Historia de los heterodoxos españoles*, 3 vols. (1880–1882).

110. Favorable biographies of Menéndez Pelayo, in addition to the Laín Entralgo works cited in note 5, include: Miguel Artigas Ferrando, *Menéndez Pelayo* (Santander, 1927), the work of a dedicated disciple; Adolfo Bonilla y San Martín, *Marcelino Menéndez y Pelayo, 1856–1912* (1914) and *La representación de Menéndez y Pelayo en la vida histórica nacional* (1912); Guillermo Lohman Villena, *Menéndez Pelayo y la hispanidad* (1957), an interesting study by a distinguished Peruvian historian; Jorge Vigón, *Menéndez Pelayo a los cién años* (1957). One of the best of the many Menéndez Pelayo anthologies is *La conciencia española* (1948), compiled by Antonio Tovar.

111. Laín Entralgo, *La generación*, pp. 62–63.

112. See Joaquín Fonseca, *Respuesta a un filósofo del renacimiento por un Tomista* (1882).

113. Sáinz Rodríguez, "Interpretación," p. 249.

114. In the early Franco regime, Sáinz Rodríguez served as minister of national education and fine arts.

115. Sáinz Rodríguez, "Interpretación," p. 247–49.

116. Labra, *Discursos*, I, p. 102.

117. See *El Siglo Futuro*, January 4, 1892, p. 1.

118. Sáinz Rodríguez, "Interpretación," p. 250.

119. Laín Entralgo, *La generación*, p. 48.

NOTES TO CHAPTER 2

1. Costa Rican writer Manuel Argüello quoted in *La Ilustración Española y Americana*, April 22, 1892, p. 252. Spanish author Adolfo Lianos Alcaraz also remarked indignantly upon the disparaging attitudes of Spanish Americans, especially Mexicans, toward Spaniards. See his *El porvenir de España en América* (México, D.F., 1878), in which he denies the possibility of establishing close ties.

2. Antonio Sánchez Moguel, "El centenario en Colombia," *La Ilustración Española y Americana*, December 8, 1892, p. 394.

3. See José Gálvez, consul of Peru in Barcelona, "Monumento a un educador español en el Perú," *Unión Ibero-Americana*, Año XXXII, no. 7 (December, 1918), pp. 11–13, and F. B. Pike, *The Modern History of Peru* (London, 1967), pp. 101–102.

4. See Pike, "Heresy, Real and Alleged, in Peru: an Aspect of the Conservative-Liberal Struggle, 1830–1875," *Hispanic American Historical Review*, XLVII, no. 1 (February, 1967), esp. pp. 64–67.

5. Liberals did at least play a major part in preparing the *Diccionario Enciclopédico Hispano-Americano*, 28 vols. (Barcelona, 1870–1878), almost unique among Spanish publication ventures at this time in that it was designed to appeal equally to Spaniards and Spanish Americans. Most of the articles on philosophy in the *Diccionario* were prepared by Urbano

González Serrano (1848–1904), a rabid republican and one of Spain's most outspoken freethinkers. Manuel Pedregal y Cañedo (1832–1896), a propagandist of democratic ideas and supporter of anticlerical causes, was another important contributor to the *Diccionario.*

6. See Mario Méndez Bejarano, *Poetas españoles que vivieron en América: recopilación de artículos biográfico-críticos* (1929), pp. 165–86. This is an important work on one aspect of early Spanish ties with Spanish America. Méndez Bejarano was a philosopher and literary critic highly regarded for his two-volume study of Spanish literature, *Literatura* (1902).

7. See Mark J. Van Aken, *Pan Hispanism: Its Origin and Development to 1866* (Berkeley and Los Angeles, 1959), pp. 117–18.

8. A typical book of this sort is Miguel Blanco Herrero, *La política de España en ultramar* (1888). An emotional glorification of the Spanish colonial period, the book implies that only Spain could help Spanish America return to a golden age; but Spain could not do this except by becoming the true Spain again and eliminating French influences and liberal tendencies.

9. See Van Aken, *Pan Hispanism,* p. 154, note 9. Rafael María de Labra, *El problema hispano-americano: discurso de . . . al inaugurar las conferencias organizadas por la Unión Ibero-Americana, 23 abril, 1905* (1906), p. 18, also notes the aversion of Spanish conservative monarchists to Spanish America, an aversion that extended into the early twentieth century.

10. Quoted in Constantino Suárez, *La verdad desnuda: sobre relaciones entre España y América* (1924), p. 22.

11. An early instance in which pro-Spanish feelings in Spanish America are seen as dependent to some degree on anti-Yankee sentiment is provided by a Labra pamphlet, *La representación e influencia de los Estados Unidos de América en el derecho internacional* (1877).

12. Van Aken, *Pan Hispanism,* p. 118.

13. See Méndez Bejarano, *Poetas españoles,* pp. 227–29.

14. Several prominent Spaniards evinced an early interest in hispanismo. Probably the most notable case is that of José Ferrer de Couto (1820–1877). Going to the Antilles in 1854 to study administrative problems there, he shortly published *Vindicación general de los hechos y administración de los españoles en el nuevo mundo.* The book concludes that although some reforms are needed, Spaniards are doing a good job of governing Cuba and Puerto Rico. Ferrer devoted much of the remainder of his life to the attempt to awaken Spanish opinion to the importance of establishing a fraternal community with Spanish America. See his *América y España consideradas en sus intereses de raza ante la república de los Estados Unidos del Norte* (Cádiz, 1859) and *Cuestiones de Méjico, Venezuela, y América en general* (1861, 2nd ed.). Journalist Gil Gelpi y Ferro spent almost as much of his life in Cuba as in Spain. In both countries he directed newspapers in which he urged closer bonds between Spain and Spanish America. His views are set forth in *Situación de España y de sus posesiones de ultramar: su verdadero peligro y el único medio de conjurarlo* (1874). One of the early Spaniards to realize that

friendship with Spanish America depended somewhat upon destroying there the prevailing Black Legend of Spanish cruelty, Gelpi y Ferro devoted a major work to this effort: *Estudios sobre la América: conquista, colonización, gobiernos coloniales y gobiernos independientes*, 2 vols. (Habana, Cuba, 1864). Alfredo Opisso, trained as a medical doctor, abandoned this profession to take up journalism on a full-time basis. From 1882 to 1900 he was the director of *La Ilustración Ibérica* (Barcelona), one of the few journals then devoting some attention to Spanish America. In the second half of the nineteenth century four other journals also reflected the spirit of hispanismo: *La América: Crónica Hispano-Americana*, founded by Eduardo Asquerino in 1857 and in publication until 1885; *El Correo de España: Revista Hispano-Americana*, published in Madrid, 1872–1874, by Rafael María de Labra and Manuel Regidor; *La Ilustración Española y Américana*, published in Madrid, 1857–1921, the most important early organ of hispanismo; and *Revista Hispano-Americana*, published in Madrid, 1866–1872, under the direction of Antonio Angulo Heredia and Labra.

15. Fabié y Escudero, *Mi gestión ministerial respecto de la isla de Cuba* (1898), pp. 19–20.

16. Albistur, *Relaciones entre España y los estados del Río de la Plata* (1861).

17. See Suárez, *La verdad desnuda*, p. 23.

18. See Serrano de Tornel, *Americanos celebres: glorias del nuevo mundo*, 2 vols. (Barcelona, 1888), dedicated to Porfirio Díaz. Another work in which Serrano de Tornel expressed her interest in America is *América y sus mujeres: estudios hechos sobre el terreno* (Barcelona, 1890).

19. See Luis Morote, *El pulso de España: interviews políticas* (1904), p. 166. See also Labra, *El congreso pedagógico hispano-portugués-americano de 1892* (1893), pp. 264–65 and *El problema hispano-americano*, pp. 19–20. On the activities of other Spaniards who saw in the abolition of slavery in Cuba a means of improving relations with Spanish America, see Arthur F. Corwin, *Spain and the Abolition of Slavery in Cuba, 1817–1886* (Austin, 1968).

20. Valera, *Cartas americanas* (1899), p. xi.

21. *Ibid.*, p. xi.

22. *Ibid.*, p. 54.

23. Valera, *Nuevas cartas americanas* (1890), pp. 194–99. Estrada had evidenced his concern for cultural ties with Spain by requesting several Spaniards to write prologues to various of his works.

24. Caro (1843–1909), a staunch Catholic and defender of the Church against the anticlericalism that characterized Colombian political life from the late 1850s to 1880, wrote prolifically on a number of subjects. His literary output also included poetry. From his youth a decided Hispanophile, Caro maintained close contact with a number of conservative literary and political figures of the peninsula. Menéndez Pelayo, an intimate friend, kept a picture of Caro in the office of his personal library building in Santander.

25. Valera, *Cartas americanas*, pp. 141–42.

26. See Armando Cotarelo y Valledor, *Bosquejo histórico de la Real*

Academia Española (1946), p. 13. A useful source of information is *Memorias de la Real Academia Española*, 6 vols. (1870–1889), and *Resumen de las tareas y actos de la Real Academia Española de 1868 a 1869* (1869).

27. Cotarelo y Valledor, *Bosquejo histórico*, p. 42. On the corresponding centers of the Real Academia in America see Edward Davis Terry, "The Academia Española and the Corresponding Academies in Spanish America, 1870–1956" (unpublished doctoral dissertation, University of North Carolina, 1959).

28. Valera, *Cartas americanas*, p. x.

29. As early as 1858 Castelar had published a famous article, "La unión de España y América," filled with sentiments of hispanismo. On Castelar's fear that the "Germanic race" threatened to engulf Hispanic people in America, see Van Aken, *Pan Hispanism*, p. 75. Unlike many liberals a warm admirer of most aspects of Spanish colonial activities in America, Castelar wrote the prologue to Carlos Gutiérrez, *Fray Bartolomé de las Casas* (1878). Castelar's interest in Spanish America is also manifested in his *Historia del descubrimiento de América*, 2 vols. (1907, and various earlier editions) and *¡Patria!* (1902, and earlier editions).

30. See La Unión Ibero-Americana, *Estatutos y reglamento* (1885).

31. In addition to *Los Dos Mundos*, Pando y Valle had been active on *La Ilustración Española y Americana*. A poet as well as a journalist, Pando expressed his early interest in America in *Galería de americanos ilustrados* (1883) and *Legítimas aspiraciones del comercio moderno* (1880). For a time in the 1890s he served as Spanish consul general in El Salvador.

32. One of the books in which Cancio Villaamil stressed the need for expanding commercial relations with Spanish America is *La Transatlántica Española: necesidad de desarrollar nuestras comunicaciones terrestres y marítimas* (1887). Staunchly conservative in his politics, even as Pando y Valle, Cancio Villaamil upon his death was succeeded in the presidency of the Unión Ibero-Americana by another stalwart of the Liberal-Conservative Party, Faustino Rodríguez San Pedro.

33. Moret's discourse was reproduced in *Unión Ibero-Americana*, Año XXI, no. 11 (November, 1907), p. 3. In a letter of October 24, 1886 to Delfín Sánchez in Mexico, Moret expressed similar sentiments: "The days of glory of the Spanish raza, still not forgotten in history, will without doubt be reborn when all those who speak the same language and profess the same religion find themselves united in this common desire for the grandeur of the Ibero-American family." See La Unión Ibero-Americana en México, *Compilación de actas, reglamentos, bases constitucionales, y demás documentos referente a dicha sociedad* (México, D.F., 1886), p. lx.

34. Labra, *El problema hispano-americano*, p. 16.

35. See La Unión Ibero-Americana, *Lista de señores socios en 31 de diciembre de 1896* (1897).

36. *Unión Ibero-Americana*, Año X (February, 1894), p. 65.

37. See William Baker Bristol, "Hispanidad in South America, 1936–1945" (unpublished doctoral dissertation, University of Pennsylvania,

1947), p. 17, and *Unión Ibero-Americana*, Año XI (February, 1894), pp. 52–53.

38. *Unión Ibero-Americana: Revista Mensual. Órgano de la Asociación Internacional* was published in Madrid from the beginning of 1886 until 1926.

39. Earlier interest had been generated by the 1888 Barcelona and the 1889 Paris Expositions. See Emilia Serrano de Tornel, *El mundo americano y la Exposición de Barcelona* (Barcelona, 1887) and Luis Bravo, *América y España en la Exposición Universal de Paris de 1889* (1889).

40. See Father José María González, *El día de Colón* (Oviedo, 1933, 2nd ed.), pp. 13–14. In this strange work, a first edition of which appeared in 1918, a Spanish priest claims credit for having originated the idea that the entire Spanish-speaking world should celebrate each October 12 as a national holiday.

41. On the events of the fourth centennial see: *El Centenario, Revista Ilustrada: Órgano Oficial de la Junta Directiva encargada de disponer las solemnidades en que han de conmemorar el descubrimiento de América*, published in Madrid in four volumes, 1891–1892; *Conferencias dadas en el Ateneo de Madrid sobre el descubrimiento de América*, 2 vols. (1892–1893); *El continente americano: conferencias dadas en el Ateneo de Madrid, cuarto centenario del descubrimiento de América*, 3 vols. (1894); *La Ilustración Española y Americana*, special edition of 1892 entitled *Homenaje a Colón, 1491–1891: IV centenario del descubrimiento de América*; Jesús Pando y Valle, *El centenario del descubrimiento de América*, with a prologue by Alejandro Pidal y Mon (1892); Alfredo Vicenti, *La celebración en España del IV centenario del descubrimiento de América* (1893). Vicenti (1854–1916), an eminent journalist who from 1907 until his death was director of *El Liberal* of Madrid, was the principal chronicler of the fourth centennial.

42. *El Siglo Futuro*, January 5, 1892, p. 3.

43. *Ibid.*, August 3, 1892, p. 1, and August 16, p. 3.

44. Labra, *El congreso pedagógico*, pp. 274–75.

45. See *Cuarto centenario del descubrimiento de América, Congreso . . . Hispano-Portugués-Americano reunido en Madrid en el mes de octubre y noviembre de 1892: Actas*, 4 vols. (1893).

46. See Real Academia de Jurisprudencia y Legislación, *El Congreso Jurídico Ibero-Americano reunido en Madrid en el año 1892: Memorias, Actas, Acuerdos* (1893).

47. See Congreso Mercantil Hispano-Americano-Portugués, Círculo de la Unión Mercantil e Industrial, *Cuarto centenario del descubrimiento de América . . . celebrado en Madrid en noviembre de 1892* (1893). Federico Rahola (1858–1919), for many years a leading figure in the attempt of Barcelona business interests to establish closer commercial ties with Spanish America, served as secretary of the Congreso Mercantil.

48. See Toribio del Campillo, *Memoria de . . . sobre las relaciones internacionales de España con los estados hispanoamericanos: Congreso Literario Hispano-Americano* (1892), and *Cuarto centenario del descubrimiento de América: Congreso Literario Hispano-Americano organizado por la Asociación de Escritores y Artistas Españoles e iniciado por*

su presidente el Excelentísimo Sr. D. Gaspar Núñez de Arce, 31 de octubre a 10 de noviembre de 1892 (1893). One of the more interesting papers at this congress was presented by Nemesio Fernández Cuesta: "Sobre los barbarismos que se han introducido en la lengua castellana, y principalmente de los galicismos e inglecismos que la afean," *Cuarto centenario . . . : Congreso Literario,* pp. 298–306. At about the same time Ceferino González, the Dominican Cardinal-Archbishop of Sevilla noted for his studies of Thomistic philosophy, presented at his reception into the Real Academia Española de la Lengua a paper stressing the importance of language in binding together the peoples of Spain and Spanish America: *Relaciones entre el habla castellana y la mística española* (1892).

49. See Labra, *El congreso pedagógico,* pp. 15, 21, 59–74.

50. This idea is stressed by Labra, who took time off from his activities in preparing for the pedagogical congress to write *Estudios de economía social: la escuela contemporánea; el problema obrero; la educación popular* (1892).

51. Ricardo Becerro de Bengoa, "Por ambos mundos," *La Ilustración Española y Americana,* January 30, 1892, p. 74, and October 30, 1892, pp. 299–303. An unidentified Colombian member of the Bogotá corresponding chapter of the Real Academia Española responded favorably to the anti-United States campaign that Spaniards had noticeably intensified in 1892. He claimed that Spanish Americans had now learned that in order to retain sovereignty and avoid becoming pawns of the most powerful New World country they would have to seek the unity of the Ibero-American world. "This is necessary not only for the survival of each Ibero-American nation but for the very survival of the Spanish raza, which because of its talent, daring, and courage is destined to dictate new laws to the world." See *Unión Ibero-Americana,* Año VIII (April, 1893), pp. 34–35. The Peruvian José Mariano Madueño advanced similar ideas in his *Asuntos hispanoamericanos* (1898). In *Mundo Latino,* a newspaper that he established in Madrid at the end of the century, Madueño also preached the necessity for Ibero-American unification to withstand the United States menace.

52. Valera, *Ecos argentinos: apuntes para la historia literaria de España en los últimos años del siglo XIX* (Buenos Aires, 1941), p. 80. The work is made up of letters Valera wrote to Argentine literary figures and that subsequently were published in newspapers and reviews of that country. In 1901 he gathered these letters together and published them as the first Madrid edition of *Ecos argentinos.*

53. *Ibid.,* pp. 178–79.

54. Castelar, "Cuba nuestra," *La Ilustración Española y Americana,* May 8, 1898, p. 270.

55. Anonymous review of Pedro Pablo Figueroa, *Historia de Francisco Bilbao: estudio analítico de introducción a la edición de las obras completas del ilustre filósofo chileno* (Santiago de Chile, 1894), in *Unión Ibero-Americana,* Año X (April, 1895), pp. 190–91.

56. This review, appearing initially in 1895, ceased publication in 1902. Assisting Altamira in its direction was the Barcelona archivist and

librarian Antonio Elías de Molins. Three other periodicals founded at this time that stressed the importance of ties with Spanish America were *Nuevo Mundo: Periódico Ilustrado*, appearing from 1894 to 1932, and two short-lived reviews, *Revista Hispano-Americana* (1898) and *Revista Política Ibero-Americana* (1895).

57. Altamira, *España en América* (Valencia, 1908), p. v. The work is largely a compilation of articles published in *España*, the organ of the Buenos Aires Asociación Patriótica Española.

58. Valera, *Ecos argentinos*, p. 20.

59. See *Unión Ibero-Americana*, Año X (January, 1895), pp. 18–19.

60. J. José Serrano, "De las relaciones Ibero-Americanas," *ibid.*, Año IX (September, 1894), p. 494.

61. See, for example, Eduardo Sanz y Escartín, *La cuestión económica: nuevas doctrinas; socialismo del estado* (1890), for a glowing account of Argentina's great economic potential.

62. See *La Ilustración Española y Americana*, March 15, 1892, p. 168, for a typical article of the period on the bright prospects of Mexican economic development and the potential of Mexican-Spanish commercial relations.

63. Donón was particularly upset that although Spain produced more olive oil than any country in the world, Spanish-American republics consumed more Italian and French than Spanish olive oil. See Donón, "Opinión comercial," *Unión Ibero-Americana*, Año X (May, 1895), pp. 222–25.

64. The notice on this appeared in *ibid.*, Año X (August, 1893), pp. 198–99.

65. See *La Unión Ibero-Americana*, Comisión permanente de relaciones comerciales, *Informe* (1897).

66. Mallada, *Los males de la patria y la futura revolución española* (1890), pp. 160–64.

67. *Ibid.*, p. 31.

68. Francisco Blanco García, *La literatura española en el siglo XIX*, 3 vols. (1891–1894), deals in vol. III with Spanish-American literature and discusses living authors.

69. See Menéndez Pelayo introduction to *Antología de poetas hispano-americanos*, 4 vols. (1893–1895), I, p. 13.

70. Ramón Menéndez Pidal states with some justification that the Menéndez Pelayo introductions would not be improved upon as comprehensive critical essays for a very long time indeed. See Menéndez Pidal, *España y su historia*, 2 vols. (1957), II, p. 603. Early in the twentieth century plans were laid for a new and revised edition of the introductions prepared by Menéndez Pelayo for the poetry anthology. Omitting all poetry selections, this work appeared in a two-volume edition (1911, 1913) with the title *Historia de la poesía hispano-americana*.

71. Menéndez Pelayo, *Antología*, I, p. 13.

72. See Menéndez Pidal, *España y su historia*, II, p. 607.

73. See Menéndez Pelayo, *Antología*, I, p. 351.

74. See Menéndez Pelayo, *Historia de los heterodoxos españoles*, VI,

p. 415, in *Obras completas*, under the supervision of Enrique Sánchez Reyes (1948).

75. Menéndez Pelayo, *Historia de los heterodoxos*, 3 vols. (1880–1882), III, pp. 537–41.

76. Menéndez Pelayo, *Antología*, I, pp. 363–64.

77. Menéndez Pelayo, *Historia de la poesía hispano-americana*, I, p. 54 in *Obras completas*.

78. *Ibid.*, I, p. 457.

79. *Ibid.*, II, p. 287. Menéndez Pelayo asserts that a bitter diatribe against Sarmiento, published by J. M. Villergas, is altogether justified. See Villergas, *Sarmienticidio, ó a mal sarmiento buena podadera* (Paris, 1853).

80. Menéndez Pelayo, "Al lector," *Historia de la poesía hispano-americana*, I, p. 4 in *Obras completas*.

81. Labra, *Discursos políticos, académicos, y forenses*, 2 vols. (1884, 1886), I, p. 73.

82. Altamira, *Cuestiones internacionales: España, América, y los Estados Unidos* (1916), p. 8.

83. "Balance geográfico de 1891," *El Siglo Futuro*, January 15, 1892, p. 3.

84. Emilia Serrano de Tornel, *Americanos celebres*, I, p. 19. Serrano de Tornel also attributed alleged Bolivian backwardness to ethnic factors. See *ibid.*, I, pp. 17–18.

85. Valera, *Cartas americanas*, pp. v–vii.

86. For example, Valera felt Argentine General Julio Roca had served his country well by exterminating many Indians. See *ibid.*, p. 61. For additional indications of Valera's anti-Indian prejudices, see *Nuevas cartas americanas*, pp. 146–47, 150.

87. Maeztu, *Defensa de la hispanidad* (1934).

88. *Ibid.*, pp. 148–52.

89. Luis Morote, *La moral de la derrota* (1900), p. 55.

90. *Unión Ibero-Americana*, Año VIII (June, 1893), p. 128.

91. Drocir de Osorno, *Cuba española: el problema de la guerra* (1896), p. 107. The author states that only Mexico favored Spain in the struggle with Cuba.

92. Castelar, "Imposibilidad de las alianzas européas," *La Ilustración Española y Americana*, April 15, 1898, p. 222.

93. See Nicolás González Ruiz, *Sánchez de Toca* (1948), a volume in the series *Los presidentes del consejo de la monarquía española, 1874–1931*.

94. See Sánchez de Toca, *Del poder naval en España y su política económica para la nacionalidad ibero-americana* (1898), pp. 317–19.

95. Labra, *Discursos*, I, p. 27 ff. and II, pp. 77–78. See also his *La crisis colonial de España, 1868–1898: estudios de política palpitante y discursos parlamentarios por . . .* (1900) and *La reforma política en ultramar, 1868–1900* (1902). For other expositions of the liberal point of view on Cuban policy see Pablo de Alzola y Minondo, *El problema cubano* (Bilbao, 1898), and *El Problema colonial contemporáneo*, with a resume by Segismundo Moret (1895). The book contains contributions

by Labra, Eliseo Giberga, Tiburcio Castañeda, José A. del Cueto, Eduardo Dolz, Rafael Montoro, and Emilio Terry.

96. Morote, *La moral de la derrota*, p. 433. The Cámara Agrícola de Alto Aragón, founded largely through the efforts of Costa, also recommended this policy and sharply condemned the war against Cuba as conducted by the Liberal-Conservative Party.

97. See C. A. M. Hennessy, *The Federal Rebublic in Spain: Pi y Margall and the Federal Republican Movement, 1868–1874* (Oxford, Eng., 1962).

98. In the year of the fourth centennial of the Columbus discovery he published his *Historia de América antecolumbina*, 2 vols. Barcelona, 1892).

99. See José Francos Rodríguez, *El año de la derrota, 1898* (n.d.), p. 23.

100. See Fabié y Escudero, *Mi gestión ministerial*, pp. 302–303.

101. R. Becerro de Bengoa, "Por ambos mundos," *La Ilustración Española y Americana*, April 22, 1898, pp. 242–44.

102. Fabié, *Mi gestión ministerial*, pp. 326–27.

103. "Lo que será Cuba bajo el yugo 'Yankee,'" *El Siglo Futuro*, January 20, 1898, p. 1.

104. Julián Manuel de Sabando, "Los Estados Unidos y Cuba," *La Ilustración Española y Americana*, August 8, 1898, p. 74.

105. See Drocir de Osorno, *Cuba española*, pp. 27–29, and *Biblioteca Popular Carlista*, Año III, January, 1897, p. 7.

106. For the congressional debates on Cuban policy see vol. X, *Congreso de Diputados: antología de las cortes de 1896 a 1898*, arranged by Francisco García Pacheco, 15 vols. (1909).

107. See Vital Fité, *Las desdichas de la patria* . . . (1899), p. 208, and Morote, *La moral de la derrota*, pp. 66–69.

108. See Joaquín Costa, *Oligarquía y caciquismo* (1901), pp. 20–21.

109. See Fité, *Las desdichas*, p. 253, and Morote, *La moral de la derrota*, p. 55, 61–2, 83.

110. Ricardo Macías Picavea, *El problema nacional* (1899), pp. 290–91.

111. *Ibid.*, pp. 277, 279.

112. See Carlos Manuel O'Donnell y Abreu, *Apuntes para la defensa del gobierno liberal-conservador desde 1895 a 1897*, 2 vols. (1902), I, pp. 76–77, 80–86. O'Donnell y Abreu (1834–1903), the Duque de Tetuán, held the foreign ministry post in the 1895–97 Cánovas del Castillo government. See also his *Responsibilidades del desastre colonial: discursos pronunciados en el senado por* . . . *al discutirse la contestación al mensaje de la corona en* . . . *1901* (1901). Also useful on this matter is Sánchez de Toca, *Del poder naval*, pp. 323–25.

113. Vázquez de Mella, *Dogmas nacionales* (1946, 2nd ed.), pp. 14–18.

114. *La Ilustración Española y Americana*, May 8, 1898, p. 262.

115. See Sánchez de Toca, *El poder naval*, pp. 331–33.

116. "Información general," *Unión Ibero-Americana*, Año XIII (January, 1898), pp. 20–21.

117. *El Siglo Futuro*, February 11, 1898, p. 1, and February 18, p. 2.

118. "Crónica general," *La Ilustración Española y Americana*, March 30, 1898, p. 182.

119. Maeztu, quoted in Diego Sevilla Andrés, *Antonio Maura* (Barcelona, 1953), p. 121.

120. Vázquez de Mella quoted in Ricardo del Arco y Garay, *La idea de imperio en la política y literatura españolas* (1944), p. 785.

121. *La Ilustración Española y Americana*, April 22, 1898, p. 230.

122. See, for example, *ibid.*, January 8, 1898, p. 2, and *El Siglo Futuro*, February 18, 1898, p. 2.

123. *Unión Ibero-Americana*, Año XIII (May, 1898), p. 215.

124. *El Siglo Futuro*, February 20, 1898, p. 1.

NOTES TO CHAPTER 3

1. Pedro Laín Entralgo, *Menéndez Pelayo: historia de sus problemas intelectuales* (1944), p. 358. On the other hand Rafael Altamira in *Psicología del pueblo español* (1902), a book begun before and completed after the disaster, sought to dispel pessimism by expressing confidence in the potential of the Spanish raza.

2. Silvela quoted in Diego Sevilla Andrés, *Antonio Maura: la revolución desde arriba* (1953), p. 133.

3. See Alberto Cólogan y Cólogan, *¿Nos regeneramos?* (1899), pp. 90–91.

4. See John B. Trend, *The Origins of Modern Spain* (Cambridge, Eng., 1934), p. 159.

5. Costa, *Reconstitución y europeización de España: programa para un partido nacional* (Huesca, 1924 ed.), p. 59.

6. Laín Entralgo, *Menéndez Pelayo*, p. 107.

7. See Luis Morote, *La moral de la derrota* (1900), pp. 64–65, and Declaration of the Unión Ibero-Americana, April 8, 1898, in *Unión Ibero-Americana*, Año XIII (June, 1898), p. 260.

8. Costa, *Reconstitución*, p. 31.

9. See *Revista de las Españas*, nos. 9–10 (May-June, 1927), p. 337.

10. Antonio María Fabié y Escudero, *Mi gestión ministerial respecto a la isla de Cuba* (1898), p. 47.

11. Morote, *La moral de la derrota*, p. 65.

12. See Ramiro de Maeztu, *Autobiografía*, vol. I in *Obras completas* (1962), p. 87. See also Vicente Marrero, *Maeztu* (1955), p. 139.

13. Ángel Ganivet, *El porvenir de España* (1946 ed.), p. 178. Ganivet, who published this work in 1898, wanted Spain to turn inward and adopt an isolationist policy only as a temporary expedient. By pursuing isolationist policies Spain could, he felt, initiate a rehabilitation process that would enable it later to turn its attention to Africa and Spanish America.

14. *Ibid.*, p. 161.

15. Laín Entralgo, *Menéndez Pelayo*, p. 124.

16. A classic plea for Europeanization is Maeztu, *Hacia otra España* (1899). See also Joaquín Pavón, *Nuestra generación se impone* (1898). Another Spaniard who agreed with Maeztu on the need for Europeaniza-

tion was the Basque literary figure José María Salaverría. Like Maeztu and indeed the majority of the men of '98 who following the disaster spoke on the need to Europeanize the country, Salaverría later changed his mind, acquired respect for Spanish traditions, and urged Spaniards to remain loyal to them. For an expression of this later mood see Salaverría, *La afirmación española: estudios sobre el pesimismo español y los nuevos tiempos* (Barcelona, 1917).

17. Maeztu, *Autobiografía*, pp. 120–22.

18. Maeztu, *Hacia otra España*, pp. 145–46.

19. Quoted in Julio Cejador, *De mi tierra* (1914), p. 9.

20. Antonio Royo Villanova, *La decentralización y el regionalismo* (Zaragoza, 1900), pp. 85–86.

21. *El Heraldo* editorial quoted in *ibid.*, p. 86. The effects of the disaster in stimulating Catalan regionalism are described in Carlos Cardo, *Histoire spirituelle des Espagnes* (Paris, 1946), p. 161, and Stanley G. Payne, "Spanish Nationalism in the Twentieth Century," *The Review of Politics*, XXVI, no. 3 (July, 1964), note 12, pp. 411–12.

22. See Costa's prologue to Royo Villanova, *La decentralización*, p. xv. Laín Entralgo, *La generación del noventa y ocho* (1956, 3rd ed.), p. 89, notes another factor contributing to separatist sentiments. Leading figures in the Generation of '98, men like Unamuno, Ganivet, Pío Baroja, Antonio Machado, Ramón Valle-Inclán, and José Martínez y Ruiz (Azorín), were of provincial birth and upon coming to Madrid developed a distinct distaste for the capital city. On the whole they regarded Madrileños as a frivolous group insensitive to the problems of Spain. On the Generation of '98 see also Manuel Tuñón de Lara, *La España del siglo XIX* (Paris, 1961), pp. 323–32, and Pierre Vilar, *Histoire de l'Espagne* (Paris, 1952), pp. 81–85.

23. Costa, prologue to Royo Villanova, *La decentralización*, pp. xvi–xvii.

24. A noted leader of the Catalan movement for greater tariff protection who frequently criticized the response of the Madrid government was Guillermo Graell. His lobbying activities in Madrid had originally won Cánovas del Castillo and the Liberal-Conservative Party to a protectionist policy. Following the disaster Graell set himself to devising means to offset the economic effects of the loss of Cuba, Puerto Rico, and the Philippines, areas to which Spain, and primarily Cataluña, had exported an estimated 500 million pesetas worth of goods annually. In his *Programa económico, social, y político para después de la guerra* (Barcelona, 1917), he reiterated the message he had constantly, and as he felt vainly, propounded since the 1890s: the need for greater protection. Similar views were expressed by the Barcelona-born José Elías de Molins, who around the turn of the century founded in his native city the daily *Protección Nacional*.

25. See *La Ilustración Española y Americana*, December 8, 1898, p. 322.

26. See Juan José Gil Cremades, *El reformismo español: Krausismo, escuela histórica, neotomismo* (1969), esp. pp. 123–45, for treatment of some of the leading figures in this movement. Jaime Vicens Vives

attributes sentiments of regionalism and separatism to the dynamic, bourgeois optimism of the Catalan generation of 1901. This contrasted sharply, he believes, with the Castilian pessimism of the Generation of '98. See his *Aproximación a la historia de España* (Barcelona, 1952), p. 199. See also his *Els Catalans en el segle XIX* (Barcelona, 1958).

27. Cólogan y Cólogan *¿Nos regeneramos?*, p. 10. The author, pp. 6–8, also stressed the need to establish lines of communication between the masses and their elected representatives. This theme is further developed in his *Reforma electoral* (1901).

28. See Javier Gómez de la Serna, *Los grandes problemas nacionales: el crédito del estado* (1901).

29. Fité, *Las desdichas de la patria* (1899), p. 316.

30. See Enrique de Tapia, *Francisco Silvela, gobernante austero* (1968), p. 247.

31. Giner de los Ríos, *Problemas urgentes de nuestra educación nacional* (1902).

32. See Trend, *The Origins of Modern Spain*, pp. 76–78.

33. See Manjón, *El pensamiento del Ave María: colonia escolar . . . establecida en . . . Granada* (Granada, 1900). Also important are Manjón's *El catequismo como asignatura céntrica* (Granada, 1913) and *Soberanía de la Iglesia* (Granada, 1903).

34. Fité, *Las desdichas*, p. 312.

35. González Posada, "Educación y enseñanza técnica," *Boletín de la Institución Libre de Enseñanza*, no. 506 (May 31, 1902), p. 134.

36. See Sela, *La educación nacional* (1900).

37. See the Tomás y Estruch pamphlet *El arte en la patria: discurso inaugural del curso 1896–1897 del Central de Artes Decorativas de Barcelona, leído por su presidente* (Barcelona, 1897).

38. By 1920 Valentí Camp had joined the Socialist Party and was president of the Ateneo Socialista de Barcelona as well as an active collaborator on various newspapers and journals. See his *La decadencia de las naciones latinas*, vol. I in the *Biblioteca Moderna de Ciencias Sociales* (Barcelona, 1901), a publication series which he directed, and *Vicisitudes y anhelos del pueblo español* (Barcelona, 1911).

39. See Lazúrtegui, *Un modelo para España: cartas alemanas* (Bilbao, 1903).

40. See Sales y Ferré, *La transformación actual de Japón: función del socialismo en la transformación actual de las naciones* (1902).

41. González Aurioles, "La literatura y las desgracias de España," *La Ilustración Española y Americana*, November 15, 1900, pp. 283–86.

42. See Feliz, *Misión social del ejército* (1907).

43. On Ramón y Cajal, see Laín Entralgo, *La generación*, and Trend, *The Origins of Modern Spain*, pp. 82–83.

44. Quoted in Fité, *Las desdichas*, p. 12–13.

45. See José Rodríguez Martínez, *Los desastres y la regeneración de España* (La Coruña, 1913).

46. See Miguel Cortacero y Velasco, *Cuestiones agrarias* (1915), in which the priest reiterates and summarizes the views he had been propounding since the turn of the century.

47. Mallada, *Los males de la patria* (1890), pp. 218–19. See also Mallada, *Cartas aragonesas* (1905).

48. See Oliván, *Por España y para España* (Zaragoza, 1899), p. 76.

49. Trend, *The Origins of Modern Spain*, p. 153.

50. See *Mercurio: Revista Comercial Hispano-Americana* (Barcelona), no. 52 (March 1, 1906), p. 757.

51. Ernesto Giménez Caballero, "La Conquista del Estado:" antología (Barcelona, 1939), pp. 28–30.

52. Altamira, *España en América* (Valencia, 1908), pp. 181–82.

53. Maeztu, *Autobiografía*, p. 69.

54. Costa, *Reconstitución*, p. 97–99.

55. *Ibid.*, p. 167.

56. For a brilliant analysis of Costa's position on Europeanizing Spain see Laín Entralgo, *La generación*, esp. p. 184. On Costa see Luis Antón del Olmet and Arturo Garcia y Caraffa, *Joaquín Costa*, in *Los grandes españoles*, 9 vols. (1913–1914); Edmundo González Blanco, *Costa y el problema de la educación nacional* (Barcelona, 1920); Gabriel Jackson, unpublished doctoral dissertation on Costa (University of Tolouse, 1952); R. Pérez de la Dehesa, *El pensamiento de Costa y su influencia en el 98* (1966); E. Tierno, *Costa y el regeneracionismo* (Barcelona, 1961). See also H. Jeschke, *La generación del 1898*, Spanish translation by Y. Pino Saavedra, prologue by G. Fernández de la Mora (1954, 2nd ed.) and *Arbor: Revista General de Investigación y Cultura*, Número Extraordinario en torno a la Generación del 98, XI, 1948.

57. Unamuno, "Sobre la tumba de Costa," *Algunas consideraciones sobre la literatura hispanoamericana* (1968, 3rd ed.), pp. 141–42. Ricardo del Arco y Garay, *La idea de imperio en la política y la literatura españolas* (1944), p. 746–47, also recognizes that Costa wanted Spain to turn toward its own, true traditions and to strengthen them so as to be able then to assimilate and synthesize foreign elements. In this Costa was not unlike Menéndez Pelayo as Carlos Arauz de Robles points out in *La vuelta al clasicismo* (San Sebastián, 1939), p. 149.

58. See Costa, *Reconstitución*, pp. 21–24.

59. *Ibid.*, pp. 19–20.

60. Costa, *Colectivismo agraria* (1898), pp. 66–67.

61. See *ibid.*, esp. pp. 3–15, 228–42.

62. Costa quoted in Azcárate, "Educación y enseñanza según Costa," *Boletín de la Institución Libre de Enseñanza*, no. 720 (March 31, 1920), p. 69. This is one of the most profound short studies ever published on Costa.

63. Macías Picavea, *El problema nacional* (1899), esp. pp. 435–44, 501. On Macías see the laudatory book by Miguel de los Santos Oliver Tolrá, *Entre dos Españas* (Barcelona, 1906). On Costa's views on elite rule see his *Oligarquía y caciquismo como la forma actual del gobierno en España* (1901), esp. pp. 62–65, 68. See also his *Quienes deben gobernar después de la catastrofe* (1900).

64. Macías Picavea, *El problema nacional*, pp. 412–13 and 389–90.

65. *Ibid.*, p. 188.

66. *Ibid.*, pp. 409–10.

67. Unamuno, *En torno al casticismo* (1916, 2nd ed.), p. 143. The work appeared first in 1895.

68. *Ibid.*, pp. 28–29.

69. See *ibid.*, pp. 140–42, and Laín Entralgo, *La generación*, p. 184 ff.

70. See Ángel Álvarez de Miranda, "El pensamiento de Unamuno sobre hispanoamérica," *Cuadernos Hispanoamericanos*, no. 13 (January-February, 1950), pp. 72–74. On all matters pertaining to Unamuno and hispanismo, it is essential to consult the masterful and exhaustive study by Julio César Chaves, *Unamuno y América* (1964). Chaves, an authority on the Generation of '98, spent five years researching this study, both in Spain and America. Providing more than the title indicates, his book is a study of one important aspect of intellectual history in Spanish America. There is a relative abundance of studies on Unamuno, one of the more satisfactory ones in English being Margaret T. Rudd, *The Lone Heretic: A Biography of Miguel Unamuno y Jugo* (Austin, 1963).

71. Unamuno, "La raza ibero-americana en la gran raza latina," *Unión Ibero-Americana, Número Extraordinario*, March 1, 1904, p. 44.

72. Unamuno essay of 1906 in *Temas argentinos* (Buenos Aires, 1943), pp. 30–33.

73. Altamira, *Mi viaje a América: libro de documentos* (1911), pp. 519–20.

74. Altamira, *Ideario político* (Valencia, 1921), pp. 12–17, from an essay written in 1900.

75. The best biography of Ganivet is Melchor Fernández Almagro, *Vida y obra de Ángel Ganivet* (Valencia, 1922).

76. Ganivet is said to have mastered Greek, Latin, French, English, German, Italian, Swedish, Russian, and Arabic.

77. Ganivet, *El porvenir de España* (1956 ed.), pp. 170–73. *El porvenir* appeared originally in the form of three long letters, published in *El Defensor* in 1898. In these letters Ganivet replied to certain criticisms that Unamuno had raised against his *Idearium español* (1896).

78. Ganivet, *Epistolario* (1904), p. 224. The *Epistolario* consists mainly of letters written from Belgium where Ganivet represented his country in a diplomatic post, 1893–1895. In these letters Ganivet dealt only fleetingly with political and social matters, concentrating primarily on literary criticism. The ten-volume *Obras completas* of Ganivet, showing the extent to which he did concern himself with philosophical as well as economic, social, political, and literary themes, were published in Madrid in 1933.

79. Ganivet, *Epistolario*, p. 173.

80. *Ibid.*, p. 224.

81. See Laín Entralgo's introduction to the 1942 edition of Ganivet, *Idearium español*, p. xii. This is the edition hereafter cited of the Ganivet work.

82. *Ibid.*, p. 133.

83. *Ibid.*, p. 211.

84. Ganivet, *El porvenir*, pp. 175–76.

85. Ganivet, *Idearium*, p. 140.

86. Ganivet, *El porvenir*, p. 168. Ganivet also saw the future of Spain

as lying in Africa. He admired the Arabs and regarded them as the instrument for spreading Spanish values into the great African interior. See *ibid.*, p. 170 ff. Costa shared in the belief that the future of Spain lay both in Africa and America. See Azcárate, "Educación y enseñanza según Costa," p. 67.

87. Ganivet, *Idearium*, pp. 179–80, 211.

88. Sánchez de Toca served as minister of agriculture, industry and commerce and as minister of the navy in Silvela cabinets between 1900 and 1903. During Antonio Maura's regime as president of the council of ministers, 1903–1904, he served as minister of justice. In 1919 he was himself president of the council of ministers. A prolific author and energetic journalist, he was active up to his death at the age of ninety-five.

89. Sánchez de Toca, *Del poder naval en España y su política económica para la nacionalidad ibero-americana* (1898).

90. *Ibid.*, pp. xxvii–lx.

91. Francisco Silvela expressed complete accord with the combined Sánchez de Toca program of naval power and hispanismo. See his prologue to *Del poder naval*.

92. *Ibid.*, p. 348.

93. Two prominent Argentine statesmen showed decided pro-Spanish sentiments as the United States intervened militarily in the Cuban issue. Ernesto Quesada, who had taught for a time at Harvard University, published *Nuestra raza* (Buenos Aires, 1900) and *El problema de la lengua en la América española* (Buenos Aires, 1900), in which he declared that Latin America in general had sympathized with Spain in its struggle with the Colossus. The United States, he said, had entered the war only as a means of gaining control over Cuba, the first step in its plans to dominate all Latin America. Roque Saenz Peña, *España y los Estados Unidos* (Buenos Aires, 1898), reached similar conclusions. In Spain, Luis de Armiñán, the Cuban-born director of *Unión Ibero-Americana*, commented with warm appreciation upon the pro-Spanish sentiments of Quesada and Saenz Peña. See Armiñán, *El panamericanismo: ¿que es? ¿que se propone? ¿como contrarrestarlo?* (1900). The same message is found in the works of the Peruvian poet José Santos Chocano and the Colombian poet-diplomat Alfredo Gómez Jaime, who early in the twentieth century represented his country in various posts in Madrid. See Chocano, *Alma América: poemas indo-españoles* (1906), with a dedication to Alfonso XIII in which the poet writes: "Oh King of the Spains! This is the New World which the Iberian legion will one day conquer; this is the world to which that legion, from across the deep ocean, gave its genius, fantasy . . . and heart." See also Gómez Jaime, *Impresiones rápidas* (1900), recording impressions of his travels through Europe and America and containing many laudatory references to Spain. For some indications of a shift toward anti-United States attitudes in Argentina, Brazil, and Chile see Allen W. Eister, *The United States and the ABC Powers, 1889–1906* (Dallas, 1950).

94. See John E. Englekirk, "El hispanoamericanismo y la generación de 98," *Revista Ibero-Americana*, II (November, 1940), pp. 323–25. In addition to Ernesto Quesada and Saenz Peña in Argentina, Paul Grou-

ssac favorably impressed Altamira with his anti-Yankee, hispanista essays. Altamira's *La Revista Crítica de Historia y Literatura Españolas, Portuguesas e Hispano-Americanas* was the mouthpiece for those Spaniards of the New and Old Worlds who desired the hegemony of Hispanic cultural values. See Altamira, "España y la literatura sudamericana," *Revista Crítica*, V, nos. 8–10 (August-October, 1900), pp. 358–66.

95. Sánchez de Toca, *Del poder naval*, p. 379.

96. Salcedo Ruiz, "Información General," *Unión Ibero-Americana*, Año X (May, 1895), p. 199.

97. Labra, *El problema hispano-americano* (1906), p. 56.

98. Mansilla, quoted in *La Ilustración Española y Americana*, May 8, 1898, p. 262.

99. Reprinted in Alberto del Solar, *Obras completas* (Paris, 1911), VI, p. 198. Solar was a Chilean hispanista.

100. Pérez de Guzmán, "Simpatías de América a España," *La Ilustración Española y Americana*, July 8, 1898, pp. 7–10. Among the Spanish Americans whom he singled out for praise because of service to the cause of hispanismo were the Nicaraguan Rubén Darío, the Peruvian José Santos Chocano, the Chilean Eduardo de la Barra, and the Colombian Laurentino Canal. Pérez de Guzmán also lauded the work in Argentina of Catalan emigrant Martín Dedeu, who had recently completed a series of articles entitled *Los dos pueblos*.

101. Ramón Arizcún, "Del sur de América," *La Ilustración Española y Americana*, June 30, 1898, pp. 383–84.

102. October 22, 1888 Valera letter to Darío in Valera, *Cartas americanas* (1889), p. 213.

103. After the 1898 trip Darío still retained some strongly anti-Spanish viewpoints. See his *España contemporánea* (Paris, 1901), made up of his dispatches from Spain to the Buenos Aires newspaper *La Nación*, which had financed his trip.

104. Englekirk, "El hispanoamericanismo," p. 335. The Spanish-American literary figures coming to Spain were associated with the modernist movement and quickly established several important Madrid periodical outlets for their poetry. While out of this development a few Spaniards, notably Enrique Diez-Canedo and Ramón Valle-Inclán, acquired lasting respect and empathy for Spanish America, for most peninsular literary figures, as Englekirk correctly points out (p. 338), interest in the New World was a passing fad. One of the better-known Spanish-American intellectuals who established close ties with Spain's Generation of '98 at the time of the disaster was Carlos Reyles. On this Uruguayan novelist-philosopher see Luis Alberto Menafra, *Carlos Reyles* (Montevideo, 1957).

105. See Maeztu, *Defensa de la hispanidad* (1934), pp. 165–70, and Marrero, *Maeztu*, pp. 618–24.

106. Francisco Gutiérrez Lasanta, *Rubén Darío, el poeta de la hispanidad* (Zaragoza, 1962), pp. 7–8, 15. The author, a conservative priest, comments further upon the electrifying effects produced in Spain by Darío's *Salutación del optimista*, written in 1905. For additional indications of Spanish attitudes toward Darío see: Guillermo Díaz Plaja, *Los grandes hombres: Rubén Darío, la vida, la obra, notas críticas* (Barcelona, 1930);

Andrés González Blanco, *Salvador Rueda y Rubén Darío* (1909) and *Escritores representativos de América* (1918); Juan González Olmedilla, *La ofrenda de España a Rubén Darío: corona lírica y artículos sobre el mismo a su muerte* (1916); Ramón Valle-Inclán, Miguel de Unamuno, Antonio Machado, et al., *Ofrenda de España a Rubén Darío* (1918); Eduardo de Ory, *Rubén Darío: al margen de su vida y de su muerte; recuerdos de recuerdos; intimidades; opiniones de la crítica; homenajes a la muerte del poeta; detalles curiosos; elogios críticos; sus poesías olivdadas* (1917). For a perceptive Spanish-American appraisal of the impact of Darío, see the study by the Peruvian Enrique Chirinos Soto, "Rubén Darío," *Actores en el drama del mundo, segunda serie* (Lima, 1967), pp. 229–46.

107. See Ramón Menéndez Pidal, *España y su historia*, 2 vols. (1957), II, p. 681.

108. Altamira did point out that a few Spanish purists might well criticize Rodó for occasional lapses in vocabulary selection. He contended, though, that this was a minor flaw. See the Altamira prologue to Rodó, *Ariel. Liberalismo y jacobinismo* (Barcelona, 1926, 3rd ed.). Almost the entirety of the Altamira prologue was written upon the initial appearance of *Ariel. Liberalismo y jacobinismo*, a separate Rodó work, is usually included with Spanish editions of the brief *Ariel*.

109. William S. Stokes, "Democracy, Freedom and Reform," in F. B. Pike, ed., *Freedom and Reform in Latin America* (Notre Dame, Ind., 1967,) p. 121.

110. Altamira prologue to *Ariel*, p. 10.

111. The book appeared in Valencia with no date of publication.

112. Goicoechea, *La obra pasada y la actual de España en América* (Montevideo, 1928), pp. 8–9. On the impact of *Ariel* in Spain, see also Englekirk, "El hispanoamericanismo," p. 336.

113. Altamira prologue to *Ariel*, p. 5.

114. Stokes, "Democracy, Freedom and Reform," p. 121.

115. On the 1900 congress see *Congreso Social y Económico Hispano-Americano reunido en Madrid el año 1900*, 2 vols. (1902), and the Rafael María de Labra pamphlet, *El Congreso Hispano-Americano de Madrid en 1900* (1904).

116. See *Unión Ibero-Americana*, Año XXVIII (February, 1914), pp. 1–2, and William Baker Bristol, "Hispanidad in South America, 1936–1945" (unpublished doctoral dissertation, University of Pennsylvania, 1947), p. 19.

117. *Boletín Oficial del Ministerio de Estado*, Año X, no. 4 (April, 1900), pp. 327–28. Because of Silvela's work as vice-president of the Junta de Patronato and as president of the organizing commission of the Hispano-American Congress formed within the Unión Ibero-Americana, Queen Regent María Cristina decorated him with the Gran Cruz de la Real y Distinguida Orden de Carlos III. Together with Silvela, Faustino Rodríguez de San Pedro and Jesús Pando y Valle, the president and secretary general respectively of the Unión Ibero-Americana, as well as Luis de Armiñán, director of the Union's official publication, played major roles in organizing the congress.

118. Among the distinguished Spanish Americans on hand were Ricardo Fernández Guardia of Costa Rica, Alejandro Deustua of Peru, Alberto Blest Gana of Chile, Santiago Pérez Triana of Colombia, and Vicente Justo Sierra of Mexico. Not all delegates were won to the cause of hispanismo. Deustua, for example, upon returning to Peru resumed the dissemination of decidedly anti-Spanish ideas.

119. In an eloquent discourse Segismundo Moret gave praise to the unity of the Hispanic community that rested upon ties of language. See Mariano Rodríguez H., "Nueva fase de la opinión pública en Colombia," *España y América*, XIV (April-June, 1907), p. 23.

120. Labra, *El problema hispano-americano*, p. 27.

121. Quoted in Julio de Lazúrtegui, *Informe y memoria presentados a las Excmas. Diputaciones Provinciales de Vizcaya, Guipúzcoa, Álava y Navarra por* . . . (Bilbao, 1923), p. 163.

122. Bristol, "Hispanidad," pp. 37–38.

123. See *Información Diplomática*, a Madrid semimonthly published by the Ministerio de Estado, no. 9 (May, 1904), pp. 52–53, 55, and Jerónimo Bécker, "Tratados políticos con la América latina," *Unión Ibero-Americana, Número Extraordinario*, March 1, 1904, p. 48. Bécker says that as a consequence of the congress, arbitration treaties were celebrated with Argentina, Bolivia, Colombia, Guatemala, Mexico, Paraguay, El Salvador, Santo Domingo, and Uruguay.

124. Pedro Martínez Vélez, "El clero y las relaciones hispano-americanas," *Unión Ibero-Americana*, Año XIX (March 1, 1904), p. 31.

125. Quoted in "Francisco Silvela," an unsigned article in *ibid.*, Año XXXVIII (January, 1924), pp. 44–45.

126. *Ibid.*, p. 45.

127. Martínez Vélez, "El Congreso Social y Económico Hispano-Americano de 1900," *España y América*, Año I, no. 8 (April 15, 1903), pp. 496–98.

NOTES TO CHAPTER 4

1. Marcelino Menéndez Pelayo, *Historia de los heterodoxos españoles*, VI, pp. 505–06 in *Obras completas*, under the supervision of Enrique Sánchez Reyes (1948).

2. Ramón Menéndez Pidal, *España y su historia*, 2 vols. (1957), I, p. 35.

3. Menéndez Pelayo, *Historia de los heterodoxos españoles*, 7 vols. (1928–1933), II, pp. 133–34.

4. Emilio Zurano Muñoz, *Alianza hispanoamericana* (1926), p. 130.

5. See the 1898 discourse by Zacarías Martínez Núñez on the three-hundredth anniversary of the death of Philip II in *Discursos y oraciones sagradas* (El Escorial, 1929, 2nd ed.), p. 106. Martínez Núñez, who delighted in recalling the glories of sixteenth-century Spain, provides further insights into Spanish conservatism in his *Sermones y discursos, conferencias y pastorales*, 2 vols. (1921).

6. Víctor Pradera, *El estado nuevo* (1941, 3rd ed.), p. 91.

7. Martínez Núñez, *Discursos y oraciones*, p. 111.

8. Ricardo Arco y Garay, *Grandeza y destino de España* (1942), p. 320. Born in Granada in 1888 and a staunch defender of traditionalism throughout his life, Arco y Garay presents views that are in line with those of Balmes, Donoso Cortés, Aparisi, Menéndez Pelayo, and Vázquez de Mella.

9. Donoso Cortés quoted in Arco y Garay, *La idea de imperio en la política y la literatura españolas* (1944), pp. 773–75. The major publication of Arco y Garay, the book goes back to Roman times in developing the thesis that Spanish nationalism is consubstantial with Catholicism and that the real basis of Spanish imperial policy was always spiritual.

10. Menéndez Pelayo, *Historia de los heterodoxos* (1928–1933), VII, pp. 514–15.

11. Miguel Artigas, *Menéndez Pelayo* (Santander, 1927), p. 168.

12. Juan Vázquez de Mella, funeral oration for Menéndez Pelayo, *Unión Ibero-Americana*, Año XXVI (May-June, 1912), p. 40.

13. Vázquez de Mella, *Dogmas nacionales* (1946, 2nd ed.), p. 19.

14. Ramiro de Maeztu, *Defensa de la hispanidad* (1934), p. 162.

15. Pedro Sáinz Rodríguez, *La tradición nacional en el estado futuro* (1935), p. 5.

16. Menéndez Pelayo, *La ciencia española*, 2 vols. (1933 ed.), I, pp. 190–91.

17. A 1915 speech of Vázquez de Mella in *Dogmas nacionales*, p. 95.

18. *Ibid.*, p. 99.

19. See Pedro Laín Entralgo, *Menéndez Pelayo: historia de sus problemas intelectuales* (1944), p. 149.

20. See Gabriel Maura y Gamazo, *Algunos testimonios literarios e históricos contra la falsa tesis de la decadencia nacional: discurso de recepción en la Real Academia Española* (1920). A son of the famous conservative leader Antonio Maura, the writer strongly disagreed with the concept of liberal historians that Spain had been decadent since the sixteenth century. This unfounded belief, he contended, had discouraged and enervated countless generations of Spaniards.

21. Ernesto Giménez Caballero, *El genio de España: exaltaciones a una resurrección nacional y del mundo* (1932), p. 35.

22. Menéndez Pelayo, *Historia de los heterodoxos* (1928–1933), VI, p. 33 ff.

23. P. Sáinz Rodríguez, *La evolución de las ideas sobre la decadencia española* (1924), pp. 56–57. The book is in the spirit of Gabriel Maura, *Algunos testimonios*.

24. See Maeztu, *Defensa de la hispanidad*, pp. 26–27, and Onésimo Redondo, *El estado nacional* (Valladolid, 1938), p. 60.

25. Vázquez de Malla, *Dogmas nacionales*, pp. 10–11.

26. Menéndez Pelayo, *Historia de los heterodoxos* (1928–1933), VII, pp. 7–8.

27. See "Sección Doctrinal, el Carlismo al alcance de todos," *Biblioteca Popular Carlista: Publicación de Propaganda* (Barcelona), Año III (January, 1897), pp. 25–30.

28. *Ibid.*, p. 15.

29. Vázquez de Mella, *Dogmas nacionales*, p. 13.

30. Menéndez Pelayo, *Historia de los heterodoxos* (1928–1933), VII, pp. 232–33.

31. *Ibid.*, VIII, p. 233, *passim*.

32. Menéndez Pelayo, *Historia de los heterodoxos*, VI, 505–508, in *Obras completas* (1948).

33. Menéndez Pelayo, *Ensayos de crítica filosófica* (1918), p. 363. A few of the many works presenting the views of conservatives on the authentic character of Spain and the true meaning of its history include: Zacarías García Villada, *El destino de España en la historia universal* (1937, 2nd ed., augmented, 1940), in which the priest who rediscovered the important Códice de Ronda of the Visigothic period expresses his conviction that Spanish nationalism arises from the country's providential role of maintaining Catholic unity in the world; Julián Juderías, *La reconstrucción de la historia de España desde el punto de vista nacional: discursos leidos ante la Real Academia de la Historia en el acto de su recepción por . . . el día 28 de abril de 1918* (1918), the essay of a conservative historian famous for combating the Black Legend and the discourse of reply by Jerónimo Bécker, an equally distinguished historian of conservative Catholic persuasions; Graciano Martínez, *Hacia una España genuina: por entre la psicología nacional* (1916), lyrical praise of the genuine, Catholic Spain by the Augustinian director of the periodical *España y América*; Salvador Minguijón, *Al servicio de la tradición: ensayo histórico-doctrinal de la concepción tradicionalista según los maestros de la contrarevolución* (1930), a major work by an intellectual-politician who sought to update traditionalist ideology and was associated with early Christian Democracy in Spain; Pedro Sáinz Rodríguez, *Las polémicas sobre la cultura española* (1919); Ángel Salcedo Ruiz, *Resumen histórico crítico de la literatura española*, 4 vols. (1915–1917), a work by a conservative deputy long active in Catholic journalism that well expresses the viewpoints of his school; Juan Tusquets, *Orígenes de la revolución española* (Barcelona, 1932), by a priest associated with Catholic Action who wrote many catechism books and led various anti-Masonry campaigns; Ángel Valbuena Prat, *El sentido Católico en la literatura española* (Zaragoza, 1940), stressing the role of Menéndez Pelayo in revising interpretations of Spanish history.

34. José Luis de Arrese, *La revolución social del nacional sindicalismo* (1940), pp. 9–10.

35. See Narciso Noguer, "Socialistas no rusos del imperio ruso," *Razón y Fe*, XII (May–August, 1905), pp. 45–48. See also Arrese, *La revolución social*, p. 39.

36. Teodoro Rodríguez, *El problema social y las derechas: nuevas orientaciones* (El Escorial, 1935), pp. 63–66. A professor at the Augustinian university at El Escorial and one of the most widely published clerical writers on the social problem, Rodríguez urged a "law and order" approach to the social problem and contended that most dissension sprang from Jewish-Masonic plots. See also his *Infiltraciones judío-masónicas en la educación Católica* (El Escorial, 1934).

37. Pablo Villada, "¿Por qué se odia a los religiosos," Razón y Fe, I, no. 1 (September-December, 1901), p. 55.

38. Antonio Vicent, Socialismo y anarquismo: la encíclica de León XIII "De Conditione . . ." y los Círculos de Obreros Católicos (Valencia, 1893), pp. 79–80.

39. Menéndez Pelayo, Historia de los heterodoxos (1928–1933), VI, pp. 102–103. Hugh Thomas, The Spanish Civil War (New York, Evanston, London, 1963), p. 27–28, writes that in the nineteenth century Spanish Masonry was actively antireligious, not merely anticlerical. Apparently in the 1880s a breach occurred between English and continental Masons when the continental brothers decided they could not tolerate any reference to God, even under the name of the "Supreme Architect," in the statutes of the order.

40. Altamira essay of 1904 in Ideario político (Valencia, 1921?), pp. 29–30.

41. Rodríguez, El problema social y las derechas, p. 47. Additional works in which Catholic conservative spokesmen condemn Judaism and Masonry include: Francisco Ferrari Billioch, Entre masones y marxistas (1929, 2nd ed.) and La masonería al desnudo: las logias desenmascaradas, with a prologue by Antonio Goicoechea, 2 vols. (Santander, 1939, 2nd ed.), two immoderate works by a Catholic journalist, novelist, and dramatist; José Huertas Lozano, ¡Yo he sido impío! Revelaciones espirituales y masónicas (1892), an exposé and condemnation of spiritualism and Masonry in Spain by a man who had been active in both before seeing the light and becoming a member of the rabidly Catholic Integrista movement; Vicente de Lafuente, Historia de las sociedades secretas antiguas y modernas en España y especialmente la Franco-Masonería, 3 vols. (Lugo, 1870–1871, republished in a one-volume Barcelona edition, 1933), a work that attributes most civil discord in Spain to Masonic plots, written by the rector of the University of Madrid following the 1876 restoration who admits (p. xv, 1933 ed.) he has difficulty in maintaining objectivity when writing about "grotesque things;" René Llanas de Niubó, Judaísmo (Valencia, 1935), which criticizes Jews for their control over many banks and virtually all the "pornographic presses" of Spain and pictures them as the natural enemies of Catholic Spain; Enrique Reig y Casanova, Sacrilegios y traidores, ó la masonería contra la Iglesia y contra España (1910), by the man who at the time taught sociology in the seminary of Toledo and who became Bishop of Barcelona in 1914, Archbishop of Valencia in 1920, and Cardinal-Archbishop of Toledo in 1922; José María Serra de Martínez, El espiritismo y sus relaciones con la masonería (Barcelona, 1934); José Torras y Bages, Catalanisme y masonisme (Barcelona, 1890), a work in which a defender of Catalan regionalism who became Bishop of Vich in 1899 argues that Masonry is thoroughly incompatible with the traditions of the patria; Jorge Villarín, Guerra en España contra el judaismo bolchevique (Cádiz, 1937).

42. Luis Marichalar y Monreal, the Vizconde de Eza, Antología de las obras del Excmo. Sr. Vizconde de Eza (1950), p. 808.

43. See Joaquín de Encinas, La tradición española y la revolución

(1958), p. 97. As a young man Menéndez Pelayo had attributed the entire Reformation to the excessive individualism that was allegedly a trait of the Teutonic race. See Laín Entralgo, *Menéndez Pelayo*, p. 143.

44. Isidro Gomá y Tomás, *Antilaicismo*, 2 vols. (Barcelona, 1935), I, pp. 3–5. Gomá y Tomás's first post in the Spanish episcopacy was as Bishop of Tarragona. He was preconized Archbishop of Toledo in 1933 and named a cardinal in 1935. *Antilaicismo* is a collection of works published principally in Catholic newspapers during the period of the second republic.

45. Encinas, *La tradición española*, p. 126.

46. Lorenzo Moret y Remisa, *Del cristianismo en España como elemento de nacionalidad* (1898), p. 124.

47. Maeztu, "El espíritu de la economía ibero-americana," *Revista de las Españas*, nos. 9–10 (May-June, 1927), p. 341. Roger E. Vekemans, the Belgian Jesuit who has served many years in Chile, created a considerable impact on Spanish-American Catholic circles in the 1960s when he argued in favor of a cultural transmutation, a process of symbiosis, in which Catholicism would incorporate and assimilate some of the characteristics originally associated with the Protestant Ethic. He saw this as the only alternative to a Marxist triumph in Spanish America. In a way Vekemans, knowingly or not, was only repeating the analysis made by Maeztu in 1927. Vekemans develops his thesis in, among other sources, "Economic Development, Social Change, and Cultural Mutation in Latin America," William V. D'Antonio and F. B. Pike, eds., *Religion, Revolution and Reform: New Forces for Change in Latin America* (New York, Washington, 1964), pp. 129–42.

48. See M. Llorens, "El P. Antonio Vicent, S.J.," *Estudios de Historia Moderna* (Barcelona), IV (1954). Raymond Carr, *Spain, 1808–1939* (Oxford, Eng., 1966), p. 456, correctly describes the Vicent approach to the social problem as being: "Restore charity and abnegation in the employer and patience and resignation in the worker."

49. See Florentino del Valle, S.J., *El P. Antonio Vicent, S.J., y la Acción Social Católica Española* (1947) and *Las reformas sociales en España* (1946).

50. Vicent, *Socialismo y anarquismo*, pp. 10–11.

51. *Ibid.*, p. 16.

52. *Ibid.*, pp. 26–27.

53. *Ibid.*, p. 81. This message of Vicent was anticipated by Father José Salamero (1835–1895), "El Padre de los Pobres," in *La crisis religiosa, causa principalísimo de la crisis social, tiene en el Catolicismo su remedio mas eficas: discurso leido ante la Real Academia de Ciencias Morales y Políticas en la recepción pública del . . .* (1890).

54. See, for example, José María González de Echevarri, *Ruina de la falsa civilización de liberalismo: la caridad cristiana, fórmula de conciliación social* (Valladolid, 1933), and Eustaquio Nieto y Martín, *Si la sociedad quiere salvarse, ha de ser en Cristo y por Cristo: carta pastoral que el Ilmo. y Rvmo. Sr. Dr. . . . Obispo de Sigüenza, dirige al clero y fieles de su diócesis en el adviento de 1919* (Sigüenza, 1919).

55. Pedro Sangro y Ros de Olano, *Crónica del movimiento de reforma*

social en España (1925), p. 40. Sangro y Ros (b. 1878), the Marqués de Guad-el-Jelú, was active in a number of social organizations, both state and private. He held several important posts in the ministry of labor and in 1930 was himself named minister of labor. Sangro y Ros also participated in Catholic Action programs serving, for example, as professor of labor legislation of the Escuela de la Acción Católica de la Mujer. He also represented Spain at various international conferences. On him see Chapter 1, note 68.

56. Graciano Martínez, "Apuntando medias y remedios," España y América, LXXV (July-August, 1922), pp. 10–11.

57. Juan Maura, Pastoral Letter of March 3, 1901, in La cuestión social: pastorales (1902), pp. 214–15.

58. For examples of this see Ramón Lloberola, S.J., La educación hispano-americana, 2 vols. (1911), on the need for Catholics to maintain a strong private educational system and to resist the tendencies toward state control over instruction; Andrés Manjón, El catequismo como asignatura céntrica (Granada, 1913, Las escuelas laicas (Barcelona, 1910), and Soberanía de la Iglesia (Granada, 1903), all defending the primacy of the Church's role in education; and José María Salvador y Barrera, Bishop of Madrid and Alcalá, El derecho cristiano y las enseñanzas de la Iglesia en sus relaciones con la instrucción pública (1915), a collection of congressional and other discourses as well as pastoral letters defending the Church's rights in the public educational structure, condemning neutral schools, and attacking the anticlerical programs of liberal leaders José Canalejas and Álvaro Figueroa y Torres, the Conde de Romanones.

59. Pedro Sanz y Escartín, El estado y la reforma social (1893), p. 248.

60. Ibid., p. 249.

61. Antonio Monedero, La Confederación Nacional Católica-Agraria en 1920: su espíritu, su organización y porvenir (1921), pp. 64–65.

62. Salvador y Barrera, "El laicismo en la enseñanza," Revista del Clero Español, no. 5 (May, 1914), pp. 321–28.

63. Speech of Ramón Nocedal to the Asociación Integrista of Madrid, reported in El Siglo Futuro, February 23, 1892.

64. T. Rodríguez, El problema social y las derechas, p. 124.

65. Arrese, La revolución social, p. 8.

66. Giménez Caballero, El genio de España, pp. 261–62, praises both Catholic traditionalists and anarcho-syndicalists for understanding that the true traditions of Spain rest upon decentralization and demand ample freedom for regional- and functional-interest groups in directing their own affairs. Traditionalists of the Catholic school as well as anarcho-syndicalists, he maintained, instinctively tended to help and to reinforce one another. Although Giménez Caballero did not point to the fact, these unlikely allies also had in common their unwillingness to accept capitalism as it evolved and as it functioned in a bourgeois setting.

67. See, for example, José Torras y Bages, El estadismo y la libertad religiosa (Vich, 1912).

68. Vicente Calatayud, "La obra de la restauración," Biblioteca Popular Carlista, Año II (December, 1897), pp. 27–28.

69. See "Sección doctrinal: el Carlismo al alcance de todos," *ibid.*, Año III (January, 1898), p. 6.

70. Vicent, *Socialismo y anarquismo*, pp. 86–87. Vicent also refers to Donoso Cortés as an early advocate of the type of decentralization that he and other Catholics were urging in the late nineteenth century.

71. Eugenio Vegas Latapié, *Romanticismo y democracia* (Santander, 1938), p. 91.

72. Maximiliano Estébanez, "Pro patria," *España y América*, Año I, no. 4 (February 15, 1903), pp. 209–16.

73. Eusebio Negrete, "Crónica de la quincena," *ibid.*, XII (January-March, 1907), pp. 465–66.

74. Pedro Martínez Vélez, "Pro patria," *ibid.*, Año I, no. 10 (May 15, 1903), pp. 99–100.

75. During the years that he spent in England (1905–1915), Maeztu returned to the Catholic faith and began to advance a program of Catholic-style decentralization based on a corporative organization. See his *Authority, Liberty and Function in the Light of the War* (London, 1916). A Spanish-language edition of this work appeared in Madrid in 1919.

76. See Sisinio Nevares, *El porqué de la sindicación obrera Católica* (1930), p. 52.

77. Severino Aznar, "El riesgo-enfermedad y las sociedades de socorros mutuos," *Revista del Clero Español*, no. 10 (October, 1914), pp. 721–34. Aznar, however, was not adverse to government aid to Catholic mutual aid societies, provided they retained their independence. See the continuation of his article in *ibid.*, no. 11 (November), pp. 801–809. Juan de Hinojosa, "Las ideas sociales de Alberto de Mun," *ibid.*, no. 13 (January, 1915), p. 75, also insisted upon Church control over private mutual assistance programs. He argued further for a corporative Cortes, based upon functional representation of semiautonomous labor and professional organizations.

78. V. Calatayud, "La obra de la restauración," pp. 25–28.

79. Monedero, *La Confederación*, pp. 194–95.

80. See José María Taboada Lago, *La Acción Católica en España*, with a prologue by Ángel Herrera y Oria (1934), p. 53, and Michael P. Fogarty, *Christian Democracy in Western Europe, 1820–1953* (Notre Dame, Ind., 1966, 2nd impression), p. 4.

81. For good insights into the organization and goals of Catholic Action, the works of three prelates are useful: Victoriano Guisasola, who later became the Cardinal-Archbishop of Toledo (Archbishop in 1913, Cardinal in 1914), *La acción social del clero: instrucción que el Excmo. y Rmo. Sr. Dr. D. . . . Arzobispo de Valencia, dirige a su amado clero diocesano* (Valencia, 1910); Enrique Reig y Casanova, *La Acción Social Católica en España: carta pastoral* (1924) and *Presente y porvenir económico de la Iglesia en España* (1908); and Ciriaco Sancha Hervás, Cardinal-Archbishop of Toledo at the time, *El kulturkampf internacional* (Toledo, 1901). Equally useful on this matter are the works of three Spanish Jesuits: Joaquín Azpiazu, *La acción social del sacerdote* (1934) and *Jóvenes y juventudes: juventudes Católicas* (1927); Gabriel Palau,

El Católico de acción (1905), La acción del sacerdote (1907), El problema de la eficacia de la Acción Social Católica en las grandes ciudades (Buenos Aires, 1917) and A los jóvenes: la gestación del ideal (Buenos Aires, 1917), the latter two works written when the sociologist-musician, who had helped form in Spain various worker syndicates as well as the Acción Social Popular (similar to the Volksverein in Germany), was living in Argentina where he taught and helped organize Catholic Action projects; and Remigio Vilariño, who wrote numerous catechism books and founded the reviews De Broma y de Veras in 1911 and Sal Terrae in 1912. See also José M. Sánchez, Reform and Reaction: The Politico-Religious Background of the Spanish Civil War (Chapel Hill, N.C., 1964), and Marie R. Madden, "Status of the Church and Catholic Action in Contemporary Spain," Catholic Historical Review, XVIII, no. I (April, 1932), pp. 19–59. Periodicals pertaining to this topic include Razón y Fe, the Jesuit journal that commenced publication in Madrid in 1901; Religión y Cultura, a Barcelona periodical published between 1908 and 1918; Revista Católica de Cuestiones Sociales, a Madrid journal appearing between 1895 and 1930; Revista del Clero Español, publicada mensualmente por el Seminario Conciliar de Madrid, beginning in January of 1914. Other journals publishing about the time of World War I and concerned with Catholic Action include: La Ciudad de Dios, an Augustinian periodical; La Paz Social; and Revista Social Hispano-Americana. Two other indispensable sources are Anuario Eclesiástico de España, 18 vols. (Barcelona, 1915–1934), and Anuario Social de España (1929). The latter study was directed by Juan Soler de Morell, S.J., and contains abundant information on Catholic worker organizations and an overall summary of Catholic Social Action programs.

82. Editorial of Revista del Clero Español, Año I, no. 1 (January, 1914), p. 8.

83. Gomá y Tomás, Antilaicismo, I, p. 285.

84. See José Gatell, "Discurso inaugural de la asociación de eclesiásticos de Barcelona para el apostolado popular," Reseña Eclesiástica (Barcelona), January, 1915, p. 105.

85. See Victoriano Guisasola, El peligro del laicismo y los deberes de los Católicos (Toledo, 1915). On Guisasola, who as Archbishop of Valencia and later as primate of Spain was a leading figure in the Church's bid to assume an important social role, see Álvaro López Núñez, Apología del Cardenal Guisasola (1923).

86. Gatell, "Discurso inaugural," p. 106.

87. Taboada, La Acción Católica, p. 148.

88. Quoted in Luis Marichalar, Antología de las obras del Excmo. Sr. Vizconde de Eza, p. 835.

89. S. Nevares, El porqué, p. 28.

90. Gomá y Tomás, Antilaicismo, I, pp. 105–107, 118, 121.

91. See Revista del Clero Español, no. 14 (February, 1915), pp. 123–124.

92. Gomá y Tomás, Antilaicismo, I, p. 139.

93. See León Martín Granizo, "A modo de prólogo: El Vizconde de

Eza y su tiempo," in Marichalar, *Antología de las obras del Excmo. Sr. Vizconde de Eza*, p. xxiii.

94. Severino Aznar, *Las encíclicas "Rerum Novarum" y "Quadragesimo Anno:" precedentes y repercusiones en España* (1941), p. 48, and Pedro Sangro y Ros, *Crónica del movimiento de reforma social*, pp. 12–13.

95. See M. A. Lugan, "Un gran obispo social, El Excmo. Sr. Dr. Laguarda, Obispo de Barcelona," *Revista del Clero Español*, no. 2 (February, 1914), pp. 140–51, a eulogistic account by a French Catholic sociologist. Laguarda, who had taught sociology at the seminary in Valencia, felt that only resolute intervention by the Church could restore social harmony and peace. He died in 1913 at the age of forty-six. On him see Narciso Plá y Deniel, *La actuación social del Obispo de Barcelona, Doctor Laguarda* (Barcelona, 1914) and *Sesión necrológica en honor de Excmo. e illmo. Sr. Dr. D. J. J. Laguarda* (Barcelona, 1914).

96. Lugan, "Un gran obispo social," pp. 145–47.

97. See Amando Castroviejo, at the time professor of economics at the University of Santiago, "Un ejemplo de acción social," *Revista del Clero Español*, no. 14 (February, 1915), pp. 238–240.

98. See S. Nevares, *El porqué*, p. 67.

99. For a description of the operation of an early syndicate founded under Catholic Action auspices in 1903, see Narciso Noguer,, " 'La Conciliación en Pamplona," *Razón y Fe*, II (January-April, 1905), pp. 78–84.

100. The Confederación Nacional Católico-Agraria was made up of fifty-eight federations and more than five thousand syndicates.

101. Sangro y Ros, *Crónica del movimiento de reforma social*, pp. 35–37. The congress also estimated that some 65,000 women were enrolled in Women's Catholic Action. As of 1934, there were an estimated 118,000 members of the Organización de Mujeres Católicas, dedicated to "combating neutral, laic, and anarchistic forces." Within Women's Catholic Action, the consiliario was "to be not just a spectator, nor even the promotor and planner, but the very soul of the organization." See *Revista Eclesiástica*, VI (1934), pp. 376–77.

102. See Joaquín de Encinas, *La tradición española*, p. 284.

103. On Catholic Action youth see Victoriano Feliz, *La conquista de la juventud obrera* (1933), *La joven de Acción Social* (1934), *Jóvenes campesinos de Acción Católica y Social* (1934), and *Manual del joven Católico* (1928). See also José María Taboada Lago, *Juventud Católica Española: los caballeros del ideal* (1928).

104. See Francisco Gutiérrez Lasanta, *Tres cardenales hispánicos y un obispo hispanizante* (Zaragoza, 1965), p. 149, and Taboada, *La Acción Católica*, p. 71.

105. Tedeschini, *Discursos y cartas sobre Acción Católica Española* (Santiago de Compostela, 1958), p. 13, a discourse pronounced in 1921.

106. The impassioned, often demagogic tone of Tedeschini is found throughout his *Discursos y cartas*. See also his *Discurso del Excmo. . . . Arzobispo de Lepanto y Nuncio Apostólico en la solemna sesión de clausura de la asamblea de las juventudes Católicas celebrada en Madrid el 30 de abril de 1924* (1930).

107. Vicent, *Socialismo y anarquismo*, pp. xxi-xxiv. In France Vicent

had fallen under the influence of Count Adrien Albert Marie de Mun and Marquis René de la Tour du Pin, Catholics who devoted much of their lives to working in behalf of Church-affiliated social justice programs.

108. The Catholic Workers' circles occasionally made attempts to organize dependent guilds (gremios) in surrounding rural regions. Membership in the agrarian guild was to consist of honorary members or protectors, wealthy and socially prominent individuals who did not actually reside in the rural areas and who in their professions were not concerned with cultivation of the land, and of regular members, men who did depend for their livelihood "upon the working of the soil," either as laborers or proprietors. See ibid., p. 288.

109. Ibid., pp. 493–94.

110. Ibid., p. 230.

111. Ibid., pp. 231–36.

112. Ibid., p. 239.

113. Ibid., pp. 263–65.

114. Ibid., p. 267.

115. See José María Gil Robles No fue posible la paz (1968), pp. 42–43. This is an extremely important work by the key figure among moderate Catholic conservatives during the second republic.

116. Ángel Herrera was the man primarily responsible for the rapidly rising presige of El Debate. Herrera bought the paper in 1915 with capital supplied by the Bishop of Madrid-Alcalá, certain Bilbao financiers, and individuals "close to the Jesuits." See Henry W. Buckley, Life and Death of the Spanish Republic (London, 1940), p. 106. Extremely active in the Church's social programs of the 1920's, Herrera came increasingly to lean toward the Christian Democratic position. During this period he may well have been one of the half dozen most important Spanish lay figures in Catholic Action and related movements. At the age of fifty-three he was ordained a priest, eventually becoming Bishop of Málaga. In the twenty-year period prior to his death in 1968, Herrera founded some 250 new elementary schools in his diocese. Unfortunately, there is no adequate biography of Herrera.

117. Monedero, La Confederación Nacional Católico-Agraria, pp. 7–13. On the Catholic agrarian movement see also Monedero, El problema de la tierra: aspecto fiscal; modificaciones en el régimen fiscal en relación con la capacidad contributiva del pequeño y el grande proprietario rural (1928); José María Azara, Apuntes sociales y agrarios (Zaragoza, 1919), an attack against usury and financial capitalism in general by a leading figure in Catholic Action's work of rural labor organization; and Sisinio Nevares, El patrón ejemplar (1936).

118. Monedero, La Confederación, pp. 18–19.

119. Ibid., p. 20.

120. Ibid., pp. 24–25.

121. When certain Andalusian landowners tried to form a Liga de Terratenientes Andaluces, limited strictly to Catholic landowners, as a means of competing against what they regarded as the dangerous joint approach of Monedero, they were blocked by Archbishop Guisasola. The primate asserted that the approach of the Andalusians was likely to

heighten class tensions and to impede the progress of Monedero's syndicates, which he described as the authentic instrument of Catholic Action. See *ibid.*, pp. 86–88.

122. By 1920 members of the Catholic Agrarian Syndicates had placed some 200 million pesetas into savings accounts and this capital was drawn upon to extend low-interest loans. See *ibid.*, pp. 70–71. In Spain as a whole, savings accounts increased from 300 billion pesetas in all reporting banking institutions to 700 million pesetas between 1898 and 1920, a period which saw the population rise from 17,974,000 to 21,280,-000. See *Unión Ibero-Americana*, Año XXXVIII (August, 1924), p. 97.

123. Monedero, *La Confederación*, p. 54.

124. *Ibid.*, p. 100.

125. *Ibid.*, p. 101.

126. *Razón y Fe*, LXXIII (September–December, 1925), pp. 305–308.

127. Sangro y Ros, *Crónica del movimiento de reforma social*, p. 36.

128. Eusebio Negrete, "Crónica de la quincena," *España y América*, XIII (January–March, 1907), p. 275.

129. According to the Ministerio de Instrucción Pública y Bellas Artes, *Estadística escolar de España* en 1908, 2 vols. (1909), there were 5,014 private Catholic schools in Spain, 24,861 public schools, 107 laic, and 91 Protestant schools. The existence of the laic and Protestant schools evoked indignant complaint from *Razón y Fe*, XXVII (January-April, 1910), pp. 450–56.

130. See V. Minteguiaga, "La real orden circular sobre las escuelas laicas," *Razón y Fe*, XXVII (January-April, 1910), pp. 450–56.

131. P. Villada, "¿Ha admitido Roma la libertad de cultos en España?" *ibid.*, XXVIII (September-December, 1910), p. 358.

132. Severino Aznar, *Impresiones de un Demócrata Cristiano*, with a prologue by Salvador Minguijón (1950), pp. 118–20. This is a revised edition of a work that appeared originally in 1930.

133. Joaquín Azpiazu, *Jóvenes y juventudes*, p. 241.

134. J. M. Salvador y Barrera, "El laicismo en la Enseñanza," *Revista del Clero Español*, no. 7 (July, 1914), p. 486.

135. Victoriano Guisasola, *Reflecciones y consejos que el Arzobispo de Valencia dirige a los maestros de instrucción primaria de su diócesis* (Valencia, 1913). See also E. Negrete, "Crónica de la quincena," *España y América*, XXXVIII (April–June, 1913), pp. 88–89.

136. See Romanones, *Notas de una vida, 1912–1931* (1947), pp. 49–51. For additional material on early twentieth-century religious issues, often involving Church-state relations, see: Joaquín Buitrago y Hernández, *Las órdenes religiosas y los religiosos en España* (1901), an impassioned denunciation of the Liberal Party's attempt to reduce the number of religious orders in Spain; Antolín López Peláez, *Injusticias del estado español: labor parlamentaria de un año* (Barcelona, 1908) and *Por la Iglesia española* (1913), an arrogant defense of alleged Church rights by the Bishop of Jaca (preconized in 1905) and Archbishop of Tarragona (preconized in 1913) as well as a prominent senator who often attacked the Eduardo Dato wing of the Liberal-Conservative Party for not being Catholic enough; Manuel Senante y Martínez, *Documentos*

parlamentarios: discursos pronunciado por . . . (1910), the views of an Integrista leader who became director of *El Siglo Futuro* upon the death of Ramón Nocedal in 1907 and represented Guipúzcoa in the chamber of deputies; Antonio Viladevall, S.J., *La voluntad nacional enfrente de jacobinismo afrancesado de Romanones y Canalejas* (Barcelona, 1907), a blistering attack against such "vile liberals" as Romanones and Canalejas, a glowing tribute to such defenders of Catholicism as Vázquez de Mella, Antonio Maura, Manuel de Burgos y Mazo, and Ramón Nocedal, and a description of the Catholic mass demonstrations against a civil marriage bill introduced by a Liberal cabinet. The anticlerical position is forcefully set forth by Jaime Torrubiano Ripoll, an excommunicated Spaniard who seemed to regard himself as his country's only reliable and sound Catholic theologian, in *La Iglesia rica y el clero pobre* (1922) and *Rebeldías: artículos sobre el problema religiosa en España*, 2 vols. (1925, 1926).

137. See Richard A. Webster, *The Cross and the Fasces: Christian Democracy and Fascism in Italy* (Stanford, Calif., 1960), p. 19.

138. *Ibid.*, pp. 52–53.

139. See Sangro y Ros, *Crónica del movimiento de reforma social*, p. 38. Sangro y Ros was in the more advanced or progressive wing of Christian Democracy, showing a decided willingness to cooperate with secular, laic forces in the social reform movement. For the important publications of members of the Grupo de la Democracia Cristiana see Álvaro López Núñez, *Inventorio bibliográfico del Grupo de la Democracia Cristiana* (1925). A valuable work on Spanish Christian Democracy is Manuel de Burgos y Mazo, *El problema social y la Democracia Cristiana*, 6 vols. (Barcelona, 1914–1930), with a prologue to the first volume by Eduardo Dato. A lifetime senator, Burgos y Mazo held important cabinet posts, including that of minister of interior. Spanish Christian Democracy suffered from serious divisiveness. Some members of the movement, among them Victoriano Flamarique and Salvador Minguijón, seemed consistently to follow Catholic Action approaches in the formative years of Christian Democracy in the peninsula. Others, among them Burgos y Mazo, Sangro y Ros, López Núñez, León Leal Ramos, and Luis Jordana de Pozas, co-operated with government agencies in working for social reform and seemed to accept some degree of secularization. In this they resembled Liberal-Conservative Party leader Dato in his position on social and political issues. Moreover, while Christian Democracy produced an advocate of liberal democracy such as Alfredo Mendizábal y Martín it also produced José Calvo Sotelo, who by the 1930s had become an authoritarian fascist type who vastly admired Charles Maurras and Action Française.

140. Aznar believed in collaborating with government agencies in the quest for social reform and thus worked alongside liberals, republicans, and anticlericals in the Instituto de Reformas Sociales. As a journalist Aznar contributed frequently to *El Debate, El Correo Español*, and *La Lectura Dominical*; in addition he founded and for a time directed *La Paz Social*. He frequently stressed that Christian Democracy developed organically from the conservative, traditionalist philosophy of Spaniards

such as Balmes, Aparisi, Donoso Cortés, Ortí y Lara, and Pidal y Mon. See, for example, his *Las encíclicas "Rerum Novarum" y "Quadragesimo Anno:" precedentes y repercusiones en España*. In the prologue to the 1950 edition of Aznar's *Impresiones de un Demócrata Cristiano*, Salvador Minguijón emphasized that his lifelong friend in the Christian Democratic movement never associated democracy with the foolish liberal notion of inorganic suffrage in which mere numbers prevail. Minguijón also asserted that the ideals of Christian Democracy finally triumphed and were implemented in the administration of Francisco Franco.

141. As early as 1905 Father Narciso Noguer published an attack against Christian Democracy, "Sobre la Democracia Cristiana," *Razón y Fe*, XII (May-August, 1905), pp. 214–17. Noguer charged that Christian Democrats rejected strict control by the ecclesiastical hierarchy. They represented, he said, the hydra of Catholic liberalism; no matter how often its head was cut off, it kept reappearing. On the other hand Francisco González Herrero's *La Democracia Cristiana como elemento para resolver la llamada cuestión social* (Cuenca, 1910) was regarded even by most opponents of the movement as a sound work that stressed the subjection of Christian Democracy to Catholic Action.

142. *Razón y Fe*, XXVIII (September-December, 1910), p. 485.

143. Review by N. Noguer of *Vista del Asesor Eclesiástico y auto de Excmo. Sr. Arzobispo de Buenos Aires, fecha 10 de abril de 1919, sobre la agrupación denominada Unión Demócrata Cristiana* (Buenos Aires, 1919) in *Razón y Fe*, LVI (January-April, 1920), pp. 103–107.

144. Fogarty, *Christian Democracy in Western Europe*, pp. 192–93. For an excellent summary of the dispute over whether Catholics should continue to form mixed circles or exclusively labor syndicates see Eugenio Madrigal Villada, *¿Sindicatos ó círculos? Un programa de acción para los Círculos Católicos como centros de organización obrera sindicalista y base de todas las demás obras económico-sociales* (Palencia, 1916).

145. Graciano Martínez, "Sana doctrina sobre sindicatos," *España y América*, LXXV (July-August, 1922), pp. 171–72, 241–43.

146. Maximiliano Arboleya Martínez, *XL aniversario de la "Rerum Novarum," Carta Magna de la justicia social*, with a prologue by Juan Bautista Luis y Pérez, Bishop of Oviedo (Barcelona, 1931), pp. 62–64. As a young priest and professor of apologetics at the University of Oviedo, Arboleya was active in forming workers' syndicates and in creating the Federación Diocesana de Sindicatos Agrarios. Attacked by some Catholics for his allegedly excessive zeal in matters of social reform, Arboleya was defended by the Cardinal-Archbishop of Toledo, Victoriano Guisasola, in the pastoral *Justicia y caridad en la organización Cristiana de trabajo* (1916). Arboleya was also an active journalist who struggled to make the Catholic press a genuinely popular medium.

147. See the introduction by the Dominican priest Luis Urbano to the Spanish edition of G. C. Rutten, *La doctrina social de la Iglesia según las encíclicas "Rerum Novarum" y "Quadragesimo Anno,"* translated by Father Cándido Fernández (Barcelona, 1936, 2nd ed.).

148. See Fogarty, *Christian Democracy in Western Europe*, p. xxv.

149. *Unión Hispano-Americana*, February, 1922, p. 19.

150. See N. Noguer, "La propiedad de lo superfluo," *Razón y Fe*, LVII (May-August, 1920), pp. 5–23.

151. Sharp divisions existed even among Spanish traditionalists who professed to represent the uncontaminated views of Balmes and Donoso Cortés and refused to collaborate with the tainted Liberal-Conservative Party. Salvador Minguijón sought to bring about certain transformations in Catholic traditionalism. His ideas were severely attacked by other traditionalists and particularly by the Integristas. Minguijón's efforts in the political realm came to an end, for the most part, with the demise of the Partido Social Popular at the outset of the Primo de Rivera dictatorship. Some of Minguijón's thinking on traditionalism and innovation is found in his *La crisis del tradicionalismo en España* (Zaragoza, 1914).

152. See E. Negrete, "Crónica," *España y América*, XIV (April-June, 1907), pp. 472–73, and Moisés Sánchez Barrado, "El clero y la política," *ABC*, June 11, 1907.

153. See "Semblanza de Víctor Pradera" by the Conde de Rodezno in Pradera, *El estado nuevo* (1941 ed.), pp. 14–15.

154. An augmented edition appeared ten years later: *Justicia social* (1910).

155. Miguel Fernández Jiménez, *El problema obrero y los partidos españoles* (Granada, 1904), p. 161.

156. See the Dato prologue to vol. I of Burgos y Mazo, *El problema social y la Democracia Cristiana*, and Vicente del Olmo, *La situación actual de España: la política de D. Eduardo Dato* (1917). There is no truly adequate biography of Dato.

157. *Mercurio*, no. 41 (April 1, 1905), pp. 400–401. In this edition the Barcelona periodical that was an important organ of hispanismo presents an excellent sketch of Dato and his political-social ideology.

158. Dato prologue to Fernández Jiménez, *El problema obrero*, pp. xxi–xxii.

159. See the interview with Dato in Luis Morote, *El pulso de España: interviews políticas* (1904), pp. 377–79.

160. Altamira, *Ideario político*, pp. 65–66.

161. Dato prologue to Fernández Jiménez, *El problema obrero*, p. xxii.

162. Dato, *Justicia social*, p. 29.

163. Dato prologue to Fernández Jiménez, *El problema obrero*, p. xxii.

164. Dato, *Justicia social*, p. 43.

165. *Ibid.*, p. 57.

166. Altamira, *Ideario político*, p. 68.

167. On Gamazo see L. Llanos de Torriglia, *Germán Gamazo, el soberbio Castellano* (1942).

168. On Maura see: Severino Aznar, *Maura y la política social* (1942), a sympathetic pamphlet-length study; Juventud Conservadora de Madrid, *El Sr. Maura y el Partido Conservador ante la opinión* (1913); Ángel Ossorio y Gallego, *Antonio Maura* (Salamanca, 1928), by a companion of Maura in the Conservative Party who repudiated Maurista ideas in the 1930s to join forces with the republicans; José Ruiz Castillo, ed., *Antonio Maura: 35 años de vida pública. Ideas, políticas, doctrinas de gobierno y campañas parlamentarias* (1953), a carefully selected anthology of Maura's

most important writings that appeared originally in a two-volume edition
in 1917; Diego Sevilla Andrés, *Antonio Maura: la revolución desde arriba*,
with a prologue by Melchor Fernández Almagro (Barcelona, 1953);
César Silió y Cortés, *Vida y empresa de un gran español: Maura* (1934).
A valuable source is *La Acción*, the Madrid newspaper that between 1916
and 1924 presented the views of Maura and his followers.

169. See Sevilla Andrés, *Maura*, p. 97.

170. See the 1915 Maura discourse in *Tres discursos de Maura sobre la
política exterior, reeditados en el centenario de su nacimiento* (1954),
p. 19.

171. See Maura, *Ideario político: extracto de sus discursos*, selected by
Juan Bautista Catalá y Gavila (1953), esp. pp. 156–57, 173–74, Sevilla
Andrés, *Maura*, p. 185, and Jesús Marañón, "Exégesis política de la
reforma local de Maura," *Ideario de Don Antonio Maura sobre la vida
local: textos y estudios; homenaje en el primer centenario de un gran
español* (1954), p. 354.

172. Father Bruno Ibeas, "El Partido Conservador: lo que ha sido,"
España y América, XL (October-December, 1913), pp. 492–93.

173. See Morote, *El pulso*, p. 444.

174. On the Juventudes Mauristas see: José Calvo Sotelo, *El proletariado ante el socialismo y el maurismo* (1915), by a member of the Juventudes destined for national prominence in the 1920s and 1930s; José
Gutiérrez-Ravé, *Yo fui un joven Maurista: historia de un movimiento de
ciudadanía*, with a prologue by Antonio Goicoechea (1945); Juventud
Maurista, *Reglamento de la . . .* (1919).

175. See Mercurio, September 1, 1905, pp. 561–62 for an excellent
sketch of Maura and a description of the polarizing effect produced in
Spanish politics by his rise to leadership of the Conservative Party.

176. Morote, *El pulso*, p. 52.

177. Juan Aragón, quoted in *España y América*, XXXVI (September-
December, 1912), pp. 565–66.

178. See Maura, *Tres discursos . . . política exterior*, pp. 23–28, *Ideario
de . . . Maura sobre la vida local*, esp. pp. 18–19, and Fernández Jiménez,
El problema obrero, p. 197.

179. Mercurio, p. 563.

180. *Ibid.*

181. Vicent, *Socialismo y anarquismo*, pp. 243–44.

182. See E. de Vargas-Zúñiga, "El problema religioso de España,"
Razón y Fe, CVIII (May-August, 1935), pp. 301–302.

183. *Anuario Eclesiástico 1926* (Barcelona, 1926), p. 42.

184. See Joaquín Azpiazu, "Un programa social Cristiano," *Razón y
Fe*, CXI (May-August, 1936), p. 152.

185. Vargas Zúñiga, "El problema religioso," pp. 296–97. See also
G. Robinot March, S.J., *Ante la apostasía de las masas* (1935, 3rd ed.),
and Francisco Pieró, *El problema religioso-social de España* (1936, 2nd
ed.). Pieró, a Dominican priest who conducted careful surveys, concluded
that only 5 percent of the rural populace of New Castile complied with
Easter duties in 1931. Hugh Thomas, *The Spanish Civil War*, p. 31,
notes that in the Basque area where the Church had remained close to

the land, with the clergy in the center of village life, the situation was different. Basque priests in 1936 claimed that 99 percent of the rural population of Guipúzcoa, Álava and Vizcaya and 52 percent of those of Basque blood living in the industrial areas were practicing Catholics. See *ibid.*, p. 54.

186. See Vargas-Zúñiga, "El problema religioso de España," cont., *Razón y Fe*, CIX (September-December, 1935), pp. 149–52. In addition to the 33,587 secular priests there were seven thousand members of the regular clergy in 1935. The ratio of priests, secular and regular, to lay Catholics was therefore still high, averaging throughout the country 1:586. In Andalusia, the ratio was 1:1,515.

187. Jaime Vicens Vives, *Aproximación a la historia de España* (Barcelona, 1952), p. 174, contends that the Church did accomplish a revival of its influence among the nobility and the bourgeoisie, a fact that enabled leftist agitators all the more successfully to depict Catholicism to the proletariat as the instrument of the accommodated classes.

188. Vargas-Zúñiga, "El problema religioso," CVIII, p. 304.

NOTES TO CHAPTER 5

1. Rafael Altamira stressed the importance that history should have for liberals. He argued that in order for Spain to become a liberal country it did not have to break with its past; rather, it had to be true to certain carefully selected traditions of its past. See his *España y el programa americanista* (1917), esp. pp. 135–41.

2. Luis Morote, *La moral de la derrota* (1900), p. 283. See also Pedro Sáinz Rodríguez, *La evolución de las ideas sobre la decadencia española* (1924), esp. p. 73, for a good analysis of the liberal interpretation on the period of the Catholic Kings. The book is a valuable study on conflicting liberal and conservative views of history.

3. Morote, *La moral*, pp. 308–309.

4. Liberals of the postdisaster era pointed back approvingly to the mid-nineteenth-century views of Emilio Castelar, who had written: "We do not have agriculture because we expelled the Moors; we do not have industry because we ousted the Jews. . . . We are an atrophied member of the world of modern culture." Castelar is quoted in Ricardo del Arco y Garay, *La idea de imperio en la política y la literatura españolas* (1944), p. 739. This book, in spite of the degree to which it reflects the author's strong conservative convictions, presents a good analysis of the liberal interpretation of Spanish history. pp. 728–71.

5. Ricardo Macías Picavea, *El problema nacional* (1899), p. 345. Earlier liberal denunciations of the Hapsburgs are found in Lucas Mallada, *Cartas aragonesas* (1905), attributing to the Flemish courtiers and courtesans who flooded the country during the early sixteenth century the moral ruin of Spain; Manuel Pedregal y Cañedo, *Estudios sobre el engrandecimiento y la decadencia de España* (1878); Felipe Picatoste, *Estudios sobre la grandeza y decadencia de España: los españoles en Italia*, 2 vols. (1887),

a work that, although denying that the Hapsburgs were tyrants or perverse men, contends they started Spain on the road to ruin by focusing attention on Europe and diverting it from America and Africa, where the nation's true destiny lay.

6. Morote, La moral, pp. 319, 334–35.

7. Interview with Labra in L. Morote, El pulso de España (1904), p. 170.

8. Morote, La moral, pp. 339–40. A typical liberal work lavishing praise upon the eighteenth-century Bourbon reformers is Juan del Nido y Segalvera, Intento de reconstruir España (1912).

9. R. M. de Labra, El problema hispano-americano (1906), p. 46.

10. See John Trend, The Origins of Modern Spain (Cambridge, Eng., 1934), p. 176.

11. Hugh Thomas, The Spanish Civil War (New York, Evanston, London 1963), p. 36.

12. See Pedro Laín Entralgo, La generación del noventa y ocho (1956, 3rd ed.), p. 61. Although the work concentrates on the 1909 "Tragic Week" in Barcelona, much material on anticlericalism in general is found in Joan C. Ullman, The Tragic Week: A Study of Anti-Clericalism in Spain, 1875–1912 (Cambridge, Mass., 1968). See also John Devlin, Spanish Anticlericalism: A Study in Modern Alienation (New York, 1966), dealing with this theme as reflected in Spanish literature.

13. Pío Baroja quoted in Laín Entralgo, La generación, p. 65.

14. Unamuno quoted in ibid., p. 107.

15. Unamuno quoted in ibid., p. 107.

16. Macías Picavea, El problema nacional, p. 229.

17. Ibid., pp. 239–40.

18. Ibid., pp. 241–42. Ángel Ganivet had earlier expressed similar viewpoints. Though he declared he was not a Catholic, Ganivet regarded Catholicism as an essential and integral part of Spain's history and the Spanish psychology, just as important, although no more so, than Seneca's stoicism and certain Arab influences. But Spanish Catholicism, he complained, had gone limp because it had not had to defend itself against competition. Ganivet saw religious toleration as the corrective to this situation. See his Idearium español (1942 ed.), pp. 26–30. See also Laín Entralgo, La generación, p. 64, and C. María Abad, "Ángel Ganivet," Razón y Fe, LXXII (May-August, 1925), p. 25.

19. Labra, Discursos políticos, académicos, y forenses, 2 vols. (1884, 1886), I, p. 385.

20. Ibid., I, pp. 9–10.

21. Ibid., I, p. 384.

22. See Mercurio (Barcelona), no. 45 (August 1, 1905), p. 426, a splendid sketch of Azcárate and his political-intellectual position.

23. Azcárate, "Neutralidad de la universidad," Boletín de la Institución Libre de Enseñanza, no. 516 (March 31, 1903), p. 371.

24. Ibid., p. 374.

25. Unamuno, "Mas sobre la crisis del patriotismo," an essay written in 1906, in Algunas consideraciones sobre la literatura hispanoamericana (1968, 3rd ed.), pp. 16–17. Unamuno objected also to what he consid-

ered the Dominican and Jesuit qualities of Castilian Catholicism, out of which emerged the insistence on "one faith, one pastor . . . , unity above all, unity imposed from above . . . and submission and obedience from those below." See his *En torno al casticismo* (1957 ed.), p. 93. So far as Spain's great humanist, classicist, and long-time rector of the University of Salamanca was concerned, Seneca's stoicism as well as Jewish and Moorish influences were just as important in shaping Spanish tradition as militant, exclusivist Catholicism.

26. See Ernesto Giménez Caballero, *Genio de España* (1932), p. 54.

27. Unamuno, "Sobre la europeización," a 1906 essay in *Algunas consideraciones*, pp. 113–14.

28. Laín Entralgo, *La generación*, p. 93.

29. Macías Picavea, *El problema nacional*, pp. 203–204.

30. Altamira, *España en América* (Valencia, 1908), pp. 214–16. Even a staunch critic of the ideology conceded the affinity of Krausism, stressing as it did the primacy of ethical and moral over material considerations, with the Spanish temperament. See the views of Ledesma Ramos as described by Santiago Montero Díaz, "Estudio sobre Ramiro Ledesma Ramos," in *¿Fascismo en España?* (1968, 2nd ed.), pp. 23–24.

31. See Adolfo González Posada, "Contestación" to Manuel García Morente, *Ensayos sobre progreso, discurso leido por . . . en la Academia de Ciencias Morales Políticas* (1932), p. 144.

32. Ahrens, a professor at the University of Gratz and later the University of Leipzig, disseminated the philosophy of Krause in France, Belgium, Spain, and South America. Some of his works translated into Spanish by his liberal admirers include: *Compendio de la historia del derecho romano*, translated by Francisco Giner de los Ríos, 2 vols. (1879, 1880); *Curso completo de derecho natural ó de filosofía del derecho*, translated by Manuel María Flamant (1864); *Curso de derecho natural*, translated and with notes by Ruperto Navarro Zamarano, 2 vols. (1841, 1842); *Enciclopedia jurídica ó exposición orgánica de la ciencia del derecho y el estado*, translated by F. Giner de los Ríos, Gumersindo de Azcárate, and Augusto de Linares, 3 vols. (1878–1880).

33. One of several works by Krause translated into Spanish by Giner de los Ríos is *Compendio de estética* (1875). The most popular Spanish edition of a Krause work was *Ideal de la humanidad para la vida*, translated and with an introduction and notes by Julián Sanz del Río (1860; 2nd ed., 1871; 3rd ed., 1904). Placed on the Index by Rome, this work has been referred to by Menéndez Pelayo, *Historia de los heterodoxos españoles*, 3 vols. (1880–1882), III, p. 736, as the banner of Spain's democratic youth. *Ideal* is certainly one of the most readable of Krause's works. It does not suffer from the obscure style that characterized his more metaphysical writings; instead it presents an often impassioned plea for human solidarity and brotherhoood based on freedom from religious fanaticism and political authoritarianism. On the other hand, in his introduction to the work and in other writings Sanz del Río emerges as a dry, tendentious, secondrate thinker. Menéndez Pelayo, *Historia de los heterodoxos*, III, p. 732, observed that it was impossible to write as badly as Sanz del Río but that fellow-Krausist Nicolás Salmerón, one-time president of the first republic

and professor of metaphysics at the University of Madrid, wrote nearly as badly. On Krausism see the essay by Ángel Ganivet in *España filosófico contemporánea y otros trabajos*, vol. IX of Ganivet's *Obras completas*, 10 vols. (1933); Juan José Gil Cremades, *El reformismo español: Krausismo, escuela histórica, neotomismo* (1969), a carefully researched, perceptive, and objective study; Pierre Jobit, *Les éducateurs de l'Espagne contemporaine: les Krausistes; lettres inédites de D. Julián Sanz del Río publiées par Manuel de la Revilla* (Paris, 1936); Juan López Morillas, *El Krausismo español: perfil de una aventura intelectual* (México, D. F., 1956), a highly favorable account; Alonso Martínez, *Movimiento de las ideas religiosas en Europa: exposición crítica del sistema krausista*, vol. IV of *Memorias de la Real Academia de Ciencias Morales y Políticas*, 14 vols. (1861–1890). References to the subject are also found in Luis Araquistain, *El pensamiento español contemporáneo* (Buenos Aires, 1962) and Luis Díaz del Corral, *El liberalismo doctrinario* (1945).

34. A decidedly hostile Menéndez Pelayo wrote that if it had not been for the confused state of his mind, into which he could fit only a very few ideas to which he then clung with zealous stubbornness, Sanz del Río would not have ignored the truly first-rate German thinkers in order to settle on an obscure sophist. According to Menéndez Pelayo, *Historia de los heterodoxos*, III, p. 715, a whole generation of Spaniards became Krausists because of the intellectual mediocrity and laziness of Sanz del Río. More than a school, the conservative writer complained, Krausism had been converted by its disciples into a lodge, a mutual aid society, a tribe. Krausists, he said, were responsible for the fact that for more than twenty years "we have suffered the tragedy of the domination, exercised with a rigor and tyranny of which foreigners can have no idea, . . . of the most mediocre disciple of Schelling, of the verbose and infecund science that is decorated with the pompous name of harmonious rationalism." See Menéndez Pelayo, *Historia de ideas estéticas* (1940), IV, p. 267.

35. See Ortí y Lara, *Krause y sus discípulos convictos de panteismo* (1864).

36. See Castro, *Resumen de las principales cuestiones de metafísica analítica* (Sevilla, 1869). At a later time Castro collaborated with Nicolás Salmerón to write *Compendio de historia universal*. Castro was an adulatory disciple of Sanz del Río. Tomás Romero de Castilla was one of the rare Spaniards who thought it possible to reconcile Krausism and liberalism in general with Catholicism. A staunch Catholic but also a follower of Castro, Romero de Castilla sought to teach a blend of Krausist and Catholic ethics at the Instituto de Badajoz. See his *La doctrina que establece el carater objetivo de las ideas y la infalibilidad de la razón no es contrario a los principios del Catolicismo* (Badajoz, 1881), *El Krausismo y la fe Católica* (Badajoz, 1883), and *Nuestro concepto de la razón y de la doctrina de Santo Tomás* (Badajoz, 1883). The Romero de Castilla position was attacked by Ramiro Fernández Valbuena, one of traditionalism's most ardent polemicists, who in 1911 became titular Bishop of Escilio, in *¿De Santo Tomás ó de Krause?* (Badajoz, 1881).

37. Salmerón became professor of metaphysics at the University of Madrid in 1869, when liberals were at the peak of their political power.

A close associate of Azcárate and Giner de los Ríos, he represented Barcelona in the chamber of deputies for a fifteen-year period preceding his death in 1908. The influence of Krausism on his social attitudes is revealed in his *La obra común de los obreros y de los republicanos* (1904).

38. Much influenced himself by Krausism, Adolfo González Posada maintained that the system was largely remade by Sanz del Río so as to suit it more fully to the Spanish temperament. The remade Krausism, he stated, emerged with the typical Spanish traits of austerity, mysticism, dreaminess, intuitional idealism, and Quijotism. Posada maintained that because traditionalists recognized the essentially Spanish character of Krausism they were all the more afraid of it, all the more passionate and hysterical in attacking it. See Posada, *España en crisis* (1923), pp. 170–75.

39. See Trend, *The Origins of Modern Spain*, pp. 40–41.

40. Pedro Sáinz Rodríguez, "Clarín y su obra," *Revista de las Españas*, nos. 9–10 (May-June, 1927), p. 309.

41. Sanz del Río, introduction to Krause, *Ideal*, p. xxviii.

42. Explanatory note of Sanz del Río to Krause, *Ideal*, p. 308. A similar view is expressed by Krause, *ibid.*, p. 76.

43. Explanatory note of Sanz del Río to Krause, *Ideal*, pp. 198–200, 208.

44. Krause, *Ideal*, p. 146.

45. Explanatory note of Sanz del Río to Krause, *Ideal*, pp. 237–38.

46. Krause, *Ideal*, p. 147.

47. Explanatory note of Sanz del Río to Krause, *Ideal*, p. 286.

48. Krause, *Ideal*, pp. 5–6.

49. Sanz del Río introduction to Krause, *Ideal*, p. xxix.

50. Krause, *Ideal*, pp. 102–104. See also p. 34 where Krause develops the notion of social harmony based on the concept that each member of society must operate in his own sphere, subordinate to the overall demands of the common good.

51. See *Ibid.*, pp. 85–86.

52. *Ibid.*, p. 65.

53. *Ibid.*, p. 138.

54. *Ibid.*, p. 105.

55. On the influence of positivism on Krausism in Spain see Gil Cremades, *El reformismo español*, pp. 183–219. See also Urbano González Serrano, *Crítica y filosofía* (1888), *Estudios de moral y de filosofía* (1888), and *Manual de psicología, lógica, y ética* (1887). González studied philosophy under Salmerón, collaborated in the Institución Libre de Enseñanza, and was a representative figure of the second epoch of Krausism during which it was influenced by positivism. The works of González show the mingling of the two ideologies.

56. See Gil Cremades, *El reformismo español*, esp. pp. 123–25, 134, 187–88, 259, stressing the organic conceptions of the Krausists and suggesting that in this they may even have anticipated the corporative state program of Catholic traditionalists. The author also indicates further points of affinity between the two philosophical-theological camps.

57. This aspect of Krausism particularly concerned Catholics who, in attacking the German system of thought as refashioned by Sanz del Río,

again and again had recourse to their claim that only Catholicism could resolve the social problem. Obviously if Spaniards came widely to believe that social stability could be maintained and the class conflict resolved on the basis of natural morality, then Catholicism would lose much of its appeal and sustain a serious setback in its endeavor to desecularize society. For a Catholic attack against Krausism on the grounds that in spite of its claims it could not eliminate the social problem but would in the final analysis contribute toward social revolution, see L. Murillo, "La ciencia y la revelación en el siglo XIX," *Razón y Fe*, I (September-December, 1901), p. 22.

58. See Giménez Caballero, *Genio de España*, p. 54.

59. Pío Baroja essay of 1903 in *Comunistas, Judíos y demás ralea* (Valladolid, 1939), pp. 153–55.

60. See Laín Entralgo, *La generación*, p. 101.

61. See Gil Cremades, *El reformismo español*, p. 261.

62. Manuel Sales y Ferré, *Problemas sociales* (1910), p. 205. At one time a student of Sanz del Río, sociologist-historian-archaeologist Sales y Ferré taught later in Sevilla and finally in Madrid, winning a chair in sociology in the capital city's university in 1899. His fame rested largely on his *Tratado de sociología*, 4 vols. (Sevilla, Madrid, 1889–1904).

63. See Father Eusebio Negrete, "Crónica de la quincena," *España y América*, XXXVI (September-December, 1912), p. 370.

64. Interview with Canalejas in Morote, *El pulso*, p. 350.

65. See *España y América*, I, no. 1 (January 1, 1903), p. 70. On Canalejas see Luis Antón del Olmet and Arturo García y Caraffa, *Los grandes españoles*, 9 vols. (1913–1914), IV, *Canalejas*, and Diego Sevilla Andrés, *Canalejas* (Barcelona, 1956). There is no thoroughly adequate biography of this fascinating figure.

66. Canalejas in a 1904 senate debate quoted in Miguel Fernández Jiménez, *El problema obrero y los partidos españoles* (1904), p. 181.

67. Fernández Jiménez, *ibid.*, pp. 181–82.

68. Severino Aznar, *Las encíclicas "Rerum Novarum" y "Quadragesimo Anno:" precedentes y repercusiones en España* (1941), p. 32.

69. See Fernández Jiménez, *El problema obrero*, p. 122, and *Mercurio*, no. 41 (April 1, 1905), p. 401.

70. For some of the Canalejas views on Church-state issues see his prologue to Juan del Nido y Segalvera, *Problemas trascendentales: estudio sobre las regalías de la corona de España* (1910).

71. The accord between Canalejas and Maura, and its potential significance had Canalejas lived, is mentioned in the interview with José María Yanguas y Messía in *Los Domingos de ABC: Suplemento Semanal*, July 13, 1969, p. 10. On the social conservatism of Canalejas, who apparently inclined favorably toward corporative concepts, see his prologue to José Cascales y Muñoz, *El problema político al inaugurarse el siglo XX: el régimen parlamentario y funcionarismo* (1902), in which he praises a book calling for political representation based on professions. One of the best sources on the political ideology of Canalejas is a book first published under his name in 1912: *La política liberal en España*. The book is made up of articles that had appeared initially in *Diario Universal* during the

summer of 1912. Although actually written by the *Diario's* director, Daniel López, they were based on extensive interviews with Canalejas and approved by him as accurately reflecting his views. A second edition of the work (Madrid, no date) contains a prologue by the younger José Canalejas, the son of the Liberal statesman.

72. E. Negrete, "Crónica de la quincena," pp. 370–72.

73. Ortega y Gasset, *España invertebrada* (1921), pp. 108, 111.

74. Posada quoted in Antonio Goicoechea, *La crisis del constitucionalismo moderno* (1925), p. 223.

75. See *Mercurio*, no. 50 (January 1, 1906), pp. 700–702, an excellent study on Romanones.

76. In his doctoral dissertation *El capital y el trabajo: ¿son armónicos ó antagonísticos?* (1861) Moret first advocated the establishment of mixed associations as a step conducive to capital-labor harmony.

77. *Mercurio*, no. 43 (June 1, 1905), pp. 472–73.

78. Adolfo González Posada, *En América: una campaña* (1911), p. 130.

79. Melquiades Álvarez, liberal statesman and head of the Partido Reformista, quoted in Morote, *El pulso*, p. 204.

80. Labra, *Discursos*, I, pp. 211–12.

81. *Ibid.*, II, pp. 376–77.

82. Emiliano Agüado in the October 3, 1931 edition of *La Conquista del Estado*, the weekly organ of a right-wing reform group during the early stages of the second republic, reproduced in *"La Conquista del Estado:" Antología* (Barcelona, 1939), p. 286.

83. Canalejas interview in Morote, *El pulso*, p. 353.

84. See the Romanones views as set forth in *Mercurio*, no. 59 (January 1, 1906), p. 702, and the Labra position as explained in *Discursos*, I, pp. 206, 212. Liberal Leader Eugenio Montero Ríos was in accord on the two-pronged approach to popular education. See *Mercurio*, no. 52 (March 1, 1906), pp. 749–50.

85. On Giner, whose *Obras completas* appeared in their first Madrid edition in 1916, see the sympathetic study of Martín Navarro, *Vida y obra de Don Francisco Giner de los Ríos* (México, D.F., 1946).

86. Giner saw positivism in Spain as in a way representing a natural outgrowth of the more objectionable features of scholasticism. See his *Estudios sobre educación*, vol. VIII in *Obras completas* (1933), pp. 12–14. The *Estudios* is made up of essays written between 1879 and 1907.

87. Pedro Sangro y Ros, *Crónica del movimiento de reforma social en España* (1925), pp. 31–33.

88. Angelina Carnicer, "En memoriam: Francisco Giner de los Ríos," *Boletín de la Institución Libre de Enseñanza*, no. 841 (May, 1930), p. 160.

89. Giner, *Estudios*, p. 187.

90. *Ibid.*, pp. 114–16.

91. See Antonio Royo Villanova, "Las obras de Giner de los Ríos," *Boletín de la Institución Libre de Enseñanza*, no. 729 (November, 1920), pp. 349–50.

92. Giner, *Estudios*, p. 187.

93. *Ibid.*, p. 115.

94. "It is never more necessary," wrote Giner, *ibid.*, p. 50, "to awaken the individual and to individualize the masses than when there has arrived at its apogee the idolatry of [social] leveling. . . ." See also Giner's apology for rule by an aristocracy of character—as opposed to an aristocracy of talent—in *ibid.*, pp. 88–94.

95. In *ibid.*, p. 275, Giner agreed with Thomas Carlyle, that the tragedy of the poor was not their poverty and the necessity of hard labor. Rather, it was that the light of their souls had been extinguished and that as a result they were concerned with things material. Giner believed the surest way to protect the principle of rule by a select elite was to educate the masses, through the study of morality, art, and poetry, to appreciate the same values venerated by the elite.

96. Giner's apparent favoring of a corporative structure was lauded by one of his disciples, identified only as C.C., who explained the master's attitudes toward syndicalism in "En memoriam: quinto aniversario de D. Francisco Giner de los Ríos," *Boletín de la Institución Libre de Enseñanza*, no. 720 (March 31, 1930), p. 95:

> If syndicalism represents the desire that our destinies be controlled by the best men, if it is a conception distinct from the badly named democratic one, Don Francisco would have been its partisan. If syndicalism . . . is opposed to the parliamentary regime, because this is the regime of incompetence, and affirms that it is to the minorities of capacity that decision-making powers correspond and not to the . . . inept majorities, Don Francisco would have applauded it. . . .

John Trend, *The Origins of Modern Spain*, p. 122, observes: "The root idea of Don Francisco in regard to this problem lay in a theory he had of the special ends and objects of life, the realization of which would demand societies specialized in the performance of these objects. It was in his conversations rather than in his writing that he developed this idea."

97. Giner believed that on the primary and secondary levels education should present as favorable a view as possible of all religious beliefs. If as the student matured he discovered a religious approach that particularly appealed to him, then and only then should he be encouraged to make a serious commitment to it. For Giner's thoughts on religion and education see his "Prolemas urgentes de nuestra educación nacional," *Boletín de la Institución Libre de Enseñanza*, no. 509 (August 31, 1902), pp. 225–28, and no. 510 (September 30, 1902), pp. 257–63. See also Felipe Alonso Bárcena, S.J., "Cultura y tolerancia," *Razón y Fe*, XCI (April-June, 1930), pp. 481–500; José Castillejo, *War of Ideas in Spain* (London, 1937), pp. 99–100; and Antonio Zozaya, "Problemas fundamentales," *Boletín de la Institución Libre de Enseñanza*, no. 839 (March 31, 1930), p. 92.

98. On the Institución, see V. Cacho Viu, *La Institución Libre de Enseñanza*, vol. I, *Orígenes y etapa universitaria* (1962). See also Manuel Bartolomé Cossío, *La enseñanza primaria en España* (1897), published under the auspices of the Museo Pedagógico Nacional, which was affiliated with the Institución Libre de Enseñanza. One of the favorite disciples of

Sanz del Río and long associated with Giner de los Ríos, Cossío exercised perhaps the main directing influence in the Institución after Giner's death in 1915.

99. In order to retain teaching posts in the days following the restoration, professors had to abide by a February 26, 1876 decree not to expound any principles in conflict with Catholic dogma and morality. The decree was rescinded in 1882 and many of the ousted professors were restored to teaching posts, although not necessarily to the ones from which they had previously been dismissed. On this see the interview with Giner de los Ríos in Morote, El pulso, pp. 4–7. See also La cuestión universitaria, 1875: epistolario de Francisco Giner de los Ríos, Gumersindo de Azcárate, Nicolás Salmerón, published in a new edition in 1967.

100. See Trend, The Origins of Modern Spain, p. 67. On the early functioning of the Institución, see Boletín de la Institución Libre de Enseñanza, no. 844 (August 31, 1930), p. 249. As of 1885, some two hundred students were enrolled in the Institución's school from the primary through the secondary level. See ibid., no. 719 (February 29, 1920), pp. 33–38.

101. See Giner, "Problemas urgentes de nuestra educación nacional."

102. See José María González de Echevarri y Vivanco, Ruina de la falsa civilización de liberalismo (Valladolid, 1933), p. 12. Moreover, a group of Catholic professors, presided over by Adolfo Bonilla y San Martín, founded the Asociación de Amigos de la Universidad to liberate the University of Madrid from the control of the Institución Libre de Enseñanza. See Severino Aznar, Impresiones de un Demócrata Cristiano (1950, 2nd ed.), pp. 136–37.

103. Revista del Clero, no. 6 (June, 1914), p. 417.

104. Alfredo Calderón, "Mal de los males," La Unión Nacional, Diario de Pontevedra, July 26, 1900, quoted in Joaquín Costa, Oligarquía y caciquismo (1901), note 64, p. 98.

105. González Posada, España en crisis, p. 41.

106. See Altamira, Ideario político (Valencia, 1921), pp. 110–11.

107. See F. Rivera y Pastor, "El estoicismo en las ideas jurídicas de Doña Concepción Arenal," Boletín de la Institución Libre de Enseñanza, no. 719 (February 29, 1920), p. 55. Rivera convincingly establishes the degree to which Azcárate was influenced by the doctrines of upper-class sacrifice, stoicism, and abnegation constantly urged by Concepción Arenal, Spain's leading nineteenth-century feminine proponent of penal reform and charitable enterprises.

108. See Gil Cremades, El reformismo español, p. xxiii, and the excellent sketch of Azcárate and analysis of his ideas in Mercurio, no. 45 (August 1, 1905), pp. 524–26. Three of Azcárate's works revealing his early interest in the social problem are: España tras la guerra (1901), El régimen parlamentario en la práctica (1885), and Resumen de un debate en el Ateneo: el problema social (1881). See also his prologue to Antonio Royo Villanova, Cuestiones obreras (Valladolid, 1910).

109. See Moret, Comisión para la mejora ó bienestar de las clases obreras (1884).

110. González Posada at the age of twenty-two in 1862 had won a

professor-of-law chair at the University of Oviedo. Prior to this he had studied both in his native Oviedo and at the Institución Libre de Enseñanza in Madrid. His interests turning increasingly toward sociology, Posada began in 1910 to teach courses in that subject at the University of Madrid. Some of his early ideas on the social problem are found in *Socialismo y reforma social* (1904) and *La reforma social en España* (1903), which he wrote in collaboration with Pedro Sangro y Ros.

111. Álvarez Buylla, born in Oviedo in 1850, was one of the leading figures in establishing the extension program of the University of Oviedo. In this work he and his collaborators sought to put into practice the ideas of Giner de los Ríos and the Institución Libre de Enseñanza on working-class education. Some of his important publications include: *El obrero y las leyes* (1905); *La protección del obrero* (1910); *La reforma social en España* (1917).

112. On the extension work conducted under the auspices of the University of Oviedo in the attempt to achieve solidarity among the different social classes see *Anales de la Universidad de Oviedo*, Año II, 1901–1903 (Oviedo, 1904) and Aniceto Sela, *La educación nacional* (1910).

113. See Canalejas, Buylla, and Luis Morote, *El Instituto de Trabajo* (1903) and Posada, *Socialismo*, pp. 223–27.

114. On some aspects of its work, see Instituto de Reformas Sociales, *Congresos sociales*, 3 vols. (1907–1910).

115. The fact that in practice labor was nearly always represented by men with socialist ideas dismayed the delegates from the capital sector, who often pursued obstructionist policies and sought to avoid the investigation and discussion of important issues. See Sangro y Ros, *Crónica del movimiento de reforma social*, p. 20.

116. See Gil Cremades, *El reformismo español*, p. 206. Among Catholics who collaborated in the work of the Instituto were Manuel de Burgos y Mazo, Álvaro López Núñez, Severino Aznar, and Pedro Sangro y Ros.

117. Posada, *España en crisis*, p. 200. Until the demise of the Institute in 1924, Posada directed its section of legislation, bibliography, and social action and took an important role in preparing nearly all the labor legislation enacted during the period. The above work describes some of his efforts in behalf of the Institute. Posada came increasingly to advocate the restructuring of Spain along corporativist lines as is seen in his *El régimen municipal de la ciudad moderna y bosquejo del régimen local en España, Francia, Inglaterra, Estados Alemanes y Estados Unidos* (1916). Julio Puyol, also called by Azcárate to collaborate in the work of the Institute, was another Spaniard of liberal leanings who admired the corporative structure. Some of his ideas on the social problem are found in *Proceso de sindicalismo revolucionario* (1919), a discourse presented before the Real Academia de Ciencias Morales y Políticas. An early work of his, *La vida política en España* (1892), is dedicated to his "illustrious teacher and dearest friend, Gumersindo de Azcárate." Still another man of corporativist leanings who collaborated in the work of the Institute was Juan Uña y Sartou. In *Las asociaciones obreras en España* (1900) he predicts an inevitable trend toward the corporative structure as a means of

rectifying the error of the French Revolution and its imitators throughout Europe in destroying the guild system.

118. On this see Adolfo Álvarez Buylla, "Las instituciones obreras en la economía contemporánea," *Boletín de la Institución Libre de Enseñanza*, no. 506 (May 31, 1902), pp. 152–53.

119. See Álvaro López Núñez, *El seguro obrero en España* (1908), published under the auspices of the Instituto de Reformas Sociales, and Ministerio de Gobernación, España: Dirección General de la Administración, *Apuntes para el estudio y la organización en España de las instituciones de beneficencia y de previsión* (1909).

120. See José Maluquer y Salvador, *Aspectos actuariales del seguro: orientaciones de los congresos internacionales de actuarios; labor española de la fraternidad actuarial, 1914–1926* (1927); *Aspectos sociales del retiro obrero* (1924); *Instituto Nacional de Previsión, 1909–1910: resumen estadística* (1910); *Modalidades de mayor integración del país en las funciones del estado* (1920); *Publicaciones del Instituto Nacional de Previsión: el sector del seguro en nuestra política económica* (1918). See also Royo Villanova, *Cuestiones obreras*, p. 177, maintaining that the Instituto Nacional de Previsión as initially conceived was altogether inadequate in scope. Similar inadequacies are pointed to by a man active in the Instituto de Reformas Sociales: Ricardo Oyuelos y Pérez, *El programa del paro involuntario en España: proyecto de caja nacional del paro forzoso* (1917).

121. Marvá was also an important official in the Instituto de Reformas Sociales and wrote many of its *Memorias*. In addition he published works dealing with inspection of labor conditions in the Instituto's drive to safeguard workers' rights and to make certain that social legislation was actually implemented. On his work with the Instituto Nacional de Previsión, see Luis Jordana de Pozas, *El Instituto Nacional de Previsión: su obra; orientaciones presentes de los seguros sociales*, with an introduction by Marvá (1925). See also Jordana de Pozas, *Publicaciones del Instituto Nacional de Previsión: elogio de D. Álvaro López Núñez* (1942).

122. See León Martín Granizo, "A modo de prólogo: el Vizconde de Eza y su tiempo," in Marichalar, *Antología de las obras de Luis Marichalar y Monreal, el Vizconde de Eza* (1950), pp. xxxii–xxxiii.

123. González Posada, *España en crisis*, pp. 35, 58.

124. See Instituto de Reformas Sociales, *Estadística de las huelgas* (1914).

125. See Jaime Vicens Vives, *Aproximación a la historia de España* (Barcelona, 1952), p. 170.

126. Joaquín Azpiazu, S.J., "Hacia la implantación del patrón de oro en España," *Razón y Fe*, LXXXIX (October–December, 1929), p. 298.

127. See *Boletín Oficial del Ministerio de Estado*, Año XXIX, no. 4 (April, 1919), pp. 282–84.

128. See Sangro y Ros, *Crónica del movimiento de reforma social*, pp. 24–26.

NOTES TO CHAPTER 6

1. Whenever the word *raza* appears in this chapter it is employed in the concept in which Spaniards consistently—but sometimes hypocritically, it seems to me—maintain they employ it. The term, that is, is used to refer to peoples who constitute a cultural community in which the most important ties are those of common traditions, history, experiences, values, and language, not those of common ethnic or biological origins. A classic expression of this Spanish view of raza is found in José Pérez de Barradas, *Los mestizos de América* (1948). One of Spain's most eminent anthropologists, Pérez seems to reject the notion of biologically inferior or superior races. He has, however, been accused of anti-Indian prejudices by spokesmen of *indigenismo* in Spanish America. (See Howard Cline's review of Juan Comas, *Ensayos sobre indigenismo* in *Hispanic American Historical Review*, XXXIV [February, 1954], p. 56.) Pérez praises the results of *mestizaje* or race mixture in Spanish America and expresses agreement with the conclusions of the distinguished Spanish medical doctor Frederico Olóriz y Aguilera (1855–1912) that the extensive mixture of diverse biological and ethnic strains consitutes one of the major strengths of the Spanish raza in the Iberian peninsula. See Olóriz, *Índice cefálico en España* (1894). Many Spaniards, however, have remained suspicious about the results of mestizaje in the Americas, tending to regard the mestizo as psychologically unstable, owing to the fact that he is, biologically, a hybrid. For an excellent, succinct summary of one influential Spaniard's attitude on the Spanish raza see the October, 1933 essay by Miguel de Unamuno, "De nuevo la raza," in Unamuno, *Obras completas* (1968), vol. IV, bearing the title *La raza y la lengua*, pp. 648–50.

2. Altamira, *España en América* (Valencia, 1908). In *Psicología del pueblo español* (1902), Altamira deals at length with the nature of the Spanish people.

3. Valera, *Nuevas cartas americanas* (1890), p. 123.

4. Martínez Vélez, "Influencia de la raza en la civilización," *España y América*, XI (October-December, 1913), p. 56.

5. See Pedro Laín Entralgo, *La generación de noventa y ocho* (1956, 3rd ed.), p. 131.

6. Pradera, *El estado nuevo* (1941, rd ed.) p. 80.

7. Menéndez Pelayo, quoted in Laín Entralgo, *Menéndez Pelayo: historia de sus problemas intelectuales* (1944), pp. 196–97. For another excellent study see Luis Granjel, *Panorama de la Generación del 98* (1959). The material on Azorín (José Martínez y Ruiz), Pío Baroja, Ramiro de Maeztu, and Miguel de Unamuno is particularly good.

8. Laín Entralgo, *Menéndez Pelayo*, pp. 218–19.

9. Telesforo García, "Ibero-americanismo," *Unión Ibero-Americana, Número Extraordinario*, March 1, 1904, p. 20. This as well as the May 1, 1904, *Número Extraordinario* of the *Unión Ibero-Americana* are works of fundamental importance for understanding the nature of early twentieth-century hispanismo.

10. Menéndez Pidal, *España y su historia*, 2 vols. (1957), I, pp. 14–15. It is my view that when dealing with national character Spaniards, even those from their country's periphery, tend to equate the traits of the populace with those of the central Castilian area. Sobriety, gravity, and seriousness may be distinguishing features of central Castile's inhabitants, but can the same be said of Spaniards in Valencia and Málaga? And, if spiritual interests do seem often to prevail over material concerns in central Spain, can the same be said of commercial, industrial Barcelona and Bilbao? Perceptive and often penetrating as well as questionable insights on Spanish character abound in Francisco de Asís Cambó, *El pesimismo español* (Barcelona, 1917); Américo Castro, *The Structure of Spanish History*, translated by Edmund L. King (Princeton, N.J., 1954) and *The Spaniards: An Introduction to Their History*, translated by William F. King and Selma Margaretten (Berkeley, Calif., 1971); Salvador de Madariaga, *Englishmen, Frenchmen, Spaniards: An Essay in Comparative Psychology* (London, 1937); Miguel de los Oliver Tolrá, *De la psicología de los pueblos hispánicos* (Barcelona, 1914); and F. Antonio del Olmet, *El alma nacional* (1915). A monumental work that throws much light on the subject is Otis H. Green, *Spain and the Western Tradition: The Castilian Mind in Literature from El Cid to Calderón*, 4 vols. (Madison, Wis., 1963–66). Another work of fundamental importance on this topic is Claudio Sánchez Albornoz, *España, un enigma histórico*, 2 vols. (Buenos Aires, 1956). The matter is also treated in H. B. Johnson, Jr., ed., *From Reconquest to Empire: The Iberian Background to Latin American History* (New York, 1970) and in Frank Paul Casa, ed., *En busca de España* (New York, 1968).

11. Unamuno, "Sobre la europeización," *Algunas consideraciones sobre la literature hispanoamericana* (1968, 3rd ed.), pp. 121–22.

12. Ganivet, *Idearium español* (1942), p. 3.

13. Menéndez Pidal, *España y su historia*, I, p. 31.

14. See Menéndez Pidal on the stoic approach to life in *ibid.*, I, p. 15. Manuel García Morente, *Idea de la hispanidad* (1947, 3rd ed., augmented, of a work originally published in Buenos Aires in 1938), p. 73, is also among the countless commentators on the Spaniard's disdain for material possessions. His work is a significant reflective inquiry into what constitutes the nature of the Hispanic *raza* as well as an analysis of the mission of the *raza* in history. It synthesizes much of the material previously written on these matters.

15. Maeztu, quoted in Francisco Moreno Herrera, *El ser de la hispanidad* (Jerez de la Frontera, 1966), pp. 16–17.

16. Lucas Mallada, *Los males de la patria* (1890), p. 132.

17. Ganivet, *El porvenir de España* (1957 ed. of a work that appeared originally in 1898), p. 179.

18. Federico de Onís, *Ensayos sobre el sentido de la cultura española* (1932), pp. 12–15.

19. See Ricardo Macías Picavea, *El problema nacional* (1899), p. 88.

20. *Ibid.*

21. See José Luis de Arrese, *La revolución social del nacional sindicalismo* (1940), p. 171.

22. *Ibid.*, p. 172.
23. García Morente, *Idea de la hispanidad*, p. 108.
24. See Laín Entralgo, *La generación*, p. 68.
25. García Morente, *Idea de la hispanidad*, p. 8.
26. Ganivet, quoted in Laín Entralgo's prologue to Ganivet's *Idearium* p. xxx.
27. García Morente, *Idea de la hispanidad*, p. 84.
28. Arrese, *La revolución social*, p. 173.
29. Valera, *Nuevas cartas americanas*, pp. 92–93.
30. Santiago Magariños and Ramón Puigdollers, *Panhispanismo, su trascendencia histórica, política y social* (Barcelona, 1926), p. 36.
31. Eugenio Sellés, "El alma de América," *Unión Ibero-Americana, Número Extraordinario*, March 1, 1904, p. 26.
32. Silvela, interviewed by Jesús Pando y Valle, *ibid.*, p. 9.
33. Labra, *El problema hispano-americano* (1906), p. 36. Similar views were later expressed by Emilio Zurano Muñoz, *Valor y fuerza de España como potencia en el concierto internacional* (1922). Zurano argues that Spain and Spanish America are part of the same whole; when separated, neither one is at its best.
34. Menéndez Pidal, *España y su historia*, I, p. 66.
35. *Ibid.*, II, p. 680.
36. See Ángel Álvarez de Miranda, "El pensamiento de Unamuno sobre hispanoamérica," *Cuadernos Hispanoamericanos*, no. 13 (January-February, 1950), pp. 57–58. In lavishly praising the novel *La gloria de Don Ramiro: una vida en tiempo de Felipe II* (1908) by the Argentine Enrique Larreta, Unamuno declared that the novelist had been altogether successful in capturing the true spirit of Spain. The reason for this, he suggested, was that Argentina, more than most Argentines realized, is Spain. No Englishman, no German, and least of all a Frenchman or an Italian, opined Unamuno, could so successfuly have understood and empathized with the Spanish spirit. See Unamuno, *Temas argentinos* (Buenos Aires, 1943), pp. 173–96. Conversely, Unamuno insisted that as a Spaniard he could understand Spanish America without ever having to visit there personally. Thus he felt eminently qualified to write on virtually all aspects of Spanish-American life even though he did not set foot in the New World. For this he was often, and with ample reason I believe, criticized by Spanish Americans.
37. November 16, 1939 discourse pronounced in the Museo de Arte Decorativo of Buenos Aires commemorating the twenty-fifth anniversary of the Institución Cultural Española, in Ortega y Gasset, *Meditación del pueblo joven* (1964), p. 65. The work consists of essays and discourses written between 1916, the date of Ortega's first visit to Buenos Aires, and 1953.
38. *Ibid.*, p. 85.
39. For an evidence of this belief see the work by the popular novelist, military writer, and artillery colonel Francisco J. de Moya y Jiménez, *Exégesis de la nacionalidad hispanoamericana* (Cádiz, 1912), esp. p. 9.
40. Discourse by Eduardo Pérez de Agudo at a June 18, 1924 banquet organized for him in Barcelona by the Spanish-American diplomatic

and consular corps, *Unión Ibero-Americana*, Año XXXVIII (August, 1924), p. 42. Pérez had just completed a series of conferences, inaugurated in October of 1923, on Spanish America.

41. Luis de Zulueta, minister of state at the time, in an address to the representatives of Spanish America at the League of Nations, stressed the "community of culture" concept. He preferred, he said, to consider this sort of community rather than to emphasize ties of race, for race connoted ethnic and biological factors and thus in its meaning had too strong a connection with material factors. On the other hand "community of culture" denoted spiritual ties and was more appropriate for describing the Spanish family in which spiritual always took precedence over material considerations. See Zulueta, "Las relaciones hispanoamericanas," *España y América: Revista Comercial* (Cádiz), no. 244 (December, 1932), p. 136. This review appeared between 1912 and 1936 and is not to be confused with the Augustinian, Madrid-published *España y América* that first appeared in 1903.

42. See Silvela interview by Pando y Valle, *Unión Ibero-Americana*, p. 10.

43. Sánchez de Toca, *Del poder naval en España y su política económica para la nacionalidad ibero-americana* (1898), pp. 385–86.

44. Francisco Gutiérrez Lasanta, *Rubén Darío, el poeta de hispanidad* (Zaragoza, 1962), p. 8.

45. See Altamira, *España en América*, p. 173, and *La Unión Hispano-Americana*, no. 63 (January 11, 1922), p. 10. Beginning publication in 1916 under the direction of the Mexican Rodolfo Reyes, this periodical was supported in part by the Madrid Centro de Cultura Hispano-Americana. The Centro was founded in 1910 under the auspices of José Canalejas. Liberal senator Luis Palomo served for many years as its president.

46. See the Pérez de Agudo discourse, *Unión Ibero-Americana*, p. 42.

47. Conde de Romanones, "La Universidad de Salamanca," *Unión Ibero-Americana*, *Número Extraordinario*, March 1, 1904, p. 27.

48. See Maura's reply to the discourse of Ricardo León y Román upon the latter's reception into the Real Academia Española de la Lengua on January 1, 1915, in León, *La voz de la sangre: ensayos españoles* (1944, 5th ed.), pp. 33–35.

49. Altamira, *España en América*, pp. 37–38.

50. Altamira, *Mi viaje a América: libro de documentos* (1911), pp. 516–17.

51. Unamuno, "Comunidad de la lengua hispánica," in *Temas argentinos*, p. 164.

52. Ibid., p. 178.

53. Unamuno's prologue to José Santos Chocano, *Alma América* (1906), p. xvii.

54. Unamuno, "Comunidad de la lengua hispánica," pp. 178–79.

55. Menéndez Pelayo, introduction to the *Antología de poetas hispano-americanos*, reproduced in *Unión Ibero-Americana*, Año XXVI (May–June, 1912), p. 19.

56. Eduardo Gómez de Baquero, "Nacionalismo e hispanismo," *Revista de las Españas*, no. 29 (March, 1929), pp. 76–77.

57. Reyes, "La IV Conferencia Panamericana," *ibid.*, nos. 20–21 (April–May, 1928), p. 165.

58. Admittedly, many conservatives would have maintained that religion was more important even than language in creating a Hispanic raza out of apparently disparate elements.

59. See, for example, the discourse presented in the Ateneo of Madrid by the respected Spanish philologist and liberal politician Manuel Rodríguez-Navas, reported in *Cultura Hispano-Americana*, no. 31, (June 15, 1919), pp. 5-6. Founded in 1912, *Cultura Hispano-Americana* was the official organ of the Centro de Cultura Hispano-Americana. See note 45.

60. Altamira, *España en América*, pp. 38–39. Menéndez Pidal, *España y su historia*, II, p. 699, agreed upon the need to defend the language: "This lovely language, the basis of spiritual fraternity [between Spain, Spanish America, and the Philippines], in which so many geniuses of the Old and New Worlds have expressed themselves; this lovely language, molded by our will, our intelligence, our sensibilities, our fantasies, has its life and its destinies in our hands." Similar sentiments are expressed by Ángel Pulido Fernández, *Desarrollo, esplendor y soberanía de la lengua española* (1921).

61. See *La Ilustración Española y Americana*, January 22, 1900, p. 38.

62. See Ricardo Becero de Bengoa, "Por ambos mundos," *ibid.*, October 22, 1900, pp. 242–43. Quesada's book was *El problema del idioma nacional* (Buenos Aires, 1900). Quesada was concerned by the influence of Italian immigrants in modifying the Spanish language in Argentina. His book was also a rejoinder to Luciano Abeille, *El idioma nacional de los argentinos* (Buenos Aires, 1899). Abeille, a French philologist of modest ability and reputation who had emigrated to Argentina, advocated the development of an Argentine national tongue distinct from Spanish. A further defense of the purity of the language was made by Quesada in *Nuestra raza* (Buenos Aires, 1900).

63. The works's full title was *Diccionario de construcción y régimen de la lengua castellana* (Paris, 1886). It carried only through the letter D. Another important work by Cuervo is *Apuntaciones críticas sobre el lenguaje bogotano* (Bogotá, 1967), revised by him just before his death in 1911. In some ways Cuervo regarded himself as carrying on the work of an earlier Spanish-American philologist, Andrés Bello. In 1847 Bello had warned that Spanish might go the way of Latin, breaking up into different tongues, unless a sustained effort was made to guard its purity. These views of Bello had been bitterly attacked by the Argentine Domingo Faustino Sarmiento. On Cuervo see Pedro Fabo, *Rufino José Cuervo y la lengua castellana*, 3 vols. (Bogotá, 1912), the work of a Spanish Augustinian living at the time in Bogotá. In it Cuervo is praised both for his ardent Catholicism and for his key role in preserving the purity of the language in Colombia.

64. Cuervo, "La lengua materna," *Unión Ibero-Americana*, Año XXXVI (September-October, 1922), pp. 46–47.

65. On this see Menéndez Pidal, *La unidad del idioma* (1944), a pamphlet-length study without pagination.

66. Bayle, "Examen de libros," *Razón y Fe*, *LXXI* (January-April, 1925), p. 102.

67. Antonio Balbín Unquera, "El gusto español clásico y el extranjero en América," *Unión Ibero-Americana*, *Número Extraordinario*, March 1, 1904, pp. 33–35.

68. Manuel de Sarlegui y Medina, discourse on his reception into the Real Academia Española de la Lengua, "Por la pureza del idioma castellano," *Unión Ibero-Americana*, Año XXVIII (May, 1914), pp. 4–6.

69. T. Navarro Tomás, "El idioma español en el 'cine' parlante," *Revista de las Españas*, nos. 48–49 (August-September, 1930), p. 420, italics added.

70. Julio Saavedra, "Lo americano en Castilla," *España y América*, XV (July-September, 1907), p. 31. Saavedra directed his criticism particularly against Julio Cejador, an important Spanish philologist who between 1900 and 1907 had published some nine books on the Spanish language. Cejador was accused of typifying the "haughty conceit" of peninsulares that led them to assume that only they were competent to pronounce upon correct languauge usage in Spanish America. On this matter see also Juan María Gutiérrez, *Cartas de un porteño: polémica en torno al idioma y a la Real Academia Española, sostenido con Juan Martínez Villegas, sequida de "Sarmienticideo"* (Buenos Aires, 1942), the statement by the Argentine Gutiérrez on his refusal to accept election to the Real Academia.

71. Unamuno, *Temas argentinos*, p. 107. In 1917 the Unión Ibero-Americana took cognizance of the resentment generated among Spanish Americans by Spanish insistence upon monopolistic control over the language. Spain, the Unión asserted, could not intervene directly in telling Spanish-American countries how to maintain the purity of the language. It could, though, perform this task indirectly by vastly increasing the export of well-written Spanish books to Spanish America. See *Boletín Oficial del Ministerio de Estado*, Año XXVII, no. 6 (June, 1916), pp. 367–69.

72. Unamuno, *Temas argentinos*, p. 107.

73. See Menéndez Pidal, *La unidad del idioma*, and *España y su historia*, II, p. 684.

74. Altamira, *España en América*, p. 171. Emilio Zurano, *Alianza hispanoamericana* (1926), pp. 10–13, 210–11, agreed upon the need for an alliance of the Spanish-speaking people in order to maintain spiritual values within and ultimately to "respiritualize the world."

75. See the Aznar essay written in 1919 in his *Impresiones de un Demócrata Cristiano* (1950, 2nd ed.), p. 138. Aznar conceded (p. 145) the possibility that at some time in the distant future hegemony over the league or new empire of Hispanic peoples might be transferred to the other side of the ocean. For at least the immediate future, however, it would have to be exercised by Spain. Along similar lines geographer and University of Sevilla professor Germán Latorre y Setién, *El panamericanismo y el porvenir de la América española* (Sevilla, 1924, 2nd ed.), p. 124, stated: "Spain, with the republics of Spanish America, should occupy in the future its natural role of older sister. . . ." Joaquín Sánchez de Toca also insisted upon Spanish hegeomony over the patria mayor of Iberian

peoples that he envisioned. See his "Ideales de patria mayor," *Unión Ibero-Americana, Número Extraordinario,* March 1, 1904, pp. 9–15.

76. Azcárate, "La fiesta de la raza," *Unión Ibero-Americana,* Año XXX (January, 1916), p. xx.

77. Vázquez de Mella, essay of 1915 in *Dogmas nacionales* (1946, 2nd ed.), pp. 174–76. Ramiro Flórez, "Aproximación hispanoamericana," *Unión Ibero-Americana,* Año XXXVIII (January, 1924), p. 50, developed ideas similar to those of Mella: "Hispanoamericanismo, this lovely word forms a part of the program of all the political parties of Spain. This lovely word, which rings so pleasantly in the ears of all Spaniards who are aware of the destinies of their country and of the future reserved to it on the other side of the Atlantic, embraces an unlimited number of aspirations, spiritual, political, and material, to the study and realization of which we must consecrate ourselves with the greatest faith and enthusiasm, because this constitutes the most agreeable, necessary, promising, transcendent end of our nation, from the international point of view."

78. Sánchez de Toca, *Del poder naval,* pp. 240–42.

79. Ramón de Basterra, "El nacionalismo mundial," *Revista de las Españas,* nos. 20–21 (April-May, 1928), pp. 147-49.

80. For indications of this see Lucas Mallada, *Los males de la patria,* p. 28; Laín Entralgo, *La generación,* p. 218; M. Rodríguez-Navas, "Concepto español del americanismo," *Cultura Hispano-Americana,* no. 39 (March, 1916), p. 38.

81. Federico Rahola, *Sangre nueva: impresiones de un viaje a la América del sur* (Barcelona, 1905), pp. 120–24. Rahola (1858–1919) served as secretary of the Congreso Nacional Mercantil, one of the many assemblies organized to celebrate the fourth centennial of the Columbus discovery in 1892.

82. González Posada, *La República Argentina: impresiones y comentarios* (1912), pp. 108–14.

83. Fernando G. del Valle y Rojas, "A mis hermanos de Ibero-América," *España y América: Revista Comercial,* no. 21 (May, 1914), pp. 350–52.

84. See *Unión Ibero-Americana, Número Extraordinario,* March 1, 1904, p. 17.

85. See Emilio Zurano, *Alianza hispanoamericana,* pp. 38–39, 67, and Pedro Sáinz Rodríguez, *La evolución de las ideas sobre la decadencia española* (1924), p. 41. Zurano further states (pp. 52–53) that only the united efforts of the Spanish raza could avert social catastrophe. If not united, then all countries of the Spanish world would fall victim, one by one, to social revolution.

86. See Jesús Pando y Valle, "El problema de la raza," *Unión Ibero-Americana,* Año XXI (November, 1907), pp. 3–6.

87. P. Martínez Vélez, "Desde el Perú," *España y América,* XXXVII (January-March, 1913), p. 153. Another conservative Catholic, Antonio Goicoechea, *La obra pasada y la actual de España en América* (Montevideo, 1928), pp. 10, 17, declared that Spain had been able to maintain social peace in the Indies because the colonial period had been a Catholic period. In collaboration with the Catholic elements of the independent

republics, Spain could, he proclaimed, lead Spanish America back to the formulas that had once assured and could again guarantee social stability.

88. "Discurso del Señor Obispo titular de Temos, Monseñor Andrea," *Unión Ibero-Americana*, Año XXXVI (May-June, 1922), p. 25.

89. Benjamín E. del Castillo, president of the Consejo Superior de Mutualidad y Previsión Social de Buenos Aires, "La cuestión social en España y América," *ibid.*, Año XXXVIII (April, 1924), pp. 54–55.

90. Labra, "La nota americana del centenario de Cádiz," *España y América: Revista Comercial*, no. 1 (September, 1921), p. 3.

91. On Giner's reaction to *Ariel*, see Luis Morote, "Las ciencias sociales en la América latina," *Unión Ibero-Americana, Número Extraordinario*, March 1, 1904, p. 51. On Altamira's, see his prologue to *Ariel* (Barcelona, 1926, 3rd ed.).

92. See the Alas prologue to Rodó's *Ariel* (Valencia, no date), pp. ix, xi, xii. Spaniards also welcomed Rodó's spirited defense of Christian charity contained in his short work of 1906, *Liberalismo y jacobinismo*, generally included in editions of *Ariel* published in Spain. Christian charity, Rodó contended, gave a new lease on life to the aristocratic concepts and social structure of the classical age. Prior to the emergence of Christian charity, the aristocracy had often been disdainful of the humble, thereby in the long run jeopardizing the elitist structure of society.

93. Rodríguez-Navas, "España y América: espiritualidad hispano-americana," *Cultura Hispano-Americana*, no. 75 (February, 1919), pp. 26–28. Similar views are expressed by two liberal disciples of Altamira, Santiago Magariños and Ramón Puigdollers, *Panhispanismo*, pp. 48–52.

94. See *Unión Ibero-Americana*, Año XXXVIII (November-December, 1924), p. 9.

95. See Reyes's speech welcoming Altamira to Mexico in Altamira, *Mi viaje a América*, pp. 378–79, and Reyes, who was living then in Bilbao, "El trabajo español en América," *La Unión Hispano-Americana*, no. 63 (January 11, 1922), pp. 8–10.

96. See José Maluquer y Salvador, "Reformas sociales en los estados Ibero-Americanos," *Unión Ibero-Americana, Número Extraordinario*, March 1, 1904, pp. 53–54.

97. See, for example, the statement by the Bishop of Jaca in *ibid.*, pp. 27–28.

98. See Goicoechea, *La obra pasada*, pp. 18–19.

99. See Carlos Badía Malacrida, *El factor geográfico en la política sudamericana* (1944, ed. of work first published in 1919), pp. 29–30.

100. See Juan Pérez de Guzmán, "Elecciones presidenciales en América," *La Ilustración Española y Americana*, July 30, 1904, p. 62.

101. See Adolfo Bonilla y San Martín, *Viaje a los Estados Unidos de América y al oriente* (1926), p. 35, the impressions of a distinguished conservative philosopher and literary critic who went to the United States for a short period in order to lecture at several universities.

102. See Magariños and Puigdollers, *Panhispanismo*, p. 94.

103. Constantino Suárez: *La verdad desnuda: sobre relaciones entre España y América* (1924), p. 49.

104. Badía, *El factor geográfico*, p. 35.

105. See *Unión Ibero-Americana*, Año XXII (April, 1908), p. 81.

106. Jesús Pando y Valle, "El programa de la raza," *ibid.*, Año XXI (November, 1907), pp. 3–4.

107. E. P. Latino, "Una catastrofe industrial," *ibid.* (October, 1907), pp. 24–25.

108. Roberto de Galaín, "¿Conquistadores ó conquistados?" *Cultura Hispano-Americana*, no. 37 (December, 1914), pp. 33–34.

109. See prologue by Alas to *Ariel*, p. xiv, and Emilio Zurano, *Alianza hispanoamericana*, pp. 85–98.

110. Pérez de Guzmán, "Elecciones presidenciales en América," p. 62.

111. Luis de Armiñán repeatedly makes this point in *El panamericanismo: ¿que es? ¿que se propone? ¿como contrarrestarlo?* (1900).

112. Magariños and Puigdollers, *Panhispanismo*, p. 117.

113. Two books that stress the menace of the United States to the political independence of Spanish America are: Ricardo Beltrán y Rózpide, *Los pueblos hispanoamericanos en el siglo XX* (1904), the work of a well-known geographer (1852–1928) who for many years was the secretary of the Real Sociedad Geográfica de Madrid, and Juan del Nido y Segalvera, *La unión ibérica: estudio crítico-histórico de este problema* (1914). *España Moderna*, a Madrid periodical published between 1889 and 1914, frequently harped on the threat of United States imperialism to the sovereignty of Spanish-American republics.

114. See *Mercurio* (Barcelona), no. 27 (February 1, 1904), p. 23.

115. See Badía, *El factor geográfico*, p. 26.

116. See Camilo Barcía Trelles, *Doctrina de Monroe y cooperación internacional* (1931), p. 73. Barcía Trelles was the first Spanish professor brought to the United States by the Carnegie Endowment for International Peace to study international law and policy. The cited work was researched by Barcía in Washington, 1928–1929. Similar observations appear in Juan Pérez de Guzmán, "Relaciones políticas entre España y las repúblicas ibero-americanas," *Unión Ibero-Americana*, *Número Extraordinario*, March 1, pp. 12–14; "Memoria presentada en el día último de diciembre de 1914 al Señor Ministro de Instrucción Pública por Luis Palomo, presidente del Centro de Cultura Hispano-Americana," *Cultura Hispano-Americana*, no. 26 (January 15, 1915), pp. 2–3; Marqués de Olivart, "Origen y desarrollo de la Doctrina de Drago y su aceptación parcial por la segunda conferencia de la paz," *Unión Ibero-Americana*, Año XXII (November, 1908), p. 21.

117. See José María González, *El día de Colón y de la paz* (Oviedo, 1933), p. 101.

118. See Gutiérrez Lasanta, *Rubén Darío*, p. 74; Eusebio Negrete, "Después del último congreso panamericano," *España y América*, Año V (January–March, 1907), pp. 33–44; and G. Latorre y Setién, *El panamericanismo*, pp. 13–14.

119. Among Spanish Americans whom Spaniards most frequently praised for recognizing the danger of the United States and the consequent need for a united Spanish raza were the Argentines Manuel Ugarte and Roque Saenz Peña, the Mexicans Rodolfo Reyes and Carlos Pereyra, the Colombian Santiago Pérez Triana, the Chilean Valentín Letelier, the

Venezuelan Rufino Blanco Fombona, the Peruvians Francisco and Ventura García Calderon, José Santos Chocano, and Javier Prado, and the Nicaraguan Rubén Darío. See, for example, Badía, *El factor geográfico*, pp. 35, 91, 128; Emilio Zurano, *Alianza hispanoamericana*, p. 173; Moya y Jiménez, *Exégesis de la nacionalidad hispanoamericana*, pp. 10–11; and *Unión Ibero-Americana, Número Extraordinario*, March 1, 1904, pp. 34–38, 51. Spaniards also praised Nicaraguan dictator José Santos Zelaya for standing up to the United States. See *Unión Ibero-Americana*, Año XXI (August, 1907), p. 9. In similar manner they praised Venezuelan dictator Cipriano Castro for his resistance to the "Machiavellian mercantilism" of the Colossus. In praising Castro, Spanish journalist A. Pando, "El General Castro, Presidente de Venezuela," *Ibid.*, Año XXI (February, 1907), p. 6, wrote: "Thanks to men such as this our raza will come to have in America the influence and power that legitimately correspond to it."

120. Armiñán, "El porvenir," *Unión Ibero-Americana, Número Extraordinario*, March 1, 1904, p. 8. Luis Palomo, president of the Centro de Cultura Hispano-Americana, in his prologue to Rufino Blanco-Fombona, *Le evolución política y social de Hispanoamérica* (1911), predicted that the triumph of the Spanish raza in its confrontation with the Anglo-Saxons in America was inevitable.

121. Alas concedes this in the prologue to *Ariel*, p. xiv, as does Badía, *El factor geográfico*, p. 35.

122. Spanish liberals were perturbed by Martiniano Leguizamón, *De capa criolla* (Buenos Aires, 1906). In this work by an Argentine, Spain is pictured as culturally backward, economically stagnant, religously fanatical, and therefore basically opposed to the liberal, modern spirit said to prevail in Argentina. Unamuno, *Temas argentinos*, p. 37 ff., conceded that this was the view which many Spanish Americans held of Spain.

NOTES TO CHAPTER 7

1. Krause, *Ideal de la humanidad para la vida*, translated by Julián Sanz del Río (1860), p. 138.

2. *Ibid.*, p. 217.

3. *Ibid.*, pp. 154–55, 219–20.

4. Antonio Goicoechea, *La crisis del constitucionalismo moderno* (1925), pp. 36–37.

5. Federico Rahola, *Sangre nueva: impresiones de un viaje a la América del sud* (Barcelona, 1905), p. 14. See also Fructuoso Carpena, *Antropología criminal* (1909). At the turn of the century Carpena had toured Cuba, Mexico, Panama, Argentina, Costa Rica, and other Spanish-American republics to spread his ideas on prison reform and criminal rehabilitation. He felt that he found a more favorable cultural climate for his reform ideas in the New World than in the peninsula.

6. Blasco Ibáñez, "Porvenir de América," *Unión Ibero-Americana*, Año XXIII (October, 1909), pp. 1–2.

7. Canalejas evidenced a deepening interest in Spanish America and

had he not been assassinated apparently would have appointed Palomo minister of the navy in one move toward inaugurating a government-supported program of hispanismo.

8. Palomo, quoted in R. García Moreno, "Emigracíon y comercio," *Unión Ibero-Americana*, Año XXII (January, 1908), p. 7.

9. December 6, 1916, discourse of Ortega y Gasset, "Impresiones de un viajero," delivered in the Instituto Popular de Conferencias, Buenos Aires, reproduced in *Meditación del pueblo joven* (1964 ed.), pp. 18–19.

10. Blanco-Fombona, "La raza latino-americana," *Unión Ibero-Americana*, Año XXIII (November, 1909), p. 1.

11. See García Moreno, "Emigración y comercio," p. 7. The Centro de Cultura Hispano-Americana, presided over by Palomo, was dedicated to preserving "in the old and the new Spains the disinterested spiritualism which seeks the sources of good and of human progress in culture, education, and integrity." See *Cultura Hispano-Americana*, nos. 140–141 (January–February, 1925), pp. 1–2.

12. Enrique Gómez Carillo, *El encanto de Buenos Aires: crónicas, cuadros y opiniones* (1921), pp. 46–47. The author, a prominent literary figure, was for a time director of *El Liberal* in Madrid. Spanish liberals delighted also in the founding of the Buenos Aires Unión Latino-Americano in the mid-1920's. Its main purposes included waging "the struggle against all influences of the Church in the public and educational life and the wide extension of obligatory and gratuitous laic or neutral education." See "Noticias Generales," *Razón y Fe*, LXXII (May–August, 1925), p. 393.

13. See *Unión Hispano-Americana*, no. 64 (February, 1922), pp. 28–30. Paraguay was also singled out for praise in 1904 because of its "dizzy rate" or economic progress. See *Mercurio*, no. 33 (August 1, 1904), p. 169. In his book *El peregrino en Indias* (1912), Ciro Bayo, a Spaniard who had spent the better part of eight years in the Oriente region of Bolivia, describes the region's vast potential wealth.

14. In *Mercurio*, the important liberal organ of hispanismo published in Barcelona (1901-1915) under the direction of Federico Rahola, Argentina and Mexico were the only Spanish-American republics to which separate sections were devoted.

15. Santiago Pérez Triana, "Crónica internacional: la lección de México," *Mercurio*, no. 31, (June 1, 1904), pp. 131–32.

16. Juan Pérez de Guzmán, "Elecciones presidenciales en América," *La Ilustración Española y Americana*, July 30, 1904, p. 62.

17. David de Monjoy, "La política de Porfirio Díaz," *Mercurio*, no. 36 (November 1, 1904), p. 254.

18. González Posada, *En América: una campaña* (1911), pp. 14–15.

19. Gómez Carillo, *El encanto de Buenos Aires*, pp. 226–29. In a similar vein there appear in *Nuestra raza: estudios biográficos de contemporáneos hispano-americanos*, edited by Saturnino Huerta-Rodrigo, M. Rey, Samuel Tena Lacén, and Segundo L. de Angulo (1907), lavishly laudatory biographical sketches of successful Spanish and Spanish-American businessmen. The work frequently alludes to the bright economic

future of Spanish America and narrates some of the rags-to-riches success stories of Spanish emigrants in the New World republics.

20. A Spaniard particularly concerned with creating a liberal image of his country in Chile was Javier Fernández Pesquero, a Madrid novelist born in 1873. Two of his important books dealing with hispanismo are *España en Chile* (Cádiz, 1910) and *El iberoamericanismo y su influencia en la grandeza de la raza latina* (Cádiz, 1908). In a similar vein are Ramón Orbea, *La reconquista de América*, with a prologue by Jesús Pando y Valle (1905) and José Plá y Casadevall, *La misión internacional de la raza hispánica*, with a prologue by the Uruguayan writer Benjamín Fernández y Medina (1928). Orbea, a Spaniard who had lived for sixteen years in Argentina, where he conducted his university studies, was commissioned by the Argentine government to undertake a study and propaganda mission in Spain. In his book, written after the tour, he describes the emergence of a new and modern Spain that will have an important economic relationship with Argentina. Plá y Casadevall, a prominent Catalan literary figure, also described a new and modernized Spain.

21. Labra, *El problema hispano-americano* (1906), p. 73. See also Labra, *América y España en el centenario de 1908* (1909), arguing that liberal Spaniards collaborated with Spanish Americans in the independence movement and asserting that liberals of the Hispanic raza must resume their fruitful cooperation.

22. Labra, *España y América, 1812–1912: estudios políticos, históricos y de derecho internacional* (1912), pp. 382–84.

23. *Ibid.*, p. 286. The University of Oviedo faculty in the early twentieth century took a leading role in the propaganda campaign to convince Spanish America that Spain was indeed undergoing transformation into a modern, progressive, liberal state. See the discourse of Rafael González de Castejón in response to the address by Faustino Álvarez de Manzón on the latter's reception into the Real Academia de Ciencias Morales y Políticas, February 12, 1911, quoted in Juan José Gil Cremades, *El reformismo español: Krausismo, escuela histórica, neotomismo* (1969), p. 203.

24. Maeztu, quoted in Javier Fernández Pesquero, *España ante el concepto americano* (1923?), p. 167.

25. See John E. Englekirk, "El hispanoamericanismo y la generación de 98," *Revista Ibero-Americana*, II (November, 1940), pp. 328–29.

26. See Gutiérrez, quoted in Rufino Blanco-Fombona, *Motivos y letras de España* (1930), p. 65 ff. On this matter see also William Baker Bristol, "Hispanidad in South America, 1936–1945" (unpublished doctoral dissertation, University of Pennsylvania, 1947), p. 72.

27. Romanones, "España Rediviva: fe en la voluntud," *Mercurio*, no. 46 (September 1, 1905), p. 559.

28. Unamuno, essay written in 1906, *Temas argentinos* (Buenos Aires, 1943), p. 23.

29. See *Mercurio*, no. 33 (August 1, 1904), p. 197.

30. See the Ramiro de Maeztu prologue to Arguedas, *Un pueblo enfermo* (Barcelona, 1909), reproduced in Maeztu, *Autobiografía* (1962), vol. I in *Obras de . . .*, pp. 197–204.

31. González Posada, *En América*, p. 84.

32. Altamira, *Cuestiones internacionales: España, América y los Estados Unidos* (1916), pp. 54–55.

33. See Altamira, *España y el programa americanista* (1917), pp. 225–29.

34. *Unión Ibero-Americana,* Año XXXVIII (October, 1924), pp. 92–98.

35. The optimistic report conceded that the deficit had increased but maintained that even in this respect Spain enjoyed an enviable position in comparison to other countries.

36. Constantino Suárez, *La verdad desnuda: sobre las relaciones entre España y América* (1924), p. 69. Migrating to Cuba in 1906 in extremely humble circumstances, Suárez made a fortune in the textile business. Subsequently he carried out an extensive campaign to end Spain's indifference toward Spanish America. In particular he sought greater government support for Spanish emigrants in Spanish America.

37. See Altamira, *Mi viaje a América: libro de documentos* (1911), p. 510.

38. *Ibid.,* pp. 24–25.

39. Altamira, *España en América* (Valencia, 1908), pp. 54–57.

40. Editorial of *El Imparcial* reproduced in Altamira, *Mi viaje,* p. 24.

41. Quoted in Altamira, *Mi viaje,* pp. 12–14.

42. Rodríguez de Armas, quoted in *ibid.,* pp. 461–62.

43. See *ibid.,* pp. 39–41.

44. *Ibid.,* p. 118.

45. Altamira continued for many years thereafter to be impressed by the strength of this spiritual affinity. See his *La huella de España en América* (1924).

46. Altamira, *Mi viaje,* pp. 510–11, 515.

47. *Ibid.,* pp. 529–32.

48. *Ibid.,* pp. 493–97.

49. *Ibid.,* p. 524.

50. See González Posada, *En América,* p. 7.

51. González Posada, *La República Argentina: impresiones y comentarios* (1912).

52. González Posada, *En América,* pp. 15–16.

53. Rodó, quoted in *ibid.,* pp. 42–43.

54. See *ibid.,* esp. pp. 68–69. Posada's continuing interest in Spanish-American cooperation in resolving social problems is evidenced by the prologue he wrote to the work of the Argentine statesman Carlos Saavedra Lamas, *Tratados internacionales de tipo social* (1923).

55. The Uruguayan José Virginio Díaz was among the many Spanish Americans who disagreed with this approach. In *Problemas sociales del Uruguay* (Montevideo, 1916) he argued that the people of the New World should aspire to better social conditions and to greater freedom than could be achieved in the tradition-bound, decadent Old World. The prevalence of this view in Spanish America was one of the greatest obstacles to hispanismo.

56. González Posada, *La República Argentina,* pp. 322–23.

57. Among the many works stressing the United States menace to

Spanish America at the time of World War I are Carlos Badía, *El factor geográfico en la política sudamericana* (1919), and Edmundo González Blanco, *Iberismo y germanismo: España ante el conflicto europeo* (Valencia and Buenos Aires, 1917). The latter study, written by a philosopher whose career was cut short by a premature death, urged a federation of Spain, Portugal, and the Ibero-American states as the only means of preserving Iberian ideals in the Western Hemisphere. Once such a confederation was formed it should, he advised, seek an alliance with Germany.

58. See Altamira, *Cuestiones internacionales*, esp. p. 15, and Labra, "Simpáticas expresiones hispano-americanistas en el senado español," *La Unión Hispano-Americana*, no. 2 (December 11, 1916), pp. 2–4.

59. By no means all liberals agreed on this approach. Federico Rahola, for example, *Programa americanista postguerra* (Barcelona, 1917), felt that no good could come from Spanish collaboration with the United States. Aurelio Ras, *Panhispania* (Barcelona, 1922), was in accord, insisting on the need for combating United States economic expansion into Spanish America so as to preserve the area's true culture. On this matter see also Germán Latorre y Setién, *El panamericanismo y el porvenir de la América española* (Sevilla, 1924, 2nd ed.), p. 46, and Bristol, "Hispanidad, pp. 34–35.

60. The liberal philologist Manuel Rodríguez-Navas provides a typical example of this viewpoint. Closely associated with Luis Palomo's Centro de Cultura Hispano-Americana, his articles published in the Centro's journal, *Cultura Hispano-Americana*, were decidedly hostile to the United States. Then, beginning in 1919, a new spirit became apparent in his writings as he came to recognize the inevitable economic predominance of the United States in Spanish America and to urge Spanish collaboration with the Colossus. As a result of such collaboration he hoped that Spain would be allowed a free rein by the United States in carrying out cultural activities aimed at protecting the spiritual values of the former colonies. Rodríguez-Navas also stressed the importance of language in maintaining ties between Spain and Spanish America. In 1918, under the auspices of the Centro, he published the *Diccionario general y técnico hispanoamericano*. Appearing in a third edition in 1924, this dictionary claimed a listing of six thousand more words than that of the Real Academia Española, being more inclined to accept new American usages and words. On this matter see *Cultura Hispano-Americana*, nos. 140–141 (January–February, 1925), pp. 4–5.

61. Santiago Magariños and Ramón Puigdollers, *Panhispanismo: su trascendencia histórica, política, y social*, with a prologue by Rafael Altamira (Barcelona, 1926), pp. 94, 105–106.

62. Altamira, "Espana, los Estados Unidos y América," *Revista de las Españas*, nos. 7–8 (March–April, 1927), pp. 175–77. A similar idea had been expressed at an earlier time by the Mexican Rodolfo Reyes in welcoming Altamira to Mexico in 1910. See Altamira, *Mi viaje*, pp. 370–71. Moreover, the former president of Colombia, Rafael Reyes developed the idea more fully in 1915. See *Cultura Hispano-Americana*, no. 29 (April 15, 1915), esp. pp. 6–10.

63. Federico de Onís, *Ensayos sobre el sentido de la cultura española* (1932), pp. 137–58.

64. *Ibid.*, pp. 169–73.

65. Prologue of Romanones to Rafael Hernández-Usera, *De América y de España: probelmas y orientaciones de 1920 a 1922* (1922), pp. 16–18. In this book the Puerto Rican Hernández-Usera contends that Spanish and United States culture were not destined to eternal conflict. To the contrary, they were becoming ever more compatible. Consequently, he urged Spanish–United States cooperation in dealing with Spanish America. The essays comprising his book first appeared as a series of articles in Madrid's leading liberal newspaper *El Sol*. On hispanismo in the United States see Miguel Romera-Navarro, *El hispanismo en Norte América* (1917), and Stanley T. Williams, *The Spanish Background of American Literature*, 2 vols. (New Haven, Conn., 1955).

66. In the 1920s Spanish socialists such as Luis Araquistain intensified their anti-Yankee fervor. See, for example, Araquistain, *La agonía antillana* (1928), and *El peligro yanqui* (1919). In appealing to Spanish Americans, then, on the ever-popular basis of anti-Yankee sentiments, Spanish liberals tended to lose out on the left to socialists and exponents of radical social change and on the right to the conservatives, who throughout the 1920's remained steadfast in their traditional anti-United States viewpoints.

67. See Ugarte's introduction to his *El porvenir de la América española: la raza; la integridad teritorial y moral; la organización interior. Edición definitiva, corregida y aumentada por el autor* (1920).

68. Indications of this approach, one which was obviously perturbing to hispanoamericanistas, were provided by José Gaxiola, *La frontera de la raza: Hispano-América* (1917), the work of a Mexican who pleads for the unity of the Latin-Indian raza in America to withstand the United States menace and who sees no need for ties with Spain, and José Ingenieros, *Para la unión latino-americana* (Buenos Aires, 1922), in which the distinguished Argentine intellectual urges unity of the Latin American republics and shows as much hostility toward Spain as toward the United States.

69. See, for example, the highly favorable articles published in the Cádiz periodical *España y América: Revista Comercial* during 1916 and 1917. Particularly significant are "El despertar de un país: México, batallador y heróico," no. 53 (January, 1917), pp. 11–12, and no. 56 (April, 1917), pp. 54–57, dealing with the pro-Revolutionary attitudes of two long-time liberal leaders in the hispanismo movement, Federico Rahola and Rafael Vehils. Also important is Salvador Rueda, "El despertar de un país: información Mexicana," no. 61 (September, 1917), pp. 127–28. Similarly sympathetic to the Mexican Revolution are Andrés Gonzáles Blanco, an eminent poet-novelist-critic, *Un despota y un libertador* (1916); his brother Edmundo González Blanco, *Carranza y la Revolución de México* (1916), and Rámon J. Sender, *El Problema religioso en Méjico*, with a prologue by Ramón Valle-Inclán (1928). Many Spanish liberals, however, as pointed out in the text, opposed the Mexican Revolution. As a group, then, even as in the case of their divided approach toward the

United States, they lost out on the left to socialists, who were steadfast supporters of the Revolution. See, for example, Luis Araquistain, *La revolución mejicana* (1928) and Teófilo Ortega, *¿Adonde va el siglo? Rusia, Méjico, España* (1931). As was also the case resulting from their divided attitudes toward the United States, Spanish liberals in their response to the Mexican Revolution were outflanked on the right by the conservatives, who consistently denounced the movement as altogether evil.

70. See Baldomero Menéndez Acebal, *Resumen cronológico de las gestiones realizadas y resultos obtenidos durante el período revolucionario, por el delegado general de la Cruz Roja Española en México* (1917), pp. 22–29.

71. Santiago Magariños, *El problema de la tierra en México y la constitución socialista de 1917* (1932), pp. 270–72, a work dedicated to the author's mother and to Rafael Altamira. In spite of his often harsh denunciations of the movement, Magariños advocated that Spain maintain a generous, tolerant attitude toward the leaders of the Mexican Revolution, perhaps even going so far as to extend credit to enable the government of Mexico to compensate Spaniards for expropriated property. Such a policy, he argued, would contribute toward Hispano-American unity, a cause he had long served.

72. *Ibid.*, pp. 279–80. See also *Unión Ibero-Americana*, Año XXXVI (March–April, 1922), pp. 2–7.

73. In defending the Revolution, *El Sol* often opened its columns to the Venezuelan Blanco-Fombona, who thought the Mexicans were well on the way to establishing a new social system that would soon extend to all of Spanish America. Blanco-Fombona's pro-Revolutionary articles published in *El Sol* and also in *La Voz* of Madrid were included in his *Motivos y letras de España*.

74. See "La situación económica y financiera de Méjico," an unsigned article in *Revista de Ambos Mundos*, an organ of classical, laissez-faire liberalism, no. 23 (August, 1930), pp. 16–17. Another liberal organ, *Cultura Hispano-Americana*, demonstrated decidedly anti-Revolutionary attitudes in the 1920s. This journal's correspondent in New York at the time was Toribio Esquivel Obregón, who had left his native Mexico in dismay over the course of the Revolution. In *Influencia de España y los Estados Unidos sobre México: ensayos de sociología hispano-americana* (1918), Esquivel Obregón, a former minister of finance (hacienda) in Mexico and a corresponding member of the Real Academia Hispano-Americana de Ciencias y Artes (Cádiz), had praised Porfirio Díaz, condemned Francisco Madero, urged Mexicans to remain loyal to their Spanish values, expressed disparaging attitudes toward the Indian, and blamed his country's ills on the propensity of its leaders to imitate the United States.

75. Magariños, *El problema de la tierra*, p. 274.

76. Manuel Mielgo, "Méjico y la tradición liberal," *Revista de las Españas*, no. 33 (May, 1929), pp. 195–96.

77. González Posada, *La república argentina*, p. 481.

78. Blas Cabrera, "La investigación científica y el porvenir de la raza

hispana," *Revista de las Españas*, nos. 13–14 (September–October, 1927), pp. 581–83.

79. See Ortega y Gasset, "El deber de la nueva generación argentina," first published in the April 6, 1924 edition of *La Nación* (Buenos Aires) and reproduced in *Meditación del pueblo joven*, pp. 29–31.

80. Unamuno, *Temas argentinos*, pp. 56–58.

81. *Ibid.*, p. 119.

82. *Ibid.*, pp. 119–20.

83. José León Suárez writing in *Revista de las Españas*, nos. 34–35 (June–July, 1929), pp. 252–53. An Argentine, León Suárez (1872–1929) visited Spain many times and felt a deep sympathy for it. He founded and for many years presided over the Ateneo Hispano Americano of Buenos Aires.

84. Rodrigo Zárate, *España y América: proyecciones y problemas derivadas de la guerra*, with a prologue by Labra (1917), p. 45. Zárate, a Peruvian army captain, was stationed in Spain during the World War I period.

85. Suárez, *La verdad desnuda*, pp. 68–69, 72–75, 77, 80.

86. Juan García Caminero, *El problema hispano-americano* (1926), pp. 95–97. García Caminero served as Spanish military attaché in several Spanish-American countries. He had little faith in the value of spiritual ties and thought Spain should concern itself almost exclusively with commercial and economic relations with Spanish America.

87. *Ibid.*, pp. 72–73,. For a description of the anti-Spanish demonstrations in Buenos Aires, see Félix Ortiz y San Pelayo, *Boceto histórico de la Asociación Patriótica Española* (Buenos Aires, 1914), p. 118. The author was for many years an important leader of the Spanish community in Buenos Aires. On the 1909 disturbances in Spain, see Salvador Canals, *Los sucesos de España de 1909*, 2 vols. (Madrid, 1909), presenting the government point of view, and Joan C. Ullman, *The Tragic Week: A Study of Anti-Clericalism in Spain, 1875–1912* (Cambridge, Mass., 1969).

88. Blanco-Fombona, *Motivos y letras de España*, pp. 301–303.

89. See the Conde de Romanones, *Notas de una vida, 1912–1931* (1947), p. 226; *Razón y Fe*, LXXI (January–April, 1925), pp. 119, 263–64, and *El Siglo Futuro*, December 1, 1924. See also Vicente Marrero, *Maeztu* (1955), pp. 466–71, describing Maeztu's bitter 1924 denunciation of Unamuno because of the latter's allegedly unprincipled attacks against the dictator.

90. Bailey W. Diffie, "The Ideology of Hispanidad," *Hispanic American Historical Review*, XXII (August, 1943), pp. 456–83, is correct in asserting that turn-of-the-century hispanismo began primarily as a Spanish liberal movement. He ignores, however, the extreme social conservatism of liberal hispanismo. When it comes to views on the proper organization of society, there is little to choose between liberal hispanismo and conservative hispanidad. There is a significant difference between the two, but it arises from religious rather than social criteria and goals. Hispanismo as advanced by liberals stressed the ties of common language and a variety of cultural factors prescinding from formal religion and was predicated upon belief in the attainment of religious toleration in a secular society.

Hispanidad, a term employed primarily by Spain's conservative Catholics, rested on the conviction that Catholicism provides the most important source of unity among members of the Hispanic raza and that a future tightening of the bonds that joined this raza depended upon a resurgence among its members of militant, uncompromising, exclusivist Catholicism.

NOTES TO CHAPTER 8

1. Fernando de Antón, "Leyes de Indias," *Unión Ibero-Americana*, Año X (September, 1895), p. 416.
2. *Ibid.*
3. Mariano Rodríguez H., "Nueva fase de la opinión pública en Colombia," *España y América*, XIV (April–June, 1907), pp. 22–23. The writer predicted the hispanismo program favored at the time by liberal statesman Segismundo Moret was doomed to failure because it sought its foundation only in the ties of common language and origin, ignoring religion, the most important of the three cardinal sources of unity between Spain and Spanish America. Ángel Álvarez de Miranda, "El pensamiento de Unamuno sobre hispanoamérica," *Cuadernos Hispanoamericanos*, no. 13 (January–February, 1950), pp. 73–74, in a similar spirit maintains that the generation of '98 failed to establish enduring and meaningful ties with Spanish America because its representative figures repudiated Catholicism, the only "true essence of the Hispanic community." For a representative sampling of other works identifying Catholicism as the essence of hispanismo see: Leopoldo Barrios Carrión, *El porvenir de las naciones iberoamericanos* (1896); Adolfo Bonilla y San Martín, *Nuestra raza española* (1926) and his introduction to J. Franscisco V. Silva, *Reparto de América española y pan-hispanismo* (1918); Luis García Nieto, *Patria y religión: Huelva y la Rábida* (Sevilla, 1920); José Mañas Jiménez, *Esquemas ideológicos sobre hispanoamericanismo* (Cádiz, 1928); Ángel Rubio and Antonio Ibot, *La conquista espiritual de América* (Sevilla, 1924); Father Adriano Suárez, *Supremo ideal hispano-americano* (Cádiz, 1918).
4. Pedro Martínez Vélez, "El clero y las relaciones hispanoamericanas," *Unión Ibero-Americana*, *Número Extraordinario*, March 1, 1904, p. 31.
5. Constantino Bayle, "El próximo congreso de las juventudes hispanoamericanas," *Razón y Fe*, LVII (September-December, 1920), p. 145.
6. At about the same time, and with a similar goal, the *Boletín Eclesiástico Hispano-Americano* was founded in Barcelona. A Madrid periodical with a similar orientation was *Revista Social Hispano-Americana*, founded shortly before World War I.
7. "Nuestro programa," *España y América*, I, no. 1 (January 1, 1903), p. 3.
8. *Ibid.*, p. 5.
9. *Ibid.*, p. 8. Unity among the clergy of Spain, let alone of Spain and Spanish America, was an elusive goal. In 1904 P. Martínez Vélez, "El clero y las relaciones hispano-americanas," pp. 32–33, lamented the tremendous gulf and even overt hostility between the regular and secular

clergy in the peninsula. The anticlericalism initiated by the laity had affected the clergy of Spain, he asserted, leading the poverty-stricken priests of rural regions to detest the more affluent members of the religious orders.

10. See José María González, *El día de Colón y de la paz* (Oviedo, 1933), pp. 42, 46.

11. "Carta del Ecuador," signed Fray M.O.M. of the Discalced Franciscans, Lima, Peru, December 7, 1897, in *El Siglo Futuro*, January 10, 1898.

12. See the unsigned review of Bernardino Izaguirre, *Biografía del Ilmo. y Rdmo. Padre Fr. José María Masía, Obispo de Loja, 1815–1902* (Barcelona, 1904), in *Razón y Fe*, XII (January-April, 1905), p. 126. See also the same periodical, XII (September-December, 1905), pp. 408–409.

13. Eusebio Negrete, "Crónica," *España y América*, XII (January–March, 1907), p. 472.

14. Negrete, "Crónica," *ibid.*, XV (July–September, 1907), p. 186.

15. "Crónicas," *Razón y Fe*, LXXXVII (April–June, 1929), pp. 365–68.

16. "Crónicas: Ecuador," *ibid.*, LXXXIX (April–June, 1930), pp. 157–64.

17. "Crónicas," *ibid.*, LXXXVII (April-June, 1929), p. 367.

18. Pablo Hernández, "La Argentina al empezar el siglo XX," *ibid.*, I (September–December, 1901), pp. 195-97.

19. *Ibid.*, p. 426.

20. See the unsigned review of Enrique B. Prack, *Los grandes problemos de la actualidad: estudios sociológicos sobre el malestar político-social del proletariado y de la justicia en la República Argentina* (La Plata, 1905), in *Razón y Fe*, XII (September-December, 1905) p. 262. In the same edition of the Jesuit journal see also "Noticias Generales," p. 132.

21. P. Villada, "La pastoral colectiva del episcopado venezolano," *ibid.*, XII (May–August, 1905), pp. 337–41.

22. T. A. Polanco, "Crónicas: Venezuela," *ibid.*, LXXXVI (January–March, 1929), p. 435. Another sign of a religious revival under the Gómez regime was the appearance in 1913 of the Catholic hispanista review *España y América*, published in Caracas.

23. Jesús María Fernández, "Crónica de Colombia," *Razón y Fe*, XLVII (January-April, 1917), pp. 370–74. For appreciative Spanish opinions on the estate of Catholicism in Colombia see also Father José Pérez Gómez, "Los padres Capuchinos y el camino del Caquetá," *España y América*, XXXVII (January–March, 1913), pp. 141–50, and Marcelino Torres, a Spanish Augustinian serving in Colombia, "D. Miguel Antonio Caro," *ibid.*, XV (July–September, 1907), pp. 226–31.

24. See Nicolás E. Navarro, a dean of the Cathedral Chapter of Caracas, *La Iglesia y la masonería en Venezuela* (Caracas, 1928), and Mary Watters, *A History of the Church in Venezuela, 1810–1930* (Chapel Hill, N.C., 1933).

25. See Herrera, "La independencia americana," originally in *Diario Español* of Montevideo, reproduced in *Cultura Hispano-Americana*, no. 36 (November, 1915), pp. 41–43. Herrera's praise of traditional Spanish

values, which he insisted rested ultimately on Catholicism, led Spanish conservatives to lionize him even as Spanish liberals at an earlier time had lionized Rodó.

26. In 1915 a Spanish Jesuit praised Chile's system of higher education for having weathered the storm of liberalism and returned to the principles originally introduced into the country by the Church during the colonial period. Because of this, he claimed, Chileans were retaining their civic virtue in an atmosphere of political and social stability. See Pablo Hernández, review of Monsignor Rainaldo Muñoz Olava, *El seminario del Concepción durante la colonia y la revolución de independencia, 1572–1813* (Santiago de Chile, 1915), *Razón y Fe*, XLVIII (May–August, 1917), p. 418 ff. See also F. B. Pike, *The Modern History of Peru* (London, New York, 1967), esp. p. 208; *Chile and the United States, 1880–1962* (Notre Dame, Ind., 1963), esp. pp. 191–94, 200–202, and "Church and State in Peru and Chile since 1840: A study in Contrasts," *American Historical Review*, LXXIII (Fall, 1967), pp. 30–50.

27. Although Pablo Hernández, "La Argentina al empezar el siglo XX," p. 198, commented in alarm on the secularism and anticlericalism of Argentina, he detected a few encouraging signs that indicated to him a future expansion of Catholic influence. For one thing, more and more citizens concerned with quality education for their children were seeking to enroll them in Catholic schools, having been disillusioned by the poor quality of instruction in public institutions.

28. Luis Rodríquez, "Cartas de América," *España y América*, I (January, 1903), pp. 62–64.

29. Rodríguez, "Cartas de América," *ibid.*, I (March 15, 1903), pp. 378–81.

30. Narciso Noguer, "Triunfos de la Acción Femenina en la Argentina," *Razón y Fe*, XLIII (September–December, 1915), pp. 493–500.

31. See Palau, *El problema de la eficacia de la Acción Social Católica en las grandes ciudades* (Buenos Aires, 1917).

32. "Noticias Generales," *Razón y Fe*, LXXII (May–August, 1925), p. 130.

33. Father José María González, *El día de Colón*, p. 16, expressed the typical Spanish Catholic view when he said the main moving force behind Columbus was always his Catholic faith and that therefore any tribute to the discoverer had to be intimately associated with Catholic Church.

34. Father M. Gorrochátegui, "Crónicas Americanas: desde el Perú," *España y América*, LXXIV (April–June, 1922), pp. 46–47.

35. N. E. Navarro, "La fiesta de la raza y la Iglesia," *Unión Ibero-Americana*, Año XXX (January, 1916), p. lv.

36. Another conservatively oriented association active in the cause of hispanismo was the Real Academia Hispano-Americana de Ciencias y Artes of Cádiz, established in 1911. On its founding see Real Academia Hispano-Americana, *Reglamento interior de la . . . aprobado en junta el 1 de abril de 1911* (Cádiz, 1911) and *Reseña de la junta solemna celebrada el 3 de enero para solemnizar el tercer aniversario de su fundación* (Cádiz, 1913). On its activities, see José Miranda y Cadrelo: *Labor de la Aca-*

demia *Hispano-Americana* (1915). See also *Real Academia Hispano-Americana de Ciencias y Artes* (Cádiz, 1929).

37. See Unión Ibero-Americana, *Fiesta de la raza* (1913). Impetus for the campaign to have October 12 celebrated as a national holiday was provided by the 1912 centennial ceremonies in honor of the Cádiz constitution. Both conservatives, such as José María González, and liberals, among them Segismundo Moret, collaborated in these ceremonies. Moret presided over the first congress of Spanish-American journalists, held in conjunction with the festivities.

38. Owing largely to the initiative of Argentine Consul Enrique Martínez Ituño, the town of Palos, from which the discoverer had departed in 1492, celebrated October 12, 1915 as *el día de la raza*.

39. Faustino Rodríguez San Pedro (1830–1925), a Conservative Party stalwart who late in the nineteenth century began his nearly thirty-year tenure as president of the Unión Ibero-Americana, was vitally interested in augmenting economic relations between Spain and Spanish America, a fact that emerges clearly in his *Junta del comercio de exportación: transportes marítimas* (1899). Perhaps to an even greater extent Rodríguez, a cabinet member on several occasions and a long-time senator noted for his interminable, soporific speeches, was interested in the cultural-spiritual side of hispanismo. On his efforts to wage a spiritual conquest of Hispanic America and to gain celebration of *la fiesta de la raza* as a national holiday throughout the Spanish-speaking world see Alberto María Carreño, "La conquista hispánica de América en el siglo XX," reproduced in *Unión Ibero-Americana*, Año XXXIV (August, 1920), pp. 3–5. See also *Mercurio*, no. 26 (January 1, 1904), p. 8, for a fine sketch of the long-term president of the Unión Ibero-Americana.

40. González, *El día de Colón*, p. 12.

41. See Francisco Gutiérrez Lasanta, *Tres cardenales hispánicos y un obispo hispanizante* (Zaragoza, 1965), pp. 174–83. Vizcarra (1879–1963) was ordained to the priesthood in 1906. Shortly after arriving in Buenos Aires he founded the Cátedra Cultura Isidoriana to provide for the religious formation of upper-class youth, as well as the Asociación del Clero Español en la Argentina. In addition he helped found the review *Criterio* and collaborated with *El Eco Español*, a Spanish-community newspaper in Buenos Aires. At the end of the civil war he returned to Spain to assist in the reorganization of Catholic Action.

42. Paz, Infanta de España, "Mi trabajo en América," *Unión Ibero-Americana*, Número Extraordinario, May 1, 1904, pp. 7–8.

43. *España y América*, I (April 15, 1903), pp. 469–72.

44. For a similar argument see Adolfo de Sandoval, *El brazo de la raza* (1921).

45. See *España y América*, I (June 1, 1903), p. 231, and *Boletín Oficial del Ministerio de Estado*, Año, VIII, no. 3 (March, 1898), p. 231. On Spanish missionary activity in Spanish America and elsewhere see also: Father Wenceslao Fernández Moro, *Cincuenta años en la selva amazónica: padres dominicanos españoles* (1952); *La misión Claretiana del Chocó, 1909–1959: cincuenta años al servico de Cristo y de Colombia* (1960); *Las Misiones Católicas: Revista* (Barcelona, 1880–1886, 1902–

1903, 1949–); *Misiones Dominicanas: Revista Publicada por Misioneros Dominicanos Españoles* (1935–1936 and later years); Elías Olazar, Obispo Vicario Apostólico de Yurimaguas, *Pioneros de Cristo en el infierno verde* (Bilboa, 1963); República de Colombia, *Informe de la Prefectura Apostólica del Chocó durante la administración de los misioneros del Inmaculado Corazón de María, 1909–1929, elaborado con motivo de la grandiosa Exposición Misional Española de Barcelona, 1929* (Barcelona, 1929); *El Siglo de las Misiones* (Barcelona, 1914–), a Jesuit periodical.

46. Constantino Bayle, "Excursión por el campo teosófico," *Razón y Fe,* LXXXVIII (July–September, 1929), pp. 6, 13.

47. See *Anuario Eclesiástico,* Año VI (Barcelona, 1920), p. 352, and *Anuario Eclesiástico, Edición Americana* (Barcelona, 1921), pp. 310, 352. Between 1910 and 1925 new Spanish missions were established in Bluefields, Nicaragua; Urubá, Colombia; Beni, Bolivia; and San Gabriel de Marañón, Peru. See *Razón y Fe,* LXXIII (September–December, 1925), p. 202. On the grounds that newly restored Franciscan missions in Ecuador, Guatemala, and El Salvador were active in "diffusing the Spanish language and love of Spain," the Spanish government in 1923 granted them a state subvention. See *Boletín Oficial del Ministerio de Estado,* Año XXXIII, no. 6 (June, 1923), p. 294.

48. *Anuario Eclesiástico, Edición Americana,* p. 310. As of 1929 it was estimated that between 1,500 and 2,000 of the total number of 2,600 Spanish priests serving in foreign lands were stationed in Spanish America. See Constantino Bayle, "El Congreso y Exposición Misionales de Barcelona," *Razón y Fe,* LXXXIX (October–December, 1929), p. 157.

49. Father Benigno Díaz, "Los Agustinos españoles en América," *Unión Ibero-Americana, Número Extraordinario,* May 1, 1904, pp. 81, 83. P. Fabo, "En defensa de la vida religiosa," *España y América,* XLI (April 1, 1914), p. 382, refers to the Spanish regular clergy in America as the true frontiersmen and the authentic welders of Spanish-American unity. Ramón Lloberola, S. J., *La educación hispano-americana,* 2 vols. (1911), expands on the need for the Catholics of Spain and Spanish America to unite in a common endeavor to assure Church control over education and to resist the liberal objective of state-controlled education.

50. Earlier, Cerro had been named "Illustrious and Favorite Son of Sucre." See *Ibérica,* XXXVII, no. 919 (March 12, 1932), p. 164. *Ibérica,* a scientific periodical published by the Jesuits in Barcelona beginning in 1914, had as one of its objectives the awakening in Spanish America of appreciation for Spain's advanced position in science.

51. *Revista de las Españas,* nos. 13–14 (September–October, 1927), pp. 640–41. Another Spanish priest on a different type of tour had also achieved notable success in Spanish America at about this time. José de Calasanz Baradat from Navarra created what was described as unprecedented religious fervor in Lima by a series of sermons that he delivered. See "Desde el Perú: algunas notas, un verdadero apóstol," *España y América,* XCII (October–December, 1926), pp. 131–33. The Spanish Dominican Luis Urbano, an important figure in his country's Catholic Action, also created a favorable impression by a sermon delivered in the

Santiago de Chile Cathedral in 1924 and published in Madrid the following year under the title *La maternidad espiritual de España*.

52. See *Revista de las Españas*, nos. 36–38 (August–October, 1929), pp. 395–96.

53. Palomo, "Congreso Cultural Hispano-Americano," *Cultura Hispano-Americana*, nos. 146–147 (July–August, 1925), p. 3.

54. See Benlloch, *Sobre la Unión Misional del Clero* (Burgos, 1922?).

55. See Fernando Soldevilla, ed., *El año político, 1924: Año XXX* (1925). This invaluable annual publication dealing with political, cultural, and social events includes in the cited edition an excellent account of the Benlloch tour.

56. See Gutiérrez Lasanta, *Tres cardenales hispánicos*, pp. 67–68. When not otherwise indicated, the account of the Benlloch tour is based on this book, esp. pp. 6, 76–77, 86, 92–93, 100–108, and *El año político, 1924*.

57. See the unsigned editorial, "América y Cardenal Benlloch," *Cultura Hispano-Americana*, nos. 148–151 (September-December, 1925), pp. 26–29.

58. Benlloch, quoted in Gutiérrez Lasanta, *Tres cardenales*, p. 117.

59. *Ibid.*, p. 125.

60. Miguel Primo de Rivera, *El pensamiento de Primo de Rivera: sus notas, artículos y discursos* (1929), p. 74.

61. "Noticias Generales," *Razón y Fe*, LXXXVII (April–June, 1929), pp. 385–87.

62. Enrique Díaz Retg, *Hacia la España nueva* (1925), praises the dictator's concern with hispanismo. See also José Antonio de Sangróniz, secretary at the time of the Unión Ibero-Americana, *Epifanía del hispanismo* (1928).

63. Primo de Rivera, *El Pensamiento*, p. 75. Conservative hispanoamericanistas were also delighted by the assistance that the Primo de Rivera regime extended to the Primer Congreso Femenino Hispanoamericano, organized in 1929 by Spain's Acción Católica de la Mujer. See "Noticias Generales," *Razón y Fe*, LXXXVII (April–June, 1929), pp. 388–89.

64. Alfonso XIII, quoted in E. Ugarte de Ercilla, "Campaña de difamación antiespañola," *Razón y Fe*, LXXII (May–August, 1925), p. 66.

65. Alfonso XIII, quoted in Diómedes Arias, "Principios básicos de la confederación iberoamericana," *España y América*, XCII (October–December, 1926), p. 441.

66. See Ugarte de Ercilla, "Campaña de difamación," pp. 48–66, an important discussion of the liberal campaign against the dictatorship and a typical example of the conservative counteroffensive.

67. During the dictatorship Juan Vázquez de Mella, well known in Spanish America and widely published in its press, served as another spokesman of conservative hispanismo. Vol. XXIII of his *Obras completas*, 29 vols. (1946), entitled *Temas internacionales*, contains much of his writing on hispanismo. At this time the young Ernesto Giménez Caballero, like José María Pemán soon to play an important part in the events leading to the founding of the Falange Española, was also emerging as an

important spokesman of right-wing hispanismo. See his *La joven España: circuito imperial* (1929).

68. See *Real Academia Hispano-Americana de Ciencas y Artes*, p. 19. Pemán's earlier interest in Spanish America is evidenced in his *Algunas consideraciones sobre la poesía hispanoamericana* (1921). For his extremely favorable attitudes toward the dictatorship see his *El hecho y la idea de la Unión Patriótica*, with a prologue by M. Primo de Rivera (1929). See also his prologue to Primo de Rivera, *El pensamiento.*

69. Pemán, *Valor de hispanoamericanismo en el progreso total humano hacia le unificación y la paz* (1927), pp. 5, 98.

70. *Ibid.*, p. 7.

71. *Ibid.*, p. 20.

72. *Ibid.*, p. 30.

73. *Ibid.*, p. 34.

74. See Andrés Pando, "Don Ramiro de Maeztu, Embajador de España en la Argentina," *Revista de las Españas*, nos. 17–18 (January–February, 1928), pp. 27–29.

75. See Vicente Marrero, *Maeztu* (1955), pp. 532–43. Members of the Nueva República group in Argentina included the brothers Julio and Rodolfo Irazusta, César Pico, Tomás Casares, Juan E. Carulla, and Ernesto Palacio.

76. El Marqués de Corvera, "Recuerdos de México," *Unión Ibero-Americana, Número Extraordinario*, March 1, 1904, pp. 42–43.

77. P. M. Blanco García, "Crónicas Americanas," *España y América*, XXXVII (January–March, 1913), p. 541.

78. "Noticias Generales," *Razón y Fe*, XLI (January–April, 1915) p. 125.

79. *Ibid.*, XLII (May–August, 1915), p. 413.

80. "Noticias Generales," *ibid.* (January–April, 1920), pp. 254–55. *Razón y Fe* (January–April, 1925), p. 232, struck the same note again in commenting upon the religious fervor demonstrated by the Mexican faithful at the just-concluded First National Eucharistic Congress celebrated in Mexico City. This fervor was taken as proof that "The Protestant Yankee dollar and the Masonic liberalism of the government cannot snuff out the Spanish inheritance in Mexico that was nourished by the blood of martyrs."

81. A. Valle, "Noticias Generales: México," *ibid.*, LXXXVII (April–May, 1929), p. 288.

82. See the special message of the editors, "Ante lo de México," *España y América*, XCI (July–September, 1926), pp. 241–42, and Father L. G. Austria, "Crónica General," *ibid.*, pp. 299–301.

83. Francisco Elguero, "Crónica de Méjico," *Razón y Fe*, LXXII (May–August, 1925), p. 385. Father M. Gorrochátegui, "Crónicas Amercanas: desde el Perú," p. 44, spoke in 1922 about the Bolshevik wave threatening to sweep over Peru. As evidence of it he pointed to the lack of respect for presidential authority and the restlessness among certain university professors who were attempting to radicalize the students.

84. P. Martínez Vélez, "El clero y las relaciones hispanoamericanas," p. 31.

85. For examples of the anti-United States tone consistently maintained by Spanish conservatives see the *Revista Crítica Hispano-americana* (1915–1919), published under the direction of Adolfo Bonilla y San Martín.

86. To some degree the differing views of liberals and conservatives vis-à-vis the United States reflected their attitudes toward World War I. Liberals, accused by conservatives for more than a century of being afrancesados, tended to favor the cause of France and the Allies. Conservatives, although not by any means with unanimity, inclined toward Germany, hoping it would serve as the instrument of providential punishment against liberal, impious, anticlerical France. For indications of this see Julio Cola, *La España de hoy* (Buenos Aires, 1916), the work of a Spaniard who spent many years in Argentina and who believed that a German victory would weaken the Anglo-Saxons and facilitate the rise of the Hispanic raza, and Edmundo González Blanco, *Iberismo y germanismo: España ante el conflicto europeo* (Valencia and Buenos Aires, 1917). The views of Heinrich Schörs, a professor of Catholic theology at the University of Bonn, had many partisans in Spain, among them Vázquez de Mella. In *La guerra y el Catolicismo* (Freiburg, 1915), translated anonymously from German, Schörs develops the thesis that a German victory would be more advantageous to the Church than the triumph of revolutionary, anticlerical France and schismatic Russia. On this matter see also Víctor Espinós Motló, *Alfonso XIII y la guerra: espejo de neutralidades, 1914–1917* (1918).

87. Luis Marichalar, *La futura política económica—exterior de España* (1917), pp. 26–27.

88. Santiago Magariños and Ramón Puigdollers, *Panhispanismo* (Barcelona, 1926).

89. Goicoechea, *La obra pasada y la actual de España en América* (Montevideo, 1928), pp. 19–20. See also Luis Izaga, S. J., "La Doctrina de Monroe: el sequndo episodio venezolano y 'el garrote grueso' de Roosevelt en Nicaragua," *Razón y Fe*, LXXXVI (January–March, 1929), pp. 193–206, and *La Doctrina de Monroe: su origen y principales fases de su evolución* (1929), maintaining that the Monroe Doctrine and the additions to it reflect the desire of the United States to absorb Spanish America and stamp out its culture. Similar attitudes are expressed by J. M. González, *El día de Colón*, pp. 28–29, and Julio Puyol in his prologue to Adolfo Bonilla y San Martín, *Viaje a los Estados Unidos de América y al oriente* (1926), p. 12.

90. Bayle, "La nueva conquista de la América española: tropas auxiliares," *Razón y Fe*, LXXII (May–August, 1925), pp. 208–209.

91. José María Salaverría, "La regresión al indio," *Revista de las Españas*, nos. 11–12 (July–August, 1927), pp. 427–28.

NOTES TO CHAPTER 9

1. Blanco-Fombona, "La raza latino-americana," *Unión Ibero-Americana*, Año XXIII (November, 1909), p. 1. A close friend of Luis Palomo, president of the Centro Cultura Hispano-Americana, Blanco-Fombona pleased Spaniards by referring to himself as a "neo-Hispanic writer" to indicate his opposition to those who claimed there was a Venezuelan national language.

2. Unamuno in a 1906 article published originally in *La Nación* of Buenos Aires, *Temas argentinos* (Buenos Aires, 1943), p. 22–23.

3. *Ibid.*, p. 105.

4. *Ibid.*, p. 103.

5. *Ibid.*, p. 106–107.

6. Marqués de Sabuz, "Julio Mancini y su última obra," *Unión Ibero-Americana*, Año XXVI (April, 1912), p. 385. Sabuz considers in this piece the work of Colombian Julio Mancini, *Bolívar et l'emancipation des colonies espagnoles des origenes a 1815*. And he states that he had lived long enough in Spanish America to understand that its people desired "pompous poems, not objective history; eloquent panegyrics, not disciplined monographs; much that is fantasy, little that is real."

7. Narciso Alonso Cortés, "España y América," *Unión Ibero-Americana*, Año XXX (March, 1916), pp. 1–2.

8. Mariano Rodríguez H., "Nueva fase de la opinión pública en Colombia," *España y América*, XIV (April–June, 1907), pp. 11–23.

9. N. Alonso Cortés, "España en América," p. 2.

10. Bernardino Corral, "¿Por qué España no ha entrado en el corazón de los americanos?" *Unión Ibero-Americana*, Año XXXII (December, 1918), pp. 30–31. Javier Fernández Pesquero, a leading member of the Spanish community in Chile, also felt that the distorted history of the Spanish colonial period contributed to the facility with which Hispanophobes in Spanish America disseminated their prejudices. See his "Nos desconocemos," *ibid.*, Año XXIII (August, 1909), pp. 9–10. Confirmation of the Fernández view is provided by Fernando Ortiz, *La reconquista de América* (Paris, 1910). A professor at the University of Habana and much later the author of the celebrated *Contrapunteo cubano del tabaco y azúcar* (Habana, 1940), Ortiz warns against the efforts of the Unión Ibero-Americana to "reconquer" the former colonies and achieve some degree of Spanish spiritual hegemony over them. He argues that the horrors of the colonial period justify Spanish America's continuing rejection of Spain. For a representative sampling of literature in the Black legend approach, see Charles Gibson, ed., *The Black Legend* (New York, 1969).

11. Antonio Goicoechea, *La obra pasada y la actual de España en América* (Montevideo, 1928), pp. 13–14.

12. See Father Zacarías Martínez, funeral oration for Menéndez Pelayo, *Unión Ibero-Americana*, Año XXVI (May–June, 1912), pp. 30–31, and Blanca de los Ríos de Lampérez, "Menéndez Pelayo," *Cultura Hispano-Americana*, no. 31 (June 15, 1915), pp. 43–50.

13. Augustín García Gutiérrez, reply to the discourse of Francisco J. de Moya y Jiménez, *Exégesis de la nacionalidad hispano-americana* (Cádiz,

1912), p. 36, on the latter's entry into the Real Academia Hispano-Americana of Cádiz. For a report on some of the efforts of this Academy to refute the Black Legend see José Miranda y Cadrelo, *Labor de la Academia Hispano-Americana* (1915).

14. Ricardo del Arco y Garay, *La idea de imperio en la política y la literatura españolas* (1944), p. 789.

15. Francisco Moreno Herrera, *El ser de la hispanidad* (Jerez de la Frontera, 1966), p. 13.

16. The thirteenth edition of this popular work was published in Madrid in 1954.

17. Juderías, in Juderías and Jerónimo Bécker, *La reconstrucción de la historia de España desde el punto de vista nacional: discursos leidos ante la Real Academia de la Historia en el acto de su recepción pública por . . . el día 28 de abril de 1918* (1918), pp. 21–22. The volume contains the entrance address of Juderías and the reply of Bécker. Staunchly conservative in his political leanings like Juderías, Bécker was a distinguished diplomatic historian who also published two important revisionist works refuting the Black Legend: *La política española de las Indias: rectificaciones históricas* (1920) and *La tradición colonial española* (1913).

18. Additional works with the same objective of dealing sympathetically with Spanish conquest and colonization include: Ricardo Beltrán y Rózpide, *España y sus Indias* (1923); Adolfo S. Carranza, *España en América* (1921); Augusto José Conte y Lacave, *La leyenda negra en la primera mitad del siglo XIX*, with a prologue by José María Pemán (1923), and *El día de la hispanidad* (1941); Nicolás Espinosa Cordero, *Historia de España en América* (1931), awarded a prize by the Madrid newspaper *ABC*; Benito Menacho, *Los pueblos crueles: lectura para emigrantes españoles—la contraleyenda negra* (México, D. F., 1925); S. Piernas Hurtado, "La casa de la contratación," *La Lectura*, May, 1907, the concluding article in a series by a University of Madrid professor of economics, arguing that Spain went bankrupt because of its great generosity and enormous expenditures in spreading civilization and establishing charitable and educational institutions in the colonies; Julián María Rubio, *La Infanta Carlota Joaquina y la política de España en América, 1808–1820* (1920). This is the first volume in the Biblioteca de Historia Hispano-americana, established as a result of the efforts of Papal Nuncio Francesco Ragonesi and enjoying the support of King Alfonso XIII. The purpose of the Biblioteca was to publish studies of the Spanish colonial system in America that would dispel old errors and myths. The editorial board included the Spaniards the Conde de Cedillo and Antonio Ballesteros and the Colombian José María Rivas Groot.

19. An early work by a liberal writer attacking the historical interpretations that later came to be referred to as the Black Legend is Manuel Pedregal y Cañedo, *Estado jurídico y social de los indios en las época de descubrimiento de América* (1892).

20. Luis Palomo, "Memoria presentada en el día último de diciembre de 1914 al Señor Ministro de Instrucción Pública por . . . , presidente del Centro de Cultura Hispano-Americana," *Cultura Hispano-Americana*, no. 26 (January 15, 1915), p. 1.

21. Labra, *El problema hispano-americana* (1915), pp. 37–39.

22. See Labra, "El problema hispano-americano," *Cultura Hispano-Americana*, no. 37 (December, 1915), p. 30. At an even earlier time than Palomo and Labra, Rafael Altamira had recognized the need to counteract the anti-Spanish prejudices so frequently found in works by Spanish Americans dealing with the colonial period. He saw to it that *España*, a periodical founded in 1904 in Buenos Aires and over whose editorial policies he exercised considerable control, published articles refuting what later came to be known as the Black Legend.

23. For typical examples of works extolling the Laws of the Indies see: Niceto Alcalá Zamora, *Reflecciones sobre las Leyes de Indias* (1935), by the man who for a time headed the second Spanish republic; Vicente Gay, *Leyes del imperio español: las Leyes de Indias y su influjo en la legislación colonial extranjera* (Valladolid, 1924), a work by a conservative professor in the Sección de Estudios Americanistas of the University of Valladolid; and Germán Latorre y Setién, *De como velaban por la moralidad en las colonias: las Leyes de las Indias* (Sevilla, 1922). A University of Sevilla professor who wrote extensively on the geography of the Indies, who participated in the first Hispano-American Congress of History and Geography, and who worked on cataloguing the Archivo General de las Indias, Latorre also refuted the Black Legend in *La separación del virreinato de Nueva España de la metrópoli* (1914).

24. Antonio María Fabié y Escudero, *Ensayo histórico de la legislación española en su estados de ultramar* (1896), p. 5.

25. Altamira, *España y el programa americanista* (1917), p. 172.

26. José Pérez de Barradas, *Los mestizos de América* (1948), again and again praises the pigmentocracy in colonial Hispanic America as an important factor contributing to the preservation of a hierarchical social order. On pigmentocracy see also Magnus Mörner, *Race Mixture in the History of Latin America* (Boston, 1967), p. 54.

27. See, for example, Diego de Saavedra y Magdalena, minister plenipotentiary of Spain in Mexico, speech in Mexico City on the fourth centennial of the establishment of the *ayuntamiento*, reported in *La Unión Hispano-Americana*, no. 63 (January 11, 1922), pp. 12–13, and the prologue of Esteban de Bilbao to Juan Vázquez de Mella, *Dogmas nacionales* (1946 ed.), esp. p. xviii.

28. See the report on Moret's talk at the conclusion of the Cádiz ceremonies in *Unión Ibero-Americana*, Año XXVI (December, 1912), pp. 10–11. See also Félix Ortiz y San Pelayo, *Boceto histórico de la Asociación Patriótica Española* (Buenos Aires, 1914), p. 133 ff., in which the conservative head of the Asociación Patriótica Española of Buenos Aires describes how he was approached by the liberal Rafael María de Labra in requesting the participation of the Asociación in the Cádiz festivities.

29. See José María González, *El día de Colón e hispanidad* (Oviedo, 1933), p. 19.

30. *España y América: Revista Comercial*, no. 6 (February, 1913), p. 82.

31. See Herrera, *España y los indios de América: memoria presentada por el Dr. . . . representante oficial de Colombia al Congreso Hispano*

Americano de Historia y Geografía reunido en Sevilla en 1914 (Bogotá, 1918), and Congreso de Historia y Geografía Hispano-Americanas celebrado en Sevilla en abril de 1914, *Actas y Memorias* (1914), pp. 100, 168–69, 225–61.

32. See William Baker Bristol, "Hispanidad in South America, 1936–1945" (unpublished doctoral dissertation, University of Pennsylvania, 1947), p. 43. Spanish–Spanish-American accord on anti–Black Legend interpretations at these congresses contributed to the publication of certain revisionist history textbooks in Spanish America. See, for example, Bernardo Portas, S. J., *Compendio de la historia de Nicaragua* (Managua, 1918). Even before this another Jesuit had published a revisionist history textbook in Argentina. See Vicente Gambón, *Lecciones de historia argentina*, 2 vols. (Buenos Aires, 1907).

33. See Irene A Wright, "The Second Congress of Hispano-American History and Geography, Sevilla, May, 1921," *Hispanic American Historical Review*, IV, no. 3 (August, 1921), p. 505.

34. See II Congreso de Historia y Geografía Hispano-Americana, celebrado en Sevilla en mayo de 1921, *Actas y Memorias* (1921), pp. 165–68. The Spanish government contributed 60,000 pesetas to help defray expenses for the second congress. In addition the Spanish government was by this time making an annual contribution to the Unión Ibero-Americana of 30,000 pesetas. The head of the organizing committee for the second congress was the Marqués de Laurencín, actively assisted by Jerónimo Bécker and Joaquín Ciriz. An important Spanish delegate was Roberto Beltrán y Rózpide, representing the Sociedad Geográfica Comercial of Barcelona. A Barcelona geographer and publicist, Beltrán y Rózpide (1852–1928), was the permanent secretary of the Real Sociedad Geográfica de Madrid. He was the author of *Los pueblos hispanoamericanos en el siglo XX* (1904), reporting on the promising conditions of Spanish-American republics in the 1901–1903 period. Subsequent volumes bearing the same title and published in 1907, 1910, and 1913 updated the material. Large sections of each of the volumes were published originally in *La Ilustratión Artística de Barcelona*. At the Second Congress of Hispano-American History and Geography, the Centro Cultura Hispano-Americana was represented by the distinguished philologist Manuel Rodrígues-Navas and the Unión Ibero-Americana by its president, the Marqués de Figueroa.

35. José María Pemán, *Valor del hispanoamericanismo en el progreso total humano hacia la unificación y la paz* (1927), p. 4. Also in 1914 the chair of American Institutions was created at the University of Madrid and assigned to Rafael Altamira.

36. See Mario Méndez Bejarano, "Para la historia de los estudios americanistas," *Cultura Hispano-Americana*, no. 79 (June 15, 1919), p. 21. See also Percy Alvin Martin, "El Centro de Estudios de Historia de América en la Universidad de Sevilla," *Hispanic American Historical Review*, XIV, no. 2 (May, 1934), pp. 245–46. The Center's periodical publication, *Boletín del Centro de Estudios Americanistas*, contained valuable bibliographical material as well as information on current research.

37. Menéndez Pelayo, *Estudios y discursos de crítica literaria e histórica*, 7 vols. (1941–1942), VII, pp. 91–92.

38. See Palomo, "Memoria presentada en el día último de diciembre," p. 2.

39. Saenz Peña had represented Argentina in Spain at the marriage of Alfonso XIII. Later he had served as Argentine minister plenipotentiary in Madrid; and, after his election as president but before his inauguration in 1910, he briefly visited Spain, being received as a conquering hero in the capital city.

40. See Ortiz y San Pelayo, *Boceto histórico*, pp. 85–90.

41. Bourne's book was published originally in New York in 1904. The Spanish translation by R. de Zayas Enríquez appeared in 1906. See *Unión Ibero-Americana*, Año XXI (March, 1907), p. 18.

42. See "Noticias Generales," *Razón y Fe*, LXXII (May–August, 1925), p. 391.

43. See Armando Cotarelo y Valledor, *Bosquejo histórico de la Real Academia Español* (1946), pp. 26, 52.

44. The Lummis work was *The Spanish Pioneers* (Chicago, 1893). It appeared in Spanish translation, *Los exploradores españoles del siglo XVI*, with a prologue by Altamira (Barcelona, 1916).

45. The Peralta work, *España y América: colección de artículos de una polémica* (San José, 1918), carried a prologue by Dr. Valeriano F. Ferraz, a Spanish educator who for some years had helped direct the Costa Rican government's Instituto Educacional in San José. Expanding its activities aimed at combating the Black Legend, the Spanish colony of San José in 1922, with the approval of the Costa Rican government, established a Junta de Extensión Cultural Española. The primary function of the Junta was to arrange for courses on the conquest and colonial period that would spread "the true history of Spain in its relations with its colonies." See *La Unión Hispano-Americana*, nos. 67–68 (May–June, 1922), p. 76.

46. Prado, *Estado social del Perú durante la dominación española* (Lima, 1894).

47. See Prado, *El genio de la lengua y la literatura castellana y sus caracteres en la historia intelectual del Perú: discurso del . . . en la reinstalación de la Academia Peruana Correspondiente de la Real Española* (Lima, 1918). See also E. Castro y Oyanguren, "Desvaneciendo la leyenda negra." *Unión Ibero-Americana*, Año XXXII (November, 1918), pp. 6–10. This article hails the conversion of Prado to hispanismo and stresses the Peruvian's insistence upon the constant Spanish preoccupation throughout the colonial period with intellectual advancement.

48. See the report on an address of Juan R. Iglesias to the Real Academia Hispano-Americana in *España y América: Revista Comercial*, Año II (January, 1913), p. 83.

49. The extremely pro-Spanish views of Gálvez are set forth in his *El solar de la raza* (Buenos Aires, 1913). See also F. B. Pike, "Identity and National Destiny in Peru and Argentina," in Pike, ed., *Latin American History: Select Problems, Identity, Integration, and Nationhood* (New York, 1969), pp. 183–87, 221–22.

50. Belmás, "Nuestra política en América," *Unión Ibero-Americana*,

Año III (May, 1916), pp. 32–35, continued in *ibid.* (June, 1916), pp. 19–20. For additional manifestations of Argentine hispanista sentiments see Arturo Costa Álvarez, *Nuestra lengua* (Buenos Aires, 1922) as well as Rafael Padilla, *España actual: exposición de sentimientos afectivos hacia esta nación* (1908) and *Sangre argentina: artículos patrióticos y políticos* (1910).

51. See Bristol, "Hispanidad," pp. 92–93, and Altamira, *La política de España en América* (Valencia, 1921), pp. 204–205.

52. See *Unión Ibero-Americana*, Año XXXVI (July–August, 1922), pp. 44–50. José León Suárez, a professor of the University of Buenos Aires and director of the Ateneo Hispano-Americano de Buenos Aires, was another Argentine hispanista who attacked the Black Legend. See his *Carácter de la revolución americana* (Buenos Aires, 1916).

53. Review by Bayle of Juan Carlos García Santillán, *Legislación sobre indios del Río de la Plata en el siglo XVI* (1928), in *Razón y Fe*, LXXXVI (January–March, 1929), pp. 181–82.

54. Eusebio Negrete, quoting a letter from an unidentified Argentine, in "Crónica," *España y América*, XIV (April–June, 1907), p. 383.

55. Valera, *Nuevas cartas americanas* (1890), p. 127.

56. Report of Marcelino Torres written from Baranquilla, *España y América*, XIV (April–June, 1907), pp. 289–97.

57. Javier Fernández Pesquero, *España ante el concepto americano* (1923), pp. 90–92.

58. Constantino Suárez, *La verdad desnuda: sobre las relaciones entre España y América* (1924), p. 97.

59. June, 1915, conference of Manuel Rodríguez-Navas in the Ateneo of Madrid, reported in *Cultura Hispano-Americana*, no. 31 (June 15, 1915). Rodríguez-Navas also complained that a large percentage of Spanish-language books imported by Spanish America each year were printed in the United States, Germany, England, France, and Germany. On the book trade see also Julio de Lazúrtegui, *El libro español en América* (Bilbao, 1919), stressing the potential commercial value.

60. See Suárez, *La verdad desnuda*, p. 27, and Fernando Bruner y Prieto, *La bibliografía general española e hispanoamericana: informe presentado a la Cámara Oficial del Libro de Barcelona* (Palma de Mallorca, 1923), pp. 5–8.

61. Suárez, *La verdad desnuda*, p. 28. On the Spanish–Spanish-American book exchange as of 1920 see also "El libro español en América," *Ibérica*, XIV, no. 352 (November, 1920), p. 292, estimating that Spain each year sent to Spanish America books worth some 8 million francs, a lamentably small percentage of the 65 million francs worth of books exported to that area by Europe as a whole.

62. Rufino Blanco-Fombona, *Mortivos y letras de España* (1930), pp. 58–59. Primarily in the attempt to increase the market for Spanish-American writers in Spain, Blanco-Fombona helped found and served as director of the Biblioteca de la Juventud Hispano-Americana. Beginning in 1919 the Biblioteca, with its headquarters in Madrid, published works on important historical personages of the New World written by Spanish-American authors.

63. Leopoldo Calvo Sotelo, *El libro español en América* (1927), pp. 12–15. According to the author, a brother of conservative statesman José Calvo Sotelo, Spain in 1925 produced a total of some 12 million books. The net value of these, in addition to the value of new editions of old works, came to some 56 million pesetas; books to the value of 28 million pesetas were exported, with about 85 percent going to Spanish America. The Spanish government in 1922 requested detailed information from its consular service in Spanish America on the book trade with Spain and the possibilities of expansion. Much of the information in Calvo Sotelo's book is based on information contained in the replies of the consuls.

64. *Ibid.*, pp. 27–28.

65. *Ibid.*, p. 47

66. In 1910 the Barcelona painter Santiago Rusiñol published his impressions on Argentina following a trip to that republic. The book, *Del Born al Plata*, was often harshly critical of Argentines, especially because of the manner in which they treated Spanish immigrants. Gregorio Martínez Sierra translated the book by the distinguished Catalan artist into Castilian: *Un viaje al Plata* (1911). A short time later the eminent Spanish writer Javier Bueno visited Brazil, Montevideo, and Buenos Aires and published a book of extremely favorable impressions: *Mi viaje a América* (Paris, 1914).

67. Quoted in Mario Méndez Bejarano, *Poetas españoles que vivieron en América: recopilación de artículos biográfico-críticos* (1929), p. 22.

68. See, for example, *Revista de Madrid: Número Extraordinario en honor de América, con motivo de las fiestas de la independencia de Argentina, Chile, y México* (1910). The *Revista de Madrid* was the organ of the Ateneo of Madrid.

69. See *Boletín Oficial del Ministerio de Estado*, Año XX, no. 4 (April, 1910), p. 247.

70. See *Razón y Fe*, XXVIII (September–December, 1910), p. 403.

71. See Peralta, *España y América*, p. 75.

72. See Menéndez Pidal, "Los romances de América," *Cultura Española*, no. 1 (February, 1906), pp. 72–111. In slightly expanded form, Menéndez Pidal published this, together with other essays, as a book. In 1958 the sixth edition of *Los romances de América y otros estudios* appeared in Madrid.

73. See Menéndez Pidal, *España y su historia*, 2 vols. (1957), II, p. 597; Carlos Badía, *El factor geográfico en la política sudamericana* (1944, 2nd ed. of a work originally published in 1919), p. 102; and José Ortega y Gasset, *Meditación del pueblo joven* (1964), p. 76. Ortega y Gasset was the second lecturer to occupy the Menéndez Pelayo chair, delivering his lectures in 1916. The courses offered by the Spaniards who held this chair were so successful that subsequently the Institución Cultural Española of Buenos Aires founded similar chairs in the universities of Rosario and Santa Fe. See Carlos Ibáñez de Ibero, *La personalidad internacional de España* (San Sebastián, 1940), p. 239.

74. See Gay, *Leyes del imperio español: las Leyes de las Indias y su influjo en la legislación colonial extranjera*.

75. See Gay's pamphlet, *Impresiones de la América española* (1915).

76. See Badía, *El factor geográfico*, p. 102.

77. By mid-1917, fifteen of the Spanish-American republics still persisted in their neutrality policies.

78. See the Marqués de Corvera, a senator in the national Cortes and former Spanish minister to Mexico, "La mejor orientación internacional de España," *La Unión Hispano-Americana*, no. 1 (November 11, 1916), pp. 4–5.

79. Romanones, quoted in Andrés Pando, "Hispano-americanismo y neutralidad," *España y América: Revista Comercial*, no. 57 (May, 1917), pp. 74–75.

80. For a typical expression of this viewpoint see "Noticias Generales," *Razón y Fe*, XLVIII (May–August, 1917), p. 543 and *ibid.*, XLIX (September–December, 1917), p. 396.

81. On the other hand, conservatives tended contemptuously to dismiss Brazil, Cuba, Panama, Bolivia, Haiti, the Dominican Republic, and Guatemala, countries committed to the Allied cause, as puppets of the United States. See Father Ángel Monjas, "La América española y la guerra europea," *España y América*, LVI (January–April, 1918), p. 42.

82. See Valentín Gutiérrez de Miguel, *La revolución argentina: relato de un testigo presencial* (1930), p. 29.

83. A. Monjas, "La América española y la guerra," pp. 94–95.

84. For indications of the pro-German sentiments of Spanish conservatives, combined often with an anti–United States viewpoint, see: Vicente Gay, "El imperialismo comercial norteamericano," *Unión Ibero-Americana*, Año XXVIII (June, 1914), pp. 16–18, and an editorial, "¡Viva México!" in *ibid.*, Año XXVIII (April, 1914), p. 1; Antonio Maura, 1916 discourses in *Tres discursos de Maura sobre la política exterior, reeditados en el centenario de su nacimiento* (1954), pp. 48–49; Father A. Lozano, review of Edmundo González Blanco, *Iberismo y germanismo: España ante la guerra europea* (Buenos Aires, 1917), in *España y América*, LVII (January–March, 1918), pp. 223–24; Father Maximiliano Estébanez, "La conflagración general del mundo," *ibid.*, LVII (January–March, 1918), pp. 233–40. On the pro-German sentiments of Juan Vázquez de Mella, see Severino Aznar, *Impresiones de un Demócrata Cristiano* (1952, 2nd ed.), pp. 218–19, and "Noticias Generales," *Razón y Fe*, XLII (May–August, 1915), p. 410.

85. Some liberals favored Spanish participation on the Allied side and were among the sixty-two intellectuals who signed a petition to this effect in 1915. Most of the signers were affiliated with the socialists or with the Radical Party of Alejandro Lerroux. In its "Noticias Generales" column, *Razón y Fe*, XLII (September–December, 1915), p. 561, dismissed the sixty-two signers as representing "neither the majority nor the best part of the men of culture and learning in Spain."

86. See the Conde de Romanones, *Notas de una vida, 1912–1931* (1947), pp. 99–128, in which he describes his pro-Allied sentiments and the bitter divisions that the war created among Spanish politicians and intellectuals. See also my Chapter 8, note 86.

87. Indications of Spanish interest in Spanish America during World

War I and the immediate postwar period are provided by Andrés González Blanco, *Escritores representativos de América* (1918) and Mario
Méndez Bejarano, *La literature española en el siglo XIX, aumentada con
un apéndice sobre la literatura hispano-americana* (1921). The appendix
dealing with the literature of Spanish America was written by Pedro
Sáinz Rodríguez, a conservative statesman-author with an abiding interest
in Spanish America. In 1918 in Barcelona, Alfredo Opisso published the
twenty-five volume *Historia de España y de las repúblicas latino-ameri-
canas*, with a prologue to the volumes on the history of Spain by Miguel
de los Santos and another for the volumes on Latin American history by
Frederico Rahola. The short volumes are popularizations not intended for
the scholar.

88. Among the peninsula's periodical organs of hispanismo published
in 1918 were: *Archivo Ibero-Americano; La Argentina* (Barcelona); *La
Argentina en Europa* (Barcelona); *Banco Español del Río de la Plata;
Boletín del Centro de Estudios Americanistas* (Sevilla); *Cultura Hispano-
Americana; España y América; España y América: Revista Comercial*
(Cádiz); *La Gaceta de España y América; Ibérica* (Barcelona); *La Ilustra-
ción Española y Americana; Mercurio: Revista Comercial Ibero-Americana*
(Barcelona); *Nuevo Mundo: Periódico Ilustrado; La Rábida: Revista
Colombina Ibero-Americana* (Huelva); *La Revista de la Raza; Revista de
la Real Academia Hispano-Americana* (Cádiz); *La Unión Hispano-Ameri-
cana, Revista Mensual: para el fomento de las relaciones económicas entre
España y las repúblicas americanas; Unión Ibero-Americana.*

89. *Raza Española: Revista de España y América* was founded in 1919
by Manuel L. Ortega, a journalist from Jerez who in 1915 had established
the Editorial Ibero-Africano-Americana. The year 1919 witnessed also the
appearance of *La Gaceta de Ambos Mundos*, founded by Julio Cola, who
had lived many years in Argentina. The following year saw the establishment of *Alma Latina* (Cádiz), a semimonthly replacing *Cuba y España*
and dealing particularly with Spanish-Cuban relations. One year later, in
1922, Juan B. Acevedo helped found the *Revista Hispano Americana de
Ciencias, Letras y Artes.*

90. The Argentine hispanista José León Suárez had also declared that
"nationalism without hispanismo in our countries of America is an absurdity." See J. Francisco Silva, review of Rafael Vehils, *Delegación parlamentaria para las relaciones con América y unión interparlamentaria
hispanoamericana* (Barcelona, 1918), *España y América*, XL (October–
December, 1918), p. 455.

91. Ríos de Lampérez, quoted in John E. Englekirk, "El hispanoamericanismo y la Generación de 98," *Revista Ibero-Americana*, II (November,
1940), pp. 331–32.

92. Vehils developed his proposal in *Delegación parlamentaria*. The
Spanish-American authors supporting him were the Argentines J. Francisco V. Silva, author of *Reparto de America espanola y pan-hispanismo*
(1918), and José León Suárez, author of *Carácter de la revolución americana*, and the Venezuelan novelist Manuel Díaz Rodríguez, author of
Motivos de meditación ante la guerra y por la hispanoamérica (Caracas,
1918). See Silva's review of the Vehils work in *España y América*, pp.

445–57. In Spain the Vehils proposal was supported by Luis Palomo and the Centro de Cultura Hispano-Americana. See *Cultura Hispano-Americana*, no. 76 (March, 1919), pp. 2–6.

93. Altamira, "La realidad de nuestra situación en América," *El Día*, August 15, 1918. Francisco Grandmontagna, an hispanoamericanista who had lived for many years in Argentina, also struck a realistic note. However absurd the situation, he wrote, it was nonetheless true that the people who had discovered Spanish America were the ones least acquainted with it. See *El Imparcial*, June 17, 1918.

94. Valera, letter of May 7, 1888, to Argentine statesman Enrique García Merou, in *Cartas americanas* (1889), p. 83.

95. See Aurelio M. Espinosa, a Stanford University professor, "El término 'América Latina' as erróneo," *Nuestra raza (ni latina ni ibera): la exposición hispanoamericana de Sevilla y el porvenir de la raza. Artículos de Doña Blanca de los Ríos de Lampérez, de don Adolfo Bonilla y San Martín, del professor Norteamericano don A. M. Espinosa, y de don Juan C. Cebrián, reproducidos de la revista "Raza Española" y otras* (1926). Espinosa's *El término "América Latina" es erróneo* was published as a pamphlet in Madrid in 1919 in a Spanish translation made by Felipe M. de Setién, another Stanford University professor; it had appeared originally in *Hispania*, the organ of the American Association of Teachers of Spanish, no. 3 (September, 1918), together with an appendix by Juan C. Cebrián, an ardent hispanoamericanista living at the time in San Francisco. On Cebrián's activities in the name polemic see Bonilla y San Martín's article, originally written in 1919, in *Nuestra raza*, pp. 34–44.

96. See *Congreso de Historia y Geografía Hispano-Americanas . . . Sevilla . . . 1914, Actas y memorias*, esp. p. 313.

97. See Andrés Pando's review of Manuel Ugarte, *El destino de un continente* (1924), in *Unión Ibero-Americana*, Año XXXVIII (January, 1924), pp. 55–56.

98. Ríos de Lampérez, "Hispanismo," a 1919 essay republished in *Nuestra raza*, pp. 15–16.

99. II Congreso de Historia y Geografía Hispano-Americanas . . . Sevilla . . . 1921, *Actas y memorias*, p. 168.

100. See *La Unión Hispano-Americana*, no. 66 (April, 1922), p. 57. The same argument was advanced at an earlier time in *Unión Ibero-Americana*, Año XVIII (December, 1914), pp. 1–2, and Badía, *El factor geográfico*, pp. 46–47.

101. J. Francos Rodríguez, prologue to C. Suárez, *La verdad desnuda*, pp. 8–11.

102. Juan García Caminero, *El problema hispano-americano* (1926), p. 85.

103. As early as the 1880s a Spanish diplomat expressed indignation when he heard Italian diplomatic representatives toast Columbus at October 12 festivities held in Spanish America. He was obliged, he said, to speak out to set the facts straight, reminding all those in attendance that the glory of the Columbus expedition belonged exclusively to Spain. See Manuel Llorente Vázquez, "Descubrimiento de América," *La Ilustración Española y Americana*, February 8, 1892, p. 83.

104. See, for example, Rafael Calzada, *La patria de Colón* (Buenos Aires, 1925), a work "proving" the Spanish origins of Columbus, written by a leader of the Spanish colony in Buenos Aires. See also Benjamín Endara, "Colón, español," *Cultura Hispano-Americana*, nos. 140–141 (January–February, 1925), pp. 25–40, in which a Colombian hispanista argues it is fully proved that Columbus was a Spaniard, born in Pontevedra. Among the sources he cites in proof of this contention is Ricardo Beltrán y Rózpide, *Cristóbal Colón y la fiesta de la raza* (1918).

105. P. Leturia, "III Congreso de Geografía e Historia Hispanoamericanas, 2–8 mayo, 1930," *Razón y Fe*, XCI (April–June, 1930), pp. 289–300.

106. See, for example, the remarks of Luis Rodríguez de Viguir, the representative for Lugo in the chamber of deputies, quoted in *Unión Ibero-Americana*, Año XXXVI (May–June, 1922), p. 44.

107. Francos, *Huellas españoles: impresiones de un viaje por América* (1921), p. 242.

108. *Ibid.*, p. 12.

109. *Unión Ibero-Americana*, Año XXXVI (February, 1922), p. 51. At the end of World War I a new agency of hispanismo came into being, the Real Academia Hispano-Americana de Ciencias y Artes de Madrid. Presided over by Gabriel Maura, the son of Conservative Party leader Antonio Maura, the association published the *Revista de la Real Academia Hispano-Americana de Ciencias y Artes de Madrid: Órgano Oficial* (1919–1924). Valentín Gutiérrez-Solana, long one of the peninsula's more active hispanoamericanistas, helped the new Academy found a corresponding center in Mexico City in 1921. Competition and conflict with the older association of the same name based in Cádiz led to the demise of the Madrid organization in 1924.

110. Message of Haya de la Torre to the president of the Unión Ibero-Americana, dated Lima, May 10, 1920, published in *Unión Ibero-Americana*, Año XXXV (June, 1920), p. 15. In contrast, the Peruvian Alberto Hidalgo, later associated with Haya in the APRA, published a virulent diatribe against Spain, *España no existe* (Buenos Aires, 1921).

111. For Aramburu's political philosophy, see his *Filosofía de derecho*, 3 vols. (1928). Aramburu belonged to the Real Academia Hispano-Americana of Cádiz.

112. See *Unión Ibero-Americana*, Año XXXVI (May–June, 1922), p. 58.

113. See Father M. Gorrochátegui, "Crónicas Americanas: desde el Perú" *España y América*, LXXIV (April–June, 1922), p. 52. The author also reported with obvious pleasure that the city council of Lima had in 1921 rechristened the Avenida Industrial the Avenida Alfonso XIII.

114. C. Suárez, *La verdad desnuda*, p. 25.

115. Unsigned article, "Iberoamericanismo: algunas consideraciones," *Unión Ibero-Americana*, Año XXXVIII (August, 1924), pp. 19–23.

116. See Cotarelo y Valledor, *Bosquejo histórico*, p. 43.

117. See *La Unión Hispano-Americana*, no. 70 (August, 1922), pp. 98–99.

118. See S. Aznar, *Impresiones de un Demócrata Cristiano*, pp. 137–41.

119. See Ibáñez de Ibero, *La personalidad internacional de España*, p. 256. Argentina and Mexico received three, and Chile two scholarships; all the other countries were awarded one each.

120. Suárez, *La verdad desnuda*, p. 89. See also Julio Cola, *Política entre España y América* (1922), an address presented at the Ateneo of Madrid.

121. *Boletín Oficial del Ministerio de Estado*, Año XXXV, no. 12 (December, 1925), p. 721.

122. José María Yanguas y Messía, minister of state, "La acción del estado en las relaciones ibero-americanas," *Revista de las Españas*, nos. 17–18 (June–February, 1928), p. 37.

123. *Ibid.*, p. 38.

124. See *ibid.*, nos. 5–6 (January–February, 1927), pp. 153–55 and nos. 29–30 (January–February, 1929), p. 80. See also Bristol, "Hispanidad," p. 107. A royal decree of May 17, 1924, also provided for establishment in Sevilla of a Colegio Mayor Hispano-Americana, where Spanish-American students would receive instruction in methods of historical, literary, and scientific research preparing them for professional careers in teaching; they were also to be offered courses in applied arts for careers in industrial designing and related fields. See *Gaceta de Madrid*, May 19, 1924. At this time, moreover, the Centro de Estudios Americanistas of Sevilla gained an augmented state subvention and Germán Latorre y Setién became its director of publications. It was further provided in the mid-1920's that the major countries of Spanish America should have residence halls in the University City planned by Alfonso XIII and Primo de Rivera and for which the king broke ground shortly before his overthrow.

125. In its expanded form the Union's journal bore the title *Revista de las Españas*. Publication began in June of 1926. The new journal replaced the *Unión Ibero-Americana* as the Union's official journal.

126. The most active corresponding associations were in Ecuador, Panama, Uruguay, and Chile. See *Revista de las Españas*, nos. 13–14 (September–October, 1927), pp. 651–52. In 1929 a new corresponding association was founded in Buenos Aires, partly owing to the impetus provided by Ambassador Ramiro de Maeztu.

127. See *ibid.*, no. 42 (February, 1930), pp. 119–20, in which José María Salaverría reports on his cultural mission financed by the Unión Ibero-Americana and urges the expansion of cultural exchange programs.

128. For indications of the accelerating tempo of cultural exchange see José Antonio de Sangróniz, *Nuevas orientaciones para la política internacional de España: la expansión cultural de España en el extranjero y principalmente en hispano América* (1925), filled with optimistic accounts of gains being made and about to be made. See also Eduardo Gómez de Baquero, *Nacionalismo e hispanismo* (1928), and various works by Valentín Gutiérrez-Solana (see note 109) including: *La gran familia hispano-americana* (1924); *Hispanoamericanismo práctico* (1925), *Mi última viaje a Cuba, Méjico, y Estados Unidos* (1929); *Optimismo hispanoamericano* (1929); and *Pro raza (¿América ó novahispania?): impostura del nombre americano; código de la raza y de la humanidad; sociedad*

de naciones hispanoamericanas; bosquejo de Carlos Pereyra (1927). The year 1927 saw the appearance of a new journal of hispanismo, the *Gaceta Literaria Ibérica-Americana-Internacional: Letras, Arte, Ciencia*, founded and directed by Ernesto Giménez Caballero. Between 1926 and 1935 Giménez Caballero also wrote the "Revista Literaria Ibérica" section for the *Revista de las Españas*.

129. Francisco Anaya Ruiz, "Hispano-americanismo lírico y práctico: una gran obra española en Colombia," *Revista de las Españas*, no. 17–18 (January–February, 1928), pp. 23–26.

130. V. A. Belaúnde discourse to the 1927 Madrid Congreso de la Prensa Latina reported in *ibid.*, nos. 11–12 (July–August, 1927), pp. 490–91. Similar sentiments were set forth in 1929 by Ecuador's minister of foreign relations, Gonzalo Zaldumbide, on the occasion of the fiesta de la raza. Ideas expressed by Zaldumbide at this time are developed more fully in his *Significado de España en América* (New York, 1933). See the Giménez Caballero tribute to the Ecuadoran statesman in *Revista de las Españas*, nos. 80–82 (April–March, 1934), p. 178.

131. See "La actualidad iberoamericana: los sucesos de Nicaragua y la solidaridad hispanoamericana," *Revista de las Españas*, nos. 5-6 (January–February, 1927), pp. 47–50.

132. See "La VI Conferencia Panamericana," *ibid.*, nos. 17–18 (January–February, 1928), pp. 51–52.

133. For indications of this see the 1915 impressions of Juan Antonio Cavestany recorded in *Unión Ibero-Americana*, Año XXX (June, 1916), p. 54; Miguel de Unamuno, "La independencia de Ibero-América," *ibid.*, Año XXXIV (July, 1920), pp. 1–2; and Ramón Orbea, *La reconquista de América* (1905), pp. 195–98.

134. On the flight and the pro-Spanish sentiments that it unleashed in Spanish America see Enrique Díaz Retg, *Glorias de la raza: raid Huelva-Buenos Aires* (1926), and Ramón Franco and Julio Ruiz de Alda, *De Palos al Plata* (1926).

135. Félix Ortiz y San Pelayo, *El "Plus Ultra" en Buenos Aires: historia de un cablegrama que no existió* (Buenos Aires, 1926), p. 45.

136. Emilio Zurano, *Alianza hispanoamericana* (1926), p. 288.

137. Quoted by Juan C. Cebrián in *Nuestra raza*, pp. 5–6. See note 95 of this chapter regarding Cebrián.

138. *Ibid.*, p. 6.

139. Ortiz y San Pelayo, *El "Plus Ultra,"* pp. 45–46.

140. *Ibid.*, pp. 88–90.

141. *Ibid.*, pp. 91–92.

142. See *Revista de las Españas*, no. 33 (May, 1929), pp. 220–22. In spite of strained Spanish-Mexican relations, Spaniards were heartened by the work of Carlos Pereyra, *Breve historia de América* (1930). In this the distinguished Mexican historian, although by no means hiding the defects of the colonial period, stressed the contributions made by Spain in America. Spaniards regarded it as an important piece of revisionist literature.

143. V. Gutiérrez-Solana, *Incomprensión del problema hispanoameri-*

cano: *discurso de . . . el día 12 de marzo de 1926 en la Real Sociedad Económica Matritense de Amigos del País* (1926), p. 5.

144. García Caminero, *El problema hispano-americano*, pp. 163–68, 180.

145. See "Noticias Generales," *Razón y Fe*, LXXI (January–April, 1925), pp. 264–65.

146. The column was "Páginas Hispano-Americanas," written by José Gutiérrez-Ravé and published in the prestigious Madrid daily *ABC*, begining with the March 16, 1928 number. On October 12, 1926, Gutiérrez-Ravé had established the short-lived Madrid weekly *Figuras de la Raza*, obtaining some financial backing for the venture from Antonio Giocoechea. Before this, the conservative journalist had inaugurated in 1919 a Hispano-American section in the Madrid newspaper *La Acción*; in 1920 he had directed the Madrid review *España y Chile*.

147. Gutiérrez-Ravé, *España en 1931* (1932), p. 83.

148. Olariaga, "Impresiones de la Argentina de un economista," *Revista de Occidente*, XX (February, 1925), pp. 232–35.

149. Father Casiano García, "De algunos textos de historia," *España y América*, XCII (September–December, 1926), pp. 3–12.

150. C. Bayle, "Crónicas: el XXVI Congreso Internacional Americanista," *Razón y Fe*, CIX (September–December, 1935), pp. 518–35. See also Lewis Hanke, *The Spanish Struggle for Justice in the Conquest of America* (Philadelphia, 1949), pp. 175–79, and "More Heat and Some Light on the Spanish Struggle for Justice in the Conquest of America," *Hispanic American Historical Review*, XLIV, no. 3 (August, 1964), p. 322; and Juan Comas, *Los Congresos Internacionales de Americanistas; síntesis histórica e índice bibliográfico general, 1875–1952* (México, D.F., 1954).

NOTES TO CHAPTER 10

1. Alfredo Vicenti, "La cruzada ultramar," *Mercurio: Revista Comercial Hispano-Americana*, no. 43 (June 1, 1905), p. 471.

2. Tirso Rodríguez, "La diplomacia en América," *Unión Ibero-Americana, Número Extraordinario*, May 1, 1904, p. 9.

3. Ricardo Beltrán y Rózpide, "Res, no verba," *ibid.*, March 1, 1904, pp. 55–56. Both extraordinary numbers of the *Unión Ibero-Americana*, March 1 and May 1, 1904, were about equally divided between articles urging cultural-spiritual ties and others that stressed the exclusive importance of economic bonds.

4. A. Ramírez Fontecha, "Panamericanismo e hispanoamericanismo," *Mercurio*, no. 57 (August 1, 1906), p. 893.

5. An earlier instance of interest in practical hispanismo is accorded by Enrique Saumell, *Comercio con la América latina: modo de propagarlo* (1902). The work urges Spanish industrialists to improve their products and to send traveling commercial agents throughout Spanish America. It also calls for more intensive efforts by Spanish diplomats and consuls to secure new markets in Spanish America.

6. Romanones, quoted in Rafael Altamira, *España y el programa americanista* (1917), pp. 77–78.

7. See *Unión Ibero-Americana*, Año XXVI (December, 1912), p. 15. The Canalejas government in 1910 created the Dirección de Comercio in the ministry of fomento (development); within the Dirección de Comercio it organized a Centro de Expansión Comercial charged with increasing commerce between Spain and Spanish America, working in collaboration with chambers of commerce both in the peninsula and the New World. The Centro was further intended to support the sending of commercial agents to Spanish America and to encourage the establishment of commercial displays and museums. Nothing came of this approach for it was abandoned by immediately succeeding governments.

8. Sanz y Escartín, "Las palabras y los hechos," *Unión Ibero-Americana*, *Número Extraordinario*, May 1, 1904, p. 27.

9. See Valentín Gutiérrez-Solana, *Incomprensión del problema hispanoamericano* (1926), p. 31.

10. The Spanish consul in Mexico in 1898 issued a disquieting report showing that because of that republic's successful program of industrialization Spanish exports to it had declined sharply. See *Boletín Oficial del Ministerio de Estado*, Año VIII, no. 7 (July, 1898), p. 607. Published on the last day of every month, the *Boletín* was established in 1891. Until 1910 it published valuable reports from overseas consuls on various aspects of Spain's foreign trade.

11. In 1898 a Centro de Información Comercial was established within the ministerio de estado. Its purpose was to coordinate efforts aimed at expanding Spanish foreign trade, especially with Spanish America. It published the semimonthly, occasionally the monthly, *Boletín del Centro de Información Comercial*.

12. Approximate exchange rates of the peseta to the dollar were: 1890, 5.3:1; 1900, 6.5:1; 1910, 5.4:1; 1920, 7.8:1; 1927, 5.9:1; 1928, 7.5:1; 1930, 9:1; See Juan Sardá, *La política monetaria y las fluctuaciones de la economía española en el siglo XIX* (1948), p. 219, 237; José Calvo Sotelo, *Mis servicios al estado: seis años de gestión* (1931), pp., 288–89; and *Revista de Ambos Mundos*, no. 25, (October, 1930), p. 53.

13. In this five-year period Spanish exports to Cuba averaged some 128 million pesetas; imports from Cuba averaged 37.8 million. Exports to Puerto Rico averaged 26.9 million pesetas and imports some 22.5 million. See Rafael María de Labra, *El problema hispano-americano* (1906), pp. 43–44, and *Unión Ibero-Americana*, Año XIII (January, 1898), p. 27.

14. Spanish exports to Cuba were valued at 56.8 million pesetas, imports at 5.3 million; exports to Puerto Rico were worth 9.8 million pesetas, imports about 3.2 million. See Labra, *El problema*, p. 44. As of 1903 the total value of Cuban trade with the United States, exports and imports, was 111 million U.S. dollars; with England it was 12.5 million dollars, with Germany 97.5 million dollars, with France 2.5 million dollars, and with Spain only 2.3 million dollars. Valuable sources for trade statistics and other economic data at this time include the following: *Anuario Estadístico de España* (1860–); *El comercio exterior de España en 1900* (no date); Dirección General de Aduanas, *Estadística general del comer-*

cio exterior de España (1895); El Economista: Revista Financiera (Madrid, 1886–), the best financial magazine; Estadística general del comercio exterior de España con sus provincias de ultramar y potentes extranjeras en 1881, prepared by the Dirección General de Contribuciones Indirectas (1889); and Unión Ibero-Americana, Memorándum dirigido al Rey de España y a los Presidentes de las Repúblicas Iberoamericanas, sobre varios asuntos culturales y comerciales, prepared by the Union's secretary Jesús Pando y Valle (1905).

15. See the March 20, 1900, report of the Spanish consul in Montevideo in Boletín Oficial del Ministerio de Estado, Año X, no. 8 (August, 1900), pp. 794–802.

16. See ibid., Año VIII, no. 3 (March, 1898), pp. 270–71, describing the efforts of Comercio Español, a commercial-cultural magazine published by the Spanish community in Buenos Aires, and a newly formed Unión Comercial de España y el Río de la Plata, to foment trade between Spain and Argentina.

17. Mercurio, no. 27 (February 1, 1904), p. 33, and no. 33 (August 1, 1904), p. 183.

18. Segismundo Moret was one of Zulueta's most voluble supporters and accused the Conservative government of neglecting commercial opportunities in Spanish America. Among those accused of indifference in exploring trade opportunities was Faustino Rodríguez San Pedro, president of the Unión Ibero-Americana and, at the beginning of 1904, minister of state in a Conservative cabinet. See the Moret speech of January 5, 1904, in the chamber of deputies, reproduced in Unión Ibero-Americana, Número Extraordinario, March 1, 1904, pp. vi-vii.

19. Mercurio, no. 31 (June 1, 1904), p. 128, and no. 39 (February 1, 1905), p. 337. Rahola (1858–1919) served as secretary of the Congreso Mercantil of 1892, organized in connection with the celebration of the fourth centennial of the discovery. In 1905 he was elected deputy to the national Cortes from Barcelona; in 1910 has was elected senator for the province of his native Gerona. In addition to his commercial interest in Spanish America, Rahola was a great admirer of that area's modernist poetry. On him see the article by Rafael Vehils, a collaborator for many years in Barcelona's program of practical hispanismo, "Rahola, Americanista," Mercurio (November 20, 1919).

20. Ibid., no. 26 (January 1, 1904), p. 1.

21. Fernández Villaverde's telegram, quoted in ibid., no. 45 (August 1, 1905), p. 542.

22. Mercurio, no. 27 (February 1, 1904), pp. 30–32, and no. 26 (January 1, 1904), pp. 11–13.

23. F. Rahola, Sangre nueva: impresiones de un viaje a la América del sud (Barcelona, 1905), provides an account of the commercial tour. A Buenos Aires edition of the work appeared in 1943.

24. See Labra, El problema hispanoamericana, p. 95.

25. Altamira, España y el programa americanista, p. 84.

26. The Sociedad was supported in its early days by the Spanish-American consular corps in Barcelona and by such Catalan business-cultural associations as La Sociedad Económica de Amigos del País, el

Círculo de la Unión Mercantil, El Consejo Provincial de Industria y Comercio, La Liga de Defensa Industrial y Comercial, La Unión de Productores de España para el Fomento de la Exportación, and El Ateneo de Barcelona. On the beginnings of the Americanista movement in Barcelona, see Rafael Vehils, *América en España: estudios americanistas en Barcelona* (Barcelona, 1910).

27. The Bilbao group with which the Sociedad reached an agreement was the Centro de Unión Ibero-Americana de Vizcaya, presided over by Julio de Lazúrtegui; in Cádiz the group was the Real Academia Hispano-Americana de Ciencias y Letras, presided over by Pelayo Quintero Atauri; in Huelva it was the Sociedad Colombina Onubenses, presided over by José Marchena Colombo, who was also the director of *La Rabida: Revista Colombina Ibero-Americana,* founded in Huelva in 1913; in Madrid it was the Centro de Cultura Hispano-Americana, of which Luis Palomo was president. For some of Quintero Atauri's ideas on hispanismo, see his reply to José Manuel Pérez, included in the latter's *La república de Colombia: rasgos generales históricos* (Cádiz, 1913), first presented as an address before the Cádiz Academy.

28. The Casa de América in addition to its other activities published books dealing with the economies and foreign trade patterns of Spanish-American republics. One such publication was Simeón Mugüerza Sáenz, *Chile: bosquejo histórico, geográfico, estadístico y comercial de dicha república* (Barcelona, 1912).

29. See Francisco de Asís Carbonell Tortós, *Bodas de oro de la casa americana, su historia* (Barcelona, 1961), pp. 10–11, an extremely valuable study. See also R. Vehils, *Los fundamentos del americanismo español y la misión oficial de la "Casa de América" en Argentina* (Barcelona, 1913).

30. "Crónica de la Quincena," *España y América,* XXXVII (January–March, 1913), pp. 83–88. See also Vehils, *Relaciones de las naciones ibero-americanas con España* (Barcelona, 1914), originally presented as an address at the VIII Curso de Expansión Comercial held in Barcelona.

31. Lazúrtegui, *Estudios de Revista Nacional de Economía: Vizcaya y América* (1920), p. 44.

32. *Ibid.,* p. 37.

33. See Labra, *El problema hispano-americano,* p. 98.

34. Lazúrtegui, *Informe y memoria presentados a las Excmas. Diputaciones Provinciales de Vizcaya, Guipúzoca, Álva y Navarra por . . . : proceso y síntesis de su viaje de estudios económicos a través de América* (Bilbao, 1923), p. 224. This section of the *Informe* consists of a reproduction of a study prepared by Lazúrtegui in 1900: *Informe de la subcomisión de la Cámara de Comercio de Bilbao relativo a la celebración de una exposición ibero-americana en Bilbao en el año de 1903.*

35. See Centro de la Unión Ibero-Americana en Vizcaya, *Pro patria* (Bilbao, 1917), an extensive report on the organization's activities, 1913–1917, with articles by leading figures in the practical hispanismo movement of northern Spain.

36. Lazúrtegui, *Estudios de Revista Nacional,* p. 44. See also his *El Comercio ibero-americano por el puerto de Bilbao,* published in 1907

(Bilbao) by the Centro de la Unión Ibero-Americana en Vizcaya, of which Lazúrtegui was then president.

37. See Lazúrtegui, *Informe y memoria*, p. 168, as well as his *La exposición nacional de artes e industriales con una sección de productos ibero-americanos en Bilbao* (Bilbao, 1906).

38. On the 1897 statistics see *El Financiero Hispano Americano*, January 29, 1909. On the 1903 figures see *Mercurio*, no. 37 (December 1, 1904), p. 292.

39. These statistics are derived from *España y América: Revista Comercial*, no. 16 (December 2, 1913), p. 256. *El Financiero Hispano Americano*, January 29, 1909, estimates total Spanish–Spanish-American commerce at 210.5 million presets but breaks it down into 152.7 million in exports, 57.8 million in imports.

40. See R. M. de Labra, "Los problemas de América," *Unión Ibero-Americana*, Año XXIII (February, 1909), p. 5. On efforts to expand Spanish trade with Uruguay and Chile see *El Comercio Español* (Montevideo, 1907–1914), the organ of the Spanish community in Montevideo, and *Monografía de la colonia española de Chile en el año de 1909* (Cádiz, 1910).

41. Labra, *Las relaciones de España con las repúblicas hispanoamericanas* (1910), an augmented edition of a work originally published in 1900, p. 92.

42. For information and statistics on economic relations between Spain and Spanish America at this time see: *Estadística General del Comercio Exterior de España* (1910, 1915–); *El Financiero Hispano Americano* (1905–1909); *La Illustración Financiera* (1908–1916, 1922–1923); Dirección General del Instituto Geográfico y Estadístico, *Reseña geográfica y estadística de España*, 3 vols. (1912–1914); *Revista de Hacienda* (1905–1936).

43. Rodrigo Zárate, *España y América: proyecciones y problemas derivados de la guerra* (1917), p. 91, estimates that Spain in 1913 supplied Spanish America with only 2.6 percent of its total imports. J. Fred Rippy, *Latin America in World Politics* (New York, 1931, revised ed.), p. 221, makes an estimate of 3.5 percent.

44. Zulueta, quoted in *Unión Ibero-Americana*, Número Extraordinario, March 1, 1904, pp. i–iv.

45. *Ibid.*, pp. xi–xii.

46. José Cárdenas, president of the Cámara Agrícola of Madrid, writing in *ibid.*, p. 65.

47. Emilio Zurano Muñoz, *Valor y fuerza de España como potencia en el concierto internacional* (1922), pp. 104–105, estimates that between 1900 and 1915 Spain imported from all parts of the world an annual average of 2,918,404 tons on foreign ships and 1,632,692 tons on Spanish ships. During the same period it exported to all parts of the world an annual average of 8,925,345 tons on foreign bottoms and 3,936,442 on Spanish ships.

48. Eusebio Negrete, "Crónica," *España y América*, XIV (April–June, 1907), pp. 91, 396. See also Ramón Orbea, *La reconquista de América* (1905), pp. 63, 126.

49. See R. Zárate, *España y América*, p. 127; J. Piernas Hurtado, "Los tratados de comercio," *Mercurio*, no. 26 (January 1, 1904), pp. 3–4; and Labra, *El problema hispano-americano*, pp. 86–87.

50. Report of the vice-consul of Spain in Concepción, February 8, 1898, in *Boletín Oficial del Ministerio de Estado*, Año VIII, no. 4 (April, 1898), p. 238.

51. See José R. de Olaso, serving at the time as consul of Argentina in Bilbao, writing on the problem of credit in *Unión Ibero-Americana*, *Número Extraordinario*, March 1, 1904, p. 72; Mariano Sabas Muniesa, a Spanish banker who presided over the commercial sessions of the 1892 congress commemorating the fourth centennial of the discovery, writing in *ibid.*, p. 58; and William Baker Bristol, "Hispanidad in South America, 1936–1945 (unpublished doctoral dissertation, University of Pennsylvania, 1947), p. 38. To improve the situation the Spanish community of Buenos Aires in collaboration with local merchants and financiers founded in 1887 the Banco Español de Río de la Plata. By 1910 it had twenty-eight branches scattered throughout the Argentine republic, fourteen of them in Buenos Aires. See Adolfo González Posada, *La República Argentina: impresiones y comentarios* (1912), pp. 42–43, and Banco Español del Río de la Plata, *Estadísticas comerciales y monetarias (1905–1906) de la República Argentina y la Républica del Uruguay* (Buenos Aires, 1908). Moreover, the Crédito Ibero-Americano, founded in 1903 owing to the impetus of the Unión Ibero-Americana, was intended to facilitate Spanish trade with Spanish America. An export-import company and bank with resources of some ten million pesetas as of 1905, it had its headquarters in Madrid and branches in Barcelona, Paris, Hamburg, and New York. By 1905 the Banco Hispano-Americano, with resources of 100 million pesetas, maintained branches in the important capitals of America and served as a clearinghouse of Spanish–Spanish-American commercial information. See Orbea, *La reconquista*, pp. 177–78.

52. See Sardá, *La política monetaria*, pp. 244–46.

53. See Altamira, *España y el programa americanista*, pp. 78–79.

54. See Orbea, *La reconquista*, pp. 32–33, 60–61, 64–74, 101–110.

55. See report of the vice-consul of Spain in Concepción, February 8, 1898, p. 237.

56. Sardá, *La política monetaria*, p. 242.

57. See Fermín Calbetón, "Política iberoamericana," *Cultura Hispano-Americana*, no. 35 (October, 1915), pp. 29–31.

58. See Maximiliano Garciá Venero, *Vida de Cambó* (Barcelona, 1952), pp. 248–49, quoting such Catalan figures as Enrique Prat de la Riba and Francisco Cambó.

59. Pedro Martínez Vélez, " 'Comunicaciones marítimas de España' y 'El comercio ibero-americano por el puerto de Bilbao,' " *España y América*, XVI (October–December, 1907), p. 313.

60. Luis Marichalar, *Antología de las obras de Luis Marichalar, el Vizconde de Eza* (1950), p. 324.

61. Duque de Ripalda, discourse of October 12, 1915, in *Unión Ibero-Americana*, Año XXX (June, 1916), p. 4.

62. Altamira, *España y el programa americanista*, p. 46. See also Alta-

mira, *Cuestiones internacionales: España, América, y los Estados Unidos* (1916). Rippy, *Latin America in World Politics*, p. 210, notes that Altamira at this period altered his previous approach to Spanish America, described as one of "pedagogical politics" based on cultural exchange programs, to give major emphasis to trade relations.

63. On Spanish hopes aroused by the opening of the canal, see: Faustino Rodríguez San Pedro, writing in the first number of *La Unión Hispano-Americana* (November 11, 1916), p. 3; *Cultura Hispano-Americana*, no. 29 (April 19, 1915), pp. 2–5; Lazúrtegui, *Estudios de Revista Nacional*, p. 44; and Father A. Monjas, "Europa y el Canal," *España y América*, XXXVIII (April–June, 1913), pp. 394–404.

64. Discourse of Senator José de Parres y Sobrino in senate sessions of June 3–5, 1916, in *La Unión Hispano-Americana*, no. 2 (December 11, 1916), p. 9.

65. Prologue by Labra to Zárate, *España y América*, pp. 31–37.

66. Another periodical of hispanismo appeared for the first time in 1916, *Boletín de la Real Academia Hispano-Americana de Ciencias y Artes* (Cádiz).

67. *La Unión Hispano-Americana*, no. 1 (November 11, 1916), pp. 2–6.

68. See Zárate, *España y América*, p. 54.

69. Lazúrtegui, *Estudios de Revista Nacional*, p. 45.

70. See "Comercio de España y las costas occidentales de la América del sur: exposición elevada a título de contribución . . . a la Junta de Iniciativas y Liga Marítima Española por D. Francisco Echaurren, encargado de negocios de Chile en Madrid," *Unión Ibero-Americana*, Año XVIII (November, 1914), pp. 23–26.

71. See *Cultura Hispano-Americana*, no. 27 (February 15, 1915), p. 6.

72. See *ibid.*, no. 29 (April, 1915), pp. 2–10.

73. On the increase of Spanish trade with the United States, see *Ibérica* (Barcelona), XIII (January 24, 1920), p. 50.

74. See Rippy, *Latin America in World Politics*, p. 221. See also Dirección General de Aduanas, *Estadística general del comercio exterior de España en 1921* (1924).

75. See *Unión Ibero-Americana*, Año XXXVI (February, 1922), pp. 28–29, and H. Gil, "La riqueza y el progreso de España," *Razón y Fe*, LXXI (January–April, 1925), p. 50.

76. See note 34. See also Lazúrtegui, *España ante el hemisferio de occidente*, 3 vols. (Bilbao, 1924–1927), a considerably expanded version of his *Informe y memoria*. Spanish economist Emilio Boix, who resided for some time in the Río de la Plata republics, was another figure active in stimulating Spanish–Spanish-American trade. See his *Los aceites en la Repúblic Argentina* (1920), *Estudio comercial sobre la república del Paraguay* (1920), *Estudio comercial sobre la república del Uruguay* (1919), and *Situación económica de la República Argentina* (1926), pamphlet-length studies prepared for the Centro de Información Comercial of the ministry of state.

77. *La Unión Hispano-Americana*, no. 79 (May, 1923), p. 87.

78. Other members of the organizing committee included Luis Palomo,

Pelayo Quintero Atauri, Abilio Calderón, Mariano Matesanz, Emilio Zurano, and Manuel Cortezo. Carlos Prast, a national senator and president of the Cámara de Comercio of the province of Madrid, was also one of the most active figures in organizing the Primer Congreso. See Carbonell Tortós, *Bodas de oro*, p. 19, and *Boletín Oficial del Ministerio de Estado*, Año XXXIII, no. 1 (January, 1923), p. 97.

79. See Pedro Albaladejo Ibáñez, "El comercio español en ultramar," *Revista de las Españas*, nos. 22–23 (June-July, 1928), pp. 270–81; Lazúrtegui, *Informe y memoria*, pp. 136–37; José Francos Rodríguez, *Acción hispanoamericana* (Sevilla, 1923); and Primer Congreso Nacional del Comercio Español en Ultramar, *Conclusiones* (1923).

80. *Boletín Oficial del Ministerio de Estado*, Año XXXIII, no. 5 (May, 1923), pp. 247–48.

81. *Ibid.*, Año XXXIII, no. 7 (July, 1923), pp. 306–309.

82. Official members of the Junta included the subsecretaries of state and of labor, commerce, and industry. Members also included the president or a representative of: El Consejo Superior de Cámaras de Comercio, Industria y Navegación; La Comisión Protectora de la Producción Nacional; El Consejo Superior Bancario; El Consejo Superior de Fomento; El Consejo Superior Ferroviario; El Consejo Superior de Emigración El Comité Oficial del Libro; La junta de Aranceles y Valoraciones; El Fomento de Trabajo Nacional; La Liga Marítima Española; La Asociación General de Agricultores de España; La Asociación Nacional de Ganaderos; La Federación de Asociaciones de la Prensa; La Compañía Transatlántica Española; El Banco de Crédito Industrial; El Comisario de Turismo.

83. Other individuals appointed to the Junta were José Francos Rodríguez, Juan Manuel Pedregal, and Pelayo Quintero Atauri.

84. See *Boletín Oficial del Ministerio de Estado*, Año XXXIII, no. 6 (June, 1923), pp. 291–92.

85. See Lazúrtegui, *Informe y memoria*, pp. 164–65.

86. Early in 1923 hispanoamericanistas were encouraged by the report of Luis Sobredo Corral, Jefe de Negociado de la Dirección General de Aduanas and a member of the Real Academia de Jurisprudencia y Legislación. Although conceding that at the moment the overwhelming preponderance of Spain's foreign commerce was with the United States, France, and Great Britain, the highly placed customs official declared that his country's true economic future lay in trade with Spanish America. All that was necessary to realize this future was for the mother country to enter resolutely and consistently upon a program of approximation and commercial-cultural copenetration with the one-time colonies. See Sobredo, "El comercio de España en las naciones iberoamericanas," *La Unión Hispano-Americana*, no. 76 (February 1, 1923), pp. 25–26. The article contains an excellent resume of the volume and commodities of trade between Spain and its principal markets in Spanish America as well as information on applicable commercial laws.

87. See *Boletín Oficial del Ministerio de Estado*, Año XXXIII, no. 10 (October, 1923), pp. 433–35, and *ibid.*, Año XXXIX, no. 7 (July, 1929), p. 515.

88. Rafael Vehils served again as secretary general for the congress. See *Acta de conclusiones de la Conferencia de Cámaras y Asociaciones Americanas de Comercio* (Barcelona, 1929), and *Memoria de la Conferencia de Cámaras y Asociaciones Americanas de Comercio, convocada por el instituto de Economía Americana y celebrada en Barcelona del 21 al 26 de octubre de 1929* (Barcelona, 1930).

89. In addition the Compañía Transatlántica provided passenger and freight service on regularly scheduled runs between Barcelona, Valencia, Málaga, Cádiz, Las Palmas, and Santa Cruz de Tenerife and Puerto Rico, Habana, Colón, Curaçao, Puerto Cabello and La Guayra; between Bilbao, Santander, Gijón, La Coruña, and Vigo and Rio de Janeiro, Montevideo and Buenos Aires. See *Revista de las Españas*, nos. 5-6 (January–February, 1927), p. 166.

90. See *ibid.*, nos. 36–38 (August–October, 1929), p. 358.

91. See Primo de Rivera, *El pensamiento de . . . : sus notas, artículos, y discursos* (1929), pp. 255–56, and *Revista de las Españas*, nos. 9–10 (May–June, 1927), p. 361. On additional aspects of practical hispanismo during the dictatorship, see Banco Exterior de España, *Proposición y programa de crédito nacional, peninsular, y americano* (1928) and Benjamín Fernández y Medina, *El Banco Exterior de España y las relaciones financieras y comerciales hispano-americanas* (1929), the work of an Uruguayan poet-journalist who vastly admired Spanish culture and served on two occasions as his country's minister to Spain. See also Antonio Palau y Dulcet, *Manual del librero hispanoamericano: inventario bibliográfico de la producción científica y literaria de España y de América latina desde la invención de la imprenta hasta nuestros días, con el valor comercial*, 7 vols. (Barcelona, 1923–1927), a formidable work intended to facilitate commerce in books between Spain and Spanish America. A second, augmented edition of the work began to appear in Barcelona in 1948, with vol. I devoted just to the letter A.

92. See Emilio Zurano, *Alianza hispanoamericana* (1926), p. 270.

93. See Luis Araquistain, "Idea de un banco interhispánico," *Revista de las Españas*, nos. 20–21 (April–May, 1928), pp. 133–35.

94. *Boletín Oficial del Ministerio de Estado*, Año XXXIII, No. 11 (November, 1923), p. 537.

95. See *ibid.*, pp. 537–38; Manuel María Sánchez Navarro, "La Exposición Ibero-Americana de Sevilla (1929–1930)," *Razón y Fe*, XC (January–March, 1930), pp. 524–26, and Julio de Lazúrtegui, ed., *El problema interna y transoceánica de España: los Congresos Americanistas y las Exposiciones de Sevilla y Barcelona en 1929–30; la educación económica, la ultramarina inclusiva de la región Vasco-Navarra y especialmente de Vizcaya* (Bilbao, 1930), published by the Centro de la Unión Ibero-Americana en Vizcaya, of which Lazúrtegui was still president. The Unión Ibero-Americana and the Centro de Cultura Hispano-Americana of Madrid, the Real Academia Hispano-Americana of Cádiz, and the Casa de América of Barcelona were among the most prominent agencies of hispanismo that assisted the authorities of Sevilla in organizing the exposition. The Casa de América also participated in preparations for the International Exposition of Barcelona that opened at the same time as the

Ibero-American Exposition. Undergoing a reorganization to enable it better to meet its expanding functions, the Casa in 1929 changed its name to the Instituto de Economía Americana.

96. See "Noticias Generales," *Razón y Fe*, LXXXVII (April–June, 1929), pp. 385–87.

97. Spanish exports to the United States in 1928 were worth 211,-958,366 pesetas; imports from the United States came to 466,478,186 pesetas. See "Noticias Generales," *Razón y Fe*, LXXXVIII (July-September, 1929), p. 178.

98. Spanish trade deficits, i.e., value of imports over exports, were as follows (in millions of pesetas): 1922, 1,400; 1923, 1,400; 1924, 1,200; 1925, 700; 1926, 500; 1927, 788. See *Revista de las Españas*, nos. 17–18 (January–February, 1927), p. 64, and *ibid.*, no. 26 (October, 1928), p. 537.

99. Almost the only exceptions are afforded by Ecuador and Venezuela. Ecuador sent to Spain between 5 and 12 percent of its total exports in each of the years from 1921 to 1932; Venezuela sent between 5 and 11 percent during the 1921-1927 period. See Bristol, "Hispanidad," p. 109. Bristol bases his figures on the annual volumes of trade statistics published by the League of Nations under different titles, beginning as *Memorandum on Balance of Payments and Foreign Trade Balances* (Geneva, 1925–).

100. On the disruption of Spanish–Spanish-American trade relations caused by the depression see Círculo de la Unión Mercantil e Industrial, *Memoria presentada por la Junta de Gobierno del . . . al día 4 de abril de 1930* (1930), and Instituto de Economía Americana, *El comercio de España con América* (Barcelona, 1935).

101. Sánchez Navarro, "La Exposición Ibero-Americana de Sevilla (1929–1930)," pp. 528–29.

102. One of the Spaniards who through the years worried the most about the consequences of exaggerated regionalism and who hoped to keep Spain united by the great ideal of a Hispano-American community was Antonio Royo Villanova. See his *El nacionalismo regionalística y la política internacional de España* (1918).

NOTES TO CHAPTER 11

1. Matías Alonso Criado, "España y América," *Mercurio*, no. 55 (June 1, 1906), p. 832.

2. See *ibid.*, no. 53 (April 1, 1906), p. 769.

3. June 6, 1916 speech of Romanones, quoted in Rafael Altamira, *España y el programa americanista* (1917), pp. 78–79. Altamira agreed in general terms with the Romanones appraisal of Spain's diplomatic-consular representation in America but noted there were some fortunate exceptions. One month and three days after the Romanones speech, Spain moved to improve the situation by raising its legation in Buenos Aires to the level of embassy.

4. Labra, *El problema hispano-americano* (1906), pp. 76–77.

5. Fernández Pesquero. *Monografía de la colonia española de Chile en el año 1909* (Cádiz, 1914), pp. 6–8. On Fernández see note 58.

6. See Labra's prologue to Rodrigo Zárate, *España y América* (1917). See also Marcelo Pujol, *España y América* (1914), a work lamenting the inadequacy in numbers, quality, and training of the Spanish diplomatic and consular corps in Spanish America.

7. First-class secretaries were assigned to the legations of Mexico City, Caracas, Asunción (the minister accredited before the Asunción government resided in Buenos Aires), Sucre, and Central America. The legations of Lima, Montevideo, Buenos Aires, Bogotá, Santiago de Chile, Caracas, Rio de Janeiro, and Central America each had the services of a second-class secretary.

8. Second-class consuls at this time were stationed in Montevideo, Rosario, Mexico City, Callao, and Panama. In addition, a vice-consul served in Buenos Aires. See *Boletín Oficial del Ministerio de Estado*, Año XXXIII, no. 1 (January, 1923), p. 5.

9. January 8, 1904 discourse of Rodríguez San Pedro, *Unión Ibero-Americana*, Año XVIII (February, 1904), pp. vii–xix.

10. See *Boletín Oficial del Ministerio de Estado*, Año XXXIII, no. 1 (January, 1923), p. 5.

11. See Valero Pujol, "Correspondencia hispano-americana," a letter of his to Jesús Pando y Valle, secretary general of the Unión Ibero-Americana, in *Unión Ibero-Americana*, Año XXI (November, 1907), pp. 18–19; January 30, 1900, report of the Spanish vice-consul in Valdivia, *Boletín Oficial del Ministerio de Estado*, Año X, no. 6 (June, 1900), p. 6; August 24, 1899, report of the Spanish consul in Rosario, *ibid.*, Año X, no. 4 (April, 1900), p. 372.

12. See *Boletín Oficial del Ministerio de Estado*, Año XV, no. 5 (May, 1905), P. 412.

13. For examples of the complaints of Spanish consuls against the inefficient and even corrupt practices of Spanish manufacturers and merchants in their dealings with Spanish America see: report of the Spanish consul in Montevideo, *ibid.*, Año VIII, no. 4 (April, 1898), pp. 354–55, and no. 9 (September, 1898), p. 850; report of the consul in Panama, *ibid.*, Año VIII, no. 10 (October, 1898), p. 924; report of the Spanish consul in Hamburg, *ibid.* (October, 1898), pp. 977–99, relating the success of German manufacturers in capturing markets in Spanish America and contrasting their advanced methods with the archaic procedures of Spanish industrialists; report of the consul in Rosario, *ibid.*, Año XV, no. 1 (January, 1905), p. 99; report of the legation in Lima, *ibid.*, Año XX, no. 8 (August, 1910), pp. 655–57.

14. August 31, 1898, report of the Spanish consul in Asunción, *ibid.*, Año VIII, no. 10 (October, 1898), pp. 931–35.

15. October 14, 1909, report of Guillermo Leyre, consul of Spain in Valparaíso, *ibid.*, Año XX, no. 2 (February, 1910), esp. pp. 109–14. A large portion of this report, especially the insistence (p. 111) that Spain had an unfavorable balance of trade with most Hispanic-American countries, is unreliable and inaccurate, evidencing a remarkable ignorance or a twisting of the facts of Spanish–Spanish-American commercial relations.

16. See *ibid.*, Año VIII, no. 6 (June, 1898) pp. 473–79. The highest-paid Spanish diplomat in Spanish America was the first-class minister plenipotentiary in Mexico, who received 51,000 pesetas in salary and expense allowance. The next highest-paid diplomats were the second-class ministers in Argentina (38,850 pesetas, combined salary and expense allowance) and Chile (37,750). This remuneration contrasts with the 87,000 pesetas paid the ambassadors in Germany and Austria, the 65,000, 62,500, 53,500, and 49,350 pesetas paid the first class ministers in the United States, Turkey, Portugal, and Belgium, respectively. Resident or third-class ministers in Venezuela and Colombia received 32,750 pesetas, in contrast to the 20,000 pesetas assigned the resident minister in Switzerland.

17. In addition the Spanish budget provided 65,625 pesetas in 1915 for the ordinary expenses of legations in Spanish America and 66,125 for the ordinary expenses of consulates. See *ibid.*, Año XXV, no. 2 (February, 1915), pp. 120–44. In terms of salary and expense allowances for personnel, the most important legations maintained by Spain in Spanish America as of 1915 were those of Buenos Aires, Habana, and Mexico City, where the respective figures were 76,300, 67,350, and 63,500 pesetas. In contrast the salary-expense total for legation personnel in Athens was 37,000 pesetas; for Berlin, it was 112,350 pesetas; for Berne, 35,000; for Brussels, 62,600; for Bucharest, 37,000; for Constantinople, 80,450; for the Hague, 38,000; for London, 115,350; for Paris, 133,450; for Rome, 86,500; for the Holy See, 82,900; for St. Petersburg, 91,850; for Stockholm, 37,700; for Tokyo, 52,500; for Vienna, 104,000; for Washington, 113,500. See *ibid.*, pp. 110-32.

18. See *ibid.*, Año XXVIII, no. 6 (June, 1919), pp. 433–35, 437, 452. By the World War I period Spain in addition allotted 50,000 pesetas for the support of commercial missions to Spanish America and 80,000 pesetas in subventions for Spanish chambers of commerce overseas, the great bulk of which were in Spanish America. See *ibid.*, Año XXVII, no. 5 (May, 1917), p. 287.

19. See Chart 5, Chapter 10.

20. See *Boletín Oficial del Ministerio de Estado*, Año XXXV, no. 7 (July, 1925), pp. 443–51.

21. Spain in 1925, in addition to its twenty-eight consul generals, first-class and second-class consuls, maintained six vice-consuls in Spanish America. See *ibid.*, Año XXXV, no. 7 (July, 1925), p. 444, and no. 4 (April, 1925), pp. 287–92. In all, Spain in 1925 was represented in Spanish America by twenty-three in the diplomatic and thirty-four in the consular service. The total of fifty-seven represented a considerable increase over the 1915 figure of forty-seven.

22. See *ibid.*, Año XL, no. 1 (January, 1930), pp. 14–24. Spain's most expensive legations in Spanish America, in terms of salary and expense allowances for personnel and building maintenance allotments were: Buenos Aires, 232,500 pesetas; Habana, 185,000; Lima, 136,000; Mexico City, 136,000; Montevideo, 136,000; and Santiago de Chile, 155,000. By way of contrast, allotments budgeted for various other foreign legations were as follows: Athens, 84,000 pesetas; Berlin, 216,000; Berne, 115,000;

Brussels, 173,000; Bucharest, 84,500; Budapest, 84,500; Copenhagen, 84,500; Cairo, 84,500; the Hague, 84,500; London, 241,000; Lisbon, 179,000; Oslo, 69,000; Paris, 281,000; Peking, 105,000; Prague, 69,500; Rome, 199,000; the Holy See, 193,000; Stockholm, 84,500; Tokyo, 141,000; Warsaw, 115,000; Vienna, 105,000; Washington, 196,000.

23. *Ibid.*, Año XL, no. 1 (January, 1930), pp. 24-37. Among the countries where Spain maintained the most extensive and most expensive consular service were Argentina, with posts in six cities and a total of eight personnel, for whom salary and expense allowances were budgeted at 182,500 pesetas; Cuba, with posts in five cities, personnel of seven, and a budget of 166,000 pesetas; Chile, with posts in two cities, three personnel, and a budget of 76,000 pesetas; Mexico, with posts in five cities, six personnel, and a budget of 133,000 pesetas. By way of contrast, Spanish consular service in various other countries was as follows: Germany, with a total of nine personnel and a budget of 181,000 pesetas; Belgium, personnel of four, budget of 76,000; China, personnel of three, budget of 56,000; the United States, personnel of eleven, budget of 266,000; France, personnel of thirty, budget of 490,000; Great Britain, personnel of sixteen, budget of 329,000; Italy, personnel of nine, budget of 175,000; Portugal, personnel of ten, budget of 168,000.

24. See *ibid.*, Año XXXIII, no. 4 (April, 1923), pp. 161–63, and Año XXXIX, no. 1 (January, 1929), pp. 44–45. The 1929 ministry of state budget also allotted 100,000 pesetas for aid in the establishment of Casas Culturales y Comerciales abroad, primarily in Spanish America.

25. Each month's *Boletín Oficial del Ministerio de Estado* contained a list of transfers and promotions of diplomatic and consular personnel. A random sampling of these lists suggests that diplomats and consular agents transferred to Spanish America generally received promotions; those transferred from Spanish America to other parts of the world most generally did not receive promotions. However, personnel transferred to Buenos Aires posts as often as not received no upgrading in rank. This may indicate that diplomatic-consular positions in Buenos Aires were considered on a par with those of European nations.

26. See *España y América: Revista Comercial*, no. 53 (January, 1917), p. 15, and *Unión Ibero-Americana*, Año XXX (July, 1916), p. 3.

27. See interview with Yanguas y Messía in *Los Domingos de ABC: Suplemento Semanal*, July 13, 1969, p. 11.

28. See William Baker Bristol, "Hispanidad in South America, 1936–1945" (unpublished doctoral dissertation, University of Pennsylvania, 1947), pp. 103–04; Labra, *Las relaciones de España con las repúblicas hispano-americanas* (1910), pp. 16–20; Ministerio de Estado: *Información Diplomática*, no. 12 (June 30, 1904), p. 82, and Zárate, *España y América*, p. 26–27. Labra, *España y América, 1812–1912* (1912), lists treaties celebrated between Spain and Spanish America from independence to 1909.

29. On the Peruvian-Ecuadoran dispute see Eugenio Montero Ríos, Gumersindo de Azcárate, Nicolás Salmerón, Eduardo Dato, Rafael María de Labra, *Los límites teritoriales de las repúblicas del Perú y el Ecuador: dictamen jurídico* (1906).

30. See *Unión Ibero-Americana*, Año XXI (February, 1907), p. 12.

31. See *Mercurio*, no. 53 (April 1, 1906), p. 769, 796, and no. 54 (May 1, 1906), p. 826. A judicious study dealing with this topic is David H. Zook, Jr., "The Spanish Arbitration of the Ecuador-Peru Dispute," *The Americas*, XX, no. 4 (April, 1964), pp. 359–75.

32. See F. B. Pike, *The Modern History of Peru* (London, 1967), p. 230

33. In 1912 a three-man Spanish mission reorganized the military academy in Guatemala; in the last years of the nineteenth century, a Spanish officer helped train the Honduran army; in 1908 a Spanish officer was employed as an instructor by the Salvadorean army, in 1912 a Spaniard helped organize the Guardia Nacional, and in 1924 a three-man mission arrived to reorganize El Salvador's Guardia Nacional; in 1916 Spain sent a two-man mission to organize a Guardia Civil in Colombia; in the same year a Spanish officer helped organize an engineers corps in Ecuador; in 1922 four officers of Spain's Guardia Civil reorganized Peru's national police force; and in 1928 a Spanish officer was engaged to teach ballistics at Chile's military academy. See *Unión Ibero-Americana*, Año XXXVIII (April, 1924), p. 29, and Enrique Fernández Heredia y Gastañaga, *Un año de misión en Bolivia*, with a prologue by Pelayo Quintero Atauri (1935).

34. Spanish hopes to use the League as a means of forging unity with Spanish America are discussed in Carlos Badía, *El factor geográfico en la política sudamericana* (1944), esp. p. 558; Camilo Barcía, "América y la Liga de Naciones," *España*, May 15, 1919; A. Fabrá Rivas, "Concepto del iberoamericanismo," *Revista de las Españas*, nos. 5–6 (January–February, 1927), pp. 58–66; José Plá, *La misión internacional de la raza hispánica*, with a prologue by Uruguayan minister to Spain Benjamín Fernández y Medina (1928); Federico Rahola, *Programa americanista postguerra* (Barcelona, 1917); Rodolfo Reyes, "La IV Conferencia Panamericana," *Revista de las Españas*, nos. 20–21 (April–May, 1928), pp. 168–69; *La Unión Hispano-Americana*, no. 76 (February 1, 1923), p. 28; *Unión Ibero-Americana*, Año XXXVIII (January, 1924), p. 77, reporting on the discourse in the chamber of deputies of future minister of state Yanguas y Messía entitled "Hispano-americanismo en Ginebra."

35. See Pike, *Chile and the United States, 1880–1962* (Notre Dame, Ind., 1963), pp. 222–23.

36. See Carlos Ibáñez de Ibero, *La personalidad internacional de España* (San Sebastián, 1940), p. 147. The author correctly notes that despite outbursts of lyricism by the peninsula's hispanoamericanistas, Spain notoriously failed to use any diplomatic means to protest United States intervention in Nicaragua, Haiti, and the Dominican Republic.

37. See Juan García Caminero, *El problema hispano-americano* (1926), p. 102, and Emilio Zurano, *Alianza hispanoamericana* (1926), p. 289. Julio de Lazúrtegui, *Informe y memoria presentadas a las Excmas. Diputaciones Provinciales de Vizcaya, Guipúzcoa, Álava y Navarra . . .* (Bilbao, 1923), pp. 126–27, also refers to the inadequacy of the Spanish diplomatic corps in Spanish America, both in quality and quantity.

38. Labra, *España y América*, p. xiv.

39. Labra, *El problema hispano-americano*, pp. 62–63. The official statistics he quotes are from the Dirección General del Instituto Geográfico y Estadístico, *Estadística da la emigración e inmigración en España, 1901–1902* (1904). Other valuable sources for emigration statistics are Consejo Superior de Emigración, *La emigración española transoceánica, 1911–1915* (1916), and *Estadística de la emigración española* (1910, 1911, 1912, 1913, 1914). The Consejo Superior de Emigración was created by the Spanish law of 1907 regulating emigration. See also Ministerio de Instrucción Pública y Bellas Artes, *Estadística de la emigración e inmigración de España en los años 1903 a 1906* (1907), and Ricardo Solier y Vilches, *La emigración española* (1919), published under the auspices of the Real Academia Hispano-Americana de Ciencias y Artes of Cádiz. A valuable article on a closely related topic is R. A. Gómez, "Spanish Immigration to the United States," *The Americas*, XIX, no. 1 (July, 1962), pp. 59–68, dealing primarily with the 1900–1924 period.

40. Labra's prologue to Zárate, *España y América*, pp. 30–31.

41. See *Unión Ibero-Americana*, Año XXVI (December, 1912), pp. 22–23.

42. *La Unión Hispano-Americana*, no. 76 (February, 1923), p. 19. The 1918 figure was the estimate of Dirección General del Instituto Geográfico y Estadístico, *Anuario Estadístico*, Año V (Madrid, 1918). According to the analysis of *Razón y Fe*, LVIII (September–December, 1920), p. 103, many Spaniards believed the population was at least 24,000,000.

43. Lazúrtegui, *Informe y memoria*, pp. 97–120.

44. On aspects of Basque emigration see Instituto Vascogado de Cultura Hispánica, *Los Vascos en la hispanidad: colección de ensayos biográficos* (Bilbao, 1964), and Félix Ortiz y San Pelayo, *Los Vascos en América* (Buenos Aires, 1915).

45. "Noticias Generales," *Razón y Fe*, LXXI (January–April, 1925), pp. 260–61.

46. See *La Unión Hispano-Americana*, no. 77 (March 1, 1920), p. 34.

47. See "Noticias Generales," *Razón y Fe*, LXXII (May–August, 1925), p. 128.

48. See Lorenzo Luzuriaga, "El analfabetismo en España," *Boletín de la Institución Libre de Enseñanza*, Año XLIV, no. 178 (January 31, 1920), pp. 9–11.

49. See Labra, *El problema hispano-americano*, pp. 66–67, and Federico Rahola, *Sangre nueva: impresiones de un viaje a América del sud* (Barcelona, 1905), pp. 165–66.

50. The most important personages in founding the Asociación Patriótica Española were Francisco Durán and Dr. Rafael Calzada. For many years the latter was a leading figure in the Spanish community of Buenos Aires. See his *Cincuenta años de América: notas autobiográficas*, 2 vols. (Buenos Aires, 1927, 1928), vols. IV and V of his *Obras completas*, the first volume of which was published in 1925. See also his prologue to Emilio F. de Villegas, *Reseña histórica del Club Español, 1852–1912* (Buenos Aires, 1912). On Calzada, see Martín Dedeu, *Nuestros hombres*

de la Argentina: Dr. Rafael Calzada (Buenos Aires, 1913, 2nd ed.).
Dedeu, a Catalan, lived for some time in Argentina.

51. See the March 1, 1898 report of the Spanish consul in Montevideo,
Boletín Oficial del Ministerio de Estado, Año VIII, no. 4 (April, 1898),
pp. 358–59, and Félix Ortiz y San Pelayo, *Boceto histórico de la Asociación Patriótica Española* (Buenos Aires, 1914). Ortiz y San Pelayo was
for years a leading figure of the Spanish community in Buenos Aires and
his *Boceto* is an extremely valuable source. On the activities of the Spanish
community in Mexico at this time see N. Ray Gilmore, "Mexico and the
Spanish American War," *Hispanic American Historical Review*, XLIII,
no. 4 (November, 1963), pp. 511–25.

52. Complaints against the discrimination suffered by Spaniards
in Mexico before Porfirio Díaz helped alter the situation are found in
Adolfo Llanos Alcaraz, *El porvenir de España en América* (México, D. F.,
1878), and *No vengáis a América* (México, D. F., 1876). Because anti-
Spanish prejudices were allegedly so strong throughout Spanish America,
the author advised Spain to abandon all interest in the former colonies.

53. See Badía, *El factor geográfico*, p. 106.

54. Saturnino Huerta-Rodrigo, M. Rey, Samuel Tena Lacén, Segundo
L. de Angulo, eds., *Nuestra raza: estudios biográficos de contemporáneos
hispano-americanos* (1907), pp. 34–35. Written in a hero-worshiping
style, the work relates the business triumphs of many Spaniards in
America. Similar in approach is Rafael María de Labra y Martínez, son of
the famous hispanoamericanista, *Los españoles contemporáneos en
América* (1915), originally presented as a Memoria to the Sección de
Ciencias Morales y Políticas of the Ateneo of Madrid. For additional
material on the Spanish community in Argentina see Juan Francisco Cor-
reas, *La inmigración española en la República Argentina* (1927); *El
Diario Español: La Fiesta de la Raza en la Argentina. Números Extraor-
dinarios dedicados a la conmemoración del 12 de octubre de 1492* (Buenos
Aires, 1928), a collection of the special numbers published by the Buenos
Aires Spanish community newspaper *El Diario Español* to commemorate
the October 12 celebrations, 1917–1928; *Los españoles en el centenario
de Bahía Blanca: reseña ilustrada del esfuerzo español en el sur de la
provincia de Buenos Aires* (Bahía Blanca, 1928); *Monumento de los
españoles: Memoria de la Comisión Española del Centenario Argentino*
(Buenos Aires, 1927). Two novels that reveal a great deal about the
Spanish immigrant communities in Argentina are Francisco Grandmontagna, *Teodoro Foronda* (Buenos Aires, 1897), and Carlos María Ocantos,
Promisión (1897). Grandmontagna was a Basque who for some time
directed the review of the Basque colony in Buenos Aires, *La Vasconía*.
At the time he wrote his novel, the Argentine Ocantos was secretary of
his country's legation in Madrid. A valuable insight is also provided in
Juan J. Marsal, *Hacer la América: autobiografía de un inmigrante español
en la Argentina* (Buenos Aires, 1969). The work is the autobiography of
J. S., helped by Marsal to write his memoirs. Born in Barcelona in 1909,
J. S. went to Argentina in 1927 and for thirty years worked there as a
carpenter. In this book he reveals his reasons for going to Argentina,
comments at length on the conditions he encountered in that country, and

explains his motives for ultimately returning to Spain. In a carefully documented appendix, Marsal deals at length with the high percentage of Spanish immigrants in Argentina who returned to their native land.

55. *Nuestra raza*, pp. 39–40. On the Spanish colony in Cuba see also *Alma Latina* (Cádiz), a semimonthly founded in 1920 dealing primarily with Spanish-Cuban relations and replacing *Cuba y España*; José María Álvarez Acevedo, with the collaboration of Miguel González Rodríguez, *La colonia española en la economía cubana*, published under the auspices of the Cámara Oficial Española de Comercio (Habana, 1937); Centro Asturiano de la Habana, *Memoria del año 1917* (Habana, 1917), providing extensive coverage on the numerous activities of an important Spanish association; and Rafael María de Labra, *Política hispanoamericana: Españoles y Cubanos después de la separación* (1916).

56. *Nuestra raza*, pp. 89–90. On the Spanish community in Mexico see also Baldomero Menéndez Acebal, *Glosa española: estudios y juicios históricos de un español residente en Méjico* (Méjico, 1939); Alberto María Carreño, *Los Españoles en el México independiente: un siglo de beneficencia* (México, D. F., 1942), and Luther N. Steward, Jr., "Spanish Journalism in Mexico, 1867–1879," *Hispanic American Historical Review*, XLV, no. 2 (August, 1966), pp. 422–33.

57. See *Unión Ibero-Americana*, Año XXXVIII (August, 1924), pp. 45–46. See also J. Peláez y Tapia, *Corona funebre a la memoria del Excmo. Sr. D. Fernando Rioja Medel, primer conde de Rioja de Neila* (Valparaíso, 1924).

58. See Javier Fernández Pesquero, *Monografía de la colonia española de Chile*, p. 211. Fernández Pesquero, a Madrid-born novelist who inclined politically toward the liberal cause, arrived in Chile at the beginning of the twentieth century. He taught in secondary schools there and founded two Spanish-community newspapers: *El Deber* and *El Heraldo de España*. A representative of the Unión Ibero-Americana in Chile and Bolivia, he founded corresponding chapters in those two republics.

59. See March 1, 1898 report of the Spanish consul in Montevideo, *Boletín Oficial del Ministerio de Estado*, Año VIII, no. 4 (April, 1898), pp. 358–59. On the Spanish colony in Uruguay see also *Los Españoles del Uruguay: contiene biografías de españoles residentes en esta república*, with a prologue by Dr. Matías Alonso Criado (Montevideo, 1918).

60. Fernández Pesquero, *Monografía de la colonia española de Chile*, p. 13.

61. *Nuestra raza*, pp. 113–14.

62. Luis Bolin, *Spain, the Vital Years* (Philadelphia, 1967), p. 70.

63. See *La Unión Hispano-Americana*, no. 64 (February, 1922), p. 20.

64. For the Valle-Inclán appraisal, see his *Tirano Banderas; novela de tierra caliente* (1922). Juan Díaz del Moral, *Historia de las agitaciones campesinos de Andalucía* (1929; 2nd ed., 1967), and more particularly Carlos Seco Serrano, director of the *Índice Histórico Español* (Barcelona), in what promises to be a definitive history of Spanish labor, have brought to light much material on the operation of Spanish anarchists, socialists, and radical labor organizers in Spanish America.

65. Baldomero Argente, "Camino de América: problemas nacionales," *Mercurio*, no. 37 (December 1, 1904), pp. 280–81. For similar justifications of emigration see Augusto B. Besada, *La emigración* (1905), and Lorenzo N. Celado, *Sobre emigración* (1909). Celado, a journalist-diplomat, was particularly interested in encouraging emigration to Brazil. He was the founder of the semimonthly *Brasil en España* and in 1910 was named vice-consul of Brazil in Madrid.

66. See "Sobre emigración," *Unión Ibero-Americana*, Año XXIII (November, 1909), pp. 5–6, and Labra, *España y América*, pp. 141–58.

67. See *Cultura Hispano-Americana*, no. 30 (May 15, 1915), pp. 26–27. Similar advice to curb emigration is found in *El problema de la emigración* (1918).

68. See M. A. Bedoya, "La confederación española de Indianos y residentes," *Unión Ibero-Americana*, Año XXXVI (March–April, 1922), pp. 13–20.

69. See Niceto Alcalá Zamora, "El idea colectivo y las fuerzas morales," *La Unión Hispano-Americana*, no. 66 (April, 1922), pp. 50–53.

70. González Posada, *En América: una campaña* (1911), pp. 19–23, 35. Similar sentiments are expressed by Rahola, *Sangre nueva*, pp. 166–67.

71. Rahola, *Sangre nueva*, p. 228.

72. See *España y América*, XV (July–September, 1907), p. 571, *Ministerio de Estado: Información Diplomática*, no. 10 (May 31, 1904), and *Mercurio*, no. 34 (October 1, 1904).

73. See Labra, *Españoles y Cubanos después de la separación* (1916), and E. P. L., "Suerte futura de la isla de Cuba," *Unión Ibero-Americana*, Año XXI (December, 1907), pp. 4–5.

74. Eusebio Negrete, "Crónica," *España y América*, XIII (January–March, 1907), pp. 281–82.

75. L. N. C., "La paz en Santo Domingo," *Unión Ibero-Americana*, Año XXI (January, 1907), p. 18.

76. See Rahola, *Sangre nueva*, p. 185.

77. Romanones, "Las tres Españas," *Cultura Hispano-Americana*, no. 35 (October 15, 1915), p. 27.

78. See Labra, *El problema hispano-americano*, p. 69, and Eduardo Sanz y Escartín, *La moneda y el cambio en España* (1905).

79. *Unión Ibero-Americana*, Año XXIII (February, 1909), p. 5.

80. Alfredo Vicenti, "El congreso hispano-americano: ponencias e informes," *La Ilustración Española y Americana*, October 30, 1900, p. 251.

81. See *España y América: Revista Comercial*, no. 16 (December, 1913), p. 255, and Juan Sardá, *La política monetaria y las fluctuaciones de la economía española en el siglo XIX* (1948), p. 241. To emigrant remittances of capital some of the major financial houses of this era owed their founding, among them the Banco Hispano Americano, founded in 1901, and El Banco Español de Crédito, founded in 1903.

82. See discourse of senator José de Parres y Sobrino in senate sessions of June 3 and 5, 1916, in *La Unión Hispano-Americana*, no. 2 (December 11, 1916), pp. 5–7.

83. Zárate, *España y América*, pp. 22, 126.

84. The lower estimate is made by García Caminero, *El problema hispano-americano*, p. 135. José Francos Rodríguez, *Huellas españolas: impresiones de un viaje por América* (1921), p. 326; "Noticias Generales," *Razón y Fe*, LXXI (January–April, 1925), p. 398; and *Cultura Hispano-Americana*, nos. 140–141 (January–February, 1925), p. 46, all agree on the higher estimate of over 500 million pesetas. Of this sum about 400 million was said to come from Spaniards living in Argentina and Uruguay, 32 million from those residing in Cuba, and about 12 million each from the Spanish colonies of Mexico and Chile. An additional 10 million was remitted by Spaniards living in Brazil and 30 million by those in the United States.

85. See García Caminero, *El problema hispano-americano*, p. 135.

86. Puyol, the secretary of the Instituto de Reformas Sociales and one of the secretaries of the 1909 Congreso de Emigración de Santiago de Galicia, played a role in the drafting of Spain's early emigration legislation.

87. See Labra, *España y América*, pp. 156–58.

88. Sangro y Ros, *Noticias útiles para el emigrante a la República Argentina* (1908). For the Primer Congreso Nacional de Emigración, Sangro y Ros prepared the *Memoria acerca de los trabajos del Congreso presentada al Instituto de Reformas Sociales* (1910). Another work of this period aimed at assisting the emigrant was Eduardo Vincenti y Reguera, *Estudio sobre emigración: guías especiales para América y Argelia* (1908).

89. *El problema de la emigración*, p. 355.

90. See Ortiz y San Pelayo, *Boceto histórico*, p. 115, and Fernández Pesquero, "Desde Chile," *Unión Ibero-Americana*, Año XXI (September, 1907), pp. 11–13.

91. See Francisco Andrés Oliván, *Por España y para España* (Zaragoza, 1899), pp. 5–6.

92. Fernández Pesquero, *Monografía estadística de la colonia española de Chile*, p. 5.

93. Toledano, *La Argentina que yo he visto* (Barcelona, 1915, 2nd ed.), pp. 12–14.

94. *Ibid.*, p. 15.

95. *Ibid.*, p. 31.

96. *Ibid.*, p. 84.

97. *Ibid.*, pp. 81, 85.

98. *El problema de la emigración*, pp. 305–09. The cheapest passage to Buenos Aires at this time was out of La Coruña. From this Galician port the one-way fare was about ninety pesetas. From other Spanish ports it averaged between 150 and 200 pesetas.

99. Beginning in January of 1917 the Asociación Española de San Rafael published in Madrid the monthly bulletin *Nuestra Emigración*.

100. See E. de Vargas-Zúñiga, "El problema religioso de España," *Razón y Fe*, CVIII (May–August, 1935), p. 135, and *El problema de la emigración*, pp. 327–30.

101. Julio Cola, *Memoria política entre España y América* (1921), p. 27. Cola lived for some time in Buenos Aires, where he founded the popular Spanish community periodical *La Gaceta de España*. Recognizing

the extent to which Spanish colonies in America had been alienated from the home government, a group of Spaniards in 1921 organized the Juventud Hispanoamericana. Its fundamental purpose was to recapture for Spain the affection of the emigrant colonies in America. It hoped to represent the interests of emigrants before the Spanish Cortes; it sought also to provide emigrant colonies with advice and information, and to encourage intellectual and cultural exchange programs. On the Juventud Hispanoamericana, which produced few tangible results, see Fernández Pesquero, *España ante el concepto americano* (1923), pp. 322–27. The Juventud Hispanoamericana was not alone in its concern to provide Spain's emigrants with some voice in the national Cortes. Justo S. López Gomara, *Un gran problema español en América* (Buenos Aires, 1915), urged direct representation for emigrants in the Cortes. López was at the time director of the *Diario Español de Buenos Aires*.

102. Valentín Gutiérrez-Solana, *Incomprensión del problema hispano-americano* (1926), pp. 21–22. Carlos Badía, *Ideario de la colonia española* (México, D.F., 1921), also complained about Spain's neglect of its emigrants and urged the extensive reform of the Spanish consulate service in America. Similar in tone is Constantino Suárez, *La desunión hispanoamericana* (Barcelona, 1917). Suárez also depicted in novels the suffering of Spanish immigrants in America: ¡*Emigrantes! dos ensayos de novela sobre emigración* (Habana, 1915); *Oros son triunfo: novela de ambiente hispanoamericano* (Habana, 1916). Another novel dealing with the suffering of Spanish immigrants in America and the disregard of their home government for them is Fernández Pesquero, *La patria del Indiano* (Santiago de Chile, 1916). Blistering attacks against the Spanish government for abandoning its emigrants to inhuman suffering in Spanish America are found in Santiago Rusiñol, *Del Born al Plata* (Barcelona, 1910), and José María Salaverría, *España vista desde la América* (1914) and *Tierra argentina: psicología, costumbres, sabores de la República del Plata* (1910). On Rusiñol, see Chapter 9, note 66. Salaverría, a Basque literary figure of considerable importance, lived for some time in Argentina. Like Badía, who served in Mexico in the Spanish consular service, like Suárez, who had faced arduous struggles as a young immigrant in Cuba, and like Fernández, a long-time resident in Chile, he knew at first hand the conditions that he exposed in his publications.

103. See note 21.

104. For the text of the law see *Boletín Oficial del Ministerio de Estado*, Año XXXV, no. 1 (January, 1925), pp. 26–67, and no. 2 (February), pp. 141–93.

105. On the attempts of the Patronato to provide school facilities for Spanish emigrant colonies in America see the interview with Yanguas y Messía, minister of state for the dictator, *Los Domingos de ABC*, p. 11, as well as *Boletín Oficial del Ministerio de Estado*, Año XXXIX, no. 1 (January, 1929), pp. 44–45, and Año XL, no. 1 (January, 1930), pp. 45–48. See also Santiago Magariños and Ramón Puigdollers, *Panhispanismo, su trascendencia histórica, política y social* (Barcelona, 1926), p. 88.

106. On Unamuno's views on the emigrant, see his *Temas argentinos* (Buenos Aires, 1943), p. 47; on Cavestany, see Fernández Pesquero,

España ante el concepto americano, p. 234. Coming to the defense of the emigrant and attacking the disparaging views of Unamuno, Cavestany, and other Spaniards, Ortiz y San Pelayo published *Españoles y españoles, ó la colectividad española en la Argentina y los visitantes españoles* (Buenos Aires, 1915) and *Vindicaciones de los españoles en las naciones del Plata* (Buenos Aires, 1917).

107. See Andrés Eloy Blanco, "El Indiano," *Unión Ibero-Americana*, Año XXXVIII (January, 1924), pp. 1–4, and Rodolfo Reyes, "El valor 'hombre' en América," *Cultura Hispano-Americana*, nos. 46–47 (July–August, 1925), pp. 15–28, in which a Venezuelan and a Mexican, respectively, express regret over the characteristic disdain that Spaniards accord the Indiano. See also Mariano Belmás, "Nuestra política en América," *Unión Ibero-Americana*, Año XXX (June, 1916), p. 24, describing the general contempt in which Indianos are held in the peninsula.

108. See Toledano, *La Argentina que yo he visto*, pp. 14, 22–23. In his estimation it was possible to succeed in Spanish America only at the price of becoming brutalized and dishonest and discarding all honor.

109. See Ortiz y San Pelayo, *Boceto histórico*, p. 32.

110. *Ibid.*, pp. 100, 110.

111. *Unión Ibero-Americana*, Año XXI (January, 1907), p. 9.

112. González Posada, "Los españoles en sud-América," *España y América: Revista Comercial*, no. 20 (April, 1914), pp. 312–13.

113. See Fernández Pesquero, *España ante el concepto americano*, pp. 286–87.

114. See Rafael Vehils, "Nuevo hispanoamericanismo," *Unión Ibero-Americana*, Año XXXVI (March–April, 1922), pp. 31–33, and *Revista de las Españas*, nos. 9–10 (May–June, 1927), p. 421.

115. See José María Salaverría, "La fiesta de la raza," *ABC*, October 12, 1916.

116. See *Revista de las Españas*, nos. 77–79 (January–March, 1934), p. 74, and nos. 85–86 (September–October, 1934), p. 431, expressing alarm over immigration restrictions in Spanish America and the drastic decline of Spanish emigration.

NOTES TO CHAPTER 12

1. See the Conde de Romanones, *Notes de una vida, 1912–1931* (1947), pp. 124–25.

2. *Ibid.*, p. 126.

3. Eusebio Negrete, "Crónica Española," *España y América*, LVII (January–March, 1918), pp. 231–32.

4. "Noticias Generales," *Razón y Fe*, LVI (January–April, 1920), pp. 121–23.

5. See Santiago Galindo Herrera, *Historia de los partidos monárquicos bajo la segunda república* (1954), p. 14.

6. See Antonio Royo Villanova, "Las obras de Giner de los Ríos," *Boletín de la Institución Libre de Enseñanza*, Año XLIV, no. 729 (November, 1920), pp. 349–52.

7. Luis de Zulueta, "Soliloquías de un español: la última esperanza," *La Libertad*, February 19, 1920.

8. González Posada, *España en crisis* (1923), p. 8.

9. *ABC*, March 21, 1918.

10. See *Revista de las Españas*, nos. 36–38 (August–October, 1929), p. 362. Galindo Herrera, *Historia de los partidos monárquicos*, p. 14, estimates that 3,280 strikes occurred in Spain during the five-year period preceding the September 23, 1923, Primo de Rivera coup.

11. Graciano Martínez, "Sana doctrina sobre sindicatos," *España y América*, LXXV (July–August, 1922), p. 241.

12. See Miguel Sancho Izquierdo, Leonardo Prieto Castro, and Antonio Muñoz Casayus, *Corporatismo: los movimientos nacionales contemporáneos* (Zaragoza, 1937), pp. 38–44. This work, written by three professors of the University of Zaragoza, presents a strong defense of the corporative organization of society, identifying corporativism with the social doctrines of the Catholic Church.

13. Jaime Vicens Vives, *Aproximación a la historia de España* (Barcelona, 1952), p. 175.

14. See José Canalejas, *La política liberal en España* (no place, no date), pp. 66–67. For a description of this work see my Chapter 5, note 71.

15. See Father Maximiliano Estébanez, "Crónica de España," *España y América*, LXXV (July–August, 1922), p. 151. Described by Estébanez as having at one point been a reactionary advocate of classical liberalism, Cambó had in 1919 become so alarmed over Spain's social-economic crisis as to abandon his earlier ideas and to advocate a state-supported social movement aimed at bettering capital-labor relations. On Cambó see Maximiano García Venero, *Vida de Cambó* (Barcelona, 1952), and the monumental study of Jesús Pabón, *Cambó, 1876–1918* (Barcelona, 1952), *Cambó, II, parte primera, 1918–1930*, and *Cambó, II, parte segunda, 1930–1947* (Barcelona, 1969).

16. See Estébanez, "Crónica de España," *España y América*, LXXIII (January–March, 1922), pp. 468–71.

17. Ortega y Gasset, *España invertebrada* (1921), p. 78.

18. *Ibid.*, p. 77.

19. *Ibid.*, p. 70.

20. *Ibid.*, pp. 61–62.

21. *ABC*, September 12, 1923.

22. Antonio Goicoechea, *La crisis del constitucionalismo moderno* (1925), p. 114.

23. See Manuel García Morente, *La idea de la hispanidad* (Buenos Aires, 1938), p. 105; Vicente Marrero, *Maeztu* (1955), pp. 333–38; Sisinio Nevares, *El porqué de la sindicación obrera Católica* (1930), p. 41; Pedro Sáinz Rodríguez, *La tradición nacional en el estado futuro* (1935), p. 24; Sancho Izquierdo, et al., *Corporatismo*, p. 74; Emilio Zurano Muñoz, *Alianza hispanoamericana* (1926), p. 70.

24. Goicoechea, *La crisis del constitucionalismo*, p. 157.

25. Sancho Izquierdo, et al., *Corporatismo*, p. 24.

26. Sáinz Rodríguez, *La tradición nacional*, pp. 21–22.

27. See Goicoechea, *La crisis del constitucionalismo*, pp. 155–56; Sáinz

Rodríguez, *La tradición nacional,* pp. 21–22; Sancho Izquierdo, *et al.,* *Corporatismo,* p. 95.

28. Maeztu, quoted in Salvador de Madariaga, "Diálogo de la intolerancia," *El Sol,* March 21, 1926.

29. García Morente, *La idea de la hispanidad,* p. 84. Similar arguments are advanced by Adolfo Bonilla y San Martín in his prologue to Goicoechea, *La crisis del constitucionalismo,* pp. 9–10, and by Eduardo Sanz y Escartín in his epilogue to Jerónimo García Gallego, *Los valores eternos de la civilización política europea y la desorientación y los errores de nuestros días* (Segovia, 1928), pp. 431–32.

30. The corporative state idea was by no means the same thing to all men. The Catholic aristocrat Luis Marichalar, the Vizconde de Eza, seemed to regard it as the best means not just for accomplishing the social objectives uppermost in the minds of most conservatives but for preserving a system of free enterprise capitalism as well. See his *La futura política-económica-exterior de España* (1917), pp. 30–31. On the other hand Ubaldo Romero Quiñones, *La revolución social* (1912), saw the corporative state as the means of accomplishing a genuine social revolution based upon what can perhaps best be described as the principles of Christian anarchism.

31. Ramiro de Maeztu was also a prominent spokesman of this school in the early twentieth century. See Chapter 4, note 75.

32. See Chapter 4, notes 168 and 171. See also the generally excellent series of essays by different authors in *Ideario de Don Antonio Maura sobre la vida local: textos y estudios. Homenaje en el primer centenario de nacimiento de un gran español* (1954), esp. pp. 289–99, 312–24.

33. See, for example, Ángel Rodríguez Pascual, *Conceptos fundamentales del problema social: su relación con la organización profesional. Discurso leído ante la Real Academia Hispano-Americana de Ciencias y Artes en el acto de su recepción pública por . . .* (Cádiz, 1926). A prolific Catholic journalist, Rodríguez Pascual was active among his Church's youth groups in Madrid. He was the founder and permanent director of the Juventud Popular Católica.

34. See Chapter 1, note 81.

35. See Maximiano García Venero, *Víctor Pradera, guerrillero de la unidad* (1943).

36. Vázquez de Mella, *Dogmas nacionales* (1948, 2nd ed.), pp. 186–93. Much of the material in this work was published originally during the World War I period and the early 1920s.

37. *Ibid.,* p. 103.

38. *Ibid.,* p. 104.

39. *Ibid.,* p. 110.

40. *Ibid.,* p. 112.

41. *Ibid.,* pp. 113–14.

42. Pradera, *Al servicio de la partia: las ocasiones perdidas por la dictadura* (1930), pp. 112–13, 222–23.

43. Pradera, *El estado nuevo* (1941, 3rd ed.), pp. 222–24. The work consists of material written mainly in the early 1930s.

44. *Ibid.,* pp. 188–89.

45. *Ibid.*, p. 200. Another formula for corporative organization is found in José Medina Echevarría, *La representación profesional en las asambleas legislativas* (Valencia, 1927).

46. On early Christian Democracy in Spain see Chapter 4, notes 139 and 140. In 1920 *El Debate*, a newspaper that often reflected the Christian Democratic viewpoint, sponsored a series of conferences on social problems in Spain and the Christian solution to them. The conferences, the texts of which appeared in *El Debate* between April and July of 1920, contain many strong endorsements by Christian Democrats of the corporative state. See also Pablo Villada, "Curso de conferencias sociales," *Razón y Fe*, LVII (May–August, 1920), pp. 273–94. Luis Jordana de Pozas, an important member of the Grupo de la Democracia Cristiana, makes a plea for the corporative state in *Problemas sociales candentes* (Subirana, 1930). The work was presented at a cycle of conferences organized by the Christian Democrats following the fall of the dictator.

47. Burgos y Mazo, *El problema social y la Democracia Cristiana*, with a prologue by Eduardo Dato, I (Barcelona, 1914), pp. 293–94, 299–300.

48. See Sancho Izquierdo, et al., *Corporatismo*, p. 82. See also Maximiliano Arboleya Martínez, *XL aniversario de la "Rerum Novarum," la Carta Magna de la justicia social* (Barcelona, 1931), pp. 119–20; Graciano Martínez, "Sana doctrina sobre sindicatos," pp. 161–72; and Salvador Minguijón, prologue to the second edition of Severino Aznar, *Impresiones de un Demócrata Cristiano* (1950), p. 21.

49. See Chapter 4, notes 144, 145.

50. On Christian Democracy's criticism of those Catholics who insisted upon Church-dominated, joint labor-capital syndicates, see S. Aznar, "El problema del trabajo a domicilio," *Revista del Clero Español*, 1915, pp. 73–74, no number or month indicated. See also Aznar, *Impresiones de un Demócrata Cristiano* (1930, 1st ed.), esp. pp. 68–73, consisting of material written in 1923. Although Antonio Monedero, president of the Confederación Nacional Católica Agraria, defended the principle of joint capital-labor syndicates, he concurred with Christian Democrats in urging the corporative state. See his *La Confederación Nacional Católica Agraria en 1920: su espíritu, su organización y porvenir* (1921), esp. pp. 56–57.

51. Goicoechea, *La crisis del constitucionalismo moderno*, pp. 219, 148–49.

52. *Ibid.*, pp. 97–98, 219–25. Among other Catholic conservatives who expressed their approval of proportional representation as conceived by Goicoechea was José Calvo Sotelo, *Mis servicios al estado; seis años de gestión. Apuntes para la historia* (1931), p. 10. To some degree this type of proportional representation had been envisioned as early as 1902 by Ángel Salcedo Ruiz, *Sufragio universal y la elección por clases y gremios* (1902), pp. 114–18.

53. A prestigious intellectual associated with early Spanish liberalism who at the same time was an advocate of the corporative organization of society was Antonio Capmany (1742–1813). See his *Centinela contra francesas* (Cádiz, 1808), in which he warns against the Napoleonic tendency to destroy guilds and other intermediary groups and *Discurso económico-político en defensa del trabajo mecánico de los menestrales*

y de la influencia de sus gremios en las costumbres populares (1778). On
the advocacy by Krause of corporative concepts see my Chapter 5,
note 50.

54. For a typical expression of liberal admiration of the Spanish
Middle Ages see Manuel Pedregal y Cañedo, *Las clases obreras: su situación en el régimen antiquo y en el moderno*, Vol. II of *La España del
siglo XIX: Coleccion de conferencias históricas*, 3 vols. (1886–1887);
*Concepto de la democracia: resumen de la discusión sostenida en la
sección de Ciencias Morales y Políticas del Ateneo de Madrid* (1882),
esp. pp. 73–74, and *El poder y la libertad en el mundo antiguo* (1878).

55. See Juan José Gil Cremades, *El reformismo español: Krausismo,
escuela histórica, neotomismo* (1969), pp. 123, 136–54, 183–219.

56. Menéndez Pidal, *España y su historia*, 2 vols. (1957), I, pp. 42–43.

57. See the October 11, 1885, discourse of Labra in his *Discursos
políticos, académicos, y forenses*, 2 vols. (1884, 1886), II, pp. 416–20.

58. See Pérez Pujol, *Dicurso de . . . al congreso nacional sociológico
convocado por el Ateneo-Casino Obrero de Valencia* (Valencia, 1883),
Historia de las instituciones sociales de España goda (Valencia, 1895),
and his prologue to Luis Tramoyeres, *Instituciones gremiales: su origin y
organización en Valencia* (Valencia, 1885).

59. See Puyol y Alonso, *La vida política en España* (1892). There
is also a strong hint of advocacy of corporative organization in the writings of Liberal Party statesman Segismundo Moret. See his *Centralización,
descentralización, regionalismo* (1906) and *Importancia política de las
clases industriales y mercantiles: causas de la decadencia y prestigio del
sistema parlamentario* (1887). See also my Chapter 5, note 6.

60. See Costa, *Reconstitución y europeización de España: programa
para un partido nacional* (Huesca, 1942 ed. of work originally published
in 1900), pp. 26–29, 62, and the unsigned article "Las cámaras de comercio españoles," *Unión Ibero-Americana*, Año XIII (December, 1898),
pp. 411–14. See in addition Luis Morote, *La moral de la derrota* (1900),
p. 671, and Rafael Altamira, *España en América* (Valencia, 1908), p. 325.
Altamira also expressed himself (p. 329) in favor of restoring "their natural liberty of action" to class and interest groups existing within the
nation.

61. See Fité, *Las desdichas de la patria* (1899), p. 337. On the general
popularity of corporativist ideas among liberals at this time see Antonio
Royo Villanova, *La decentralización y el regionalismo*, with a prologue
by Joaquín Costa (Zaragoza, 1900), pp. 47–48. Royo Villanova himself,
however, rejected corporativism in favor of municipal autonomy.

62. Cascales y Muñoz, *El problema político al inaugurarse el siglo XX:
el régimen parlamentario y funcionarismo* (1902), pp. 3–4, 107–20.

63. See Juan Luis de Simón Tobalina, "La representación corporativa
en los proyectos de Maura," in Maura, *Ideario*, pp. 485–92, 505–508,
510–12. See also my Chapter 5, note 71.

64. Canalejas prologue to Cascales y Muñoz, *El problema político*, p. 4.

65. González Posada, article of 1917 reproduced in his *España en
crisis*, pp. 17–19. Another liberal—although he had begun his political
career as a conservative—who favored corporative organization at this

time was the controversial Santiago Alba. See his *Problemas de España* (1916).

66. Posada, *España en crisis*, pp. 165–66. See also Chapter 5, note 117.

67. See Chapter 5, notes 85, 86, 88, 91, 94, and 95.

68. Giner, quoted in Posada, *España en crisis*, pp. 163–64. See also my Chapter 5, note 96.

69. Even an apologist for the Socialist Party, who sang the praises of universal education and thought that an educated electorate could wisely choose a lower house on the basis of inorganic universal suffrage, made a strong case for a corporative senate. See Juan Sánchez Rivera, *El sufragio universal y el parlamentarismo* (1928).

70. Antonio Zozaya, "Problemas fundamentales," *Boletín de la Institución Libre de Enseñanza*, Año LIV, no. 839 (March 31, 1930), p. 94.

71. Primo de Rivera, *El pensamiento de . . .; sus notas, artículos y discursos*, with a prologue by José María Pemán (1929), p. 36. A sketchy survey of this period is found in Dillwyn F. Ratcliff, *Prelude to Franco: Political Aspects of the Dictatorship of General Primo de Rivera* (New York, 1957).

72. Primo de Rivera, *El pensamiento*, p. 37.

73. *Ibid.*, pp. 75–76.

74. See the prologue by Antonio Goicoechea to Calvo Sotelo, *La voz de un perseguido*, 2 vols. (1933, 1934), I, p. x. For favorable treatments of Calvo Sotelo see Eduardo Aunós Pérez, *Calvo Sotelo y la política de su tiempo* (1941), and Eugenio Vegas Latapié, *El pensamiento político de Calvo Sotelo* (1941).

75. Simón Tobalina, "La representación corporativa en los proyectos de Maura," pp. 507–508.

76. Calvo Sotelo, *Mis servicios al estado*, pp. 8–9.

77. Simón Tobalina, "La representación," p. 508. See also *Estatuto municipal: decreto ley de 8 de marzo de 1924*, with a prologue by Calvo Sotelo (1924).

78. Calvo Sotelo, *Mis servicios al estado*, pp. 54–55, concedes that this was a serious mistake.

79. Primo de Rivera, *El pensamiento*, pp. 74, 360.

80. *Ibid.*, p. 361. These ideas were developed at some length by Primo in two 1923 *Manifiestos*, one directed to the working classes, another to the management-capital sector, and included in *ibid.*, pp. 119–23.

81. For the ideas of Eduardo Aunós, who in his corporative beliefs considered himself to be following the precepts of *Rerum Novarum*, see his: *Epistolario, 1916–1941: cartas político-literarios* (1941); *España en crisis* (Buenos Aires, 1942); *El estado corporativo* (1928); *Itinerario histórico de la España contemporánea* (Barcelona, 1940); *La reforma corporativa del estado* (1935). As many Spaniards in the Catholic social justice movement, Aunós was influenced by the Marquis René de la Tour du Pin, an early French advocate of the corporative organization of society. See La Tour du Pin, *Hacia un orden social Cristiano*, translated into Spanish and with an introduction by Eduardo Aunós (1936). Aunós served as minister of justice in the early Franco administration and in 1942 undertook a voyage to Argentina to strengthen ties between that country and

Spain. See his *Argentina, el imperio del sur* (Buenos Aires, 1944). Antonio Aunós Pérez was also a leading apologist for the corporative state. See his *El nuevo derecho corporativo* (1929) and *Principios de derecho corporativo* (Barcelona, 1929). In 1926 he founded the Barcelona quarterly *Revista Social*. Four years later in the same city he founded the monthly *Información Corporativa*.

82. José María Taboada Lago, *La Acción Católica en España* (1934), p. 151, claims that the basic idea for the comité paritario originated with Jaime Balmes.

83. See Sancho Izquierdo, et al., *Corporatismo*, pp. 166–67.

84. Romanones, *Notas de una vida, 1912–1931*, p. 216. See also Arboleya Martínez, *XL aniversario de la "Rerum Novarum,"* p. 114, who talks of the co-opting of the socialist labor unions and of the degree to which, under the dictatorship, they accepted the traditional Catholic concept of corporativism. He further claims that during this period liberals came around to the Catholic view on the corporative state.

85. Vázquez de Mella, *Dogmas nacionales*, pp. 56–58.

86. See Pradera, *Al servicio de la patria*, pp. 19–20.

87. *Ibid.*, pp. 53–57.

88. Maura's sons also opposed the dictatorship and have written books critical of Primo de Rivera. See Gabriel Maura y Gamazo, *Bosquejo histórico de la dictadura*, 2 vols. (1930), and, with Melchor Fernández Almagro, *Por qué cayó Alfonso XIII: evolución y disolución de los partidos históricos durante su reinado* (1948); and Miguel Maura y Gamazo, *Así cayó Alfonso XIII* (México, D.F., 1962). José Sánchez Guerra, for a brief time the head of the Conservative Party, also opposed Primo de Rivera and went into voluntary exile shortly after the establishment of the dictatorship. See his *Al servicio de España* (1930).

89. Pradera, *Al servicio de la patria*, pp. 374, 376–78. Pradera in addition (pp. 401–11) accused Primo of failing to achieve decentralization and of abandoning his early ideas in favor of municipal and regional autarquía, that is, semi-autonomy within a decentralized political structure. See also Pradera's prologue to Ignacio Estruch y Díaz de Lara, *Política salvadora* (1934).

90. Manuel de Burgos y Mazo from the outset opposed the dictator. See his *Al servicio de la doctrina constitucional* (1930) and *La dictadura y los constitucionalistas*, 4 vols. (1934–1935).

91. On the alleged fascist leanings of Eduardo Aunós Pérez, who is described as an idolater of Mussolini, see Jerónimo García Gallego, *Los valores eternos*, pp. xxxi, 373–86.

92. See Joaquín Azpiazu, "Hacia la implantación del patrón de oro en España," *Razón y Fe*, LXXXIX (October–December, 1929), pp. 289–310, arguing for a policy of government decentralization so as to encourage economic productivity; Galindo Herrera, *Historia de los partidos monárquicos*, pp. 17–18; Isidro Gomá y Tomás, *Antilaicismo*, 2 vols. (Barcelona, 1935), I, pp. 123–28; Ángel Rodríguez Pascual, *Conceptos fundamentales del problema social*, pp. 23–25.

93. S. Nevares, *El porqué de la sindicación*, pp. 87–88.

94. See *Boletín Oficial del Ministerio de Estado*, Año XXXIX, no. 7 (July, 1929), p. 496.

95. For an example of the sort of objections that Catholics raised to the favored status that Primo de Rivera conferred on the UGT see Carlos Ruiz del Castillo, *El conflicto entre el comunismo y la reforma social* (1928).

96. J. García Gallego, *Los valores eternos*, pp. 373–86.

97. See *ibid.*, esp. pp. xii, xxxi, xxxiv.

98. For works in the spirit represented by the Liga, see Francisco Villanueva, *La crisis de la democracia* (1927) and *El momento constitucional: crónica de actuaciones públicas y privadas para salir de la dictadura en España* (1929).

99. García Gallego, *Los valores eternos*, p. xxi.

100. Severino Aznar, quoted in "Crónicas Generales," *Razón y Fe*, XCI (April–June, 1930), p. 361.

101. Pedro Rico, "Crisis Bilbaína: una crisis comercial," *Revista de Ambos Mundos*, no. 22 (July, 1930), pp. 17–19.

102. Baldomero Argente, "Del momento: hogares sin pan," *ibid.*, no. 30 (March, 1931), p. 85.

103. Moreno Nieto, quoted by Juan Manuel Ortí y Lara in his introduction to the Spanish edition of Franz Hitze, *El problema social y su solución* (1880).

104. Maximiliano Estébanez, "Sagasta," *España y América*, I (January 15, 1903), pp. 107–108. See also Joaquín de Encinas, *La tradición española y la revolución* (1958), p. 129.

105. Donoso Cortés, *Obras completas de* . . ., II (1946), p. 311–12.

106. Sáinz, Rodríguez, *La tradición nacional*, p. 14.

107. Gonzalo Fernández de la Mora, "Artículos de Gregorio Marañón," *Mirador Literario, Crónica Semanal de las Letras, ABC*, January 23, 1968, p. 6.

108. Baldomero Argente, "Ante el momento político," *Revista de Ambos Mundos*, no. 33 (June, 1931), pp. 3–5.

NOTES TO CHAPTER 13

1. Severino Aznar, "Noticias Generales," *Razón y Fe*, XCI (April–June, 1930), p. 77.

2. See José M. Sánchez, *Reform and Reaction: The Politico-Religious Background of the Spanish Civil War* (Chapel Hill, N.C., 1963), pp. 73, 78. A succinct summary of these events and of the entire period of the second republic is Joaquín Arrarás, *Historia de la segunda república española*, abbreviated text (1965), esp. pp. 7–20. Also valuable is Ricardo de la Cierva, *Historia de la guerra civil española, antecedentes: monarquía y república, 1898–1936* (1969), esp. pp. 138–51, and Richard A. H. Robinson, *The Origins of Franco's Spain: The Right, the Republic and Revolution, 1931–1936* (Pittsburgh, 1970). A valuable study concentrating on the CEDA, the Robinson book appeared too late to allow for inclusion of some of its material in the text of my work.

3. Sánchez, *Reform and Reaction*, p. 111.

4. *Ibid.*, p. 128. For indications of the type of opposition that Catholics waged to the anticlerical programs of the second republic see: Cultura Española, *Los Católicos y la república* (1934); Rafael García y García del Castro, Bishop of Jaen, *¿El Catolicismo en crisis?* (1935); Gabino Márquez, S.J., *Errores actuales que se hallan extendidos en España causando gravísimos estragos en el pueblo Catótico expuestos y refutados* (1935); E. Allison Peers, *Spain, the Church and the Orders* (London, 1939) and *The Spanish Tragedy, 1930–1936: Dictatorship, Republic, Chaos*, (New York, 1936); Jesús Requejo San Román, *El Cardenal Segura* (1932?) and *De la revolución española: los Jesuitas*, with a prologue by Ángel Herrera y Oria (1932); Monsignor Juan Tusquets, *Orígenes de la revolución española* (Barcelona, 1932).

5. Isidro Gomá y Tomás, *Antilaicismo*, 2 vols. (Barcelona, 1935), I, p. 141. On Goma see my Chapter 4, note 44.

6. Teodoro Rodríguez, *El problema social y las derechas: nuevas orientaciones* (El Escorial, 1935), pp. 20–21.

7. Pedro Sáinz Rodríguez, *La tradición nacional en el estado futuro* (1935), p. 18.

8. *Ibid.*, pp. 3–4.

9. See José María Gil Robles, *No fue posible la paz* (1968), pp. 45–46. This is an indispensable source, written by the leader of the rightist CEDA (which will be discussed later) and one of the most important political figures of the second republic.

10. T. Rodríguez, *El problema social*, p. 111.

11. Ramón Serrano Suñer, *De la victoria y la postguerra: discursos* (1941), p. 79. A brother-in-law of Francisco Franco, Serrano Suñer was an important figure in rightist circles and in the Falange during the second republic. See Ángel Alcázar de Velasco, *Serrano Suñer en la Falange* (1941).

12. T. Rodríguez, *El problema social*, p. 43.

13. Juan Bautista Luis y Pérez, Bishop of Oviedo, prologue to Maximiliano Arboleya Martínez, *XL aniversario de la "Rerum Novarum," la Carta Magna de la justicia social* (1931), pp. 7–9.

14. José María Taboada Lago, *La Acción Católica en España* (1934), p. 125.

15. *Ibid.*, pp. 90–91.

16. For sources revealing the anti-semitic spirit of the period see Chapter 4, note 41.

17. Pío Baroja, *Comunistas, Judíos y demás ralea* (Valladolid, 1939), p. 66. The work is made up mainly of articles published before the civil war .

18. *Ibid.*, pp. 69–70.

19. See Vicente Marrero, *Maeztu* (1955), pp. 555–56. For Maeztu's political thought at this time see his *Liquidación de la monarquía parlamentaria* (1957) and *El nuevo tradicionalismo y la revolución social* (1959), vols. XII and XXI, respectively, in *Obras de. . . .* See also Gonzalo Fernández de la Mora, *Maeztu y la teoría de la revolución* (1956).

20. See "Semblanza de Pradera" by the Conde de Rodezno in Pradera, *El estado nuevo* (1941, 3rd ed.), esp. pp. 12–15.

21. Sáinz Rodríguez was the director of the library maintained by Acción Española.

22. On the views of Goicoechea at this time see his *Ciclo de conferencias sobre temas culturales y políticos* (1931).

23. On the views of Vegas Latapié at this time see his *Escritos políticos* (1940) and *Romanticismo y democracia* (Santander, 1938, 2nd ed.).

24. On Acción Española see Luis María Anson, *Acción Española* (Zaragoza, 1960), and Ignacio Estruch y Díaz de Lara, *Política salvadora*, with prologues by Antonio Goicoechea and Víctor Pradera (1934).

25. Acción Española was published sporadically from 1931 to 1936. The Conde de Santibáñez del Río was one of its principal editors. A representative sampling of the periodical's articles is found in "*Acción Española:*" *Antología* (Burgos, 1937).

26. See Maeztu, *Autobiografía* (1962), Vol. I in *Obras de. . . .* See also Santiago Galindo Herrera, *Historia de los partidos monárquicos bajo la segunda república* (1954), pp. 71–72.

27. Maeztu, *Autobiografía*, p. 322.

28. Sáinz Rodríguez, *La tradición nacional*, pp. 41–42, 46.

29. Pradera, *El estado nuevo*, pp. 151–61.

30. See E. Giménez Caballero, *Genio de España: exaltaciones a una resurrección nacional y del mundo* (1932), p. 170; Galindo Herrera, *Historia de los partidos*, pp. 44–45; and Melchor Fernández Almagro, *Historia de la república española, 1931–1936* (1940), p. 199.

31. One of the principal directors of the Comunión Tradicionalista Carlista was Manuel Fal Conde, a man who had enjoyed considerable success in organizing Carlist forces in Andalusia. On him see *Fal Conde y el requeté juzgados por el extranjero* (Burgos, 1937). On the Carlists at this time see also Galindo Herrera, *Breve historia del tradicionalismo español* (1956); Román Oyarzún, *Historia del Carlismo* (Bilboa, 1939); and Manuel Senante y Martínez, *Verdadera doctrina sobre acatamiento la resistencia a los poderes ilegítimas y de hecho: la política tradicionalista* (1932).

32. On Renovación Española see Francisco Moreno Herrera, the Marqués de Eliseda and later Conde de los Andes, *Fascismo, Catolicismo y monarquía* (1935).

33. On this see Gabriel Jackson, *The Spanish Republic and the Civil War, 1931–1939* (Princeton, N.J., 1965), pp. 179–80.

34. Ramiro Ledesma Ramos, *¿Fascismo en España?; Discurso a las juventudes de España*, with a study on Ledesma by Santiago Montero Díaz (1968), p. 64. These two works by Ledesma, written in 1935 and published separately at that time, appeared in a combined edition in 1968. All citations of these works correspond to the later edition.

35. For an expression of this point of view see Francisco Bergamín, "La organización corporativa en España," *Revista de Ambos Mundos*, no. 18 (March, 1930), pp. 3–16.

36. See Galindo Herrera, *Historia de los partidos*, pp. 85–86.

37. See Gil Robles, *No fue posible la paz*, p. 438.

38. A central thesis of Ledesma Ramos in ¿Fascismo en España? is that there were fascist types, not fascists, in Spain.

39. An excellent revisionist article emphasizing the complexity of fascism and the inclusion in it of certain socially revolutionary elements is Roland Sarti, "Fascist Modernization in Italy: Traditional or Revolutionary?" The American Historical Review, LXXV, no. 4 (April, 1970), pp. 1029–1045.

40. On Cambó, see Chapter 12, note 15.

41. See Cambó, En torno del fascismo italiano (Barcelona, 1925), pp. 183–85. Another of Cambó's important works is Las dictaduras (1929).

42. Cambó, En torno del fascismo, pp. 42–46, 177.

43. Ibid., pp. 207–18. In a similar vein see Felipe Ferrer Calbetó, Los factores económicos y el momento político Catalán (Barcelona, 1933) and Nacionalismo económico español, with a prologue by José Calvo Sotelo (Barcelona, 1934).

44. See Eduardo Aunós Pérez, Calvo Sotelo y la política de su tiempo (1941), esp. p. 136.

45. See Galindo Herrera, Historia de los partidos, pp. 120–21, and Gil Robles, No fue posible la paz, pp. 150–51.

46. See April 25, 1935 article by José Antonio Primo de Rivera in Obras de . . ., edición cronológico, compiled by Agustín del Río Cisneros (1966, 4th ed.), pp. 532–33.

47. See Miguel Sancho Izquierdo, Leonardo Prieto Castro, Antonio Muñoz Casayus, Corporatismo: los movimientos nacionales contemporáneos (Zaragoza, 1937), pp. 175–76.

48. See Calvo Sotelo, La voz de un perseguido, 2 vols., vol. I with a prologue by Antonio Goicoechea, vol. II with a prologue by José María Pemán (1933, 1934), II, pp. 306–307. On Calvo Sotelo's defense of capitalism see ibid., I, pp. 20–21, and his El capitalismo contemporáneo y su evolución (1935).

49. Calvo Sotelo, Mis servicios al estado: seis años de gestión. Apuntes para la historia (1931), p. xiii.

50. Calvo Sotelo, La voz de un perseguido, I, p. 56.

51. Calvo Sotelo, quoted in Gil Robles, No fue posible la paz, p. 819.

52. On Calvo Sotelo's anti-Masonry prejudices see ibid., pp. 169–70.

53. An influential maverick group of rightists, including Miguel Maura y Gamazo, son of the long-time Conservative Party leader, repudiated monarchical principles and attempted to form an alliance of conservative republicans. See Calvo Sotelo, La voz de un perseguido, I, pp. 260–61, and Galindo Herrera, Historia de los partidos, pp. 26–28. Republican Catholics, among them Alfredo Mendizábal y Martín and José María Semprún y Gurrea, published between 1933 and 1936 the Madrid periodical Cruz y Raya: Revista de Afirmación y Negación. Many of the men associated with Cruz y Raya supported the republic during the civil war. See Alfredo Mendizábal, The Martyrdom of Spain: Origins of a Civil War, translated by C. H. Lumley with an introduction by Jacques Maritain (New York, 1938).

54. On Gil Robles see Juan Arrabal, José María Gil Robles: su vida,

su actuación, sus ideas (1933), and José Gutiérrez-Ravé, *Gil Robles, caudillo frustrado* (1967).

55. On Herrera see Chapter 4, note 116. Some of his political-social ideas during this period are found in his *La posición de la derecha española en la política actual: discurso pronunciado . . . en el Teatro Apolo de Valencia, 21 de diciembre, 1931* (1932) as well as in the *Boletín de la Asociación Católico-Nacional de Propagandistas*, published in Madrid, 1933–1935. Herrera was president of the Asociación.

56. On Acción Popular see José Monge y Bernal, *Acción Popular: estudio de biología política* (1936).

57. See Galindo Herrera, *Historia de los partidos*, p. 52.

58. Gil Robles, *No fue posible la paz*, p. 92.

59. See Michael P. Fogarty, *Christian Democracy in Western Europe, 1820–1953* (Notre Dame, Ind., 1957), pp. xix–xx.

60. Gil Robles, *No fue posible la paz*, p. 810. On the CEDA see also Francisco Casares, *La CEDA va a gobernar* (1934), and *CEDA Órgano de la Confederación Española de Derechas Autónomas*, published in Madrid, 1934–1935.

61. Gil Robles, *No fue posible la paz*, pp. 48–50.

62. *Ibid.*, pp. 821–22.

63. *Ibid.*, pp. 27–28.

64. Interesting material on the collaboration between the CEDA and the Radical Party is found in Alejandro Lerroux, *Mis memorias*. Originally published in Buenos Aires when Lerroux was in exile there, *Mis memorias* appeared in a Madrid edition in 1963. Another useful work by Lerroux, the controversial head of the Radical Party, is *La pequeña historia: apuntes para la historia grande vividos y redactados por el autor* (Buenos Aires, 1945).

65. See Herrera's prologue to Taboada Lago, *La Acción Católica*, pp. 5–7. See also Juan Hervás, *La Acción Católica y la política* (1936).

66. Even the CEDA's advocacy of political accidentalism evoked the fury of the far right. See Galindo Herrera, *Historia de los partidos*, pp. 106, 139, and Gil Robles, *No fue posible la paz*, pp. 381–88.

67. See Gil Robles, *No fue posible la paz*, p. 438.

68. Indispensable sources for the Falange are *FE*, the official weekly founded in Madrid in December of 1933, and *Arriba*. Published as a weekly beginning in March of 1935, *Arriba* was the official organ of the FE-JONS.

69. There is vast biographical material on José Antonio, undoubtedly the most compelling and colorful figure that the Spanish nationalist movement produced. A few of the many laudatory studies on him include: Emiliano Agüado, *José Antonio* (1942); José Luis de Arrese, *El estado totalitario en el pensamiento de José Antonio*, with a prologue by Raimundo Fernández Cuesta (1945), an important work written by an early member and a leading economic theoretician of the FE who later helped tame the Falange for the Franco regime, denying that José Antonio desired a totalitarian state; Francisco Bravo Martínez, *José Antonio: el hombre, el jefe, el camarada* (1940), the work of a man who was a personal collaborator of José Antonio and who later held important posts

in the Franco administration; Manuel Fuentes Irurozqui, *El pensamiento económico de José Antonio Primo de Rivera*, with a prologue by José María Gutiérrez de Castilla (1957), a sound study by an eminent Spanish economist; Nicolás Gonzáles Ruiz, *José Antonio, biografía e ideario* (1940) with a prologue by Pilar Primo de Rivera, José Antonio's sister; Luis Gutiérrez Santa María, *Hacia José Antonio* (Barcelona, 1958); Felipe Jiménez Sandoval, *José Antonio: biografía apasionada* (1963), considered the standard biography by many of José Antonio's admirers; Ramón Serrano Suñer, *Semblanza de José Antonio joven* (Barcelona, 1958), a brief but penetrating study. A more recent biography of José Antonio is Adolfo Muñoz Alonso, *Un pensador para un pueblo* (1970). Various editions of the complete works of José Antonio have appeared, beginning with a 1939 Barcelona volume. I have found the most useful edition to be *Obras de José Antonio Primo de Rivera: edición cronológico*, compiled by Augustín del Río Cisneros (see note 46). This is the volume henceforth cited as *Obras* in all references to José Antonio.

70. In 1933 José Antonio had collaborated on the newspaper *El Fascio* and had shown favorable inclinations toward fascism. By late 1934, however, he had come to deny the applicability of fascistic models to Spain. See his *Obras*, p. 995. See also José Luis de Arrese, *La revolución social del nacional sindicalismo* (1940), p. 35, for a convincing denial that the FE was a fascist organization. Originally completed in 1936 and awaiting only the prologue to be provided by José Antonio, this work did not appear in print until after the civil war. Especially in explaining the economic aspects of national syndicalism, the work is far less utopian and considerably more disciplined and closely reasoned than the pronouncements of José Antonio on economics.

71. On the elitism of José Antonio see the admirable study by Stanley G. Payne, *Falange: A History of Spanish Fascism* (Stanford, Calif., 1961), p. 29. In this section Payne notes the influence that the elitist theories of Ortega y Gasset exercised over José Antonio. Ortega y Gasset had given a new exposition of his elitist views in *La rebelión de las masas* (1932).

72. On the JONS see Francisco Guillén Salaya, *Anecdotario de la J.O.N.S.* (San Sebastián, 1938). See also "*J.O.N.S.*:" *Antología*, selection and a prologue by Juan Aparicio (Barcelona, 1939), consisting of readings from a periodical founded by Ledesma Ramos.

73. See the anonymous introduction to *Redondo: vida, pensamiento, obra* (Valladolid, 1941?), pp. xvi–xviii, an anthology of Redondo's writings. See also the introduction by an unidentified writer to *Redondo, Caudillo de Castilla: fragmentos de sus artículos periódicos y discursos* (Valladolid, 1937), p. 5, another anonymously edited work of Redondo's writings.

74. For indications of the esteem in which rightist circles tended to hold Germany at this time see Miguel Artigas, *Aspectos del hispanismo en la Alemania actual* (1929), and Vicente Gay, *De Alemania: recuerdos de un estudiante* (Barcelona, 1935). See also Gay's *Ideales de la nueva edad: la revolución nacionalsocialista* (Barcelona, 1934) and *Qué es el socialismo, el marxismo, y el fascismo* (Barcelona, 1934).

75. "To think of an adaptation in Spain of what Mussolini and Hitler

have conceived for their respective countries," Redondo wrote on November 20, 1933, "is to fall into the same vice that we denounce in our enemies." See *Redondo: vida*, p. lxx. See also Redondo, *El estado nacional* (Valladolid, 1938), pp. 116, 156–58, a work made up of representative writings originally published in *Libertad*, 1931–1932, and in *Igualdad*, a review that replaced *Libertad* when the latter was briefly suppressed.

76. Redondo, *El estado nacional*, pp. 78–81.

77. *Ibid.*, pp. 65–66.

78. Redondo, *Caudillo de Castilla*, p. 104.

79. *Ibid.*, p. 106.

80. *Ibid.*, pp. 148–49. In this thesis Redondo seems to have anticipated the "rural transformation" ideas to which various developmental experts began to turn in the late 1960s.

81. *Ibid.*, p. 154.

82. Redondo, *El estado nacional*, pp. 21–22, a selection written in December, 1931.

83. *Ibid.*, p. 124.

84. Works of the egocentric Giménez Caballero, who often claimed a role more important than the one he actually played in the founding of the JONS, include *La Falange: hecha hombre iconquista del del estado!* (Salamanca, 1937), *La nueva catolicidad: teoría general sobre el fascismo en Europa y en España* (1933), in which he envisions the contribution by Spain of a spiritual quality to German national socialism and Italian fascism, and *Los secretos de la Falange* (1939). See also his prologue to Pío Baroja, *Comunistas, Judíos*, claiming Baroja as a precursor of fascism in Spain—a role that the celebrated novelist denied.

85. See *"La Conquista del Estado:" Antología* (Barcelona, 1939), with a valuable prologue by Juan Aparicio describing the group, of which he was a member, that collaborated on this weekly. The *Antología* consists mainly of the writings of Ledesma Ramos.

86. On Ledesma see Emiliano Aguado, *Ramiro Ledesma en la crisis de España* (1943), Juan Aparicio, *Ramiro Ledesma, fundador de las J.O.N.S.* (1942), Santiago Montero Díaz, *La universidad y los orígenes del nacionalsindicalismo* (Múrcia, 1939) and "Estudio sobre Ramiro Ledesma Ramos" in Ledesma, *¿Fascismo?; Discurso*, pp. 13–36.

87. For Ledesma's principal criticism of fascism, see his 1935 *Discurso a las juventudes de España*, in *¿Fascismo?; Discurso*, esp. pp. 294–99. In this section he complains about the privileged status of the reactionary bourgeoisie in Italian fascism, noting that Italy had not moved to weaken the great fortresses of financial capital, of the bourgeoise industrial tycoons, and of the great landlords.

88. Ledesma *¿Fascismo?; Discurso*, p. 97.

89. See the Aparicio prologue to *"La Conquista del Estado,"* p. xiii.

90. *"La Conquista del Estado,"* pp. 4–5, reproducing the manifesto in which the founders of the weekly explained their ideology.

91. *Ibid.*, p. 5.

92. *Ibid.*, pp. 212–213.

93. *Ibid.*, pp. 6–7.

94. *Ibid.*, p. 213.

95. See Ledesma, ¿Fascismo?; Discurso, pp. 148–58.

96. The Obras completas of Ruiz de Alda were published in Barcelona in 1939.

97. On the ideology of the FE–JONS see José Pemartín, Qué es "lo nuevo:" consideraciones sobre el momento español presente (Sevilla, 1937); Julián Pemartín, Primera lección sobre el concepto jerarquía: coloración falangista (1939?) and Teoría de la Falange (1941), and José Pérez de Cabo, Arriba España, with a prologue by José Antonio (1935).

98. José Antonio's prologue to La dictadura de Primo de Rivera juzgada en el extranjero (1931), in Obras, pp. 9–13.

99. March 16, 1933 article of José Antonio, Obras, pp. 37–38.

100. August 27, 1934 article of José Antonio, ibid., p. 294.

101. March 28, 1935 article of José Antonio, ibid., p. 461.

102. "La Conquista del Estado," pp. 61–64.

103. Redondo, El estado nacional, p. 114.

104. José Antonio, Obras, pp. 566–67.

105. Ledesma, ¿Fascismo?; Discurso, p. 62.

106. Redondo, El estado nacional, p. 42.

107. Ibid., p. 50 .

108. Ibid., pp. 46–47.

109. December 7, 1933 article of José Antonio, Obras, p. 92.

110. See ibid., pp. 933–38. Ledesma, ¿Fascismo?; Discurso, pp. 196–97, notes that in the days immediately following its formation, the FE–JONS recruited many former Marxists.

111. José Antonio, Obras, pp. 192–93, 869.

112. On José Antonio's appeal to small landowners, individual proprietors, and artisans, see his May 19, 1935 discourse, ibid., pp. 562–64.

113. According to Redondo, El estado nacional, pp. 32–33, no less important than the struggle against communism was the campaign against the treason of bourgeois capitalism to the authentic values of the Spanish state.

114. February 13, 1936 article of José Antonio, Obras, pp. 882–83.

115. Arrese, La revolución social, p. 141.

116. Ibid., pp. 51, 142.

117. Ibid., p. 144.

118. Whether José Antonio gradually evolved into a proponent of social revolution because of ideological convictions, the viewpoint to which I personally subscribe, or simply because he tried to establish ties with the right and having failed in this turned against it, is debatable. On the matter see Gil Robles, No fue posible la paz, p. 442, note 59.

119. February 6, 1936 article of José Antonio, Obras, p. 787.

120. April 9, 1935 conference of José Antonio, ibid., pp. 507–508.

121. Arrese, La revolución social, p. 221.

122. José Antonio, admittedly, is quite vague in explaining this aspect of national syndicalism, but I believe I am intepreting his position accurately. If so, then there is a great deal of similarity between the ideology of the Spanish Falange and of Chilean Christian Democracy. The "communitarian society," long urged by Chile's Christian Democrats, is one in which the distinction between capital and labor is to be removed by

combining the two functions in the same individuals. In this light, the fact that Chile's Christian Democrats called their political party, founded in 1937, the Falange is readily understandable and altogether logical. See F. B. Pike, *Chile and the United States, 1880–1962* (Notre Dame, Ind., 1963), pp. 259–61.

123. Arrese, *La revolución social*, p. 92.

124. March 3, 1935 conference of José Antonio, *Obras*, pp. 426–27. See also the November 21, 1935, José Antonio article, *ibid.*, pp. 737–38. In the explanation of national syndicalism offered by Arrese, *La revolución social*, pp. 68–71, 95, laborers, technicians, and capitalists in each industry would be organized into one guild or syndicate. The syndicate itself would then determine the share of profits to be assigned the three sections comprising it. Eventually as workers received a part of their share of the profits in the form of company securities, the capital-labor distinction would disappear. Enterprises that operated at a loss would receive from the government enough money to guarantee workers a living wage, with funds for this purpose coming from the excess profits earned by other productive sectors of the economy.

125. Arrese, *La revolución social*, p. 223.

126. March 3, 1955 conference of José Antonio, *Obras*, p. 427.

127. See the October 29, 1933 speech of José Antonio, *ibid.*, pp. 66–67. Ledesma Ramos maintained that in the present epoch of history Spain required the positive action, the participation, of the masses in the great enterprises that the state initiated. "But there must be hierarchical order and a powerful state to instill a new discipline in the masses through a syndical economy." See Montero Díaz, quoting Ledesma, "Estudio sobre Ramiro Ledesma Ramos." pp. 32–33.

NOTES TO CHAPTER 14

1. Riva Agüero, an eminent historian who had spent much of the 1920s in Spain and who in 1932 ceremoniously announced his return to the Catholic Church, was prime minister for the military dictator Óscar R. Benavides in 1934. After brief service in this post he resigned, rather than sign a divorce law passed by Congress. See F. B. Pike, *The Modern History of Peru* (London, New York, 1967), pp. 258, 270. Riva Agüero's discourse in Lima in which he recanted his liberal beliefs and announced his return to the Church was published in Spain under the title *Un discurso notabilísimo del Dr. José de la Riva Agüero y Osma: conmovedora retracción de un intellectual peruano* (1933).

2. P. Martínez Vélez, "La fundación de Lima y el sentido de su centenario," *Revista de las Españas*, nos. 87–88 (November–December, 1934), pp. 476–77.

3. José María Taboada Lago, *La Acción Católica en España* (1934), p. 32.

4. Ramiro de Maeztu, quoted in Vicente Marrero, *Maeztu* (1955), p. 582.

5. Eugenio Vegas Latapié, *Romanticismo y democracia* (Santander, 1938), pp. 180–81.

6. *Ibid.*, pp. 183–184, in which the author praises the Nicaraguan Pablo Antonio Cuadra for understanding that only Spanish, Catholic values and traditions could save Spanish America from communism. Alberto Martín Artajo, who served as Spanish minister of foreign affairs, 1945–1955, praises not only Cuadra for his understanding of this truth but also the Peruvians Felipe Barreda Laos, Víctor Andrés Balaúnde, José de la Riva Agüero, and Alberto Wagner de Reyna; the Ecuadoran José María Velasco Ibarra; the Argentine Mario Amadeo; the Chilean Osvaldo Lira; the Mexican José Vasconcelos; and the Uruguayan Luis Alberto de Herrera. See Martín Artajo, *Hacia la comunidad hispánica de naciones* (1956), p. 8. Spaniards were also favorably impressed by the hispanista work of the Chilean Víctor de Valdivia, *El imperio iberoamericano* (Santiago de Chile, 1930). For additional material on Spanish Americans who responded positively to hispanidad in the early 1930s see Marrero, *Maeztu*, pp. 474–95.

7. On the origins of the term *hispanidad* see Ricardo del Arco y Garay, *La idea del imperio en la política y literatura españolas* (1944) p. 787.

8. This thesis is advanced by Ramón Serrano Suñer, *De la victoria y la postguerra: discursos* (1941), pp. 167–68.

9. Vegas Latapié, *Romanticismo*, pp. 177–78. Along similar lines see Taboada, *La Acción Católica*, p. 29, dealing with the alleged communist takeover in Mexico. In 1934 the Mexican secular priest Xavier Navarro, in an article published in Madrid, warned his religious brothers in Spain about the attempt of Marxist-Masonic forces to stamp out religion in the New World republic. Unless Spaniards were on guard, he implied, they would soon be in the same plight as Mexicans. See Navarro, "Crónica de México," *Revista Eclesiástica: Órgano del Clero de Habla Española*, VII (1934), pp. 306–17.

10. "Crónicas, México," *Razón y Fe*, CVII (January–April, 1935), pp. 239–54. On the alleged Marxist threat in Cuba see *ibid.*, p. 567. Ramiro de Maeztu, *Defensa de la hispanidad* (1934), p. 173, contended that Uruguay, under the influence of secularism fostered by two-time President José Batlle y Ordóñez (1903–1907, 1911–1915) had become a center of Marxist activity.

11. This is an underlying contention in Emiliano Zurano Muñoz, *España, madre de América* (1935). Francisco Gutiérrez Lasanta, *Juan Vázquez de Mella, el verbo de la hispanidad* (1961), pp. 45–46, traces this idea, so common during the 1930s, back to the World War I period, attributing its origin in part to Vázquez de Mella.

12. Raymond Carr, *Spain, 1808–1939* (Oxford, Eng., 1966), p. 606, note 2, observes that in arguing against anticlerical Article 26 of the republican constitution a deputy to the constituent Cortes asserted that suppression of the Spanish friars would mean the replacement of the Spanish language by English in Spanish America.

13. For an excellent treatment of Maeztu, including a bibliography of his works and works on him and impressions and appreciations written

by leading Spanish and Spanish-American intellectuals, see the special edition of *Cuadernos Hispanoamericanos*, nos. 33–34, 1952.

14. An interesting but short-lived periodical dedicated to expounding these views was *Hispanidad: Revista Quincenal de Ciencias, Artes . . . y Economía* (1935–1936).

15. Maeztu, *Defensa de la hispanidad*, pp. 155–65.

16. *Ibid.*, p. 59.

17. *Ibid.*, p. 73.

18. *Ibid.*, p. 67.

19. *Ibid.*, pp. 52–53.

20. *Ibid.*, p. 211.

21. Sessions of the congress extended from the seventh to the fourteenth of October. The title of the Gomá y Tomás discourse was "Apología de la hispanidad."

22. See F. Gutiérrez Lasanta, *Tres cardenales hispánicos y un obispo hispanizante* (Zaragoza, 1965), p. 15.

23. October 12, 1934 discourse of Gomá y Tomás in his *Antilaicismo*, 2 vols. (Barcelona, 1935), II, pp. 30–31.

24. *Ibid.*, p. 13.

25. *Ibid.*, p. 17.

26. *Ibid.*, p. 33.

27. *Ibid.*, p. 10.

28. *Ibid.*, p. 19.

29. *Ibid.*, p. 25.

30. *Ibid.*, p. 39.

31. See Gutiérrez Lasanta, *Tres cardenales*, p. 24.

32. October 12 discourse of Gomá y Tomás, pp. 42–44.

33. *Ibid.*, p. 48.

34. See Santiago Margariños, *El problema de la tierra en México y la constitución socialista de 1917* (1932), p. 277.

35. *La decadencia de occidente*, translated by García Morente, was published in Madrid in 1922 in the *Biblioteca de Ideas del Siglo XX* series directed by José Ortega y Gasset.

36. García Morente, *Idea de la hispanidad* (1961), pp. 9–11. (The original edition of this work was published in Buenos Aries in 1938.)

37. *Ibid.*, p. 13.

38. *Ibid.*, pp. 14–15.

39. *Ibid.*, pp. 43–48.

40. See García Morente, *Ensayos sobre el progreso* (1932). The work consists of a discourse read before the Academia de Ciencias Morales y Políticas, to which Adolfo González Posada delivered the reply.

41. García Morente, *Idea de la hispanidad*, pp. 16–17.

42. *El Diario Ilustrado* of Santiago de Chile, December 16, 1935, quoted in J. M. Gil Robles, *No fue posible la paz* (1968), p. 381.

43. Giménez Caballero, *La nueva catolicidad: teoría general sobre el fascismo en Europa y en España* (1933). In the period after the civil war Giménez Caballero became one of the most ardent spokesmen of hispanidad. See his *Amor a Argentina ó el genio de España en América*

(1948). In the 1960s he served as his country's ambassador to Paraguay. On him see Chapter 13, note 84.

44. Giménez Caballero, *Genio de España: exaltaciones a una resurrección nacional y del mundo* (1932), pp. 123–24.

45. *Ibid.*, pp. 129–30.

46. Giménez Caballero, *La nueva catolicidad*, p. 175.

47. *Ibid.*, p. 177.

48. Giménez Caballero, *Genio de España*, p. 151.

49. *Ibid.*, p. 210.

50. *Ibid.*, p. 250.

51. *Ibid.*, p. 262.

52. *Ibid.*, pp. 132–33.

53. *Ibid.*, p. 131.

54. Giménez Caballero, *Los secretos de la Falange* (1939), p. 34.

55. Giménez Caballero, *La nueva catolicidad*, p. 181.

56. Giménez Caballero, *La joven España: circuito imperial* (1929), p. 16.

57. Giménez Caballero, *La nueva catolicidad*, p. 52.

58. Giménez Caballero, "Revista Literaria Ibérica," *Revista de las Españas*, nos. 80–82 (April–March, 1934), p. 178.

59. "*La Conquista del Estado:*" *Antología* (Barcelona, 1939), pp. 94, 136.

60. *Ibid.*, p. 6.

61. See Redondo, *El estado nacional* (Valladolid, 1938), pp. 162–63.

62. *Onésimo Redondo: vida, pensamiento, obra* (Valladolid, 1941?), pp. lxvii–lxviii.

63. Redondo, *El estdo nacional*, p. 101.

64. Giménez Caballero, *Secretos de la Falange*, p. 19. On this matter see also H. Rutledge Southworth, "The Spanish Phalanx and Latin America," *Foreign Affairs*, XVIII, no. 1 (October, 1939), pp. 148–52.

65. June 24, 1935 article of José Antonio, *Obras de José Antonio Primo de Rivera: edición cronológica*, compiled by A. del Río Cisneros (1966, 4th ed.), pp. 601–602.

66. José Luis de Arrese, *La revolución social del nacional sindicalismo* (1940), p. 185. Raimundo Fernández Cuesta, quoted in *ibid.*, p. 167, also stressed that national syndicalism was a program for the entire Hispanic world, as did Juan Beneyto Pérez, *España y el problema de Europa: contribución a la historia de la idea de imperio* (1942), p. 285. Both Fernández Cuesta and Beneyto Pérez were important figures in the Falange.

67. Arrese, *La revolución social*, pp. 185–86.

68. Arco y Garay, *La idea de imperio*, p. 801, and José Antonio, *Obras*, p. 339.

69. April 18, 1935 article of José Antonio, *Obras*, p. 527.

70. See Chapter 3, notes 85–87.

71. Arrese, *La revolución social*, pp. 42–43.

72. December 7, 1933 article of José Antonio, *Obras*, p. 85. On Falange dreams of international power based on Spanish-American unification see also Falange Española de las Juntas de Ofensiva Nacional

Sindicalista, *El imperio de España* (Valladolid, 1937?), and Eugenio Montes, *La obra de la unidad* (Burgos, 1937).

73. "Información española e hispanoamericana: España, situación política," *Revista de las Españas*, nos. 77–79 (January–March, 1934), p. 17. The Unión at this time still received a government subvention of 40,000 pesetas.

74. See *Boletín Oficial del Ministerio de Estado*, Año XLV, no. 7 (July, 1935), p. 578. In the late 1920s the Casa de América had been reorganized as the Instituto de Economía Americana and had played a significant part in organizing the 1929 exposition in Sevilla. See Chapter 10, notes 28, 29, and 95.

75. "Información española e hispanoamericana," pp. 73–74.

76. Some of the effects of the depression on emigration to Spanish America are discussed by José Sánchez Guerra, an important Conservative Party leader, in *Plan de emigración*, with a prologue by Gregorio Marañón (1930).

77. Gil de Monforte, "Carta de Cuba: repatriaciones," *Revista de Ambos Mundos*, no. 39 (December, 1931), pp. 9–11. See also Severo Gómez Núñez, "La emigración y los emigrantes," *ibid.*, pp. 21–23.

78. See Chapter 10, Chart 6.

79. The decline is all the more startling when the depreciation of the peseta is taken into account. In 1929 the exchange rate was generally in the vicinity of 7.5 to the dollar. In the early 1930s, although subject to frequent fluctuations, the rate was generally in the proximity of 10:1.

80. The source for these statistics is Carlos Ibáñez de Ibero, *La personalidad internacional de España* (San Sebastián, 1940), pp. 137, 142–43. See also the valuable study by Vicente Torente and Gabriel Manueco, *Las relaciones económicas de España con Hispanoamérica* (1953). About two-thirds of this lengthy book written by two officials in the Spanish diplomatic service is devoted to statistical tabulations of trade between Spain and Spanish America for the 1931–1936 and 1946–1948 periods. Imports and exports are listed by commodity and according to country, volume, and value. Even as earlier workers in the field of practical hispanismo, Torente and Manueco were far from satisfied with the existing extent of commercial ties between Spain and Spanish America.

81. See *España y América: Revista Comercial*, no. 276 (August, 1935), p. 86.

82. *Boletín Oficial del Ministerio de Estado*, Año XLV, no. 6 (June, 1935), p. 624.

83. José Pérez Cepeda, "Vida marítima: nuestras comunicaciones con América," *España y América: Revista Comercial*, no. 273 (May, 1935), p. 52.

84. See "Bloque Ibero-Americano," *ibid.*, no. 275 (July, 1935), p. 75.

85. Figures for 1935 are compiled on the basis of information in *Boletín Oficial del Ministerio de Estado*, Año XLV, no. 7 (July, 1935), pp. 654–61. On 1930 statistics see Chapter 11, note 23.

86. A random sampling shows that consular personnel in Germany stood at the same number in 1935 as in 1930. In Austria consular personnel increased by two during this five-year period and in Turkey the

number rose from three to four; in Belgium personnel was cut back by one; in Bulgaria it was augmented by one; in China it was reduced from three to two; in the United States, from eleven to nine; in France, from thirty to twenty-eight; in Great Britain, from sixteen to fourteen; in Italy, from nine to eight; in Portugal, from ten to nine. See *Boletín* as cited in note 85.

87. See Fernández Heredia y Gastañaga, *Un año de misión en Bolivia* (1935), pp. 5–6.

88. *Ibid.*, pp. 278–89, 364–66.

89. In spite of the disastrous consequences of the military mission, the Chaco War afforded Spain the opportunity to play a constructive role in New World affairs, for Julio Álvarez del Vayo, Spanish ambassador to the League of Nations, presided over the commission that the Council of the League sent to the scene of contention in the attempt to end hostilities. An *Informe de la Comisión del Chaco* was published in Madrid in May of 1934.

90. Zulueta, "Las relaciones hispanoamericanas," *España y América: Revista Comercial*, no. 244 (December, 1932), pp. 135–37.

91. Niceto Alcalá Zamora, who was both a prime minister and a president of the second republic, was also interested in the cultural-spiritual side of hispanismo as is evidenced in his *Reflecciones sobre las Leyes de Indias* (1935).

92. See Chapter 8, note 63.

93. See *Revista de las Españas*, nos. 80–82 (April–May, 1934), p. 195.

94. *Boletín Oficial del Ministerio de Estado*, Año XLIII, no. 1 (January, 1933), p. 11. The government of the republic also allotted some of its tight funds to a useful bibliographical project. This resulted in the publication of the *Catálogo de las bibliotecas españolas en las repúblicas hispano-americanas* (1934) under the auspices of the Junta de Relaciones Culturales of the Ministerio de Asuntos Exteriores.

95. William Baker Bristol, "Hispanidad in South America, 1936–1945" (unpublished doctoral dissertation, University of Pennsylvania, 1947), p. 47.

96. See Percy Alvin Martin, "El Centro de Estudios de Historia de América en la Universidad de Sevilla," *Hispanic American Historical Review*, XIV, no. 2 (May, 1934), pp. 245–46.

97. In 1933 Spain and Brazil raised their legations to embassy status.

98. See *Revista de las Españas*, nos. 80–82 (April–May, 1934) p. 196. L. E. Smith, *Mexico and the Spanish Republicans* (Berkeley, Calif., 1955), is an important study of this subject.

99. See *Revista de las Españas*, nos. 80–82, p. 206.

100. In Germany, Belgium, China, France, Italy, Japan, and Poland diplomatic personnel was reduced by two between 1930 and 1935; in the United States it was reduced by one, in Great Britain by four. Moreover, diplomatic representation before the Holy See was reduced by two, constituting a one-third reduction. Figures for 1935 are compiled on the basis of information in *Boletín Oficial del Ministerio de Estado*, Año XLV, no. 7 (July, 1935), pp. 645–53. Figures for 1930 are taken from *ibid.*, Año XL, no. 1 (January, 1930), pp. 24–37.

101. Information is based on sources cited in above note.
102. See Chapter 8, note 25.
103. See note 1.
104. The diplomat was Benjamín Cohen, Chilean chargé d'affaires in Washington at the time of the Roosevelt inauguration. See F. B. Pike, *Chile and the United States, 1880–1962* (Notre Dame, Ind., 1963), pp. 238–39.
105. *El Imparcial*, Santiago de Chile, December 29, 1933.
106. See Chapter 7, note 67.
107. Ugarte, "El crepúsculo del imperialismo yanqui," *Revista de las Españas*, nos. 83–84 (July–August, 1934), pp. 257–60.
108. Camilo Barcía Trelles, *Puntos cardinales de la política internacional española* (Barcelona, 1939), p. 234. On Barcía see Chapter 6, note 116.

NOTES TO CHAPTER 15

1. Labra, *El problema hispano-americano* (1906), p. 7.
2. Badía Malacrida, *El factor geográfico en la política sudamericana: memoria redactada . . . en 1919* (1944, 2nd ed.), p. 55.
3. Valera, *Cartas americanas* (1889), p. 90.
4. Menéndez Pelayo, quoted in José María Taboada Lago, *La Acción Católica en España* (1934), p. 183.
5. For a typical expression of the viewpoint that Spanish America is in a period of formation, see Emilio Zurano Muñoz, *Apuntes para la organización económica entre los pueblos hispánicos* (no date), p. 158.
6. Unamuno, *Temas argentinos* (Buenos Aires, 1943), pp. 59–60.
7. Camilo Barcía Trelles, *Puntos cardinales de la política internacional española* (Barcelona, 1939), pp. 196–97.
8. Bruno Ibeas, "La cuestión religiosa en Méjico," *España y América*, XCII (October–December, 1926), pp. 162–63.
9. "Boletín Canónico," *Razón y Fe*, XXVII (May–August, 1910), pp. 236–37.
10. Unamuno, *Temas argentinos*, pp. 55–56.
11. Unamuno, "Sobre la literatura hispanoamericana," an essay written in 1905, in *Algunas consideraciones sobre la literatura hispanoamericana* (1968, 3rd ed.), p. 100.
12. Ángel Álvarez de Miranda, "El pensamiento de Unamuno sobre Hispanoamérica," *Cuadernos Hispanoamericanos*, no. 13 (January–February, 1950), pp. 58–59.
13. *Ibid.*, p. 71.
14. See the December 6, 1916 discourse of Ortega y Gasset, "Impresiones de un viajero," delivered in the Instituto Popular de Conferencias, Buenos Aires, in *Meditación del pueblo joven* (1964), pp. 21–22.
15. Ortega y Gasset, "Ictiosauros y editores clandestinos," originally published in the Buenos Aires review Sur in November of 1937 and included in *Meditación*, p. 66.

16. Writing on this matter, Pedro Sáinz Rodríguez, *La evolución de las ideas sobre la decadencia española* (1924), p. 42, asserts that Spaniards in the colonial period were split on the racial issue. On one hand stood Bartolomé de las Casas, who believed in racial equality, and on the other Juan Ginés de Sepúlveda, who justified the conquest on the basis of the superiority of the Spanish over the Indian race. The Bolivian Gustavo Adolfo Otero, *Figura y carácter del Indio* (Barcelona, no date), p. 32, is typical of those who insist that the paternalistic humanitarianism of Las Casas vis-à-vis the Indian was inspired by the Dominican friar's belief in the inferiority of the native and the subsequent need to protect him through special devices. On some eighteenth-century Spanish attitudes on the Indian and the entire question of the raza in America, attitudes which remained remarkably consistent in the twentieth century, see Anthony Tudisco, "The Land, People and Problems of America in Eighteenth-Century Spanish Literature," *The Americas*, XII, no. 4 (April, 1956), pp. 363–84, and "America in Some Travelers, Historians, and Political Economists of the Spanish Eighteenth Century," *ibid.*, XV, no. 1 (July, 1958), pp. 1–22.

17. On "pigmentocracy" see Chapter 9, note 26. Spanish attitudes on race had also been shaped to some degree by Count Gobineau. On Gobineau's possible influence on Menéndez Pelayo, see Pedro Laín Entralgo, *Menéndez Pelayo: historia de sus problemas intelectuales* (1944), pp. 196–201.

18. Father Paulino Díaz, "Cartas de América," *España y América*, Año I, no. 8 (April 15, 1903), p. 516.

19. F. J. Simonet, "Misión providencial de la Iglesia Católica y de la nación española en el descubrimiento del nueva mundo," *El Siglo Futuro*, October 18, 1892, p. 2.

20. Ortega y Gasset, *Meditación*, p. 100.

21. Pemán, *Valor del hispanoamericanismo en el progreso total humano hacia la unificación y la paz* (1927), p. 5.

22. *Cultura Hispano-Americana*, no. 32 (July 15, 1915), p. 30, editorializing on the death of Porfirio Díaz and maintaining that he had understood how to govern the type of people that constituted the Mexican populace.

23. In 1899 Maeztu had commented on the Spanish assumption of the ethnic inferiority of the Indian but had denied that he shared this assumption. See Vicente Marrero, *Maeztu* (1955), p. 62.

24. Maeztu, "El espíritu de la economía ibero-americana," *Revista de las Españas*, nos. 9–11 (May–June, 1927), p. 341. Mexican philosopher-historian Edmundo O'Gorman in *The Invention of America: An Inquiry into the Historical Nature of the New World and the Meaning of its History* (Bloomington, Ind., 1961) attributes Spanish America's hostility to innovation and its lack of concern with material development not to Indian but to Spanish characteristics.

25. Santiago Magariños, *El problema de la tierra en México y la constitución socialista de 1917* (México, D. F., 1932), p. 274.

26. Menéndez Pelayo, *Historia de la poesía hispano-americana*, 2 vols. (1911, 1913), I, pp. 124–26.

27. Antonio María Fabié y Escudero, *Ensayo histórico de la legislación española en sus estados de ultramar* (1896), p. 12.

28. Father Casiano García, "De algunos textos de historia," *España y América*, XVII (October–December, 1926), p. 190. One-time prime minister and president of the second republic Niceto Alcalá Zamora also assumed that Spaniards, in mixing with the Indians, had caused all elements of Indian culture to disappear. See José Jacinto Rada, secretary of the legation of Peru in Spain, "Hispanoamericanismo," *España y América: Revista Comercial*, no. 275 (July, 1935), pp. 80–81.

29. Spaniards were also disdainful toward Spanish America because of the abundance of Negro elements in some of the republics. Rather typically Menéndez Pelayo, *Historia de la poesía*, I, p. 312, referred to the Blacks of the Dominican Republic as "elements refractory to all European races and civilization."

30. Alfredo Vicenti, an influential journalist and the chronicler of the 1900 Congreso Hispano Americano, expressed a widespread view when he recommended Spanish emigration to America as the best means of improving the hybrid race of that area. See Vicenti, "El Congreso Hispano-Americano: ponencias e informes," *La Ilustración Española y Americana*, October 30, 1900, p. 251. On this matter see also Chapter 6, note 1.

31. P. Martínez Vélez, "Influencia de la raza en la civilización," *España y América*, XL (October–December, 1913), pp. 57–58.

32. Unamuno, *En torno al casticismo: cinco ensayos* (1957, 4th ed.), p. 13. In this work Unamuno also argues (p. 143) that the masses of Europe are similar because they share a common protoplasm. The differences among the European nations he attributes to historical influences. It seems clear that, given his views on racial mixture, Unamuno did not feel that Spaniards and Spanish Americans shared a common protoplasm. In another work, "Sobre la europeización," in *Algunas consideraciones*, p. 125, Unamuno asserted: "spiritual mestizaje is an infecund hybridism."

33. See Álvarez, "El pensamiento de Unamuno," p. 60.

34. *El problema de la emigración* (1918), pp. 370–72.

35. M. A. Bedoya, "La confederación española de Indianos y residentes," *Unión Ibero-Americana*, Año XXXVI (March–April, 1922), pp. 18–19.

36. Lazúrtegui, *Informe y memoria presentadas a las Excmas. Diputaciones Provinciales de Vizcaya, Guipúzcoa, Álava y Navarra* . . . (Bilbao, 1923), p. 79.

37. Latorre y Setién, *El panamericanismo y el porvenir de la América española* (1924, 2nd ed.), pp. 83, 90. Latorre stated (pp. 5–6) that he would affirm neither the absolute superiority of the white race, as Gobineau did, nor the absolute equality of all races. Races at different points in their evolution, he contended, developed certain characteristics that other races, at their particular stage of progress, possessed to a much lesser degree. He maintained that the white race had developed certain characteristics, especially of an intellectual and moral type, that had propelled it to a degree of civilization which was "very superior to that of its sister races."

38. Chilean journalist Carlos Silva Vildósola, writing in *El Mercurio* (Santiago de Chile), February 20, 1914, as quoted in Javier Fernández Pesquero, *España ante el concepto americano* (1923), pp. 155–56.

39. "Benomar," "El futuro problema iberoamericano: los cuatro peligros," *Revista de las Españas,* nos. 7–8 (March–April, 1927), pp. 210–11.

40. Hildebrando Castro Pozo, *Renuevo de peruanidad* (Lima, 1934), pp. 21, 26–27.

41. Luis E. Valcárcel, *Tempestad en los Andes* (Lima, 1927), p. 116.

42. César Góngora P., "La geografía humana del Perú," *Letras: Órgano de la Facultad de Letras de San Marcos* (Lima), first quarter, 1936, p. 15.

43. See *Revista de la Universidad Católica del Perú,* XIII, nos. 4–5 (July–August, 1940), pp. 439–40.

44. Chocano, *Alma América: poemas indo-españoles,* with a prologue by Unamuno (1906), p. vii.

45. For a brilliant discussion of various aspects and manifestations of this New World feeling see Arthur P. Whitaker, *The Western Hemisphere Idea: Its Rise and Decline* (Ithaca, N.Y., 1954).

46. Argentine poet-pensador Leopoldo Lugones, quoted by José María Salaverría, "El suspicaz excesivo," *Revista de las Españas,* nos. 29–30 (January–February, 1929), pp. 3–4.

47. Blanco-Fombona, "La raza latino-americana," *Unión Ibero-Americana,* Año XXIII (November, 1919), pp. 1–2.

48. Blanco-Fombona, *Motivos y letras de España,* (1930), pp. 69–70.

49. Palacios, quoted in *ibid.,* pp. 71–72.

50. See William Baker Bristol, "Hispanidad in South America, 1936–1945" (unpublished doctoral dissertation, University of Pennsylvania, 1947), p. 95; Earl T. Glauert, "Ricardo Rojas and the Emergence of Argentine Cultural Nationalism," *Hispanic American Historical Review,* XLIII (1936), pp. 1–13; F. B. Pike, ed., *Latin American History: Select Problems, Identity, Integration, and Nationhood* (New York, 1969), pp. 183–84, 186.

51. José Uriel García, *El nuevo Indio: ensayos indianistas sobre la sierra surperuana* (Cuzco, 1937, 2nd ed.), pp. 86–87, 95, 97, 107–108.

52. See also Vasconcelos, "Palabras de un gran hispanófilo," *España y América: Revista Comercial,* no. 155 (July, 1925), p. 75, and "Hacia la liga de naciones de habla española," *ibid.,* no. 157 (September, 1925), p. 102. In a way Vasconcelos was simply continuing the tradition of certain Mexican positivists in exalting their country's mixed, mestizo race. Generally, the glorification of mestizaje came later to other Spanish-American countries. For a sampling of some of the writings of Peruvians who extolled the mestizo "race," regarding it as an improvement over the Spanish component in it, see Pike, ed., *Latin American History,* pp. 183, 200–204.

53. See the 1939 Ortega y Gasset conference presented in Argentina, *Meditación,* pp. 99–109.

54. Rodolfo Reyes, "El valor 'hombre' en América," *Cultura Hispano-Americana,* nos. 46–47 (July–August, 1915), pp. 16–17.

55. The best general survey of the subject is Arthur P. Whitaker and

David C. Jordan, *Nationalism in Contemporary Latin America* (New York, 1966).

56. Augusto Barcía, en enthusiastic hispanoamericanista, in 1922 advanced the contention that was typical of his school. "Ties of race," he asserted, "are always stronger than the accidental ones of geography." See his "El hispanoamericanismo," *Unión Ibero-Americana*, Año XXXVI (March–April, 1922), p. 46. At about the same time José Francos Rodríguez, also a dedicated hispanoamericanista, insisted that all really important ties among peoples must be based on ethnic factors. See his *Huellas españolas: impresiones de un viaje por América* (1921), p. 342.

57. According to a Cuban diplomat, Latin America's attraction toward the United States arose in part from the strong anti-European sentiment that was so much a part of the New World's intellectual tradition. See Orestes Ferrara, Cuban ambassador to the United States at the time, *El panamericanismo y la opinión europea* (Paris, 1930). See also Ángel del Río, *The Clash and Attraction of Two Cultures: the Hispanic and Anglo-Saxon Worlds in America*, translated from the Spanish and edited by James F. Shearer (Baton Rouge, La., 1965).

58. For the adverse reaction of Francos to the Brum statements, see *Huellas españolas*, pp. 340–42.

59. See the address of Brum, who prior to becoming his country's president had gained international prestige as Uruguay's minister of foreign relations, "Solidaridad americana," originally presented at the University of Montevideo and published in *Unión Ibero-Americana*, Año XXXIV (July, 1920), esp. pp. 11–13. In a way Brum's ideas on hemisphere solidarity anticipated the mutual defense system established in the 1930s and expanded in the mid- to late 1940s into the Organization of American States. Brum (pp. 16–17) urged the establishment of a continental league. "This league," he stated, "will expand the spirit of Monroeism to preclude territorial conquest not only from Europe but from within the continent as well. . . . There is no reason why such a league cannot exist and function within the League of Nations, but it will have precedence in matters affecting the peace of the American continent."

60. Lugones, quoted in "Noticias Generales," *Razón y Fe*, LXXII (May–August, 1925), pp. 127–28.

61. Valle-Inclán, *Tirano Banderas: novela de tierra caliente* (1968, 7th ed.), p. 35. The work appeared originally in 1922.

62. This is the description of Uruguayan writer Edgardo Ubaldo Genta, "Crisis en Iberoamérica," *ABC*, June 1, 1969, p. 5.

63. See Leopoldo Zea, *The Latin American Mind*, translated from the Spanish by James H. Abbott and Lowell Dunham (Norman, Okla., 1963), pp. 224–25.

64. This statement was made by the Peruvian intellectual Javier Prado, *Estado social del Perú durante la dominación española* (Lima, 1941, 2nd ed.), p. 206. The work appeared originally in 1894. On Prado see my Chapter 9, note 47.

65. For a discussion of how Chilean upper classes gained the support of and co-opted the middle sectors see F. B. Pike, "Aspects of Class

Relations in Chile, 1850–1960," *Hispanic American Historical Review*, XLIII (February, 1963), pp. 14–33.

66. Claudio Véliz, "An Historical Introduction," in Véliz, ed., *Latin America and the Caribbean: A Handbook* (London, 1968), pp. xxi–xxiii.

67. See Marrero, *Maeztu*, p. 505.

INDEX OF NAMES

471

Atlantic
Ocean

DOMINICAN REPUBLIC
San Juan
PUERTO RICO

bean Sea

Santa
mingo

GUIANAS

Amazon R.

Orinoco R.

Caracas
ENEZUELA

Orinoco R.

tá
OMBIA

Quito
ECUADOR
Guayaquil

81
83
85
88